The Cognitive Foundations
of Personality Traits

EMOTIONS, PERSONALITY, AND PSYCHOTHERAPY

Series Editors
Carroll E. Izard, *University of Delaware, Newark, Delaware*
and
Jerome L. Singer, *Yale University, New Haven, Connecticut*

A Continuation Order Plan is available for this series. A continuation order will bring delivery of each new volume immediately upon publication. Volumes are billed only upon actual shipment. For further information please contact the publisher.

The Cognitive Foundations of Personality Traits

Shulamith Kreitler
and
Hans Kreitler

Tel Aviv University
Tel Aviv, Israel

PLENUM PRESS • NEW YORK AND LONDON

Library of Congress Cataloging in Publication Data

Kreitler, Shulamith.
   The cognitive foundations of personality traits / Shulamith Kreitler and Hans
Kreitler.
       p.   cm. — (Emotions, personality, and psychotherapy)
   Includes bibliographical references.
   ISBN 0-306-43179-3
   1. Personality and cognition. I. Kreitler, Hans. II. Title. III. Series.
BF698.9.C63K74   1989   89-38261
155.2′3 — dc20   CIP

© 1990 Plenum Press, New York
A Division of Plenum Publishing Corporation
233 Spring Street, New York, N.Y. 10013

Printed in the United States of America

To

Solomon E. Asch and Florence Asch

for a quarter-century of

inspiring and heartwarming friendship

Preface

Hardly anything in psychology is as irking as the trait concept. Psychologists and laypersons alike use primarily adjective trait-names to characterize and even conceptualize the individuals they encounter. There are more than a hundred well-defined personality traits and a great many questionnaires for their assessment, some of which are designed to assess the same or very similar traits. Little is known about their ontogenetic development and even less about their underlying dynamics. Psychoanalytic theory was invoked for explaining the psychodynamics underlying a few personality traits without, however, presenting sufficient empirical evidence for the validity of these interpretations. In a reductionistic vein, behaviorally inclined psychologists have propounded the thesis that all traits are acquired behaviors. Yet, this view neither reduces the number of personality tests nor explains the resistance of traits to modification by means of reward and punishment.

Dissatisfied with these and some other less well-known approaches to personality traits, we decided to explore whether applying our psychosemantic theory of cognition to the trait concept would do better. The way we had to follow was anything but easy. This book presents the results of our long explorations: a new definition of traits, an explanation of trait dynamics in terms of meaning, a specification of trait characteristics that allows us, for example, to compare traits or to determine whether a given personality disposition is a trait or is not, the amazing fact—even for us—that one relatively simple test can be used for assessing each of the 120 best known and well-studied personality traits, and many more applications and demonstrations of the new conception of traits.

In the first part of the book (Part I), we present and analyze various problems and difficulties besetting the conventional trait concept (Chapter 1). Then we describe the new meaning-based approach to cognition, emphasizing its major assumptions, tenets, concepts (e.g., *meaning, meaning profile,* and *meaning variable*), implications, and the new assessment tools it has generated, mainly the assessment of meaning. Following this presentation, we proceed to the theoretical rationale leading to the cognitive conception of personality traits (Chapter 2). This conception was tested in a series of over 40 empirical studies of personality traits. The major findings and conclusions of these studies in regard to personality traits are described in Chapters 3 to 8. The conclusions concern issues, such as the nature of traits (Chapter 3), how traits function (Chapter 4), and the relations of traits to overt behavior (Chapter 8). The problems concerning traits raised in Chapter 1 are answered in Chapter 7 in the framework of the new meaning-based trait concept, on the basis of the extensive research findings.

The second part of the book (Part II) is devoted to empirical studies of traits based on applying the new cognitive approach, implemented by the assessment of meaning. An introductory section discusses the methodological and procedural issues common to all the studies. The 22 presented studies were selected because they deal with 76 common traits of different kinds (e.g., emotional, cognitive, and social), illustrate a wide range of different applications of the new conception, and demonstrate its contributions to resolving specific problems concerning particular personality traits, such as extroversion, Machiavellianism, external and internal control, and sensation seeking.

The third part of the book (Part III) focuses on practical applications of the new conception of personality traits to issues such as trait assessment, trait comparisons, and the construct validity of traits. The illustrations are based partly on studies of the Minnesota Multiphasic Personality Inventory, the Jackson Research Form, and different anxiety scales. In particular we show how one test, the assessment of meaning, can provide information about trait scores. Each of the chapters of Part III includes precise instructions for working with the new trait concept. The information necessary for applying the new concept to the assessment of personality traits is summarized in Appendix B.

Owing to the amazing number of publications, psychologists often lack the time to read a professional book from cover to cover. Therefore, it seems advisable to point out what is essential to understanding, as well as what is likely to be of special interest to different professional groups.

To our mind, reading Part I is absolutely necessary for obtaining an adequate understanding of the new trait concept, its dynamics, its theoretical and practical implications, and the extent of its potentialities. Chapter 6, however, may be skipped by those readers who either are not particularly interested in methodological aspects or trust that the authors have done a proper job.

The studies described in Part II may be interesting and, we hope, even important to psychologists who are actively involved in research in personality in general or personality traits in particular, as well as to those who want to learn more about one or another of the discussed traits. Both groups are advised to read the introductory section and then those studies that deal with the traits in which they are particularly interested.

Part III is specifically designed for researchers and practitioners. Chapter 10, which describes in detail how to assess traits by means of the meaning test, is essential reading for both. The other chapters deal with more specific applications focusing on issues of identifying traits (Chapter 11), characterizing trait scales and factors (Chapter 12), and using the meaning system for validation (Chapter 13). Any of these may be read either by investigators who are interested in the discussed issue or by those who would like to use the detailed examples as inspiration for exploring further applications of the new system.

A preface would hardly be complete without expressions of thanks to all those who have helped in making this book possible. Out of the many, we would like to mention in particular the workers of the Tel Aviv Computation Center for having contributed their expertise and time; Professor William McGuire of Yale University for his unswerving encouragement and help; and our students at Tel Aviv University, especially Mr. Gadi Breier, Ms. Iris Drexler, and Dr. Talma Lobel, whose data constitute a part of the broad research base for the new conception; Mrs. Orna Hamilis, the graphic art designer at Tel Aviv University, who has volunteered to prepare Figure 1; as well as the many others whose critical remarks over the years have led us toward an increasing clarity of conception. We would finally like to thank those at Plenum, namely Eliot Werner, Margaret Ritchie, and Robert Freire, for their contributions in the course of bringing this volume to publication.

Contents

I

The Trait Concept

Traits: The Embattled Concept

DOING SOMETHING ABOUT TRAITS

Mark Twain is quoted as having said that everybody talks about the weather and suffers from it, but nobody does anything about it. Indeed, this is no longer quite so true. We have become adept at defending ourselves against it and are even beginning to do something about changing it.

In many respects, traits are like the weather. We complain about them, and we suffer from their deficiencies, but so far, very little has been done about changing this exasperating state of affairs. Maybe it is time to do something about traits. And this is what this book is all about.

Unfortunately, we cannot present our suggested solution in full armor at this point. The reason is that, even if we did, it could not be understood or applied or tested by the reader. Its presentation requires a description of trait ailments and of the theoretical concepts we brought to bear on this issue, as well as of our methodology, tools, studies, and applications, all of which have made possible the formulation of the new trait concept. But though we cannot present the solution in this section, we can at least characterize, to some extent, the kind of solution it will be.

First and foremost, the solution is based on a cognitive approach to traits. In itself, this basis should not be very surprising in view of two known facts. The first is that, in recent years, large bodies of data have accumulated indicating the crucial role of cognition in domains of basic importance in personality, including motivation (Weiner, 1972), emotions (Schachter, 1964), self-control (Mischel, 1974), self-regulation (Zivin, 1979), social perception (Cohen, 1981; Higgins, Herman, & Zanna, 1982; Miller, 1980), psychopathology (Landfield & Leitner, 1980), and behavior change (Beck, 1970; Mahoney, 1974; Meichenbaum, 1977). There is also increasing evidence that cognitive variables—such as cognitive complexity (Harvey, Hunt, & Schroder, 1961), cognitive-control or perceptual-style factors (Gardner, Holzman, Klein, Linton, & Spence, 1959; Gardner & Long, 1962; Klein, 1970), and cognitive differentiation (Witkin, Lewis, Hertzman, Machover, Meissner, & Wagner, 1954), rigidity (Rokeach, 1960)—affect behavior that is not necessarily cognitive. The second fact is the increased "cognitivization" of the domain of personality proper (Mischel, 1979; Pervin, 1983). Different investigators have called for the application of cognitive approaches to issues in personality or have ventured attempts in this direction (e.g.,

Bowers, 1973; Cantor, 1981; Forgus & Shulman, 1979; Golding, 1977; Hamilton, 1983; Rogers, 1981).

Though cognitive concepts have been used both by critics (Cantor & Mischel, 1977) and by supporters (Buss & Craik, 1984) of the trait approach, the cognitive approach has often been seen as inimical to traits (Cantor & Kihlstrom, 1982). Nevertheless, the bonding of cognition with traits was not very far off. Yet, what may be surprising is the kind of cognitive processes we brought to bear on the problem, the way in which we reached the new conception, and the unexpected conclusions that it generated.

Another characteristic of our solution is that it deals with traits as structural-functional units and sheds light on what they are and how they work.

And finally, a third characteristic of our suggested solution is that it actually seems to salvage traits that, in recent decades, have increasingly become an endangered species.

In the different sections of this chapter, we introduce traits and describe some difficulties that have resulted in the present predicament of the concept of trait.

TRAITS IN PERSONALITY

The trait approach constitutes one of the commonest, oldest, and most characteristic approaches to personality. A trait is essentially a relatively stable tendency or feature characteristic of an individual. A construct like this has been with us since the early beginnings of theorizing about people by Greek philosophers and Indian thinkers. Mischel (1976) dated the origins of this approach to as far back as the "beginnings of language" (p. 13), and Meili (1968) noted that "even quite young children learn to use the names of traits correctly without knowing anything about psychology, except implicitly" (p. 213). Indeed, most of the descriptive terms about people that we have in language are trait names. Despite their fairly conservative criterion for identifying traits, Allport and Odbert (1936) showed that trait names comprised 4.5% of the 400,000 terms in the 1925 edition of Websters *New International Dictionary of the English Language*. Thus, whenever we talk of people nonprofessionally, and very often even when we discuss them professionally, we use traits directly or refer to them indirectly.

In psychology, traits have been identified and studied in very different domains of behavior (e.g., aggressiveness), emotions (e.g., fearfulness), cognition (e.g., closed-mindedness), motivation (e.g., level of aspiration), expressiveness (e.g., expansive movements), interpersonal behavior (e.g., friendliness), personal style (e.g., rigidity), and so on. Different terms are sometimes used to refer to traits, such as *internal dispositions, intrapsychic features of personality, psychic structures, mental structures, cognitive styles, personality tendencies, personality variables, styles,* and *orientations* (e.g., Alker, 1972; Allport, 1937; Wachtel, 1973). Common to the different contents and labels is the conception of stable individual characteristics.

In personality theories, traits have been used to answer two basic questions: Of what does personality consist? And why do people behave as they do (i.e., consistently, and differently from others)? Thus, traits have traditionally fulfilled two roles, as units of structure or building blocks and as explanatory constructs. The first role is evident in the common definition of personality as the sum total of traits or the individual's "unique pattern of traits" (Guilford, 1959). Traits are the basic and dominant if not sole units in the personality theories of Cattell (1965), Eysenck (1953), and Allport (1961), and they are important units in such different personality theories as those of Freud (Abraham, 1927, 1954; Freud, 1925, 1950; Jones, 1923a,b), Jung (1923), Fromm (1947), Adler (1964), and Sheldon (1942). Moreover, traits are the basic variables assessed by most personality inventories including Cattell's 16 PF (16 Personality Factors), the Minnesota Multiphasic Personality Inventory (MMPI), the California Psychological Inventory (CPI), the Guilford-Zimmerman Temperament Survey (GZTS), and the Edwards Personal Preferences Schedule (EPPS), to mention just a few. As explanatory constructs, traits have figured dominantly in such basic comprehensive theories as those of Eysenck (1953), Cattell (1965), Guilford (1959), and Allport (1961), as well as in more restricted theoretical frameworks devoted to the study of specific traits, for example, field dependency (Witkin, Dyk, Faterson, Goodenough, & Karp, 1962), authoritarianism (Adorno, Frenkel-Brunswick, Levinson, & Sanford, 1950), or reflection and impulsivity (Kagan, 1966). As may be surmised, the two roles—building blocks and explanatory constructs—are not mutually exclusive. More often than not, traits serve both functions.

Meili (1968) suggested that traits are direct perceptions representing definite aspects of the personality; as such, they are primary units "preceding reflexion and psychological analysis and constituting the raw material of scientific work" (pp. 212–213). It is probably the case that direct impressions of this kind form the basis for the perception of other people, but it is not the case that traits are indispensable to a theory of personality. The trait-based theories constitute a major trend in the study of personality, but not the only trend. Following the terminology suggested by Bo Ekehammar (1974), we consider traits the clearest and most central manifestation of personologism in personality theory.

TRAITS IN THE QUAGMIRE

Since the mid-1970s traits have come under an increasingly intense attack from different quarters. The various arguments have converged sufficiently so that they can be summed up in a series of issues. Most of them arose precisely because traits had been used in so many theories and had been studied so widely in previous decades. We will review these issues in order to clarify the problems attendant on the construct of traits. These are the problems we have tried to resolve by applying our concept of meaning to the study of traits.

A convenient point of departure for presenting the disputed issues is Allport's definition of traits (1961). This is the best known modern definition, which has often served as a focus for further elaboration or as a target for dissent. Allport defined a trait as a "neuropsychic structure having the capacity to render many stimuli functionally equivalent, and to initiate and guide equivalent (meaningfully consistent) forms of adaptive and expressive behavior" (p. 347). This definition emphasizes that a trait is a structure, that it causes behavior, and that its dynamic potential consists in reflecting or forming a unity of meaning. Allport further explained that the unity of meaning exists in regard to both responses and stimuli:

> It is only the repeated occurrence of acts having the same significance (equivalence of response) following upon a definable range of stimuli having the same personal signifi-

cance (equivalence of stimuli) that makes necessary the inference of traits and personal dispositions. (p. 374)

Do traits exist? The strongest controversy was evoked by Allport's statement that traits actually exist and cause behavior. Some (e.g., Cattell, 1950, 1965; Guilford, 1959) have maintained that traits are merely theoretical constructs, abstractions devised by researchers for the sake of describing and explaining behavior. Others (Heider, 1958; Icheiser, 1949; Jones & Nisbett, 1971; Mischel, 1968, 1969) have said that traits are in "the eye of the beholder," characterizing the view that outside observers may have of another person's behavior.

The "outside observer" is evidently just a common person and not necessarily a researcher, as maintained by Cattell and Guilford. However, because researchers are also observers, the thesis that traits are the impressions of observers turns out to be a paraphrase or extension of the older conception of traits as constructs devised for explaining behavior. Moreover, Cattell (1977) showed that the viewpoints of researchers (objective-test data and questionnaire data) and of lay observers (rating-scale data) on traits are correlated and reveal similar information about an individual. Thus, Stagner (1976) suggested that traits are "generalized expectancies that certain consequences can be expected from contact with certain categories of stimuli" (p. 122) and hence "may be viewed as a cognitive pattern either within the person observed or within the observer" (p. 115). Usually, however, the emphasis has been on the observer as the source of the trait. As Kelly (1958) noted somewhat facetiously but clearly, "If I say that Professor Cattell's head is 'discursive,' everyone looks over at him, as if the proposition had popped out of his head instead of out of mine" (p. 40).

As attributions by the observer, traits may be further specified as internal attributions made either when the information available about the behavior(s) is characterized by high consensus, high consistency, and high distinctiveness (Kelley, 1967) or when the behavior deviates from that expected in a given situation (Jones & Davis, 1965). The implication often accompanying views of this kind is that the attributions confound judgments with reality (D'Andrade, 1970) and are often subject to biases, distortions, and unwarranted pressures toward consistency with the established schema (Cantor & Mischel, 1977; Jones, Kanouse, Kelley, Nisbett, Valins, & Weiner, 1971; Schweder, 1975). The logical conclusions of this view are that traits constitute "the fundamental attributional error" (Ross, 1977) and that personality is perceptions (Fiske, 1974). Thus, at present, the epistemological status of traits is unclear. In contrast to Allport's thesis that traits actually exist as "neurophysic structures," some have claimed that they exist merely as forms of perception, whereas others have maintained that traits have no more than a nominal status because they are just labels or convenient abstractions.

What do traits include? A second problem, closely allied to the issue of traits' existence, concerns what traits include, or what they consist of. Allport (1961) emphasized that traits are "generalized action tendencies," "predispositions to act" that embrace two or more interdependent habits. Many of his examples fit this thesis (e.g., rioting, writing protests, and joining the Ku Klux Klan), but many do not (e.g., humor, honesty, fear of capitalism, insight, and holding various attitudes). Of course, this second set of examples could be bound indirectly to actions, but this would introduce a confusion into the concept of trait that would be hard to combat.

Furthermore, Allport also ascribed to traits the motivational function of initiating and guiding actions. The lack of clarity concerning the manifestations of traits has remained a characteristic feature of the concept. Some researchers (e.g., Cattell, 1965; Eysenck, 1947) developed theories accounting, to a certain degree, for the broadened range of trait manifestations. In any case, any run-of-the-mill definition of traits may include references to attitudes, values, opinions, feelings, emotional reactions, moods, aspirations, wishes, actions, habits, or tendencies and any arbitrary number of these. In comparing definitions of two traits given by Jackson and by Gough and Heilbrun, Fiske (1978) deplored the difficulty of deciding whether "feelings of inferiority" mentioned in one definition correspond to "exposes himself to situations where he is in an inferior position" mentioned in the other (pp. 7–8). To our mind, the problem is even more basic: Do "feelings of inferiority" belong at all to the range of manifestations of a trait, and if so, how are they related to other manifestations, notably the strivings, attitudes, and actions commonly associated with "feelings of inferiority"?

How do traits interact? A third point in Allport's definition that evoked opposition was the suggested implication that traits are independent entities. Hall and Lindzey (1957, p. 267) noted that behavioral acts are the product of several traits and that, hence, it is necessary to describe how the operation of a trait depends on the nature and state of other traits. Cattell (1965) studied the interaction of traits statistically, as parameters in regression equations. There is, however, no principle in addition to trial and error that guides the identification of the traits that enter into a specific equation. Others have assumed much more fuzzy interactions of traits in relatively stable frameworks often called *types*. Sometimes *type* represents merely the finding that individuals characterized by a high or low value on one trait have corresponding high or low values on one or more other traits (London & Exner, 1978). Thus, the issue of cooperation of traits is rephrased as coexistence within the framework of one individual person. In other cases, the different traits are assumed to express an underlying tendency (e.g., Erikson, 1950; Freud's character types in Fenichel, 1945), but there is no specification of whether and how they coact. Neither can such specifications be found in the theses of those who have studied the statistical grouping of traits into higher level clusters often called *second-order factors* (e.g., Eysenck, 1947) or in the conceptualizations offered by those personologists (including Allport or Kelly) who feel uneasy about types as stultifying concepts inimical to individuality.

How are traits organized? A fourth point on which psychologists have disagreed with Allport or elaborated on his view concerns the generality and organization of traits. Essentially, the problem is on what level of generality or abstractness traits exist or are to be defined. Whereas Allport distinguished between common traits and unique traits ("personal dispositions"), as well as between cardinal, central, and secondary traits on the basis of their decreasing generality, others have distinguished between surface traits and source traits (Cattell, 1950), personality dimensions and traits (Eysenck, 1953), and so on.

What are the contents of traits? A fifth focus of disagreements concerns the content of traits. Guilford (1959) suggested behavior traits and somatic (physical makeup) traits; Cattell (1965) distinguished between dynamic traits (goals), ability traits, and temperament traits (concerned with energy and emotional reactivity); and so on. Dependent on the content of traits is the issue of their number. Counts of trait names in language run into the thousands. Allport and Odbert's conservative list (1936) contains 17,953 words describing personality characteristics. In practice, psychologists work with a smaller number: Allport's list (1966) of Jenny's central traits included only 8; Cattell (1965) opted for 16 primary traits; in the CPI, there are 18 scales; the original MMPI scales do not exceed 9; the EPPS assesses 15; the GZTS measures 10 traits; Eysenck (Wilson, 1977) was satisfied with 3; Norman (1963) suggested 5; and London and Exner (1978) noted that there are at present at least 13 popular and influential traits, each of which has been the focus of a body of research. Out of despair or in a mood of optimism, London (1978) suggested "a definition-measurement-methodology committee" as the best resolution to this confusing state of affairs (p. 161). Essentially, the problems of what kinds of traits have to be distinguished and how many traits there are arose because there is no agreed-upon theoretical and operational definition of traits. Hence, the resolution of these problems depends on establishing criteria for determining what a trait is and how it is to be assessed operationally.

In what sense are traits structures? A sixth point concerns the nature of the trait as a structure. If it is a structure, then it should consist of some distinguishable components interrelated in some fashion. Allport (1961, p. 373) talked about a "neuropsychic" structure, which may mean that the elements or the special relations between them or both are neural or psychic or both. Each alternative may form the basis for a full-fledged theory. Cattell (1950) spoke of the trait as a "mental structure," but again, he left the issue fairly ambiguous. Some have assumed that the elements of traits are actual specific responses (e.g., Cattell, 1950, and Eysenck, 1953). Others have emphasized that the elements must be habitual responses, that is, habits.

How are traits related to other concepts? A seventh point of controversy concerns the relations between the trait and other related concepts, mainly attitude (or value), habit, cognitive style, response set, and personal disposition. Allport (1961) himself drew some distinctions. He regarded personal dispositions as traits that are peculiar only to the individual, and that thus correspond to what Cattell (1965) called unique traits as against common traits. Allport assumed that habits differ from traits in being less general in the situations appropriate to them and in the responses to which they lead. Again, an attitude is like a trait and differs from it only in often being bound to a certain object or class of objects and in including evaluation of the object. But when an attitude is bound to many different objects, and when the evaluation element is less prominent, an attitude would be indistinguishable from a trait. Again, Allport treated value orientations as being suspiciously akin to traits.

The distinction between traits and the mentioned concepts of disposition, habit, attitude, and value, as well as the further concepts of cognitive style and response set, is also far from clear in the writings of other personality theorists and researchers. Cognitive style or cognitive control is often presented as a trait limited to cognitive tasks (Gardner, 1962), whereas response style is usually defined as a trait limited to test and performance, and response set as a trait limited to a specific test form (Jackson & Messick, 1962). In a later version of the theory, Allport (1966) himself veered toward the conclusion that "traits . . . include long-range sets and attitudes, as well as such variables as 'perceptual response dispositions,' 'personal constructs' and 'cognitive styles.'" (p. 3). But while emphasizing the similarities, he remained fully cognizant of the need to define the differences: "There are . . . refinements of differences between trait, attitude, habit, sentiment, need, etc. Since these are all inside tendencies of some sort, they are for the present occasion all 'traits' to me" (p. 9). We have illustrated the difficulty in drawing these various distinctions in order to emphasize the need for a comprehensive framework that will make it possible to define the differences among these and other related concepts.

How are traits related to other personality constructs? The eighth issue is: How do traits relate to personality constructs, mainly need, belief, and the basic core motivations? Maddi (1968, p. 290) deplored the fact that Allport had neglected to specify the relationship between traits and the appropriate functions. Allport himself (see Evans, 1971) voiced the opinion of many when he claimed that a trait must ultimately be related to the total pattern of personality of which it is a part. The only question is how this integration is to be attained. Liebert and Spiegler (1978) emphasized that, because the trait approach in general lacks a theoretical base, traits have to be placed in some "foster home" (pp. 299–300). This approach calls for interrelating traits with other personality variables, but the trait concept is not geared for this. The problem becomes particularly evident when traits are put to work as factors in the explanation of behavior. At this point, one often encounters statements like "whether a specific action occurs depends on a complex interaction among traits, beliefs, desires, motives, goals, etc." (Hirschberg, 1978, p. 63). The difficulty of integrating traits with other personality variables does not mean that traits should be discarded but that the solution can come only through embedding traits and other constructs in a broader theoretical framework that allocates a specific function to traits and shows how they interrelate with other constructs.

How are traits related to behavior? The final and ninth point is the knotty issue of the relation of traits to behavior. We have not put it at the end of the list because it is in any way less important than the other issues. Quite the contrary. In a sense, it could be viewed as the most central issue concerning traits. In recent years, this view has been increasingly voiced both by supporters and critics of the trait approach. Nevertheless, we have delayed its presentation to the end, so as not to let it overshadow other aspects of traits that are not exclusively bound to the problem of traits' relation to behavior.

As already mentioned, traits have always been conceived of as related to behavior. Allport (1961) assumed that traits "initiate and guide behavior" (p. 373). This is a very strong and demanding assumption. Others have settled for more modest claims. One possibility is the "summary view" of traits (Mischel, 1968; Shweder, 1975; Wiggins, 1973), according to which ascribing a trait to a person merely affirms "that a certain corresponding form of behavior has occurred in the person, frequently or relatively frequently in the past—perhaps with the implication in some sense that the same frequency may be expected to continue" (Brandt, 1970, p. 25). Another possibility is the dispositional view of traits (Alston, 1975; Brandt, 1970; Hirschberg, 1978) that emphasizes the dependence of trait manifestations on the occurrence of appropriate conditions, without, however, assuming that traits necessarily cause behavior.

Beyond the theoretical aspect of the issue there are the empirical findings, which are most disturbing. Geis (1978) provided a careful summary statement: "Paper-and-pencil personality tests that use self-report, trait-descriptive items will relate to the behavior problematically, at best" (p. 135). Two problems have converged to produce this disturbing state of affairs. One is that self-report measures do not, as a rule, correlate with overt molar behavior (Argyle & Little, 1972; Kendon & Cook, 1969; Mann, 1959; Porter, Argyle, & Salter, 1970). But as Campbell and Fiske (1959) noted, whereas questionnaires do not correlate with behavior measures, they often correlate with other questionnaires. These may be of the self-report kind as well as of other kinds, assessing judgments, values, and so on. The fact that trait questionnaires hardly correlate with behavior is in itself sufficiently discouraging, but it is only part of the story. The other part is that, even on this level, the relations found are not always what one expects them to be. Take, for example, internal versus external control. Predictions about conformity and resistance to external pressures are fairly straightforward and have been partly confirmed, but most of the accumulated data refer to responses that are only tenuously related to the original formulations. For example, internals were found to need more time before they reached a decision (Rotter & Mulry, 1965) and to favor persuasion over coercion in dealing with a hypothetical problem worker (Goodstadt & Hjelle, 1973). Some *post hoc* explanation, sometimes presented as a hypothesis, can be found for any correlation, but the possibility to present such an explanation does not disconfirm the conclusions stated by Meehl (1967) that large proportions of existing data in personality are absolutely equivocal in meaning, and by Golding (1978) that most of the empirical data "dangle in a vacuum theoretically and bear little or no relation to the theory they supposedly corroborate" (p. 77).

Another problem is that behavior is not as consistent as the concept of trait would lead us to believe. Indeed, it is not at all consistent, at least as it appears to most researchers. The problem is of paramount importance in the study of personality at large, because without intraindividual consistency, there can hardly be interindividual differences and certainly no basis for upholding a unit such as a trait.

Indeed, the problem has been with us since Hartshorne and May (1928, 1929; Hartshorne, May, & Shuttleworth, 1930) showed, in a by now classic study, that honesty is a situation-specific trait or behavior rather than a general personality disposition. The study may not have been methodologically perfect, but the findings turned out to be right after all. Over the years, consistency of behavior has been investigated by psychologists in different populations (e.g., normals and psychiatric patients), different age groups, different behaviors, different methodologies (e.g., ratings by others, self-reports, and observations of behavior), and different research paradigms (e.g., correlational studies, factor analyses, and multidimensional analyses of variance). Over time, an overwhelming mass of data has accumulated, and it shows that what was true of the honesty of schoolchildren is true of other behaviors in other contexts too (e.g., Bowers, 1973; Dudycha, 1936; Ekehammar, 1974; Endler, Hunt, & Rosenstein, 1962; Fiedler, 1971; Fiske, 1971, pp. 180–191, Chapter 8; Mischel, 1976; Moos, 1970; Nelsen, Grinder, & Mutterer, 1969; Newcomb, 1929; Trickett & Moos, 1970). Further, even when there are some significant transsituational correlations between behaviors, they are so low (often around .30) that their practical value is severely limited (Mischel, 1968, p. 38).

Psychologists were not very quick in drawing the obvious conclusions about the scientific status of traits and general tendencies in behavior, but when they did draw conclusions, the message was very clearly stated (e.g., Endler & Magnusson, 1974; Mischel, 1969, 1976; Pervin, 1968; Vernon, 1964, 1973). Mischel, who often gets credit for having revived the issue, stated it very clearly but, as shown elsewhere (S. Kreitler & H. Kreitler, 1983, 1984, 1989c), in a too rash form:

> behavior . . . is specific to the situation: response patterns even in highly similar situations often fail to be strongly related. Individuals show far less cross-situational consistency in their behavior than has been assumed by trait-state theories . . . behavior tends to be extremely variable and unstable. (Mischel, 1968, pp. 177–178)

Allport (1966) was aware of the inconsistency, and this awareness may have been a reason that he added to his trait theory that "acts, and even habits, that are inconsistent with a trait are not proof of the nonexistence of the trait" (p. 1). Yet, he had no remedy for the problem and remained content with the suggestion that "the variability induced by ecological, social, and situational factors" should be brought to mesh with traits through "an adequate theory" (p. 9). Moreover, his suggestion, designed to preserve the concept of trait, introduces an element of confusion: How much inconsistency is consistent with a trait? And what kind of inconsistency is consistent with a trait?

Both problems—namely, the apparent unrelatedness of traits to behavior and the low cross-situational consistency in behavior—are of central importance to psychology in general and to personality theory in particular. Moreover, both involve contradictions in research findings, on the one hand, and psychological theories, as well as the intuition based on daily life experience with people, on the other hand.

Several attempts have been made to support the trait concept despite findings that show traits and behavior to be unrelated or only minimally related. Here are some of the more typical arguments:

1. Because in some cases, with certain kinds of measures, self-reports and overt behaviors, as observed by others, have been found to converge (e.g., Pinneau & Milton, 1958), it is clear that relations exist and have only to be investigated with the proper methodology (Argyle & Little, 1972).

2. Since correlations with external measures may be attenuated for statistical reasons (mainly low reliability), improving the reliability of behavioral measures would facilitate demonstrating relations of traits to behaviors (Block, 1963, 1964; Byrne & Holcomb, 1962; Humphreys, 1960).

3. Failures to detect relations between traits and behaviors may have been due to a research paradigm that focused on examining correspondences between single traits and single behaviors, whereas the desirable procedure is to focus on relations between combinations of traits and specific behaviors (Argyle & Little, 1972; Craik, 1969), or between traits and global measures of behaviors (Argyle & Little, 1972), or between traits and more extended samples of behavior (Epstein, 1977, 1979).

Arguments of a different order have been raised to support traits despite the evidence that there is low cross-situational consistency in behavior and that behavior is situation-specific. Here are some examples of these arguments:

1. Inconsistency may be merely phenotypical, whereas consistency may be characteristic of the genotype (Lazarus, 1971).
2. There are many different types of inconsistency (e.g., spatial, temporal, absolute, and relative), in some of which inconsistency has been found to be

less than in others, so that a systematic search for consistency should be continued (Block, 1977; Magnusson, Duner, & Zetterblom, 1975).

3. Some inconsistency in behavior should be expected because people change over time (Block, 1971).

4. Consistency is higher in self-report data and in data derived from observers' evaluations (personality ratings), particularly when the evaluations are global statements based on different kinds of information about the subject, than it is in objective data on behavior in standardized laboratory situations, which is admittedly low in consistency (Block, 1977, 1981). Thus, personality research should be based on the former rather than on the latter kind of data.

5. Consistency can be expected only among respondent measures or among operant measures of behavior and not between respondent and operant measures (McClelland, 1981).

6. Mediating variables on a higher level of abstractness or generality have to be introduced if the underlying consistencies are to be uncovered (e.g., Golding, 1977).

7. Modifier variables have to be introduced so that the total sample can be divided into subgroups, in some of which consistency would be manifested (Grooms & Endler, 1960; Kogan & Wallach, 1964).

8. Although inconsistency is not characteristic of behavior, it may have occurred in studies because the investigated behaviors were not significant and salient to the subject; because the context may have been unfamiliar to the subject; because the subject may have been in a psychopathological state, such as paranoia, that leads to extreme contrasting behaviors; and so on (Block, 1968).

9. Inconsistency is characteristic mainly of low scorers on behavior measures, and not of high scorers (Vaughan, 1977).

10. The often-reported inconsistency has been claimed to be the result of statistical errors due to inadequate sampling of behaviors and to using inappropriate total variance terms in computing the percentage of variance reflecting individual differences (Epstein, 1977).

The large number of these arguments reveals how tenuous the position of trait psychologists has become. Most of the arguments are weakly supported, refer to rare or unlikely contingencies, or are programmatic in nature. The evidence for specific and circumscribed types of consistency or of trait–behavior relations is scarce and raises more questions than it answers, for it is evident that the trait concept can neither predict these findings nor even account for them *ad hoc* without the help of assumptions that are external to the trait concept. Further, Block's data (1977) about consistency in self-report and observers' data were enthusiastically espoused by Mischel (1977) as further evidence that traits are in the eye of the beholder. Again, the various arguments that restrict consistency to some level or score or measure have failed so far to establish convincingly how much variability is consistent in a stable trait. Finally, these arguments, as well as the suggestions about working with combinations of traits and introducing moderator variables, still await the elaboration of a theory that will spell out how this is to be done.

THE EIGHT QUESTIONS

The disputed issues we have reviewed above may best be summarized in a series of eight questions, which have guided our research and theorizing in this domain. We present them here to serve as a bridge between the questions raised in this chapter and the answers we will attempt to provide following the description of our theory and findings (see Chapter 7). The questions are:

1. What is a trait and what is the epistemological and existential status of the trait concept? (See the first issue above.)
2. What are the typical manifestations of traits? (See the second issue above.)
3. What are the similarities or differences between traits as well as between traits and related concepts? (See the seventh issue.)
4. What are the attributes of traits? (See the fourth issue.)
5. Are there different kinds of traits? (See the fifth issue.)
6. What is the structure of traits? (See the sixth issue.)
7. How do traits function? (See the third issue.)
8. What is the relation of traits and behavior? (See the eight and ninth issues.)

These issues or questions do not reflect any specific conception about traits. They have been suggested mainly to summarize the controversies concerning traits and to facilitate the presentation of our major findings and conclusions about traits.

It is evident that the questions raised above are not fully independent of each other. The conception that an investigator has about, say, the nature of traits affects to some extent her or his hypotheses about the manifestations of traits. Nevertheless, the answer given to one question does not completely determine the answers to the other questions; it merely restricts the range of the possible further answers. Hence, it is justifiable to deal with each question separately and not only in relation to the other questions. Thus, the questions outline a trail that leads from the controversies to the suggested resolutions, but it is neither a linear trail nor a very short one.

Toward a Solution

THE UNDERLYING LEVEL

Not every concept that has fallen into the quagmire of discarded scientific ideas should be allowed to rot there along with Ptolemaic epicycles, Newtonian corpuscles, flogiston, ether, McDougall's sentiments, Freud's quantitative but never quantified libido, and other celebrities of our scientific past. Even if we were willing to disregard the awe-inspiring longevity of the concept of personality traits, its current importance in the perception and evaluation of the self and others as well as in the shaping of social relations would be incentive enough to undertake a further attempt at its rehabilitation.

In the empirical sciences, situations of this kind are not unusual. Every so often, apparent inconsistencies have been shown to be regular, explainable, and predictable through a shift to a deeper and more comprehensive level of theorizing. Sometimes, this deeper level was already available and had only to be adapted to the issues at hand, as in the case of quantum mechanics. Examples closer to our present subject are the adoption of Christian von Ehrenfels's Gestalt principle by Max Wertheimer and Wolfgang Köhler to explain learning and productive thinking or the adoption of Pavlov's principle of conditioning by the behaviorists to explain the emergence of modified or new behaviors. In other cases, the deeper level has not been known and has had to be discovered—quarks and genetic structures, as well as depth psychology. To take one example, Freud's unconscious and preconscious processes had to be discovered before they could be applied to an explanation of personality disorders.

Thus in the present attempt to rehabilitate the endangered trait concept, we adopted a deeper level theory originally developed for the understanding of cognitive processes, as well as of their involvement in the formation of human behavior. As is sometimes the case with new ideas, the theory in question focuses on a concept that, for a long time, has been anathema to most psychologists, as relativity and probability were to physicists in the early nineteenth century. Learning theorists have considered this concept an epiphenomenon, perception psychologists have found it too mentalistic, most cognitive psychologists have skillfully avoided it, and phenomenologists, while recognizing its importance, have discussed it in a fog of aesthetically appealing, but vague, language. The name of the concept is *meaning*.

When meaning is presented in the unoperational terms of most philosophers or is dwarfed by Charles Osgood's reduction to three dimensions, its psychological significance is not apparent. To grasp the extent of its importance, one has to recognize that cognitive content is not merely a collection of manipulable items that can be inserted into the grammatical slots resulting from phrase–structure analysis or the application of transformational rules, but an active agent guiding human thought and affecting emotions and behaviors. It is this insight that has induced us to develop an empirically based theory of meaning that has made possible the satisfactory characterization and quantification of cognitive content (S. Kreitler & H. Kreitler, 1968; H. Kreitler & S. Kreitler, 1976, Chapter 2).

Different studies have shown that applying the new concepts and strategies derived from the system of meaning provides insight into cognitive performance on a broad range of tasks. For example, when we know the ability or tendency of subjects to make use of particular meanings, we are able to predict whether these subjects will solve problems that require overcoming functional fixedness (Arnon & Kreitler, 1984), whether they will evidence conservation in line with Jean Piaget's *decalage* or not (S. Kreitler & H. Kreitler, 1987b), what kinds of aspects they will consider in constructing plans (S. Kreitler & H. Kreitler, 1986a), and how well they will perform on cognitive tasks, such as analogies (S. Kreitler & H. Kreitler, 1988c), recalling specific classes of words and sentences (H. Kreitler & S. Kreitler, 1989a), comprehending particular texts (S. Kreitler & H. Kreitler, 1985b), or planning specific actions (S. Kreitler & H. Kreitler, 1987b,c). Moreover, it has been demonstrated that training in missing or rarely used meaning variables that have been identified as relevant to a particular task improves the cognitive performance of subjects—adults as well as retarded children—on this task (H. Kreitler & S. Kreitler, 1977; S. Kreitler & H. Kreitler, 1989b).

Thus, we have learned, step by step, that meaning is not merely an aspect of cognitive contents but an important concept in its own right that fulfills a basic role in cognition at large. The evidence was so massive and convincing that we ventured to define cognition as the meaning-processing system, that is, the system that assigns, stores, combines, manipulates, transforms, learns, and sometimes produces meanings. As we discovered later, it even influences, to some extent, the meanings it processes.

The idea that led to the studies reported in this book was that meaning variables could well constitute the formative understructure of personality traits. This idea was initiated by casual observations indicating the involvement of meaning in trait-inconsistent behaviors. Take, for instance, the miser who will not buy for himself a needed pair of warm gloves because he considers it a shameful waste of money, but who buys an expensive house because he regards this purchase as good investment. Or take the student who frustrates his teachers and friends by being late, yet comes on time to meet a lecturer who is known to be chronically late and who is highly embarrassed over her lateness. In both cases, behaviors that appear to be trait-inconsistent are consistent with the meaning underlying each of the traits: property and an increased quantity of money in the case of the miser, superiority and attention provoking in the case of the student. Observations of this kind were complemented by findings of studies. An experiment showed that anxiety scales correlated significantly with a pattern of meaning variables (S. Kreitler & H. Kreitler, 1985a), and that changing some of these meaning variables brought about a decrease in the subjects' level of anxiety (S. Kreitler & H. Kreitler, 1987a).

When we considered together the correlations of meaning with anxiety and the above-mentioned correlations of meaning with different cognitive variables, we were struck by three features that seemed crucial. First, the correlations all made sense and were interpretable in the context studied. Second, the correlations occurred in patterns rather than singly, which may be expected in view of the complexity of the variables studied (e.g., S. Kreitler and H. Kreitler, 1985a). And third, the correlations indicated the likely impact of meaning on the variables studied. This conjecture was based on the above-mentioned evidence that changing the relevant aspects of meaning led to expected changes in the variables studied. All three features led us to assume that meaning constellations and processes constitute the understructure of human predispositions and inclinations and hence could provide a more profound and powerful conception of personality traits.

Familiarity with our meaning system is required for an understanding of our hypotheses, of the procedures applied in testing them, and of the eventual application of the findings to salvaging the trait concept, as well as of the contribution of our studies to a more precise definition of 76 personality traits and a more economical method of trait assessment. Indeed, there is hardly a domain of psychological inquiry that would not benefit from a modicum of psychosemantic knowledge. We believe that familiarity with the basic concepts of meaning, meaning variables, and their dynamics may prove to be as essential to psychological research in general and to the study of personality in particular as familiarity with mathematics is to research in physics.

THE MEANING SYSTEM

Basic Assumptions

Many philosophers, linguists, and other investigators in the human disciplines have been convinced for ages that meaning is of central importance in human action and life. This conviction in itself, however, does not make it possible to assess meaning so as to study its effects and to manipulate it experimentally. Psychologists, in their turn, have devised different methods of assessment (e.g., Deese, 1965; Osgood, Suci, & Tannenbaum, 1958) that are operational, but that are too limited in their conceptual and methodological scope to allow for the study of meaning in all its depth and breadth. The meaning system that we have developed is designed to bridge the two approaches, in order to provide a method for the assessment of meaning that would potentially do justice to the conception of meaning as basic in human behavior.

The collection and elaboration of data were guided by several assumptions based on general information about meaning in different domains of psychology:

1. Meaning is essentially communicable. This assumption was based on the evidence that the majority of meanings are learned from others directly or indirectly, and that misunderstandings concerning meanings can be resolved by discussing meanings. Hence, most people may be considered adept at communicating and comprehending meaning on an interpersonal basis.

2. There may be two modes of meaning: the lexical interpersonally shared meaning and the personal-subjective meaning. This assumption reflects a common distinction concerning meaning that has been drawn by many investigators (Jung,

1964; Ogden & Richards, 1949; Werner & Kaplan, 1963), and that corresponds to the experience of individuals who communicate meaning.

3. Meaning is referent-bound. This assumption reflects the intuition of most philosophers and linguists that meaning is always the meaning of something, although they have differed in their specification of what this "something" is. We have called it the *referent* simply because meaning refers to it.

4. Meaning is essentially multifaceted. This assumption reflects the evidence that the meaning assigned to a particular input is often very rich and variegated (Bolinger, 1968), indeed, so much so that some parts of it may even be changed, further elaborated, generalized, or transferred (Osgood, 1964, pp. 701–712).

The first assumption (i.e., communicability) made it possible for us to construct the standard experimental situation for the sake of data collection, and it has led us to instruct the subjects to use common means of human communication. The second assumption (i.e., lexical and personal meaning) underlies the different sets of instructions to the subjects that we have used. The third assumption (i.e., referent-boundedness) led us to anchor our meaning research in a rich variety of referents, both verbal and nonverbal. The fourth assumption (i.e., multifacetedness) underlies our approach to data coding and analysis.

Derivation of the Meaning System

The basic variables of the system were derived from empirical data designed to provide a maximally comprehensive coverage of the major aspects of meaning (H. Kreitler & S. Kreitler, 1982; S. Kreitler & H. Kreitler, 1968, 1987c). Accordingly, there was a large range of variation in subjects and stimuli. Approximately 1,000 subjects participated. They varied in age (from 2 to over 80 years), gender, mental health (normals, hospitalized schizophrenics, neurotics, and various brain-damaged patients), level of intelligence (average, particularly gifted and creative individuals, different degrees of mental retardation), educational level (illiterate subjects to those who held high university degrees), socioeconomic level (low, medium, and high), profession (more than 260 different professions were represented on all levels), and cultural backgrounds (within Israel, there were samples from Far Eastern, Middle Eastern, European, and American backgrounds, and from outside Israel, there were American, South American, and Japanese samples). No less varied were the stimuli. They included words of diverse content and form classes, representative of the major types mentioned in the thesaurus and texts of traditional or modern grammer, word combinations, phrases, and sentences; longer verbal texts, such as paragraphs, scenes of plays, short stories, and records of group discussions or committee sessions; drawings of simple and of complex objects, geometrical figures, graphical signs, and cultural or religious symbols; real objects; photographs of scenes, paintings, and sculptures; scenes from films; musical pieces; actual situations that subjects had observed or in which they had participated; and so on.

Our basic experimental task consisted of asking the subject to communicate the meaning of a standard set of stimuli to an imaginary other (of the subject's choice) who does not know the meaning of the stimuli but who can understand communications in any form of expression. In line with the particular kind of meaning studied (lexical, personal, or both), the instructions requested the subjects to communicate "the common conventional meaning . . . which is known and accepted by most people," the "most personal meaning that the stimulus (specified) has for you," or both kinds of meaning. We also assessed personal tendencies toward either kind of meaning by not specifying the kind of meaning to be communicated.

For analysis of the data, the subjects' responses were divided into units of meaning. A unit included two elements. One was the carrier of meaning, to which the meaning was assigned. This element might be the input or any aspect of the input. Because this element was not necessarily identical to the input, we called it the *referent*. The other element was the assigned meaning. It consisted of a specific communication of some content about the referent, and we called it *meaning value* (for a more precise definition, see "Meaning Dimensions" in the next section). For example, if the input was *car* and the subject's response was "Buicks are the best," the referent was *Buicks* and the meaning value was *the best*. Thus, the referent was the thing about which the subject communicated something, and the meaning value was the communication about the referent. In order to identify the referent, we asked, "About what does the subject communicate?" In order to identify the meaning value, we asked, "What does the subject communicate about the referent?"

THE MEANING VARIABLES

Analysis of the data made possible the characterization of meaning in terms of four sets of variables. These variables characterize the meaning unit and its elements. We now describe the four sets and their characteristics, which are necessary for understanding the studies and conclusions in later parts of this book.

Meaning Dimensions

Meaning dimensions (*Dim*) are general categories of content that characterize meaning communications by specifying the aspect of the input to which the communication refers. The meaning dimensions were derived by asking, in regard to the subject's responses, questions like, "What does the subject communicate about the referent?" "What kind of information about the referent is stated?" These questions were answered only in terms of the stated content without consideration of the veridicality of the content or the means of expression used by the subject. The questions provided a ready tool for identifying units within the subject's response and for labeling these units. A unit was defined as any response or part of a response communicating something specific about the referent, characterizing it in some particular way, or answering some implicit question about it. If the referent is considered a "subject," the communicated content can be considered a predicate. The various predicates, characterizations, or specifications were first labeled in general terms and then classified according to similarities or common elements in the labels. For example, different labels—such as "describes why the referent occurred," "specifies the antecedents of the event," and "communicates the conditions under which the referent is likely to occur"—were grouped together into one class called "Antecedents and Causes." Thus, the grouping of the labels into classes was guided by common characterizing elements, such as causes, functions, and sensory qualities. The classes themselves are called *meaning dimensions*, whereas the units of response are called *meaning values*.

There are 22 empirically defined meaning dimensions:

Dim 1. Contextual Allocation: The superordinate system of items or relations to which the referent belongs or of which it forms part, or the concept or abstract superordinate class whose member it is. Embedding the referent in some concrete system or classifying it in some abstract class often involves labeling and naming, for example, *eye,* "a part of the body, an organ"; *walk,* "a word, a verb, a movement"; *Mary,* "a girl, a female"; *Genesis,* "a book of the Bible"; *God,* "belongs to religion."

Dim 2. Range of Inclusion: The members of the class that the referent designates or for which it could serve as a label or superordinate concept, or the items and parts that the referent includes. It is possible to distinguish between two subdimensions: range of inclusion in a more conceptual sense (i.e., members of the class that the referent denotes; *Dim* 2a) and in a more concrete sense (i.e., the constituting parts of an object or the elements that make up a concept; *Dim* 2b). Examples might be *body,* "head, shoulders, legs," and so on (*Dim* 2b); *day,* "Sunday, Monday," and so on (*Dim* 2a); *amphibia,* "frogs, newts, and salamanders" (*Dim* 2a); *art,* "painting, music, film, and dance" (*Dim* 2a); *book,* "Asimov's science fiction, thesaurus" (*Dim* 2a); *house,* "doors, walls, floors" (*Dim* 2b); *wisdom,* "knowledge and power of reasoning" (*Dim* 2b).

Dim 3. Function, Purpose, or Role: The uses to which the referent is usually put, or the usual activity (or activities) that it does or that may be done with it and that suggest its utility more indirectly, for example, *watch,* "it shows the time"; *and,* "it combines two phrases"; *marriage,* "serves to satisfy basic human needs, hostility no less than sexuality"; *eating,* "helps one to stay alive."

Dim 4. Action and Potentialities for Action: The action(s) that the referent does or can do, or action(s) that others do or can do with it or to it, and that do not represent the referent's function, purpose, or role. Active actions or potentialities for actions (*Dim* 4a) can be distinguished from passive actions or potentialities for actions (*Dim* 4b). For example, *man,* "moves, breathes, consumes, reproduces, and kills" (*Dim* 4a); *table,* "can be folded up" (*Dim* 4b); *cat,* "climbs trees" (*Dim* 4a) and "you can feed it" (*Dim* 4b).

Dim 5. Manner of Occurrence or Operation: The stages, processes, acts, instruments, means, organs, and so on that constitute the operation or manifestation of the referent or that are involved in its occurrence; the manner in which the referent actually occurs, operates, or is realized, for example, *eating,* "it is done with knife, fork, and spoon"; *walk,* "first you lift one leg off the ground and place the other on its toes, then you place the first leg further forward, and so on"; *fire,* "can be produced by a match"; *democracy,* "candidates are elected in conventions," and so on.

Dim 6. Antecedents and Causes: The causes (e.g., physical, physiological, chemical, or social) of the referent; the necessary and/or sufficient conditions for the referent's existence, occurrence, or operation; antecedents of whatever nature and order preceding the referent more-or-less immediately, which are involved directly or indirectly in some way (by, e.g., natural law, legal ruling, or accidental prior occurrence) in bringing about the referent or in enabling its occurrence; reasons, rationales, raisons d'être, or motives for the referent's existence, occurrence, or operation. Examples might be *eating*, "due to hunger"; *anger*, "it is evoked through recalling how your boss insulted you"; *rain*, "it rains because water evaporates from the oceans"; *war*, "happens for economic and political reasons."

Dim 7. Consequences and Results: Consequence, results, or effects, of whatever nature and order, that derive directly or indirectly, in any manner (e.g., intentionally, accidentally, or by natural law or legal ruling) from the referent's existence, occurrence, or operation, or that even merely take place after the referent's occurrence. Examples might be *war*, "many dead and a lot of destruction"; *tired*, "one goes to bed"; *love*, "the sorrow of parting"; *why*, "after asking it, you often get an answer."

Dim 8. Domain of Application: The items (e.g., people, objects, states, or events) to which the referent is or could be applied; the items with which it interacts or that are affected through it; in linguistic terms, the entities that can be assigned to the referent as subjects or as objects (direct or indirect) in answering questions like, "Who (what) does (did) it" "To whom (what) can the referent be assigned?" "Of whom (what) can it be predicted?" "With or in regard to whom (what) is it done?" "Who (what) is concerned with it?" and "Who (what) uses it?" When the referent is a verb, the meaning values of this dimension can be characterized grammatically as specifying, on the one hand, the agent or the performer or the "experiencer" (Chafe, 1970) of the action or, on the other hand, the agentive, the dative, the objective (Fillmore, 1968), or the benefactive (Platt, 1971) cases of the role of the "patient" (Chafe, 1970) that is, the person or thing affected by the action or acting as its recipient. When the referent is some property, the meaning values specify the noun or the modified entity in a phrase consisting of a noun and modifiers. It is possible to distinguish between meaning values that serve as subjects of the referent (*Dim* 8a) and those that serve as direct or indirect objects (*Dim* 8b). Examples might be *sex*, "performed with persons of other or same gender, rarely with animals" (*Dim* 8b); *beautiful*, "it applies to women and the weather" (*Dim* 8a); eat, "fruit, meat" (*Dim* 8b), "all living creatures do it" (*Dim* 8a).

Dim 9. Material: The material(s) of which the referent is or could be made or of which it consists, for example, *table*, "is made of wood, metal, and sometimes plastic materials"; *sea*, "consists of water or of oxygen and hydrogen atoms"; *dream*, "has no substance."

Dim 10. Structure: The interrelations between the parts or elements of the referent; the placement or position of the elements relative to one another or to a more general system of representation; the organization of the material, processes, or other composing entities or system variables (abstract or concrete) on the visible or molar level or at any submolar level. Examples might be *empire*, "like a pyramid with the ruler on top, satellite figures around her or him, satellite states still lower, and the people anywhere at the lowest level"; *gas*, "an unordered mass of molecules";

world, "a disorganized structureless system"; *car*, "a motor in the front or the rear connected with a gasoline tank and two pairs of wheels."

Dim 11. State and Possible Changes in State: The actual, potential, or possible state(s) of the referent at any point in time, and changes that could occur in its state under specified or unspecified conditions, for example, *water*, "evaporates in heat, freezes in cold, but cannot be broken"; *god*, "exists"; *man*, "may be strong or weak, healthy or sick, alive or dead"; *Mary*, "weak and dependent"; *walk*, "it appears in various forms like *walking, walks,* and *walked.*"

Dim 12. Weight and Mass: The weight or mass of the referent, expressed in standard units of measurement or in terms of estimates (of, e.g., heaviness or inertia), absolute or relative, for example, *baby*, "may weigh 6–7 pounds"; *rock*, "it is heavy."

Dim 13. Size and Dimensionality: The size of the referent in standard units of measurement or in terms of estimates, absolute or relative; the number of the referent's dimensions. Examples might be *atom*, "it is smaller than a molecule"; *Earth*, "its diameter is approximately 12,750 kilometers"; *house*, "has three dimensions"; *tree*, "it is high and sometimes very wide."

Dim 14. Quantity and Number: The quantity, number, or frequency of occurrence of the referent, expressed in standard units of measurement or in terms of estimates, absolute or relative. Examples might be *world*, "there is only one of its kind"; *human being*, "has fewer specimens than a virus".

Dim 15. Locational Qualities: The place, address, or domain in which the referent exists, occurs, lives, operates, is located, can be found, and so on, expressed in standard units of measurement or in terms of estimates, relative to other objects or events or in terms of some standard reference system. Examples might be *Rockefeller Center*, "in Manhattan"; *I*, "here"; *sun*, "is located in a side-branch of our galaxy"; *orange*, "is placed between the yellow and the red in a color circle"; *food*, "in the refrigerator or the supermarket"; *coming*, "moving toward the listener".

Dim 16. Temporal Qualities: The time at which the referent exists or existed; the referent's age; the duration, timeliness, durability, continuity, or other temporal properties of the referent's occurrence or operation expressed in standard units of measurement or in terms of estimates, relative or absolute. Examples might be *John*, "5 years old"; *happiness*, "lasts for seconds or minutes"; *party*, "there was one last Friday."

Dim 17. Possession and Belongingness: The actual or potential possessions of the referent as well as to whom (or what) the referent belongs or may belong. Possessions (i.e., what belongs to the referent; *Dim* 17a) and belongingness (i.e., to whom or what the referent belongs; *Dim* 17b) may be distinguished as subdimensions, for example, *house*, "it is owned by the landlord or the tenants" (*Dim* 17b); *cat*, "I have one" (*Dim* 17b); *Mr. B.*, "he's rich, he owns several houses" (*Dim* 17a).

Dim 18. Development: The ontogenetic or phylogenetic development of the referent over extended periods in the past, including the referent's personal history, origin, physical evolution, or historical forerunners; the manner in which it was made or shaped to take its present form; how it has become what it is now; and its expected or usual or possible development in the future. Examples might be *bride*, "first, she was a baby, then a lively teenager, then a dreaming girl, and now she takes the ring"; *buying*, "it is the modern version of exchange and will be replaced in the future by an arrangement in which everyone will simply take from the common pool whatever he or she needs."

Dim 19. Sensory Qualities: The sensory qualities that characterize the referent, that is, those that others perceive in the referent and that the referent experiences or could experience. The sensations evoked in others through the referent (*Dim 19a*) and those experienced by the referent (*Dim 19b*) can be distinguished as subdimensions. Further subdivisions of sensations of either kind are visual sensations (e.g., *table*, "can be seen"); color and brightness (including hue and saturation, e.g., *sky*, "blue or gray"); form and shape (e.g., *pen*, "long and pointed"); auditory sensations (including sound and tone); tactile sensations (e.g., *silk*, "smooth"; *thorn*, "prickly"); taste; temperature (e.g., "cool," "warm," "32°C"); smell and odor; internal sensations (e.g., "pain," "nausea," "aches," "burning sensations," "imbalance," "heart rate," "difficulties in breathing," "arousal"); transparency; pressure and elasticity (including rigidity); and moisture (e.g., "dry," "wet," "humid"). Examples might be *knife*, "has an elongated shape, its blade is smooth, is cool to the touch, and has no odor when clean" (*Dim 19a*); *fetus*, "does not sense colors and forms but probably has auditory, kinesthetic, and thermal sensations" (*Dim 19b*).

Dim 20. Feelings and Emotions: Feelings, emotions, and moods that the referent evokes or may evoke in others and those that the referent experiences or could experience. The feelings evoked in others (*Dim 20a*) and those experienced by the referent (*Dim 20b*) may be distinguished as subdimensions, for example, *exam*, "most people detest it" (*Dim 20a*); *monster*, "frightens children" (*Dim 20a*) and "probably enjoys seeing how scared they are" (*Dim 20b*); *peace*, "you can only hope for it" (*Dim 20a*).

Dim 21. Judgments and Evaluations: The judgments, opinions, beliefs, attitudes, values, or evaluations others hold in regard to the referent, and those the referent himself or herself can hold. Those evoked by the referent in others (*Dim 21a*) and those held by the referent (*Dim 21b*) may be distinguished as two subdimensions, for example, *law*, "most of it is bad and unjust and the rest is superflous" (*Dim 21a*); *Mr. X*, "believes in psychology and UFOs" (*Dim 21b*); *but*, "the single indispensable item of communication."

Dim 22. Cognitive Qualities and Actions: Cognitive qualities (e.g., "bright," "witty," "silly," "IQ") and actions (e.g., "thinking," "recalling," "imagining in fantasy") evoked by or through the referent in others (e.g., "evoking fantasy," "reminding," "convincing") and those that characterize the referent himself or herself. The evoked cognitive qualities and actions (*Dim 22a*) and those characteristic of or enacted by the referent (*Dim* 22b) can be distinguished as subdimensions, for example, *street*, "makes me think and daydream" (*Dim* 22a); *Dr. Z*, "is generally dumb but has a good memory" (*Dim* 22b).

General Remarks about the Meaning Dimensions

The first remark concerns the comprehensiveness of the meaning system. It will be noted that some of the 22 meaning dimensions resemble definitions of meaning suggested by other investigators. For example, the dimension "Action" (*Dim* 4) resembles the behaviorist definition (e.g., Skinner, 1957); the dimension "Consequences and Results" (*Dim* 7) resembles the definition of meaning implied by Pavlov (1927); the dimension "Manner of Occurrence or Operation" (*Dim* 5) resembles the operational definition of meaning (Bridgeman, 1927); the dimension "Function, Purpose, or Role" (*Dim* 3) resembles Wittgenstein's emphasis (1953) on "use" as the core of meaning; and the dimension "Judgments and Evaluations" (*Dim* 21) resembles the meaning factor "Evaluation" identified by Osgood, Suci, and Tannenbaum (1958), whereas the meaning dimensions "State" (*Dim* 11) and "Action" (*Dim* 4) resemble the factors "Potency" and "Activity," respectively, defined by these investigators.

There are, however, major differences between these approaches and ours, the first concerning the stuff of which meaning is made. Whereas other approaches characteristically assume that meaning actually consists of actions, emotions and so on, our approach emphasizes that meaning is cognitive content, that is, *representations* of action, emotions, and so on. Second, concerning comprehensiveness, other approaches limit meaning to what we consider one, two, or three meaning dimensions, whereas our approach is, in principle and in method, more comprehensive (especially in view of the additional sets of meaning variables). The greater comprehensiveness of our system is, however, due not to eclecticism but to the application of a more fundamental conception of meaning that has allowed for the derivation of the other "definitions" as partial aspects of meaning.

The second remark concerns relations between the meaning dimensions. The order in which the 22 dimensions are presented above is random. However, sometimes it may be important to consider the meaning dimensions from the point of view of their interrelations (e.g., see Study 14 in Chapter 9).

The circular model of meaning dimensions presented in Figure 1 is a structure called *radex* (Schlesinger & Guttman, 1969; S. Kreitler and H. Kreitler, 1989a).[1] It shows two characteristics of meaning dimensions: (1) proximity, which is represented in terms of placement along the circumference of the circle, and (2) generality or specificity of meaning values within each meaning dimension, which is represented along the radii of the circle. Proximity is the theme of the present remark (generality is dealt with in the third remark).

The circular model shows that meaning dimensions differ in the degree of their proximity. The dimensions that are closest to each other are placed in adjoining positions on the circle's circumference; those most distant are placed in opposite locations on the circle's circumference, being removed 180 degrees from each other.

---

[1]Thanks are due to the late Professor Louis Guttman for his advice and to Joseph Glickson for his help in computations concerning the radex.

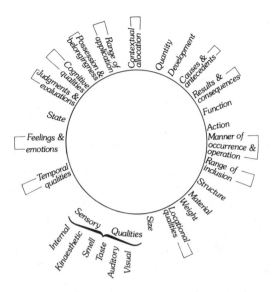

Figure 1. The circle of meaning dimensions. This figure represents schematically the circumplex model of meaning dimensions based on the data available to date. Some of the relations are still tentative.

The proximity order is based on four independent sources of information that have provided largely overlapping findings (S. Kreitler & H. Kreitler, 1985b):

1. Content analyses of meaning communications showed that meaning values sometimes shared the characteristics of two meaning dimensions; for example, the meaning value "boring" concerning a film as referent shares characteristics of "Feelings and Emotions" (*Dim* 20a) and of "Judgments and Evaluations" (*Dim* 21a). In Figure 1 such dimensions are placed in adjoining positions.

2. Correlations between meaning dimensions across subjects showed that some meaning dimensions were more closely correlated than others. In Figure 1, such meaning dimensions are placed closer to each other than other dimensions less closely intercorrelated. Dimensions found by factor analysis to be diametrically opposed were located in Figure 1 at the end points of radial axes, notably "Contextual Allocation" (*Dim* 1) and "Sensory Qualities" (*Dim* 19) or "Action" (*Dim* 4) and "Feelings and Emotions" (*Dim* 20).

3. Studies of the development of meaning showed that, in some cases, the differentiation between two dimensions sets in later than that between other dimensions; for example, children at the age of 4 hardly distinguish between "Function," "Consequences," and "Action," which are placed close to each other in Figure 1, but they already distinguish well between, say, "Action" and "Feelings and Emotions," which are located in Figure 1 at a distance from each other.

4. Several empirical studies of cognitive functions based on hypotheses using the relative proximities of meaning dimensions according to the circle of Figure 1 have yielded results that fully confirmed the hypotheses, and that thus lent further support to the circle model (S. Kreitler & H. Kreitler, 1986b, 1987e, 1988c; Kreitler, Drechsler, & Kreitler, 1988).

The third general remark concerns the level of abstractness of the meaning dimensions. It will be noted that, in some cases (e.g., *Dim* 21 and *Dim* 22), sub-dimensions are listed. Subdimensions are groupings of meaning values that share some common characteristic(s) of content in addition to the characteristics of the meaning dimension shared by all meaning values subsumed under that dimension. The listed subdimensions were defined on the basis of developmental studies (S. Kreitler & H. Kreitler, 1987c,e) showing that the subdimensions were initially used as distinct dimensions and were only gradually integrated into a common category. However, we mentioned subdimensions only when they provided more information than the integrated dimension. The same is true of the subdivisions in the dimension "Sensory Qualities." It is evident that there is a continuum of decreasing generality, from the label of the meaning dimension, through subdimensions, and through further subdivisions down to a highly specific meaning value. Despite the relations between the levels, each level contributes a unique aspect to the characterization of the meaning value of this level, so that the application of subdimensions (and/or subdivisions) cannot replace the application of the total dimension. The decision to consider subdimensions and/or subdivisions in addition to the meaning dimension itself depends on the hypotheses of the particular study (see also S. Kreitler & H. Kreitler, 1988b).

The fourth and last remark concerns the dynamic aspects of the manifestations of meaning dimensions. It will be noted that meaning dimensions can be conceived of not only as categories of contents but also as thought processes. For example, the dimension "Antecedents and Causes" corresponds to processes of casual thinking, "Contextual Allocation" to processes of classification or categorization, "Consequences and Results" to processes of inference and implication, and so on. From a static point of view, meaning dimensions can be regarded as categories for coding the manner in which a meaning value characterizes a referent. From a dynamic point of view, they are strategies for the retrieval of cognitive content and its formulation into meaning values according to the respective dimensional rule. Yet each meaning dimension functions also as a retrieval strategy for its own previously formed meaning values for reassignment to the original referent or assignment to another referent. Both the more static and the more dynamic conceptions of meaning dimensions can be applied simultaneously in the same domain of investigation; we used this approach in some of the studies reported in this book (e.g., Studies 7, 11, and 12). In such cases, the meaning dimension that characterizes the process is called the *major meaning dimension*, whereas the meaning dimension(s) characterizing the content in regard to which the process is applied is called the *auxiliary dimension*. For example, a cognitive task that requires the classification of emotional stimuli may be characterized in terms of "Contextual Allocation" as a major dimension and "Feelings and Emotions" as an auxiliary dimension.

Types of Relation

Types of relation (*TR*) characterize the manner in which a meaning value of any meaning dimension is related to the referent. The relation may be more-and-less immediate and may involve different processes. Statically seen, types of relation are nonevaluative merely descriptive categories for coding the directness of the relations between the referent and the meaning value, or, dynamically seen, strategies for establishing more or less direct and complex relations between the referent and meaning value. Four major kinds of types of relation were defined on the basis of the data, each including two or more variants that may be coded in addition to the overall type of relation:

TR 1. The Attributive Relation: The meaning values are related to the referent directly as qualities, features, properties, events, actions, or other characteristics. The two variants are (1) the substantive relation (*TR* 1a), in which meaning values are presented as qualities or properties of the referent, viewed as a concrete or abstract substance (i.e., a static substance–quality relation), for example, *book*, "it is full of information, it has a cover, it is often on a shelf," and (2) the actional relation (*TR* 1b), in which meaning values are presented as characteristics or properties dependent on the activity of the referent, viewed as a concrete or abstract agent, or "doer" (i.e., a more dynamic doer–action relation), for example, *book*, "provides a lot of information, is bound with a cover, is placed on a shelf."

TR 2. The Comparative Relation: The meaning values are related to the referent indirectly through the mediation of another referent, which is typically on a level of generality or abstractness similar to that of the original referent, sometimes without even stating the actual meaning values. The four variants are (1) the relation of similarity (*TR* 2a), which includes identity or synonymy, equivalence, match, and similarity in some specified, unspecified, or implied sense (e.g., isomorphism or homeormorphism), for example, *moon*, "like the earth"; *perfection*, "like happiness, both are fictions"; (2) the relation of dissimilarity (*TR* 2b), which includes difference, mismatch, contradiction, contrast, reversal, inversion and antonymy, for example, *day*, "the opposite of night"; *breathing*, "different from sleeping"; (3) the relation of complementarity (*TR* 2c), which includes reciprocity, for example, *Friends*, "help each other"; and (4) the relational relation (*TR* 2d), which consists of stating the meaning value in a manner that implies some other meaning value or referent serving as a standard for comparison explicitly (i.e., in explicitly comparative terms like *higher than* and *best*) or implicitly (i.e., in apparently noncomparative terms like *high* and *wide*) (Bierwisch, 1967; Sapir, 1944), for example, *New York*, "the craziest and noisiest city in the world"; *highway*, "a wider and busier street than the regular ones, including more lanes in each direction."

TR 3. The Exemplifying-Illustrative Relation: The meaning values relate to the referent as examples. The three variants are (1) an exemplifying instance (*TR* 3a), which presents the meaning value through an object, an event, an animal, or a person assigned the role of example for the referent or some aspect(s) of the referent; instances might be *red*, it is the color of the dress (the dress is actually pointed out); *evil*, "war"; *if*, "one may say 'if you don't come, I'll be sad'"; (2) an exemplifying situation (*TR* 3b), which presents the meaning value through the image of a situation that is richer in details than an exemplifying instance, may depict some activity, and may even suggest some duration but lacks dynamism and development, for example, *playing*, "a child sits on the floor doing things with toys"; *motherhood*, "a woman with a baby in her arms"; (3) an exemplifying scene (*TR* 3c), which presents the meaning value through an unfolding situation or story or a sequence of events, structured in a scenodynamic way, with dynamism and duration, for example, *aggression*, "the kids were playing in the yard, then they split into two groups and played war, beating one another, and then when they got really heated up with the game, they caught a cat and tortured it to death."

TR 4. The Metaphoric-Symbolic Relation: The meaning values are drawn from domains that do not, as a rule, belong strictly to the referent's conventional spheres of connotation or denotation but relate to the referent metaphorically, through the intermediation of another referent, mostly more concrete or specific than the original referent. The four main variants are (1) the relation of interpretation (*TR* 4a), which consists of presenting some nonconventional interpretation of the referent stated in abstract terms, for example, *happiness*, "that which can never be found in whatever is found"; (2) the conventional metaphor (*TR* 4b), which uses a meaning value that is itself a metaphoric idiom, for example, *love*, "to have a broken heart"; (3) the metaphor proper (*TR* 4c), which consists of presenting some information about the referent through a relatively concrete instance, situation, or scene that does not belong to the referent's conventional spheres of connotation or denotation, for example, *wisdom*, "like a cool drink on a hot day"; *love*, "an intense glow of light"; (4) the symbol—a particular kind of complex metaphor—which includes several features of similarity between the metaphoric image and the original referent, among which there is at least one pair of contrasting features reflecting a problem that is resolved through the metaphoric image (S. Kreitler, 1965; H. Kreitler & S. Kreitler, 1972c), for example, *love*, "it is like a river that constantly changes and renews itself yet remains always the same."

Modes of Meaning: The modes of meaning include (1) the lexical mode (*Lex Mode*), in which the lexical or interpersonally shared meaning is defined by the attributive and the comparative types of relation, and (2) the personal mode (*Pers Mode*), in which the personal or subjective meaning is defined by the exemplifying-illustrative and the metaphoric-symbolic types of relation.

This distinction is based on empirical findings that showed that the lexical mode predominates when subjects are asked to communicate interpersonally shared conventional meaning, whereas the personal mode predominates when they are asked to communicate subjective meanings (Kreitler, Kreitler, & Wanounou, 1988c). The types of relation defining the modes determine further characteristics in which the modes differ, for example, concreteness, imaginal character, extent of personal references, and interdependence among the meaning values. The distinction resembles, in some respects, the distinctions between socialized and egocentric meanings (Piaget, 1948), external and internal meanings (Vygotsky, 1962), symbolic and emotive meanings (Ogden & Richards, 1949), lexicalized meaning and sense (Werner & Kaplan, 1963), or signs and symbols (Cassirer, 1953; Jung, 1964). Thus, statically seen, modes indicate whether the meaning value characterizes the referent conventionally (lexical mode) or unconventionally (personal mode). From the dynamic point of view, they are strategies for the selection of meaning values and, to a lesser extent, may codetermine the selection of meaning dimensions and types of relation, for example, the personal mode elicits the metaphoric type of relation.

Forms of Relation

The forms of relation (*FR*) characterize the relation of meaning values to referents from the logical-formal point of view. Thus, statically seen, forms of relation are evaluative categories for the meaning-value referent relations, or dynamically seen, they are strategies that denote whether and to which extent a meaning value characterizes the referent, for example, whether it is, it is not, or it is either this or that. The forms of relation are:

1. *Assertion or Positive Relation (FR 1):* The meaning value refers positively to the referent, for example, *table*, "a piece of furniture."
2. *Negative Relation or Denial (FR 2):* The meaning value is related to the referent negatively, for example, *Yoga*, "it is not a religion."
3. *The Mixed or Restrictive Relation (FR 3):* The positive relation of meaning value to the referent is restricted in terms of range, frequency, circumstances, intensity, and so on, for example, *apple*, "sometimes red"; *winter*, "may be cold."
4. *Conjunction (FR 4):* At least two stated meaning values apply jointly to the referent, for example, *home*, "where you live and feel at ease."
5. *Disjunction (FR 5):* Of the two stated meaning values, only one applies to the referent but not both (i.e., the disjunction is exclusive), at least not without further restrictions of time, place, and so on, for example, *baby*, "is either awake or asleep."
6. *Obligatory Relation (FR 6):* The meaning value is related to the referent necessarily (somewhat in the manner specified by deontological logic), for example, *law*, "must be obeyed."
7. *Double Negation (FR 7):* Both of at least two stated meaning values are jointly related negatively to the referent, for example, *happiness*, "neither exists nor should be aspired to."
8. *Combined Positive and Negative Relation (FR 8):* Of two jointly stated meaning values, one applies positively while the other, not necessarily a contrasted one, applies negatively, for example, *sun*, "it is a medium-sized but not an old star."

A grouping of the forms of relation into positive and negative ones (see Appendix A) conforms to the view of traditional logic that admits only assertion and negation as basic forms but does not obviate the need to code separately each category that highlights a unique aspect of forms of relation.

Shifts in Referents

In coding meaning values in terms of dimensions, types, and forms of relation, it is important to consider the actual referent of the response, which is rarely identical to the referent presented by the experimenter and often changes from one meaning value to another. It is, in principle, possible to distinguish between initial shifts in referents (*SR*), which describe the shifts from the initial referent presented by the experimenter to the first actual referent of the subject (e.g., the presented referent is *coconut*, but the subject refers from the start to "the wooden shell of the coconut") and shifts in the course of actual meaning assignment (e.g., from "wooden shells" to "hollow barks"). Initial shifts can be distinguished only if there is a presented referent with a clear identification, sharp outlines, and a conventional interpersonally accepted label (e.g., an object or a word). Otherwise, it makes sense to speak, not of initial shifts, but of referent(s) specification by the subject as the first stage of meaning assignment. However, because an initial shift can also be considered a shift in regard to a previous referent (i.e., the one presented by the experimenter), the difference between the two kinds of shifts is not essential. Therefore, we combined the lists of the two varieties of shifts in referents into one list. When viewed statically, shifts in referents can be considered as indicators of the kind and amount of cognitive flexibility, whereas in dynamic terms, they are strategies for extending the scope of meaning assignment. The list of shifts in referents is:

1. *The actual referent is identical to the presented referent (SR 1)*; for example, the presented referent is *car*, and the subject's actual referent is *car*.
2. *The actual referent is the negation (the inverse or opposite) of the presented referent (SR 2)*; for example, the presented referent is *love* but the subject responds to *hate*.
3. *Actual referent is a part of the presented referent (SR 3)*; for example, the presented referent is *car*, and the actual referent is *tires* or *Volvo*.
4. *The referent is the whole or a part of a previous meaning value (SR 4)*; for example, the presented referent is *TV*, and the response is "A machine that shows films for entertainment." In this response, "shows films" is both a meaning value of *machine* and a referent for *entertainment*.
5. *The actual referent is the presented referent combined with a previous meaning value (SR 5)*; for example, the presented referent is *submarine*, and the first response is "It can be yellow." In the further response, the actual referent may be *the yellow submarine*.
6. *The referent is a combination of several previous meaning values (SR 6)*; for example, the presented referent is *to eat*, and the response is "You can eat bread, spaghetti, rolls; all these carbohydrates make you fat." In this response, *all these carbohydrates* is a referent reflecting a combination of three previous meaning values (i.e., bread, spaghetti, rolls).
7. *The actual referent is related to the presented or previous referent only by some association (SR 7)*; for example, the presented referent is *home*, and the actual referent is *my cats*, the probable association being that cats stay in the home.
8. *The actual referent is a grammatical variation of the presented referent (SR 8)*. This can occur when the presented referent is a word and the variations involve shifts in terms of parts of speech, that is, across the categories of noun, verb, adjective, adverb, gender, number (singular and plural), tenses, declensions, and so on; for example, the presented referent is *to eat*, and the actual referent may be *ate*, *eating*, or *having eaten*.
9. *The actual referent is the presented referent treated as a label (SR 9)*. This can occur when the presented referent is a word or some other conventional sign and involves a shift from the contents denoted by the label to the characteristics of the label itself (e.g., its elements, sound or color, or etymological features).
10. *The actual referent is not related in any obvious way to the presented or the previous referent (SR 10)*. That is, the relation, neither explained nor implied by the

available information, may represent a sudden leap (short-circuiting) from one sphere to another or may derive from an unreported chain of associations; for example, the presented referent is *street*, and the subject responds to *pen*.

On the basis of unanimous judgments by six independent judges (three graduate students and three Ph.D. psychologists), the 10 shifts were grouped into two classes: relatively smaller shifts (Nos. 1, 3, 4, 5, and 8) and relatively larger shifts (Nos. 2, 6, 7, 9, 10). Because most of the *SR* variables refer to initial shifts, the extent of the shifts may be expected to reflect the degree of acceptance of interpersonally established reality (see also S. Kreitler & H. Kreitler, 1986b).

A BRIEF INTERIM SUMMARY

Meaning analysis is focused on coding various aspects of directly or indirectly presented meaning communications. The two major elements of such a communication are the referent and the meaning value. Together, they form a meaning unit. The content of the meaning value is analyzed in terms of meaning dimensions. The relation of the meaning value to the referent is analyzed in terms of types of relation (including modes of meaning) and forms of relation. The referent is characterized in terms of its relation to the previous referent, including the referent presented by the experimenter (referent shifts). Appendix A presents a standard list and code of the meaning variables, which the reader will need to consult often in the course of reading the book. Appendix C presents instructions for coding materials in terms of the meaning system.

At first glance, the number of meaning variables may seem bewildering, but if one considers the functions of the presented variables, one may end up wondering whether the list is long enough. The meaning variables are designed to serve as tools for assessing all sorts of human communications of meaning, verbal and nonverbal, and hence to enable the characterization and analysis of all content in all kinds of contexts. In view of the variety, richness, and diversity of manifestations of human content, it may appear surprising that 22 meaning dimensions proved sufficient for the task. However, the list includes further sets of variables designed to characterize modifiers of the expressions of the content and transformation of the referents.

Yet, the test for the adequacy of the system is the evidence, mentioned earlier, of the role of these meaning variables in the cognitive functioning of individuals (H. Kreitler & S. Kreitler, 1983, 1984d, 1989; S. Kreitler & H. Kreitler, 1984a, 1985b, 1987b,c,d,e, 1988c, 1989b,c). A system that enables insight into the cognitive processes involved in a whole array of cognitive and noncognitive tasks must necessarily be fairly complex. In addition, when considering the length of the list, it is important to emphasize the manner in which it is used. It constitutes an inventory of all the variables relevant to scoring the meaning communications of all human beings about all kinds of stimuli. Yet, in scoring one meaning communication of one person, it is necessary to use only a few of the variables. By the same token, no cognitive act by any human being involves all the processes corresponding to these variables. Accordingly, the list is long because (1) it is comprehensive; (2) it is designed for the assessment of an exceedingly rich and complex domain; and (3) it constitutes a complete system from which selections are drawn that characterize a particular communication, content, or cognitive act.

Finally, lest the reader become discouraged, it should be noted that our students regularly learn to apply the meaning system to the actual coding of materials in a matter of several hours. Understanding the system is much less demanding in time and effort. To our mind, the investment is worthwhile because the meaning system provides tools for exploring the whole array of personality traits and situations and enables important insights into their role in human behavior.

THE MEANING PROFILE

As mentioned in the first section of this chapter, the communicability of meaning and its frequently discussed role in interpersonal communication should not mislead us into overlooking its various intrapersonal functions. Meaning not only constitutes the basis of cognition, defined above as the meaning-processing system, but also influences phenomena like emotions, which despite the compelling evidence (e.g., Frijda, 1986), are still discussed without explicit reference to meaning. Imagine the following situation: While you are walking on a crowded street, someone bumps into you and, instead of uttering the habitual phrases of apology starts shouting insulting words at you. It is very likely that you will become angry, too. Yet, upon closer observation, you realize that the person is blind. Would not the sudden change in the meaning of the situation at once modify your emotion? According to the evidence accumulated in our laboratory, this change in meaning would bring about a change in the emotional reaction. Similarly, the information that there is free coffee and cake at the cafeteria may stimulate your appetite. Then again, it may not if you get the further information that the coffee is cold and the cake moldy. The intentional triviality of these examples underscores not only the general intrapersonal importance of meaning, but also the almost tragic neglect by psychologists (for a long time, us included) of the study of meaning, meaning processes, meaning impacts, and meaning potentials. An important key to studies of this kind is the meaning profile.

A meaning profile is a summary statement about a series of scored meaning communications. When the statement summarizes the coded meaning responses given by one individual to different inputs, then we call it the individual's meaning profile. There are two further kinds of meaning profiles. One is the meaning profile of a specific input, which summarizes the meaning communications of many individuals in regard to that input (e.g., a situation or a poem). Another is the meaning profile of a group, which summarizes the meaning communications of many individuals in regard to many inputs. In this book, we discuss only the individual's meaning profile.

Just as X-ray and ultrasound images of skeleton and muscles do not show all the movements that the client may perform, so the meaning profile does not reflect the myriad meaning values that a subject may be capable of producing or retrieving. What the profile shows are the meaning dimensions, types of relations, and forms of relations between the referent and the meaning values, as well as the kinds of referent shifts the subject is likely to use. This information reflects the basic content

characteristics and the essential features of content elaboration that, to the best of our knowledge, constitute the nuclei of cognitive processes that span the whole gamut of cognitive acts, from guided attention and input identification to complex cognitive skills including creativity (see references in the first section of this chapter and in following chapters). In short, the meaning profile informs us about the subject's meaning potentials.

The meaning profile is obtained by summing the subject's scored responses to the meaning questionnaire. The meaning questionnaire requests the subject to respond to a standard set of 11 terms: *to create, street, life, bicycle, feeling, to take, friendship, art, to murder, sea (ocean)*, and *telephone*. The terms were selected, on the basis of extensive pretests, as those that together provide opportunities for the evocation and application of all meaning variables. The subjects receive the list of terms together with the following standard instructions:

Questionnaire of Meaning

In this questionnaire there is a list of words. Your task is to communicate the meaning of each word. Imagine there is someone (you may choose any person you want) who does not know the meaning of the particular word but understands language and other forms of expression, such as drawings or gestures. Please communicate to that person the meaning of each word—both the generally accepted meaning (what it means in general) and the personal meaning (what it means to you personally).

You may use any means of communication you consider adequate—words, drawings, descriptions of drawings, movements, etc. The main thing is that the other person will learn what each word means in general and to you.

Please, do not use translations into other languages and do not write merely associations, but try to express the meanings—both general and personal.

For special purposes there are two further versions of the instructions, one emphasizing the "general meaning" and the other the "personal meaning." Both versions are identical to the standard version in the first three sentences, after which the "general meaning" version continues thus:

Please communicate to that person the generally accepted meaning of each word, so that most of those who know the meanings of the words would agree with what you write or describe.

You may use any means of communication you consider adequate—words, drawings, descriptions of drawings, gestures, etc. You may also try to express the meaning in different ways. The main thing is that the other person will learn what the general meaning of each word is.

Please do not use translations into other languages and do not write merely associations, but try to focus only on the general meaning and to communicate it as precisely and completely as you can.

The version of instructions for "personal meaning" continues thus after the first three sentences of the standard version:

Please communicate to that person the personal meaning of each word for you, that is, what the word means to you personally.

You may use any means of communication you consider adequate—words, drawings, descriptions of drawings, gestures, etc. You may also try to express the meaning in different ways. The main thing is to "open up," as it were, to the different words, and to communicate the personal meaning of the words so that the other person will know what they mean to you personally.

Please do not use translations into other languages and do not write merely associations, but try to focus only on the deepest and truest meaning of the words to you and to communicate it as precisely, clearly, and completely as you can.

Regardless of the specific set of instructions used, the meaning communication of one input consists mostly of several meaning units (i.e., combinations of referent plus meaning value). Each meaning unit is coded on all four sets of meaning variables, one from each set. The coding on the variables of each set is independent of that on other sets. Thus, the analysis of one meaning unit consists of assigning to it four parameters: one meaning dimension, one type of relation, one form of relation, and one referent shift. The summing of the coded responses of one subject across all inputs on each meaning variable separately yields the individual's meaning profile. Thus, the meaning profile is the set of frequencies with which the subject uses each of the meaning variables in responding to the meaning questionnaire. (For information about intercoder and test–retest reliability, see the introductory remarks in Chapter 9. Appendix C presents instructions for coding the meaning questionnaire.)

In itself, the individual's meaning profile is merely a test result indicating the meaning potentials of a particular subject. But when considered in conjunction with the well-supported assumptions about the various functions of meaning, the meaning profile provides information that may be useful in various domains of psychological research. These domains may be as many and varied as the functions and influences of what was earlier designated vaguely as the underlying level. Meaning is probably not the deepest level underlying mental processes, but for the time being, it is the deepest and most profound we know.

ZIGZAGGING TOWARD A HYPOTHESIS

Active and Passive Mastery of Meaning Variables

Sometimes the gap between a promising idea and a testable hypothesis is amazingly wide. In the present case, we had to evaluate and reevaluate former studies in different fields, zigzagging between different considerations, until we stumbled on a previously overlooked phenomenon that proved to be the key element of a new and more efficient trait concept.

The extensive research that led us to the development of the meaning system showed that mentally normal subjects made active use of from 11 to 17 or 18 meaning dimensions as well as of some forms and types of relation. But the use of inputs with strong demand characteristics, direct questioning, and the administration of some coaching or brief training showed that these subjects were capable of understanding inputs coined in terms of meaning variables that they did not use habitually or proficiently. Thus, it became evident that these subjects had a passive command of all or almost all meaning variables. Doing better or worse on cognitive tasks (see the first section of this chapter "The Underlying Level") was found to be correlated with the active and proficient application of task-relevant meaning variables, but not with passive command. The same held true for the positive and significant correlation of IQ scores with the number of different meaning variables over which the subject had active command. The absence of both passive and active command over the majority of meaning variables was found only in several retarded individuals and, to some extent, in brain-damaged patients (H. Kreitler & S. Kreitler, 1977; S. Kreitler & H. Kreitler, 1989a). Because relatively mild means, such as changes in inputs or moderate manipulations, sufficed to induce normal individuals to make *ad hoc* use of all meaning variables, the distinction between an active and a passive command of meaning variables relates more to function than to potential.

This conclusion was highlighted by the results of a microgenetic study, which actually indicated to us the "where" and "what" of a possible relationship between traits and meaning variables. The study dealt with the identification of microgenetically presented visual inputs: words, line drawings, black-and-white photographs, color paintings, and color photographs (S. Kreitler & H. Kreitler, 1977, 1984a). Normal adult subjects were requested to identify the inputs that were presented tachistoscopically in a series of exposures with gradually increased duration, illumination, and clarity of focus. In the beginning of the first phase of identification, all subjects used at least one of the three most relevant meaning dimensions, that is, "Sensory Qualities" (i.e., brightness), "Locational Qualities," and "Quantity," and, in addition, applied the dimension of "Contextual Allocation" in their attempts to specify the referent, even though mostly in a vague form (e.g., "it is something").

Homogeneity of applied meaning dimensions also characterized the further steps of the first phase: "Sensory Qualities" (i.e., form) and "Structure," followed by "Sensory Qualities" (i.e., color) and "Size." The first phase ended with primary input identification (e.g., a triangle or a human figure). In the second, and particularly the third, phases of identification, the subject began to elaborate on the input in increasingly personal terms, using many meaning dimensions. In the second phase, there was still some similarity in the perceptions of different individuals, but this similarity depended on the general class of the referent that the subject identified. For example, subjects who identified human referents reported meaning values along the dimensions of "State" and "Action." In contrast, subjects who identified nonhuman referents concentrated predominantly on meaning values of the dimension "Structure." However, the highest degree of personal elaboration of the inputs was found in the third phase, and it was here that the correlations were highest between the subjects' meaning profile and the meaning variables that the subject applied in elaborating on the perceived inputs. In other words, the meaning variables used most frequently in the meaning test were those applied most frequently in the extended input elaboration. For example, in the case of 95% of the subjects, one of the three most frequently used meaning dimensions in the meaning profile was applied in the third phase of the microgenetic elaborations.

Preferred Meaning Variables

It was at this point that we first began to consider the utility of a distinction between the meaning potential of a person and his or her meaning preferences. The difference became highly salient through a replication of the microgenetic study, carried out not with normal subjects but with chronic hospitalized schizophrenics (Kreitler & Kreitler, 1986b). From the first phase onward, these subjects tended to distort the input, to ignore its demand characteristics, to assign primarily personal meanings, and even to invent new inputs. But many of them found an opportunity, sometimes in the third stage, or even after concluding the identification task, to let us know that they knew what the input was. For example, one patient said, "You wanted me to see a triangle but it was the grotesque mask that the group therapist usually wears," or "If it had not been for the voices commanding me otherwise, I might have succeeded in reading the word, which I think was *guitar*." Reexamination of the patient's performance on the input identification task in conjunction with their meaning profiles showed that most of the distortions by the schizophrenics were due not to deficiencies in their meaning potentials but to an exaggerated use of preferred meaning-assignment tendencies.

Still, without any clear notion or even a hunch about the psychological significance of meaning preferences, but somehow attracted by the concept, we first decided on its more precise definition. We defined *preferred meaning variables* as those meaning variables whose frequencies appear in the highest quartile or in the lowest quartile of the frequency distribution in the subject's meaning profile. The former are to be designated as positive meaning preferences or positive meaning-assignment tendencies; the latter, as negative meaning preferences or negative meaning-assignment tendencies.

In line with this definition, we recoded the previously obtained meaning profiles of adult subjects who had performed the meaning test under special conditions. In one of these studies, originally designed to check the test's consistency over time, the subjects ($n = 55$) responded to the same standard questionnaire three or four times, in intervals ranging from 5 to 20 weeks. In another study, the subjects ($n = 60$) responded to the questionnaire first under regular conditions and then again a week later, after having heard a two-hour lecture about the meaning system and all its variables. In a further study, subjects ($n = 30$) took the meaning test once without any time limitation (the usual duration of the test is 25–30 minutes) and then again with a severe time limitation (i.e., 8 minutes). In another study, the meaning test was completed by a group of subjects ($n = 40$) once under normal conditions and once under distracting conditions of noise and commotion.

Two further variations were tested. One included changes in the standard list of words so that the subjects ($n = 30$) responded not only to the original list but also to lists of inputs varying, to different degrees, from the standard list. Another variation included changes in the response format, so that the subjects ($n = 30$) responded on one occasion in the free-expression form of the original test and on another occasion by selecting responses or completing partial responses from a list containing responses or examples of responses along all meaning variables.

The results of all these studies showed that individual meaning preferences, both the positive and the negative ones, were amazingly stable across the different conditions. They recurred in 81%–100% of the cases despite changes in conditions, inputs, and response formats, whereas the meaning variables with medium frequency in the individual's meaning profile had a much lower rate of recurrence (40%–65%). Further, training of meaning variables (e.g., Arnon & Kreitler, 1984; Ensenberg, 1976; S. Kreitler & H. Kreitler, 1987a, 1989b; Lahav, 1982) indicated that the positive and negative meaning preferences were less susceptible to experimental changes and manipulations than the medium-frequency meaning variables.

On the Track of Function

The function of meaning preferences was still an enigma. Rereading our studies on meaning and cognitive functioning, we found that, in every case, the decisive factor in successful performance was the availability of the task-relevant meaning variables in the subject's meaning profile rather than positive or negative meaning preferences. Thus, for example, planning requires, among other meaning variables, the availability of the meaning dimension "Manner of Occurrence and Operation." The likelihood that a person would successfully complete a series of planning tasks increased if this dimension was included in his or her meaning profile, regardless of whether it was positively preferred. Of course, an overlap of preference and task relevance proved to constitute a particularly favorable antecedent of successful cognitive functioning in that task (S. Kreitler & H. Kreitler, 1987b,c).

The first glimmer of an idea about the possible function of meaning preferences arose in conjunction with a study of the content and considerations characterizing the plans formed by subjects (S. Kreitler & H. Kreitler, 1986a). For example, different individuals may consider emotional impact or formal functional arrangements or financial implications or aesthetic aspects, and so on. This content proved to be independent of the quality of the plan itself. More important, it was correlated highly with the individual's preferred meaning variables. Again, children tended to pursue their curiosity by using, for exploration, means corresponding to their preferred meaning-assignment tendencies—for example, manipulation, if they had a preference for the meaning dimension "Action," or observation, if they had a preference for the meaning dimension "Sensory Qualities" (S. Kreitler & H. Kreitler, 1986c). We felt that it was not a coincidence that the preferred meaning variables affected cognitive performance more in a relatively unstructured framework than they did in a structured task.

However, a stronger lead emerged from the behavior prediction studies. When we rechecked the material of more than 40 successful predictions of human overt behavior, carried out in line with the theory of cognitive orientation (H. Kreitler & S. Kreitler, 1976, 1982), we found no significant correlations of preferences for meaning variables with the executed overt behaviors. Indeed, no correlations should have been expected, because of the gap in level of generality between the meaning variables and the behaviors. The meaning variables are on a more general level than the predicted and executed behaviors, for example, giving up smoking after behavioral therapy, coming on time, doing better or worse after success and after failure, or reacting to an anxiety-evoking situation either with danger control or with fear control (see in Chapter 3, "Behavioral Manifestations of Meaning Preferences"; S. Kreitler & H. Kreitler, 1984c, 1989c).

Fortunately, we did find some significant correlations, which, though neither impressively high nor theoretically surprising, led our considerations in a promising direction. These medium-level correlations showed that individual meaning preferences were related to the matrix of beliefs that constitutes the core of our procedure of behavior prediction. This matrix we call the *cognitive orientation cluster* (CO cluster), and it consists of four kinds of beliefs that the individual holds: (1) beliefs concerning one's goals; (2) beliefs concerning norms, rules, and standards; (3) beliefs about oneself; and (4) general beliefs, that is, about the environment and other people. Together, these beliefs orient the individual toward a particular act of overt behavior that will be carried out provided that particular conditions specified by the CO theory are met. The conditions include the availability of an adequate behavioral program, the absence of a competing CO cluster, and, most important, support of the same behavior by at least three of the four kinds or components of beliefs.

We regard belief as a unit of cognitive content that consists of at least two meaning values related by a third; for example, in the belief "John loves Mary," the related meaning values are *John* and *Mary*, and the relating meaning value is *loves*.

Because all beliefs, regardless of their behavioral direction, consist of meaning values, preferred meaning variables are more likely than other meaning variables to influence belief formation and belief retrieval. This is why the preferred meaning variables were correlated to some extent with CO clusters but not with the actual behaviors.

As already mentioned, CO clusters are manifestations of behavioral inclinations that, pending sufficient belief support, may produce a behavioral intent, which, in turn, may be executed by the adoption of a behavioral program. However, the term *behavioral inclination* has often been used in the definition of traits (Cattell, 1965; Eysenck, 1970; Pervin, 1980). In which respect, then, do CO clusters differ from traits, and how are they similar? It was this question that eventually set our theorizing on the right track.

It was obvious from the very start that CO clusters and traits differ in their specificity and their potential for behavior predicting. CO clusters are input-initiated; that is, they are retrieved or formed for the sole purpose of coping with the given input situation. Moreover, the behavioral inclination reflected by the CO cluster points to a particular act in which only the how of performance remains unspecified. Thus, the correlations of CO clusters with individually preferred meaning-assignment tendencies can be only marginal. In contrast, the same trait can be activated by a wide range of different input situations, and the so-called trait-specific manifestations are manifested by a wide range of different behavioral acts. Therefore, one can expect the impact of underlying meaning preferences to be almost unlimited, perhaps even to such an extent that traits can be defined in terms of underlying meaning preferences. However, it would be justified to suggest such a definition only if it could be shown (1) that the definition entails satisfactory explanations of all trait manifestations, and (2) that the definition holds in regard to all known personality traits.

Some Assumptions and the Hypotheses

Could meaning preferences be expected to do this very demanding job? Could it be shown that they fulfill the requirements for entering into a new definition of traits? The odds appeared considerable. One main problem seemed to us to be the multiplicity of trait manifestations. Each of the better studied personality traits, and probably some of the others too, is known to have a great variety of manifestations, often inconsistent with each other. Hence, a single preferred meaning-assignment tendency cannot suffice to account for all or even some of these manifestations, particularly the contradictory ones. We had to assume that several meaning variables—a pattern or group, sometimes perhaps even several subgroups—would be required in order to do justice to each trait. Furthermore, because the traits differ, we assumed that the patterns of meaning variables had to be unique.

Beyond these assumptions, the major remaining question was: Which are the meaning variables relevant to traits? Conclusions based on previous studies concerning typical manifestations of meaning variables could provide only fragmentary and limited information and unreliable hints. It seemed obvious that answers could be obtained only through a broad-ranged set of empirical studies focused on this problem. We were aware of the possibility that the answers obtained could invalidate our expectations totally or partially. In the former case, no trait-specific groups of meaning preferences would be found for any of the commonly assessed personality traits; in the latter case, they would be found for some, but not all, traits. In both cases, the result would be the same: The old quagmire would merely be replaced by a new one, and the whole effort would be wasted. Nonetheless, the idea of preferred meaning-assignment tendencies as the dynamic agents underlying traits was sufficiently tempting for us to undertake these risks.

Eventually we formulated the following two hypotheses:

1. Each of 76 of the better known and most commonly assessed personality traits will correlate with a unique pattern of preferred meaning variables.

2. The patterns of meaning variables correlated with the traits will increase our understanding of the nature and dynamics of traits in general and of the functioning of each of the studied traits in particular. Thus, the findings would help to provide satisfactory answers to the questions posed in Chapter 1.

The project designed to provide the answers was structured so that it included 22 studies, each devoted to one or several traits (see Part II). Each study was expected to fulfill three functions: (1) to provide information relevant to testing the two hypotheses stated above; (2) to contribute to the resolution of some problem concerning the relation of meaning variables and traits (e.g., does the pattern of interrelations of a trait with meaning variables differ from the meaning assigned by the subjects directly to the label of a trait?—Study 10); and (3) to contribute, through the application of meaning, to the resolution of some problem specific to the studied trait or group of traits (e.g., are there two subtypes of external control?—Study 12).

Common to all the studies was the administration of the meaning test and one or more trait questionnaires to the participating subjects. This procedure enabled assigning to each subject a meaning profile, on the one hand, and trait scores, on the other hand. The correlations between the profiles and the scores were expected to provide the major results relevant to testing the hypotheses. The first hypothesis was expected to be confirmed if the correlations showed (1) that each trait was related to more than one preferred meaning variable, and (2) that the pattern of meaning variables related to each trait constituted a unique combination of meaning variables.

The testing of the second hypothesis required the comparison of the characteristics of each assessed personality trait with the manifestations of the meaning variables that would be correlated with the trait. The second hypothesis was expected to be confirmed if the comparisons yielded correspondences that (1) increased insight into the nature and functioning of at least the majority of the studied traits and (2) provided information relevant to traits in general.

By now, it is clear that we expected our project to yield two sets of findings: those pertaining to the trait concept in general and those pertaining to specific traits in particular. We will first discuss the findings that shed light on traits in general because this is the major theme of this book, and because dealing first with this theme will facilitate the later discussion of particular traits.

The Trait and Its Constituents

THE MAJOR FINDING

The results of 22 studies, in which 1,811 subjects participated, show that each of the 76 common personality traits correlates with a pattern of preferred meaning variables which is unique in its composition. This major finding deserves to be stated at the outset so as to serve as a guideline for the discussion in the subsequent chapters of Part I. The results of Studies 1–20 are summarized in Table 1 (Studies 21 and 22 served for control and further elaboration). At a later date—after completion of Parts I and II of the manuscript—the project was extended to two further sets of traits, those assessed by the Minnesota Multiphasic Personality Inventory (MMPI) and Jackson's Personality Research Form (PRF) scales (see Part III). The findings from these sets confirmed the conclusions obtained in the studies presented in Part II and served to extend them and to demonstrate their application. There is thus sufficient evidence for the generality of our findings. Moreover, as shown in this and the following chapter, conceiving of each trait in terms of its underlying meaning preferences widens our understanding of traits and explains many of the trait manifestations that were before regarded as inconsistent. Therefore, we feel justified in defining traits as unique patterns of meaning preferences or, in more dynamic terms, as patterns of preferred meaning-assignment tendencies.

Before describing the patterns of meaning preferences and their implications, it may be important to note that the patterns were found to be stable across different samples (e.g., in Studies 3 and 4), across different measures for the same trait (e.g., in Studies 8 and 9), and to some extent even across meaning questionnaires that included stimuli different from those included in the standard meaning questionnaire (e.g., in Studies 3 and 4). Moreover, when the subjects were asked about the meaning of a particular trait, their answers did not correspond to the preferred meaning variables constituting this particular trait (Study 10). Likewise, comparisons showed that the patterns of preferred meaning variables constituting the trait were not related to the explicit content of the items included in the questionnaire on the same trait, except in some cases when the explicit content of the items referred directly to particular dynamic features of the trait (Studies 15 and 17). This finding indicates that the patterns corresponding to the traits are identical neither with the subjects' stereotypical or more personal conceptions of the trait nor with the face validity of the traits' scales.

According to the best of our professional knowledge, no artifact is involved in our recurrent finding that each trait corresponds to a pattern of preferred meaning-assignment tendencies, both positive and negative. This finding indicates that trait measures reflect the tendencies of subjects to process external inputs as well as internal stimulation by preferential use or avoidance of particular meaning dimensions, types of relation (between referents and meaning values), stimulus-referent relations, and forms of relation (between referents and meaning values). Hence, when we say that a person has a certain trait or scores high on some scale that measures the trait, what we are, in fact, saying is that the person characteristically or preferentially applies or does not apply certain meaning-assignment tendencies. Let us give some examples of single meaning-assignment tendencies bound to different traits, though they should not be mistaken for traits. Thus, we found that a person who has the trait of hypochondriasis tends to apply the meaning dimension "Sensory Qualities" (particularly "Internal Sensations") (Study 10); a person who scores high on Machiavellianism tends to apply the meaning dimension "Function, Purpose, and Role" (Studies 3–5); an authoritarian individual tends not to apply the qualified, restrictive form of relation (Study 13); and an impulsive person tends not to apply the meaning dimension "Consequences" (Study 10).

However, no person tends to apply only one meaning-assignment tendency and no trait consists of the preference for only one meaning variable. A major element in our definition of traits is the term *pattern*. This indicates operationally that each of the studied traits was correlated with several meaning preferences. This finding in itself explains why the effects of traits are often so generalized. The pattern also has structural implications for the functioning of traits.

The pattern consists of specific strong and weak meaning-assignment tendencies. When an individual's score is high on some trait, the meaning-assignment tendencies that constitute that trait characterize the individual; that is, they are the meaning-assignment tendencies preferred (positively or negatively) by the individual. What are meaning-assignment tendencies?

MEANING-ASSIGNMENT TENDENCIES

Every normal adult engages continuously in meaning assignment and has active or at least passive command of all or almost all aspects of the meaning system (Chapter 2). Meanings are assigned partly in line with the label meaning of inputs, and partly in line with individual preferences. Label meaning includes specific meaning values attached to some input by convention. For example, the label meaning of a cup includes the meaning value "used for drinking," and the label meaning of the question "What color is grass?" strongly provokes reference to the meaning value "green." By definition, label meaning is shared by members of a particular culture. Accordingly, label meaning is learned and admits of relatively little variation. Meaning assigned in line with individual preferences depends to a much greater extent on the individual but not exclusively so. It also depends on circumstances, at least in the sense that it requires cues to which meaning values of the preferred meaning variables could be applied. But it is not determined by semantic conventions or demand characteristics of inputs and their content. Hence, it admits of individual differences.

Preferred meaning-assignment tendencies depend on individual habits. As stated earlier (Chapter 2), the frequency with which a preferred tendency is applied differs from the frequencies of other meaning variables in the subject's meaning profile and in the population to which the subject belongs. Preference for a meaning variable can be assessed best under conditions that do not emphasize label meaning, including the specific demand characteristics of inputs. The standard procedure for assessing meaning in general (Chapter 2) approximates these conditions most closely. Accordingly, a positive preference for a meaning variable corresponds operationally to a high (i.e., upper-quartile) frequency of a certain meaning variable in the subject's meaning profile. In contrast, a negative preference corresponds to a low (i.e., lowest-quartile) frequency of a certain meaning variable in the subject's meaning profile.

When we have diagnosed, on the basis of the individual's meaning profile, that the individual has a preference for a particular meaning variable, this diagnosis indicates that the individual applies the particular meaning variable with a high frequency to inputs of different kinds (i.e., tends to assign meaning values to inputs in terms of that meaning variable, notes meaning values corresponding to that meaning variable, and so on). When a positively preferred meaning variable forms part of the pattern of meaning variables corresponding to a trait, the score of the trait is correlated positively with the particular meaning variable.

A negative preference or nonpreference for a meaning variable is diagnosed on the basis of a low frequency of that meaning variable in the subject's meaning profile. Hence, negative preference indicates that the individual is cognitively able to apply that meaning variable but applies it relatively less frequently than he or she applies other meaning variables. In practice, a negative preference for a meaning variable makes it likely that the individual will not tend to apply the particular meaning-assignment tendency if it is not specifically called for by the input's label meaning, and that the individual may sometimes even actively avoid its application (as shown, for example, in Study 2). Accordingly, having a negative preference for a meaning variable means that the individual tends not to apply to inputs meaning values in line with that meaning variable, tends to disregard cues suggesting meaning values relevant to that meaning variable, deemphasizes regular manifestations of that meaning variable, and so on. When a negatively preferred meaning variable forms part of the pattern of meaning variables corresponding to a trait, the score of the trait is correlated negatively with the particular meaning variable.

MANIFESTATIONS OF MEANING-ASSIGNMENT TENDENCIES

In view of our definition of traits as particular patterns of meaning-assignment tendencies, the major question becomes, then, what it is that we learn about an individual when we have established the meaning-assignment variables characteristic of her or him. Studies 1–22 (see Part II and also Appendix B) show the kind of statements that may be made about individuals who prefer one or another meaning variable. For example, a person who applies preferentially the meaning dimension "Judgments and Evaluations" (say, *Dim* 21a) tends to be concerned with values, judgments (Study 2), and moral standards (Study 6); has a high superego strength and a strong sense of duty; is conscientious and critical of others as well as of himself or herself (Study 6); and so on. Again, an individual who does not apply this dimension (or who has a trait that correlates negatively with "Judgments and Evaluations," *Dim* 21a) tends to react psychopathically, does not worry about the judgment of others (Study 6), often disregards the evaluations of others (Study 1), readily changes opinions and attitudes in response to persuasion, is uninhibited (Study 6), is uncritical in endorsing statements (Study 8), and so on.

The above examples constitute instances of what we call manifestations of a preferred or nonpreferred meaning-assignment variable. We found specific manifestations for each meaning variable, often supported by the findings of more than one study and by complementary results in regard to the preferred and nonpreferred use of the meaning variable. In the case of only very few meaning variables were the available data limited. To our mind, this scarcity is due merely to insufficient current information and suggests the need for specific investigations of these variables. The data concerning any particular variable are never contradictory but always repetitious or complementary, a fact that greatly increases the validity of the findings. All the results of our investigations about the manifestations of meaning variables in the sphere of traits proper (Studies 1–22) are summarized in Appendix B.

Findings of the kind presented in Appendix B make it possible to explain in greater detail and specificity what is actually meant when we say that an individual prefers or does not prefer a certain meaning variable. Each meaning variable denotes a specific, characteristic complex of processes and domain of operation that define that meaning variable. For example, the comparative types of relation are defined by various processes of comparison and matching, and their domain of operation is the relation between meaning values and their referents. Similarly, the meaning dimension "Function" is defined by the processes involved in deducing or inducing statements about function, purpose, and role, and its domain of operation is the sphere of content corresponding to functionality. Meaning values are the specific manifestations of the processes and domain of operation particular to the meaning variable. Hence, each meaning variable defines a specific set of meaning values and constitutes a rule for generating meaning values of a particular kind. In this way, each meaning variable points to the use of a particular procedure or set of rules for identifying and interpreting inputs or internal phenomena. It demarcates a particular area or aspect of perception and constitutes a particular approach to external and internal reality based on representing it cognitively in a manner that is unique to that specific meaning variable.

In view of these remarks, it is clear that a positive preference for a meaning variable indicates concretely that the individual has available a relatively large store of meaning values characterized by the specific meaning variable or is able to retrieve or construct such meaning values with relative ease. Hence, an individual with a positive preference for a certain meaning variable tends to use meaning values reflecting that meaning variable in perception and cognition. Thus, such an individual may be expected to assign meaning values of the preferred variable to inputs of all kinds, if such an assignment is at all possible. As a result, in that individual's meaning assignments, meaning values corresponding to the preferred meaning variable will recur often, will be salient, and will fulfill an important role. Further, the individual will be attentive to situational cues suggesting the preferred meaning variables and will be particularly sensitive to aspects of phenomena that correspond to or could correspond to the preferred meaning variables (see, for example, Study

5). For instance, if an individual's meaning profile indicates a positive preference for, say, the meaning dimension "Feelings and Emotions," the individual has a set for attending to cues suggesting this dimension and will perceive them as major aspects or referents of a situation (S. Kreitler & H. Kreitler, 1986c).

An individual with a positive preference for a certain meaning variable will also be interested in issues involved in the general domain described in terms of meaning values of the preferred meaning variable. As a result, he or she will be better informed about these issues, will know more about them, will more often think about them, will consider them more frequently and more carefully, will inquire about them, or will be otherwise concerned with them (e.g., with values and judgments when the preferred meaning variables is "Judgments and Evaluations," with causes when the preferred meaning variable is "Antecedents and Causes," or with metaphors when the preferred meaning variable is the metaphoric type of relation).

Because a positively preferred meaning variable also provides preferred coding categories, a person with a positive preference for a meaning variable will use meaning values corresponding to that variable in attempting to comprehend situations, events, and other people's behavior and character or in explaining herself or himself to others (S. Kreitler & H. Kreitler, 1984a,b, 1985b). It is needless to emphasize that, when the individual has a low or negative preference for a certain meaning variable, all the above-mentioned manifestations, as well as others discussed below, occur rarely if at all, because of either the weakness of the underlying tendency or an active attempt to avoid it.

The increased availability of meaning values corresponding to the preferred meaning variable is also reflected in a greater facility and a higher level of cognitive performance in domains of content corresponding to the preferred meaning variable. For example, the person may have more associations of meaning values reflecting the preferred variable, may comprehend with greater ease material relevant to the preferred variable, will recall better inputs such as data and texts in the domain of content defined by that variable, and will, in general, operate cognitively with greater proficiency and readiness with materials corresponding to the preferred than to the nonpreferred meaning variables (H. Kreitler & S. Kreitler, 1989; S. Kreitler & H. Kreitler, 1987b,c,e, 1988, 1989b,c).

Further manifestations of preferred meaning-assignment tendencies exemplify the more dynamic aspect of meaning variables. As mentioned, each meaning variable not only characterizes a specific domain of content—as shown by the above examples—but also represents a particular kind of cognitive process or strategy. Thus, the meaning dimension "Causes and Antecedents" corresponds to the processes of causal reasoning, the meaning dimension "Contextual Allocation" corresponds to classifying and grouping, the comparative type of relation *difference* corresponds to comparing focused on differentiating and contrasting, and the form of relation "Conjunction" corresponds to the processes of summating and bonding.

Accordingly, when there is a preference for a certain meaning variable, the processes corresponding to that variable occur with greater frequency and facility. Hence, a person with a preference for a meaning variable performs better and on a higher level in tasks that depend on the involvement of one or more processes corresponding to the preferred meaning variable than a person who has no such preference. For example, subjects with a preference for the meaning dimension "Structure" (*Dim* 10) were found to perform better on tasks that require awareness of structural qualities (Study 1), perceptual closure tasks, and tasks that consist of finding hidden words and pictures (i.e., detecting specific structures against a background noise—Study 6, Factor 6). Likewise, individuals with negative preference for the comparative type of relation *difference* were found to have difficulty in tasks of discrimination (Study 8). Again, individuals with a negative preference for the meaning dimension "Feelings and Emotions" (*Dim* 20b) were found to have less fluency in responding to inputs with an emotional rather than a nonemotional connotation (Study 6, Factor 18). Finally, subjects with a negative preference for the meaning dimension "Range of Inclusion" (*Dim* 2a) coupled with a positive preference for the dimension "Contextual Allocation" (*Dim* 1) were found to tend toward overinclusion (Study 1). These examples show that some of the manifestations of a preferred meaning variable are what would be considered cognitive functioning.

The large number of different manifestations of any meaning variable indicates the centrality of the construct of the meaning variable and its dynamic impact as an underlying factor. The fact that each meaning variable may be treated both as content and as process greatly increases the range of its potential effects. Further, most tasks are fairly complex and require the involvement of more than one meaning variable. The recurrent activation of a meaning-assignment tendency in various contexts serves to enhance its differentiated aspects. The frequent activation, in turn, also strengthens the meaning-assignment tendency and increases the likelihood of its involvement in further contexts.

Incidentally, the conclusion about the self-strengthening of meaning-assignment tendencies implies that the gap between positively and negatively preferred meaning-assignment tendencies does not remain constant over time. The reason is that the frequent activation of the positively preferred meaning-assignment tendency strengthens it, whereas the relatively rare activation of the negatively preferred one does not change its status. Hence, the gap between the differentially preferred meaning-assignment tendencies becomes larger and more pronounced in the course of time.

MEANING PREFERENCES AND BELIEFS

The manifestations of preferred meaning-assignment tendencies mentioned up to now consist of effects in which meaning values reflecting the preferred variable as content or process are involved in a most direct way. There are, however, further kinds of manifestations of preferred meaning variables revealed by the studies on traits (see Part II) and listed in Appendix B. These further kinds also depend on the meaning values, corresponding to the preferred variable, as all manifestations of the meaning variable necessarily do, but in a less direct manner than the manifestations discussed earlier. They seem to be fewer in number than the earlier manifestations, but this impression may reflect the bias of investigators rather than any property of the phenomena involved. Be that as it may, it is important to sort these further manifestations and to identify them for what they are. Essentially, they seem to comprise two phenomena: beliefs and behaviors. We will deal with the first in the present section, and with the second in the next one.

Beliefs are units of content that include what are commonly called assertions, attitudes, preferences, opinions, statements of value, judgments, and so on. It was found that subjects who preferred a certain meaning variable acquired or developed beliefs in domains of content that corresponded to the preferred meaning variable. For example, subjects who preferred the meaning dimension "Function, Purpose, or Role" (*Dim* 3) were found to have a functional approach and to value efficiency and practicality (Studies 3 and 6). Likewise, subjects who preferred the meaning dimension "Action" (*Dim* 4a) evaluated sports positively. Again, subjects who preferred the meaning dimension "Cognitive Qualities" (*Dim* 22a) stressed the importance of theories and basic ideas (Study 6, Factor 9), whereas subjects who preferred the illustrative-exemplifying type of relation *scene (TR* 3c) liked dramatics (Study 6). Finally, subjects with a negative preference for the meaning dimension "Judgments and Evaluations" (*Dim* 21a) showed little or no concern about moral or social values (Studies 2 and 4).

Findings of this kind could be expected. As a belief consists of at least two meaning values joined by a third meaning value (Kreitler & Kreitler, 1976, pp. 89ff), meaning values constitute the raw materials of beliefs. In fact, a belief could be regarded as a generalization of the meaning-assignment tendency, for it is produced by joining a meaning value to some referent. The chances of such a joining are particularly high in the case of preferred meaning variables, because of the increased frequency of using meaning values corresponding to the preferred variables. It is obvious that a meaning variable does not determine what a person who prefers it and uses meaning values corresponding to it will believe about a certain phenomenon, but it guides that person's thinking toward a specific kind of considerations and reflections. This guidance in a specific direction is made possible by the particular orientative function of meaning values in regard to perception and thinking in general. Accordingly, if we have three individuals, two of whom have a positive preference for the meaning dimension "Feelings and Emotions" and one who has a negative preference for this dimension, then it is likely that the former two will have preformed beliefs concerning feelings whereas the latter would not. But the former two may still have very different beliefs about feelings; for example, one may hold that "Feeling disturbs one's peace of mind and disrupts one's clarity of reasoning," whereas the other may believe that "Feelings help to reinstate psychological balance and reveal truths hidden from regular reasoning."

Likewise, a preferred meaning variable does not determine whether the person would turn the initially temporary bond between the meaning value and the referent into a more permanent belief. Yet, the chances of this are high because a person with a preference for a meaning variable is likely to be recurrently more attentive to cues suggestive of the preferred variable and to be repeatedly more concerned with issues relevant to it. Thus, one possibility is that the individual will be more often confronted with evidence bearing on the original belief or its variations. If this evidence does not lead to the discarding of the belief, it may eventually bring about its strengthening.

Another possibility is that the individual will be led more often to form various beliefs with meaning values corresponding to the preferred meaning variable. This process may eventually lead to the formation of a permanent belief, by abstraction from the specific referents mentioned in these specific beliefs and by generalization to some superordinate class of meaning values. The two possibilities may account for the formation of permanent beliefs in domains corresponding to preferred meaning variables.

Beliefs may be more general or more specific. Appendix B lists instances of both kinds. For example, preference for the meaning dimension "Quantity and Number" (*Dim* 14) was related positively to a general functional-utilitarian attitude (Study 15), and also to an appreciation of precise standards in personal, legal, and other spheres (Study 2). Beliefs become specific when one or more additional meaning values are brought to bear on the original two or three meaning values of the core belief. For example, "I like thinking" becomes increasingly specific through the addition of meaning values such as "about philosophical issues" (*Dim* 8b), "in the evenings" (*Dim* 16), and "particularly if there is no need to reach any conclusions" (*Dim* 7) (H. Kreitler & S. Kreitler, 1976, Chapter 13, Studies I and II).

Thus, specific beliefs are often the product of the interaction of several meaning variables. For example, an attitude of disregard for the implications of the statements that one makes and the positions that one has espoused (found to be typical of extroverts, Study 1) is the product of low preference for two meaning dimensions: "Consequences and Results" and "Judgments and Evaluations." In keeping with this analysis, we actually found that extroversion is correlated negatively with both these meaning dimensions (Study 1). Similarly, subjects high in externality (external = internal [EI] control, Study 11) were reported to be unconcerned with assigning blame to specific agents. This attitude reflects the absence of a specific belief about causality in the domain of values. As expected, we found that EI is correlated negatively with the meaning dimensions "Causes and Antecedents" (*Dim* 6) and "Judgments and Evaluations" (*Dim* 21b). It is plausible to assume that beliefs which seem to be related somewhat indirectly to the corresponding meaning variable are the product of more than one meaning variable. For example, it was found that externals ("EI Control," Study 11) believe the world is unpredictable and ruled by chance. This belief involves meaning values of the meaning dimensions "Consequences" and "Actions." In Study 11, we indeed found that externality was correlated negatively with the meaning dimensions "Consequences and Results" (*Dim* 7) and "Actions" (*Dim* 4).

Some of the more general beliefs listed as manifestations of meaning variables are part of a larger grouping of beliefs such as a conception of world. For example, the concern with possessions that is correlated with the meaning dimension "Possessions and Belongingness" (*Dim* 17b) may be part of a conservative outlook (Study 1), part of a functional-exploitive orientation (Study 3), or subservient to a striving for power, prestige, and status (Study 4). In such cases, the belief is often the product of meaning values of different meaning variables. A similar conclusion applies when the belief itself is so general that it could serve as a label for some larger grouping of beliefs. Examples of such general superordinate orientations are realism, interest in the environment, and acceptance of given circumstances found to be correlated with the attributive type of relation (*TR* 1) (Studies 1, 6, 7, 8, and 10) or the complementary approach of subjectivity found to be correlated with a preference for the illustrative-exemplifying (*TR* 3) and the metaphoric-symbolic (*TR* 4) types of relation (see Appendix B). Such generally orientative beliefs sometimes appear in single trait names, like *realistic, worldly, shrewed,* and *optimistic.*

In sum, there is ample evidence of a relationship between preferences for meaning-assignment tendencies and belief formation, especially if we focus on the general domain in which the subject is likely to form beliefs rather than on the specific content of the beliefs. From the viewpoint of this relationship, beliefs resemble the other listed manifestations of meaning-assignment tendencies. However, from the viewpoint of their form and function, they resemble regular traits less than the cognitive content of the kinds commonly called attitudes, opinions, values, and judgments. Therefore, if beliefs form the major bulk of a trait's manifestations, it is perhaps justified to consider the trait a pseudotrait, closer to an attitude than to a full-fledged trait.

BEHAVIORAL MANIFESTATIONS OF MEANING PREFERENCES

Behaviors constitute a subset of the potential manifestations of meaning variables. It is a small subset and includes partly actual behaviors (such as drug taking), partly tendencies toward more inclusive classes of behaviors (such as assertiveness), and partly characteristics that could apply to a variety of actions (such as conscientiousness or punctuality).

Because even full-fledged traits indicate merely inclinations toward particular behaviors, the relation between a preferred meaning-assignment tendency and overt behavior can, at best, be only marginal and indirect. As already mentioned in Chapter 2, meaning variables and behaviors differ in their levels of generality. In addition, they are separated from each other by a long chain of intervening psychological events, including belief retrieval, Cognitive Orientation (CO) cluster formation, emergence of a behavioral intent, and adoption of a behavioral program. In this chain, each link may exert a modifying influence, as specified by the theory of cognitive orientation (H. Kreitler & S. Kreitler, 1976, 1982), so that there is a further increase in the psychological gap between meaning assignment and behavior. As a result, it is unlikely that meaning variables could yield reliable predictions of overt behavior.

If, however, we reverse our considerations by starting with the executed behavior and thinking backward, the picture is slightly modified. The reason is that specific behaviors, especially if frequent, presuppose the availability of particular meanings or are more likely to occur if these meanings are strong and influential, as in the case of preferred meaning-assignment tendencies. For example, delay of gratification was shown to be related positively to the meaning dimension "Temporal Qualities" (*Dim* 16—Study 11). The dimension "Temporal Qualities" was also related to a particular aspect of action in general, namely, its speed (Studies 1 and 6). Another example refers to behaviors like gambling and drug consumption (Study 15). *A posteriori* it is almost self-evident that they are related to a negative preference for the meaning dimension "Consequences and Results" (*Dim* 7).

It goes without saying that a great many people who have never gambled or taken drugs may still have a negative preference for "Consequences and Results." Thus, the mentioned correlations of meaning variables with behaviors do not provide a reliable basis for predicting behavior. But they may still have considerable explanatory value. Indeed, to some extent, this is also true of our trait concept in general. The pattern of underlying meaning preferences predicts the trait and points to its typical manifestations. Although the underlying pattern of meaning preferences does not provide reliable predictions of human overt behavior, it shows behavioral inclinations and reveals their cognitive roots. Thus, it constitutes a reliable and economic instrument for diagnosing traits, and by virtue of its explanatory power, it may eventually pave the way for trait modification.

In sum, we defined *trait* as a pattern of preferred meaning-assignment tendencies and showed that an underlying pattern of this kind was found for all of the better-known personality traits (Table 1). Then we focused on various meaning preferences in order to exemplify what they reveal about typical manifestations of meaning-assignment tendencies. This analysis led to the conclusion that each preferred meaning variable corresponds to a set of manifestations in perception and cognition, with extensions to the spheres of beliefs and actions. Hence, a trait consists of a pattern made up of all the sets of manifestations corresponding to the meaning variables defining the particular pattern. Yet, so far, we have not discussed the characteristics of trait patterns in general (see Chapter 5). This discussion has to be postponed until more has been said about trait dynamics and interaction.

Table 1. Distribution of Significant Correlations of the Traits (in Studies 1–20) with Meaning Variables[a]

Meaning variable	Exvia (Cattell)	Extroversion (Eysenck)	CPI scales																		Mach IV	n power	16 PF						
			Do	Cs	Sy	Sp	Sa	Wb	Re	So	Sc	To	Gi	Cm	Ac	Ai	Ie	Py	Fx	Fe			1	2	3	4	5	6	7
Dim																													
1	+	+																			−		+	+		+	+		+	
2a		−																												
2b																													+	
2a + b																												+		−
3																					+	+								+
4a																						+				+		+	+
4b														−								+			+		−		+	+
4a + b	+																												−
5																									+	+			
6	−	−																											
7																					−								
8a			+		+	+	+				+			+			−				−	+							
8b				−																		+							
8a + b					+	+					+											+							
9	+							−	−																				
10		+							−													+						−	
11																	−	−			−	+						+	−
12											−																		
13						−					−																		
14	+	−						+	+												+	+	+		+				
15	−	−				−				−											+	+			+	−		−	
16	−	−														−				−				−	−	−	−	−	
17a		+																			+	+			−				
17b		+			−																	+					+	+	
17a + b		+																				+							
18		+																			+						+	−	+

(continued)

Table 1. *(Continued)*

Meaning variable	Exvia (Cattell)	Extroversion (Eysenck)	Do	Cs	Sy	Sp	Sa	Wb	Re	So	Sc	To	Gi	Cm	Ac	Ai	Ie	Py	Fx	Fe	Mach IV	n power	1	2	3	4	5	6	7
																			CPI scales		**Mach IV**		**16 PF**						
Dim																													
19a	−	+																	+				−		−	−		−	+
19b		−																					+			−	−		−	
19a + b		+																					+			−			−	+
20a																				−			+	+	−			+		+
20b				+																			+					+		
20a + b								−															+					+		
21a	−	−																				+	+	−	−		−	−	−	
21b	−	−				−					−	−									+	+	−	−				−	
21a + b		−												−									+	−	−					+
22a											−									−		+		−	−				+
22b																	+			−				+				+
22a + b	+	+																										−		
No. of dif. Dim																					+									
Dim																														
TR		+						+	+			+				+						+		+		−		+		
1a																								+				+		
1b																														
1a + b	+																				+							−		
2a				+				+	+			+										+	−				+			
2b			+	+			+						+											+				−		
2c			+	+	+		+						+	+	+	+							−						
2d		+		+	+	+	+						+	+	+	+													
2a + b + c + d			+										+		+	+													
3a	−		+	+	+		+						+	+	+								−	−	−			+	
3b					+		+							+	+	+								−					
3c																							−						
3a + b + c																													
4a				+			+																−		+	−			
4b		−													+						+	−	−		+		−	

	Total
4c	23
4d	31
4a+b+c+d	11
No. of dif.	16
TR	16
Lex mode	18
Pers mode	10
FR	24
1	11
2	4
3	4
4	2
5	4
6	8
7	9
8	15
FR$_{pos.}$	13
FR$_{neg.}$	7
SR	10
1	2
2	13
3	11
4	17
5	11
6	13
7	12
8	11
9	24
10	15
SR$_{near}$	
SR$_{far}$	
No. of dif. SR	
No. of meaning values	
Ratio of m. values to m. dim.	
Total	

(continued)

Table 1. (*Continued*)

Meaning variable	16 PF																			Myers-Briggs									
	8	9	10	11	12	13	14	15	17	18	19	20	21	22	23	24	25	26	27	Extro-version	Sensa-tion	Thinking	Judging	Approval motive	Ego strength	Anality	Cleanliness, order	Hypochond.	Avarice
Dim																													
1				−	+															−	−			+		+		−	
2a			+																			+					+	+	
2b					+																	+							
2a + b																				+	+		+						
3	+	−	+		+					+										+	+				−	+		−	
4a	+	+	+		+			−	−			−	−				−	−	−	+	+							+	
4b		−			−	−		+	−	−	+	−	−		−										−			+	+
4a + b	+	−						−	−	−			−							+						+			
5		+	+		+		+				+										+		+				−	+	
6		−			+		+					−							−		+		+					+	+
7					+		+								−								+						
8a															+	+				+			+	+		+	+	+	+
8b	+				+		+								+								+				+	+	+
8a + b	−				+		−								+	−				+	+		+			+	+	−	
9															+	+					+				+		+		
10		−			+		+					−								+	+								
11	+			+	+		−														+				+				
12	−	−														−				+	+		−	−	+	+	−	+	
13			−	−									−							−			+	+	+	+			
14			+									−				−			−				−	+	+	+	+		+
15				+				+	+				−			+					+				+	+			
16			+							−			−	−		−	−	−	−	−			+	+		+	+		
17a																−	−	−							+	+	+		+
17b				+					+							+				−					+	+	−		+
17a + b																										+			+
18	−	−								−		−				+					+				−		−	−	
19a	−	−	−									−									+					−	+	−	+
19b	−	+	+	+			+		+	−		−		−							−				+	−	−	+	−
19a + b	−	−								−		+	+	−						−	−			−	−	−	+	−	

20a			−	+	+																			+			+		
20b		+		+			−		+			+	+	−			−	+								+			
20a + b		+					−			−			−	−			−	−							−				
21a			−	+	+	−	+	+	+	−		+	+	−						−		+		−			+	+	
21b		−	+																										
21a + b				+					+	−	−											+							
22a		+		+				+	+	−		+	+	−		−					−			−		+	+		
22b	+				−		−	+					+								−								
22a + b		+		+			−	+	+	−		+	+	−							−				−				
No. of dif. *Dim*				+						−																			
TR																													
1a					+																	+			+				
1b					+												+												−
1a + b					+				−					+						+	+			+	+			−	
2a			−			+															+	+	+			−	−		
2b	+		+	+	+	+			+													+		−					+
2c		−				+				+				+				+				+	+	+	+	+		−	
2d								+	+													+	+						
2a + b + c + d		−				+																+	+					+	
3a			+	+		+			+			+		−						+		−		−					
3b		−			−								+				+					−				−			
3c	−	−	−				+																						
3a + b + c			−										+				−							−	−	+	−	+	
4a			−													−						+		−					
4b					+			+	+				+	−			−				−	−			−	+			
4c		+			+						+		+		+	+					−			+					
4d	−	−	−				+																						
4a + b + c + d											−		+				−							−	−	+	+		
No. of dif. *TR*			−		+		+			+	+	−	−			+										−			
Lex mode																						+							
Pers mode																						−							

(*continued*)

Table 1. (*Continued*)

Meaning variable	16 PF																			Myers-Briggs									
	8	9	10	11	12	13	14	15	17	18	19	20	21	22	23	24	25	26	27	Extro-version	Sensa-tion	Thinking	Judging	Approval motive	Ego strength	Anality	Cleanliness, order	Hypochond.	Avarice
FR																													
1																				+									
2																												+	
3																							+						
4																							+						
5																							+		.				
6																													
7																							+						
8																							+						
FR_pos.																													
FR_neg.																							−						
SR																													
1	+						+						+								+								
2	+	−	−		−							−											+						
3			+												−						+				−			+	
4					+																								
5		−	−				+				+		+								−		+				+		
6											+		+														+		
7		−	−				+						+												−		+		
8	+						+						+														+		
9		−			+																								
10		−																							−				
SR_near																−													
SR_far																				+									
No. of dif. SR							+																						
No. of meaning values	−	−																											
Ratio of m. values to m. dim.																													
Total	17	25	25	13	23	7	20	9	15	12	7	15	23	11	7	10	10	6	2	14	23	16	20	16	16	21	21	23	11

Meaning variable (Dim)	Impulsivity	EI control	Authoritar.	Dogmatism	Cog. activity Jancke-Boucsein	Ideation. activ. pref.	Mot. activity pref.	Sens. seeking (SSS)	Thrill & adv. seeking (SSS)	Experience seeking (SSS)	Disinhibition (SSS)	Boredom susceptibility (SSS)	Bem: Mascul.	Bem: Femin.	Bem: Androg.	Bem: Soc. des.	Intolerance of ambiguity	LPC scores	Sum: Pos. cor.	Sum: Neg. cor.	Total
1				+	+	+							−		+			+	14	5	19
2a			−	+	−	−		−		−							+		5	5	10
2b	−			+				−		−			+		+	+			5	2	7
2a + b	+	−		+	−	+		+	+	+					−				3	4	7
3				−	+			+										−	16	7	23
4a					−		+			−	+	+		−	+				14	9	23
4b					−							−		+					8	14	22
4a + b		−			−						+						−		7	6	13
5	+			−			+							+	+		−	+	10	5	15
6	−	−	−	+	−	−		−	−										9	4	13
7		−							−									−	7	13	20
8a		−		−										+	+		+	+	11	4	15
8b				−											−		+	+	11	2	13
8a + b				−						+								+	10	1	11
9		+	−				+		+				+			+	−	+	11	8	19
10	−	−			+	+			−		−			+	−				11	5	16
11		+	+		+	+	+			+			+	+				+	14	6	20
12		+	+	+						+									5	6	11
13							+			+									6	7	13
14				−		+	+		+	+							+		18	3	21
15					−					+									8	7	15
16	+	−								+	+			+	+		+		11	19	30
17a	+	−		+										−	−				8	6	14
17b	−			−				+				−		+	+				9	4	13

(continued)

Table 1. (*Continued*)

SSS (Sens. seeking, Thrill & adv. seeking, Experience seeking, Disinhibition, Boredom susceptibility)

Meaning variable	Impulsivity	El control	Authoritar.	Dogmatism	Cog. activity Jancke-Boucsein	Ideation. activ. pref.	Mot. activity pref.	Sens. seeking	Thrill & adv. seeking	Experience seeking	Disinhibition	Boredom susceptibility	Bem: Mascul.	Bem: Femin.	Bem: Androg.	Bem: Soc. des.	Intolerance of ambiguity	LPC scores	Sum: Pos. cor.	Sum: Neg. cor.	Total
Dim																					
17a + b		+			+	+					+					+			11	0	11
18		+	+		−						−		−		+	−			7	7	14
19a		+	+							+	+						−		11	9	20
19b		+	+										−			−			11	14	25
19a + b					−								−		+	−			4	8	12
20a	+						−		−									+	9	5	14
20b	+															−	−	+	12	7	19
20a + b	+					−												+	5	9	14
21a		−		+		+		+	−	+			−	+	+			−	15	15	30
21b						+								+	+				9	7	16
21a + b				+					−				−	+	+			−	8	10	18
22a						+				+			−						12	12	24
22b				+		+			−					+	+				8	6	14
22a + b			+						−			+	−		+				10	8	18
No. of dif.																	−	+	5	3	8
TR																					
1a		−	−			+									+			+	11	1	12
1b		−							+						+			+	7	1	8
1a + b					+	+									+		+	+	12	2	14
2a	−		−												+		−	+	10	8	18
2b						+								−			−	+	16	5	21
2c				+	+													−	24	3	27
2d						+							−	+	+				16	3	19
2a + b + c + d		−				+	+								+				7	3	10

	C1	C2	C3	C4	C5	C6	C7	C8	C9	C10	C11	C12	C13	C14	C15	C16	C17			
3a	+	+		+	+		−			−	−	−	−			+		16	12	28
3b	+		−						+				−		+	+	+	13	6	19
3c																		4	5	9
3a + b + c						+	−		+			+	−					4	7	11
4a		−											+			+	+	6	5	11
4b													+			+		13	9	22
4c		+		+		+			+				+				+	16	1	17
4d									−			+	−		+		+	4	8	12
4a + b + c + d	+	+		+	+	+	−		+	−			+				+	10	5	15
No. of dif. TR	+	+			+						+				−			20	4	24
Lex mode			+					+										3	0	3
Pers mode																		0	1	1
FR																				
1		−	+	+	+							+	+					13	0	13
2													−					13	2	15
3						−												8	6	14
4																		1	1	2
5								+	+									10	4	14
6																		1	0	1
7								−					−					1	0	1
8								+										5	0	5
FRpos.													+				+	0	2	2
FRneg.															+			2	0	2
SR																				
1		+					−		−	−		−	−		−	+	+	4	8	12
2								−							+			5	8	13
3		+	+			−				+	+		−					9	9	18
4				+	+		+				+	+	−			−		10	3	13
5												+	+	−		+	−	9	2	11
6		−							+							+		11	2	13
7									+							+		10	5	15
8				+		−		+	+				−	+		−		9	7	16

(continued)

Table 1. (Continued)

Meaning variable	Impulsivity	El control	Authoritar.	Dogmatism	Cog. activity Jancke-Boucsein	Ideation. activ. pref.	Mot. activity pref.	Sens. seeking	Thrill & adv. seeking	Experience seeking	Disinhibition	Boredom susceptibility	Bem: Mascul.	Bem: Femin.	Bem: Androg.	Bem: Soc. des.	Intolerance of ambiguity	LPC scores	Sum: Pos. cor.	Sum: Neg. cor.	Total
SR								SSS													
9		+	−		−														3	3	6
10		+	+														−		7	5	12
*SR*near							+							+	+				4	3	7
*SR*far													−						0	1	1
No. of dif. *SR*			+		−		+							+	+		−		5	5	10
No. of meaning values																			9	2	11
Ratio of M. values to M. dim.					−										+				1	1	2
Total	18	31	20	20	36	25	15	11	12	24	13	10	19	20	35	10	26	23	730	441	1171

aThe signs + and − in the table denote positive and negative correlations. Blanks in the table denote the absence of significant correlations. (FR variables were not coded for the 16 PF.) The traits in the headings are listed in the order in which they appear in Studies 1–20 (e.g., the first two traits appear in Study 1, the CPI scales in Study 2, etc.) of Chapter 9. (The same order appears in Table 2.)

Trait Dynamics

MEANING ASSIGNMENT

Whereas Chapter 3 presented a definition of traits and explained its major constituents, this chapter focuses on how the different elements combine and actually function. This discussion will make our treatment of traits more dynamic and process-oriented.

Our starting point is the conception that traits function as patterns of meaning-assignment tendencies. We described in Chapter 3 how each meaning variable in the pattern prompts the use of specific meaning values to characterize inputs in a way that produces, through the intervention of different processes, an array of manifestations in different contexts characteristic of that meaning variable. Every meaning variable has a potentially large range of manifestations. Some of them could be singled out and identified as primarily cognitive (e.g., a preference for the meaning-variable comparative type of relation facilitates performance on tasks of discrimination), others as socially oriented (e.g., a preference for the meaning dimension "Domain of Application" reflects an interest in human beings), still others as emotional-temperamental (e.g., a preference for the meaning dimension "Sensory Qualities" indicates concern with sensory experiences, including attentiveness to internal sensations and physiological processes), and so on. These distinctions reflect mainly methodologies and biases of research rather than dynamic differences of psychological import. All the different manifestations are implemented by the process of meaning assignment and depend more on inputs and meaning preferences than on differences in underlying processes. Thus, despite the traditional approach which treats them as different, the meaning system reveals their common dynamic background and allows us to regard them as elements within one framework.

The different manifestations of a meaning variable depend on the major function of the particular meaning variable, which is to guide the meaning assignment to inputs in a specific way or direction. Indeed, Allport's thesis (1961) that a trait is a structure "having the capacity to render many stimuli functionally equivalent" (p. 347) can hardly be implemented by processes other than those constituting meaning assignment. For it is only meaning-assignment tendencies that can render inputs equivalent or nonequivalent in terms of their psychological effects.

No meaning-assignment tendency can function alone without other meaning-assignment tendencies of specific kinds. As may be recalled, meaning assignment is realized in the form of meaning values, each of which is characterized by belonging to a certain meaning dimension, manifesting a certain type of relation and a specific form of relation, and by being bound to a particular referent that is related in a specific manner to the presented input. Hence, several meaning-assignment tendencies are necessary to fully characterize any single meaning value. In dynamic terms, this conclusion indicates that any act of meaning assignment involves the activation of several meaning variables, that is, at least one meaning dimension, one type of relation, one form of relation, and one stimulus-referent relation. In principle, any meaning variable of one kind—say, a meaning dimension—can function together with any meaning variable of another kind. In mentally normal individuals, the main restrictions are imposed by label meanings (concerning in particular the primary identification of inputs and their demand characteristics), and by the positive and negative preferences of the individual. Some of our findings show that individual preferences may even affect the identification of the input (Study 5; H. Kreitler & S. Kreitler, 1983; S. Kreitler & H. Kreitler, 1984a,b, 1986c, 1989c). Individual preferences concern not only specific meaning-assignment tendencies but also combinations of such tendencies.

Another characteristic of meaning assignment is that more than one specific meaning value can be characterized by the same meaning variables. For example, the meaning values "square" and oblong" of the referent *a room* are equivalent in terms of the meaning dimension ("Sensory Qualities: Form"), the type of relation (attributive), and form of relation (positive) characterizing them. This clarifies how constancy is possible amidst variety and change. Because a meaning variable is on a higher level of generality or abstractness than a meaning value, it can accommodate meaning values that differ in specific, more concrete characteristics. For example, an individual may note on one occasion a happy child, on another occasion a sad lady, and on a third occasion a jealous husband or an angry boss. The specific content of these meaning values is different, but they are all meaning values of the meaning dimension "Feelings and Emotions." The constancy across situations is accounted for by the meaning assignment tendency of the individual; the variety across situations is accounted for by the changing inputs. Thus, if we conceive of a meaning-assignment tendency as a dynamic tendency that shapes the internal representations of inputs, it is possible to see how a modicum of objectivity is preserved despite the subjectivity of meaning assignment. The resolution of the apparent paradox is possible because the specific meaning value is the product of the individual's more general meaning-assignment tendency acting on inputs. It is this dynamic complementary interaction that enables a person to express herself or himself and to grasp the world-as-given in one and the same act.

INTERACTION WITHIN THE TRAIT PATTERN

In defining a trait as a pattern rather than as a structure of meaning preferences, we indicated that the meaning-assignment tendencies seem to retain functional autonomy and can therefore be discussed one by one. Nonetheless we have ample evidence of interactions among meaning variables within the trait pattern. However, our data consist, on the one hand, of the results of meaning tests and what is known about meaning variables, and, on the other hand, of the results of trait questionnaires and what is generally known about their trait manifestations. This overall design does not allow for a detailed discussion of the mechanics of interactions within the trait pattern, in particular of whether the interactions occur on the level of meaning-assignment tendencies or on the level of meaning values. This question will be taken up in a forthcoming book about personality theory (S. Kreitler & H. Kreitler, 1989c). Our present findings point toward several kinds of interactions within the trait pattern, resulting in a modification of the central trait manifestation. By *modifying* we do not mean that one meaning variable influences another meaning variable. As mentioned earlier, we cannot at present discuss the "how" of interaction. Instead, the term *modification* relates to a common input of two or more meaning variables and serves merely as a general description of outcome, though not of process.

An example based on comparing the findings of Studies 2, 3, and 6 may demonstrate what is meant by the term *modification*. Let us compare (1) subjects who were high in tolerance, particularly tolerance of the ideas and opinions of others (California Psychological Inventory (CPI), Scale Tolerance (To), Study 2); (2) subjects who were high in Machiavellianism (Study 3); and (3) subjects who were high in Cattell's Factor G, which is often interpreted as reflecting sociopathy. We will find that all three groups of subjects were very low on the meaning dimension "Judgments and Evaluations" (*Dim* 21); that is, they shared a pronounced negative preference for this meaning dimension. Disregard for values and judgments is one of the most obvious and important features of psychopathy. Yet, the subjects high in tolerance did not exhibit pronounced psychopathic inclinations, which is not surprising if we take into account that they had positive preferences for the *mixed* form of relation (*FR* 3) (e.g., they often applied "sometimes" or "to some extent") and the *complementary* type of relation (*TR* 2c). The former preference suggests a tendency to qualify, and the latter suggests a tendency toward a balanced approach, based on cooperation and mutuality. In addition, both together indicate hesitation, even difficulty in making a general, unqualified, and binding statement.

In contrast, in the subjects who scored high on Machiavellianism, the negative preference for "Judgments and Evaluations" was paired with a positive preference for "Consequences and Results" (*Dim* 7) as well as for "Function, Purpose, and Role" (*Dim* 3). Therefore, they tended to evaluate inputs not in terms of values, but in terms of eventual outcomes and possibilities for manipulation. Thus, in contrast to psychopaths, they were well-organized, realistic, and exploitative manipulators, but they shared with psychopaths a low concern about morality.

Finally, in individuals with psychopathy or psychopathic tendencies, the negative preference for the meaning-assignment tendency of "Judgments and Evaluations" was coupled with a disregard for "Consequences" (*Dim* 7) and a negative preference for "Domain of Application" (*Dim* 8), which includes also low concern for other human beings. Hence, they manifested the well-known psychopathic syndrome of amorality, an unrealistic disregard for the results of their actions, and low consideration even of those people whom they pretended to love.

The interaction within the pattern consists of matching various manifestations corresponding to the meaning-assignment tendencies of the pattern against each other. The resulting modification may take different forms. A strengthening occurs when two or more meaning variables are similar in their typical manifestations. For example, take the metaphoric-symbolic type of relation *metaphors* (*TR* 4c) and the stimulus-referent variable of shifting to a referent related to the input by association (*SR* 7). The former indicates a tendency to generate meaning values that are not strictly within the sphere of content commonly associated with the referent, whereas the latter indicates a tendency to shift associatively from the presented stimuli to referents that do not have an obvious relation to these stimuli. The elements common to these two meaning-assignment tendencies are a deviation from the given inputs and their transformation into something less obvious and familiar. Hence, in individuals who have positive preferences for both meaning-assignment tendencies, as high scorers on external control (Study 11) or on Experience seeking (a subscale of sensation seeking) (Study 15), the common elements would be intensified, and their manifestations would be more salient than in individuals who have a positive preference for only one of these meaning-assignment tendencies; for example, high scorers on "Tolerance of Ambiguity" had a preference only for metaphors (Study 18), whereas high scorers on hypochondriasis had a preference only for deviating associatively from the input (Study 10).

Another form of modification is a weakening or even a suppression of some manifestations of a meaning variable. This is likely to occur when the typical manifestations of two or more meaning variables in the pattern are incongruent. For example, a preference for the attributive type of relation (e.g., *TR* 1a) indicates concern with interpersonally shared reality, whereas a preference for the metaphoric type of relation (e.g., *TR* 4c) indicates focusing on internal and subjectively experienced reality. When an individual has positive preferences for both, as, for example, the high scorers on androgyny (Study 17), the manifestations of one or both of these meaning-assignment tendencies may be weakened. The weakening is relative to the strength of the manifestations in individuals who have a preference for only one of these meaning-assignment tendencies. Again, the manifestations of which meaning-assignment tendency would undergo weakening depends on the other tendencies represented in that pattern.

A third possibility is that the interaction of manifestations of at least two meaning variables in the pattern leads to a transformed manifestation that is, to some extent, different from both. It is likely that transformation is the most common kind of modification in trait patterns. Take, for example, a preference for the meaning dimension "Structure" (*Dim* 10). If the individual has, in addition, preferences for, say, "Contextual Allocation" (*Dim* 1) and "Cognitive Qualities" (*Dim* 22), the preference for "Structure" would probably be manifested in dealing with theoretical systems, producing abstract models, or analyzing mathematical structures. But if the individual has, in addition to preferring "Structure," preferences for, say, "Locational Qualities" (*Dim* 15), it is likely that the preference for "Structure" would be manifested through interest in navigation, geography, or other concrete formations.

Because the product of the interaction is, in all three cases, different in some respect from the original components, this kind of interaction may be expressed formally in the following way:

$$a \times b \rightarrow K$$
$$a \times c \rightarrow L$$

where a, b, and c denote the original components, and K and L the products of the interactions that may be an enhancement, a weakening, or another transformation based on selecting and integrating.

It is evident that this kind of interaction within the pattern between different meaning-assignment tendencies is actually an extension of the interaction described in Chapter 3 as occurring between different manifestations of the same meaning-assignment tendency.

SUBSTITUTION

Another dynamically important characteristic of patterns of meaning-assignment tendencies is that they make it possible for different meaning variables to implement functions that are equivalent to some degree.

There are many examples of alternative meaning variables in the studies of Part II (see Appendix B). For instance, the different exemplifying-illustrative types of relation could substitute for each other to some extent. Lack of concern for interpersonal reality could be implemented by preferences for several of the personal types of relation (*TR* 3 and/or *TR* 4) or by a low preference for several of the lexical types of relation (*TR* 1 and/or *TR* 2), or it could be bolstered by a preference for the former and a rejection of the latter (e.g., Study 13). Or again, concern with the individual's internal world, as contrasted with interest in external reality, could be implemented (1) by preferences for one or more of the meaning dimensions "Sensory Qualities" (*Dim* 19b), "Feelings and Emotions" (*Dim* 20), "Judgments and Evaluations" (*Dim* 21), or "Cognitive Qualities" (*Dim* 22); (2) by negative preferences for any of the meaning dimensions reflecting concern for external reality, for example, "Domain of Application" (*Dim* 8b), "Weight and Mass" (*Dim* 12), "Size" (*Dim* 13), "Quantity" (*Dim* 14), or "Locational Qualities" (*Dim* 15); or (3) by both kinds of tendencies (e.g., Studies 15 and 17).

The kind of relation between meaning variables in the pattern that was described above can be expressed formally in the following way:

$$a \longrightarrow M$$
$$b + c \rightarrow M$$
$$d \times e \rightarrow M$$

where a, b, c, d, and e designate the original meaning variables and M designates some quality common to one or more manifestations of meaning variables, acting singly (i.e., a), in combination (i.e., $b + c$) or in interaction with each other (i.e., $d \times e$).

There is good reason to believe that the more meaning variables point to the same direction, the stronger would be the corresponding manifestations (see Study 22). But as the degree of this kind of redundancy is kept low in most patterns, it is likely that a selection is made. We have been able to identify two principles that probably guide this selection. One principle we call the *multifunctionality of meaning variables*. Out of several alternatives for implementing some tendency, the meaning variable selected for a pattern is likely to be one that has some function also in regard to another tendency relevant to the pattern, or one that at least does not clash with the meaning variables implementing another tendency of the pattern. For example, in the pattern for authoritarianism (Study 13), the tendency toward concreteness could be implemented to a certain extent either by a high preference for the comparative type of relation *difference* (*TR* 2b) or by a low preference for the comparative type of relation *similarity* (*TR* 2a). It is the latter that actually occurs in the pattern for authoritarianism. We tend to attribute it to the fact that the former could not be selected because it corresponds to low conformity, whereas authoritarians tend toward high conformity (Study 13).

STRUCTURAL IMPACTS

A third dynamic feature of patterns, in addition to interaction and substitution, is subservience to holistic features of the pattern: different meaning-assignment tendencies in the pattern contribute singly or together to facilitating or promoting some property characteristic of the pattern as a whole or an important part of it. For example, the pattern of ego strength (Study 8) consists of a variety of meaning variables, many, if not all, of which could potentially contribute to enhancing ego strength, for example, (1) a disregard for emotional cues in general and bodily sensations in particular, which make for emotional control, and internal stability; (2) a disregard for cognitive properties, which like the former, reflect lack of concern with the internal world; (3) a deemphasis on subjectivity through a negative preference for the types of relation of the personal mode (*TR* 3 and *TR* 4); (4) a positive preference for different meaning dimensions that reflect interest in external reality (i.e., *Dim* 13, "Size" and *Dim* 14, "Quantity") and in people (*Dim* 8b, "Domain of Application"); and (5) an emphasis on the types of relation of the lexical mode (*TR* 1 and *TR* 2, the attributive and comparative types of relation). These different meaning-assignment tendencies may all support or contribute to ego strength, besides the different roles they could fulfill in other spheres of the functioning individual. They are equivalent insofar as they may all promote ego strength.

The described phenomenon utilizes, to some extent, the potentiality for alternation inherent in meaning variables (see above), but it rests mainly on a selective enhancement of some manifestations of the meaning variables in the pattern, because of the impact of the whole structure of which they form a part. This form of interdependence seems to be one of the earmarks of a pattern that is a structure. In view of its function, we suggest calling it *conjoint facilitation*.

Formally, conjoint facilitation could be expressed in the following way:

$$a + b \longrightarrow N$$
$$a + c \longrightarrow N$$
$$a + b + c \rightarrow N$$
$$b + c \longrightarrow N, \text{ etc.}$$

where a, b, and c designate the original components in different combinations, and N designates the product of their conjoint facilitation.

The importance of conjoint facilitation becomes apparent when we consider the rich variety of contexts with which an individual is confronted and in which she or he has to respond and act. The wide variety of meaning-assignment tendencies promoting ago strength ensures that the individual who has this pattern will be able easily and naturally to assign to a rich variety of inputs in different situations meanings reflective of ego strength and promoting ego strength. Thus, in a pattern, different meaning-assignment tendencies may substitute for each other and replace one another in different contexts according to the characteristics of different inputs.

The possibility of conjoint facilitation has important implications. First, it explains the consistency and the stability of a "trait" despite variation in responses. Second, it suggests that a trait may become stronger through time. The reason is that the individual learns to apply the meaning-assignment tendencies constituting the pattern to an increasingly large and variegated range of inputs. And third, it explains why an individual may act in keeping with a trait pattern although she or he may prefer or avoid not all of the meaning variables that constitute it (examples are provided in Studies 12 and 13). The conclusion that a trait may be functionally viable even when fewer than all of the meaning variables in its meaning pattern are preferred (or avoided) opens important methodological possibilities in research because it enables selecting subjects with a particular pattern of meaning-assignment tendencies on the basis of preferences for fewer than 100% of the relevant meaning variables (see above studies). Further, by the same token, it also suggests why different individuals may resemble each other in some trait although they do not share all the meaning variables defining the pattern.

It is noteworthy that the pattern of preferred meaning variables is activated in a manner that contributes to its own strengthening. Different studies indicate that the subjects tended to detect in situations cues that corresponded to their positively preferred meaning-assignment tendencies. For example, subjects high in Machiavellianism, the pattern of which includes preferences for "Function" (*Dim* 3) were particularly attentive to cues suggesting function (i.e., cues that were suited to triggering their preferred meaning-assignment tendencies) and might even assume them when they were not actually there (Study 5). Similarly, subjects who scored high on anality were found to assign specific meaning values to inputs along meaning variables included in the pattern correspondong to anality, particularly when the referents were related meaningfully to anality (Study 9). In further studies clarifying the elaboration of complex inputs (Kreitler & Kreitler, 1989c), the subjects tended to assign meaning to situations in terms of their preferred meaning-assignment tendencies and identified as major referents of a situation those that specifically corresponded to their preferred tendencies. Identifying referents of this kind allowed the subjects to activate the pattern of their preferred meaning-assignment tendencies. This recursive process of repeated activation of the pattern may be expressed formally in the following way:

$$(a + b)^0 \rightarrow P^0 \rightarrow (a + b)^1 \rightarrow P^1 \rightarrow (a + b)^2 \rightarrow P^2, \text{ etc.}$$

where a and b indicate originally preferred meaning variables, P indicates some aspect of the meaning assigned to the input, and the exponents indicate a regular enhancement of both members of the loop over time.

THE PRESERVATION OF REALITY TESTING

However, the recursive loop does not imply that preference for certain meaning variables necessitates distorting or overlooking inputs that do not lend themselves readily to meaning assignment in terms of the preferred meaning variables. Paradoxically, the main guarantee against such a hopelessly solipsistic loop is not the ability that every normal adult has to apply, if required, meaning-assignment tendencies that may not be preferred. The main guarantee is actually built into the pattern of the preferred meaning-assignment tendencies in the form of the multiple meaning variables that the pattern includes. Because a pattern of preferred meaning variables includes several meaning variables (indeed, 13–14 on the average) and because every individual has more than one pattern of preferred meaning variables, it is evident that an individual has at his or her disposal a sufficiently large number of preferred meaning variables to accommodate, without distortion, the different inputs encountered in a great variety of contexts. The wide range of possibilities of assigning meaning in line with preferred meaning variables can be especially appreciated when we recognize that the number of meaning variables involved in any specific act of meaning assignment is limited.

Of course, a pattern of meaning-assignment tendencies is almost never applied as a pattern all at one time. Rather, one or more meaning variables of the pattern are selectively applied in any specific act of meaning assignment. This selective application raises the question of how the selection of meaning-assignment tendencies in different situations takes place. We will mention here particularly those regulating factors that depend mainly on traits as patterns of preferred meaning variables (the issue has further aspects that are dealt with in a forthcoming book on personality— S. Kreitler & H. Kreitler, 1989c). One such factor is the subclusters of preferred meaning variables within the larger pattern (e.g., Studies 12, 16, and 19). Subclusters may represent groupings of meaning variables bound particularly to a specific kind of inputs among those relevant to the pattern as a whole. For example, the pattern corresponding to intolerance of ambiguity includes one subcluster for coping mainly with ambiguous cues whose ambiguity is due to their contradictoriness, and another subcluster for coping mainly with ambiguous cues whose ambiguity is due to their susceptibility to multiple identifications (Study 19).

Another regulating factor may be groupings of preferred meaning variables focused on dealing with a specific class of inputs. In one study (S. Kreitler & H. Kreitler, 1989c), two such groupings were isolated, both focused on assigning meanings to cues related to human beings, their acts, and their behavior. One grouping seemed to mediate what has come to be called *situationist attributions;* another, *dispositionist attributions*. Such groupings do not correspond to traits but may cut across traits. Because an individual has several patterns of preferred meaning variables, and because a grouping can be identified as existing and can operate even when there are fewer than all meaning variables defining it (see above), it seems likely that individuals apply meaning variables characteristic of groupings of this kind in assigning meaning to specific inputs.

A third determinant is based on the selective role played by auxiliary meaning dimensions, that is meaning dimensions used in assigning meaning to subsidiary referents (e.g., when the input is *human being* and the given meaning is "working all the time," then "Temporal Qualities" is an auxiliary meaning dimension characterizing the subsidiary referent *Working*; see Chapter 2). We found (S. Kreitler & H. Kreitler, 1988f) that the major meaning dimension characterizing the situation meaning evoked in all subjects a certain set of meaning dimensions, out of which the subjects applied consistently a certain limited selection of dimensions in regard to issues defined by particular auxiliary meaning dimensions. This selection was characteristic of one or more individuals and varied in line with the auxiliary meaning dimensions. For example, when the task was explaining people's behavior (i.e., the major meaning dimension was "Causes and Antecedents") and the description of the specific situation included an "Evaluation," one group of subjects consistently used meaning values of "Emotions" in order to "explain" the act, whereas when the description of the specific situation included a statement of "Consequences," the same subjects consistently used meaning values of "Cognitive Qualities." Hence, it seems that specific combinations of meaning values of referents, along major and auxiliary meaning dimensions, regulate the evocation of one or another meaning-assignment tendency in given conditions.

A GLIMPSE OF THE INTERACTION BETWEEN TRAITS

Until now, we have discussed mainly processes characteristic of single patterns of preferred meaning-assignment variables. It is, however, evident that traits coexist—or, rather, cooperate—within the individual. Where the traditional concepts of traits may find it hard to account for the manner in which different traits interact, the conception of traits as patterns of meaning-assignment tendencies provides readily for this possibility. Indeed, as all traits consist essentially of the same conceptual units of psychological elements, it is hard to see how they could possibly not interact. Study 22 showed that when the preference for one and the same meaning variable forms a part of two separate patterns of meaning-assignment tendencies that an individual has, this meaning variable produces a stronger effect than when the preference for the meaning variable forms a part of only one pattern. Again, in the latter case, the effect is stronger than when the meaning variable is not preferred within the framework of any of the two examined patterns, or when in one pattern there is a positive preference for it and in another a negative preference. The combinations of effects showed the interaction to be fairly linear. It is noteworthy that the interaction among different patterns of preferred meaning variables appears to be an extension of the interaction within the patterns between different manifestations of the same meaning variable as well as between different meaning variables.

TRAITS AND BEHAVIOR

If behavior is interpreted as any response of an individual on any level (e.g., verbal, emotional, cognitive, or physiological), then traits are no doubt closely related to behavior. In the chapters about the nature and dynamics of traits (Chapters 2 and 3), we dwelt lengthily on the manifestations of meaning-assignment tendencies that include a rich variety of responses in different domains, mainly perceptual, cognitive, experiential, and behavioral. The most controversial of these has been the domain of overt behaviors because the bulk of research findings indicated both that traits in general did not correspond well to overt behaviors and that overt behaviors tended to be inconsistent across situations (Chapter 1). More precisely, trait-related behavior is sometimes consistent across situations and sometimes it is not, even though the situations may seem to researchers to be similar or identical. What, then, is the relation of traits and human behavior?

A profound answer to this question is beyond the scope of this book—first, because it requires that the nature and impacts of situations be studied and discussed to the same extent (S. Kreitler & H. Kreitler, 1989c) as the nature and dynamics of traits have been in this book; second and mainly, because the common consideration of traits and situations requires a new conception of how traits and situations interact and of how these interactions combine with the processes involved in shaping overt behavior, as specified in the theory of cognitive orientation (H. Kreitler & S. Kreitler, 1976, 1982). An initial outline of the suggested solution to the problem of behavioral inconsistencies has been presented before (Kreitler & Kreitler, 1983), and a fuller presentation is available elsewhere (S. Kreitler & H. Kreitler, 1989c). At present, we restrict the discussion to a particular aspect of meaning assignment, which, though it constitutes merely a partial solution, is of great relevance to any comprehensive resolution of the trait–behavior problem (see also Chapters 6, 7, and 8).

In order to sharpen the problem, let us recapitulate: If everyday observations had not supported the notion of a relationship between traits and behaviors, the classical trait concept would not have survived for 2,500 years. Yet, if traits were a reliable indicator of human overt behavior (at least within situations), hundreds of articles and dozens of books—this book included—would not have been written. Therefore, it is justified to inquire what the material presented up to now contributes to an eventual solution of the nagging problem of trait–behavior inconsistencies.

The point to be made entails an important aspect of meaning assignment that has not been discussed up to now. Therefore, it would be advisable to briefly recapitulate the procedure by which we found the meaning preferences underlying each of the studied personality traits. As may be recalled, we compared the trait scores of groups of subjects with their meaning-assignment tendencies and let the significant correlations guide us to the patterns of meaning preferences underlying the different traits. However, we noticed that the meaning profiles of the subjects often included meaning preferences that were not integrated into the framework of any of their traits. These meaning preferences sometimes differed across subjects, sometimes were even shared by subjects who scored high and those who scored low on the same trait. The low homogeneity in the distribution of these meaning preferences in itself was not amazing, because from our previous studies of various cognitive processes and skills we knew that meaning preferences and cognitive capacities, including intelligence, functional fixedness, planning abilities, and so on, cut across personality traits. In sum, because we define traits not merely as preferred meaning-assignment tendencies, but as specific clusters of preferred meaning-assignment tendencies, we found in almost every person meaning preferences that did not underlie any of that person's traits. In this respect, these meaning preferences were isolated.

The common impact of the trait pattern usually overrides the impact of isolated meaning-assignment tendencies, but it does not always eliminate it. A slight fluctuation of attention resulting in a somewhat different evaluation of a familiar situation, the emergence of an interfering though only peripherally attended-to association, or the introduction of an internal input like thirst or fatigue into the cognitive system—all these may activate one or another of the trait-independent meaning-assignment tendencies that may cause a spontaneous and transient modification of the usual trait manifestations.

Because the meaning repertoire of an individual contains more meaning variables than those functioning within the framework of that person's traits, there is always the chance of trait-inconsistent behaviors. It appears to us that the probability of such an event is not high enough to explain all or most of the trait-inconsistent behaviors recorded by personality researchers. Therefore, the transient impacts of isolated meaning-assignment tendencies, important as they are, can render merely a partial solution to the problem of behavioral inconsistencies of trait manifestations. As mentioned, a satisfactory solution presupposes, in addition to considering isolated meaning preferences, also a reevaluation of the impact of situations and, last but not least, consideration of the processes postulated by the cognitive orientation theory (H. Kreitler & S. Kreitler, 1976) and shown to provide reliable predictions of human overt behavior. This conclusion about the involvement of additional factors may prove disappointing only for those who expect traits to be determinants of human overt behavior rather than tendencies that contribute to the shaping of covert and overt behavior.

TRAIT DYNAMICS AND INTERACTIONS: A BRIEF SUMMARY

This chapter deals with the dynamics of traits as patterns of meaning-assignment tendencies. The major processes discussed above describe how the different manifestations of positively and negatively preferred meaning variables interact within and between patterns. These interactions account for the manner in which the meaning-assignment tendencies, constituting a pattern, bring about actual effects in the perceptual, cognitive, experiential, and behavioral spheres. The interactions also show how a preference for a meaning-assignment tendency may be gradually strengthened (by the recursive loop), and may indicate the basis for the stability of the pattern (by means of alternation and conjoint facilitation), and for the applicability of the pattern to a broad range of inputs (mediated by the multiplicity of meaning variables and their selective application).

In particular, the different forms of interaction, substitution, and conjoint facilitation demonstrate the structural properties of the pattern of preferred meaning variables. Indeed, although themselves being dependent on these properties, they help in specifying in what ways the set of preferred meaning variables corresponding to a trait is actually a structure. The discussion in this section leads to the specification that the patterns are structures insofar as the different meaning-assignment tendencies of which they consist affect one another through interactions, contribute to the enhancement of properties characteristic of the pattern as a whole, manifest qualities through the impact of interaction with other meaning variables and the embeddedness within the pattern, and are equipotential to the extent that they may alternate with and replace one another to some extent. Thus, it may be claimed that traits represent an organizational principle of meaning variables on the level of the individual in addition to the principle of the circle of dimensions characteristic of the system of meaning as a whole.

Finally, it was mentioned that meaning-assignment tendencies that do not belong to one of the individual's trait patterns may account for some trait-inconsistent behaviors but do not provide sufficient explanation for the full range of these behaviors.

Characteristics of the Trait Pattern

THE USES OF TRAIT CHARACTERISTICS

Up to now we have discussed the patterns underlying traits in terms of preferred meaning-assignment tendencies, the dynamics of these patterns, and their interactions, emphasizing repeatedly that each pattern corresponds uniquely to one of the studied personality traits. However, trait patterns have additional characteristics that are less dependent on specific meanings and hence less content-bound. These characteristics can be used for the further specification of traits and would thus enable trait comparisons, grouping traits into categories, identifying types of traits, detecting subclusters within single traits, and differentiating between the patterns underlying the hitherto recognized traits and patterns underlying constructs or phenomena that do not qualify as traits. The last is of particular importance in distinguishing between traits and nontraits and in characterizing the relations of traits to cognate constructs, including habits, attitudes, predispositions, motives, and so on. A refinement and extension of the characteristics may eventually enable defining new traits that have not yet been detected.

In pursuing the mentioned tasks, from comparisons to trait "inventions," different subsets of the characteristics may be selected. Sometimes, one or two characteristics would suffice; at other times, the whole set would have to be applied.

The brief listing of the uses of trait characteristics clarifies that they constitute a major instrument for trait research that would shed further light on the psychological role and impacts of traits.

THE SEVEN TRAIT CHARACTERISTICS

The seven characteristics have been derived one by one through exploration of the patterns of meaning assignment tendencies corresponding to the different traits. The exploration was designed to highlight features which would enable identification of each trait as unique and as a member of the class of traits. Hence, though largely heuristic, the derivation of the features was guided by a combination - different in each case - of theoretical expectations and methodological principles. As a result, the list includes both obvious and less obvious characteristics, on different levels of complexity. The method of derivation does not, however, provide any guarantee for the completeness of the list.

1. Specificity

Each pattern of preferred meaning-assignment tendencies corresponding to a trait is a unique combination, and each of the meaning variables has a unique set of manifestatons that can be considered the unique contribution of that variable to personality dynamics. In order to learn about a trait, it is necessary to examine, one by one, the meaning variables in the pattern, their manifestations (see Chapter 3 and Appendix B), and their interactions (see Chapter 4). This empirically derived notion underlies the characterization of the 76 traits and the comparisons of traits presented in the studies of Part II. Accordingly, characterizing a trait consists of explicating singly and in combination the manifestations of the meaning variables that constitute the trait's pattern. The result is a specification of which major manifestations are characteristic of the trait in terms of processes and the domains of operation of these processes. For example, impulsivity (Study 10) was described as being focused on concern with emotions, functionality, and the present concrete situation, coupled with a disregard for consequences and implications, alternatives, comparisons, structure, possession, and so on.

Similarly, a comparison of traits rests on the thesis that all similarities and differences between traits are ultimately reducible to similarities and differences in the meaning variables constituting the patterns underlying these traits. This conclusion has made possible comparisons, for example, of neuroticism and psychoticism (Study 6) and of authoritarianism and dogmatism (Study 13), or two measures of preferences for cognitive activity (Study 14).

2. Two Levels of Generality

A second characteristic of trait patterns refers to the level of generality of the manifestations of the meaning variables in the pattern. Some of the listed manifestations of meaning variables (Appendix B) appear to be of a more general kind (e.g., for *Dim* 16, "Temporal Qualities," concern with time and speed), and some seem to be far more specific (e.g., for *Dim* 8, "Domain of Application," concern with human beings as participants in actions and situations).

Differences in the level of generality of trait manifestations are typical of the whole domain. It is to be noted that our validational data had to be taken from different studies carried out by investigators who were interested in behaviors at different level of generality. Thus, if according to some study subjects low in "Consequences and Results" are devoted to gambling (Appendix B), this does not indicate that the manifestations of "Consequences and Results" (*Dim* 7) are more specific than those of, say, "Temporal Qualities" (*Dim* 16). Rather, the gambling tendency may simply be a specific manifestation of a more general risk-taking and adventurous tendency. Similarly, concern with human beings (correlated with *Dim* 8, "Domain of Application") is a specific manifestation of the more general concern with what or who is involved, regardless of whether inanimate or animate units are concerned (see Appendix B, *Dim* 8).

However, emphasis on some specific manifestations of a general tendency could be a convention or bias shared by many researchers in some domain and may even be institutionalized in the framework of that discipline. Thus, investigators in personality may share the bias that concern for human beings is more important and revealing about individuals' personality than concern with, say, the kind of furniture in a room or plants in a garden, which may also be noticed by an individual high in "Domain of Application" (*Dim* 8). The emphasis on sociability mediated by "Domain of Application" (*Dim* 8) could be an example of a convention of this type, which, far from being arbitrary, is rooted in basic assumptions of the field of personality.

These observations were designed to help distinguish actual differences in the level of generality of manifestations from fortuitious ones. The criterion for distinguishing between actual and fortuitous differences is based on testing whether the correlations of traits with meaning variables are improved when the meaning variables are defined more narrowly. If the correlations are improved, then it is likely that the differences are actual. If they are not, then the differences are most probably fortuitious. Broader and narrower definitions refer to the distinction between meaning variables and subvariables, whereby the former are more general than the latter. For example, the regular meaning dimension "Feelings and Emotions" (*Dim* 20) is more general than the subdimensions "Feelings and Emotions Evoked by the Referent" (*Dim* 20a) and "Feelings and Emotions Experienced by the Referent" (*Dim* 20b). Similarly, the exemplifying-illustrative type of relation (*TR* 3) is more general than the subtypes exemplifying instance (*TR* 3a), exemplifying situation (*TR* 3b), and exemplifying scene (*TR* 3c) (see also Chapter 2, "The Meaning Variables"). It is evident that the meaning system provides to some extent the possibility of defining variables on the level of greater or lesser specificity, as seems appropriate for the general domain of study. Thus, when one is studying the meaning of sensations, it would be more informative to deal with specific subdimensions of "Sensory Qualities" (*Dim* 19) (e.g., sensations of smell and taste) than to lump them all together.

Guided by this principle, we used meaning variables on two levels of generality because the findings revealed meaningful relations on the more specific level, too. For example, the findings showed that there was a consistent difference between "Sensory Qualities of the Referent" (*Dim* 19a), "Feelings and Emotions of the Referent" (*Dim* 20a), "Judgments and Evaluations of the Referent" (*Dim* 21a), and "Cognitive Qualities of the Referent" (*Dim* 22a) and the corresponding "Sensory Qualities by the Referent" (*Dim* 19b), "Feelings and Emotions by the Referent" (*Dim* 20b), "Judgments and Evaluations by the Referent" (*Dim* 21b), and "Cognitive Qualities by the Referent" (*Dim* 22b). Whereas the former referred to concern with sensations, emotions, evaluations, and cognitions of others, the latter focused on sensations, emotions, evaluations, and cognitions of oneself. In some cases, it was even meaningful to study specific sensory subsubdivisions.

As subvariables have more specific manifestations than regular variables, a trait defined primarily in terms of subvariables may be considered bound more to specific contexts and to be manifested in specific, readily recognizable ways than a trait defined primarily in terms of regular variables. Differences between regular and subvariables are particularly clear in regard to meaning dimensions and types of relation. We tested our assumption by comparing more specific traits, like Cattell's primary factors, with more general traits like Cattell's secondary factors in regard to differences in the number of correlations with meaning variables (Study 6). The obvious expectation is that the mean difference between the number of correlations with the 29 subvariables (of dimensions and types of relation) and 12 regular corresponding variables should be larger in the primaries than in the secondaries. Indeed, this is precisely the finding obtained ($\bar{X}$ = .07, SD = .05; $\bar{X}$ = .002, SD = .011, respectively; t = 5.07, df = 23, p < .001). This finding shows that more specific traits are correlated relatively more with subvariables than the more general traits.

As may be expected, overall, according to the data presented in Table 1, the 29 subvariables were correlated with more traits ($\bar{X}$ = 17.34, SD = 55.73) than the 12 corresponding regular variables ($\bar{X}$ = 12.75, SD = 3.22; (t = 3.26, df = 39, p < .01). This finding indicates that many of the studied traits tended to have fairly specific manifestations. Again, it is a matter of relative emphasis because all studied traits were correlated with both subvariables and regular variables. For example, a comparison showed that the "cognitive" traits[1] were correlated with more of the regular variables ($\bar{X}$ = 2.06, SD = .56) than the "emotional-temperamental" traits ($\bar{X}$ = 1.50, SD = .63; t = 2.55, df = 26, p < .05) but did not differ from them in the frequency of correlations with subvariables ($\bar{X}$ = 7.63, SD = 2.47; $\bar{X}$ = 6.14, SD = 2.05; t = 1.83, df = 26, n.s.) (see Tables 2 and 3 for the definition of the trait groups). These findings are in keeping with the general characterization of "cognitive" traits as more general than the "emotional-temperamental" traits. (For all personality traits, the mean proportion of correlations with general meaning variables is .44).

3. Structure

Structure is a further characteristic of traits. By definition, each trait pattern can be regarded as a structure because its constituent meaning variables correlate with each other to a higher extent than they do with meaning variables that are not part of the pattern. However, beyond this overall structural characteristic of every trait, cluster analysis revealed, in many traits, substructures that were found to have considerable psychological significance. The substructures consist of groupings of meaning-assignment tendencies or meaning values within the pattern underlying the trait. Up to now, we have identified three kinds of subclusters, each contributing to the solution of a hitherto unresolved problem of personology (in general) and trait research (in particular).

The first kind of substructure suggests a further explanation for inconsistencies in trait manifestations (see also Chapter 8, "Traits and Behavior"). For example, Studies 11 and 12, which dealt with internal-external (IE) control, revealed two subclusters of internal control and two subclusters of external control. The two subclusters of internal control share several meaning variables that reflect manifestations characteristic of internality (i.e., the acceptance of enterprising action), but they differ from each other in regard to those meaning variables that reflect how internality is implemented. Whereas the meaning variables constituting one subcluster (i.e., the meaning dimensions "Action" and "Domain of Application") indicate a kind of internality based on and evoked by considering actions and the involvement of people in situations, the meaning variables constituting the other subcluster (i.e., the meaning dimensions "Temporal Qualities," "Locational Qualities," "Structure," and "Development") indicate an internality focused on considering more impersonal features of situations. Not surprisingly, the former is more prototypical of internality than the latter.

Similarly, the two subclusters of externality share several meaning variables that reflect manifestations characteristic of externality (i.e., rejection of enterprising action), but they differ from each other in further meaning variables indicative of the manner in which externality is implemented. One subcluster is defined by meaning dimensions such as "Sensory Qualities," "Weight and Mass," and "Material," which reflect focusing on perceptual properties of situations, whereas the other subcluster is defined by the meaning dimensions "Actions" and "Domain of Application," which reflect focusing on the human beings involved in the situation and on what they do.

The similarities and differences in meaning variables between the four subclusters of IE made possible the arrangement of the four subclusters along a continuum, with the two extreme forms of internality and externality at the poles and the two intermediate forms in between. The continuum highlighted the differences between the two extreme subclusters and the similarities between the intermediate ones as well as between subclusters of each kind. It allowed for distinguishing between variables characteristic of the trait as a whole and those bound to only one or another of its forms of realization. Last but not least, the subclusters enabled us to explain why questionnaire scores of internality or externality do not suffice to predict consistent trait manifestation.

A similar example concerns the need for Power (n Power). Two subclusters were uncovered within the pattern of n Power (Study 4). They differed in the dynamics underlying the trait. One subcluster was primarily actional-functional, the other emotional-evaluative. The distinction made possible resolving the problem of relations between n Power and Machiavellianism.

Intolerance of ambiguity presents a third example of this kind of subcluster. Whereas the subclusters of internal-external control and those of n Power were defined in terms of meaning dimensions alone, subclusters of intolerance of ambiguity included other meaning variables, too (Study 19). In this case, the three subclusters differed in the type of ambiguity to which they were relevant (i.e., ambiguity deriving from multiple interpretations, or from difficulties in identifying and categorizing, or from contradictory cues). Accordingly, the focal constituents of the subclusters were also different: the first was defined by a negative preference for certain meaning dimensions, the second by positive preference for certain meaning dimensions as well as some variables of stimulus-referent relations, and the third only by variables of types of relation and forms of relation.

The nature of the described subclusters within traits is not yet completely clear. They could represent specific nuclei within the larger pattern, bound to particular inputs or contexts. This possibility seems to apply to the subclusters of internal-external control. Such subclusters could exist in the same individual and would be activated alternately in line with the characteristics of the inputs. Yet, subclusters could also be conceptualized as representing subsets of meaning-assignment tendencies anchored in one or more specific meaning variables. This possibility seems to apply to the subclusters of n Power and intolerance of ambiguity. Such subclusters could appear as variants of a trait and would be less likely to occur in the same individual.

The second hitherto observed kind of subcluster consists of preferred meaning values that belong to preferred meaning variables and are preferentially assigned to referents (inputs) with a related label meaning, for instance, "bad odors" would be assigned to *dirt*, "very dangerous" to *a knife* or *a handgun*. Thus, there is a relation by meaning between the preferred meaning values, the preferred meaning dimensions, and the evocative referents. An illustrative example is provided by Study 9. It showed that subjects with a strong inclination toward cleanliness and order repeatedly used specific meaning values in regard to particular referents related to cleanliness and order. The meaning values were along positively preferred meaning variables, which, in fact, belong to the pattern of the trait of cleanliness and order, and the referents were selectively chosen from an array of referents that could also be relevant to the issue of cleanliness and order. Paying special attention to some inputs while selectively ignoring or neglecting others is a common feature in individuals concerned with cleanliness and order. Even in the pretests we conducted for Studies 8 and 9, we got information about one subject whose obsession with cleanliness was restricted to his body, his clothes, and his books, while his room was often in chaotic disarray and cluttered with dirt; or about another subject who could not bear a speck of dirt on his shirt but did not mind drinking out of a filthy cup. Thus, without taking into account these highly specific subclusters of preferred meaning values, validation research would register trait-inconsistent behavior.

We found (Study 9) that there were three conditions promoting a preference for specific meaning values: (1) the strength of the trait, (2) the relevance of the referents, and (3) the belonging of the meaning variables characterizing the meaning values to the pattern defining the trait. It is likely, although we still have no empirical proof, that these conditions can also be met with regard to other traits. Traits concerning the management of money are likely candidates. Examples of selective misers or selective spendthrifts come readily to mind, as, for instance, a stingy housewife who frequents the most expensive beauty parlor, a miser who cuts down on food but not on gold jewelry, or a spendthrift who saves on home electricity by using only low-voltage bulbs. However, pending further research, it would not be justified to regard subclusters of preferred meaning values as the most frequent cause of trait-inconsistent manifestations.

The third—and, in many respects, the most interesting—kind of subclusters consists again of meaning variables and hence is on the same level of generality as the first kind of subclusters. Yet, in contrast to the other two subclusters, a subcluster of the third kind shows up in the framework of different traits without changes in its composition and may also be found outside the framework of trait patterns. If it occurs within a trait pattern, its meaning variables are preferred. But if it is not related to a trait (i.e., if it does not overlap with a trait pattern), then one or more of its constituents may not be preferred, as is true of some cognitive clusters we found. The most intriguing subcluster of this kind is probably projection. We found it first when studying the meaning background of defense mechanisms (S. Kreitler & H. Kreitler, 1989c), and we fully identified it in the context of authoritarianism (Study 13). In the same context, we also found subclusters related to the manifestations of denial and concreteness. Another subcluster differentiated between maturational levels in the sense of Werner (Study 14). Because each of the subclusters consists of several meaning variables, their manifestations are likely to be rather specific. Moreover, they may be revealed with different degrees of strength or salience, in line with the number of their meaning variables that are preferred by the individual. It is likely that more subclusters of this kind exist. Be that as it may, more research is required for any definite interpretation of all the functions of these subclusters. On the basis of the available data, we can only express our impression that the third mentioned kind of subcluster is of potential importance in understanding the relations of traits and psychopathology.

In sum, up to now, we have found four types of trait structures:

1. Traits whose pattern of preferred meaning assignment tendencies includes no subclusters below the level of overall functioning.
2. Traits with subclusters of preferred meaning assignment tendencies, some of which may function alternatively.
3. Traits with subclusters of preferred meaning values.
4. Traits whose subclusters of meaning assignment tendencies cut across different traits and may even be found outside any known trait pattern.

4. Meaning Variables of Different Kinds and Their Proportions in the Pattern

It is of importance to examine how many of the four kinds of meaning variables (meaning dimensions, types of relation, forms of relations, and referent-shift variables) are represented in the trait patterns. Most of the traits were correlated with several kinds of meaning variables: 27% were correlated with all four kinds, 41% with three kinds, 31% with two kinds, and 1% (i.e., one trait) with only one kind. Thus, it seems characteristic for patterns of preferred meaning variables underlying traits (i.e., for 68% of the patterns) to include meaning variables of three or four kinds. This characteristic results in stability of the pattern and increases the versatility of its manifestations. In the patterns of all traits, the proportions of meaning dimensions, types of relation, referent shifts, and forms of relation were 54.75%, 25.75%, 12.57%, and 5.9%, respectively.

Further, different traits or groups of traits may differ in the proportions of the four kinds of meaning variables in the patterns. This characteristic is important because not only different meaning variables but also different kinds of meaning

Table 2. Differences between Three Groups of Traits in the Frequency of the Kinds of Meaning Variables to Which They Are Related[a]

Variable: Mean of correlation	Mental-health traits (a)	Emotional-temperamental traits (b)	Social-interpers. traits (c)	F ($df = 2/35$)	Significant dif.: Groups (a) & (c) (q_r)
Meaning variables	19.60	15.50	12.92	3.60*	3.93*
	(3.44)	(5.82)	(5.68)		
Meaning dimensions	12.80	9.00	6.47	4.15*	4.28*
Types of relation	4.80	3.71	4.26	.43	
Stimulus–ref. relations	1.80	1.93	.84	2.15	
Forms of relation	.00	.71	1.00	1.09	

[a]For (a), (b), and (c) the numbers are means except for those in parentheses, which are SDs. Mental-health traits include neuroticism, psychoticism (Cattell's 16 PF, Study 6), ego strength, anality (Study 8), and hypochondriasis (Study 10). Emotional-temperamental traits include impulsivity (Study 10), the four factors of sensation seeking (Study 15), Factors 1, 2, 4, 6, 8, 11, 15, and 17 of the 16 PF (Study 6), and the Wb scale of the CPI (Study 2). Social-interpersonal traits include the need for approval (Study 8), Machiavellianism (Studies 3–5), need for power (Study 4), social desirability (Studies 8, 17), LPC (Study 20), scales Do, Cs, Sy, Gi, Ac, and Py of the CPI (Study 2), and Factors 3, 5, 13, 22, and 25 of the 16 PF (Study 6). The selection of traits for the three groups was done out of the total list of 76 traits assessed in Studies 1–20 (Part II), by three independent judges who were professors of psychology. Only traits about which all judges agreed were included in the groups. There were three further groups of traits about which there was no unanimity. They were later combined into "cognitive traits" after analyses showed they did not differ in the seven trait characteristics (see text and Table 3, note a).
*$p < .05$.

Table 3. Comparison of the Observed and Expected Distributions of Different Kinds
of Meaning Variables in Different Groupings of Traits[a]

Meaning variables		Mental-health traits (a)	Emotional-temperam. traits (b)	Social-interpers. traits (c)	Cognitive traits (d)	χ^2
Meaning dimensions	Obs.	64	126	123	138	
	Exp.	45.58	101.03	112.31	128.75	15.29**
Types of relation	Obs.	24	52	81	78	
	Exp.	23.38	51.81	57.60	66.03	11.70**
Stimulus–ref. relations	Obs.	9	27	16	43	
	Exp.	15.19	33.66	37.43	42.91	16.11**
Forms of relation	Obs.	0	10	19	15	
	Exp.	12.85	28.49	31.67	36.30	30.51***
χ^2 (all four kinds) ($df = 3$)		22.83***	19.49***	27.87***	15.33**	
χ^2 (only first three kinds) ($df = 2$)		9.98*	7.49*	22.80**	2.83	
Prop. of correlations with meaning dim.[b]		.66	.59	.51	.50	$F = 2.78$ ($p = .06$)
Prop. of correlations with TR, FR, and SR		.34	.41	.49	.50	
Mean prop. of positive to negative correlations[c]		1.15 (.62)	1.71 (1.54)	5.16 (6.42)	3.07 (4.55)	$F = 2.23$ ($df = 3/50$) ($p < .10$)

[a]For the traits included in groups (a), (b), and (c) and the method of selection, see Table 2. Cognitive traits included intolerance of ambiguity (Study 18), internal-external control (Study 11), three scales of the Myers-Briggs Indicator (Thinking, Judging, Intuition; Study 7), Ideational Activity Preference Score and the Jancke-Boucsein Cognitive Activity Score (Study 14), authoritarianism, dogmatism (Study 13), several CPI scales (Fx, Tu, Ai, Ie; Study 2), and several factors of the 16 PF (Factors 12, 23, 24; Study 6). These traits were grouped together after analyses showed that the following three groups initially identified by our judges did not differ in any of the variables mentioned in the text: the group of "cognitive style" variables (CPI: Fx; intolerance of amiguity; EI control); the group of attitude variables (CPI: To; 16 PF: 12; authoritarianism; dogmatism); and the group of cognitive activity variables (Myers-Briggs: Thinking, Judging, and Intuition; CPI: Ai, Ie; 16 PF: 23, 24; Ideational Activity Pref.; Jancke-Boucsein Cog. Activity Score).
[b]Groups (a) and (b) do not differ significantly from each other; neither do groups (c) and (d). But each of the groups (a) and (b) differs significantly from each of the groups (c) and (d) at the .05 level.
[c]None of the differences between the groups are significant by the Newman-Keuls procedure. However, when group (a) is combined with (b) ($\bar{X} = 1.56$, $SD = 5.66$), the difference between them is significant ($t = 2.60$, $df = 52$, $p < .05$).
*$p < .05$.
**$p < .01$.
***$p < .001$.

variables seem to have different manifestations. Thus, their proportions could help in characterizing different groups of traits.

For the purpose of illustration, we compared prominent groups of traits (Tables 2 and 3; see note *a* to Table 2 and note *a* to Table 3). Table 3 shows that in the four groups of traits (i.e., mental-health traits, emotional-temperamental traits, social-interpersonal traits and cognitive traits), the frequencies of correlations with the four kinds of meaning variables deviate from chance. Such deviations provide important information about the most prominent manifestations of the traits. For example, Table 3 shows that mental health traits and emotional-temperamental traits are correlated with more meaning dimensions and with fewer of the other kinds of meaning variables than social-interpersonal traits or cognitive traits (see also Table 2 about the significantly larger number of meaning dimensions related to mental-health traits than to social-interpersonal traits). This may explain why the former have clearer manifestations in domains and issues that are obviously related to contents, whereas the latter have clearer manifestations in aspects of style and more formal processes. This difference between the two groups of traits is not a matter of either-or but rather of relative emphasis. The finding, however, is a contribution that clarifies the difference between the traits that have traditionally been identified as personality traits and those that have traditionally been called cognitive style variables. It is apparent that both are traits but differ in the relative composition of the meaning variables of which their pattern consists. The meaning system provides a unitary framework for accommodating both types as mere examples of a great variety of different kinds of traits that could exist. Furthermore, it shows that each trait is some kind of integration of the different kinds of meaning-assignment tendencies and enables us to specify in which particular respects a trait resembles the traditional personality traits or the cognitive style traits. This specification would, however, require analyzing the particular meaning-assignment tendencies involved in each case.

5. Positive and Negative Components

The pattern of a trait may be defined through both positive and negative correlations with meaning-assignment tendencies. Table 5 shows that, on the whole, for the 76 traits, there were almost twice (1:1.71) as many positive correlations as negative ones (more so for variables of types of relation and forms of relation than for meaning dimensions and variables of stimulus–referent relations). This preponderance of positive correlations indicates that traits in general consist more of tendencies to respond in certain ways than of tendencies not to respond in certain ways. This conclusion is convincing both intuitively and psychologically.

The fifth characteristic may also be used for comparing traits and expressing differences among traits. Further, different groups of traits may be characterized by different proportions of positive and negative correlations in their patterns of meaning-assignment tendencies. A comparison of groups of traits classified by contents (see note *a* to Table 2 and note *a* to Table 3) shows that the preponderance of positive over negative correlations tends to be larger in regard to social-interpersonal traits and cognitive traits than in regard to emotional-temperamental traits and mental-health traits (Table 5). It is noteworthy that, again, just as in regard to the criterion of proportion of correlations with the four kinds of meaning variables (see above, fourth characteristic), the social-interpersonal traits are grouped together with the cognitive traits, whereas the emotional-temperamental traits are grouped together with the mental-health traits. Here, too, the differentiation makes sense psychodynamically because personality traits in the spheres of emotions and mental health can be expected to involve more avoidance and repression tendencies than, on the one hand, social traits, which are more directly oriented toward action (which promotes positive more than negative tendencies), and on the other hand, cognitive traits, which do not involve as much need for avoidance. Hence, it appears that the two groups of traits—those that refer to emotions and mental health versus the social and cognitive ones—differ from each other.

A detailed examination of the 76 traits reveals that, in the patterns of 24 traits (i.e., 32% of all studied traits), there are more negative than positive correlations with meaning variables. These traits may be characterized as consisting dynamically

Table 4. Distribution of the Positive and Negative Significant Correlations of the Traits in Studies 1–20 with Meaning Variables in Terms of Kinds of Meaning Variables

Meaning variable	Exvia (Cattell)	Extroversion (Eysenck)	Do	Cs	Sy	Sp	Sa	Wb	Re	So	Sc	To	Gi	Cm	Ac	Ai	Ie	Py	Fx	Fe	Mach IV	n power	PF 1	PF 2	PF 3	PF 4	PF 5	PF 6	PF 7
Dim Pos.	5	9	1	1	3	2	2	1	1		2			1		1	1		1	1	7	21	3	1	4	4	6	6	11
Dim Neg.	6	8		1		3		2	2	1	3	1		2		1	2	1	2	3	3	3	3	8	6	5	2	10	3
TR Pos.	1	2	5	7	5	1	7	2	3			3	6	5	7	5	1				1	3		3	1	3	1	2	3
TR Neg.	1	1																					2	5	2	2	1	5	
FR Pos.			3	1	3	4	4	1	1	1	3	1	4	4	2			1											
FR Neg.								3	3			1																	
SR Pos.	1	3	1	1	2	1	3				2		2	2		1													
SR Neg.	1	1						2	3	2		1	1	1					1									6	2
No. of meaning values Pos.			1	1			1																						1
No. of meaning values Neg.			1	1																									
Total Pos.	7	14	11	11	13	8	17	4	5	1	7	4	12	12	9	7	2	1	1	1	8	24	3	5	7	8	8	9	18
Total Neg.	8	10	1	1	3	3	7	8	8	1	3	3	1	3		1	2	1	3	3	3	7	5	13	9	8	3	22	5
Overall	15	24	12	13	11	17	13	10	13	4	10	7	13	15	9	8	4	2	4	4	11	24	8	18	16	16	11	31	23

(CPI scales: Do, Cs, Sy, Sp, Sa, Wb, Re, So, Sc, To, Gi, Cm, Ac, Ai, Ie, Py, Fx, Fe; PF 1–7 = 16 PF)

Meaning variable	16 PF																			Myers-Briggs									
	8	9	10	11	12	13	14	15	17	18	19	20	21	22	23	24	25	26	27	Extroversion	Sensation	Thinking	Judging	Approval Motive	Ego Strength	Anality	Cleanliness, Order	Hypochond.	Avarice
Dim Pos.	4	7	8	9	10	2	7	5	7	1	1	5	6	4	4	3		7		6	10	4	7	4	3	11	13	10	8
Dim Neg.	5	8	5	2	2	2	5	2	3	9	1	7	7	7	1	3	5	4	2	4	5			4	5	3	2	6	1
TR Pos.	1	1	2	2	7	5	3	2	4	2	2	1	5	2	1	2	2	1	1	2	2	8	4	3	3	4	1	2	2
TR Neg.	2	5	6		1			1	1		1	1	1	2		1	3				2	4		5	3	3	2	2	1
FR Pos.																				1			5					1	
FR Neg.																													
SR Pos.	4		1	2	2		4				2		4								2		3				3	2	
SR Neg.		3	3		1							1			1	1					2		1		2				
No. of mean values Pos.							1													1									
No. of mean values Neg.	1	1																											
Total Pos.	9	8	11	11	5	5	7	7	3	5	5	6	15	2	5	5	2	2	2	10	14	12	19	7	6	15	17	15	9
Total Neg.	8	17	14	2	2	2	2	2	9	2	2	9	8	9	2	5	8	4	2	4	9	4	1	9	10	6	4	8	2
Overall	17	25	25	13	7	7	9	9	12	7	7	15	23	11	7	10	10	6	4	14	23	16	20	16	16	21	21	23	11

(continued)

Table 4. *(Continued)*

Meaning variable	Impulsivity	El control	Authoritar.	Dogmatism	Cog. activity Jancke-Boucsein	Ideation. activ. pref.	Motor activ. preference	SSS Sens. seeking	SSS Thrill & adv. seeking	SSS Experience seeking	SSS Disinhibition	SSS Boredom susceptibility	Bem: Mascul.	Bem: Femin.	Bem: Androg.	Bem: Soc. des.	Intolerance of ambiguity	LPC scores	Total
Dim Pos.	7	7	6	10	5	10	6	4	2	11	5	2	3	10	13	3	5	11	368
Dim Neg.	4	9	3	7	9	3	1	3	9	3	2	2	8	2	4	4	6	5	272
TR Pos.	5	4	2	1	7	7	2		1	4		1	3	3	10		4	6	212
TR Neg.	1	3	2		4	1	1	2		1		2	1	1		1	3	1	89
FR Pos.	1		1		2	1				1	3			1	2	1			54
FR Neg.			1		2						1		1				3		15
SR Pos.		6	2	1	1	2	4	1		3	1	1		2	4	1	2		86
SR Neg.		2	2	1	5	1	1	1		1	1	2	3				3		61
No. of meaning values Pos.			1											1	1				9
No. of meaning values Neg.																			3
Total Pos.	13	17	12	12	15	20	12	5	3	19	9	4	6	17	30	5	11	17	729
Total Neg.	5	14	8	8	20	5	3	6	9	5	4	6	13	3	4	5	15	6	440
Total Overall	18	31	20	20	35	25	15	11	12	24	13	10	19	20	34	10	26	23	1,169

Table 5. Comparisons of Different Kinds of Meaning Variables

Meaning variables	No. of cor.	Mean of cor. per variable[a]	Pos. cor.	Neg. cor.	Sig. of dif. (z values)	No. of cor. expected[b]	Sig. of deviation from exp. (z values)
1. Meaning dimensions	640	16.41 (5.38)	368	272	3.75***	543.67	2.77**
2. Types of relation[c]	301	15.05 (7.26)	212	89	7.04***	278.84	.88
3. Stimulus–referent relations	147	11.31 (4.82)	86	61	1.98*	181.19	1.83 ($p = .07$)
4. Forms of relation	69	6.90 (6.27)	54	15	4.58***	153.30	−5.59***
Special variables[d]	12	—	9	3	1.45	13.84	−.17
Total	1,169	—	729	440	8.42***	315.00	22.14***
Significance of differences	Dev. from expected[b]: $\chi^2 = 71.64$*** Dev. from equal distr.: $\chi^2 = 663.48$***	$F = 9.29$*** ($df = 3/79$) *variables:* 1. & 4. $q_r = 6.90$** 1. & 3. $q_r = 3.48$* 2. & 4. $q_r = 6.02$** 3. & 4. $q_r = 3.42$*					

[a]The numbers in parentheses are standard deviations. The significance of differences between variables was tested by the q_r statistic according to the Newman-Keuls procedure.

[b]The expected frequencies were computed on the basis of the percentages of the four kinds of variables, i.e., 46.99%, 24.10%, 15.66%, and 13.25% for meaning dimensions, TR, SR, and FR, respectively. "Special variables" were not included. They were not included in any of the chi-square computations. The deviation from the expected for "special variables" was computed by calculating their expected frequency out of a total of meaning variables that included it, too (i.e., 84 and not 83, the number used for calculating the expected frequencies of the other variables). The deviation from the expected for the total was computed by calculating the expected frequency of 5% significant correlations out of the total number of correlated variables (i.e., 84 meaning variables × 75 traits (not counting LPC, Study 20) = 6,300 correlations; 5% = 315.00).

[c]Includes the variables "lexical mode" and "personal mode" because they are defined in terms of TR.

[d]Includes the variable "number of meaning values."

primarily of tendencies not to respond to external inputs and internal stimulation in certain ways. For example, a set of variables like Cattell's 16 PF tends to include more traits in the patterns of which there are more negative than positive correlations (16 out of 26, i.e., 46%) than a set of variables like the CPI (4 out of 18, i.e., 22%) (see Table 4; see also Studies 2 and 6). Though the difference is not significant ($z = 1.64$, $p < .10$), the proportions suggest at least some tendency for the 16 PF relative to the CPI to assess a greater number of traits involving more avoidance than positive response tendencies.

However, it is again a matter of relative emphasis. Most traits (93%) are correlated both positively and negatively with meaning variables (the exceptions are five traits that correlated only positively) and differ merely in the proportion of these two kinds of correlations.

6. Number of Meaning Variables in the Pattern

This simple characteristic provides a rough index of the size of the pattern. Table 5 shows that the number of meaning variables in the trait pattern varies from 2 (for two CPI scales that would perhaps not qualify at all as traits, i.e., *Py* and *So*, Study 2) to 36 (the Boucsein-Jancke Scale of Cognitive Activity, Study 14). The median is at 14.5 and the mean is at 13.85 ($SD = 6.71$) meaning variables per pattern. It may not be superfluous to note that, because every meaning variable can be involved in more than one trait pattern, one pattern, even when it includes many meaning variables, does not exhaust the possibilities of the system.

The frequency distribution is fairly regular: 25% of the traits were correlated with 2–10 meaning variables, 50% with 11–20, and 25% with 21–36. The distribution is essentially normal, with 70.6% of all traits falling in the range of $\bar{X} \pm 1\ SD$. The normal shape of the distribution suggests that the distribution we obtained is probably stable and may be used for purposes of comparing the patterns of different traits or groups of traits. For example, the mean number of meaning variables in the 18 CPI scales is 9.22 (Study 2); in the 16 PF, it is 14.77 (Study 6); and in the sensation-seeking scale and its four factors, it is 13.80 (Study 15). In all these cases the patterns fall in the range of $\bar{X} \pm 1\ SD$. More deviant cases are represented by external-internal control (31 meaning variables, Study 11) or androgyny as measured by Bem (35 meaning variables, Study 17).

In view of the range of variation in the number of meaning variables in different trait patterns, it is plausible to assume that traits related to more meaning variables are stronger (i.e., have more manifestations in a greater number of different contexts than traits related to fewer meaning variables). The studies in Part II indicate some probable determinants of differences in the number of variables in the patterns.

One determinant may be inheritability. Traits with a large, identifiable genetic component tend to be related to more meaning variables than those with a lower genetic component (this was shown for the CPI scales, Study 2, but not for the 16 PF factors, Study 6).

A second determinant is the age at which a trait becomes manifest. It was found that traits that become manifest only on the adult level, in the early 20s, were related to more meaning variables than traits that are manifest from childhood on (Study 6).

A third determinant is the state of the trait in the specific life period at which it is assessed. Traits that were generally on the increase at the age at which the subject were tested were related to more meaning variables than traits that were, at that time, stable or decreasing (Study 6).

A fourth determinant is the abstractness or level of generality of the trait. Traits that reflect second-order factors in terms of a factor analysis and hence are more abstract or general are related to fewer meaning variables than first-order factors (Study 6).

A fifth determinant may be the structural complexity of a trait. Patterns of traits in which two or more relatively autonomous subclusters were identified (e.g., the patterns corresponding to internal-external control, Studies 11–12, or to intolerance of ambiguity, Studies 18–19) included a larger number of meaning variables than patterns of traits in which no subclusters were evident (Table 5).

A sixth determinant is the content of the trait. A comparison of the traits of different groups (see note *a* to Table 2 and note *a* to Table 3) shows that emotional-temperamental traits are related to more meaning variables than social-interpersonal traits (see Table 2). Because in another context (S. Kreitler & H. Kreitler, 1989c) it was found that measures of beliefs are related to more meaning variables than are measures of behavior, one could perhaps generalize that traits bound more closely to the internal world of cognition and emotions tend to be related to more meaning variables than traits like the social-interpersonal ones that are bound more closely to specific behaviors.

There are, however, also several factors that were found not to affect the size of the pattern, for example, the regularity of the changes in the trait across ages, the degree to which the trait tends to be changed by life events, or the correspondence of the trait as assessed by a questionnaire to parallel traits detected in objective test data or ratings by observers (Study 6).

7. Coherence

The term *coherence* refers to the degree of organization or cohesion characterizing the trait pattern. Admittedly, it is a controversial feature that, at present, rests more on intuitive evaluation than on precise measurement. On analysis, some patterns appeared to be highly coherent and consistent. It was evident that coherence does not depend on the number of meaning variables in the trait pattern or on the complexity of its structure. In a coherent pattern, it was clear (1) what role each meaning variable fulfilled in the pattern and (2) how the meaning variables of the pattern were related to each other and to the overall characteristic(s) of the trait indexed by that pattern. Sometimes, the variables in the pattern tended to group around a small number of clearly detected themes that subserved the total structure. Take, for example, the pattern for androgyny as defined by Bem (Study 17). By comparing the pattern with the allied patterns indexing feminity, masculinity, and social desirability, the meaning variables in the androgyny pattern could be readily identified as those that underlay profemininity, those that manifested anti-masculinity, and those that revealed the low level of the tendency to submit to social desirability. The set of meaning variables corresponding to the need for approval provides another example of a pattern coherent in and through each of its parts. In this case, however, the coherence seemed to be based primarily on the reflection of the total structure in each of the elements. Be that as it may, it was mostly easy to describe the "organized" patterns in a few words or even to assign to them a label.

In contrast, there were patterns that impressed us as somewhat disjointed in the sense that they consisted of several tendencies, each pointing in a different direction, with no sharply delineated or readily identified overall structure. The patterns for traits like anality (Study 8) or extroversion in Eysenck's sense (Study 1) could serve as examples for the less organized structures we observed.

Of course, there is no reason to assume that the traits with patterns low in coherence are functionally less viable than those with patterns high in coherence. Probably, the contrary is true, as those low in coherence would have a greater variety of manifestations that could become evident in different contexts. But those high in coherence would have a different kind of "advantage." It is likely that the clear structure that characterizes them either reflects some culturally familiar stereotype(s) or may become such a stereotype. Hence, an individual who is characterized by a trait pattern high in coherence would be readily identified as having the trait, for example, as being a hypochondriac, a miser, a tough guy, or an authoritarian.

CONCLUDING REMARKS AND AN EXTENDED TRAIT DEFINITION

In this chapter, we have discussed seven major characteristics of the trait pattern: specificity, levels of generality, structure, the relative proportions of the four kinds of meaning variables, positive and negative components, the number of meaning variables in the pattern, and coherence. While introducing these characteristics, we referred frequently to trait comparisons and groupings of similar traits and, in the case of structure, also to detecting subclusters within the trait pattern. Yet, we did not mention trait identification. This omission was not accidental. Each of the characteristics or several of them together can be used for comparing traits. Their choice depends on the particular purpose of the study, and as will be discussed in Chapter 7, many domains of psychological inquiry are likely to benefit from a reliable method of comparing traits. Also, grouping can be carried out in line with one or another characteristic, though some may seem better suited to the task than others. But as long as we compare traits or groups of traits, we stay within the well-circumscribed sphere of traits.

In contrast, trait identification carries us beyond the sphere of traits proper, for it involves the need to examine constructs from related spheres—attitudes, personality dispositions, cognitive tendencies or habits, defense mechanisms, motives, emotions, and so on—to compare them to traits or, rather, to the characteristics of trait patterns, and to evaluate how far they resemble trait patterns or differ from them. If these constructs from related spheres resemble traits sufficiently they can be considered as traits. Hence, the task requires applying simultaneoulsy several of the seven characteristics of trait patterns, setting up criteria for the evaluation of resemblance, and considering the dynamics and functions of traits in a variety of contexts. These requirements can be met better after some familiarity with the working of particular traits has been gained (Part II). Therefore, the description of the procedure will be postponed to Part III. Meanwhile, we will suggest tentatively an extended trait definition, based on the seven described characteristics of trait patterns: A trait is a unique pattern of preferred meaning-assignment tendencies, within a limited numerical range, which are often more positive than negative, are on two levels of generality, include representatives of all three or four kinds of meaning variables in specific proportions, may be structurally complex, and reflect a characteristic grouping of perceptual, cognitive, emotional, and attitudinal manifestations. (For values operationalizing the different criteria, see pp. 74–81, 86, or 304.)

A Methodological Interlude

PURPOSE

The system of meaning plays a dominant and crucial role in the empirical findings and the theoretical conclusions that constitute the stuff of which this book is made. All the studies reported in Part II are based on applying the system of meaning, and all the answers we provide to the questions raised in regard to traits (Chapter 7) are couched in terms of the system of meaning. The system of meaning is a set of various variables, grouped and interrelated in different ways. Being a system implies that it has different properties that characterize it as a whole, beyond those that attach to one or another of its constituents (i.e., meaning variables). For example, there is in the system a certain distribution of meaning variables of different kinds. Properties like these could affect the results obtained when applying the system of meaning. Thus, to continue the previous example, one could wonder whether the distribution of variables in the system determined the distribution of meaning variables in the trait patterns. If the answer to this and similar questions were positive, the validity of our assessment tool and the basis for our conclusions would be seriously impaired. It is evident that the potentially worrisome properties of the meaning system are the trait-irrelevant ones that could exert a distorting impact on the composition and other characteristics of the trait patterns.

It is therefore legitimate to raise the question whether it is likely that the properties of the system of meaning have affected or biased our explorations into the meaning patterns underlying traits. The purpose of this interlude is to cope with this question.

It is called an interlude because it constitutes a break in the ordered flow of presentation. It is located at this point in the exposition because it forms a bridge between the chapter immediately preceding it and the one following it. Indeed, it serves as a kind of appendix to Chapter 5, which dealt with the characteristics of trait patterns, and as a necessary introduction to Chapter 7, which summarizes our answers to questions raised about traits.

TESTING FOR BIASES

The procedure we have adopted in order to examine whether the properties of the meaning system have affected our results rests on two major assumptions. The first is that, given no specific indications based on the meaning system, the chance expectation is that each meaning variable or each particular grouping of these variables would appear equally in the whole set of assessed traits. The second assumption is that, given specific indications based on the meaning system, the chance expectation is that each meaning variable or each particular grouping of these variables would appear according to these indications in the whole set of assessed traits. Accordingly, when the first assumption applies, bias would be indexed by a significant deviation from chance in favor of any meaning variable or a particular grouping of these variables. In contrast, when the second assumption applies, bias would be indexed by the absence of a significant deviation from the distribution specified in line with the properties of the meaning system.

It is evident that the two assumptions are complementary from the point of view of testing for biases. In each case, either the one or the other applies, in line with the specific bias tested for.

QUESTION 1: IS THERE A BIAS PRO OR CONTRA ANY PARTICULAR MEANING VARIABLE?

From the viewpoint of the system of meaning, there is no indication that any particular meaning variable should occur in trait patterns more frequently than any other. Hence, the first assumption applies (see "Testing for Biases" above). This conclusion does not, however, imply that all meaning variables should be correlated with the same number of traits. A more plausible expectation is represented by the normal distribution.

The summary table of the 76 trait patterns (Table 1) shows that every single meaning variable was correlated with at least some traits and that no meaning variable was correlated with all traits. The mean number of traits with which the meaning variables were correlated was 13.99 (SD = 6.50), the median was 11.50, and the range was 1–29. The distribution had a slight positive skewness (Sk = 1.15) but did not deviate significantly from the normal distribution.

Because meaning dimensions, types of relation, forms of relation, and referent-shift variables differ in their frequencies within the meaning system, the above conclusions had to be tested also in regard to each of the four kinds of meaning variables separately. The mean number of traits correlated with meaning dimensions was 16.41 (SD = 5.38) and the range was 7 (for Dim 2a+b) to 29 (for Dim 16); the mean for types of relation was 15.05 (SD = 7.26) and the range was 8 (for TR 1b) to 28 (for TR 3a); the mean for forms of relation was 6.90 (SD = 6.27) and the range was 1 (for FR 6 and FR 7) to 15 (for FR_{far}); and the mean for referent-shift variables was 11.31 (SD = 4.82) and the range was 1 (for SR_{far}) to 19 (for SR 3). None of the four distributions deviated significantly from the normal distribution.

In conclusion, there seems to be no bias pro or contra any specific meaning variable from the viewpoint of its chances to be included in any trait pattern.

QUESTION 2: DID THE CHARACTERISTICS OF THE MEANING SYSTEM BIAS THE DISTRIBUTION OF THE MEANING VARIABLES IN THE TRAIT PATTERNS?

The four kinds of meaning variables are represented in the system of meaning with different frequencies. Meaning dimensions constitute 46.99% of the variables in the system, types of relation constitute 24.10%, forms of relation constitute 15.66%, and referent-shift variables constitute 13.25%. Therefore, in order to examine whether these frequencies determined the frequencies of the meaning variables in the trait patterns, it was necessary to compare the distribution of the meaning variables of the four kinds in the trait patterns, not merely with the chance expectation of equal frequencies but with their distribution in the meaning system. Only if the distribution in the trait patterns deviates significantly from the distribution in the meaning system are we justified in concluding that the findings concerning trait patterns are not determined by the properties of the meaning system in this respect.

A comparison of the distributions showed that the four kinds of meaning variables occurred in the trait patterns in frequencies that deviated significantly not only from the chance expectation of equal frequencies (Table 5, Column 1) but from their frequencies in the meaning system (Table 5, Column 2). This result indicates that the observed patterns of intercorrelations are not determined by the characteristics of the meaning system.

It is of interest to examine in greater detail in which respects the distribution of the four kinds of meaning variables deviates from their distribution in the meaning system. Table 5 shows that, in the patterns of all 76 studied traits, correlations with meaning dimensions and types of relation (TR) are more frequent than correlations with shift of referent variables (SR) and forms of relation (FR). This conclusion is supported by different analyses. For example, correlations with meaning dimensions are more frequent than expected by chance, their mean is higher than the mean of correlations with SR or FR variables, and they occur in 97.3% of all traits (they are missing only in two California Psychological Inventory [CPI] scales). The least frequent are correlations with FR variables: their frequency deviates massively from the expected and they occur in only 36% of the traits. SR and TR variables are in between the extremes. SR variables are somewhat less frequent than expected, but they occur in 69.3% of the traits. TR variables have precisely the expected frequency, their mean does not differ significantly from the mean of correlations for dimensions, and they occur in 93.3% of the traits.

QUESTION 3: WAS THERE ANY BIAS IN THE CHANCES OF ANY GROUPING OF MEANING VARIABLES TO BE INCLUDED IN THE TRAIT PATTERNS?

This question could be handled best by examining various groupings of meaning variables within the four kinds of meaning variables. The groupings reflect different points of view and were not necessarily formed for the sake of the study of traits. The assumptions concerning chance expectations conformed mostly to the first assumption (of equal occurrence; i.e., see below, A, B, D, E, F, and G), and in one case (i.e., C) to the second assumption.

A. Within Meaning Dimensions: Orientation toward External and Internal Reality. Focusing on external reality or the internal reality is one of the hallmarks of different types of personality. Even a cursory view reveals that some of the meaning dimensions appear to reflect an orientation toward the more objective reality—for example, the meaning dimensions "Material" (*Dim* 9) or "Sensory Qualities" (*Dim* 19a)—whereas others reflect an orientation toward the internal and more subjective reality, for example, the meaning dimensions "Feelings and Emotions" (*Dim* 20a,

20b, 20a+b) or "Cognitive Qualities" (*Dim* 22a, 22b, 22a+b). Given that the selection of the 76 traits studied in Part II was not biased, if there is no bias in the meaning dimensions we may expect an equal involvement in the trait patterns of meaning dimensions orienting externally or internally.

In order to examine this issue, two groups of meaning dimensions were formed in line with the judgment of two psychologists who were not involved in the project and who worked independently. They were provided with explanations of the meaning system and the two orientations and then were asked to categorize the meaning dimensions into three groups: those that reflected orientation to external reality, those that reflected orientation to internal reality, and those that were irrelevant to these categories. The resulting groups of meaning dimensions included only those for which the two psychologists provided fully identical judgments. Thus, the group of meaning dimensions reflecting the external orientation included *Dim* 3, *Dim* 4a, *Dim* 4b, *Dim* 4a+b, *Dim* 8a, *Dim* 8b, *Dim* 8a+b, *Dim* 9, *Dim* 12, *Dim* 13, *Dim* 14, and *Dim* 19a, whereas the group of meaning dimensions reflecting the internal orientation included *Dim* 19b, *Dim* 20a, *Dim* 20b, *Dim* 20a+b, *Dim* 21a, *Dim* 21b, *Dim* 21a+b, *Dim* 22a, *Dim* 22b, and *Dim* 22a+b. The number of traits with which the meaning dimensions in each group were correlated was counted. A comparison of means showed that the two groups did not differ significantly in the number of correlated traits (for "external": $\bar{X} = 16.67$, $SD = 4.70$; for "internal": $\bar{X} = 19.00$, $SD = 5.03$; $t = 1.11$, $df = 20$, n.s.).

B. Within Meaning Dimensions: Quarters of the Meaning Circle. As described in Chapter 2 ("The Meaning Variables"), the meaning dimensions fall into a circular arrangement approximating the circumplex model. This arrangement reflects various degrees of proximity in content, co-occurrence, and developmental course. It could be argued that meaning dimensions closer to each other along the circle represent groupings and hence have higher chances of entering trait patterns than groupings in other parts of the circle. In order to examine this issue, it was necessary to subdivide the circular model. We did it in line with factors derived from factor analyses in different samples. These analyses revealed four recurrent bipolar factors (see Figure 1). The first factor is defined approximately by the polarity of "Contextual Allocation" (*Dim* 1) and "Sensory Qualities" (*Dim* 19b); the second is defined approximately by the polarity of "Action" (*Dim* 4) and "Feelings and Emotions" (*Dim* 20); the third is defined approximately by the polarity of "Causes" (*Dim* 6) and "Temporal Qualities" (*Dim* 16); and the fourth is defined approximately by the polarity of "Possessions and Belongingness" (*Dim* 17) and "Structure" (*Dim* 10).

We wanted to partition the circle into four quarters because more parts would represent sections too small for the comparisons we planned to make, and because we had evidence from previous studies about the psychological meaningfulness of quarters of the circle (S. Kreitler, Drechsler, & H. Kreitler, 1985a, 1988). Thus, we decided to partition the circle of meaning dimensions into two separate sets of four quarters, one in line with the first two factors and the other in line with the latter two factors. The rationale for the pairwise combination of factors were differences between the two sets of factors: (1) the first two factors account for a larger part of the variance than the latter two factors, and (2) the first two factors are manifest already in data obtained from children 6–8 years old, whereas the latter two factors do not become manifest before the age of 14–16 years.

It is noteworthy that each pair of factors yields four quarters of the circle that lend themselves readily to characterization. Thus, the first pair yields the following four quarters: (1) conceptual-causal aspects: *Dim* 1, *Dim* 14, *Dim* 18, *Dim* 6, *Dim* 7, and *Dim* 3; (2) actional-objective aspects: *Dim* 4, *Dim* 5, *Dim* 2, *Dim* 10, *Dim* 9, *Dim* 12, *Dim* 15, and *Dim* 13; (3) experiential aspects: *Dim* 19, *Dim* 16, and *Dim* 20; and (4) evaluative aspects: *Dim* 11, *Dim* 21, *Dim* 22, *Dim* 17, and *Dim* 8.

The second pair of factors yields the following four quarters: (1) conceptual-identificatory aspects: *Dim* 17, *Dim* 8, *Dim* 1, *Dim* 14, and *Dim* 18; (2) actional-functional aspects: *Dim* 6, *Dim* 7, *Dim* 3, *Dim* 4, and *Dim* 5; (3) material-sensory aspects: *Dim* 2, *Dim* 10, *Dim* 9, *Dim* 12, *Dim* 15, *Dim* 13, *Dim* 19, and *Dim* 16; and (4) experiential-evaluative aspects: *Dim* 20. *Dim* 11, *Dim* 21, and *Dim* 22.

Thus, according to each of the two partitions, there are 6–13 meaning dimensions in each quarter (counting the subdivisions and their additions). For each partition, we compared the mean number of traits with which the meaning dimensions in the quarter were correlated. The results for the quarters of the first partition were $\bar{X}$ = 17.83 (SD = 3.66), $\bar{X}$ = 14.08 (SD = 5.14), $\bar{X}$ = 18.71 (SD = 6.82), and $\bar{X}$ = 16.15 (SD = 5.37), respectively, and for the quarters of the second partition, $\bar{X}$ = 14.11 (SD = 3.44), $\bar{X}$ = 18.00 (SD = 4.55), $\bar{X}$ = 15.33 (SD = 7.02), and $\bar{X}$ = 18.00 (SD = 5.10), respectively. The mean differences were not significant in either of the two partitions. These findings indicate that the structure of the circular model, when examined in quarter chunks, does not affect the chances of the meaning dimensions to be involved in the trait patterns.

C. Within Meaning Dimensions: Adjoining Proximities on the Meaning Circle. The circular model of meaning dimensions represents relative proximities among the dimensions (see Chapter 2, "The Meaning Variables"). It was shown above that, when the proximities were grouped into quarters, there was no effect of proximity on correlations with the whole sample of traits. However, one may further inquire whether the fact that meaning dimensions are placed in adjoining positions along the circle (i.e., they have relatively the highest degree of similarity) does not affect their chances to be included in the pattern of the same trait. More specifically, if one meaning dimension is correlated with a trait, would not this fact increase the chances of the adjoining meaning dimensions, on its right and left along the circle, to be correlated with the same trait? If the answer were positive we would have evidence of the "spread of effect" in meaning dimensions. Evidence for such an effect would, however, detract from the validity of our findings about trait patterns.

This issue was examined specifically in Study 14 (Part II) in regard to the tendencies of cognitive or of motor activities. We examined whether the meaning dimensions immediately adjoining a meaning dimension correlated with a trait have a higher than chance probability to be correlated with that trait. The findings showed that the occurrence of such correlations did not deviate significantly from chance (for details, see Study 14 and Table 29). Hence, it is justified to conclude that proximity between meaning dimensions did not bias the detected relations between meaning dimensions and traits.

D. Within Types of Relation: The Four Types. The four types of relation represent major categories of relating cognitive content to referents (see Chapter 2, "The Meaning Variables"). Each highlights a different set of processes that may play a crucial role in the shaping of personality and its manifestations. The four types of relation are the attributive, the comparative, the exemplifying-illustrative, and the metaphoric-symbolic. If there is no bias from the viewpoint of the system of meaning, the four types of relation should prove to be correlated with the same number of traits. The mean number of traits correlated with the attributive type of relation was 11.33 (SD = 3.05), with the comparative 18.20 (SD = 5.76), with the exemplifying-illustrative 16.25 (SD = 8.14), and with the metaphoric-symbolic 15.50 (SD = 5.07). The differences were not significant (F = 1.03, df = 3/13, n.s.). Hence there was no bias with respect to the involvement of the four types of relation in trait patterns.

E. Within Types of Relation: Modes of Meaning. As mentioned before (Chapter 2, "The Meaning Variables"), the modes of meaning are defined in terms of a binary grouping of the types of relation: the lexical interpersonally shared meaning mode is defined by the attributive and comparative types of relation, whereas the personal-subjective mode is defined by the exemplifying-illustrative and the metaphoric-symbolic types of relation. Is there a bias in favor or disfavor of one or another of the modes of meaning insofar as correlations with traits are concerned? The chance expectation is equal numbers of correlations of traits with the two modes. Hence, the first assumption applies again (see "Testing for Biases" in this chapter). The mean of correlations with the lexical mode was 14.56 (SD = 7.05), and with the personal mode 14.50 (SD = 7.51). The difference was not significant. It is therefore justified to conclude that there is no bias in regard to the modes of meaning.

F. Within Referent-Shift Variables: Shifts Near and Far. The referent-shift variables can be readily grouped into those that represent transformations of referents closer to the original input (i.e., SR_{near}: SR 1, SR 3, SR 4, SR 5, SR 6, SR 8) and those that represent transformations of referents further from the original input (i.e., SR_{far} SR 2, SR 7, SR 9, SR 10). The salience of one or another grouping of referent-shift variables in trait patterns has important implications in regard to personality manifestations in general and in regard to reality testing in particular. Hence, it is important to check whether there is, in trait patterns, a bias pro or contra one or another grouping of referent shifts.

The mean of correlations with traits for close shifts was 12.57 (SD = 4.20) and for far shifts 9.60 (SD = 6.02). The difference was not significant (t = .95, df = 10, n.s.). Hence, it is justified to conclude that there is no bias in regard to close and far shifts of referent.

G. Within Forms of Relation: Assertion and Negation. The two major groupings of forms of relation are the assertive (i.e., FR_{pos}: FR 1, FR 3, FR 4, FR 5, FR 6) and the negating (i.e., FR_{neg}: FR 2, FR 7) kinds of forms of relation. The personality manifestations of these two kinds of forms of relation are highly different. Therefore, it is important to test whether there is, in trait patterns, a bias pro or contra any of these kinds of forms of relation.

The mean of correlations with traits for the assertive forms of relation was 5.33 (SD = 6.66), and for the negating forms of relation 6.80 (SD = 7.05). Hence, it is justified to conclude that there is no bias in regard to assertive and negating forms of relation.

SOME GENERAL CONCLUSIONS

In this interlude, we tested whether there were any biases affecting our data because of properties built into the meaning system. We raised different questions and applied a variety of tests. The findings are complementary, and they all support the following conclusion: It is unlikely that any trait-irrelevant characteristics in the meaning system as a whole or in any of its parts have affected the correlations between the meaning variables and the personality traits. In a more positive formulation of the same conclusion, each correlation of a trait with a meaning variable reflects the dynamics of the trait and may therefore be used to promote understanding of that trait in particular and of personality traits in general.

The Answers: A Summary of Contributions

ANSWERING THE QUESTIONS

After discussing the plight of the trait concept (Chapter 1), we posed a series of questions and suggested that, if proper and scientifically sound answers could be given to these questions, the trait concept would reemerge from its present controversial state. When it becomes free from the serious problems that have bogged it down, its potentialities as an explanatory concept may be further examined and expanded. We think that our findings provide the required answers. As a matter of fact, most of them were given in the previous chapters, whereas some will be substantiated by the studies presented in Part II and the applications discussed in Part III of this book. There are two reasons that we have answered the questions already rather than saving them for the final chapter, perhaps as a concluding reward for the persistent reader who will pursue this road with us to its very end. One is that, though the answers are pertinent to each single trait, they relate directly to the problems of the trait concept that have already been discussed. Second, keeping in mind the answers, or at least their gist, may help in counterbalancing the mass of details of the 22 studies in Part II and could provide a frame of reference for trait testing and trait research (Part III). Be that as it may, one of the better known of "Murphy's laws" states that, when there is a problem, it always helps to know the solution. By the same token, if there is a solution, it is better to know it sooner than later. For the sake of clarity, we repeat the questions and answer them one by one.

QUESTION 1. WHAT IS A TRAIT AND WHAT IS THE EPISTEMOLOGICAL AND EXISTENTIAL STATUS OF THE TRAIT CONCEPT?

Though derived from a new theoretical approach to cognition, our definition of *trait* is heuristic in the sense that it was developed in line with 76 common personality traits. However, it could and—for the sake of a neat classification—it should be made normative so as to enable eventually excluding those phenomena that deviate appreciably from the observed values (for example, in the case of meaning, those that deviate by more than one or two standard deviations). We defined a trait as being a uniquely composed and thus trait-specific pattern of preferred meaning-assignment tendencies that—owing to their singly and/or interactively exerted influence on input identification, input elaboration, belief formation and belief retrieval—are bound to specific perceptual, cognitive, and behavioral manifestations. Most often, the pattern consists of meaning variables of three or four kinds in specific proportions. The kinds more likely to occur are meaning dimensions and types of relation, and those less likely to occur are stimulus-referent variables and forms of relation. Meaning dimensions are often overrepresented, and forms of relation are often underrepresented. Typically, there are more positive than negative meaning preferences in the trait pattern. The mean number of meaning variables in the pattern is 13.85 ($SD = 6.71$). Thus, the pattern underlying a particular trait is a unique trait-specific combination of meaning preferences. In addition, the patterns underlying different traits may differ from each other—and often do—with respect to their level of generality, their structural features, their relative proportions of the different kinds of meaning variables, their relative frequencies of positive and negative meaning preferences, the number of meaning assignment tendencies in the pattern, and their coherence or degree of organization.

In line with McGuire's methodological suggestions (1983), it may be advantageous to examine this new trait concept from the viewpoint of its intrinsic and extrinsic characteristics. The epistemological analysis of the intrinsic characteristics of this trait concept shows that it is internally consistent (1) because all its components are meaning variables, and (2) because their interactions result in mutual strengthening or weakening. The fact that the suggested trait concept is based on a new approach to traits, which is cognitive, and on a new approach within the cognitive framework itself, which is meaning-anchored, testifies to the novelty of the concept. Further, because every trait pattern contains only constituents that proved to be significantly correlated with the trait, the trait concept is parsimonious. Owing to the specificity of the pattern of meaning variables underlying each trait, the concept deserves to be regarded as sufficiently specific to represent what it stands for. The list of seven trait characteristics (Chapter 5) further increases the specificity of the concept by enabling discriminations between traits and other tendencies and habits in the domains of personality and cognition. As for the concept's elegance, we leave the judgment to others. It is evident that the concept also has an empirical basis (see Part II), the major characteristic required of personality concepts by Fiske (1978).

The most important extrinsic characteristic of the suggested trait concept seems to be its empirical *refutability*. One could refute it, for instance, by showing that individuals whose meaning profile contains the same pattern of preferred meaning-assignment tendencies do not have the same trait (as would be indicated by our findings) but different traits. A refutation of this kind presupposes the measurement of traits by the same instruments we used in Parts II and III. More recently, Karl Popper's followers expect a good concept (or theory) to survive empirical refutation by *post hoc* adaptation or immunization (Albert, 1985). This procedure is exemplified by what was done to uphold Keppler's laws of elliptical planetary orbits. The deviations observed in these orbits were eventually interpreted as deflections due to the gravitational impact of another planet. Because our trait concept has been derived from a general conception of cognition and cognitive processes, it is likely that it has this kind of survival capacity and could be immunized. Whether it should be is more a question of scientific decency and taste.

Last but not least, the intrinsic parsimony of our trait concept has its extrinsic or pragmatic repercussion in regard to assessment. The concept enables us to use one single test, that is, the Meaning Questionnaire, to measure the same phenomena whose measurement up to now required the use of a great many trait questionnaires.

Finally, it may not be superfluous to note that our trait concept also stands up well to a fairly new criterion, with mixed intrinsic and extrinsic features, that has recently been emphasized in personality research: the power to give rise to further theoretical conceptions (Maddi, 1980). As will be indicated in the next chapter and in greater detail in a forthcoming book (S. Kreitler & H. Kreitler, 1989c), our trait concept has paved the way for developing a comprehensive cognitive theory of personality.

As for its existential status, our trait concept shares its existential problems with other psychological concepts. That is, it is as "real" as instincts, according to the ethological definitions of Tinbergen (1951) or Lorenz (1969); conflicts, according to the topological definition of Kurt Lewin (1936); plans, according to the information-processing definition of Miller, Galanter, and Pribram (1960); behavioral intents, according to the cognitive-orientational definition of H. Kreitler and S. Kreitler (1976); schema, according to the genetic-epistemological definition of Piaget (1951); and so on. We can diagnose it, we can measure it, and, last but not least, we can discuss it with some conviction that we know what we are talking about. Again, like instinct, conflict, plan, behavioral intent, schema, hunger, love, or gravitation, meaning-assignment tendencies are not given to direct observation. What can be observed are their manifestations. The terms *preference* and *pattern* as used by us designate quantitative concepts derived from measurement and supported by statistical findings.

QUESTION 2. WHAT ARE THE TYPICAL MANIFESTATIONS OF TRAITS?

It is an amazing peculiarity of our trait concept that it allows for "inventing" or constructing new traits without an *a priori* reference to their manifestations. Select 8–20 meaning variables, let them be of three or four kinds, assume that about two thirds are positively preferred, whereas one third is negatively preferred, and postulate at least some interactions between them, and you have not only a hypothetical trait but also ample information about its most likely manifestations, as presented in Appendix B. The importance of this modest thought experiment is threefold: (1) it indicates the general validity of our trait concept; (2) it suggests a strategy for trait research; and (3) most relevant in the present context, it emphasizes our well-substantiated claim that the so-called trait manifestations are due mainly to the specific meaning-assignment tendencies in the pattern and, to a lesser extent, to their interactions.

As already indicated, Appendix B lists the hitherto identified manifestations of meaning variables, including several that resulted from interactions of meaning variables. The majority are manifestations of those meaning variables that appeared as preferred meaning-assignment tendencies in one or more trait patterns. Others are manifestations known to us from our studies of cognitive functioning and skills. The procedures used to obtain these data are explained in the introduction to Part II and are exemplified by the 22 studies presented in Part II.

The identified trait manifestations include a variety of reactions, such as perceptual, cognitive, attitudinal, experiential, and behavioral. Most of the manifestations are in the cognitive sphere and consist in susceptibility to certain classes of inputs and direct and indirect input elaborations, as well as outcomes of these.

Appendix B can be used profitably only in conjunction with meaning profiles because they indicate which are the preferred meaning-assignment tendencies whose manifestations have to be looked up. Given this easily available information, merely consulting Appendix B may resolve some of the obstinate problems haunting trait research.

Take the case of the approval motive (Part II, Study 8). It was often assumed that approval seeking consists in a special concern about and a craving for a positive evaluation by others. Observations, however, were not always consistent with this thesis, which is focal in the understanding of the approval motive. The reason becomes evident from the meaning profile of the high scores on the approval motive questionnaire. It includes a positive preference for the meaning subdimension "Feelings and Emotions Evoked in Others" (*Dim* 20a) but not for the meaning dimension "Judgments and Evaluations." According to Appendix B, the manifestations of the subdimension *Dim* 20a include special concern about emotional acceptance by others, which may or may not imply positive evaluation by others. This finding explains why the postulated concern about positive evaluation by others occurred with such disturbing inconsistency.

Similarly, a logically consistent and apparently justified concept extrapolation led to the assumption that extroverts have a particularly high tolerance of pain (Part II, Study 1). Validation research carried out with common electrodermal and thermal stimuli yielded inconsistent results (Part II, Study 1). A glance at the negative preference of extroverts for the meaning subdimension "Sensory Qualities of Referent" (*Dim* 19b) reveals that a sweeping generalization is not justified. Extroverts have a negative preference specifically for thermal sensations but not for kinesthetic and dermal ones. Hence, they may be expected to evidence higher tolerance of pain when the stimuli are thermal than when they are electrothermal. Because of phenomena like these, Appendix B also lists manifestations of subdimensions, whenever available.

A further example hinges on the manifestations of the four kinds of meaning variables. The manifestations of meaning dimensions are revealed predominantly through concern with content, whereas those of the other kinds of meaning variables are revealed mainly through concern with formal, stylistic, and modificational aspects. This characterization of the major manifestations of kinds of meaning variables could have helped to settle the controversy concerning the nature of dogmatism: whether it is essentially a striving for extremes, right or left, or a devotion to the right-wing ideology (Part II, Study 13). The former view characterizes dogmatism as a matter of style; the latter, as a matter of content. Noting the preference for meaning dimensions evidenced by high scorers on dogmatism reveals at a glance that it is more a matter of content than of style, more ideology than extremism. Authoritarianism is, however, a more complex story (Part II, Study 13).

Our last example is focused on anality (Part II, Study 8). One important question concerning a trait like anality is whether it is a direct reflection of fixations in the anal stage (in line with Freud's developmental scheme), or whether it is anchored mainly on the so-called sublimatory level. If Freud was right in his contention that manifestations like concern with possessions, functionality, and time indicate a higher sublimatory level than concern with smell and touch, then anality is strongly modified by sublimation. The basis for our conclusion is the finding that high scores on anality correlate positively with the meaning dimensions "Possessions" (*Dim* 17), "Function" (*Dim* 3), and "Temporal Qualities" (*Dim* 16), and negatively with the "Sensory Qualities" subdimensions "Tactility" (*Dim* $19a_4$) and "Smell" (*Dim* $19a_7$). Again, the manifestations of these meaning-assignment tendencies can be found in Appendix B. This appendix provides, for the time being, a satisfactory answer to the question concerning trait manifestations. In the future, it may be extended by new findings about the manifestations of the meaning variables in a broad range of domains ranging from cognition to personality.

QUESTION 3. WHAT ARE THE SIMILARITIES OR DIFFERENCES BETWEEN TRAITS AS WELL AS BETWEEN TRAITS AND RELATED CONCEPTS?

Trait comparisons are usually performed between concepts that have already been identified as traits by some rule or procedure. Comparisons of traits with other constructs are usually performed between traits that have been identified as such and other constructs whose nature may be more or less clear. Some of the latter are often called *habits, attitudes, inclinations, predispositions, tendencies, personal styles, temperamental features,* even *emotions* and *motives,* or more generally, *psychological* or *social-psychological constructs.*

The goals of trait comparisons may be to identify precisely in which respects two or more traits resemble or differ from each other, which traits resemble each other more than they resemble other traits, where the differences between common groups of traits lie, and so on. The goals of comparisons between traits and other constructs often resemble the goals of intratraits comparisons. They are usually designed to allow the specification of points of similarity or difference between the traits and the nontraits or to allow the discovery of constructs that resemble one or several traits more than they resemble others. Yet, in addition, the new suggested trait concept enables one also to use extratrait comparisons in order to identify traits among variables that are not usually conceived as traits or to discriminate more sharply between traits and nontraits (e.g., Kreitler, Kreitler, & Carasso, 1989). In any case, intratrait and extratrait comparisons may be expected to contribute appreciably to the deepening of our understanding of traits.

Both intratrait and extratrait comparisons are lines of research that can hardly be performed without the new trait concept. As already mentioned, the seven characteristics of traits, discussed in Chapter 5, provide the major means of conducting these comparisons.

The kind of conclusions provided by trait comparisons may be illustrated through some of the findings we obtained by applying mainly the first of the seven characteristics (specificity), which is also the only nonformal one. For instance, a comparison of neuroticism and psychoticism as defined by Cattell showed that they differ in the strategies available for deviating from interpersonally shared reality

(Part II, Study 6). Whereas neuroticism consists largely in focusing on specific content (as indexed by the meaning dimensions), psychoticism is manifested more in types of relation (e.g., symbolization) and stimulus-referent relations that mediate transformations of the input.

Another comparison was carried out between two correlated measures of preferences for cognitive activities (Part II, Study 14). The underlying patterns of meaning-assignment tendencies showed that high scorers on one scale (Stein and Craik's Ideational Activity Preference Score) were concerned with cognitive activities because of a positive interest in this particular sphere, whereas high scorers on the other scale (Janke-Boucsein's Cognitive Activity Score) were concerned with cognitive activities because of a low preference for motor activities and for other aspects of reality.

A comparison of the four scales of the Myers-Briggs Type Inventory (Part II, Study 7) indicated that the scales "Feeling" and "Thinking" differ primarily in types of relation, the former assessing the personal mode of meaning, the latter, the lexical mode, whereas the other scales differ in other meaning variables. The differences between the scales "Sensation" and "Intuition" revealed that they are amazingly complementary, almost mirror images of each other.

Again, the comparison between subjects high on external or internal control (Part II, Studies 11–12) showed that both were concerned with enhancing their grasp of reality but in different ways, the former by focusing on specific content (e.g., sensory qualities and material), the latter by low preference for the strategies that define the personal mode of meaning.

Comparisons of three traits—the approval motive, ego strength, and anality—were used for uncovering the common core of these traits, in an attempt to identify their common dynamics (Part II, Study 8).

Finally, another comparison of traits showed that social desirability resembled masculinity, whereas, contrary to expectations, androgyny did not consist of features shared by masculinity but of preferences for features typical of femininity and a low preference for features typical of masculinity (Part II, Study 17). This last example also demonstrates the usefulness of the pattern of meaning variables for studying the dynamics of stereotypes in traits.

The above examples show how comparisons of the meaning variables in different trait patterns help in specifying the similarities and differences of the different traits. Considering in addition the proportion of identical or similar meaning variables in the different trait patterns enables us to understand, as well as to predict, the extent of the correlation between them (e.g., Part II, Studies 8 and 14). The same principle can be extended to groups of traits forming statistically defined factors or types. This principle was applied in regard to curiosity behaviors and generated a procedure for the systematic specification of the nature of factors (S. Kreitler & H. Kreitler, 1986c; see Chapter 12, "Characterizing Factors").

Also, similarities and differences between traits and other constructs may be expressed in terms of one or more of the seven trait characteristics. For example, a comparison of the pattern of meaning-assignment tendencies corresponding to seven anxiety scales with the set of features characteristic of traits showed that the patterns underlying the anxiety scales resembled the trait patterns in three respects (i.e., the number of meaning variables in the pattern, the inclusion of meaning variables of four kinds, and deviations of these from the chance distribution) but differed from them in another respect (i.e., in the proportion of the different kinds of meaning variables) (S. Kreitler & H. Kreitler, 1985a). This comparison provided insight into the issue of whether anxiety, even so-called trait anxiety, is a trait. It showed that anxiety is highly similar to traits, yet not identical to them. The major difference between anxiety and traits is that the anxiety patterns have an exaggerated salience of meaning dimensions, namely, concern with specific content at the expense of other meaning variables. Hence, anxiety can be best characterized as a traitlike pattern of meaning-assignment tendencies (see also Chapter 11 and Chapter 12, "Comparing Traits").

QUESTION 4. WHAT ARE THE ATTRIBUTES OF TRAITS?

This is a double question because it relates to traits in general and to each trait in particular. The attributes common to all traits are outlined in our definition of trait and are specified in the list of the seven trait characteristics: specificity, two levels of generality, structure, kinds and proportions of different meaning variables, positive and negative constituents, number of meaning-assignment variables, and coherence (Chapter 5). Notably, all characteristics refer to the pattern of meaning-assignment variables and are related to the trait by means of the concept that views the pattern as underlying the trait.

In addition, each trait, being by definition unique, should have specific attributes. Most of these attributes are determined by the meaning-assignment tendencies of the pattern of that particular trait, whereas some result from interactions and hence may be the product of a mutual strengthening or weakening of trait manifestations (Chapter 4). It is possible that there are more complex kinds of interaction, based, for instance, on qualitive modifications that may bring about manifestations beyond those listed in Appendix B. So far, we have not encountered them in our studies, but with the refinement of observations, what today is viewed as a remote possibility may tomorrow be the focus of intense research.

QUESTION 5. ARE THERE DIFFERENT KINDS OF TRAITS?

As often mentioned, our trait concept constitutes a framework for integrating all kinds of personality traits, but it also provides criteria for spelling out similarities and differences among traits, which, in turn, could be used for the systematic classification of traits (Chapter 5). The choice of specific criteria for grouping depends on the purpose of the classification. A psychologist influenced by the structuralist anthropology of Lévi-Strauss may choose subclusters of meaning variables or levels of generality as guiding principles in classifying the traits of natives, whereas a psychologist excited about cultural anthropology of the kind advocated by M. Mead or R. Benedict may strive to class the traits in terms of common meaning dimensions or even in line with the salience of particular meaning values. Again, if the purpose is to establish a classification based on the range of the trait's manifestations, perhaps the number of meaning variables in the pattern would be an appropriate criterion; but if the purpose were to set up classes of traits based on internal cohesion, then coherence would probably be the adequate criterion.

Actually the seven characteristics provide for 10 criteria because each of five of the characteristics supplies one criterion, whereas the third characteristic, "Structure," provides three structural criteria (i.e., the existence of subclusters of meaning variables, subclusters of meaning values, and cross-trait subclusters), and the fourth characteristic, "Meaning Variables of Different Kinds and Their Properties in the Pattern," provides two criteria (i.e., the number of kinds of meaning variables and their proportions). If one considers the seven characteristics or the 10 criteria and in addition the meaning variables themselves with their specific manifestations, it seems likely that the means available for systematic trait classification probably surpass the meaningful requirements for classification on the part of psychologists. Yet, there is a price to pay for this multipurpose classification potential. Our meaning concept neither points toward nor implies a particular grouping of traits as the most desirable or useful one. Thus, it cannot offer a definite answer to this traditional but obviously imprecise, perhaps even ill-conceived, question about different kinds of traits.

Therefore, there seem to be three alternatives for coping with this issue. One would derive from the characteristics of traits as defined in terms of the meaning system. It could be called the *trait-based hypothetical approach* and would generate suggestions to classify traits, for example, in line with their structural features, or relative proportions of positive and negative preferences, or relative proportions of the four kinds of meanings variables in the pattern. Each classification of this type would have to be tested for its meaningfulness or the range of phenomena for which it could account.

Another alternative would derive from the characteristics of the meaning system. It could be called the *meaning-based hypothetical approach* and would generate suggestions to classify traits, for example, in line with positive preferences for meaning dimensions located close to one another or placed in specific quarters of the circumplex model (see Figure 1 in Chapter 2; Chapter 6), or according to the salience of one or another or both modes of meaning in the patterns. Also, the meaningfulness of these "traits" would have to be tested.

The third alternative would consist in applying the different means provided by our trait concept for examining the validity of existing trait classifications. It could be called the *realistic post hoc approach,* and it leads to the kind of comparisons we carried out in regard to the common classification of traits into mental-health traits, emotional-temperamental traits, social-interpersonal traits, and cognitive traits (see Chapter 5 and Tables 2 and 3). We found that these groups of traits differed, for example, in terms of levels of generality, proportions of positive and negative preferences, and proportions of the four kinds of meaning variables. The observed differences shed light on characteristics of these groups of traits, for example, concern with specific content in mental-health traits versus concern with stylistic aspects in cognitive traits. These differences also indicated a further internal classification into mental-health and emotional-tempermental traits, which corresponds to a widely shared intuition that, up to now, could not be confirmed (see also Chapter 12, "Identifying the General Class of Traits").

In sum, the new trait concept enables us to set up classifications of traits, suggests such classifications, and makes possible the testing of existing classifications. At present, it is justified to conclude that there are different kinds of traits, but before more research is done, it is premature to venture a statement about the most comprehensive, useful, or best-founded classification, if any.

QUESTION 6. WHAT IS THE STRUCTURE OF TRAITS?

Because structure is one of the seven characteristics of traits that were discussed in Chapter 5, reference to that section would suffice as an answer, were it not for the fuzzy nature of structure. Despite or because of its frequent use in so many domains of human knowledge, structure is such a multifaceted concept that its criteria are anything but univocal. In which respect, then, does our trait concept qualify as a structure? Concomitance of components in general and of meaning-assignment tendencies in particular does not necessarily make them into a structure, even when their impact is common. We did demonstrate interaction of the trait constituents (Part II, Study 22), yet we did not demonstrate it in regard to each trait, nor did we show that it takes place whenever the trait is invoked. The same holds true for subclusters, because we did not check them in regard to all traits. Both interaction and internal organization would be generally accepted criteria of structure.

Many psychologists, however, consider oversummative qualities or whole effects as the earmarks of structure (Köhler, 1947; Piaget, 1970). This criterion was already highly valued by Plato and was resurrected by the Graz and Berlin schools of Gestalt psychology. Though demonstrated in hundreds of well-controlled experiments, it has not remained unchallenged, mainly because there are no univocal measures for wholeness. Attneave's interesting suggestion (1954) that gestalts be assessed in terms of redundancies would at best distinguish only between good and bad gestalts (and even only insofar as probability calculations can be carried out reliably, which is rarely the case); but this approach would not distinguish between the presence or absence of a gestalt (i.e., a structure). More important, the Attneave's measure is unfit for dealing with structures formed by content variables because of the abyss between information measurements and meaning (H. Kreitler & S. Kreitler, 1976, Chapter 2; Miller, 1965). Even in regard to visual gestalts, all attempts to prove their "objective" existence—for example, by observing isomorphic cortical representations—have failed. Hence, wholeness remains an experiential fact, a concept or thought product that, notwithstanding sporadic protestations from the behaviorist camp, most investigators accept as something that, if at all admitted, can only be grasped, because it cannot be detected by analyzing the parts of the whole.

Long before the advent of scientific psychology, traits were perceived as distinct trends or inclinations with given labels, notwithstanding occasional variations in their manifestations. Even extroversion and introversion, as originally described by Jung, have intuitively convincing whole characteristics that have survived to some extent despite the fogging impact of the Eysenckian dichotomous cloud of low-level correlations. Yet, Eysenck's admirable tenacity in showing what goes with what, as well as Cattell's broad-ranging and depth-sounding factor analyses, will eventually make it necessary to find clear distinctions between the nucleus and the periphery of each trait, the former carrying its whole characteristics, and the latter describing the boundaries of its varying manifestations.

Our data provided evidence of three kinds in regard to the "whole properties" of the trait pattern. One concerns the functioning of the trait pattern. The pattern mostly functions through a selective application of some of its constituents so that a part of the pattern represents the whole.

The second kind of evidence concerns the unique combination of constancy and change represented by the trait pattern. The pattern consists of preferred meaning-assignment tendencies that remain constant despite changes in its manifestations due to (1) selective evocation; (2) interactions; and (3) learning and development. The changes due to selective evocation and interactions may be of short duration, but some may persist and produce more lasting configurations. The changes due to learning and development are slower and last longer. They consist in a gradual elaboration and differentiation of the available manifestations as well as in the acquisition of new ones, and sometimes in canceling or suppressing old ones. The constancy of the pattern despite the changes in the manifestations exemplifies most convincingly the fact that the pattern is a gestalt and, as such, is different from the sum of its parts.

Finally, the third line of evidence concerns the internal organization of the pattern. It is best reflected in the seventh characteristic of trait patterns, which we called coherence (Chapter 5, "Coherence"). It was designed to express the peculiar subservience of the parts to the whole, which renders it possible for the whole to transcend the sum of its parts and for each of the parts to represent the whole.

The three mentioned lines of evidence for the whole qualities of the trait pattern are hardly independent. Rather, they complement each other or express differentially complementary aspects of the same theme. Together, they seem to justify the conclusion that the trait pattern is a structure.

If, however, we broaden the range of criteria for structure, there is a longer list of features demonstrating the structural properties of the trait pattern. Our findings show that most of the 76 studied trait patterns have at least one of the features, each of which is generally accepted as indicating structure. These are (1) interactions within the pattern or between patterns or both; (2) levels manifested through subclusters of meaning variables or of meaning values; (3) the alternative functioning of subclusters; (4) the occasional emergence of subclusters that are related to each other symmetrically or even as mirror images (e.g., Part II, Studies 12 and 17); (5) coherence; and (6) stability of the pattern despite variations in manifestations.

In testing whether the pattern of a particular trait constitutes a structure, one should first check the pattern for each of the above-mentioned features. If none of these holds, we still have recourse to experiential and cognitive whole perception. However, if even these props fail us, we had better check whether the particular trait was not fathered by a statistical artifact and born by the need for publication.

QUESTION 7. HOW DO TRAITS FUNCTION?

Notwithstanding its structural features and perhaps its whole characteristics, the trait, if defined as a pattern of preferred meaning-assignment tendencies, should not be expected to function as a directed force, a vector with a univocally determined direction. Traits are not even bundles of forces in spite of observable results and ample evidence of interactions. Apparently, mental phenomena and concepts cannot be adequately discussed in physical terms. In the cognitive sciences and the currently dominant brand of cognitive psychology, the physicalism is blurred by drawing flowcharts with arrows and using terms like *input, output, feedback,* and *control*. But this computer-related lingo is not less mechanistic than Freud's hydraulic-drive model or Tolman's switchboard. Terms like *meaning, meaning variables,* and even *meaning preferences* are indeed less physicalistic, but when we start discussing their functioning, we are back at a mechanics that has shaped the greater part of our dictionary. In a certain sense, process-oriented psychologists are even more mechanistic than physicists because, unlike the latter, they cannot still use the language of mathematics, which hitherto has been too limited, too concept-poor, and too precise for expressing what they have to say.

Aware of these conceptual and linguistic limitations, we regard the trait pattern as a set of guiding principles that, through concomitantly or alternatively dominant subsets of meaning-assignment tendencies, influences perception, orientation, experiencing, formation of attitudes, judgments, and beliefs, as well as behavioral decisions or choices. The term *influences* does not require invoking a physical force or smuggling it in through the back door. Because cognitive processes, from input identification (i.e., perception) to making a behavioral decision, are merely meaning manipulation carried out on the level of meanings, the influence in question can be understood in the sense that we understand or believe we understand the influence of an adjective on a noun. Meaning modifies meanings. A word like *dumb* may modify our concept of *politician*. Indeed, cognitive psychology can hardly live up to its name as long as it does not provide an explanation for this kinds of influence, kicking this ball instead into the playground of semanticists and linguists. As regards the influence of traits on the processes that occur between situational inputs or internal stimulation and behavioral output, we may have conceived some of the involved meaning processes but require for their discussion the framework of a broader theory of personality (S. Kreitler & H. Kreitler, 1989c). Because the pattern of meaning-assignment tendencies that we call *trait* is involved in several of the major nodes or junctions from input to output, it exerts, as each point, a direct impact on the ongoing processes as well as an indirect one through the results and directive influence of the processes impacted at previous or parallel stages.

The studies presented in Part II have shed some light on the manner in which traits function. The process is essentially one of meaning assignment, which depends on a referent and meaning values in constant interdetermination. In the process, both the referent and the meaning values undergo changes in various respects (e.g., in contents, extent, the type and form of relations between them, and function). Because the trait pattern includes multiple meaning-assignment tendencies, it may potentially be evoked in a wide variety of situations. Hence its broadrange applicability. The trait pattern may sometimes function as a whole unit, but probably rarely. More often, it functions through the selective application of some of its constituent meaning-assignment tendencies that are evoked in line with the different properties of inputs or situations. As noted, the determination of referents is part of the meaning-assignment process, but the identified referents themselves guide the further evocation of meaning values. The selection may apply to the meaning-assignment tendencies themselves or to their manifestations or to both.

The meaning-assignment tendencies of the trait pattern may function in parallel; they may bring to the fore particular subclusters of meaning-assignment tendencies or even of meaning values; and they may operate by way of interactions that may increase or decrease a particular trend of meaning variables or subcluters, and that may sometimes even produce a modified trend. The interactions may take place on the level of the meaning-assignment tendencies but more often they apply to the manifestations of these tendencies. Yet, even if some of these interactions may still be difficult to analyze, the unique combination of preferred meaning-assignment

tendencies called a *trait* provides information about the more frequent trait manifestations and suggests explanations for those trait manifestations that are generally
considered inconsistent, though they are consistent with meaning preferences in the
trait pattern. Other inconsistencies are due to the complex relationship between
traits and the evocation of overt behaviors, discussed below.

QUESTION 8. WHAT IS THE RELATION OF TRAITS AND BEHAVIOR?

One need not be a behaviorist to be greatly concerned by the problem posed by
human behavior. The concern is shared by researchers, therapists, educators, and
counselors with the most varied theoretical biases, as well as advisers in different
domains and private citizens, all of whom focus on the behavior of individuals or
groups and many of whom regard behavior as the best expression of human nature.

Because we are often affected more directly by what a person does than by what
he or she perceives, thinks, dreams, feels, or wants, we not only pay special attention to overt behaviors but frequently regard them as the ultimate test of what we as
individuals hoped, feared or expected, or of what we as professionals hypothesized
or predicted. Therefore, it is not surprising that, in addition to dynamic and descriptive personality theories, which were often expected to account for behavior, concepts within personality theories (e.g., conditioning and defense mechanisms or
attitudes) have also been evaluated according to their relation to behavior. This
emphasis on behavior is particularly common and particularly misguided in regard
to traits. Many thoughtful personality researchers, from Allport to Mischel, have
emphasized that the relation of traits to behavior, as well as other similar relations,
can be clarified only in the framework of a comprehensive theory of personality and
personality functioning. In other words, just as every high-school student may be
expected to know that the relation of our moon to the planet Venus can be clarified
only by applying Newton's theory of gravitation or a more recent field concept,
students of personality should be aware of the difference between listing behavioral
manifestations of traits or trait constituents and the elucidation of the relation of
traits to overt behavior.

So far, we have done only the listing. Will we abstain from attempting the
elucidation? No and yes. This is a book about traits, their nature, their dynamics,
how to study them experimentally, how to assess them, and how to use the new
trait concept in research. Far more is required for a theory of personality. The
psychological status of the situations, the dynamics of trait–situation interaction, the
cognitive determination of emotions and motivation, and the nature of the self—
these are the main issues but still not all of the issues that will have to be dealt with.
In this book, there is no space for their thorough treatment.

However, our trait concept would be badly served if it were suddenly aban-
doned in the cold of a psychological void. Moreover, its applicability would be
jeopardized if no indication were given of how to deal with the obstinate problem of
behavioral consistencies and inconsistencies. We will address this problem in the
following chapter, and in doing so, we will expand somewhat on the laconic answer
that has so far been given to the question of this section: The relation of traits and
behavior is essentially indirect and highly complex.

Traits and Human Behavior

A SYSTEMS APPROACH

Whether one still cherishes the slightly tautological notion that traits are merely behavioral inclinations or accepts our definition of traits as patterns of preferred meaning-assignment tendencies, the relationship between the overt behavior and the inferred black-box process stands in need of clarification. Where, when, and how do traits influence behavior?

Bridging the conceptual gap between the new trait concept and human behavior requires a process-oriented theory of behavior evocation that outlines explicitly all the stages that allow for interactions between trait-bound meaning variables and the other agents involved in the shaping of behavior. Luckily, the already-mentioned theory of cognitive orientation (CO) proved to be appropriate for this purpose. We say "luckily" because when we first conceived of the feasibility of a cognitive theory of normal and abnormal behavior (H. Kreitler & S. Kreitler, 1965, 1967) and then gradually developed it concomitantly with the theory of meaning (H. Kreitler & S. Kreitler, 1972b, 1976, 1982), we did not in any way foresee our eventual involvement in personality theory in general and in the trait problem in particular.

To be sure, the CO theory is neither a process-oriented conceptualization of personality nor a blueprint of all personality functions. Starting with some basic assumptions, it describes a system that receives stimulating inputs from the external and internal (i.e., physiological) environment, elaborates these inputs, and shapes different kinds of outputs, the major one being human behavior. Focusing exclusively on the cognitive aspects of input–output elaboration, the CO theory could be rejected and ignored *a priori* by those psychologists who deny the functional effectiveness of cognitive processes, were it not that the theory succeeded so well in predicting overt human behavior and in providing a method for its controlled modification.

The CO theory can be experimentally disproved or may be eventually superseded by a theory more successful in predicting and modifying behavior. For the time being, however, it provides the best known framework for coping with the problem at hand.

So far in this book, we have mentioned the CO theory several times, describing briefly one or another aspect as needed in some context. Now we are in need of a more detailed, though still highly condensed, outline of the major processes and stages of behavior evocation for discussing more elaborately the sequence of possible trait impacts on the eventually resulting molar behavior. We define *molar behavior* as an observable act or sequence of acts initiated by a behavioral intent and terminated in line with it. The behavioral intent, in turn, is very much like the tendency reflected in the striving for completion evoked by interrupting a behavioral sequence (Lewin, 1936).

THE COGNITIVE ORIENTATION THEORY

The basic tenet of the CO theory is the testable assumption that human behavior above the level of innate reflexes is guided by the orientative impact of cognitive content and cognitive processes. In line with this assumption, it is expected (1) that the theory will describe the relevant agents and processes intervening between input (i.e., external or internal stimulation) and behavioral output; (2) that knowledge about these processes and constellations, or at least the major ones, will yield reliable predictions of the output behavior; (3) that the experimental production of change in one or more of the presumably predictive processes or constellations would modify the output behavior in line with the change and would thus demonstrate a causal relation of the former to the latter; and (4) that some evidence can be adduced for the major stages of these black-box processes. More than 40 studies performed in the framework of the CO theory with normal or schizophrenic adults and with normal or retarded children indicate that this theory fulfills the stated requirements (H. Kreitler & S. Kreitler, 1965, 1967, 1969, 1970, 1972a, 1972b, 1976, 1981, 1982; S. Kreitler & H. Kreitler, 1987c, 1987e, 1988a; Kreitler & Chemerinski, 1988; Kreitler, Kreitler, & Zigler, 1974; Kreitler, Maguen, & Kreitler, 1975; Kreitler, Schwartz, & Kreitler, 1987; Kreitler, Shahar, & Kreitler, 1976; Kreitler, Kreitler, & Carasso, 1987; Lobel, 1982; Westhoff & Halbach-Suarez, 1989; Zakay, Bar-El, & Kreitler, 1984; Ziv-Av, 1978).

It goes without saying that a comprehensive presentation of a theory like this would not only take up a lot of space but, because of its many details, might blur the general overview required for the present purpose. Therefore, we will summarize only the major stages between input and output that may have some bearing on the relation of traits to molar behavior. (For an overview of the theory, see also the flowchart in Figure 2).

Given external or internal stimulation that, in terms of a certain threshold, differs from hitherto ongoing stimulation, this input it subjected to "meaning action," a procedure for primary input identification, which utilizes a number of meaning values along a few, probably preselected meaning dimensions (e.g., "Sensory Qualities," "Locational Qualities," and "Contextual Allocation"), that were shown to be constant across subjects (H. Kreitler & S. Kreitler, 1986; S. Kreitler & H. Kreitler, 1984a). Focused, as it were, on Pavlov's famous metaphorical question "What is it?" the process of meaning action continues until the input is identified as (1) a signal for a defensive or adaptive reflex or for a conditioned response; (2) a signal for molar action that, as such, stands in need of a more extensive elaboration of its meaning than is warranted on this primary level; (3) irrelevant to the present situation and therefore not further attended to or elaborated unless for eventual memory registration; or (4) new or particularly significant according to specific criteria and hence as a signal for the elicitation of an orienting reflex, which may, in turn, provide further meaning values sufficient to identify the input in line with one of the other alternatives, 1 or 2 or 3.

Meaning action is the initial phase of meaning assignment. It differs from later phases in having a more limited range, in being more focused on input characteristics, and in providing less scope for individual preferences in meaning. Nevertheless, we consider meaning assignment one continuous evolving process, in contrast to Broadbent (1958) and others (Anderson, 1975, Chapters 2 and 3), who have separated early input analysis from later stages of input elaboration. Conceptually, meaning action culminates in initial meaning (or limited meaning) that provides for input identification. Operationally, meaning action is terminated when one of the actions indicated by alternative 1, 2, or 3 has been taken. On this level, there is no decision making, but a full or quasi-automatic selection between meaning-bound alternatives, each of which has its preestablished behavioral program for guiding output action.

The transition from the submolar to the molar level occurs under one of the following three conditions: (1) when, despite improved perception due to the orienting reflex, the input has not been identified sufficiently to inhibit this reflex (i.e., when the question "What is it?" could not be answered satisfactorily); (2) when the elicited adaptive, defensive, or conditioned response has proved to be insufficient to cope with the input (e.g., when narrowing the eye pupils or blinking did not suffice to remove the unpleasantness caused by a strong source of light); and (3) when, according to the initial meaning, the input is known as a signal for an act of molar behavior (e.g., when the input has been identified as the ringing of a telephone that has to be answered).

The transition to the molar level is brought about by activating more comprehensive and elaborate processes of meaning assignment called *meaning generation*. Meaning generation constitutes the second phase in the sequence of behavior evocation. It is focused on the metaphoric question "What does it mean and what does it mean to me and for me?" and is designed to clarify the input's behavioral relevance. As compared with meaning action, meaning generation has as its referent not only the input but also the meaning assigned to the input in the course of meaning action; it uses a greater number of meaning dimensions and a larger variety of types and forms of relation; it includes the personal mode in addition to the lexical mode; and it operates with more complex meaning values called *beliefs*. A belief is defined as a cognitive unit that consists of at least two meaning values related to each other by another meaning value or by syntax (e.g., "I love flowers"). Because they are independent units, including their referent as a part of themselves, they are potentially orientative (i.e., relevant in regard to behavior as well as other domains of human functioning with which we do not deal in this context). Beliefs are behaviorally orientative when they indicate some action directly (e.g., "I want to eat" indicates eating) or in conjunction with other beliefs (e.g., "Today it is July 16" indicates the action of calling my friend when conjoined with the belief "My friend's birthday is on July 16").

Meaning generation culminates in bringing to the fore:

1. One or more beliefs indicating that the input situation, as hitherto identified and elaborated, does not require further attention. In this case the process terminates with memory registration or without it; or

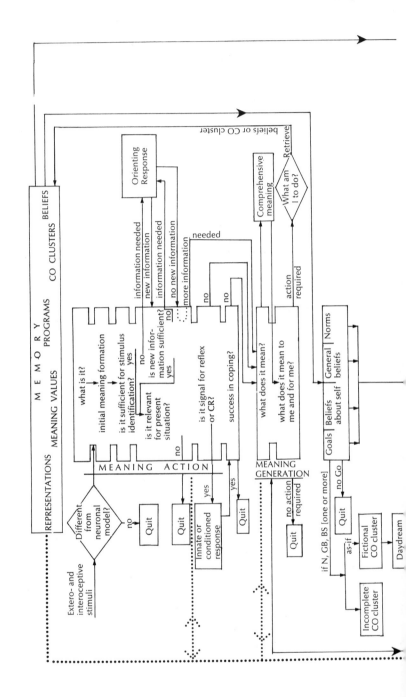

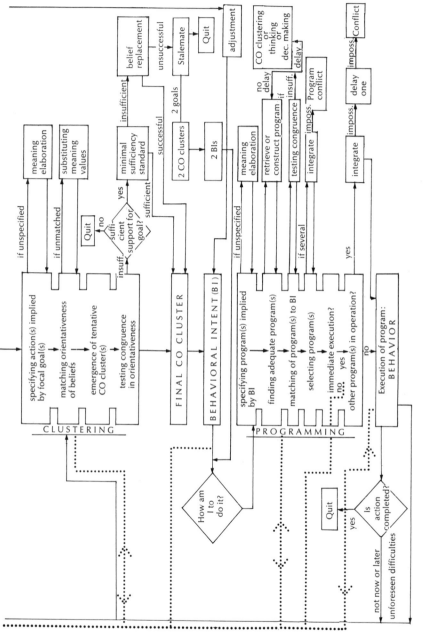

Figure 2. Schematic presentation of the main processes postulated by the cognitive orientation theory. (Reprinted from H. Kreitler and S. Kreitler, *Cognitive Orientation and Behavior*, pp. 160–161. Copyright 1976 by Springer Publishing Company, Inc., New York.)

2. One or more beliefs indicating one or several courses of action. In this case, the process of input elaboration continues in so different a manner that we regard it as the onset of the third phase in the sequence of behavior evocation.

The third phase is focused, as it were, on the metaphorical question "What will I do?" It consists in the meaning elaboration of the course(s) of action that have emerged. The belief(s) embodying the course(s) of action serves as a focal belief(s). The meaning elaboration in this stage takes the form of retrieving or constructing beliefs of four types that relate to the course(s) of action. The four types of beliefs are:

1. *Beliefs about Goals (Go)*. Formally, the belief consists of the meaning value *I*, as subject, linked to one or more meaning values by a meaning value that reflects the relation of being desired, which may be positive (wanted) or negative (rejected). The goal may be general (e.g., "I want to be happy"), particular (e.g., "I want to divorce Linda"), permanent (e.g., "I want to live"), or transient (e.g., "Now I want to eat").

2. *Beliefs about Self (BS)*. Formally the belief consists of the meaning values *I*, as subject, linked to one or more meaning values by a meaning value that reflects a factual relation (i.e., is so or is not so). Beliefs of this type express information about oneself, such as one's habits, inclinations, actions, feelings, sensations, and abilities in the present, past, or future (e.g., "I am ambitious," "I do not take moral rules too seriously," or "Next year I will still be living in this town").

3. *Beliefs about Norms and Rules (N)*. Formally, the belief consists of a non-I meaning value, serving as subject, linked to one or more meaning values by a meaning value that reflects a normative relation (should, ought, should not, or ought not). Beliefs of this type express ethical, aesthetic, social, and other rules and standards (e.g., "One should help one's neighbors," "People should not be too fat," or "One should walk cautiously on frozen snow").

4. *General Beliefs (GB)*. Formally, the belief consists of a non-I meaning value, serving as subject, linked to one or more meaning values by a meaning value that reflects a factual relation (i.e., is so or is not so). Beliefs of this type express information about people, objects, events, concepts, situations, or any aggregate or aspects of these in the past, present, or future (e.g., "People lie a lot," "Worrying is the cause of a lot of trouble," or "Cheaters are frequently very successful").

The evoked beliefs of the four types relating to the various aspects of the examined behavior undergo interactions within and across the belief types in a manner that eventually results in the pooling of beliefs in line with their orientational directionalities. Thus, there arise groupings of beliefs that support the indicated course of action, negate it, or are neutral in regard to it. The crucial comparison, however, is within the framework of a belief type between beliefs that support the action and those that negate it. The grouping that has the majority of beliefs comes to represent the particular belief type in the given context. Thus, each belief type turns into a CO component with a specific orientational directionality.

The interaction of the four CO components gives rise to a tentative cluster of beliefs that we call the *CO clusters*. Within the CO cluster, each of the four components functions like a single belief representing the componential majority. If the focal course of action is supported by all four CO components, the CO cluster becomes final, and a *behavioral intent* in line with the supported behavior will ensue. The same outcome may be expected also when only three CO components support the action if there is no competing course of action and if the CO component that does not support the focal course of action is neutral, rather than negative, in regard to it. When no final CO cluster can be formed, the clustering is resumed by replacing beliefs, modifying meanings of beliefs, or shifting the referent to another course of action if available. The process continues until a CO cluster can be formed or it is established that the required degree of congruence cannot be attained. When there is a stalemate, with two CO components supporting the indicated course of action and the other two opposing it, failure in attaining congruence may result in the formation of two CO clusters, with opposing behavioral implications, each of which is anchored in a course of action supported by beliefs of all four CO components. The outcome of such two competing CO clusters would be two competing behavioral intents, a constellation called *intent conflict*.

There are several kinds of unoperational CO clusters, major among which are (1) the incomplete CO cluster, which occurs when one CO component is missing because of the absence of pertinent beliefs, and (2) CO clusters induced by a focal belief that relates to an imaginative as-if performance (e.g., daydreaming) or a cognitive activity like problem solving. Most CO clusters are not *ad hoc* productions but are retrieved in an almost complete state and are merely adjusted to the prevailing conditions.

The product of a full-fledged CO cluster is the behavioral intent. This is the construct that provides the answer to the metaphoric question of the third phase "What will I do?" Its emergence also marks the beginning of the fourth phase, which is focused on the question "How will I do it?" The answer to this question manifests itself in a *behavioral program*. Behavioral programs are hierarchically ordered and sequentially structured detailed instructions for the execution of a motor act. Without a behavioral program, no action can occur, and no behavioral intent can be implemented. Behavioral programs are bileveled structures that include a program scheme, akin to an overall strategy, and an operational program, which is bound with the physiological details of operations. Summarizing the findings of many investigators, we distinguish among four kinds of programs from the viewpoint of their origin: (1) *innate programs* that underlie primarily but not exclusively submolar reactions like reflex behavior and classical conditioned responses; (2) *programs that are partly innate and partly acquired,* guiding instinct behavior in the sense of Tinbergen (1951) and Lorenz (1969), actions like walking, swimming, making love, basic defense mechanisms, and phonetic articulation of language; (3) *learned programs* that guide most common behaviors characteristic of the individual, like writing, driving, dancing, thinking, and traveling; and (4) *ad hoc constructed programs* that are made up for the purpose of some action when no ready-made adequate program is available.

Unless innate factors or prior learning have chained a particular behavioral intent to a specific behavioral program, meaning elaboration of the intent in the context of the present situation of action is needed for the retrieval of programs followed by the selection of the program with the best match, or for constructing a new program. The selection or construction is mostly bound to adjusting the program to the prevailing conditions. The adjustments may vary from minimal changes to sizable modifications equivalent to programming. Conflicts may arise between two programs, both of which seem adequate to implement the same behavioral intent, or between a new program and one in the course of execution. *Program conflicts* of this kind are often resolved by special programs for conflict resolution that range from simple tricks (e.g., flipping a coin) to defense mechanisms and complex procedures for decision making.

The final phase consists of behavior itself, whose execution is subject to cognitive control through the program scheme and the behavioral intent. Thus, not even the execution of the behavioral program is automatic. Moreover, renewed CO clustering and even further meaning generation may be required for coping with contingencies like danger signals or a mismatch between the expected and the achieved results of the action. Hence, there is good reason to assume that the processes delineated by the CO theory function almost premanently during waking life and probably to a certain extent during sleep, too.

TRAITS AND BEHAVIOR EVOCATION

Incomplete as this summary is, it may suffice for an examination of where, in the course of behavior evocation, traits may exert some impact on molar action. To the best of our understanding, comparing an input with the immediately preceding stimulation (i.e., with its representation in the sensory register or with the "neuronal model"—Sokolov, 1958) and registering change in line with a match–mismatch criterion leave hardly any leeway for the interference of preferred meaning-assignment tendencies. In principle, the situation could be different in regard to initial input identification carried out by "meaning action." Indeed, already in this stage, some schizophrenics apply meaning variables that are completely unsuited to the task of meaning action (H. Kreitler & S. Kreitler, 1986). In contrast, the above-mentioned cross-subject concordance of meaning dimensions applied to primary input identification does not support the notion of trait interference in this stage, insofar as laboratory research is concerned. In real-life situations, a set-induced tendency to ignore inputs of a particular kind (e.g., specific visual or olfacory stimuli) may inhibit meaning action to such an extent that even previously established conditioned responses do not occur. We have some vague indications that these kinds of negative or positive perceptual sets are bounds to a particular meaning value. The meaning value, in turn, may belong to a positively or negatively preferred meaning dimension and, in the latter case, could substitute for the meaning action. Yet, all in all, the impact of input characteristics is so dominant that the influence of trait-bound meaning variables can be regarded as marginal.

As mentioned, meaning assignment for the sake of input identification is a progressively unfolding process. This is manifested most clearly in the stage of "meaning generation," in which more and more meaning variables are used, and meaning values are increasingly replaced by larger units, particularly by beliefs. Thus, more opportunities arise for idiosyncratic uses of meaning, and therefore, the chance of trait-bound influences increases. As mentioned earlier, preformed beliefs ready to be retrieved are one of the manifestations of positively preferred meaning variables (Chapter 3). As compared with other stages in the course of molar behavior evocation, meaning generation has the fewest constraints limiting interference through meaning preferences. For instance, in the course of meaning generation, a miser is likely to make extensive use of the meaning dimension "Possessions" and hence may discover in a situation some opportunities or possibilities for gain, loss, or waste. In more general terms, preferred meaning variables are more readily available and therefore are more frequently applied than others. Thus, preferred meaning dimensions have more meaning values than less preferred meaning dimensions, or perhaps the other way round: having more meaning values, preferred meaning dimensions are more salient and can be used more frequently. Our findings showed the abundance of meaning values in preferred dimensions but did not indicate which of the two alternatives hold.

Nevertheless, we found that even strong trait impacts may be reduced or entirely checked by strong demand characteristics in the interpersonally shared aspects of situation meaning. For example, danger situations evoke meaning dimensions like "Consequences," "Function," and "Feelings and Emotions," even if these meaning dimensions do not belong to any of the subject's traits. There is evidence that even weaker impacts than danger may curb the application of preferred meaning-assignment tendencies, which are the constituents of traits. The dependent variable of the study—extremity of responses to items of a personality inventory—was shown to be a content-bound manifestation of the meaning that the subject assigns to the whole questionnaire (S. Kreitler & H. Kreitler, 1981). The extremity of subjects' responses to a self-report questionnaire assessing beliefs about oneself and one's goals was found to be determined by two kinds of factors: the correctness of the item as perceived by the subject and nonrelevant factors, which included the correspondence of the item's content to a meaning dimension preferred by the subject. Whereas the perceived correctness accounted for 58% of the variance, the correspondence to a preferred meaning dimension accounted for only 9%. The impact was larger in the case of items perceived as correct than in the case of those perceived as incorrect. For purposes of comparison, it may be worthwhile to note that the other nonrelevant factor tested (i.e., social desirability) accounted for a very similar percentage (8%) of the variance (S. Kreitler & H. Kreitler, 1984b). These findings suggest that the impact of preferred meaning-assignment tendencies, singly or in patterns, on meaning generation is limited by the interpersonally shared aspects of the situation meanings.

To the best of our hitherto acquired knowledge, the process of CO cluster formation has its own dynamics that leave no leeway for direct trait interference. The principle guiding belief selection is orientative directionality relative to the orientativeness of the currently dominant focal belief, which most often is a goal belief. The beliefs of the four types either orient in the same direction as the focal belief, thus supporting it, or orient in another direction, thus weakening it. To be sure, this is a rather crude simplification of CO clustering. But because it has served us well in our predictions of behavior, and because it is also the best we know, we must sustain this simple, essentially procedural notion until a more refined one is available.

Nonetheless, studies that are presented in our forthcoming book about personality (S. Kreitler & H. Kreitler, 1989c) showed that subjects produce more CO clusters in line with their dominant traits than CO clusters with no trait relation. We assume that the reason is the above-mentioned abundance of trait-related beliefs. Being more numerous than non-trait-related beliefs, the trait-related beliefs are more readily available for CO clustering.

A closer relation was observed between traits and a particular kind of CO cluster, namely, incomplete CO clusters, especially those that induce daydreaming. Though this observation is not directly relevant to our present concern with the trait–behavior relation, it may have indirect implications concerning this relation. If empirical proof is found for Singer's plausible conjecture (1966) that at least some daydreams affect future behaviors, this proof would provide an additional explanation of the relative frequency of trait-related CO clusters.

Because the behavioral intent is merely the tendency or the vector reflecting the behavioral direction of the CO cluster, neither theoretical reasoning nor experimental findings lend any support to the notion of trait interference in intent formation.

On the other hand, there is empirical evidence that traits affect program construction and selection. In studies of planning in children and in adults (S. Kreitler & H. Kreitler, 1987b,c). it was found that planning capabilities depend on specific meaning-assignment tendencies and are enhanced if these tendencies are preferred. More important, we also found that the structure of the formed plan, its nature, the employed strategy, and the considerations that underlie it—all these correspond clearly to preferred meaning-assignment variables grouped in trait-similar patterns (S. Kreitler & H. Kreitler, 1986a, 1987c).

The two mentioned studies showing trait interference in program selection dealt specifically with planning. We cannot, however, mention further evidence about the impact of traits on program selection from our many behavior prediction studies for the simple reason that most of these studies were done before we embarked on the trait project and therefore did not attend to trait-relevant information. Moreover, in experimental situations not specifically designed for studying program selection, fewer behavioral programs may be available than in real-life situations. Considering program retrieval and selection from our present point of view, we assume that, in this stage of behavior evocation, traits have a fair chance of influencing overt behavior. The reason is that, in the course of their life, individuals develop or acquire more and more behavioral programs in line with one dominant trait or another. This is what is usually meant by *habit formation*. Behavioral habits are also influenced by factors other than traits (mainly education) and social or environmental conditions. Thus, habits need not necessarily be trait-bound. Nevertheless, because the behavioral program determines not "what" to do but "how" to do it, there is frequently some margin for trait involvement.

In sum, the well-substantiated claim that the CO theory renders reliable predictions of human overt behavior without any reference to traits does not negate the influence of traits on the different processes of behavior evocation. Though minimal in meaning action (the stage of primary input identification), the involvement of trait-bound meaning-assignment tendencies is rather obvious in the stages of meaning elaboration and belief retrieval, as well as in program selection or *ad hoc* program formation. However, even a very pronounced trait dominance in one stage does not imply trait dominance in one or more of the following stages. Nor does a trait's dominance in the selection and adoption of programs eliminate the impact of the behavioral intent on program choice. In other words, traits influence human molar behavior, and thus, human molar behavior may show the influence of traits, but one cannot be expected to predict the other.

THE ISSUE OF BEHAVIORAL CONSISTENCY

One of the most puzzling outcomes of psychological reductionism is the consistency problem, or more precisely, the two mutually inconsistent expectations that overt behavior will be consistent with situations or that overt behavior will be consistent with traits. A great deal of work and money were wasted on demonstrating behavioral consistency according to one or the other position. But the results have remained inconsistent in a devious manner, devious because they were consistent enough to encourage the protagonists of both positions to continue their research efforts, but sufficiently inconsistent for the eventual frustration of both parties. Indeed, after more than 125 years of scientific psychology and the contributions of James, Freud, Thorndike, the Gestalt school, Hull, and Piaget to the increasingly complex picture of mental functioning, it is difficult to believe that two so simplistic notions could have survived in the intellectually challenging domain of personology. But as they did survive, it may be instructive to apply the CO theory to exploring under which conditions behavior may be consistent with the situation or with traits and how likely these constellations are.

In an article with the telling title "The Consistency of Behavioral Inconsistencies" (S. Kreitler & H. Kreitler, 1983), we assumed two different situations and used the four stages of behavior evocation, as outlined by the CO theory, to construct a schema showing the constellations required for maximally similar (virtually identical) behaviors in the two situations, maximally dissimilar behaviors as well as different degrees of similarity or dissimilarity in the evoked behaviors. Because in this schema the two different situations are kept constant, all the variations in behavior depend on initial input identification (meaning action), input elaboration (meaning generation plus retrieval or formation of beliefs), CO clustering resulting in intent formation, and adoption of a behavioral program assumed to be equivalent to the resulting molar behavior.

Figure 3 shows that, as regards traits, the two most radical combinations are

No. of combination	Factors of the CO theory			
	Initial meaning	Comprehensive meaning	CO cluster and behavioral intent	Behavioral program
1	S	S	S	S
2	S	S	S	D
3	S	S	D	S
4	S	D	S	S
5	D	S	S	S
6	S	S	D	D
7	S	D	D	S
8	D	D	S	S
9	S	D	S	D
10	D	S	S	D
11	S	S	D	S
12	S	D	D	D
13	D	D	D	S
14	D	D	S	D
15	D	S	D	D
16	D	D	D	D

Figure 3. Schematic representation of conditions for consistency and inconsistency in overt behavior in different situations. *Key:* CO, cognitive orientation; S, similar; D, different. (Reprinted with slight modifications from H. Kreitler & S. Kreitler, "The consistency of behavioral inconsistencies," *Archives of Psychology*, 1983, vol. 135, pp. 199–218; the figure is reprinted from page 216.)

either that each of the four stages is entirely dominated by traits (Combination 1) or that none of the stages is dominated by traits (Combination 16). In the first case, the molar behavior would be maximally similar in the two different situations; in the latter case, it would differ maximally from one situation to the other according to their respective situational impacts. To the best of our knowledge, both cases are utterly unlikely. However, it is important to note that each of the two behavioral outcomes, represented in Figure 3 by the behavioral program (D or S), is identical with the output behavior of seven other combinations. In other words, it would be erroneous to view situation-consistent output behavior or trait-consistent output behavior as proof of the validity of one theoretical position or the other. The argument that people cannot be expected to adopt a behavioral program that is not in line with their behavioral intent ignores observations in psychopathology, business, schools, and politics (H. Kreitler and S. Kreitler, 1989b). Moreover, it still leaves for each alternative three combinations in which the behavioral program is in line with the intent.

In sum, behavioral consistency is a concept too simple-minded to do justice to the complexities of situation impacts and trait effects. Even if granted equal recognition and equal standing, the trait–situation pair restricts our understanding of input elaboration and eventual response formation in a distorting manner. The same holds true when we focus merely on the evocation of molar behavior. The theory of cognitive orientation may be applied to these issues but was developed explicitly to trace the processes between input and output regardless of whether the output is a conditioned response, a memory entry, the decision not to react, a daydream, the onset of problem-solving activity, or an observable act of molar behavior (see Figures 3.1, 4.1, 5.1, and 6.1 in H. Kreitler & S. Kreitler, 1976). Thus, this theory is a very broad framework that must frequently be amended by subroutines, as in the case of decision making (Zakay, 1976) or planning (S. Kreitler & H. Kreitler, 1987b,c).

Being only one of the possible outcomes of the involved chain of processes, molar behavior does not provide reliable information about the processes of behavior evocation. Neither would its consistency of inconsistency with either traits or situations confirm or disconfirm one of these hypotheses. Therefore, it might be better for personology if we recognized that consistency of molar behavior is neither a substitute for nor a reliable indication of lawfulness of molar behavior. The lawfulness we are after is a lawfulness in terms of a comprehensive theory of personality, which, we hope, can be developed by combining the CO theory with the new trait concept, our semantic conceptualization of situations, and reasonable assumptions about the what and how of interactions. Whether a theory constructed along these lines will be psychologically pertinent and useful will be judged by its explanatory power, its testable predictions, and, last but not least, its ability to integrate the major theories of personology.

BEYOND THE TRAIT–BEHAVIOR RELATION: THE IMPORTANCE OF A TRAIT CONCEPT

For more than half a century, behavior was regarded as so important and focal that a great many introductory textbooks define psychology as the science of human behavior, sometimes qualifying the term *behavior* by adding the vague words *overt and covert.* Notwithstanding the rapid decline of behaviorism, *behavior* is still so influential a catchword that many psychologists may be inclined to ask, "If trait assessments do not reliably inform us of how the person will behave, what else are traits good for?" A more precise formulation of this question would read, "Are there psychological phenomena that cannot be approximately described and explained without recourse to a trait concept?" These questions, which are certainly not new, have attained additional pertinence and topicality in view of our trait research. This research revealed preferred meaning-assignment tendencies to be the constituents of traits and thus generated an additional question: "Why, then, not drop altogether the notion of patterns and their trait designations and instead focus research efforts exclusively on the underlying meaning processes?"

It is evident that the answer to the last question is more general and hence should be given first. Just as the discovery of atoms did not render the concept of molecules obsolete, and the discovery of particles did not eliminate the notion of atoms, traits cannot be replaced by their constituent elements without our losing sight of important psychological phenomena and functions. Substituting meaning-assignment tendencies for traits would result in the reductionist fallacy that consists not in an awareness of underlying levels but in a blindness for structures and their holistic impact. The "nothing-but" thesis is misguided regardless of whether it crowns the physiological, behavioristic, psychoanalytic, or cognitive approaches. The reason is that what account for a trait are not merely the preferred meaning-assignment tendencies within the pattern but their concomitance and interactions. Without these wholeness effects, meaning-assignment tendencies would be almost as unsuited to characterizing people as a mere mixture of two-thirds hydrogen and one-third oxygen would be for quenching thirst. There is ample evidence of the whole characteristics of traits (see in Chapter 7, "What Is the Structure of Traits?"), for example, the frequent finding that a subject may score high on a trait even if one or another meaning-assignment tendency of that trait pattern is missing in the subject's meaning profile.

The whole properties of the pattern of meaning-assignment tendencies are thus the major reason for preserving the trait label. Another reason may be the utility of the trait label as a handy and practical bridge between the sphere of meaning, which is still unfamiliar to many, and the lore of everyday language and the traditional jargon of psychology. This bridge may also be of help in exploring the manifestations corresponding to meaning-assignment tendencies. Because many empirical findings have accumulated in regard to traits, this material can be used to expand information about the yet unexplored manifestations of meaning-assignment tendencies.

In approaching the major subject matter of this section (the psychological functions or tasks of the trait concept), it may help to reemphasize the traditional argument underlying many approaches in personology: All of us perceive ourselves, as well as other human beings, as individuals who, notwithstanding shifts in molar behavior, thoughts, attitudes, emotional reactions, and so on, exhibit and preserve psychological identity and overall consistency, usually called individuality. These consistencies across situation meanings probably derive from various sources, such as physiological peculiarities, cognitive habits (not to be mistaken for cognitive style), enduring beliefs, permanently stored and frequently retrieved CO clusters, and habitual behavioral programs. Yet, personality traits are the most significant source, partly because of their influence on these other factors mentioned in the former section), but mainly because of their well-attested resistance to environmentally and developmentally induced change in adulthood (Bloom, 1964; Brim & Kagan, 1980).

Indeed, development does not stop entirely during adulthood. Ideas, cognitive skills, emotional reactions, behavioral programs manifested in molar behaviors, and so on undergo modifications during the course of a lifetime. And we assume, although we do not know yet for certain, that these changes are due to slight shifts in meaning preferences. But traits seem to be the major stabilizing factor responsible for the preservation of personal identity. Therefore, we suggest accepting traits as the most basic explanatory concept of individual consistency so far, even if they are occasionally or frequently inconsistent with molar behavior.

The acceptance of traits as an identify-stabilizing factor may be facilitated by recalling that our new trait concept not only answers questions unanswered by former conceptions of traits in general and specific traits in particular, as shown in this and the former chapter, but also liberates the trait from its former primarily descriptive existence as well as from its isolation within the turbulence of psychodynamics. The conception of traits as specific patterns of preferred meaning-assignment tendencies makes it possible to study the functioning of traits and to explain the dynamic influence of traits on molar behavior, as well as to investigate their functional relations to other processes, such as input identification, thinking, learning, and the cognitive manifestations of depth-psychological constellations and dynamics.

There is no doubt that personality theory has to encompass much more than traits. But we cannot imagine a theory of personality without a workable trait concept, just as we cannot imagine describing and conceptualizing people without frequent recourse to their dominant traits.

II

Studies on Traits

Studies on Traits

GOALS OF THE STUDIES

Whereas Part I of the book was designed to introduce the new theoretical conception of traits, it is the purpose of Part II to provide the empirical foundations of this new conception. Accordingly, Part II presents 22 studies about traits, each of which deals with one or more specific traits. The number of studies reported here is so high because the studies fulfill different roles in regard to the new conception of traits. One is the straightforward role of providing support for the new theoretical conception. The support can take various forms, for example, empirical confirmation of predictions drawn from the new conception or findings increasing the plausibility of one or another assumption. It is difficult to decide how much support a new conception needs. It is generally agreed that "the more the better," especially when we are dealing, as in the present case, with a very new conception. Despite the 22 studies, there can be little doubt that many more studies are still needed to firm up different aspects of the new conception, to fill up holes, and to eliminate loose ends, even before it becomes subject to the regular fate of new constructs, which is further development and transformations.

Beyond strict support, the studies were also expected to provide answers to at least some of the questions that arise, as a rule, in the wake of a new conception. The basic conception is that each trait corresponds to a pattern of meaning variables that can be assessed by means of a meaning questionnaire. Accordingly, we attempted in different studies to deal with such questions as "Does it make a difference if the meaning questionnaire focuses on personal or lexical or unspecified meaning?" (Study 4); "Is the pattern of interrelations of a trait with meaning variables identical to the meaning assigned by the subjects directly to the label of the trait?" (Study 10); "Does the pattern correspond more to theoretical considerations that underlie the construction of the scale than to validational research findings?" (Study 7); "Does the pattern correspond more to the assumed unconscious dynamics of the trait or to its so-called sublimated exterior?" (Study 8); and "How do traits interact?" (Study 22). Answering questions of this kind require many studies. Thus, each study deals with one or more traits and, in addition, with a more general problem concerning traits in general or trait research.

The studies also had a third role that is of basic importance to the implementation of the theoretical conception. The studies were designed to serve as an exploratory means of learning about the relation between meaning variables and their manifestations. Information about these manifestations is crucial for turning the new conception of traits into an actual tool for personality assessment and research. Obtaining this information required analyzing a great number of interrelations between trait scores and specific meaning variables. Therefore, it was necessary to carry out studies with many traits, especially because the number of meaning variables is so high and each has specific manifestations. Because administering many trait scales to the same sample reduces the reliability of the subjects' responses, we had to use different samples, to each of which very few trait scales, mostly only one, were presented.

A related role of the studies was to provide information about the patterns of meaning variables corresponding to a great number of traits. Indeed, in order to support the claim that a trait corresponds to a pattern of meaning variables, it would suffice to present one case of such correspondence; and in order to support the stronger claim, which we make, that each trait corresponds to a unique pattern of meaning variables, it would suffice to present the two different patterns corresponding to two different traits. But for psychology, and mainly for psychologists, it would be far from sufficient. One reason is that there are many different traits and each trait constitutes a minitheory with its own characteristic measurement instruments, variables, issues, and adherents who often do not deal with other traits theoretically or practically. The other and main reason is that the usefulness of the meaning questionnaire as a single instrument for the assessment of many traits depends on the availability of information about the patterns of meaning variables corresponding to a great number of traits. Therefore, we considered it necessary to make our point more than once and to provide a rich variety of patterns of meaning variables corresponding to a broader selection of traits than that required strictly by the canons of proof and disproof.

A fifth role of the studies emphasizes the contribution of the new trait conception to traits. This role derived from our conviction that, in science, usefulness or the ability to resolve unresolved issues or new problems is one of the criteria for evaluating a new conception. Examples of such problems are "Why are extroverts more sensitive to pain induced electrically than thermally?" (Study 1); "Why, contrary to expectation, have n Power and Machiavellianism not been found to be correlated?" (Study 4); "How do authoritarianism and dogmatism resemble and differ from each other?" (Study 13); "What are the unique characteristics of the four factors of sensation seeking?" (Studies 15 and 16); "What is the impact of stereotypes on established traits like masculinity or relatively new productions like androgyny?" (Study 17). Pursuing answers to these and other problems has also made it possible to illustrate some new procedures in this emergent sphere of personality research, for example, the comparison of patterns of meaning variables (Studies 10 and 13; for examples of more procedures see Part III).

We have mentioned five roles that the studies fulfill in regard to the new conception of traits. This multiplicity of roles explains why it was not enough to report in a summative form patterns of intercorrelations between trait scores and meaning variables instead of presenting the studies as we do. The multiplicity of roles also explains why each of the 22 studies fulfills more than one role. Each mostly provides information about the pattern of meaning variables of at least one trait and, in addition, addresses itself to a further problem that concerns the theory, traits in general, or some specific trait(s).

ORDER OF PRESENTATION

The 22 studies are presented roughly in the chronological order in which they were carried out. This order implies that, to some extent, the results of earlier studies affected the hypotheses, design, procedures, and forms of interpretation applied in later studies. As noted, the studies were designed for, among other roles, clarification of the manifestations of the meaning variables and the provision of information about the meaning patterns corresponding to specific traits. Thus, the manifestations of meaning variables found in earlier studies were rechecked and applied in later studies. Consequently, responses that, in earlier studies, were merely hypothesized or assumed to be manifestations of a meaning variable, if supported by data were accepted in later studies as actual manifestations of that meaning variable. Also, the patterns corresponding to traits examined in earlier studies were sometimes compared to the patterns of traits examined in later studies. Moreover, the cumulative data about characteristics of the patterns of meaning variables corresponding to traits served to define tentative standards characterizing the patterns that were applied to testing the patterns of specific variables so as to determine whether these variables were trait-similar or trait-dissimilar (e.g., Study 13 and Chapter 11). In addition, it is evident that specific issues could be addressed only after certain preceding ones had been settled in previous studies. For example, subclusters within patterns of meaning variables could be examined (e.g., Studies 12 and 19) only after the essential characteristics of the regular patterns were identified. Again, the issue of trait interaction could be addressed (Study 22) only after the characteristics of traits as autonomous units were examined.

These remarks are meant mainly to emphasize that the 22 studies form a body of research; that is, they not only share several common goals but, together, support several common conclusions, many of which were presented in Part I. Nevertheless, the studies are reported so that each can be read and understood independently of the others. All necessary references to previous studies are mentioned in their context, so that each study is a self-contained unit that deals with specific problems. Even the order of the studies is not binding for the reader, who may select his or her itinerary and preferred spots for skipping or tarrying.

GENERAL GUIDING PRINCIPLES

Three general assumptions served as hypothetical guiding principles underlying problems raised in regard to specific traits in one or more of the studies. One assumption was that traits represent psychological units on some level of conceptualization. It appeared to us that this unit has proved sufficiently useful in different frameworks of psychology and sufficiently neutral theoretically to deserve an attempt to clarify its nature and functioning. Again, our attempt was not designed to support any specific trait theory or personality theory based on traits, but merely to clear up our trait concept, which has a good potential for serving as a more-or-less general unit, a building block for theories, or raw material for conceptualization in different contexts.

Another assumption was that the meaning system is vitally relevant to traits and therefore could contribute to resolving basic issues that have plagued traits. Hence our major strategy of studying traits through their interrelations with meaning variables. The guiding questions underlying our analyses of these interrelations were "What do these interrelations indicate about traits in general?" "How do the findings correspond to what is already known about this specific trait?" and "What can the interrelations contribute to resolving problems that have arisen in regard to this specific trait?"

A third assumption was that each meaning variable is unique in its potential contribution to traits. Hence the emphasis we place on each interrelation of a trait score to a single meaning variable. In keeping with the general characteristics of meaning variables found in other contexts (S. Kreitler & H. Kreitler, 1984a, 1985b, 1987c), we assumed that meaning variables differ in the spheres of contents and the specific processes in which they are manifested, as well as in the relative degree to which they reflect contents and processes. For example, under most circumstances, meaning dimensions reflect contents and processes to a similar degree, whereas other kinds of meaning variables (i.e., types of relation, forms of relation, and referent shifts) tend more to manifest with greater salience the process aspect. Hence, in the interests of simplified terminology and at the expense of precision, we sometimes refer to meaning dimensions as relatively content-determined and to other kinds of meaning variables as relatively content-free. In keeping with the common conception that regular traits are more content-bound than cognitive style variables, we expected by way of a general hypothesis that meaning dimensions would play a relatively larger role and the other kinds of meaning variables (e.g., referent shifts) a relatively smaller role in regular traits than in the cognitive style variables (e.g., Studies 6 and 13).

THE STUDIED TRAITS

The 22 studies deal with 76 different traits. In addition, in Part III, the 10 clinical scales and the 3 validity scales of the Minnesota Multiphasic Personality Inventory (MMPI), as well as the 22 traits of the Personality Research Form (PRF), are examined (Chapters 11 and 12). The studied traits were selected to represent a very broad range of different traits, for example, social traits (e.g., several of the California Personality Inventory (CPI) scales, Study 2; Machiavellianism, Studies 3–5; Least-Preferred-Co-worker score, Study 20), temperamental traits (e.g., several of the 16 Personality Factors scales) standard personality traits (e.g., extroversion, Study 1; approval motive, Study 8), cognitive style traits (e.g., intolerance of ambiguity, Studies 18 and 19; external-internal control, Studies 11 and 12), traits of attitudes (e.g., dogmatism and authoritarianism, Study 13), Freudian traits (e.g., anality, Study 8), Jungian traits (i.e., feeling, thinking, sensation, and intuition assessed by the Myers-Briggs Type Indicator, Study 7), traits assessed by questionnaire (e.g., Machiavellianism, Studies 3–5) and by ratings of external observers (e.g., leadership, ability to decide, ability to withstand stress, Study 21), traits that have been researched a lot (e.g., extroversion-introversion, Study 1; hypochondriasis, Study 10) and traits that have hardly been investigated at all (e.g., avarice, Study 10), traits that have elements of social stereotypes (e.g., masculinity and femininity, Study 17), motivational traits (e.g., n Power, Study 4), traditional traits (e.g., ego strength, Study 8) and relative newcomers on the scene (e.g., sensation seeking, Studies 15 and 16), traits that form part of multitrait instruments (e.g., CPI, Study 2; 16 PF,

Study 6; MMPI, Chapter 11; PRF, Chapters 11 and 12) and "loners" (e.g., authoritarianism, Study 13), bipolar traits (e.g., external-internal control, Studies 11 and 12; preferences for ideational activities, Study 14) and unipolar traits (e.g., Janke-Boucsein Cognitive Activity Score, Study 14), and so on. In very few cases, we selected the same traits assessed by different scales so as to provide the possibility of comparison of the patterns of meaning variables correlated to each of them (e.g., see social desirability in Studies 8 and 17 and Chapter 12). The purpose of the broad selection of traits was to provide a stable basis for the conclusions to be drawn (see list, for example, in Table 1).

The list of studied traits shows that we examined a fair sample of the sphere of personality traits and included representatives of the best known traits that enjoy a broad-base consensus as personality traits.

SOME FEATURES OF METHOD COMMON TO THE STUDIES

The number of subjects in the 22 studies was 1,811 (with an additional 334 in the studies reported in Chapter 10, 11, and 12). The range was 37 to 248 subjects in the different studies. As specified in each study, they were mostly students at universities, teacher seminaries, or schools (elementary, junior high, and senior high); enlisted soldiers; teachers; and others in the age range of 13–54 years. No subjects with known mental or cognitive abnormalities participated in any of the studies. In all but one study (Study 21), subjects of both genders participated. The exception was made necessary by the purpose of the study. In none were gender differences detected. The subjects were asked to participate either on a voluntary basis or, in the case of students, in the framework of the standard requirements for students participating in certain courses. Only three subjects refused to volunteer or to participate when approached.

In most studies, the subjects were administered a measure of one or more traits and a meaning questionnaire so that we could examine the interrelations between the trait score and the meaning variables. In all cases, when measures of traits and meaning were administered, special precautions were taken to prevent effects of the one on the other (e.g., they were administered separately, in different sessions, with an interval of at least days but mostly weeks or even months, and in random order). The measures were scored by different individuals who knew nothing of the study beyond the scale or questionnaire they scored.

The standard trait measures used were Hebrew versions, translated from English (or in one case, from German, Study 14) and pretested by others or by us, as indicated in the text.

Unless otherwise specified, meaning was assessed by the standard meaning questionnaire with instructions that did not refer to a specific kind of meaning (i.e., lexical or personal), and with standard 11 terms (i.e., *to create, street, life, bicycle, sea, telephone, feeling, art, to murder, friendship,* and *to take*). Exceptions include, for example, Study 3, in which three meaning questionnaires with different instructions were used, and the number of stimulus words was fewer than in the standard version (for detailed instructions for the meaning questionnaires, see "The Meaning System," Chapter 2).

The meaning questionnaire was scored according to the standard procedure that has been elaborated in previous studies (H. Kreitler & S. Kreitler, 1976; S. Kreitler & H. Kreitler, 1968; this book, Chapter 2). Essentially, it consists in identifying in the meaning communications meaning units, each of which includes a referent and a meaning value, and scoring each of the meaning units in terms of the four sets of variables: meaning dimensions, types of relation, forms of relation, and referent shift variables (see Chapter 2 and Appendixes A and C). Thus, each meaning unit got four scores, one on each set of variables. The scores were summed across all meaning units in the subject's responses to the questionnaire. These summed scores constituted the subject's meaning profile (see "The Meaning Profile," Chapter 2). The meaning questionnaires were scored according to a standard manual (see Appendix C). The intercoder reliability was found to be very high for the meaning questionnaires in different samples of subjects and different pairs or triads of scorers (range of r: .92 to 1.00). The test–retest reliability of the meaning questionnaires over intervals of 3 weeks to 12 months for adult subjects was found to be in the range of .88 to .96 (for the different meaning variables) (S. Kreitler, 1965; S. Kreitler & H. Kreitler, 1968, 1985a, 1987c).

Unless otherwise indicated, in all studies the score of each meaning variable in a subject's meaning profile was a proportion of the frequency of meaning values of that variable out of the total of meaning values produced by the subject in response to the whole meaning questionnaire. This pretested procedure was used in order to eliminate the distorting effects of individual differences in fluency.

ON THE TRACK OF MANIFESTATIONS OF MEANING VARIABLES

Manifestations of meaning variables are a major constituent of our new conception of traits. They form the core of the dynamics of this conception and enable the use of the meaning questionnaire for the assessment of traits (Chapter 10). As mentioned, the 22 studies in Part II served as our major tool for identifying the manifestations of meaning variables in the sphere of personality. In our investigation of these manifestations, we applied two complementary methods. One method consisted of proceeding from the manifestations to the meaning variables. Thus, we first noted the different findings concerning a given trait that were obtained in independent research on this trait. We treated these findings conceptually as hypothetical manifestations of meaning variables and predicted to which meaning variables the trait score would be correlated.

In our predictions, we were led both by previous findings concerning the manifestations of meaning variables in the spheres of cognition and personality (e.g., H. Kreitler & S. Kreitler, 1986, 1989a; S. Kreitler & H. Kreitler, 1985a, 1986a,b,c, 1987a,b,c,d,e, 1988a,b,c,d, 1989a,b,c) and by theoretical assumptions (see Chapter 2). The major assumptions were that each meaning variable has a set of manifestations, that these manifestations are unique to the meaning variable, and that, at least in the case of meaning dimensions, the manifestations are shaped by the sphere of the content denoted by the meaning dimension (e.g., materials in the case of "Material," *Dim* 9, or locations in the case of "Locational Qualities," *Dim* 15). Accordingly, in line with the first method, we expected that a trait like low ego strength (Factor C of the 16 PF), which is characterized by evasion of responsibilities and instability in attitudes, would be correlated negatively to the variable "Judgments and Evaluations" (*Dim* 21a and *Dim* 21b), which presumably represents concern with rules, standards, and personal values (Study 6). If the negative correlation actually occurred, we regarded its occurrence as a confirmation of the hypothesis about the specific manifestations of the variable "Judgments and Evaluations" (*Dim* 21a and *Dim* 21b). Again, we expected that a trait like conformity would be correlated negatively with the comparative type of relation difference (*TR* 2b) because this meaning variable is presumably involved in noting differences between oneself and others (Study 2). The occurrence of the negative correlation served as confirmation of the hypothesis about the specific manifestations of the difference type of relation (*TR* 2b).

The second method consisted in proceeding from the meaning variable to its manifestations. Thus, we first noted with which meaning variable a specific trait was correlated. Then, we specified—on the basis of previous findings and assumptions, as stated above—the particular expected manifestations of this meaning variable and hypothesized that the trait is related to variables that correspond to these manifestations. Accordingly, we searched the literature for published studies about the relation of the particular trait to the specific variables (e.g., Studies 1 and 11). Let us take as an example the case of a trait found to be correlated positively with the meaning dimension "Feelings and Emotions" (*Dim* 20). We concluded (or in the case of other meaning variables, often assumed) from previous studies that high scorers on "Feelings and Emotions" are concerned with emotions, are sensitive to emotional cues, respond emotionally, and so on. Consequently, we inferred that high scorers on the trait found to be correlated with "Feelings and Emotions" would also have the noted characteristics. We regarded published studies about the trait showing that high scorers actually had the expected characteristics as a confirmation of the claim that the noted characteristics are manifestations of the particular meaning variable.

It is obvious that these two methods complement each other fully. Whereas the first is based on moving, as it were, from the data to the meaning variable, the second is based on moving from the meaning variable to the data. In order to learn as much as possible about the manifestations of a meaning variable, it is necessary to apply both of these methods. Thus, the choice of which method to begin the exploration with is merely a matter of convenience.

The two methods suffer from similar difficulties. As noted, the implementation of both methods depends on published studies about the different traits. The findings in these studies are often phrased in different terminologies, or even different "languages." It may therefore be difficult to compare the relevant findings of different investigators. We solved this difficulty by juxtaposing the findings so that readers can judge for themselves whether our judgment that the findings bear on the same point was sound. Different findings concerning any specific trait are juxtaposed in the framework of the study focusing on that trait, whereas the findings concerning the same meaning variable across different traits are juxtaposed in the framework of Appendix B.

Another difficulty is that the different published studies were carried out by investigators who were not familiar with the meaning system and the present project. Therefore, it may sometimes be difficult to relate the observations to expectations about specific manifestations of meaning variables. We solved this difficulty by preserving as much as possible the original language of the findings as presented by the different investigators, without interpreting them or transforming them to our own language. This strategy forced us to limit ourselves primarily to clear-cut findings about immediate manifestations of meaning variables because ambiguities are at a bare minimum in such findings. For example, when we deal with the manifestations of a meaning variable such as "Possessions and Belongingness (*Dim* 17), findings concerning immediate manifestations (i.e., concern with possessions, money, valuables, and so on) can hardly be controversial—at any rate, much less than findings about possible indirect and more far-flung manifestations (e.g., attempts to "possess" people by controlling them or dominating them). In any case, we undoubtedly gained in clarity and reliability but may have lost in the breadth of the range of manifestations of the meaning variables. Even if the latter is the case and there are indirect manifestations with which we did not deal, we still consider it desirable in the first stage of a new venture to establish clearly the immediate range of effects before moving on to effects further from the origin.

The two methods share a further problem, which is the availability of studies about the different manifestations of meaning variables in regard to different traits. In some cases, no studies had been performed, either because no investigator happened to think about those specific manifestations or because they did not seem interesting or important. In the case of some traits and some meaning variables, this possibility definitely seemed likely. But it is also possible that relevant studies have been performed and we did not locate them. We would like to assure the reader that such a failure of omission—if it has occurred—has not been deliberate and is the effect, not of any controllable bias, but of limitations on the material available in libraries or reference compendia and review articles. Wherever they were available, we have cited disconfirming data as fully as confirming data. Moreover, where material is missing (for whatever reason), we have suggested that specific studies be performed to clarify the point.

The two mentioned methods have a prominent strength, which happens to be precisely identical to their weakness. It is their "dependence on published studies about the different traits," "carried out by investigators who were not familiar with the meaning system and the present project" (quoted from the above discussion about weaknesses). This dependence on external sources of data is a very strong guarantee of the absence of any conceivable bias in the data. As noted, we quoted equally confirming and nonconfirming studies.

The two major complementary methods for interpreting patterns of intercorrelations were supplemented by two further methods. One consisted in examining the findings about the correlation with any meaning variable and the data about the manifestations of this variable within the larger context of the whole pattern of intercorrelations with meaning variables as well as the data about their manifestations. Examining the finding within its context entailed the application of one or more techniques, for example, (1) analyzing the similarities and differences of the specific finding and others in the same pattern; (2) considering possible inconsistencies; (3) examining the possibilities of mutual strengthening or neutralization, alternative functioning, substitution, and replacement through other meaning-assignment tendencies; (4) analyzing the occurrence of a correlation with a particular meaning variable in view of other alternatives; and (5) considering the possibilities of groupings of meaning-assignment tendencies and subclusters within the larger pattern. Analyses in line with these techniques shed light on the plausibility of the finding and on the specific form and role it has in regard to a particular trait.

The other method consisted in comparing findings concerning the manifestations of meaning variables across different traits. For example, if in one study a certain meaning variable was shown to correspond to, say, rigidity, a check was made to see whether in another study this variable also corresponded to rigidity or to a similar variable if allowance was made for differences in terminology. The most complete presentation of this cross-checking is provided in Appendix B, which brings together all the different findings concerning each of the meaning variables. Cross-checking may greatly enhance the validity of a finding. In fact, it is the only safe guarantee we have against accidental and faulty results.

We call the first of these supplementary methods *examining in context* and the second, *cross-checking by traits*. The first is based on our assumption that meaning is a system and traits are interactive structures. The second simply expresses our faith in the cumulative nature of science.

NOTES ON INTERACTIONS

Our new conception of traits emphasizes not only manifestations of single meaning variables but also interactions among them. Yet, the methods described so far for hypothesizing, discovering, and identifying manifestations of meaning variables seem to be focused on the single meaning variable or a single manifestation of a meaning variable. This impression is correct to a certain extent. Whereas the described methods could, in principle, be applied to the study of single manifestations as well as interactions among them, most of the applications actually deal with single manifestations of meaning variables. The main reason is the available material about traits, which mostly concerns separate responses.

Nonetheless, we have made a good start also with regard to the study of interactions, through a convergent analysis from two directions. One direction started with the available data about traits. Some of the findings concerned responses that, on analysis, seemed to be the products of interactions between two meaning variables. Overinclusion is a case in point. When we looked for the meaning variables corresponding to this tendency—found to be characteristic of extroverts (Study 1)—it became apparent that both "Contextual Allocation" (*Dim* 1) and the subdimension "Range of Inclusion: Classes" (*Dim* 2a) were involved, the first as a positive preference, responsible for "inclusion," and the latter as a negative preference, for the "*over*inclusion." This hypothesis was checked by examining whether the pattern of intercorrelations between the trait score and the meaning variables actually included *both* a positive correlation with "Contextual Allocation" (*Dim* 1) *and* a negative correlation with "Range of Inclusion: Classes" (*Dim* 2a). The hypothesis was considered confirmed only if both expected correlations occurred.

It should, however, be noted that we always adopted a minimalist criterion; that is, if a finding about a trait could be viewed as corresponding either to one or to two meaning variables, in the interests of economy we always preferred the correspondence to only one meaning variable. This principle reinforces the validity of those cases we identified as products of interactions.

The other direction started with the meaning variables observed to be correlated with a trait score. Looking for possible interactions between meaning variables, we regularly set up hypotheses about likely products of such interactions. For example, if we observed in the pattern a positive correlation with "Function" (*Dim* 3) *and* a negative correlation with "Judgments and Evaluations" (*Dim* 21a), we inferred a likely interaction in the form of ruthless pursuit of egotistical goals and searched the literature for relevant observations about the trait in question (see Studies 3 and 4).

In addition to these two systematic procedures for the examination of interactions, we also looked for interactions on an *ad hoc* basis, mainly under the following conditions. One was inconsistencies between our expectations and the published findings about the traits. For example, if a pattern included a positive correlation with the meaning dimension "Consequences" (*Dim* 7) but there was no evidence that the trait assessed concern with implications, we examined the pattern of correlations with the trait for another meaning variable that could interact with the high score on "Consequences" (*Dim* 7) and that could produce another characteristic. For example, if the high score on "Consequences" (*Dim* 7) interacted with a high score on "Sensory Qualities," particularly those perceived by the referent (*Dim* 19b), the result could be a tendency toward hypochondriasis, which thrives on a magnification of the possible results of any bodily disturbance; but if it interacted with a high score on the metaphoric-symbolic type of relation, the result could be an enhanced tendency toward imaginative constructions.

Another condition that led to *post hoc* examinations of interactions was the comparison of patterns corresponding to different traits. If we found the same meaning variable in two patterns corresponding to two traits, we looked, in both cases, for the same manifestation of that meaning variable. If we did not find the same manifestation in both traits, we tended to suspect that an interaction was involved in shaping the manifestations.

The identified interactions are mentioned in Appendix B. The fact that their number is lower than that of noninteractive manifestations suggests that there is still work to be done on interactions among manifestations of meaning variables.

STUDY 1: EXTROVERSION IN QUESTIONNAIRE AND MEANING[1]

Purpose and Hypotheses

One purpose of this study was to examine and compare the interrelations with meaning of two questionnaire measures of extroversion: Cattell's and Eysenck's. Although both presumably assess the same construct, the two investigators have emphasized differences (Cattell, 1973, p. 183; White, Eysenck, & Soueif, 1969). Cattell (1973, pp. 182–184) defined exvia-invia as a second-order factor based on primary factors defined in terms of scores in the 16 PF self-report questionnaire (the relevant primaries are Factors 1, 3, 4, 6, and 13, Study 6, Table 17), and corresponding to a specific first-order factor based on behavioral data (Factor U.I.32—Hundleby, Pawlik, & Cattell, 1965, pp. 292–302). Cattell considered susceptibility to social inhibition the core of exvia-invia and assumed that it is higher in inviants because they have genetically a greater autonomic responsiveness to threat stimuli that has become relatively strongly conditioned to social stimuli. Eysenck (1967) defined extroversion-introversion as a personality trait measured directly by a questionnaire (the Eysenck Personality Inventory [EPI]), and as being due to individual differences in

[1]This study was done with Talma Lobel.

the functioning of the reticular activation system. He assumed that introverts are in a state of higher arousal and hence are more susceptible to conditioning that is reflected in more restrained behavior.

This brief summary demonstrates that the nature of the differences, if any, has not yet been sufficiently sharply delineated to allow for the testing of specific hypotheses about them. The fact that the two measures have been found to intercorrelate (White, Eysenck, & Soueif, 1969) is also not of much help because an intercorrelation does not specify which particular aspects are shared by the two measures and which are not. There are different incompatible findings about the two measures, but as there are also incompatible findings about any of the single measures separately (e.g., Wilson, 1977, p. 205), it is difficult to decide which incompatibilities are fortuitous and which reflect hard-core differences. Thus, a second purpose of this study was to use the meaning system as a tool for exploring differences between the two measures of extroversion.

However, because there are several findings common to the two measures, we used them as guidelines for stating hypotheses about both measures. Accordingly, we expected, first, that extroversion-introversion would be correlated positively with "Sensory Qualities" (*Dim* 19) because both schools assume that the extrovert has a "strong stimulus hunger" (Eysenck, 1967, p. 163) and "reacts abundantly to stimuli" (Hundleby, Pawlik, & Cattell, 1965, p. 295).

Second, we expected extroversion-introversion to be correlated negatively with "Judgments and Evaluations" (*Dim* 21) because investigators of both schools found that extroverts often disregard rules and norms (Cattell, 1973, p. 183), tend to break institutional regulations of all kinds, engage in antisocial behavior (Allsopp & Feldman, 1974), suffer less from social anxiety (Morris, 1979, p. 86), are less susceptible than introverts to moral considerations, notice injustice less often, cheat more on impulse or for the sake of cheating (Stephenson & Barker, 1972), and more often land in prison or even return to it as recidivists (M. Eysenck, 1974b). Further, when abnormal, extroverts tend to manifest psychopathic and criminal behavior. In contrast, introverts tend more easily to learn rules and inhibitions and to acquire a strict superego and, when abnormal, often develop syndromes like anxiety states, obsessions, and schizophrenia, which testify to their overconcern with rules and norms (Eysenck, 1953, 1965, 1970a). Further, the hypothesis also holds if we focus on the cognitive aspects of "Judgments and Evaluations" (*Dim* 21). Again, both schools emphasize that extroverts do not prefer, as introverts do, "reflectiveness, introspection, abstract-intellectual pursuits" (Morris, 1979, p. 41), or thoughtfulness, and that, under duress, they use even less than introverts the more "intellectual defense mechanisms" (Morris, 1979, p. 77). These negative preferences are a direct manifestation of Eysenckian extroversion and perhaps a more indirect manifestation of Cattellian exvia (resulting from lower inhibition of action tendencies) (Cattell, 1965, p. 126; Hundleby *et al.*, 1965, pp. 144ff).

Third, we expected extroversion-introversion to be correlated negatively with "Results and Consequences" (*Dim* 7) because low concern with consequences and implications seemed to be the feature common to the following findings in the two schools: As compared to inviants, exviants were found to be less aware of dangers, less cautious, less critical in regard to themselves, and highly optimistic (Hundleby *et al.*, 1965, p. 295), and to have "a slap-dash readiness to accept a quick and questionable solution" (Cattell, 1965, p. 126). Further, as compared to introverts, extroverts were found to be risk lovers (Cameron & Myers, 1966; Lynn & Butler, 1962; Ves-

Table 6. Significant Correlations of Two Extroversion Measures with Meaning Variables

Measure of extroversion	Significant correlations with meaning variables
Exvia-invia, based on the 16 PF (Cattell & Eber, 1964)	Dim 1, .30**; Dim 5, .29*; Dim 7, −.23*; Dim 10, .24*; Dim 14, .28*; Dim 15, −.24*; Dim 16, −.62**; Dim 19b, −.32**; (19b$_8$, −.54***); Dim 21a, −.30**; Dim 21b, .36**; Dim 21a + b, −.35**; no. of dif. m. dim., −.26*; TR 1a + b, .29*; TR 3a, −.32**; SR$_{near}$, −.30**; SR 8, .36**.
Extroversion (Eysenck's MPI)	Dim 1, .23*; Dim 2a, −.31**; Dim 4a, .23*; Dim 7, −.24*; Dim 12, .23*; Dim 15, −.23*; Dim 16, −.32**; Dim 17b, .25*; Dim 17a + b, .26*; Dim 18, .24*; Dim 19a, .34**; (19a$_2$, .34**; 19a$_3$, .30**; 19a$_5$, .35**; 19a$_6$, .29*; 19a$_7$, .39***); Dim 19b, −.51***; (19b$_6$, −.32**; 19b$_8$, −.42***); Dim 19a + b, .23*; Dim 21a, −.37**; Dim 21b, −.30**; Dim 21a + b, −.28*; no. of dif. m. dim., −.24*; TR 1a, .40***; TR 3c, .23*; TR 4b, −.30**; SR 4, −.30**; SR 7, .23*; SR 10, .23*; no. of dif. SR, .23*.

Note. For the code of the meaning variables, see Appendix A.
  *$p < .05$.
 **$p < .01$.
***$p < .001$.

tewig, 1977); to be more impulsive, less reflective, and less fearful (Eysenck, Hendrickson, & Eysenck, 1969); to be inclined to ignore the possible unpleasant consequences of their behavior (Gray, 1973); to be prone to minor accidents (Craske, 1968), and so on.

Fourth, we expected extroversion-introversion to be correlated positively with the lexical mode of meaning (particularly the attributive type of relation, TR 1, as there was no empirical basis for expecting a salience of the comparative type of relation, TR 2, in extroverts) and to be correlated negatively with the personal mode of meaning. The rationale was the findings about the realism of extroverts and their social orientation (Hundleby et al., 1965, p. 295; Morris, 1979, p. 86) as contrasted with the orientation of introverts toward the inner world (Wilson, 1977). Again, we assumed that types of relation rather that meaning dimensions would manifest the above difference because no findings suggested the salience of dimensions like "Feelings and Emotions" (Dim 20) or "Cognitive Qualities" (Dim 22) in introverts.

Method

The subjects were 72 undergraduates in psychology and the social sciences at Tel Aviv University (28 males and 44 females), in the age range of 22–31 years.* They were administered separately, in random order, the three questionnaires: Cattell's 16 PF (see Study 6), Eysenck's EPI (Eysenck & Eysenck, 1964), and the standard meaning questionnaire (11 stimulus words).

Results and Conclusions

Table 6 shows that the first hypothesis was confirmed only in regard to "Sensory Qualities" characterizing the referent (Dim 19a) and only in regard to Eysenck's

*The age range is so high because Israeli students enter the university only after obligatory military service.

measure. Eysenckian extroversion is correlated with visual (form and shape), auditory, gustatory, thermal, and olfactory sensory qualities. The findings are impressive and vindicate Eysenck's claim that extroverts are attentive to stimuli. Not so Cattellian exviants. This finding indicates that Hundelby et al.'s above-quoted claim (1965, p. 295) that extroverts react abundantly to stimuli is an inadequate interpretation of their findings about what they call the extroverts' "cognitive plasticity." Yet, even more surprising at first glance are the negative correlations with "Sensory Qualities" perceived by the referent (*Dim* 19b) and particularly with "Internal Sensations" (*Dim* 19b$_8$). These negative correlations are common to both Eysenckian and Cattellian extroversion and are the highest in both patterns. The correlations indicate that extroverts attend, less than introverts, to sensory experiences and particularly internal sensations. The findings become less surprising if we note that *Dim* 19a probably deals primarily with sensory qualities, whereas *Dim* 19b deals with the accompanying sensations or sensory experiences. This distinction implies that there may be a difference between noting the sensory qualities of things and focusing on experiencing these qualities. Accordingly, extroverts would prefer to note sensory qualities but would deemphasize the experiential aspect, particularly of internal sensations.

The conclusion that extroverts attend less to sensory experiences is confirmed by the findings that they tend less toward hypochondriasis and sleeplessness (Eysenck, Hendrickson, & Eysenck, 1969) and suffer less from psychosomatic disease (Sainsbury, 1960). Further, they are repressors; that is, they tend to ignore adjustment problems, stress, and different negative emotions, in contrast to the sensitizers (i.e., introverts), who tend to emphasize and even exaggerate them (Bryne, 1964; Cohen & Oziel, 1972; Dana & Cocking, 1969; Geen, 1976; Lester, 1976). Morris (1979) who viewed the correlation of extroversion-introversion with repression-sensitization as "one of the most robust findings in the current literature on personality traits" (p. 77), noted that it is unclear whether extroverts are aware of fewer problems or tend to talk less about them. Our finding indicates that lower awareness is probably the case. Again, most impressive are the findings that show extroverts to have a higher pain tolerance (Hill, 1975; Ludvigh & Happ, 1974), as well as higher sensation thresholds and pain thresholds (Haslam, 1966; Lynn & Eysenck, 1961; Schalling & Levander, 1964). Notably, Lynn et al. and Haslam used a thermostimulator for pain, whereas Schalling et al. used a regular electrical pain device. Because by our findings extroverts have low sensitivity to thermal sensations (see negative correlation with *Dim* 19b$_6$), it is not surprising that the former found stronger effects than the latter. Eysenck linked the higher persistence of extroverts to their relative insensitivity to pain (Costello & Eysenck, 1961; Singh, Gupta, & Manocha, 1966). In addition, several studies show that Eysenckian extroverts have higher sensory thresholds than introverts (e.g., for auditory inputs, S. Smith, 1966; gustatory stimuli, Fisher, Griffin, & Rockey, 1966; electrical vestibular stimulation, Dzendolet, 1963).

The cited empirical findings confirm the conclusion drawn from the negative correlation with "Sensory Qualities" perceived by the referent (*Dim* 19b). Hence, it would not seem presumptuous to use our results to suggest solutions to some unresolved issues of the relation between arousal level and extroversion. In the Cattellian camp, there seems to be a lack of clarity about the relation of reactivity and arousal to exvia-invia. Whereas Cattell (1973, p. 183) clearly stated that exviants have a genetically lower autonomic reactivity (they are high on Parmia and low on Threctia, Factor 6, Study 6; for definition see Table 16), Hundleby *et al.* 1965) stated that "exvia originates in . . . higher temperamental ardor (more intensive emotions which are readily overtly expressed)," whereas "invia . . . is caused by higher temperamental apathy" (p. 298). The state of affairs is not more encouraging in the Eysenckian camp. Here, the problem is not clarity (the claim that extroverts have a lower arousal level is unequivocal), but the empirical confirmation. Whereas measures of arousal under regular conditions and various laboratory tests did not support Eysenck's claim (Gale, 1973), various predictions about the responses of extroverts and introverts to manipulations that involve transient changes in arousal levels (e.g., threats of shocks, drugs, and vigilance tasks) did confirm the predictions (Claridge & Herrington, 1963: M. Eysenck, 1974a,b; Haslam, 1966; Shagass, 1956).

To our mind, the resolution of this paradox arises from our findings about the inattention of extroverts and the pronounced attention of introverts to sensory experiences in general and to internal sensations in particular. These findings suggest that the manipulation of arousal by drugs and other transient changes in arousal would attract the attention of introverts more than that of extroverts, so that the former would tend to react to them more than the latter. Thus, much larger changes in arousal would be needed to attract the attention of extroverts and to disturb them than would be needed to attract the attention of introverts. Hence, we suggest that extroverts and introverts differ in their tendencies to note sensory experiences, and particularly internal sensations. The difference is conceptualized best in terms of thresholds and not in terms of reactions to stimulation when eventually processed. This assumption would correspond to the many observed facts (Eysenck, 1967; Eysenck & Eysenck, 1969, Chapter 7; Hundleby *et al.*, 1965, pp. 292–302) without the necessity of assuming differences in intrinsic or steady-state levels of arousal that probably do not exist.

Further, in a purely speculative way, we suggest that our conclusion may be relevant also to the controversial issue of the relation of extroversion to sociability. Despite decades of research, it is still an open question whether extroverts are at all sociable and whether the sociable impression they make is due to their interest in people or to other causes (e.g., to tendencies to maintain cortical arousal, decrease anxiety, and exercise assertiveness (Carrigan, 1960; Hundleby *et al.*, 1965, p. 295; Wilson, 1977). We found no positive indications suggesting that extroverts are interested in people (e.g., there were no correlations of extroversion with "Domain of Application," *Dim.* 8a, which indicates interest in people; see Study 2). Therefore, we tend to interpret the disregard of extroverts for internal sensory experiences of referents as indicating that they are not particularly interested in the internal world of other people. Hence, they are probably intrinsically less interested in people than they may superficially appear.

The findings concerning the second hypothesis are again partly unexpected. Both measures of extroversion correlate negatively, as predicted, with "Judgments and Evaluations" about the referent (*Dim* 21a). But concerning "Judgments and Evaluations" of the referent (*Dim* 21b), only the Eysenckian measure correlates negatively, whereas the correlation of the Cattellian measure is positive. These findings imply that both Eysenckian and Cattellian extroverts disregard evaluations by others. The difference between them is that the former also disregard their own judgments whereas the latter note them to advantage. This conclusion is largely confirmed by empirical findings. Eysenckian extroverts were found to be more inclined to change their judgments under prestige suggestions (Sinha & Ojha, 1963), to change their evaluation of paintings after being informed of the painter's name (Mohan & Mohan, 1965), to conform with peers' urging to undertake antisocial acts (Rim & Seidendross, 1971), to be sexually more permissive (Eysenck, 1976), and to favor a pragmatic, nonidealistic, tough-minded approach to issues (Eysenck, 1954). In contrast, the Cattellian exviant has "little authority submission," "little authority suggestibility," and "less tendency to agree" (Hundleby et al., 1965, pp. 301–302, Items 246, 35, and 152).

The third hypothesis about a negative correlation with "Consequences and Results" (Dim 7) was confirmed equally for both measures. Concerning the fourth hypothesis, about the relations with modes of meaning, the data tend to confirm the expectation. Both measures are correlated positively with the attributive type of relation (TR 1) and negatively with one of the types of relation that constitute the personal mode, though not with the same one: the exviants deemphasize the exemplifying-illustrative type of relation (TR 3), and the extroverts the metaphoric-symbolic one (TR 4). Notably, the positive correlation of extroversion with the exemplifying scene (TR 3c) is confirmed by the finding that extroverts tends to describe events dramatically (Forrest, 1963). Thus, this correlation may reflect more a style of presentation.

There are further findings common to both measures, which is to be expected in view of the high correlation between them ($r = .62$, $p < .01$). First, both measures were correlated positively with "Contextual Allocation" (Dim 1). This meaning dimension stands for generalizing, abstracting, and categorizing. The observed correlation thus corresponds to the findings showing that, on a free recall task, extroverts clustered words together on the basis of semantic categories at a higher rate than introverts (Schwartz, 1975), retrieved more quickly items corresponding to given category names (M. W. Eysenck, 1974a,b), and, on a word classification task, grouped together more words (Hundleby et al., 1965, p. 301, Item 706). It is of interest to note that, in extroverts, there is an accompanying negative correlation with "Range of Inclusion: Classes" (Dim 2a) that reflects low differentiation in categorizations. Together, the tendency to generalize (reflected by Dim 1), coupled with low concern for differentiations between categories (reflected by Dim 2a), may account for the overinclusion of extroverts (Payne, 1973, p. 460) or their "slight confabulatory tendency" (Hundleby et al., 1965, p. 295). The positive correlation with "Contextual Allocation" and negative with "Range of Inclusion" may also explain why extroverts are superior in short-term recall. Because they are more concerned with identifying the common characteristics of things that allow for lumping them together than with distinguishing features, they may find it easy to bind stimuli to each other through multiple cues that facilitate immediate recall. However, long-term recall requires other cognitive strategies that extroverts do not master or apply as well as introverts do (see below).

Second, in both scales, extroversion was correlated negatively with the number of different meaning dimensions used, a finding that may indicate a tendency to prefer or limit oneself to a narrower range of meanings. The evidence for this interpretation is clear, though indirect. In learning, extroverts tend to stick to older cognitive habits when they interfere with newly learned ones (Hundleby *et al.*, 1965, p. 295), and in problem-solving, their performance declines appreciably from the first to the last third of the task (Eysenck, 1959). Both effects may be due to a restricted number of dimensions. Further, there is evidence that the number of different dimensions reflects the degree of elaboration to which inputs are subjected (S. Kreitler & H. Kreitler, 1989b). Thus, the use of a low number of different dimensions by the extroverts may explain why their learning or recall of material over long time periods is worse than that of introverts (M. Eysenck, 1977, Chapter 8). Because conditioning also represents long-term learning, the lower number of meaning dimensions that extroverts habitually use may provide an alternative to the explanation in terms of arousal that is commonly given to the low conditionality of extroverts. However, as noted above, there are other determinants in the meaning profile that may explain why extroverts are superior in learning over short-term periods (see above).

Third, both scales show that extroverts tend to use varied referents. This tendency may account for the variability of responses that was found to be characteristic of extroverts. Extroverts have low perceptual rigidity (Canestrari, 1957), low rigidity in thinking (Eysenck & Eysenck, 1962; Watson, 1967; White, 1968), high intrapersonal variability (Eysenck, 1947), high variation in sexual partners (Wilson & Nias, 1975), high variety-seeking on monotonous tasks (Hill, 1975), low persistence (Payne, 1973, p. 472), high alternation behavior (Eysenck, 1967), more fluctuations of reversible figures, and more changes in choice-of-viewing situations (Wilson, 1978). Further, exviants were found to have larger variability in simple reaction times, less persistence, and more "cognitive plasticity" (Hundleby *et al.*, 1965, p. 301, Items 263 and 402, p. 295). Further, the tendency to vary referents may account partly for the finding that extroverts learn better when subjected to a "discovery" approach that allows more freedom in selecting and defining referents than the formal "reception" approach does (Leith, 1974). It is possible that the tendency to vary referents contributes also to the lower performance of extroverts on vigilance tasks that require focusing on one or more specific referents (see references below). As noted below, low vigilance may also depend on the low use of the dimension "Range of Inclusion: Classes" (*Dim* 2a). Thus, the performance of extroverts on vigilance tasks may serve to illustrate the product of interaction between two meaning dimensions. In sum, it may be of interest to note that the tendency to vary referents could be viewed as a major determinant of what has often been called the extrovert's *stimulus hunger* (Gale, 1969).

Also common to both scales are negative correlations with locational and temporal qualities. Both indicate low performance on tasks that require attention to location or time. The expectation about locational performance was confirmed by findings indicating that extroverts make more mistakes (of line crossing, entering blind alleys, etc.) on maze tasks (Foulds, 1951; Foulds & Caine, 1958; Gibson, 1965; Payne, 1973, p. 465) and have lower scores on tasks that require the crossing of slanted lines (Hundleby *et al.*, 1965, p. 301, Item 16a). Our expectation concerning temporal performance is fully in accord with Eysenck's assumption about the lower arousal state of extroverts. Claridge (1967), Venables (1966), and others (Payne, 1973, p. 471; Tizard & Venables, 1957; Venables & O'Connor, 1959) found that speed is positively correlated with cortical arousal and is lower in extroverts. Most of the direct evidence also supports this conclusion. Studies showed that, compared to normals or introverts, extroverts err more in time estimation (i.e., negative time error) (Eysenck, 1967, pp. 145–146), are more impulsive (i.e., plan ahead less), have lapses of attention on tasks that require waiting for delayed or infrequent signals (Hundleby *et al.*, 1965, p. 301, Item 5; Thackray, Jones, & Touchstone, 1974; Wilson, 1977, pp. 184–185), and tend to react slower than introverts on some tasks (Hundleby *et al.*, 1965, p. 302, Item 420a). However, there seems also to be contradicting evidence about the greater speed of extroverts on other tasks, for example, a test that measures speed of aesthetic decision (Hundleby *et al.*, 1965, p. 302, Items 684), speed of decision on the length of lines, the matrices test, and mazes tasks (Eysenck, 1967, pp. 160–163). On purely hypothetical grounds, it seems plausible to ask whether the greater speed of extroverts on these tasks is due to their better ability to decide freely without undue anxiety, or to their readiness to take risks and settle for solutions that are less than perfect.

Finally, some findings are specific only to one scale. Most of them are of interest because they highlight various interrelations of the scales with other variables. Thus, the positive correlation of Eysenck's scale with "Actions" (*Dim* 4) underscores the fact that extroversion includes "activity" as a definable cluster. Again, the positive correlation of Eysenck's scale with "Possessions" (*Dim* 17) is notable because concern with possessions is part of the conservative orientation found to be characteristic of extroverts (Eysenck & Wilson, 1976, pp. 195, 202). It is of interest to note that Eysenck's scale is correlated negatively with "Range of Inclusion: Classes" (*Dim* 2a). This finding suggests only weak tendencies for analyzing, discriminating, and differentiating. The low use of this dimension may be one reason that extroverts were found to perform less well on vigilance and detection tasks, which require differentiating sharply between stimuli (Bakan, 1959; Harkins & Geen, 1976; Krupski, Raskin, & Bakan, 1971; Tune, 1966). It may also account for the finding that extroverts are less disturbed than introverts by competing responses (Howarth, 1969). Because they focus less on the features distinguishing between the different responses, they may be less bothered by them. Further, the positive correlation of Cattell's measure with "Structure" (*Dim* 10) is confirmed by the finding that exviants have higher scores on tasks that require seeing objects in unstructured drawings, gestalt completion, and arithmetic reasoning and logic (Hundleby *et al.*, 1968, pp. 302–301, Items 282, 146a, and 275).

In sum, the study showed that the correlations between meaning variables and the extroversion scores correspond with high accuracy to the independent findings of many studies. Further, the meaning variables bound with the scores provided insights into the nature of extroversion and into differences between the two measures of extroversion. The disregard of extroverts for sensory experiences and particularly internal sensations, their preference for varying the referent, and their tendencies to emphasize the lexical and to deemphasize the personal mode of meaning exemplify insights into the nature of extroversion. The differential concern of extroverts with sensory qualities, the coping with their own judgments and beliefs, the activity structure, and their attitudes toward possessions exemplify insights into the differences between Eysenck's and Cattell's measures of extroversion. The findings have also served to shed new light on some of the intriguing issues concerning extroversion, such as superior short-term recall and inferior long-term recall, as well as pain sensitivity to electrical more than to thermal stimuli.

STUDY 2: THE MEANING PATTERNS OF THE CALIFORNIA PSYCHOLOGICAL INVENTORY[2]

Purposes and Hypotheses

The major purpose of this study was to test several hypotheses about relations between specific variables of meaning and personality traits. A secondary purpose was to explore further nonpredicted relations between meaning variables and personality traits so as to increase our information about the personological implications of meaning variables. The California Psychological Inventory (CPI) seemed to us the personality test best suited to attaining our objectives for the following reasons.

First, it is presumed to assess some of the traits in which we were particularly interested, for example, sociability. In the CPI manual, Gough (1969b) clearly stated: "Its scales are addressed principally to personality characteristics important for social living and social interaction . . . of socially functioning individuals" (p. 5). Second, it is presumed to assess both personality traits and more cognitive predispositions, such as intellectual efficiency, which enabled us to test a broader range of hypotheses. Third, it was designed primarily and originally for use with normal populations, that is, the kind of populations that we primarily intended our conclusions to fit. Fourth, all investigators agree that many of the 18 scales of the test do not measure relatively independent personality dimensions or traits (Megargee, 1972, pp. 115–117). Even Gough's original descriptions of the scales clearly indicate the overlap. All factor analyses showed that the test is highly redundant (Crites, 1964; Crites, Bechtoldt, Goldstein, & Heilbrun, 1961; Mitchell & Pierce-Jones, 1960; Thorndike, 1959). This conceptual redundancy suited our purpose well because it enabled us to test some of our hypotheses across more than one scale. Fifth, the test is remarkably straightforward in interpretation. Indeed, its face validity often converges toward its construct validity. This property made it easier to use in testing our hypotheses. Sixth, the interpretation of the test is based on considering each property discretely rather than in interaction with other properties. This characteristic, again, is a help in testing hypotheses about meaning variables related to the various indicated properties. Seventh, the test is homogeneously based on agreeing to or rejecting items that are formally beliefs about oneself (Kreitler & Kreitler, 1976). This unity in structure and content helped us to test relations between meaning variables and beliefs about the self. And eighth, the many validity studies in regard to this test lend our conclusions a sounder empirical basis.

The range of hypotheses was limited at the start by the properties known to be assessed by the CPI and by the available validation material about the CPI known to us. Thus, the following list of hypotheses represents those we considered it possible to test in the present context rather than those that could and should be tested about the personological implications of various meaning variables.

Accordingly, we had 11 major hypotheses:

1. We expected sociability to be positively correlated with the meaning dimension "Domain of Application" (*Dim* 8a). The rationale was that sociability requires attention to the identity of the participants in a situation or an event. An individual interested in other people, for whatever reason, may be expected to be concerned

---

[2]This study was done with Iris Drexler.

with identifying them and with finding out who is who, who did what, which event or object or action applies to whom, and so on. This may not be the single requirement or manifestation of sociability, but it is an indispensable one. Correspondingly, an active lack of interest in human beings should be manifested in a negative correlation with "Domain of Application."

2. We expected concern with one's values, opinions, and judgments to be positively related with the meaning dimension "Judgments and Evaluations" (*Dim* 21b), and we expected active lack of concern with one's values to be negatively related to this meaning dimension. Again, the rationale was simple. Individuals who care for values should be concerned with the corresponding meaning dimension, and vice versa. Concern with values may be manifested by an explicit endorsement of values and an insistence on being guided by them, whereas low concern with values may take, on the one hand, the form of tolerance or liberalism and, on the other hand, even the form of certain types of criminality, for example, those that involve an intentional breaking of rules or an ideologically rooted anarchism. Many other forms of criminality involve strict adherence to rules. Be it as it may, it is imperative to emphasize that concern with rules cannot be considered the cause of criminality, which is a molar behavior—indeed, a style of life. Further, a negative correlation with a meaning dimension is to be distinguished from the absence of a correlation. Whereas the former presumably involves an active stance of negating, overlooking, or annulling the effect of the relevant domain of content, the latter probably indicates merely lack of particular concern with the specific domain. Hence, the absence of a correlation with the meaning dimension "Judgments and Evaluations" may reflect indifference toward this domain, which is the attitude routinely entertained by many nondelinquents as well as by a fair number of delinquents.

3. We expected concern with one's cognitive properties and activities to be correlated positively with the meaning dimension "Cognitive Qualities" (*Dim* 22b); and we expected active overlooking of one's own cognitive properties or the cognitive reactions and functioning of others to be correlated negatively with the referent's "Cognitive Qualities (*Dim* 22b) and "Cognitive Qualities" evoked in others (*Dim* 22a), respectively. Active lack of concern with the cognitive qualities and responses of oneself or of others was assumed to be manifested by a denial or an intentional overlooking of these properties. The rationale for the hypothesis was straightforward: An individual concerned with using or demonstrating his or her cognitive potential may be expected to have more meaning values in this dimension than an individual who is indifferent to this domain and especially one who is intent on disregarding the cognitive potential or even dissimulating it.

4. Along the same lines, we expected concern with feelings and emotions to be correlated positively with the meaning dimension "Feelings and Emotions" (*Dim* 20b), and we expected an active lack of concern (i.e., denial or intentional overlooking of one's emotional state) to be negatively correlated with this meaning dimension. The CPI enabled us to test only the second part of this hypothesis, because none of its scales purportedly measures active concern with emotions.

5. We expected concern with actions to be correlated positively with the meaning dimension "Actions" (*Dim* 4, and particularly *Dim* 4a), and we expected active lack of interest in actions to be correlated negatively with this meaning dimension. This hypothesis indicates that concern with actions (i.e., with what one does, what

others do, and what is done) is to be distinguished from the rather temperamental quality of activity and dynamism. The meaning profile reflects conceptualizations and not temperament.

6. We expected flexibility and tolerance of ambiguities to be correlated negatively with the meaning dimensions "Contextual Allocation" (*Dim* 1) and "Belongingness" (*Dim* 17b). The complementary part of this hypothesis about rigidity could not be tested with the CPI, which does not expressly measure it. The rationale of this hypothesis was that flexibility requires lack of concern with classifying items, things, qualities, and people into strictly differentiated categories, and with allocating each of them precisely into the category or sphere where it supposedly belongs. We assumed that "Contextual Allocation" reflects the more abstract aspect of this tendency, whereas "Belongingness" reflects its more concrete manifestations.

7. We expected the tendency to resist pressures toward conformity to be correlate positively with the different kinds of the comparative type of relation (*TR* 2a, *TR* 2b, *TR* 2c, and *TR* 2d) and particularly with the type of relation *difference* (*TR* 2b). The rationale was that the ability not to yield to conformity pressures requires—as a necessary though not sufficient condition—the tendency to compare one's response with that of others, to consider differences (*TR* 2b), and possibly to weigh alternatives to similarity (*TR* 2a) that include complementariness (*TR* 2c; e.g., "Whereas they respond in this way, I respond in the complementary way") and relationality (*TR* 2d; e.g., "Being a son he behaves as a son, and being his parent I should not behave as he does, but as a parent"). Thus, the different comparative types of relation may represent different forms of implementing the tendency to withstand pressures toward conformity. Further, it is plausible that the comparative type of relation "difference" plays a central role in facilitating firmness in view of conformity pressures because lack of conformity seems to involve primarily acceptance of differences between one's responses and responses of others.

8. We expected the tendency toward defiance or contrariness in interpersonal relations to be correlated positively with the comparative type of relation *difference* (*TR* 2b). The rationale was that contrariness requires—as a necessary but not sufficient condition—the tendency to emphasize differences.

9. We expected creativity to be correlated positively with the personal mode of meaning (i.e., the exemplifying-illustrative and metaphoric-symbolic types of relation). This hypothesis is based on several studies showing that the personal mode of meaning plays a crucial role in creativity as assessed by different instruments (Ensenberg, 1976; H. Kreitler & S. Kreitler, 1983, 1989a; Lahav, 1982). Some of the studies were correlational, and others showed the effects on creativity of manipulating the personal mode of meaning.

10. We expected a sense of duty and the tendency to cooperate with others to be correlated positively with the total number of meaning values (i.e., responses) in the subject's meaning profile. The rationale is straightforward: Because the number of required responses is not specified in the instructions for the meaning questionnaire, producing a high number of responses may reflect a particular orientation toward cooperation.

11. The last hypothesis was of a completely different order. It dealt with the relation of meaning variables to traits with a relatively larger or smaller "degree of genetic determination," following the term coined by Loehlin and Nichols (1976, p. 26). The hypothesis was that traits with a relatively larger genetic determination would be related to more meaning variables than traits with a relatively smaller

genetic determination. Presentation of the hypothesis was made possible by the existence of two independent studies assessing the heritability of CPI scales (Gottesman, 1966; Loehlin & Nichols, 1976). Because the hypothesis dealt with relative degrees of genetic determination, we felt that it could be stated and tested regardless of whether one assumes a greater (H. Eysenck, 1973) or a lesser role (Loehlin & Nichols, 1976) for genetics in human personality. We expected traits with a larger heritability to be related to more meaning variables for three reasons. First, we assumed such traits have clearer, stronger and more homogeneous manifestations in a greater number of individuals and thus would be more readily related to other variables. Second, we assumed such traits would be manifested at earlier developmental stages and thus would have a better chance to be related to more other variables. And third, studies showed that personality test items with a strong genetic component tend to cluster more clearly than other items (Horn, Plomin, & Rosenman, 1976); that is, they exist more often in patterns that increase the chances of interrelations with other variables (see also Study 6, third hypothesis).

Method

The number of subjects was 85: 42 women and 43 men in the age range 17–20 years. They were partly high-school students ($n = 30$), partly enlisted soldiers ($n = 28$), and partly university students ($n = 27$). Each of these subsamples included an almost equal number of men and women. They were administered the CPI (translated and adapted to Hebrew; Levin & Karni, 1970) and the standard meaning questionnaire (11 stimulus words). The CPI was administered in group sessions, and the meaning questionnaire was answered at the subject's convenience within a specified time period. The two questionnaires were administered separately as different tasks, at different times, and in random order. They were presented as research tasks, and participation was voluntary with no rewards. There were no significant differences between older and younger subjects (17 and 18 versus 19 and 20) or the genders.

For the testing of the hypotheses, it was necessary to determine independently of the meaning analysis which CPI scales presumably assess the different relevant qualities. This determination was made on the basis of two sources of material: the manifest content of the items in the scales and the validation studies mentioned in Gough's CPI manual (1969b/1975), in Megargee's CPI handbook (1972), or reported in journals and other publications (as specified).

Thus, the actual procedure of testing the hypotheses consisted of first setting up a table of correlations between the meaning variables (each expressed as a ratio of the subject's total number of responses) and the CPI scales, and then comparing the actual correlational findings with the predictions. A fit between the prediction and the findings required, first, that the obtained correlations be those predicted for the specific meaning variable, and second, that the correlations obtained for the particular meaning variable be only those that were predicted and not others as well. This strict criterion is necessary to ensure that the obtained correlations actually confirm the stated hypotheses. This major stage of analyzing the data was supplemented by a subsidiary stage that was performed later and consisted in examining *ad hoc* further relations between CPI scales and meaning variables that were obtained but had not been predicted.

Table 7 specifies which CPI scales were assumed to assess the different person-

Table 7. California Psychological Inventory (CPI) Scales
Regarded as Assessing Specific Personality Variables[a]

Personality variable	CPI scales by which assessed	Rationale	Remarks
Hypothesis 1: Sociability	*Do, Sy, Sp, Sa, Cm*	*Do, Sy, Sp,* and *Sa* assess sociability and interpers. adequacy (Gough, 1969b); these scales load highly on a factor reflecting social poise or extroversion (Mitchell & Pierce-Jones, 1960; Pierce-Jones, Mitchell & King, 1969; Shure & Rogers, 1963), social confidence and drive (Leton & Walter, 1962), extroversion (Gendre, 1966), self-acceptance and outgoingness (Springob & Struening, 1964), person orientation (Nichols & Schnell, 1963), and interpers. effectiveness (Bouchard, 1969); these scales correlate with factors A, E, F, and H of the 16 PF, which indicate outgoingness and social participation (Megargee, 1972, p. 120) and the sociability scale of the Guilford-Zimmerman Temperament Survey (GZTS) that reflects liking social activities, entering into conversations, seeking social contacts, etc. (Guilford, Zimmerman, & Guilford, 1976, pp. 6, 47); items of these scales refer to sociability and interest in people. *Cm* is included although not saturated on the sociability factor (Mitchell *et al.*, 1960) because items (e.g., Item 348) reflect interest in being with others and resembling them; conventionality involves interest in others; a Smallest Space Analysis showed *Cm* to be close to the *Do, Sy,* and *Sa* scales (Karni & Levin, 1972). *Sc* included because high scorers describe themselves as "considerate" and "dependable" as against "impulsive," "self-seeking," and "individualistic" (Megargee, 1972, pp. 261–262), and many of its items (e.g., Items 174, 276, 66, 81, 102, 114, 173, and 183) reflect consideration for others that suggests indirectly interest in others; correlated zero with social intro-	*Cs* not included although saturated on sociability factor (Mitchell *et al.*, 1960), because explicitly designed to assess "ambition and self-assurance that leads to status" (Gough, 1968, p. 61) and its items do not refer to sociability. *Wb* not included although mentioned by Gough (1969b) together with the "social" scales, because the content of its items, its purpose, and its correlations with other tests do not indicate that it assesses sociability.

Table 7. (*Continued*)

Personality variable	CPI scales by which assessed	Rationale	Remarks
		version (MMPI) and negatively with timidity (16 PF) but positively with friendliness and personal relations (GZTS) (Gough, 1975).	
Active lack of interest in people	*Ie*	High scores indicate concentration on intellectual pursuits; the items do not reflect sociability and the only socially oriented items are cognitively loaded (Nos. 188, 200)	
Hypothesis 2: Concern with values, opinions, and judgments	*Cs*	*Cs:* Its items (e.g., 103, 160) reflect literary and artistic interests and "social conscience" (Megargee, 1972, p. 46; e.g., Item 190); high scorers tend to possess at home objects like books and phonographs (Gough, 1949) and to describe themselves as "progressive" (Megargee, 1972, p. 261), an adjective reflecting values.	*Re* and *So* not included because, despite their labels, the content of their items and their intercorrelations with other tests indicate that they do not actually assess values.
Active lack of concern for values, opinions, and judgments	*Sp, To*	*Sp:* Assesses behavior in line with values and accepted morality; high scorers are characterized by "broadminded unstuffy attitudes about social rules and prohibitions" and "an outright rejection of the Protestant ethic with its emphasis on duty, conformity and moderation" (Megargee, 1972, p. 50); they admit that they do not follow the rules and even enjoy not following them (Items 14, 58, 69, 96, 98, 150, etc.) and describe themselves as "pleasure-seeking," "unconventional," "uninhibited," and "spontaneous" (Megargee, 1972, pp. 261, 265), i.e., they do not care very much for their own values or those of others; the scale discriminates not only bet. nonusers and users of marijuana but also between nonusers of over 3 years and initial nonusers who became users in the course of 3 years (Kay, Lyons, Newman, Mankin, & Loeb, 1978). *To:* Designed to identify "permissive, accepting and nonjudgmental social beliefs and	

(*continued*)

Table 7. (*Continued*)

Personality variable	CPI scales by which assessed	Rationale	Remarks
		attitudes" (Gough, 1969b) (e.g., Item 67), i.e., acceptance of people regardless of their opinions and values; it is correlated negatively with the F scale (Gough, 1975; Jensen, 1957) and other measures of prejudice (Gough, 1969b; Young, Benson & Holzman, 1969) and positively with the scales E, O, F, and P of the GZTS, which indicate tolerance of others, even of hostile action and domination (Guilford *et al.*, 1976, pp. 6–7, 46)	
Hypothesis 3: Concern with one's cognitive properties and actions	*Ie*	*Ie*: Designed to assess "the adequacy and effectiveness with which a subject employs his intellectual resources" (Gough, 1969b); items reflect interest in books, discussion, science, poetry, etc. (Items 50, 122, 152, 228, 269, 283, 399, etc.); high scorers describe themselves in cog. terms, e.g., reasonable, intelligent, sophisticated, clearthinking, and logical (Megargee, 1972, pp. 261, 265); scale correlates positively with intelligence (Aiken, 1963; Gough, 1969b, 1975, pp. 24, 34; Purkey, 1966; Southern & Plant, 1968) and with giftedness (Lessinger & Martinson, 1961) and gradepoint average (Bendig & Klugh, 1956; Flaherty & Reutzel, 1965; Gough, 1964a,b), even when IQ controlled (Gill & Spilka, 1962; Gough, 1963; Morgan, 1952; Snider & Linton, 1964); correlates with achievement on tasks of some intellectual challenge, e.g., performance in air-trafficcontrol course (Trites *et al.*, 1967), in an academic setting (Dicken, 1963), and in militarypolice-training courses (Hogan, 1970; Rosenberg *et al.*, 1962), but not males' completion of elementary-education courses or student teaching (Durflinger, 1963a,b).	
Active overlooking of one's cognitive properties and actions	*Fe*	*Fe*: Designed to assess psychological feminity-masculinity (Gough, 1966; Gough, Chun, & Chung, 1968; Hase & Goldberg, 1967),	

Table 7. (*Continued*)

Personality variable	CPI scales by which assessed	Rationale	Remarks
		and its items (e.g., 65, 78, 240) express the social stereotype of femininity, i.e., sensitive, modest, withdrawing from achievements (self-descriptions as "warm, meek, weak, and self-denying," Megargee, 1972, pp. 263, 265), the acceptance of which is bound with underplaying intellectual qualities (Maccoby & Jacklin, 1974, Ch. 3); scale correlates negatively with *Ie* (Megargee, 1972, pp. 206–207) and 4 measures of intellectual functioning (Gough, 1975, p. 34).	
Lack of concern with cognitive properties and actions evoked in others	*Fe, Sc, Cm*	*Fe:* Reasons similar to those presented for *Fe* above, i.e., a "submissive," "warm" woman is supposed to care for the emotional responses and well-being of others rather than their cognitive responses (see Item 58). *Sc:* High scorers are characterized by a self-effacing modesty, particularly in cognitive domains (they deny tendency to boast or show off; see Items 4, 42, 78, 81, 102, 231, 267, 292) and describe themselves as modest and self-denying (Megargee, 1972, pp. 261, 265); scale correlates neg. with General Culture Test, Guilford Creativity Battery, General Intelligence (16 PF), and Achievement (Edwards Personal Preference Schedule) (Gough, 1975), but as high scorers nevertheless rely on judgment, etc. (Items 149, 170, 174), we inferred that, though they may care about cognition, they do not care about evoking favorable cognitive responses in others. *Cm:* A measure of "contented normativism" (Shure & Rogers, 1963) and "inflexible conformity" (Pierce-Jones et al., 1962). We assumed subjects who adhere to platitudes (e.g., Item 348) tend to actively overlook cog. responses; scale correlates negatively with 5 measures of intellectual functioning (Gough, 1975, p. 34).	

(*continued*)

Table 7. (*Continued*)

Personality variable	CPI scales by which assessed	Rationale	Remarks
Hypothesis 4: Denial of one's emotions	Wb	Wb: Scale is designed to identify dissimulators, i.e., those who intentionally deny emotional states and problems (Gough, 1975); majority of items refer to denials of common emotions— e.g., fear, jealousy, annoyance, and dislike of some people (Items 15, 309, 344, 351, 372, 375, 425)—and of autonomic sensations often involved in emotions (Items 308, 313); further items denote denials of common actions expected of people who deny emotions, e.g., quarreling with family, playing sick, and being touchy on some subjects (Items 70, 191, 236, 276); high scorers describe themselves as "inhibited," "calm," and "poised" (Megargee, 1972, pp. 261, 265); scale correlates negatively with Welsh's (1952) and Taylor's (1953) anxiety scales and positively with emotional stability (GZTS) & superego strength, harria (tough-mindedness), adequacy, and low ergic tension (16 PF) (Gough, 1975, p. 35), indicate emotional aloofness and restraint[b]	Gi: Although items denote denials, scale was not included because the denials focus not on emotions in particular but on socially disapproved attitudes and actions; indeed, high scorers describe themselves as "worrying" (Megargee, 1972, p. 266).
Lack of concern with emotional responses of others	Fe	Fe: Scale correlated negatively with 4 measures of social acuity, including empathy, which involves sensitivity to others' emotions (Gough, 1975, p. 34); positive correlations of the scale with factors I, M, and O (16 PF) (Gough, 1975, p. 34) suggest egocentric focusing on self and hence perhaps lack of conern for others; accordingly, Fe correlated positively with social introversion (MMPI) (Gough, 1975, p. 34).	Cm: Although also correlated negatively with social acuity measures (Gough, 1975), it was not included because the low acuity is bound with consideration for others rather than egocentrism.
Hyposthesis 5: Concern with actions	Sa	Sa: High scorers described themselves as "bossy, demanding, dominant, enterprising" (Megargee, 1972, pp. 261, 265); items of the scale (Items 21, 179, 185, 219) emphasize activity and hard work; high scorers succeed in military training programs	Do: Despite correlation with Gen. Activity (GZTS), etc., not included because activities of high scorers are mainly cognitive and verbal. Scale identifies well leaders in

Table 7. (*Continued*)

Personality variable	CPI scales by which assessed	Rationale	Remarks
		(Elliott, 1960; Rosenberg *et al.*, 1962) and are more often active as social leaders (Carson & Parker, 1966; Gough, 1969a; Holland & Astin, 1962; Johnson & Frandsen, 1962); scale correlated positively with general activity (GZTS) and factors E, H, and F (16 PF), which indicate impulsivity, assertiveness, and energetic activity (Gough, 1975), suggesting concern with activities.	situations capitalizing on verbal fluency and persuasion, e.g., student leaders elected to presidency of a college org. (Jonson & Frandsen, 1962) or Ss behaving dominantly in a problem-solving task (Altrocchi, 1959; Smelser, 1961) but not leaders of the actional type, e.g., fire captains (Olmstead & Monachesi, 1956) and high-school leaders in extracurricular activities (Carson & Parker, 1966; Gough, 1969a, b).
Hypothesis 6: Flexibility and tolerance of ambiguity	*Fx, Ai, Sp*	*Fx*: Scale was designed to identify flexible, adaptable individuals, changeable in outlook and temperament (Gough, 1968, 1969b), and was developed as a scale of rigidity validated against observer ratings of rigidity and scores on Ethnocentrism and F (Authoritarianism) scales (Gough, 1951a); most items express tolerance of the uncertain, undetermined, unresolved, unclear, unorganized, etc. (Items 305, 326, 329, 340, 354, 357, 363, 364, 361, 377, 387, 397, 400, 404, 408, 451, 458); high scorers describe themselves as "fickle," "independent" (Megargee, 1972, p. 263); loaded on a factor called *flexibility* (Crites *et al.*, 1961; Springob & Struening, 1964), *capacity for independent thought and action* (Mitchell *et al.*, 1960; Gendre, 1966; Shure & Rogers, 1968), or *adaptive autonomy* (Parloff *et al.*, 1968); negligible correlations with social desirability scales (Edwards & Marlow-Crowne) but high with Q_1 ("experimenting") (16 PF) (Gough, 1975). *Ai*: Scale designed to identify individuals likely to succeed when	*Fx*: On the basis of nonsignificant findings about the relations of *Fx* to mirror tracing, Stroop's Color Naming (Hill, 1960), and creativity ratings (Garwood, 1964; Helson, 1967a), Megargee (1972, p. 90) concluded "that ... *Fx* ... does correlate negatively with ... rigidity, but ... fails to relate positively to ... flexibility." The evidence seems to us irrelevant: the role of flexibility in creativity is doubtful, and the other measures are behavioral and controversial indices of rigidity. Yet Megargee's claim fits our goal of testing the neg. cor. of *Fx* to rigidity.

(*continued*)

Table 7. (*Continued*)

Personality variable	CPI scales by which assessed	Rationale	Remarks
		independence of thought and creativity are required (Gough, 1953a,b); many items refer to tolerance of ambiguity and anti-dogmatism (Items 3, 5, 41, 116, 139, 204, 237, 255); high scorers succeed better in courses requiring unconventional approaches and independent thought than in courses requiring conformance (Domiro, 1968); like *Fx* (Domiro, 1968), loaded on CPI factor of flexibility, only low correlation with social desirability and high with Q_1 experimenting (16 PF).	
		Sp: High scorers reject traditional social rules regardless of whether it concerns a party or business (e.g., Items 5, 96, 275); scale correlated negatively with O and positively with Q_1 (16 PF) (Gough, 1975, p. 35), i.e., scale assesses "resilience" and tolerance of unclarities that stimulate exploration. (No specific validating studies are available.)	
Hypothesis 7: Strong tendency not to yield to conformity pressures (nonconformity)	*Do, Cs, Sy, Sp, Sa, Ai*	*Do, Cs, Sy, Sp, Sa*, and *Ai*: On the basis of item content and self-descriptive adjectives (Megargee, 1972, pp. 261–266), these scales assess self-assurance, particularly in social contexts that are of main relevance to conformity; *Cs, Sy, Sp, Sa*, and *Ai* contain items directly reflecting rejection of conventional attitudes; *Ai* assesses by design achievement in settings rewarding independence of thought, and many of its items indicate rejection of conventional attitudes (e.g., Items 3, 41, 255)	
Weak tendency not to yield to conformity pressures (conformity)	*Re, So, Wb, Cm, Ac, Gi, Fe*	Conformity involves socialization and acceptance of conventional standards: *Re* and *So* directly assess socialization and acceptance of conventional regulations (Gough, 1975); *Cm* and *So* are loaded on a factor of conventionality (Megargee, 1972, pp. 113–115); *Fe* assesses (by design,	

Table 7. (*Continued*)

Personality variable	CPI scales by which assessed	Rationale	Remarks
		item content, self-descriptive adjectives of high and low scorers, and validation studies; Gough, 1975; Megargee, 1972, pp. 261–266) acceptance of the stereotypical roles of genders; *Ac* assesses "achievement via conformance"; *Gi* assesses the tendency to produce a good impression by describing oneself as conforming to accepted standards in general; and *Wb* assesses the tendency to present oneself as conforming to standards of mental and physical health in particular (Megargee, 1972, pp. 52–53).	
		The assumptions about the relations of CPI scales to conformity were tested by means of the results of correlations between conformity and the CPI in seven different samples: Crutchfield (1955), Hase & Goldberg (1967), Harper (1964), and Tuddenham (1959). The mean of samples showing nonconformity was 2.33 per scale for those we viewed as assessing nonconformity, and .43 for those viewed as assessing conformity. The mean cor. coefficients with nonconf. were $-.33$ and $-.03$ for the former and latter scales, respectively.[c] In both cases, the differences were sig. at $p < .01$.	
Hypothesis 8: Tendency toward defiance or contrariness	Sp, Sa, Gi, Ai, Cs	*Sp:* High scorers tend to be verbally aggressive; like to use, attack, and manipulate people (Megargee, 1972, p. 79), and check items showing they did not care about keeping the rules (Items 93, 150, 275). *Sa:* High scorers do not openly contradict accepted rules but "manifest a comfortable and imperturbable sense of personal worth" (Gough, 1968, p. 63) and a "capacity for independent thinking and action" (Gough, 1969b, p. 10). *Gi:* High scorers defy the rules by	

(*continued*)

Table 7. (*Continued*)

Personality variable	CPI scales by which assessed	Rationale	Remarks
		which a person is expected to have at least some human frailties, and they exhibit a mask of unperturbed perfection (see purpose, items, and validation, in Gough, 1975).	
		Ai: Scale assesses independent thinking and rejection of dogmatism, even when it involves unpopular opinions (e.g., Item 255) (Gough, 1975).	
		Cs: High scorers manifest defiance by not accepting the social status quo, i.e., by being "ascendant and self-seeking" (Gough, 1975, p. 10) and striving to improve their status (see Item 94); Gough (1975, p. 10) described them as nonconventional and nonstereotypical; they describe themselves as "independent," "opportunistic," and "individualistic" (Megargee, 1972, pp. 261, 264).	
		Sp, Sa, Gi, Ai, and *Cs*: Share characteristics facilitating defiance: low anxiety (neg. cor. with Welsh's (1952) and Taylor's (1953) anxiety scales; high ego strength (pos. cor. with Barron's ego-strength scale); "unshakable nerve . . . unanxious confidence . . . to the point of being insensitive of approval or disapproval by others when a group is not going along with him so that he may evoke antipathies and distrust" (Cattell & Eber, 1962, p. 17) (neg. cor. with factor O of 16 PF); high levels of restraint (except *Cs*) and emotional stability (pos. cor. with these scales of the GZTS); pos. cor. with dominance on the EPPS (except *Ai*) (Gough, 1975, p. 35).	
Hypothesis 9: Higher creativity	*Do, Sp, Fx, Cs, Sy, Sa, Ai*	The criterion was primarily empirical. We relied on the findings of the following studies about the relation of CPI to creativity: Barron (1965); Garwood (1964); Gough (1969b); Helson (1967a,b); Helson and Crutchfield (1970); Holland and Astin (1962); MacKinnon (1964);	

Table 7. (*Continued*)

Personality variable	CPI scales by which assessed	Rationale	Remarks
		McDermid (1965); and Parloff and Datta (1965). The number of samples studied in these studies was 14—for some scales, 13 (the samples and the relations of the scales to creativity are presented in Megargee, 1972, pp. 236–238). Only sig. relations were considered. An index reflecting relatedness of a scale to creativity was constructed by counting the number of independent samples in which a scale was found to be related positively to creativity and subtracting from it the number of samples in which it was found to be related negatively to creativity.[d]	
		Scales were defined as indicating creativity if their index of relatedness to creativity was at least +2. For the listed scales, the indices were 5, 4, 4.33, 2, 3, 2, 2.66, respectively ($\bar{X} = 3.28$, $SD = 1.10$).	
		Also, by purpose and content of items, the scales with a high index of relatedness to creativity seemed to assess creativity in different forms; e.g., one may expect Fx to indicate creativity "since research has shown the creative person to be innovative . . . able to break away from past patterns and perceive new relationships" (Megargee, 1972, p. 90); Ai assesses mainly "achievement in settings where independence of thought, creativity . . . were rewarded" (Megargee, 1972, p. 76).	
Lower (or no) creativity	*Ie, Py, Fe, Wb, Re, So, Sc, Gi, Cm, Ac, To*	Scales were defined as indicating low or no creativity if their index of relatedness to creativity (Megargee, 1972, p. 76) was lower than +2. For the listed scales, the indices were 1.66, 1.33, 1.33, −2, −1, −1, −6.66, −1.66, −3.33, −2, and −1, respectively ($\bar{X} = -1.30$, $SD = 2.27$). The difference between the mean of indices of the scales high and low in creativity is significant ($t = 11.17$, $df = 16$, $p <$	

(*continued*)

Table 7. (*Continued*)

Personality variable	CPI scales by which assessed	Rationale	Remarks
		.001); also, by purpose and content of items, scales with a low index did not seem to assess creativity, e.g., *Gi, Cm,* and *Fe* because of their emphasis on conventionality (Gough, 1975).	
Hypothesis 10: A sense of duty and a tendency to cooperate with others	*Do, Cs, Sa, Cm, Ac*	*Do:* High scorers describe themselves as "responsible" (Megargee, 1972, p. 261) and "have an element of dogged persistence and a sense of duty" (Megargee, 1972, p. 40); many items (Nos. 57, 167, 233, 235, 253, 295, 303, 304, 315, 319, and 379) express sense of duty and cooperation in social domains; the interest of high scorers in having authority over people (Gough, 1975; Items 31, 53, 179, 202, 359, 376, 403, 412, 443, and 448) involves an emphasis on responsibility and cooperating with others for the sake of being accepted as a leader; high scorers are verbally fluent (describe themselves as talkative—Megargee, 1972, p. 265 also see Items 267 and 346). *Cs:* High scorers have the capacity to achieve status (Gough, 1975), and this presumably requires social attitudes emphasizing responsibility and the need for cooperating with others in relevant social contexts (see Items 167, 186, 190, 233, and 287); high scorers are "effective in communication" (Gough, 1975, p. 10. *Ac:* High scorers describe themselves as "conscientious" and "responsible" (Megargee, 1972, p. 262); scale identifies individuals who attain what is expected of them efficiently and dutifully (Gough, 1975, p. 23); items express sense of duty, obedience, meeting expectations of others (e.g., Items 125 and 260) *Sa, Cs,* and *Do:* Scales are loaded on a factor of CPI scales identified as "interpersonal effectiveness" (Bouchard, 1969), which suggests cooperation with others.	*Gi:* Though the scale assesses tendency to produce good impression, it was not included as high scorers do not cooperate in the test situation; on the contrary, they fake intentionally. *Re:* Describe themselves as "conscientious" and "responsible" (Megargee, 1972, p. 261) and have a sense of duty (Gough, 1969b). Yet, not included because there is no indication of amiable cooperation (e.g., in training as soldiers, they walk almost as fast when alone as when watched—Kohfeld & Weitzel, 1969) and of doing more than is strictly expected of them.

Table 7. (*Continued*)

Personality variable	CPI scales by which assessed	Rationale	Remarks
		Sa: Scale includes "a cluster of items [that] emphasizes the value of hard work, attention to duty and consideration of others" (Megargee, 1972, p. 51) (Items 86, 112, 185, 198, 247); high scorers describe themselves as "talkative" and "argumentative" (Megargee, 1972, p. 265).	
		Cm: High scorers "fake good" (Gough, 1975, pp. 16–17) and "have an overly conventional attitude" (Gough, 1975, p. 71); i.e., they overdo cooperation; they describe themselves as "conscientious" and "responsible" (Gough, 1975, p. 262); scale is loaded on a factor labeled "conventionality," "inflexible conformity to conventional standards" (Bouchard, 1969; Pierce-Jones *et al.*, 1962); Items 348, 350, 371, 374, and 447 emphasize duty, responsibility, and consideration for others.	

[a]Number of items in parentheses refer to the numbers of the items in the California Psychological Inventory (CPI) scale in the standard CPI booklet (Gough, 1960). For the code of the CPI scales, see Table 8.

[b]The assumption that *Wb* assesses denial of one's emotions may help to resolve the apparent contradiction between findings that show that high scorers on *Wb* are healthier than low scorers (Canter, 1963; Goodstein, Crites, Heilbrun, & Rempel, 1961; Gough, 1969b) and findings that show no difference in mental health between high and low scorers (Lorei, 1964; Stewart, 1962). Megargee (1972, p. 52) mentioned Gough's suggestion that *Wb* assesses a state rather than a trait but was skeptical about it. So are we. A simpler explanation is that denial of emotional states is not a measure of mental health but may enhance the appearance of either health or sickness.

[c]Concerning the coefficients in Crutchfield's study see Table 1.8, fn 2.

[d]Every sample in which a CPI scale was related positively to creativity was counted as +1, whereas a sample in which a CPI scale was related negatively to creativity was counted as −1. The exception was the study by Parloff and Data (1965), who reported their findings in terms of differences between means of the high-creative vs. moderate-creative, high-creative vs. low-creative, and moderate-creative vs. low-creative. Each significant difference was counted as .33 points. No attempt was made to combine the findings in terms of the strength of relation, because of the different measures of creativity and statistical methods used in the studies.

ality variables involved in Hypotheses 1–10 and presents the empirical and theoretical rationale underlying these assumptions. As noted, whenever the published material concerning the CPI scales made it possible, we set up hypotheses about positive concern and the corresponding lack of concern with some domain (e.g., Hypotheses 1, 7, and 9). This was not possible in all cases (e.g., Hypotheses 4 and 5). The CPI scales of higher and lower heritability (Hypothesis 11), according to different criteria (based essentially on the index of heritability and on interclass correlations between two random samples of identical and fraternal twins), are presented in Table 10. The data used for testing this hypothesis consisted of material published independently by Gottesman (1966, Tables 1 and 2, p. 203), who studied 147 pairs of twins in Grades 9–12 (79 pairs of identical twins, 34 male and 45 female; and 68 pairs of fraternal twins, 32 male and 36 female), and by Loehlin and Nichols (1976, Table 4–1, p. 27, and Appendix B-37), who studied 807 pairs of twins, 17 years old (490 pairs of identical twins, 202 male and 288 female; and 317 pairs of fraternal twins, 124 male and 193 female). These were the only available data concerning the heritability of separate CPI scales. Other studies (i.e., Horn, Plomin, & Rosenman, 1976) did not use the CPI scales as units.

Results and Conclusions

Table 8 shows that the number of significant correlations of CPI scales with meaning variables ($n = 169$) deviates significantly ($z = 7.26$, $p < .001$) from the number of significant correlations expected by chance (18 CPI scales × 65 meaning variables = 1,170 correlations, 5% of which—i.e., 58.5—could be expected to occur by chance). The range of significant correlations for the different scales was 2 (for So and Py) to 17 (for Sa), the mean per scale was 9.28, and the $SD = 9.30$.

The significant correlations involved all four types of meaning variables (41 with meaning dimensions, 57 with types of relation, 24 with stimulus-referent relations, an 41 with forms of relation). The distribution deviates significantly from chance ($\bar{X} = 49.21$, $df = 3$, $p < .001$). The reason for the large chi-square value is that there were more correlations with type of relation (TR) and form of relation (FR) variables and fewer correlations with meaning dimensions than expected by chance. The number of correlations with variables of shifts in referent (SR) was about that expected on the basis of a chance distribution. The form of the distribution suggests that CPI scales may resemble cognitive style traits more than "emotional" and other so-called personality traits (see Tables 2 an 3).

Results Concerning the Hypotheses

Hypothesis 1: Table 8 shows that there are positive significant correlations between the meaning dimension "Domain of Application" (Dim 8a) and each of the six CPI scales assumed to assess sociability: Dominance (Do), Sociability (Sy), Social Presence (Sp), Self Acceptance (Sa), Communality (Cm), and Self Control (Sc). There are no other positive correlations with "Domain of Application." Further, there is one negative correlation with "Domain of Application," and this is for the Intellectual Efficiency (Ie) scale, as predicted.

Hypothesis 2: Table 8 shows that there are, as predicted, positive significant correlations between "Judgments and Evaluations" (Dim 21b) and the Capacity for Status (Cs) scale, and negative significant correlations between Dim 21b and the scales Social Presence (Sp) and Tolerance (To). There are no other significant correlations of this meaning dimension with other scales.

Hypothesis 3: Table 8 shows that, as predicted, there is a positive significant correlation between "Cognitive Qualities" (Dim 22b) and the Intellectual Efficiency (Ie) scale, a negative significant correlation between Dim 22b and the Femininity (Fe) scale, and negative significant correlations between Dim 22a and the scales Femininity (Fe), Self Control (Sc), and Communality (Cm). There are no other significant correlations of "Cognitive Qualities" with CPI scales.

Hypothesis 4: Table 8 shows that, as predicted, Sense of Well Being (Wb) is correlated negatively with "Feelings and Emotions" of the referent (Dim 20b),

Table 8. Significant Correlations of CPI Scales with Meaning Variables

CPI scales	Meaning variables
Dominance (*Do*)	*Dim* 8a, .39*; *TR* 2c, .69*; *TR* 2d, .83*; *TR* 3a, .56*; *TR* 3b, .81*; no. of diff. *TR*, .65*; *SR* 6, .79*; *FR* 2, .92*; *FR* 3, .86*; *FR* 4, .99*; no. of m. values, .33*.
Capacity for Status (*Cs*)	*Dim* 8b, −.35*; *Dim* 21b, .92*; *TR* 2a, .89*; *TR* 2b, .87*; *TR* 2c, .85*; *TR* 2d, .50*; *TR* 3b, .80*; *TR* 4c, .57*; no. of diff. *TR*, .76*; *SR* 4, .39*; *FR* 1, .85*; no. of meaning values, .40*.
Sociability (*Sy*)	*Dim* 8a, .51*; *Dim* 9, .44*; *Dim* 14, −.41*; *TR* 2c, .68*; *TR* 2d, .58*; *TR* 3a, .38*; *TR* 3b, .67*; no. of diff. *TR*, .53*; *SR* 3, .99*; *SR* 6, .91*; *FR* 2, .96*; *FR* 4, .92*; *FR* 5, .99*.
Social Presence (*Sp*)	*Dim* 8a, .55*; *Dim* 9, .47*; *Dim* 15, −.40*; *Dim* 17a, −.64*; *Dim* 21b, −.95*; *TR* 2b, .78*; *SR* 3, .98*; *FR* 1, .37*; *FR* 2, .77*; *FR* 3, .86*; *FR* 5, .98*.
Self Acceptance (*Sa*)	*Dim* 4a, .35*; *Dim* 8a, .40*; *TR* 2b, .96*; *TR* 2c, .92*; *TR* 2d, .87*; *TR* 3a, .60*; *TR* 3b, .99*; *TR* 4c, .62*; no. of diff. *TR*, .85*; *SR* 6, .49*; *FR* 1, .58*; *FR* 2, .60*; *FR* 3, .86*; *FR* 5, .98*; no. of m. values, .38*.
Sense of Well-Being (*Wb*)	*Dim* 9, −.64*; *Dim* 14, .39*; *Dim* 20b, −.44*; *TR* 1a, .40*; *TR* 2c, .46*; *SR* 3, −.99*; *SR* 6, −.72*; *FR* 1, .50*; *FR* 2, −.65*; *FR* 3, −.84*; *FR* 5, −.97*.
Responsibility (*Re*)	*Dim* 9, −.57*; *Dim* 10, −.81*; *Dim* 14, .47*; *TR* 1a, .37*; *TR* 2c, .49*; no. of diff. *TR*, .37*; *SR* 3, −.89*; *SR* 6, −.54*; *SR* 8, −.69*; *FR* 1, .68*; *FR* 2, −.39*; *FR* 3, −.82*; *FR* 5, −.98*.
Socialization (*So*)	*Dim* 16, −.36*; *FR* 1, .52*.
Self Control (*Sc*)	*Dim* 8a, .44*; *Dim* 9, .62*; *Dim* 13, −.48*; *Dim* 14, −.46*; *Dim* 22a, −.90*; *SR* 3, .97*; *SR* 6, .72*; *FR* 2, .83*; *FR* 3, .85*; *FR* 5, .95*.
Tolerance (*To*)	*Dim* 21b, −.90*; *TR* 1a, .45*; *TR* 2c, .48*; no. of diff. *TR*, .38*; *SR* 3, −.89*; *FR* 1, .82*; *FR* 3, −.80*.
Good Impression (*Gi*)	*TR* 2a, .91*; *TR* 2b, .97*; *TR* 2c, .75*; *TR* 3a, .72*; *TR* 4c, .54*; no. of diff. *TR*, .71*; *SR* 3, .99*; *SR* 6, .49*; *SR* 8, −.73*; *FR* 1, .69*; *FR* 2, .63*; *FR* 3, .89*; *FR* 5, .97*.
Communality (*Cm*)	*Dim* 4b, −.43*; *Dim* 8a, .49*; *Dim* 22a, −.89*; *TR* 2c, .84*; *TR* 2d, .67*; *TR* 3a, .46*; *TR* 3b, .82*; no. of diff. *TR*, .60*; *SR* 3, .98*; *SR* 6, .79*; *SR* 8, −.94*; *FR* 1, .39*; *FR* 2, .88*; *FR* 3, .92*; *FR* 5, .98*; no. of m. values, .36*.
Achievement via Conformance (*Ac*)	*TR* 2b, .81*; *TR* 2c, .78*; *TR* 2d, .94*; *TR* 3a, .67*; *TR* 3b, .92*; *TR* 4c, .48*; no. of diff. *TR*, .50*; *FR* 1, .42*; *FR* 5, .82*; no. of m. values, .37*.
Achievement via Independence (*Ai*)	*Dim* 17a, −.66*; *TR* 1a, .47*; *TR* 2a, .80*; *TR* 2b, .90*; *TR* 2c, .58*; *TR* 3b, .51*; *SR* 1, .39*; *FR* 1, .86*.
Intellectual Efficiency (*Ie*)	*Dim* 8a, −.48*; *Dim* 13, −.49*; *Dim* 22b, .56*; no. of diff. *TR*, −.48*.
Psychological Mindedness (*Py*)	*Dim* 13, −.56*; *FR* 5, −.88*.
Flexibility (*Fx*)	*Dim* 1, −.48*; *Dim* 17a, −.64*; *Dim* 19a, .46*; *SR* 8, −.73*; no. of m. values, .41*.
Femininity (*Fe*)	*Dim* 4a, .49*; *Dim* 20a, −.55*; *Dim* 22a, −.94*; *Dim* 22b, −.61*.

Note. For the code of the meaning variables, see Appendix A.
*$p < .001$.

whereas Femininity (*Fe*) is correlated negatively with "Feelings and Emotions" evoked by the referent (*Dim* 20a). This meaning dimension (*Dim* 20) is not related negatively with any other scale.

Hypothesis 5: Table 8 shows that there is a positive significant correlation between the Self Acceptance (*Sa*) scale and the dimension "Actions" (active) (*Dim* 4a), as predicted. However, there are two further correlations that can be explained only *post hoc*. One is the negative correlation of Communality (*Cm*) with "Actions" (passive) (*Dim* 4b), which reflects, perhaps, the necessity of not attending to actions in order to preserve the rigid conformity found associated with high scoring on this scale (Gendre, 1966, p. 38; Mitchel & Pierce-Jones, 1960). The other is the positive correlation between Femininity (*Fe*) and "Actions" (*Dim* 4a), which reflects, perhaps, the concern of high scorers with actions of a certain type (i.e., actions that can qualify as proper for the social role espoused by the individual). There are far too few data to support any of these explanations.

Hypothesis 6: As predicted, Table 8 shows, for the Flexibility (*Fx*) scale, negative significant correlations with "Contextual Allocation" (*Dim* 1) and "Belongingness" (*Dim* 17a), and for the scales of Achievement via Independence (*Ai*) and Social Presence (*Sp*) significant negative correlations only with "Belongingness." The latter two scales were not correlated with "Contextual Allocation."

Hypothesis 7: The hypothesis was tested by comparing the number of correlations with the comparative types of relation in the meaning patterns of the CPI scales that were viewed as assessing high nonconformity with the number of correlations in those viewed as assessing low nonconformity. The means are 2.5 and 1.43, respectively ($p < .05$). Further, a correlation with the *difference* comparative type of relation (*TR* 2b) occurred on the average in .83 and .71 of the scales, respectively ($p < .05$). These findings fully support the hypothesis.

However, as information was available about the relation of all scales to conformity (i.e., yielding to pressure in Asch-type settings—Megargee, 1972, p. 228), we subjected the hypothesis to a further and stricter test, also using all the information about scales concerning which we had no hypothesis. We compared the number of samples in which nonconformity was found and the mean correlation coefficients with nonconformity for CPI scales correlated with different numbers of comparative types of relation. Table 9 (lower part) shows that the higher the number of comparative types of relation correlated with the scale, the more samples there were in which high scorers on the scale manifested nonconformity and the stronger the manifestation of the nonconformity. The relation between the number of comparative types of relation correlated with the CPI scale and nonconformity of high scorers on that scale is linear and consistent. These findings lend full support to our hypothesis.

The same results are obtained if we first divide the CPI scales into those that were found to assess nonconformity in at least one sample up to a maximum of five samples (i.e., *Cs, Ai, Do, Sy, To, Py, Sp, Re, Ac*, and *Fx*; for the code names see Table 8), and those that were found not to assess nonconformity or to assess conformity in at least one sample (i.e., *Sa, Wb, Sc, Ie, So, Gi, Cm*, and *Fe*) and then compare them in the number of comparative types of relation with which they are related ($\bar{X} = 1.70$, $SD = 1.45$, and $\bar{X} = 1.00$, $SD = 1.25$, respectively; $t = 2.19$, $df = 16$, $p < .05$).

Further, comparisons of nonconformity for scales correlated with each type of relation separately and those not correlated with it show (Table 9) that each of the

Table 9. Summary of Relations between the Comparative Types of Relation and Nonconformity[a]

Comparative type of relation (TR)	Occurrence of correlation with comparative TR			No occurrence of correlation with comparative TR		
	No. of CPI scales	Mean no. of supporting studies per scale[b]	Mean of cor. coeffic. per scale[c]	No. of CPI scales	Mean no. of supporting studies per scale[d]	Mean of cor. coeffic. per scale[d]
Similarity	3	3	−.24	15	.87**	−.16**
Difference	6	1.83	−.27	12	1.00*	−.13**
Complementariness	11	1.64	−.19	7	.57**	−.15
Relational	7	1.57	−.27	11	1.18*	−.12**
No. of comp. TR with which scale is correlated:						
4 or 3	5	2.00	−.23			
2 or 1	6	1.17	−.18			
0	6	.50	−.10			

[a]The presented means are based on adding the number (or correlation coefficients) of the positive findings and subtracting the number of significant negative ones.
[b]Each study counts as one sample. The samples were studied by Crutchfield (1955), Harper (1964), Hase and Goldberg (1967), and Tuddenham (1959). The total number of samples was seven.
[c]A negative correlation indicates nonconformity. As Crutchfield (1955) reported negative correlations "ranging from −.30 to −.41" without specifying which CPI scale got which coefficient, we followed Megargee's procedure of assigning to all scales the lowest coefficient.
[d]In the mean number of supporting studies, each study counts as one sample. The significance levels are based on t tests calculated between the means of the corresponding columns.
*$p < .05$.
**$p < .01$.

comparative types of relation contributes to a strengthening of nonconformity: the contribution of the similarity, difference, and relational types of relation is about equal, whereas that of the complementary type of relation is the weakest. Hence, although it is obvious that difference (TR 2b) is correlated with nonconformity as predicted, similarly high correlations characterize two of the other comparative types of relation, so that, by this test, the difference type of relation does not play a particular role in nonconformity.

The findings seem to suggest that, because any one or more of the comparative types of relation could promote nonconformity, if the specific scale or trait is oriented toward nonconformity the particular comparative type(s) of relation with which it will be correlated would depend on the other characteristics of the trait or, rather, of the pattern of meaning variables underlying it.

Hypothesis 8: Table 8 shows that all four predicted scales are correlated positively with the difference comparative type of relation (TR 2b). However, a further scale, Achievement via Conformance (Ac), was also correlated positively with the difference comparative type of relation (TR 2b). On a *post hoc* basis, one may only suggest that the element of defiance in high scorers on this scale consists in their insistence on achievement that may set them apart from their group. Although this interpretation is shaky, there is evidence that the Ac scale shares with the other four scales correlated with the difference type of relation (TR 2b) all the characteristics mentioned as facilitating defiance (i.e., negative correlations with Welsh's and Taylor's anxiety scales and Factor D of the 16 PF, and positive correlations with Barron's ego strength, with emotional stability, and restraint on Guilford–Zimmerman Temperament Survey, and dominance on the Edwards Personal Preference Schedule). Thus, the suggestion that the *Ac* scale also measures some kind of defiance is not very farfetched.

Hypothesis 9: The hypothesis was tested by comparing the mean number of meaning variables of the personal mode of meaning (i.e., the exemplifying-illustrative and the metaphoric-symbolic types of relation) which correlate with CPI scales considered as assessing higher creativity and those scales viewed as assessing lower or no creativity. The means were 1.43 (SD = 1.28) and .55 (SD = .95) for the two groups, respectively. The difference between the means was significant (t = 3.38, df = 16, p < .01), as predicted in Hypothesis 9.

For the sake of control, three further comparisons between the two groups were made: (1) a comparison of the means of the number of meaning variables of the lexical mode (i.e., the attributive and comparative types of relation) with which the two groups were correlated ($\bar{X}$ = 2.29, SD = 1.38, and $\bar{X}$ = 1.27, SD = 1.22, respectively; t = 1.54, df = 16, n.s.); (2) a comparison of the mean ratio of variables of the lexical and personal modes of meaning with which the two groups were correlated ($\bar{X}$ = 1.57, SD = 1.18, and $\bar{X}$ = 1.45, SD = 1.66, respectively; t = .39, df = 16, n.s.); and (3) a comparison of the mean number of meaning variables with which the two groups were correlated ($\bar{X}$ = 10.86, SD = 3.75, and $\bar{X}$ = 8.18, SD = 4.45, respectively; t = 1.24, df = 16, n.s.). As noted, none of the comparisons yielded significant differences. Hence, the finding that CPI scales related to creativity are correlated with a larger number of meaning variables of the personal mode than the scales unrelated to creativity is a specific finding (see the nonsignificant difference between the groups in variables of the lexical mode) and, moreover, is not an artifact reflecting a larger number of correlated meaning variables in general.

The two groups of scales were correlated only with the following three kinds of meaning variables of the personal mode: exemplifying instance (*TR* 3a), exemplifying situation (*TR* 3b), and metaphor (*TR* 4c). There were no significant differences between the groups of scales in the means of any of the three variables. Hence, what characterizes the CPI scales related to creativity is the preference for the personal mode in general and not for any specific meaning variable of that mode in particular.

Hypothesis 10: Table 8 shows that, as predicted, the scales Dominance (*Do*), Capacity for Status (*Cs*), Self Acceptance (*Sa*), Communality (*Cm*), and Achievement via Conformance (*Ac*) are correlated positively with the total number of responses given to the meaning questionnaire. However, a further scale, Flexibility (*Fx*), is also correlated with the number of responses, although we did not predict it to be so. The flexibility of the high scorers on this scale could have been a factor facilitating the increase in the number of produced meaning values.

Hypothesis 11: Table 10 shows that, as predicted, according to all five criteria based on whole sample data, CPI scales with a relatively high heritability were correlated with a significantly larger number of meaning variables than scales with a relatively low heritability. Whereas the mean of the former was in the range of 10.6–14.3, the mean of the latter was in the range of 6.0–7.8. Table 10 also shows that the differences become larger and more significant when the criteria are clearer and tougher (compare the findings of Criteria 1–3 with those of Criteria 4–5). The findings fully support the hypothesis.

Table 10. Comparison of Number of Meaning Variables Correlated with CPI Scales High and Low in Heritability

	High herit.			Low herit.			
Criteria	n	M	SD	n	M	SD	t
Gottesman's (1966) findings. High herit.: $H > .35$ (scales Sy, Do, Sa, Sp, Gi) Low herit.: $H < .32$ (scales: all except Sy, Do, Sa, Sp, Gi)	5	13.00	2.45	13	7.85	4.34	3.16**
Gottesman's (1966) findings. High herit.: H value sig. by F at least 1.55 (scales: Sy, Do, Sa, Sp, Gi) Low herit.: H value nonsig. F value 5 lowest (scales: Fx, Ac, Wb, Ie, Ai)	5	13.00	2.45	5	7.60	3.05	3.09*
Loehlin & Nichol's (1976) findings. High herit.: Dif. in interclass correlations bet. 2 subsamples of identical twins lower than that bet. 2 subsamples of fraternal twins (scales: Sy, Sa, Wb, Re, Sc, To, Gi, Cm, Ac, Py, Fx) Low herit.: If difference in former larger than in latter (scales: Cs, So, Ai, Ie, Fe)	11	10.64	4.57	5	6.00	3.58	2.20*
High herit.: Scales of high herit. according to 1st and 2nd criteria above (scales: Gi, Sy, Sa) Low herit.: Scales of low herit. according to 1st and 2nd criteria above (scales: Cs, So, Ai, Ie, Fe)	3	14.33	2.34	5	6.00	3.58	3.97**
High herit.: Scales of high herit. according to 2nd and 3rd criteria above (scales: Gi, Sy, Sa) Low herit.: Scales of low herit. according to 2nd and 3rd criteria above (scales: Ai, Ie)	3	14.33	2.34	2	6.00	2.83	3.44*

*$p < .05$.
**$p < .01$.

Additional Findings

In addition to the findings cited above that were based on *a priori* hypotheses, Table 8 shows further relations between specific traits and meaning variables. These relations are presented as *post hoc* hypotheses that stand in need of further confirmation. We will concentrate primarily on relations that occur across several CPI scales.

First, the three scales Sociability (*Sy*), Social Presence (*Sp*), and Self Control (*Sc*) are positively correlated with the meaning dimension "Material" (*Dim* 9), and the two scales Sense of Well Being (*Wb*) and Responsibility (*Re*) are negatively correlated with it. This pattern of correlations suggests that the meaning dimension "Material" reflects a practical, down-to-earth attitude toward life that combines realism with openness to life, tolerance of others, and readiness for enjoyment. It is conceivable that this cluster of qualities is related to concern with the constituents and materials out of which things are made. Perhaps it is not accidental that materialism, matter, and material seem to have been derived from the same etymological root. The particular blend of properties noted above seems to be characteristic of high scorers in Sociability (Sy; enjoys social interactions, feels that he or she is a good mixer, is tolerant of others), Social Presence (Sp; enjoys social interactions, rejects stuffy and conservative attitudes, is tolerant and practical), or Social Control (Sc; realistic, controlled, rational, practical). We do not find this blend of properties in other CPI scales. Again, it is plausible to assume that high scorers on Sense of Well-Being (Wb) and Responsibility (Re) actively reject these same qualities, the former because of the tendency to preserve poise and peace of mind, and the latter because of a strong concern with duty and self-discipline.

Second, there is a negative correlation between the meaning dimension "Size" (Dim 13) and the three CPI scales Intellectual Efficiency (Ie), Psychological Mindedness (Py), and Self Control (Sc). An analysis of the items of these three scales readily reveals a common element that they do not share with other CPI scales: emphasis on reason and the intellect. The Intellectual Efficiency scale (Ie) is a kind of intelligence measure. High scorers clearly indicate their interest in and enjoyment of intellectual pursuits (Megargee, 1972, pp. 80ff.). Similarly, high Self Control (Sc) scorers emphasize that thought and reason are the best solution to problems and a safeguard against impulsivity and trouble (Megargee, 1972, p. 65 ff). Likewise, high scorers on Psychological Mindedness (Py) put a premium on intellectual pursuits and insights, such as doing research, and describe themselves as "logical" or "sharp-witted" (Megargee, 1972, pp. 87, 267). The pattern of intercorrelations of these three scales with other personality variables (Gough, 1969b, p. 35) reveals tendencies toward an independent, critical, analytical stance: all three scales are positively correlated with ego strength on the MMPI and Barron's scale and dominance and autonomy on the EPPS, and negatively with Welsh's and Taylor's anxiety scales; they are also correlate positively with Factors N and Q_1 and negatively with Factor O on the 16 PF (i.e., the high scorers tend to be experimenting, critical, and intellectually independent; see also Table 16). Concern over "Size" may reflect a superficial approach and a certain measure of intellectual "laziness." This may be the reason for the negative correlation of the "intellectual" scales with the dimension "Size."

Third, two scales are positively correlated with the meaning dimension "Quantity" (Sense of Well-Being, Wb, and Responsibility, Re) and two (Sociability, Sy, and Self Control, Sc) are negatively correlated with it. We venture to suggest that the dimension "Quantity" (Dim 14) reflects some degree of concern with standards, personal for the high scorers on Sense of Well-Being (Wb) and more legal-social for the high scorers on Responsibility (Re). Accordingly, a negative correlation with this dimension would reflect an active rejection of fixed standards in favor of more flexible adaptation according to changing contexts, an approach that high scorers on Sociability (Sy) and Self Control (Sc) could have in common. Support for this interpretation is provided also by the positive correlations of these two scales with Factors H, N, and O on Cattell's 16 PF, which indicate that high scorers are "ready to try new things . . . can be careless of detail . . . [are] intellectual, unsentimental . . . [have] an approach akin to cynicism . . . [are] resilient" (Cattell & Eber, 1962; see also Table 16).

Finally, we would like to venture one last hypothesis concerning the cluster of correlations with the negative (*FR* 2), mixed (*FR* 3), and disjunctive (*FR* 5) forms of relation. We call it a cluster because there are five CPI scales (*Sp, Sa, Sc, Gi,* and *Cm;* for the code names, see Table 8) correlated positively with all three variables; two scales (*Wb* and *Re*) correlated negatively with all three; and seven scales (*Cs, So, Ai, Fe, Fx, Py,* and *Ie*) correlated with neither of them. It seemed likely that similar correlations with so many different scales reflect a general disposition, more like a scheme or generalized style than a specific trait.

An examination of the scales correlated positively and negatively with the cluster suggests that the cluster underlies a general disposition to adjust to external reality through efficient and persistent activity. This tendency is fairly obvious in regard to the five scales correlated positively with the cluster: two of them, Self Control (*Sc*) and Good Impression (*Gi*), are highly loaded on a factor of CPI scales identified as "disciplined effectiveness" (Genre, 1966; Parloff *et al.,* 1968), whereas two others, Social Presence (*Sp*) an Social Acceptance (*Sa*), are highly loaded on a factor identified as "dominance-adjustment by control of external reality" (Crites *et al.,* 1961). Activity in the "real" world and persistence seem to be the elements common to these scales. The tendency toward persistence in such activities seems to be missing in the seven scales not correlated with the cluster. They are all loaded on a factor identified as "intellectual functioning" (Bouchard, 1969) or "capacity for independent thought and action" (Genre, 1966; Mitchel *et al.,* 1960). The emphasis on intellectual concerns may counterbalance the persistence in actual action. Again, in the two scales correlated negatively with the cluster, there is an emphasis on adapting to some standard rather than to reality as such, and this by means other than persistence, that is, by denying in oneself anything that seems to contradict the standard Sense of Well-Being (*Wb*) or by disciplining oneself in a moral sense of Responsibility (*Re*).

Some General Conclusions

The study demonstrated a method for analyzing the patterns of meaning variables corresponding to traits. It showed that, by examining the motivational, cognitive, and behavioral implications of meaning variables and by testing them against extraneous, independently validated criteria, it is possible to establish the contribution of different variables in the meaning profile to the dynamics of the individual's personality. A most important finding that holds across all meaning variables is that a high frequency of meaning values corresponding to a meaning variable of the individual's meaning profile indicates that the individual preferentially applies the particular meaning variable to external and internal inputs and uses it in meaning assignment. In contrast, low frequency of meaning values in the meaning variable reflects—at least, in normal, cognitively unimpaired individuals—an overlooking of the particular meaning variable in meaning assignment.

Every CPI scale was found to be correlated with meaning variables. The scales differ, however, in the number of their intercorrelations with meaning variables. One determinant of the differences was shown to be the relative heritability characteristic of the scale.

In most cases, the studied meaning variables had the predicted personality manifestations. The findings support the following conclusions: "Range of Application" (*Dim* 8a) is related to degree of sociability and concern about others; "Judgments and Evaluations" (*Dim* 21b) is related to degree of concern over one's values; "Cognitive Qualities" is related to degree of concern over one's cognitive functioning and properties (*Dim* 22b) or over the cognitive properties and responses of others (*Dim* 22a); "Feelings and Emotions" is related to degree of concern with one's feelings and emotions (*Dim* 20b) or with the emotional responses of others (*Dim* 20a); "Contextual Allocation" (*Dim* 1) and "Belongingness" (*Dim* 17b) are related to degree of flexibility and tolerance of ambiguity; the four comparative types of relation (*TR* 2a, *TR* 2b, *TR* 2c, and *TR* 2d) are related to extent of resistance to pressures toward conformity; the difference comparative (*TR* 2b) type of relation is related to degree of aggressive contrariness in interpersonal contexts; the personal mode of meaning (*TR* 3a, *TR* 3b, *TR* 3c, and *TR* 4a, *TR* 4b, *TR* 4c, *TR* 4d) is related to degree of creativity; and the total number of meaning values in the meaning questionnaire is related to the degree of sense of duty and cooperation.

The following further findings seem plausible but stand in need of additional confirmation: "Actions" (*Dim* 4a) may be related to degree of concern with one's actions and activities; "Material" (*Dim* 9) may be related to a practical, realistic, tolerant, down-to-earth openness toward life; "Size" (*Dim* 13) may be related to the degree of a somewhat shallow, intellectually lazy approach; "Quantity" (*Dim* 14) may be related to degree of concern with standards; and the negative, mixed, and disjunctive forms of relation (*FR* 2, *FR* 3, and *FR* 5) as a cluster may be related to persistence in physical activities in one's environment.

The above summary indicates that the manifestations of meaning variables in personality tend to be a straightforward extension of the contents and processes characteristic of the demain denoted by the specific aspect of meaning. This conclusion, which will be explored in further studies (Studies 3–21), may be of great importance in the use of the meaning profile in personality testing (see Appendix B).

It should, however, be recalled that the relations of meaning variables to specific personality variables, as indicated in this study, do not exhaust the range of effects and manifestations of a meaning variable. A meaning variable may be involved in facilitating or inhibiting a whole set of functions. Some of these functions may be manifested in other domains, particularly in the purely cognitive domain; others may be manifested also or primarily in a more indirect manner, through the effects (i.e., reinforcement or inhibition) that they exert on other personality and cognitive variables. Such interactions within the meaning profile may be a reason for attenuations of relations between a trait and a meaning variable.

For the sake of illustrating interactions between meaning variables, we will take a CPI scale as the unit constituting the space within which the interaction occurs. Lack of concern with judgments, values, and beliefs (*Dim* 21) coexists in the scale Tolerance (*To*) with the complementary type of relation (*TR* 2c), whereas in the scale Social Presence (*Sp*), it coexists with a practical approach, sociability, and a general disposition toward adjustment through persistent activities in physical reality. Thus, it is plausible to expect that, in the former case, the lack of concern with values and beliefs would give the flavor of tolerance, and that, in the latter case, it would give the flavor of indifference and low regard for beliefs and opinions in general. Again, tolerance of ambiguity (*Dim* 17a) coexists in the scale Achievement via Independence (*Ai*) with the tendencies toward defiance and originality in thinking, whereas in the scale Social Presence (*Sp*), it coexists with sociability, a practical approach, and persistent physical activities. One may expect tolerance of ambiguity to be manifested, in the former case, primarily in the domain of cognitive operations and in the latter case, in the domain of physical activities in the actual environment. In any case, these examples were designed to suggest that different aspects of meaning may interact within the framework of the individual's world.

STUDY 3: MEANING AND MACHIAVELLIANISM[3]

Purpose and Hypotheses

This study focused on the relations between Machiavellianism (Christie & Geis, 1970) and meaning variables. There were three reasons that we chose Machiavellianism. One was that Machiavellianism seems to be a trait that combines a set of specific beliefs (i.e., reflecting a low evaluation of people) with particular behavioral strategies (i.e., for the manipulation of people) (Christie, 1978; Christie & Geis, 1970; Golding, 1977) in contrast to other traits that are mostly assumed to reflect either beliefs (e.g., internal-external control) or behaviors (e.g., rigidity). Second, the interactions of Machiavellianism with different situations have been extensively studied, and its manifestations have been shown to depend largely on specific situational cues (Christie, 1978; Christie & Geis, 1970). Third, the measure of Machiavellianism was shown to be correlated with at least one social desirability measure (Christie & Geis, 1970, p. 19), a fact that makes it difficult to interpret the subjects' responses at face value. For these three reasons, it seemed to us particularly challenging to study the constellation of meaning-assignment tendencies bound to Machiavellianism.

Because of the many studies that have been conducted on Machiavellianism, it was possible to set up several hypotheses about the relations of *Mach* (the measure commonly used to assess Machiavellianism) and different meaning variables. The list of hypotheses was expected not to be exhaustive but to represent only a sample. We had two hypotheses. The first was that Mach would be correlated positively with the meaning dimension "Function, Purpose, and Role" (*Dim* 3). The rationale was that a functional approach seemed to be characteristic of high-*Mach* subjects in different experimental situations. In describing the behavior of high-*Mach* subjects, experimenters unanimously checked the item "characteristically pushes and tries to stretch the limits; sees what he can get away with" (Geis, 1970, p. 133). In her summary of Machiavelli's advice, Geis (1970) mentioned as the first point "Do what works—whatever works—regardless of ethical considerations" (p. 30). And later, she elaborated, "In the 'do what works' approach . . . the emphasis seems to be less on the 'what' is to be done, and more on the 'works'" (p. 133). Or again, "They [high *Machs*] appear to aim at achieving the possible and adapt their tactics to the specific conditions of the situation at hand" (Geis & Christie, 1970, p. 303). This is indeed the essence of the functional approach. Different findings about high-*Mach* subjects fully bear out this expectation. A most obvious example is the observation that high *Machs* differ from low *Machs* in situation that enable interaction with people but not in impersonal situations like picking up from photographs facial cues identifying the winners in a contest (Geis & Christie, 1970). This difference between

[3]Thanks are due to Shmaryahu Sheppes for his help in administering the questionnaires to the male subjects.

interpersonal and impersonal situations is to be expected if a functional approach plays a paramount role.

The second hypothesis was that Machiavellianism would be negatively correlated with the meaning dimension "Consequences and Results" (*Dim* 7). At first glance, this hypothesis may seem strange in regard to subjects presumably intent on the instrumental, self-interested exploitation of people and situations. On the other hand, however, it seems to be a more plausible hypothesis than the alternative that high *Mach*s do not care for values and norms. Two sets of observations led us to expect a negative correlation with the meaning dimension "Consequences and Results." One set consisted of the findings that show high *Mach*s to be apt to take risks. Rim (1966) found that high *Mach*s tended to have initially high scores on risk taking and were the influencers in the group discussion that led to a shift of the whole group toward greater risk. Further, Edelstein (1966) found that the behavioral differences between high and low *Mach*s were significantly stronger in situations with higher risk. The second set of findings indicated that high *Mach*s were apparently unconcerned about discrepancies between their opinions and behaviors, did not change their attitudes when involved in a dissonance, and were unaffected by refutations of their position (Bogart, Geis, Levy, & Zimbardo, 1970; Feiler, 1967; Geis & Christie, 1970; Harris, 1966) although they upheld ideological positions no less than low *Mach*s (Geis, Weinheimer, & Berger, 1970). To our mind, disregard of consequences is the element common to risk taking and to a nonchalant attitude toward contradictions and discrepancies.

As noted, we expected further relations with meaning variables. In addition, we used this study to examine the problem of whether there were differences between the findings concerning Machiavellianism yielded by meaning questionnaires using three types of instruction: instructions designed to elicit lexical meaning, personal meaning, or unspecified meaning. Because traits are a personality variable bound with internal experience and "cognitions" (Geis & Christie, 1970), it could be argued that meaning elicited through instructions designed to evoke personal meaning would provide data more akin to the questionnaire score. On the other hand, it could also be argued that the concept of traits combines information about internally guided behavior in an externally shaped context and hence would be more closely related to meaning based on a questionnaire designed to elicit lexical meaning or unspecified meaning. This study was designed to explore the problem in regard to the concrete issue of Machiavellianism.

Method

The subjects were 87 individuals in the age range of 18–23. There were 46 men, all enlisted for the regular military service, and 41 women matched in age and educational level, all students in technical schools and teachers' seminars. The subjects were administered the *Mach* IV questionnaire (translated into Hebrew and pretested for comprehensibility) and three separate questionnaires of meaning: one designed to elicit personal meaning, one designed to elicit lexical meaning, and one without any specifications. Each questionnaire included five stimuli: an abstract noun (one of the following: *tension, confidence,* or *independence*), a concrete noun (one of the following: *water, air,* or *soil*), a verb (one of the following: *to create, to run,* or *to inquire*), an adjective (one of the following: *dirty, complex,* or *red*), and an adverb (one of the following: *quickly, cautiously,* or *lightly*). The selection of the stimuli for the three questionnaires was random, and it varied across subjects. The four question-naires were administered in random order, different for different subjects, in four group sessions, three to four days apart.

Results and Conclusions

Table 11 shows that, as predicted in the first and second hypotheses, Machiavel-lianism is correlated positively with the meaning dimension "Function" (*Dim* 3) and negatively with the meaning dimension "Consequences" (*Dim* 7). Additional find-ings are highly significant negative correlations with "Causes" (*Dim* 6) and positive correlations with "Locational Qualities" (*Dim* 15) and "Possessions" (specifically "Belongingness," *Dim* 17b).

The negative emphasis on "Causes" corresponds well with the negative empha-sis on "Consequences" and the positive concern with "Function." All three, and particularly the latter, make it possible to understand some of the apparent contra-dictions in the findings concerning Machiavellianism. For example, in the question-naires, high *Machs* admitted more hostility and dishonesty than low *Machs* but did not necessarily behave in a more hostile manner in actual situations and did not actually lie and cheat more (Christie & Geis, 1970, pp. 307–308). Further, high *Machs* declared that they did not value verbally voiced opinions very much (e.g., they advocate lying, giving false reasons for requests, and flattering) but did not change them when under pressure of dissonance (Christie & Geis, 1970, pp. 296–297). Again, high *Machs* claimed commitment to rules and values as strongly as the low *Machs* but did not let it interfere in their bargaining with people (Christie & Geis, 1970, p. 308). High *Machs* claimed they preferred balanced situations but took nice advantage of unbalanced ones to promote their interests (Christie & Geis, 1970, p. 308). Similarly, high *Machs* succeeded better than low *Machs* in manipulating people but were not better in judging people on a cognitive task (Christie & Geis, 1970, pp. 286–294).

Table 11. Significant Correlations of *Mach* IV with Meaning Variables[a]

Lexical meaning		Personal meaning		Unspecified meaning	
Dim 3	.45***	Dim 3	.38***	Dim 3	.58***
Dim 6	−.39***	Dim 6	−.18 (p < .10)	Dim 6	−.35***
Dim 7	−.31**	Dim 7	−.32**	Dim 7	−.38***
Dim 15	.37***	Dim 11	−.18 (p < .10)	Dim 14	.21*
Dim 17a	.28**	Dim 14	.23*	Dim 15	.36***
Dim 17a + b	.28**	Dim 17a	.35***	Dim 17a	.32**
Dim 20b	.18 (p < .10)	Dim 17a + b	.35***	Dim 17a + b	.33**
Dim 20a + b	.18 (p < .10)	TR 1a + b	.18 (p < .10)	Dim 20b	.18 (p < .10)
TR 4a + b + c + d	.19 (p < .10)	No. of m. values	−.19 (p < .10)	Dim 20a + b	.20 (p < .10)
				TR 1a + b	.22*

[a]For the sake of comparison across the three kinds of questionnaires of meaning, the table also presents correla-tions significant only at the .10 level. In order to prevent a biased presentation, the table includes all correlations significant at the .10 level and not only those that are of special interest from the viewpoint of comparisons (e.g., *Dim* 6). For the code of the meaning variables, see Appendix A.
*$p < .05$.
**$p < .01$.
***$p < .001$.

Geis and Christie (1970) suggested several reasons for these inconsistencies, some of which are situational (e.g., Machiavellianism is facilitated by face-to-face interaction and by conditions that allow for improvisation) and some dispositional (e.g., high *Mach*s more than low *Mach*s are oriented toward cognitions rather than persons and resist social influence). In view of these arguments, based on comparing studies with positive and negative findings, Christie (1978, p. 118) even drew the general conclusion that traits should be studied in the context of situations that elicit the relevant behaviors. This is one possibility. In view of our findings about the meaning variables correlated with Machiavellianism, it seems to us more economical to consider the behaviors of high *Mach*s in terms of functionality. They may change their attitude, approach, an behavior because under different conditions, different things seem to them to be useful. Their disregard for "Consequences" and "Causes" may be of great help in enhancing the pursuit of functionality. Geis and Christie (1970) noted that high *Mach*s "appear less influenced by what they themselves have just said or done" (p. 297). Further, we assume that the high *Mach*s' preference for "Function" may affect their behavior through corresponding beliefs that they have gradually acquired (see Chapter 2). In any case, what makes the Machiavellians apply the functional approach is not a particular characteristic in the situation but specific meaning-assignment tendencies that depend on the dominance of particular meaning dimensions in the individual's meaning profile. Study 5 shows that this functional approach does not actually depend on eliciting situational cues, as it is manifested even in the absence of such cues, but that its manifestations are guided by the cues.

The high correlations of Machiavellianism with "Locational Qualities and "Possessions" fit well into the overall pattern but were not predicted because of a lack of specific, relevant data about these tendencies. Concern with "Location" and "Possessions," particularly "Belongingness," just as the weaker concern with "Quantity," may be expected of individuals intent on exploiting the interpersonal potentialities of situations and on "bargaining it out," if possible. Concerning "Possessions" specifically, two points may be of interest. First, studies have shown that the involvement of monetary stakes in experimental games elicited more Machiavellianism in the high *Mach*s than in the low *Mach*s (Christie & Geis, 1970, Chapters 9 and 10). Thus, high *Mach*s are not uninterested in possessions. Second, concern with possessions is characteristic of subjects with a high need for power (McClelland, 1975; Winter, 1973), which is involved in Machiavellianism in some form (see Study 4).

The weak correlation with the meaning dimension "Feelings and Emotions" (*Dim* 20) is of particular interest in view of the controversy over the relations of Machiavellianism to emotional involvement. At first glance, it may seem that high *Mach*s "play it cool" and shy away from investing affect where it can be foregone. Yet, different studies have suggested that this view is too superficial. High *Mach*s do not tend to let affects irrelevant to the issues at stake dictate their tactics; rather, they invest affect in issues that are of importance in the present context (Geis & Christie, 1970, p. 288; Geis & Levy, 1970; Geis, Weinheimer, & Berger, 1970). Hence, what may seem externally to be "coolness toward other people" may instead be "detachment from their own ideological positions" (Geis & Christie, 1970, p. 295). Moreover, in terms of GSR (galvanic skin response) recordings in the course of a neutral task, they were not more cool than the low *Mach*s (Oksenberg, 1964). The indication we obtained that Machiavellianism is related to the dimension "Feelings and Emotions," specifically the referent's emotions (*dim* 20b) and not emotions that the referent evokes in others (*Dim* 20a), is of particular interest in this controversy. It supports the view that high *Mach*s may "play it cool" but are not cool.

Concerning the comparison of findings based on lexical, personal, and unspecified meaning questionnaires, Table 11 shows that the three questionnaires provided essentially the same information concerning the major findings (about the meaning dimensions of "Function," "Consequences," "Causes," and "Possessions"). The differences concern weaker correlations (i.e., with the meaning dimensions of "Quantity" and "State"). There is no strong evidence that particular relations between the *Mach* and meaning variables depend on the specific meaning questionnaires. Indeed, the correlation with "Locational Qualities" occurred only on the lexical and unspecified questionnaires, which may seem to be expected, but other findings are less "typical" (e.g., the correlations with "Emotions" also occurred only on the lexical and unspecified questionnaires). The small differences among the three sets of findings may be due to the differences in stimuli in the three questionnaires. Also, in purely quantitative terms, the three types of questionnaires did not differ. They were correlated with *Mach* almost to the same extent (i.e., the numbers of significant correlations with meaning variables based on the lexical, personal, and unspecified questionnaires were 9, 9, and 10, respectively). The impressive consistency of the three sets of findings suggests that no specific set of instructions is superior in this case. However, the issue is to be further studied, as the consistency may reflect, to some extent, a characteristic of Machiavellianism. (Study 21 deals with the same issue in another context.)

STUDY 4: NEED FOR POWER AND SOME MORE MACHIAVELLIANISM

Purpose and Hypotheses

This study had three purposes. One was to examine the constellation of meaning variables that is bound to the need for power (*n* Power) as defined by Winter (1973) and McClelland (1975). The second was to explore the possibilities of identifying specific subtypes within a larger constellation of correlations between a personal disposition and meaning variables. The third was to replicate the study on Machiavellianism and meaning (Study 3) with a meaning questionnaire based on different stimulus words.

Our interest in the *n* Power was evoked primarily because of its strong motivational and cognitive aspects. Motivationally it can be viewed as a striving for certain goals or the disposition to be affected by certain kinds of incentives, so that the goals and the incentives are formulated in terms of specific cognitions, for example, feeling powerful (McClelland, 1975, p. 17) or concern about having impact, prestige, or power (Winter, 1973, p. 250). Cognitively it can be viewed as "enduring, recurring, and retrievable associated cognitive clusters (Winter & Stewart, 1978, p. 396), focused mainly on goals and cognitions concerning relevant instrumental actions, memories and feelings (Winter, 1973, Chapter 1; Winter & Stewart, 1978). Due to this broad range of manifestations, we expected *n* Power to be related to a pattern of meaning variables like the other traits.

The scoring system for *n* Power and various findings about the relations of *n* Power to different behaviors led us to expect some specific correlations with meaning variables. The major ones were the following: (1) a positive correlation with "Action" (*Dim* 4a) because actions are a major element in the scoring of power imagery (Winter, 1973, p. 73) and characterize occupations and hobbies like sports preferred by individuals with high *n* Power (Winter, 1973, Chap. 4); (2) positive correlations with "Feelings and Emotions," particularly those evoked in others (*Dim* 20a; because arousing strong affect in others is a major element in the scoring of *n* Power) and also with those experienced by the person (*Dim* 20b; because high *n* Power is characterized by affective intensification of ordinary experiences; Winter and Stewart, 1978, pp. 409–410); (3) a positive correlation with "Judgments and Evaluations" (particularly *Dim* 21a) because explicit concern about reputation is a major element in the scoring of *n* Power (Winter, 1973, p. 73); (4) positive correlations with "Domain of Application" (*Dim* 8a and *Dim* 8b) because high scorers on *n* Power have been found to be concerned with the specific kind of people involved in different situations (e.g., high scorers differentiate in their relationships between people in their inner circle and those outside, or between people of higher status and others; Winter, 1973, pp. 115–118), and with the particular nature of the things they collect or own (Winter, 1973, pp. 125ff.); (5) positive correlations with "Possessions" (*Dim* 17) because high scorers on *n* Power have been found to have possessions as a source of power, status, and prestige (McClelland, 1975, pp. 10, 15–17; Winter, 1973, pp. 127–128); and (6) positive correlations with "Sensory Qualities" (particularly *Dim* 19b, "Sensory Qualities" perceived by the referent) because high scorers on *n* Power have been found to suffer from and complain about various physical symptoms (McClelland, 1975, p. 66; McClelland & Jemmott, 1982; McClelland, Locke, & Williams, 1982). These expectations formed our first set of hypotheses. However, we expected more correlations to occur than those we could predict.

The second purpose had to do with the possibility of identifying subtypes of *n* Power on the basis of subclusters of meaning variables. Two kinds of considerations guided us in this attempt. The first kind was based on the scoring system and the findings about the different manifestations of *n* Power. The scoring system includes three different criteria for scoring: "strong rigorous actions which express power," "actions that arouse strong affect in others," and "explicit concern about reputation and position" (Winter, 1973, p. 73). The description of these criteria (Winter, 1973, Appendix I) indicated the possibility that the first corresponds to the meaning dimensions "Action" (*Dim* 4a) and "Possessions" (*Dim* 17), the second to the meaning dimensions "Feelings and Emotions" (*Dim* 20a) and "Domain of Application" (particularly *Dim* 8a), and the third to the meaning dimensions "Judgments and Evaluations" (*Dim* 21a), "Domain of Application" (particularly *Dim* 8b), and perhaps "State" (*Dim* 11). The possibility that there might be three clusters of *n* Power was supported by Winter's findings about different manifestations of *n* Power. Winter (1973) found that some manifestations were more characteristic of certain social classes than others (pp. 133–136), whereas some were vicarious manifestations (pp. 132–141) and hence did not necessarily occur in the same individuals who engaged in the direct manifestations.

The second set of considerations was based on the intriguing finding that *n* Power is not correlated with Machiavellianism (Winter, 1973, p. 94, cited the correlation between *Mach* V and *n* Power as −.22, nonsignificant in a sample of 46 people).

The finding is intriguing because it runs counter to intuition, counter to some findings, and counter to theoretical arguments. Intuition leads us to expect that individuals high in *Mach* are concerned about gaining and using power. The findings show that, in some basic respects, subjects high in *n* Power resemble subjects high in *Mach:* both tend to gain positions of leadership in the studied context of small groups, and to initiate as well as control the structure of the groups (Christie & Geis, 1970, pp. 140–149, 309–311, 356–358; Winter, 1973, Chapter 4), and both express hostility toward others (Golding, 1978; Winter, 1973, Chapter 4). The theoretical arguments are mainly that if high-*Mach* subjects are not concerned with gaining and wielding power, what else could they be concerned with? Similarly, if high–*n* Power individuals, with their tendencies to compete and succeed, are not Machiavellian to some degree, what else could they be? Winter (1973, p. 18) argued that Machiavellianism is a "sentiment" about the nature of power in human nature and "a particular style of exercizing power," and that these are simply different from a disposition to strive for power. Winter's arguments seemed to us to confirm our suspicion that *n* Power and Machiavellianism should be related. Hence, we hypothesized that only one of the three clusters of *n* Power that we tentatively defined would be related to *Mach*.

Thus, the second set of hypotheses was that there are subclusters within *n* Power defined by the relative prominence of different meaning variables. We defined them tentatively and exhaustively as follows: Cluster A would include "Action" (*Dim* 4a), "Function" (*Dim* 3), and "Possessions" (*Dim* 17); Cluster B would include "Feelings and Emotions" (*Dim* 20a) and "Domain of Application: Subject" (*Dim* 8a); and Cluster C would include "Judgments and Evaluations" (*Dim* 21b), "Domain of Application: Object" (*Dim* 8b), and "State" (*Dim* 11). Further, we hypothesized that only the first cluster would be related to *Mach* because of the similarity of this subcluster to the constellation of meaning variables that was found to be correlated with *Mach* (Study 3).

The third purpose was to replicate Study 3. We hypothesized that the results obtained in this study with a different meaning questionnaire would not differ from those reported in Study 3. The reason was that the results would depend on meaning dimensions that are relatively abstract categories of content and hence might be expected to remain stabile despite variations in meaning values.

Method

The subjects were 65 individuals in the age range of 18–23. There were 35 men, all enlisted in active military service, and 30 women who were students in professional schools and teachers' seminars. They were administered—in random order in three separate group sessions, five to six days apart—the three following questionnaires: the standard meaning questionnaire (with 11 stimulus words), the *Mach* IV questionnaire (see Study 3, "Method"), and a measure of *n* Power that included four pictures like those on the Thematic Apperception Test, with the instructions to write about each a story specifying what is happening, who the people are, what has happened earlier, what the people think and want, an what will happen (for pictures and detailed instructions, see McClelland, 1975, Appendix 1B). The coding of *n* Power was done, in line with Winter's manual (1973, Appendix 1), by two coders with an intercoder reliability of $r = .89$.

In examining clusters within the larger correlation matrix, we followed a modified procedure derived from the method designed by Holzinger and Harman (1941).
The procedure consisted in classifying all the correlations of *n* Power with meaning
dimensions into three clusters and comparing the mean of correlations within the
clusters with the mean of correlations with variables outside the cluster. Within
clusters, only significant correlations were included. Each correlation was included
in only one cluster. The value and sign of the correlations were considered. Subdimensions (e.g., *Dim* 8a and *Dim* 8b), but not additions based on them (e.g., *Dim*
8a+b), were considered separately because of their theoretical importance. We started with the variables hypothesized to be within the three clusters and added others
in line with the correlations between the meaning variables themselves (i.e., we
added to each cluster correlations with those meaning variables whose mean correlations with the meaning variables in the cluster were highest) until all the significant
correlations with *n* Power were included.

Results and Conclusions

Table 12 shows that, as expected, *n* Power is related to meaning variables. These
are mostly meaning dimensions, and their range is broad. The correlations include
those predicted—with the meaning dimensions "Action," "Domain of Application," "Feelings and Emotions," "Judgments and Evaluations," "Possessions," and
"Sensory Qualities"—in addition to others. Some of these others correspond to
descriptions of *n* Power provided by McClelland (1975). Thus, the correlations with
"Contextual Allocation" (*Dim* 1) and "Structure" (*Dim* 10) may indicate that high
scorers on *n* Power are aware of organizations and superordinate structures (Mc-
Clelland, 1975, pp. 10, 45); and the correlation with conventional metaphors (*TR* 4b)
corresponds to tendencies to deal with symbols of power or prestige and other
vicarious satisfactions (e.g., prestige possessions, reading and viewing pornographic
and sport materials, and belonging to larger organizations; (McClelland, 1975, Chap.
1). The findings show that like other traits, *n* Power is related to a constellation of
meaning variables.

Table 13 shows that the correlations between *n* Power and meaning variables are

Table 12. Significant Correlations of *n* Power and *Mach* IV with Meaning Variables

Personality variable	Significant correlations with meaning variables
n Power	*Dim* 1, .24*; *Dim* 3, .30*; *Dim* 4a, .51***; *Dim* 8a, .36**; *Dim* 8b, .33**; *Dim* 8a + b, .34**; *Dim* 10, .27*; *Dim* 11, .33**; *Dim* 14, .24*; *Dim* 15, .45***; *Dim* 17a, .29*; *Dim* 17b, .37**; *Dim* 17a + b, .33**; *Dim* 19b, .27*; *Dim* 20a, .26*; *Dim* 20b, .23*; *Dim* 20a + b, .25*; *Dim* 21a, .49***; *Dim* 21b, .30*; *Dim* 21a + b, .36**; *Dim* 22a, .36**; *TR* 1b, .25*; *TR* 2b, .27*; *TR* 4b, .30*.
Mach IV	*Dim* 3, .60***; *Dim* 6, −.31*; *Dim* 7, −.39**; *Dim* 11, .24*; *Dim* 15, .35**; *Dim* 17a, .30*; *Dim* 17a + b, .32**; *TR* 1a, .24*.

Note. For the code of the meaning variables, see Appendix A.
*$p < .05$.
**$p < .01$.
***$p < .001$.

Table 13. Three Clusters of *n* Power Based on Correlations of *n* Power with Meaning Variables

Cluster	A	B	C	B and C
Meaning variables in cluster	Dim 4a, Dim 17a, Dim 17b, Dim 3, Dim 14, Dim 15	Dim 20a, Dim 8a, Dim 19b, Dim 20b	Dim 21, DIm 8b, Dim 21b, Dim 22a, Dim 11, Dim 1, Dim 10	Dim 8a, Dim 8b, Dim 1, Dim 10, Dim 19b, Dim 20a, Dim 20b, Dim 21a, Dim 21b, Dim 22a
Mean of correlations within cluster[a]	.35	.28	.32	.30
Mean of correlations outside cluster[a]	.21	.22	.20	.19
B coefficients[b]	1.58	1.22	1.64	1.61

[a]In computing means of correlations, the *r* values were converted to *z* values. The reported values are *r* values. The ratios are based on the corresponding *z* values. Therefore, the ratios are lower than those that would be obtained by using the unconverted *r* values. The means refer to correlations with *n* Power.
[b]The minimum significant value of the B coefficient was set arbitrarily at 1.30 (Holzinger & Harman, 1941).

classifiable into clusters. Of the three hypothesized clusters, two were confirmed: the one originally defined by "Action" and "Possessions" and the one originally defined by "Evaluations" of others. The cluster originally defined by evoked "Emotions" was not confirmed. In view of these findings, we continued the process of clustering, following the same criteria as earlier, and reclassified the data into two clusters (Table 13, Cluster A and B + C). The change led to a combination of the second and third clusters, which, in fact, makes good sense psychologically insofar as power manifestations based on evoking specific emotional reactions in others seem to be closely related to manifestations based on evoking specific evaluations in others. Thus, we found two clusters within *n* Power: an actional-functional one and an evaluative-emotional one. These clusters were defined on the basis of the meaning-assignment tendencies underlying *n* Power, and we suggest viewing them as subtraits. The present study provides one kind of support for the psychological reality of these subtraits in terms of their relation to Machiavellianism. Table 14 shows that only in subjects high and low in Cluster A were *n* Power and *Mach* scores related significantly (81.5% of the subjects had the predicted combination of scores, i.e., high in both or low in both), whereas in subjects high and low in Cluster B, *n* Power and *Mach* scores were unrelated (only 33.8% of the subjects had the predicted combination scores).

Finally, Table 14 shows that the present study replicated fully the results of Study 3 concerning the relations between Machiavellianism and meaning variables.

In sum, the study showed that *n* Power is related to specific meaning variables, and that these are classifiable into two clusters. The findings enabled a clarification of the relations between *n* Power and Machiavellianism by showing that only one of the clusters of *n* Power is related to *Mach*. In general, *n* Power was shown to be related to a broader range of meaning variables than *Mach*.

Table 14. Distribution of *n* Power and *Mach* IV Scores in Subjects High and Low
in Two Clusters of Meaning Dimensions

n Power[a] *Mach*[b]	High		Low		Significance
	High	Low	High	Low	
Cluster A (action-function)					
High[c] (*n* = 38)	31	2	4	1	53 vs. 12 (pro vs. anti hypothesis) $z = 4.96, p < .0001$
Low (*n* = 27)	—	3	2	22	
Cluster B (eval.-emotion)					
High[c] (*n* = 28)	9	12	3	4	22 vs. 43 (pro vs. anti hypothesis) $z = -2.48, p < .05$
Low (*n* = 37)	4	5	15	13	

[a]High and low in *n* Power were defined in terms of above or below the group's mean ($\bar{X} = 5.72$), respectively.
[b]High and low in *Mach* were defined in terms of above or below the group's mean ($\bar{X} = 70.58$), respectively.
[c]Subjects high in Cluster A were defined as those who had above the mean frequencies in 3–6 of the meaning dimensions defining the cluster; subjects low in Cluster A were those who did not. Subjects high in Cluster B were defined as those who had above the mean frequencies in 5–10 of the meaning dimensions defining the cluster; subjects low in Cluster B were those who did not.

STUDY 5: THE FUNCTIONALITY OF MACHIAVELLIANS

Purpose and Hypotheses

The purpose of this study was to test a hypothesis about the responses of subjects based on their meaning profile. As Studies 3 and 4 showed that Machiavellianism is highly correlated with the meaning dimension "Function" (*Dim* 3), we hypothesized that subjects high in *Mach* would respond to a situational manipulation based on function more than subjects low in *Mach*; that is, they would increase a response more if told that increasing it would be functional, and they would decrease it more if told that decreasing it would be functional. The testing of this hypothesis was important in exploring how traits become manifested and how meaning-assignment tendencies interact with the meanings of inputs.

Method

The subjects were 60 individuals, 30 men (enlisted soldiers) and 30 women (students in a teacher's seminar) in the age range of 18–24. They were administered the *Mach* IV (see Study 3, "Method") and were divided into high in *Mach* (*n* = 30) versus low in *Mach* (*n* = 30) on the basis of the group's mean ($\bar{x} = 69.03$). Then, the high-*Mach* subjects and the low-*Mach* subjects were divided randomly into three groups each, one of which got the positive-function manipulation, one of which got the negative-function manipulation; the third group served as a control. The assignment of the manipulations to the groups was random. Thus, the design was bifactorial; one factor (the *Mach*) had two levels, and the other (the function manipulation) had three levels. The number of subjects in each group was 10. The task, administered in group sessions, was to describe in writing some locality in the country in as much detail as possible. This task was chosen because it was assumed that most of the subjects would be motivated to cooperate on a neutral task of this kind (H. Kreitler & S. Kreitler, 1976, p. 102), that all the subjects could perform it, that it allowed for individual differences, and lent itself well to the manipulation.

The subjects were first administered the task with the regular instructions only and were allowed to work on it for 10 minutes. Then the manipulation was administered, and the subjects were asked to go on until stopped and, in any case, to wait until the session was over. The positive-function manipulation consisted in remarking vaguely that detailed descriptions could be helpful to the subjects by revealing the subjects' positive characteristics; the negative-function manipulation consisted in remarking vaguely that detailed descriptions might not always be helpful to the subjects because they would not necessarily reveal positive characteristics of the subjects; the control manipulation consisted in simply remarking vaguely, "Well, you are working on the task." We made the manipulation vague and weak in order to test whether it would be picked up by the subjects who were assumed to be sensitive to it. The subjects were asked, presumably for standardization, to make a sign on their pages every 5 minutes when the time was written on the blackboard. The dependent variable was the difference in the number of lines written in the last 10 minutes and the first 10 minutes.

Results and Conclusions

A preliminary test showed that the six groups did not differ significantly from each other in the means of the number of lines written in the first 10-minute period. Hence, it would be safe to conclude that the observed effects are attributable to the manipulation. The two-factor analysis of variance showed that, whereas the main effects attributable to the Mach ($F = 2.70$, $df = 1/118$) and to the manipulation ($F = 2.93$, $df = 2/118$) were not significant, the interaction between the *Mach* and the manipulation was significant ($F = 3.06$, $df = 2/118$, $p < .05$).

An examination of the means of the different groups (Table 15) indicates that the interaction reflects several findings: the difference between the effects of the positive

Table 15. Mean Difference Scores of Subjects High and Low
in *Mach* Subjected to Three Kinds of Manipulations

Groups[a]	Positive function $\bar{X}$	Negative function $\bar{X}$	Control $\bar{X}$
		Manipulations	
High *Mach*	11.31	−6.02	7.50
	(a)	(b)	(c)
Low *Mach*	3.24	−1.26	2.82
	(d)	(e)	(f)

[a]By the Newman–Keuls procedure (Winer, 1971, pp. 196ff.) Group *a* differed significantly ($p < .05$) from *b, d, e,* and *f*; Group *c* differed significantly ($p < .05$) from *b, e,* and *f*; Group *d* differed significantly ($p < .05$) from *b*; and Group *f* differs significantly ($p < .05$) from *b*.

function and the negative function was significant only in the high-*Mach* group; the difference between the negative function and the control was significant only in the high-*Mach* group; and the only significant difference between the high-*Mach* and the low-*Mach* subjects was in the positive function. More generally, the findings show that, as predicted, the high-*Mach* subjects picked up the cues of functionality suggested by the experimenter and reacted to them as expected, whereas the low-*Mach* subjects did not do so. Of course, the study does not tell us whether they did not pick up the cues or whether they did but did not react to them in the same way as the high *Mach*s. However, the findings show something that was unexpected: The high-*Mach* subjects in the control conditions increased their productivity almost as much as the high-*Mach* subjects in the positive-function group, so that the difference between these two groups was not significant. This finding implies that high *Mach*s tend to act as if functionality is involved even when no explicit cues of this kind are actually presented. Because in most testing situations productivity is an asset, the high *Mach*s of the control group naturally assumed, in line with their functional approach, that increased productivity might be instrumental, or at least not detrimental.

The findings shed some light on the interaction between meaning dimensions and situational cues. In the context of this study, the situational cues did not actually elicit the functional approach, and they were perhaps not even necessary for its manifestation; rather, they guided the form of the manifestation, that is, an increase or a decrease in productivity.

STUDY 6: CATTELL'S PERSONALITY FACTORS AS PATTERNS OF MEANING VARIABLES[4]

Purpose and Hypotheses

The 16 Personality Factors (PF) Test devised by Cattell was of special interest to us in our attempt to explore the interrelations between meaning and personality traits. There were three reasons. First, the test was developed as a comprehensive measure of personality (Cattell, 1965; Cattell & Eber, 1964) and provides information about each of 16 basic personality factors or source traits (see Table 16). The measured traits are of different kinds and generality and hence provided an opportunity to test hypotheses about specific relations between meaning variables and specific types of personality traits. Second, the personality factors defined by the 16 PF are based on extensive factor-analytic research and are rooted in the three complementary kinds of data, from questionnaires, from ratings, and from directly measured behaviors. Thus, it is possible to test various predictions about the intercorrelations of the factors with meaning variables and learn more about the personological manifestations of the meaning variables. Third, a lot of information has been collected by Cattell and his co-workers about many different aspects of the 16 factors. Thus it is possible to compare different classifications of the factors in terms of their interrelations with meaning variables. These comparisons could contribute to extending our understanding of the patterns of meaning variable related to traits.

[4]Thanks are due to Talma Lobel, who kindly made available to us the data on the scores on the 16 PF of part of the subjects.

Table 16. List and Brief Descriptions of the Personality Factors
Assessed by Cattell's 16 Personality Factors (PF) Test

No. of factor in text and tables of Study 6	Label and description of factor: High score versus low score
	Primary (first-order) factors:
1	Affectothymia–Sizothymia (Factor A) (Warmth: warmhearted, outgoing, participating vs. reserved, detached, aloof)
2	Higher Ego Strength–Lower Ego Strength (Factor C) (Emotional stability: stable, mature, faces reality vs. emotionally unstable, easily upset, changeable)
3	Dominance–Submissiveness (Factor E) (Ascendance: assertive, aggressive, competitive vs. obedient, docile, accommodating)
4	Surgency–Desurgency (Factor F) (Impulsivity: enthusiastic, heedless, expressive, open vs. sober, serious, concerned, cautious)
5	Stronger Superego Strength–Weaker Superego Strength (Factor G) (Group conformity: conscientious, persistent, responsible, concerned about moral standards vs. disregards rules, fickle, self-indulgent, undependable)
6	Parmia–Threctia (Factor H) (Boldness: adventurous, daring, socially bold, risk-taking, carefree vs. shy, timid, threat-sensitive, careful)
7	Premsia–Harria (Factor I) (Emotional sensitivity: sensitive, dependent, gentle, tender-minded vs. tough-minded, practical, hard)
8	Protension–Alaxia (Factor L) (Suspiciousness: jealous, suspecting, dogmatic vs. trusting, permissive, conciliatory)
9	Autia–Praxenia (Factor M) (Imagination: imaginative, interested in ideas, generally enthused vs. practical, conventional, prosaic)
10	Shrewdness–Artlessness (Factor N) (Poise, sophistication: astute, worldly, socially polished, smart, insightful, artful vs. naive, natural, socially unskilled, forthright)
11	Guilt Proneness–Untroubled Adequacy (Factor O) (Tendency to guilt and anxiousness: apprehensive, self-reproaching, worrying, sensitive to disapproval vs. placid, self-confident, is not afraid, impenitent)
12	Radicalism–Conservatism (Factor Q_1) (Rebelliousness: experimenting, liberal, free-thinking vs. conservative, tolerant of traditional difficulties and shortcomings)
13	Self-Sufficiency–Group Adherence (Factor Q_2) (Self-sufficiency: relies on oneself, prefers to reach one's own decisions, resourceful vs. group dependent sociably, prefers to follow group decisions)
14	High Strength of Self-Sentiment–Low Self-Sentiment Integration (Factor Q_3) (Ability to control anxiety: controlled, compulsive, has will power vs. lax, uncontrolled, careless of social rules, does not channel energy well)
15	High Ergic Tension–Low Ergic Tension (Factor Q_4) (Free-floating anxiety: tense, driven, irritated, high-strung vs. relaxed, composed, calm, unfrustrated)

(continued)

Table 16. (*Continued*)

No. of factor in text and tables of Study 6	Label and description of factor: High score versus low score
	Secondary (second-order) factors:
16	Exvia–Invia (not included in Study 6; see Table 6)
17	Anxiety–Adjustment
18	Cortertia (Tough Poise)–Pathemia
19	Independence–Subduedness
20	Neuroticism: High, Low
21	Psychoticism: High, Low
22	Leadership: High Low
23	Creativity: High, Low
24	Academic Achievements: High, Low
25	Conformity: High, Low
26	Degree of Correspondence between Subject's Profile and the Norm: High, Low

Note. Each of the primary factors is followed by a short description of the factor and by adjectives characterizing individuals typical of the positive (first mentioned) and negative (second mentioned) aspects of the factor. The descriptions are modelled after Cattell and Eber (1962, 1964) and Karson and O'Dell (1976). Factor B of the primary factors has not been presented because it assesses "Intelligence," a factor irrelevant to the purposes of Study 6.

The first and major hypothesis of this study was that the predominant characteristics of the different personality factors would be correlated with corresponding meaning variables. This hypothesis included many specifications for the different personality factors and their varied manifestations. Our major guidelines for setting up the specific hypotheses were provided by the ample material about the personality factors presented in the numerous publications of Cattell and his co-workers. We relied mainly on the following sources: Cattell (1965, 1973), Cattell and Eber (1964), Cattell, Eber, and Tatsuoka (1970), Cattell and Scheier (1961), Hammond (1977), Ishikawa (1977), Wilde (1977), and Hundleby, Pawlik, and Cattell (1965) for material about those factors of the 16 PF that had been found to be strongly, recurrently, and unambiguously related to objective data factors.

For the sake of a concentrated presentation of our findings and in order to avoid repetition, we will postpone the full exposition of the findings and their rationale to the section "Results and Conclusions" and limit ourselves at this point to merely illustrating the kind of specific hypotheses we had. Thus, in the framework of the first hypothesis, we expected, for example, Factor 1 (Affectothymia-Schizothymia), first, to be correlated positively with "Feelings and Emotions" (particularly *Dim* 20a) because individuals with a high score have "accessible emotions" (Cattell & Eber, 1964, p. 10), are warm in emotional reactions, and are concerned with interpersonal relations (Cattell, 1973, p. 158), that is, the affective responses of others; and second, to be negatively correlated with "Judgments and Evaluations" because sociopaths score high on this factor, whereas low scorers have a critical-judgmental attitude, emphasize ideation and evaluation (Cattell, 1973, p. 158), and stand by their ideas (Cattell, 1973, p. 257). Or we expected the factor of Shrewdness-Artlessness to be correlated positively with the comparative type of relation *difference* (*TR* 2b) because it was found that high scorers on this factor tended to be competitive (Cattell, 1973, p. 172), that is, concerned with comparisons and mainly differences.

Our further hypotheses referred to differences in the frequency of interrelations with meaning variables between factors having different characteristics. The second hypothesis was that second-order factors would be related to fewer meaning variables than primary or source factors. The theoretical rationale was that second-order factors are more abstract than primary factors and hence are bound less directly than these to the actual, ongoing meaning-assignment processes. In fact, an average of only 60%–70% of the variance of all the known primary factors is accounted for by Cattell's second-order factors (Cattell, Eber, & Delhees, 1968; Gorsuch & Cattell, 1967). The methodological rationale was that second-order factors are defined by their saturation on several primary factors and hence that some of the meaning variables correlated with the latter may be canceled in the process of combining the scores.

The third hypothesis was that personality factors with a larger estimated heritability factor (Cattell, 1973, Chapter 5) would be related to more meaning variables than factors with a lower heritability index. The rationale was the assumption that factors with higher heritability have manifestations of greater variety and strength or at earlier ages than other factors and hence may be expected to become related more readily or over time, in a stable manner, to more meaning variables. It may be recalled that a similar hypothesis concerning CPI scales was confirmed by the findings of Study 2.

The fourth hypothesis was that factors with regular age trends (i.e., steady increase, decrease, or no change) are related to more meaning variables than factors with irregular age trends (i.e., with ups and downs). The rationale was that a regular trend would favor the production of a broad range of interrelations with the other steady characteristics of the individual.

The fifth hypothesis was that factors whose strength was increasing in the age range of 20–30 years would be related to more meaning variables than factors whose strength was decreasing or remained steady in the age range 20–30 years, which was the age range of our subjects. The rationale was that, if the strength of a factor is increasing, it is more likely to be involved in more personality manifestations and thus would become related to a greater number of meaning variables.

The sixth hypothesis was that factors with consistent manifestations from early childhood onward would be related to a broader range of meaning variables than factors that were first manifested clearly in young adulthood. The rationale was that, in the course of the long period of time from early childhood, there would be ample opportunity for a factor to become related to a variety of meaning variables in different, yet recurrent, contexts. We expected the time period to be of greater importance in facilitating relations with meaning variables than the attention drawn to the factor through its occurrence at a later period.

The seventh hypothesis was that factors that tend to be demonstrably affected in their strength by different events in the individual's life (e.g., marriage, frustrations on the job, or leaving the parents' home) would be related to a greater number of meaning variables than factors that do not tend to be so affected. The rationale was that changes in the strength of a factor would tend to bring its manifestations into focus and hence would increase its chances of becoming related to a great many meaning variables.

The eighth hypothesis was that factors corresponding to factors identified clearly in ratings by others who know the individual would be related to a larger number of meaning variables than factors that correspond to no such factors or to weakly identified factors. The rationale was that correspondence to factors in rating data indicates that a factor is manifested in overt interpersonal behavior noticeable by external observers. Hence, this factor may be assumed to have variegated manifestations and is more likely to be related to meaning variables than a factor with fewer manifestations in overt interpersonal behavior.

The ninth hypothesis was similar to the eighth in its rationale but dealt with correspondence to factors identified in behaviors assessed by means of standardized measures (called "objective data" by Cattell and his co-workers). Again, we expected factors corresponding to more objective-data factors to be related to a greater number of meaning variables than factors corresponding to fewer such factors.

Method

The subjects were 72 undergraduates in psychology and the social sciences at Tel Aviv University (28 men and 44 women), in the age range of 22–31 years. They were administered, in random order, the standard meaning questionnaire (11 stimulus words) and Cattell's 16 PF (in a standardized Hebrew version) in small-group sessions, on separate occasions, five to seven days apart.

The first and major set of hypotheses was examined by testing the predicted correspondences between the correlations of each factor with specific meaning variables and findings about high and low scorers on that factor, derived from different published sources. These findings were established independently of our correlational study, and hence, the correspondences cannot be assumed to be artifactual.

Hypotheses 2–9 were tested by comparing the number of meaning variables related to different classes of factors. The classes were defined in terms of criteria specified either in the text (for Hypothesis 2) or in the footnotes to Table 19 (for Hypotheses 3–9).

Results and Conclusions

The number of significant correlations of Cattell's primary and secondary personality factors with the meaning variables exceeded the number expected by chance. It formed 20.26% of the total of possible correlations (24.5% for the primaries and 14.48% for the secondaries; see Table 18). The range of significant intercorrelations was 5 (Factor 26) to 31 (Factor 6), the mean was 15.35, and the $SD = 7.18$. Table 18 also shows that the personality factors were correlated with the three kinds of meaning variables coded in this study. For all the personality factors involved, the distribution of correlations with meaning dimensions, types of relation, and shifts in referent deviated significantly from the expected on the basis of chance (in line with the distribution of variables in the meaning system, pp,. 92–93, $\chi^2 = 19.31$, $df = 2$, p < .001) but did not deviate significantly from the expected in patterns corresponding to traits, p. 79, $\chi^2 = 4.03$, $df = 2$, n.s.; expected distributions were adjusted for the absence of FR variables in this study).

Table 17 shows that each personality factor was correlated with several meaning variables. The mean of intercorrelations as 17.42, with a range that ran from a low of 8 (for Factor 13) to a high of 39 (for Factor 6). This finding in itself supports our basic conception that a trait may profitably be conceptualized as a constellation of meaning-assignment variables preferred by the individual and may thus be applied by

Table 17. Significant Correlations between Cattell's Primary and Secondary Personality Factors and Meaning Variables[a]

Personality factors	Meaning variables
Primary factors: Factor 1	*Dim* 1, .23*; *Dim* 14, .28*; *Dim* 20a, .35**; *Dim* 21a, −.25*; *Dim* 21b, −.23*; *Dim* 21a + b, −.24*; *TR* 2a, −.23*; *TR* 4b, −.29*; *SR* 5, −.29*; no. of dif. *SR*, −.23*.
Factor 2	*Dim* 4b, .23*; *Dim* 16, −.25*; $(19a_{li}, −.23^*)$; *Dim* 19b, −.39***; $(19b_8, −.38^{***})$; *Dim* 20b, −.23*; *Dim* 21a + b, −.25*; *Dim* 22a, −.25*; *Dim* 22b, −.23*; *Dim* 22a + b, −.29*; no. of dif. *Dim*, −.28*; *TR* 1b, .29*; *TR* 1a + b, .38***; *TR* 2c, .24*; *TR* 2d, −.23*; *TR* 3a, −.26*; *TR* 3a + b + c, −.24*; *TR* 4b, −.28*; *TR* 4a + b + c + d, −.29*; *SR* 8, .26*.
Factor 3	*Dim* 1, .23*; *Dim* 5, .24*; *Dim* 14, .23*; *Dim* 15, .24*; *Dim* 16, −.42***; *Dim* 17a, −.24*; *Dim* 19a, −.24*; $(19a_4, −.28^*)$; *Dim* 19b, −.32**; $(19b_8, −.40^{**})$; *Dim* 19a + b, −.28*; *Dim* 22a, −.25*; *TR* 3c, −.28*; *TR* 4c, .27*; *SR* 3, −.25*; *SR* 6, .23*; *SR* 8, .25*.
Factor 4	*Dim* 1, .24*; *Dim* 4a, .35**; *Dim* 4b, −.36**; *Dim* 5, .28*; *Dim* 15, −.38***; *Dim* 16, −.45***; *Dim* 19b, −.29*; $(19b_8, −.30^{**})$; *Dim* 21a, −.30**; *Dim* 22a + b, .33**; *TR* 2b, −.25*; *TR* 3a, −.26*; *TR* 3a + b + c, .28*; *TR* 4b, .25*; *TR* 4a + b + c + d, .25*; *SR* 4, −.24*; *SR* 8, .36**.
Factor 5	*Dim* 3, .32**; *Dim* 16, −.25*; *Dim* 17b, .29*; *Dim* 17a + b, .31**; $(19a_{li}, −.24^*)$; *Dim* 21a, .27*; *Dim* 21b, .36**; *Dim* 21a + b, .27*; *Dim* 22a, −.26*; *TR* 2c, .24*; *TR* 4a, −.25*; no. of dif. *SR*, .23*.
Factor 6	*Dim* 1, .25*; *Dim* 2b, .23*; *Dim* 4a + b, .25*; *Dim* 5, .28*; *Dim* 9, −.23*; *Dim* 10, .23*; *Dim* 15, −.23*; *Dim* 16, −.40***; *Dim* 17a + b, .23*; *Dim* 18, −.25*; *Dim* 19a, −.26*; $(19a_1, −.37^{**}; 19a_2, −.23^*; 19a_3, −.27^*; 19a_4, −.38^{***}; 19a_6, −.32^{**}; 19a_7, −.32^{**}; 19a_8, −.38^{***})$; *Dim* 19b, −.38***; $(19b_8, −.28^*)$; *Dim* 19a + b, −.25*; *Dim* 21a, −.23*; *Dim* 21a + b, −.25*; no. of dif. *Dim*, −.27*; *TR* 1b, .25*; *TR* 1a + b, .39***; *TR* 2b, −.26*; *TR* 2a + b + c + d, −.26*; *TR* 3c, −.42***; *TR* 4b, −.25*; *TR* 4d, −.32**; *SR* 2, −.32**; *SR* 3, −.28*; *SR* 7, −.30**; *SR* 8, .28*; *SR* 10, −.30**; SR_{near}, −.25*; no. of dif. *SR*, −.28*; no. of m. values, −.36**.
Factor 7	*Dim* 3, −.29*; *Dim* 4a, .32**; *Dim* 4b, .35**; *Dim* 4a + b, .32**; *Dim* 5, −.26*; *Dim* 12, −.50***; *Dim* 16, .23*; *Dim* 18, .38***; *Dim* 19a, .28*; $(19a_1, .30^{**}; 19a_3, .30^{**}; 19a_4, .29^*; 19a_6, .42^{***}; 19a_7, .38^{***}; 19a_8, .27^*)$; *Dim* 19a + b, .26*; *Dim* 20b, .28*; *Dim* 22a, .23*; *Dim* 22b, .25*; *Dim* 22a + b, .24*; *TR* 3c, .40***; *TR* 4c, .40***; *TR* 4d, .44***; *SR* 2, −.40***; *SR* 3, −.30**; *SR* 7, .38***; *SR* 10, .38***; no. of dif. *SR*, .23*; no. of m. values, .39***.
Factor 8	*Dim* 4a, .24*; *Dim* 4a + b, .25*; *Dim* 9, −.23*; *Dim* 11, .32**; *Dim* 12, −.42***; *Dim* 18, −.34**; *Dim* 19a, −.38***; $(19a_1, .38^{***}; 19a_3, −.32^{**}; 19a_4, −.38^{***}; 19a_6, −.40^{***}; 19a_7, −.39^{***}; 19a_8, −.35^{**}; 19b_{li}, .25^*)$; *Dim* 19a + b, −.38***; *Dim* 22b, .42***; *TR* 2b, .35**; *TR* 3c, −.45***; *TR* 4d, −.44**, *SR* 1, .26*; *SR* 2, .45***; *SR* 7, .48***; *SR* 10, .38***; no. of m. values, −.38***.
Factor 9	*Dim* 3, −.41***; *Dim* 4a, .36**; *Dim* 4b, −.24*; *Dim* 5, .23*; *Dim* 7, −.25*; *Dim* 12, −.48***; *Dim* 18, −.40***; *Dim* 19a, −.34**; $(19a_1, −.38^{***}; 19a_3, −.23^*; 19a_4, −.32^{**}; 19a_6, −.50^{***}; 19a_7, −.44^{***}; 19a_8, −.49^{***})$; *Dim* 19b, .40***; $(19b_8, .24^*)$; *Dim* 19a + b, −.38***; *Dim* 20b, .39***; *Dim* 20a + b, .25*; *Dim* 21b, −.35**; *Dim* 22a, .33**; *Dim* 22a + b, .45***; *TR* 2c, −.26*;

(*continued*)

Table 17. (*Continued*)

Personality factors	Meaning variables
	TR 2a + b + c + d, −.32**; *TR* 3b, −.23*; *TR* 3c, −.46***; *TR* 4c, .40***; *TR* 4d, −.48***; *SR* 2, −.42***; *SR* 7, −.45***; *SR* 10, −.42***; no. of m. values, −.25*.
Factor 10	*Dim* 2b, .23*; *Dim* 3, .34**; *Dim* 5, .34**; *Dim* 7, .29*; *Dim* 12, −.30**; *Dim* 14, .28*; *Dim* 16, .28*; *Dim* 18, −.23*; *Dim* 19a, −.26*; (19a$_1$, −.26*; 19a$_3$, −.27*; 19a$_4$, −.23*; 19a$_6$, −.28*; 19a$_7$, −.30**; 19a$_8$, −.29*); *Dim* 19b, .39***; (19b$_8$, .35**); *Dim* 20a, −.25*; *Dim* 21a, −.26*; *Dim* 21b, .29*; *TR* 2a, −.28*; *TR* 2b, .32**; *TR* 3a, .26*; *TR* 3c, −.32**; *TR* 3a + b + c, −.23*; *TR* 4a, −.26*; *TR* 4d, −.38***; no. of dif. *TR*, −.23*; *SR* 2, −.33**; *SR* 4, .33**; *SR* 7, −.32**; *SR* 10, −.34**.
Factor 11	*Dim* 1, −.28*; *Dim* 14, −.23*; *Dim* 16, .46***; *Dim* 19b, .38***; (19b$_8$, .52**), *Dim* 20a, .32**; *Dim* 20b, .23*; *Dim* 21a, .56***; *Dim* 21a + b, .32**; *Dim* 22a, .26*; *Dim* 22a + b, .25*; no. of dif. *Dim*, .28*; *TR* 2b, .36**; *TR* 3a, .34**.
Factor 12	*Dim* 1, .32**; *Dim* 2b, .28*; *Dim* 4a, .24*; *Dim* 4b, −.25*; *Dim* 6, .23*; *Dim* 7, .29*; *Dim* 9, .37**; *Dim* 10, .28*; *Dim* 11, .28*; (19b$_3$, .25*); *Dim* 20a, .25*; *Dim* 21a, .32**; *Dim* 22b, −.26*; *TR* 1a, .32**; *TR* 1b, .26*; *TR* 1a + b, .29*; *TR* 2b, .29*; *TR* 3b, −.25*; *TR* 4b, .24*; *TR* 4c, .23*; no. of dif. *TR*, .25*; *SR* 1, −.28*; *SR* 5, .25*; *SR$_{near}$*, .36**.
Factor 13	*Dim* 4a + b, −.25*; (19a$_0$, −.30**); *Dim* 21a, −.31**; *TR* 2a, .32**; *TR* 2b, .30**; *TR* 2c, .24*; *TR* 2a + b + c + d, .24*; *TR* 3a, .23*.
Factor 14	*Dim* 5, .25*; *Dim* 6, .32**; *Dim* 7, .35**; *Dim* 10, .23*; *Dim* 11, .28*; *Dim* 12, −.23*; *Dim* 19a, .24*; (19a$_1$, .27*; 19a$_3$, .26*; 19a$_4$, .23*; 19a$_6$, .25*; 19a$_7$, .23*); *Dim* 20b, −.45***; *Dim* 20a + b, −.40***; *Dim* 21a, .41***; *Dim* 22b, −.25*; *Dim* 22a + b, −.25*; *TR* 3c, .26*; *TR* 4d, .26*; no. of dif. *TR*, .28*; *SR* 2, .25*; *SR* 7, .25*; *SR* 10, .23*; no. of dif. *SR*, .23*; no. of m. values, .25*.
Factor 15	*Dim* 4a, −.30**; *Dim* 4b, .28*; *Dim* 4a + b, −.24*; *Dim* 21a, .26*; *Dim* 22a, .35*; *Dim* 22b, .25*; *Dim* 22a + b, .43***; *TR* 2d, .26*; *TR* 4b, .28*.
Secondary factors: Factor 17	*Dim* 4a, −.26*; *Dim* 4b, −.23*; *Dim* 4a + b, −.24*; *Dim* 16, .32**; *Dim* 19b, .26*; (19b$_8$, .25*); *Dim* 20b, .26*; *Dim* 21a, .28*; *Dim* 21a + b, .28*, *Dim* 22a, .35**; *Dim* 22a + b, .32**; *TR* 1a + b, −.30**; *TR* 2b, .25*; *TR* 2d, .23*; *TR* 3a, .25*; *TR* 4b, .25*.
Factor 18	*Dim* 3, .28*; *Dim* 4b, −.23*; *Dim* 16, −.52***; *Dim* 19b, −.29*; (19b$_8$, −.25*); *Dim* 20a + b, −.23*; *Dim* 21a, −.27*; *Dim* 21a + b, −.24*; *Dim* 22a, −.28*; *Dim* 22a + b, −.23*; no. of dif. *Dim*, −.24*; *TR* 2c, .39***; no. of dif. *TR*, .24*.
Factor 19	*Dim* 5, .24*; (19a$_1$, −.23*); *Dim* 21a + b, −.32**; *TR* 4c, .40***; *TR* 4a + b + c + d, −.26*; no. of dif. *TR*, .29*; *SR* 6, .24*; *SR* 8, .26*.
Factor 20	*Dim* 4b, −.28*; *Dim* 5, −.23*; *Dim* 8a, −.25*; *Dim* 12, −.24*; *Dim* 16, −.49***; *Dim* 18, −.25*; *Dim* 19a, −.26*; *Dim* 19b, .30**; (19b$_8$, .36**); *Dim* 20b, .28*; *Dim* 21a, .32**; *Dim* 22a, .29*; *Dim* 22a + b, .26*; *TR* 3a, .26*; no. of dif. *TR*, −.25*; *SR* 1, −.25*.

Table 17. (Continued)

Personality factors	Meaning variables
Factor 21	*Dim* 4a, −.35**; *Dim* 4b, −.28*; *Dim* 4a + b, −.26*; *Dim* 11, −.29*; *Dim* 14, −.27*; *Dim* 16, −.35**; *Dim* 19b, .23*; *Dim* 20b, .29*; *Dim* 20a + b, −.26*; *Dim* 21a, .26*; *Dim* 22a, .28*; *Dim* 22b, .26*; *Dim* 22a + b, .32**; *TR* 3b, .39***; *TR* 3a + b + c, .27*; *TR* 4b, .38***; *TR* 4c, .25*; *TR* 4a + b + c + d, .26*; no. of dif. *TR*, −.24*; *SR* 2, .26*; *SR* 7, .28*; *SR* 9, .31**; *SR* 10, .23*.
Factor 22	*Dim* 16, −.48***; *Dim* 19b, −.27*; (19b$_8$, −.23*); *Dim* 20b, −.28*; *Dim* 20a + b, −.26*; *Dim* 21a, −.36**; *Dim* 22a, −.31**; *Dim* 22a + b, −.25*; *TR* 1a + b, .24*; *TR* 2c, .24*; *TR* 3a, −.28*; *TR* 4b, −.25*.
Factor 23	*Dim* 4b, −.26*; *Dim* 8a, .28*; *Dim* 8b, .23*; *Dim* 8a + b, .24*; *Dim* 10, .23*; (19a$_2$, −.25*; 19a$_6$, −.23*); *TR* 4c, .45**; *SR* 3, −.25*.
Factor 24	*Dim* 10, .23*; *Dim* 13, −.24*; *Dim* 15, .25*; *Dim* 16, −.23*; *Dim* 17a + b, .24*; *Dim* 22a, −.26*; *TR* 4a, −.27*; *TR* 4c, .46***; no. of dif. *TR*, .25*; no. of dif. *SR*, −.30**.
Factor 25	*Dim* 4a, −.24*; *Dim* 13, −.23*; *Dim* 16, −.27*; *Dim* 20b, −.28*; *Dim* 20a + b, −.27*; *TR* 1b, .25*; *TR* 3b, .23*; *TR* 3a + b + c, −.20*; *TR* 4b, −.26*; *TR* 4a + b + c + d, −.25*.
Factor 26	*Dim* 4a, −.25*; *Dim* 7, −.23*; (19a$_0$, −.24*); *Dim* 20b, .36**; *Dim* 20a + b, −.36**; *TR* 2c, .25*.

^{a}For the code of the personality factors see Table 16. The pattern of correlations with Factor 16 (Exvia-Invia) was not presented here because it was presented in Table 6. For the code of the meaning variables, see Appendix A. *FR* variables were not coded.
*$p < .05$.
**$p < .01$.
***$p < .001$.

Table 18. Distribution of Correlations of Cattell's Personality Factors with Different Meaning Variables

No. of correlations^a	Primary source traits ($n = 15$)			Secondary traits ($n = 10^b$)		
	No.	Percent out of maximum possible	Percent out of total of correlations	No.	Percent out of maximum possible	Percent out of total of correlations
Total	316^c	24.50		137	14.48	
With variables of dimensions ($n = 55$)	211	25.58	66.77	92	15.21	67.15
With variables of *TR* ($n = 18$)	65	24.07	20.57	34	17.17	24.82
With variables of *SR* ($n = 12$)	35	19.44	11.08	11	8.33	8.03

^{a}Distribution of variables in percentages: 64.71% of variables dealing with meaning dimensions, 21.18% with types of relation, and 14.12% with stimulus-referent relations.
^{b}Exvia-Invia (see Table 6) and Anxiety (S. Kreitler & H. Kreitler, 1985a) were included in the list.
^{c}This total includes five correlations with the variable "no. of meaning values," which is not included in the classification in the table. Secondary traits did not correlate with this variable.

him or her when conditions allow. However, the real test of our major hypothesis consists not in a sheer count of correlations but in their being related dynamically to the major characteristics known about the factors. Let us turn to a brief examination of the pattern of correlations with meaning variables characteristic of each factor (see Table 17).

Factor 1: The positive correlation with "Feelings and Emotions" (*Dim* 20a) corresponds to the findings that high scorers on this factor have "accessible emotions" and warm emotional responses and are concerned with interpersonal relations (e.g., are attentive to people and ready to cooperate and are thus attentive to others' emotional reactions; Cattell, 1973, p. 158; Cattell & Eber, 1964, p. 10). The negative correlations with "Judgments and Evaluations" (*Dim* 21) correspond to the findings that low scorers have a critical, judgmental attitude and emphasize ideation and evaluations (Cattell, 1973, pp. 159, 257). The schizoid tendencies of the low scorers may also be revealed in the negative correlations with metaphors and with the common referent shift variable of combining the referent with a previous meaning value (*SR* 5).

Factor 2: The negative correlations with "Sensory Qualities" characterizing the referent (*Dim* 19a), "Sensory Qualities" perceivable by the referent (*Dim* 19b), "Feelings and Emotions" experienced by the referent (*Dim* 20b), "Judgments and Evaluations" (*Dim* 21), and "Cognitive Qualities" (*Dim* 22) and with the types of relation of the personal mode (*TR* 3 and *TR* 4) correspond to the description of the low scorers as being "emotional," "showing general emotionality," "worrying" (*Dim* 20), being changeable in attitudes, evading responsibilities, getting into fights (*Dim* 21), being unstable and easily annoyed by external inputs (*Dim* 19a, *TR* 3), and being inclined toward hypochondriasis (*Dim* 19b and *Dim* $19b_8$) (Cattell, 1973, p. 258; Cattell & Eber, 1964, p. 12). The negative correlation with "Judgments and Evaluations" (*Dim* 21) corresponds to the findings that the factor is particularly high in psychopaths (Cattell, 1973, p. 161). Conversely, the different negative correlations may be interpreted as revealing the particular dynamics of maintaining ego strength (i.e., not being overly concerned with sensations, emotions, etc.).

Factor 3: The negative correlations with "Sensory Qualities" (*Dim* 19a and *Dim* 19b), "Cognitive Qualities" (*Dim* 22), and the exemplifying type of relation (*TR* 3) correspond to the findings that low scorers are expressive, unstable, easily upset, and hypochondriacal (with *Dim* $19b_8$, $r = -.40$), but in contrast to low scorers on Factor 2, they tend to use only the exemplifying type of relation (*TR* 3) and not the metaphoric-symbolic one (*TR* 4) as well; that is, they are less disposed to espouse predominantly the personal mode. "Contextual Allocation" (*Dim* 1), "Manner of Occurrence and Operation" (*Dim* 5), and "Metaphors" (*TR* 4c) were found to be high in creative individuals (H. Kreitler & S. Kreitler, 1983, 1989a; S. Kreitler, H. Kreitler, & Wanounou, 1987, 1988). Thus, the positive correlations with these variables and perhaps also with the referent shift to a combination of several meaning values (*SR* 6) as well as the negative correlation with the referent shift to a part of the input (*SR* 3) correspond to the findings about high scorers' being unconventional (Cattell & Eber, 1964, p. 12) and particularly creative (Cattell, 1973, p. 163). Perhaps the positive correlations with "Quantity" and "Locational Qualities" reflect the reality orientation of these subjects.

Factor 4: The negative correlation with "Judgments and Evaluations" (*Dim* 21a) corresponds to the findings that high scores indicate an unconcerned happy-go-lucky approach (Cattell & Eber, 1964, p. 13), are high in psychopaths (Cattell, 1973, p. 164) and even criminals (Hundleby et al., 1965, p. 319, reported the latter about factor U.I. 35, which correlates consistently with surgency as defined in Table 16; ibid., p. 318) and in individuals impervious to social suggestion (Hundleby et al., 1965, pp. 188–189, about factor U.I. 21 correlated with surgency). The correlations with "Actions" (Dim 4; positive with Dim 4a, and negative with Dim 4b) correspond to the findings that high scorers are active, tend to act out, and have a general physiological pattern of high activity (Hundleby et al., 1965, p. 191). The interpretation of this correlation is further supported by the finding that the factor is low in periods of low physical activity due, for example, to sickness (Cattell, 1973, p. 164; Cattell & Eber, 1964, p. 13). The positive correlation with "Cognitive Qualities" (Dim 22) reflects the cognitive alertness of the high scorers, whereas the negative correlation with internal sensory qualities (Dim 19b) corresponds to the hypochondriacal tendencies of the low scores (Cattell & Eber, 1964, p. 13).

Again, as in Factor 3, we find the combination of positive correlations with "Contextual Allocation" (Dim 1), "Manner of Occurrence and Operation" (Dim 5), and the exemplifying type of relation (TR 3) characteristic of creativity (Cattell, 1973, pp. 163–164). Of particular interest is the negative correlation with the difference type of relation (TR 2b), which corresponds to the tendency of high scorers "toward agreement responses (or, to be more precise, away from disagreement responses)" (Hundleby et al., 1965, p. 189).

An intriguing finding is presented by the negative correlation with "Temporal Qualities" (Dim 16). It is intriguing because it apparently contradicts the findings about this factor, that is, quickness (Cattell & Eber, 1964, p. 13), speed of social judgment and of perceptual judgment, and fast tempo in general (Hundleby et al., 1965, pp. 189–190). But the evidence is not unambiguous. Hundleby et al. (1965, p. 189) not only suggested that the speed of social judgment may be due to the tendency to agree, and that the speed of perceptual judgments was shown only on very simple tasks, but found this trait also to be positively correlated with another factor that is characterized precisely by slow speed and slower reaction time when the signals for the response are presented irregularly (Hundleby et al., 1965, pp. 318–321, factor U.I. 35). Further, high scorers have been described by others not only as "energetic" but also as "placid" (Hammond, 1977, p. 60). Moreover, this factor may also be involved in temporal qualities, when it is interpreted as assessing "long circuiting of ergic satisfaction" (Cattell & Eber, 1964, p. 13) or "the renunciation of immediate satisfaction in the interests of attaining relatively remote goals" (Hundleby et al., 1965, p. 322). This competing interpretation suggested by Cattell corresponds precisely to the negative correlation we found. The renunciation increases with age, when the factor decreases in strength.

Factor 5: The positive correlations with "Judgments and Evaluations" (Dim 21) correspond to the findings that high scores indicate superego strength, regard for moral standards, and conscientiousness (Cattell & Eber, 1964, p. 13). Also, the factor is particularly low in psychopaths. Despite lack of evidence on the point, the positive correlations with "Possessions" (Dim 17b) are to be expected of subjects who regard themselves as the guardians of manners and morals (Cattell & Eber, 1964, p. 13). The positive correlation with "Function" (Dim 3) corresponds to the findings that high scorers prefer efficient people to other companions and succeed at tasks that require a functional approach (Cattell & Eber, 1964, p. 13). The negative correlations with the exemplifying-illustrative (*TR* 3) and metaphoric-symbolic (*TR* 4) types of relations, as well as with "Cognitive Qualities" (*Dim* 22), are in line with this efficient, practical approach, which sets a premium on organization and concentration.

Factor 6: This factor is described as a temperamental trait reflecting "an over-responsive sympathetic nervous system," a high "autonomic activity level," and a "constitutional insusceptibility to inhibition" (Cattell & Eber, 1964, p. 14). This characterization corresponds to the finding that this factor was related to more meaning variables (39) than any other factor (see also the correlation with the number of meaning values). The positive correlation with "Action" (*Dim* 4a) corresponds to the findings that high scorers are "active" and responsive (Cattell & Eber, 1964, p. 14). The negative correlation with "Judgments and Evaluations" (*Dim* 21a) corresponds to the findings that high scorers are uninhibited, carefree, impulsive, and unworried about the judgment of others (Cattell & Eber, 1964, p. 14; Cattell, 1973, pp. 167–168), and that high scores are frequent in sociopaths (Cattell, 1973, p. 167). The negative correlation with internal sensations (*Dim* 19b$_8$) corresponds to the basic characteristic of the high scorers of not being affected by threats and danger signals. Moreover, high scorers are described as "thick skinned" (Cattell & Eber, 1962, p. 15) and were found "to remain relatively unaffected by distraction" (Hundleby *et al.*, 1965, pp. 166–168; for high scorers on U.I. 19, which correlates consistently with Parmia-Threctia, see p. 164), as would be expected from the long series of negative correlations with sensory qualities (*Dim* 19a). Perhaps their ability "to face wear and tear in dealing with people and . . . situations without fatigue" (Cattell & Eber, 1964, p. 15) is related to the negative correlation with perceivable "Sensory Qualities" (*Dim* 19b).

High scorers are described as careless of detail (Hundleby *et al.*, 1965, pp. 166–168), a characteristic that may be reflected in the negative correlation with the exemplifying-illustrative type of relation (*TR* 3). Further, most impressive are the findings that high scorers are good in mathematics (Hundleby *et al.*, 1965, p. 167) and in perceptual closure tasks, in logical consistency of attitudes, and in finding hidden words and pictures (Hundleby *et al.*, 1965, p. 172, Items 146a, 146b, 206, 65, 198, 170) (see positive correlations with "Structure," *Dim* 10); have a high ability to suggest classifications (ibid., Item No. 3; see correlation with "Contextual Allocation," *Dim* 1, and "Range of Inclusion," *Dim* 2b); and are not particularly or consistently fast (Hundleby *et al.*, 1965, pp. 172–175, Items 176, 288, 5, and 6a, b, c; see negative correlation with "Temporal Qualities," *Dim* 16).

Factor 7: Cattell and Eber (1964, p. 15) described the high scorer thus: impractical (negative correlation with "Function," *Dim* 3); "acts on sensitive intention" (see positive correlation with "Sensory Qualities," *Dim* 19a); "imaginative in inner life and daydreams" (see positive correlations with "Feelings and Emotions," *Dim* 20b; "Cognitive Qualities," *Dim* 22; and the metaphoric-symbolic type of relation, *TR* 4); artistically oriented (*TR* 4); "dependent, seeking help" (i.e., concerned with evoked actions; see correlation with "Passive Action," *Dim* 4b); loves dramatics and is "theatrical" (Cattell, 1973, p. 258) (see positive correlation with "Exemplifying Scene," (*TR* 3c!) and is "subjective" (see positive correlations with the exemplifying and metaphoric types of relation, TR 3 and TR 4, of the personal mode and with shifts to associational or unrelated referents, SR 7 and SR 10, that reflect the subjective shaping of the referent). Cattell (1973, pp. 169, 258) further emphasized that the high scorer has a "predisposition to emotional sensitivity," "lives by feelings," and "expects affection" (see the positive correlation with "Feelings and Emotions," *Dim*

20b); acts on intuition (Cattell, 1973, p. 258; see correlation with "Cognitive Qualities," *Dim* 22); and is flighty (see again the correlation with "Sensory Qualities," *Dim* 19a). To these qualities, one may add the slow tempo found by Hundleby *et al.* (1965, pp. 136–137; Factor U.I. 16 correlates negatively with Factor 7, p. 134).

Factor 8: The "withdrawn," "brooding," "suspicious" qualities of the high scorers (Cattell & Eber, 1964, pp. 15–16), as well as their "higher inner tension" and tendency to "dwell on frustrations" (Cattell, 1973, p. 260), are reflected in the positive correlations with "Cognitive Qualities" (*Dim* 22) and "Sensory Qualities" (*Dim* 19b) and in the negative correlations with the different sensory qualities of *Dim* 19a. Yet, the high scorers are not closed off from reality, as witnessed by the positive correlations with "Action" and "State." Their prominent tendency to project (Cattell, 1973, p. 169) is reflected in the positive correlation with the stimulus-referent relations that indicate reversal (!) and in the choice of referents loosely related to the stimulus. Further, the high scorer "declines to be generous in giving information to others in a test situation" (Cattell & Eber, 1964, p. 16), as is reflected in the negative correlation with the total number of meaning values.

Factor 9: The high scorers are described as nonpractical (Cattell & Eber, 1964, p. 16) and "easily seduced from practical judgment" (Cattell, 1973, p. 260; see negative correlation with "Function," *Dim* 3); unconventional and frivolous (Cattell, 1973, p. 260) and "indifferent with regard to existing 'good taste' and to what is generally considered appropriate or inappropriate" (Hundleby *et al.*, 1965, p. 313, about U.I. 34, which correlates with Factor 9, Hundleby *et al.*, 1965, p. 311; see also the negative correlation with "Judgments and Evaluations," *Dim* 21a); accident prone (Cattell, 1973, p. 171) and not concerned about possible consequences of actions or events (Hundleby *et al.*, 1965, pp. 312–313, 316–317, Items 711, 731, 732; Cattell & Eber, 1964, p. 16; also see negative correlation with "Consequences," *Dim* 7); emotionally oriented (Cattell, 1973, p. 260; "enthused, with occasional hysterical swings" (Cattell, 1973, p. 260; see the positive correlation with "Feelings and Emotions," *Dim* 20b and *Dim* 20a+b); creative (Cattell, 1973, p. 260); see the positive correlation with "Manner of Occurrence," *Dim* 5, and metaphors); having a rich and intense internal or imaginative life (Cattell & Eber, 1964, p. 16; see also the positive correlations with "Cognitive Qualities," *Dim* 22, and the metaphoric type of relation, *TR* 4); "absorbed in ideas," "interested in . . . theory, basic beliefs," and "enthralled by inner creations" (Cattell, 1973, p. 260; see also the positive correlations with "Cognitive Qualities," *Dim* 22); self-absorbed (Cattell & Eber, 1964, p. 16; positive correlation with *Dim* 19b but negative with *Dim* 19a), yet active (Cattell & Eber, 1964, p. 16; positive correlations with "Action," *Dim* 4). Notably, Cattell (1973, p. 171) emphasized that high scorers have "a greater intensity of images [*Dim* 19b] and ideas [*Dim* 22] relative to sensory stimuli" (negative correlation with *Dim* 19a). Perhaps, also, the high arousal level of high scorers (Hundleby *et al.*, 1965, p. 313) is reflected in the positive correlation with *Dim* 19b. Concern with internal stimulation could bring about increase in arousal (Study 1).

Concerning the approach to reality, Cattell and Eber (1964) wrote that high scorers are unconcerned with everyday matters, "are concerned with essentials and oblivious of particular people and physical realities" (p. 16). Yet, these tendencies are due to their emphasis on inner life and not to being unrealistic. Cattell (1973, p. 121) noted that they act within reality and, when frustrated, do not become unrealistic but increase their daydreaming. The meaning profile corresponds to these observations: there are negative correlations with the exemplifying-illustrative type of relation, which reflects concern with concrete instances and situations, in addition to the pattern of inner-directedness noted above. Nevertheless, the negative correlations with the distortive shifts in referent (*SR 2, SR 7,* and *SR* 10) suggest that there is no tendency to distort reality.

Factor 10: Cattell (1973, p. 172) wrote, "The pattern is one of shrewd competitiveness [positive correlation with difference, *TR* 2b; negative with similarity, *TR* 2a] in which personal gain often plays a role" (positive correlation with "Function," *Dim* 3). High scorers are analytical (correlation with "Range of Inclusion," *Dim* 2b); experienced, worldly, and realistic (Cattell & Eber, 1964, p. 16; negative correlations with two *TR* 3 and two *TR* 4 variables that reflect the personal mode, negative correlations with several shifts in referent variables reflecting distortion of reality, and positive correlation with the commonest shift in referent variable, namely, shifting to the previous meaning value, *SR* 4); cynical and hardheaded (Cattell & Eber, 1964, p. 16) (negative correlation with "Exemplifying Scene," *TR* 3c, which reflects dramatization); and shrewd and calculating (Cattell & Eber, 1964, p. 16) as well as "artful and devious" (Cattell, 1973, p. 260; positive correlation with "Consequences," *Dim* 7). The realism, coupled with the analytical and calculating approach, may underlie the "sophistication and deviousness" (Cattell, 1973, p. 179) for which high scorers are notorious. Further, in small groups that deal with problem solving, they are "rated high in keeping to the point" (Cattell, 1973, p. 172; see negative correlations with the far shifts in referents, *SR* 7 and *SR* 10); they have mental flexibility (Hundleby *et al.,* 1965, p. 167; see also p. 164 about Factor 10 and U.I. 19; correlation with "Manner of Occurrence," *Dim* 5); are not distractible (Hundleby *et al.,* 1965, p. 167; negative correlations with "Sensory Qualities," *Dim* 19a, and the different sensory subcategories); tend to be precise and calculating (Cattell & Eber, 1964, p. 17; Hundleby *et al.,* 1965, p. 167; positive correlation with "Quantity," *Dim* 14); are emotionally detached, "disciplined" (Cattell, 1973, p. 260), and "unsentimental" (Cattell & Eber, 1964, p. 17; negative correlations with "Feelings and Emotions," *Dim* 20); and have "a certain criticalness of others while maintaining a rather more complacent view of oneself" (Hundleby *et al.,* 1965, p. 167; positive correlation with *Dim* 21b and negative with *Dim* 21a). Further observations that correspond to the negative correlation with "Judgments and Evaluations" (*Dim* 21a) include the deviousness and the tendency "to cut corners" (Cattell, 1973, pp. 172, 260).

Factor 11: The findings that high scorers have high standards of conformity to rules and a strong sense of duty, emphasize judgments, claim that "people are not as moral as they should be," are "scrupulous," are sensitive to the approval and disapproval of others (Cattell, 1973, p. 260), and tend to feel guilty and not to be sociopaths (Cattell & Eber, 1964, pp. 17–18) correspond to the positive correlations with "Judgments and Evaluations" (*Dim* 21a). Further, the findings about their moodiness (the high scorer is "worrying, anxious, depressed, cries easily, easily touched, overcome by moods"; Cattell, 1973, p. 260) correspond to the positive correlations with "Feelings and Emotions" (both *Dim* 20b and *Dim* 20a, with a greater emphasis on the latter, as is to be expected in view of their tendency toward phobias). The trend toward internalization of problems, with the resulting overfatigue, insomnia, and especially hypochondriasis (Cattell, 1973, p. 260) is reflected in the positive correlation with "Sensory Qualities" (*Dim* $19b_8$). Again, the tendencies toward brooding and fantasy are reflected in the positive correlations with "Cognitive Qualities" (*Dim* 22).

Concerning the correlations with "Temporal Qualities" (*Dim* 16), "Quantity" (*Dim* 14), and difference (*TR* 2b), no direct validating information was available, so we used indirect findings reported by Hundleby *et al.* (1965) on objective factors with which Factor 11 was correlated to some degree. These are the factors Hundleby *et al.* named: U.I. 22, U.I. 24, U.I. 25, U.I. 26, and U.I. 35. According to the information about three of these five factors, high scorers on Factor 11 should be fast in responding, whereas according to the other two factors (U.I. 25 and U.I. 26), they should be, on the whole, slower. Thus, the finding is not quite conclusive. Concerning numerical ability (*Dim* 14), according to three factors, high scorers on Factor 11 should have low numerical ability (in one factor, the findings are ambiguous; in another, there are no data). Thus, it appears that a negative correlation with "Quantity" (*Dim* 14) suggests low numerical abilities. Finally, according to all five factors, the conformity of high scorers on Factor 11 (i.e., measured by suggestibility to authority and by a tendency to agree) should be low. The positive correlation with the comparative type of relation of difference (*TR* 2b) corresponds precisely to this expectation (see Study 2).

Factor 12: The high scorer is described as "skeptical and inquiring regarding ideas either old or new" (Cattell & Eber, 1962, p. 17). This doubting attitude and particularly the sensitivity to inconsistencies (Cattell & Eber, 1962, p. 17) may be reflected in the positive correlations with "Causes" (*Dim* 6) and "Consequences" (*Dim* 7). Again, the concern with "experimenting with problem solutions" (Cattell & Eber, 1964, p. 18) may be reflected in the correlation with "Causes" (*Dim* 6). Further information (Cattell & Eber, 1964, p. 18) indicates that high scorers tend to be interested in science (perhaps the correlations with "Material," *Dim* 9, "Structure," *Dim* 10, and "State," *Dim* 11, are relevant in this context), and in analytical thought (see correlations with "Contextual Allocation," *Dim* 1, and "Range of Inclusion," *Dim* 2b); often hold radical attitudes in social and political matters and are in general critical (correlation with "Judgments and Evaluations," *Dim* 21a); tend to be interested in the new (perhaps the correlation with the difference type of relation, *TR* 2b, is relevant); and on the whole are fairly realistic (see the correlations with the attributive type of relation, *TR* 1, and the small shifts in referent, *SR* $_{near}$). According to indirect information (based on the objective factor U.I. 28, with which Factor 12 is correlated negatively; Hundleby *et al.*, 1965, pp. 263–270), high scorers are nonconformists (see the correlation with the difference type of relation, *TR* 2b). The negative correlation with "Cognitive Qualities" (*Dim* 22a) may seem surprising at first but becomes less so in view of the observation that high scorers are "skeptical . . . regarding ideas" and "more inclined to experiment in life generally" (Cattell & Eber, 1962, p. 17). At least in groups, they "have a high participation count" (Cattell, 1973, p. 174; positive correlation with "Action," *Dim* 4a). It is possible to interpret the positive correlation with active "Action" (*Dim* 4a) and the negative one with passive "Action" (*Dim* 4b) as reflecting a combination favorable for the occupations common in high scorers: executives, directors, and politicians have to be both active and particularly attuned to actions evoked in others.

Factor 13: The major characteristics of the high scorers are that they are not concerned about social approval, conventions, and fashions and set themselves apart from the group. They "discount public opinion" and "go about their own way," having no need for the agreement or support of other people (Cattell & Eber, 1964, p. 18). These findings correspond to the negative correlations with "Judgments and Evaluations" (*Dim* 21b) and the positive correlations with the comparative type of relation (*TR* 2). The negative correlation with "Action" is not consistent with the described characteristics of this factor.

Factor 14: The major properties of the high scorers (Cattell & Eber, 1964, pp. 18–19) are foresight, considerateness of others, effectiveness in raising and solving problems, and the ability to set up a consistent set of standards (all these characteristics imply the positive correlations with "Causes," *Dim* 6, and "Consequences," *Dim* 7); conscientiousness and emphasis on social approval and "social reputation" (Cattell, 1973, p. 177; see the positive correlation with "Judgments and Evaluations," *Dim* 21a); a sense of structure that is evident in their mathematical skill, interest in science, and preference for administration (Cattell, 1973, p. 176; see the positive correlation with "Structure," *Dim* 10); emotional self-control (see the negative correlations with "Feelings and Emotions," *Dim* 20b); and a general openness to reality (perhaps it is reflected in the positive correlations with "Sensory Qualities," *Dim* 19a).

Factor 15: The major findings about high scorers are that they are unable to discharge their energies adequately in action and hence suffer from general imbalance and worrying (Cattell & Eber, 1964, p. 19). This conception corresponds to our findings of a negative correlation with "Action" (*Dim* 4a) and positive correlations with "Judgments and Evaluations" (*Dim* 21a) and "Cognitive Qualities" (*Dim* 22). These findings reveal the characteristic worrying and tension to be of a cognitive rather than an emotional nature.

Of the second-order factors, we will discuss here only Factors 17–21 because Factor 16 is discussed elsewhere (Study 1), and because too little independent and consistently replicated published information about Factors 22–26 is available so far.

Factor 17 (loaded positively on Factors 11, 15, and, to some degree, 8 and negatively on Factors 2, 6, and 14): Cattell called this factor "Anxiety" and conceived of it "as a product of mutually-interacting primaries" (1973, p. 185). The major characteristics of anxiety are traceable to the original primaries. This factor was found to correlate highly with a specific factor based on objective-behavior data (U.I. 24, Hundleby *et al.*, 1965, pp. 220–232). The negative correlations with "Action" (*Dim* 4; as in Factors 2 and 8) correspond to the findings that high scorers are inhibited in acting (through insecurity or high moral standards) and hence suffer from unreduced drive strength (Hundleby *et al.*, 1965, pp. 222–225). The tendency to espouse high evaluative standards (as in Factors 2, 6, and 11) is reflected in the positive correlations with "Judgments and Evaluations" (*Dim* 21) and corresponds to various findings; for example, the anxious were found to admit more common frailties or "sins" than the average, to be more severe in criticism, to be more critical in evaluating the performance of others, to adopt extreme viewpoints, to make better ethical choices in story completion, and to fluctuate less in attitudes (Hundleby *et al.*, 1965, pp. 230–232, Items 219, 116a, 116b, 133, 67a, 330, and 31). The positive correlation with "Temporal Qualities" (as in Factors 2, 6, and 11) suggests increased speed in performance. This implication is supported by many findings; for example, high scorers perform faster in forming objects with putty, in arm circling, and in leg circling (Hundleby *et al.*, 1965, pp. 230–232, Items 982, 270, and 269). Indeed, the greater speed is also implied by Cattell's conception of anxiety as being bound with a higher drive-state (Hundleby *et al.*, 1965, p. 225; see also the loading on Factor 15) and is consistent with other common conceptions of anxiety as a state of generalized drive (Farber, 1954) or of "heightened arousal and heightened attention" (Gray, 1979, p. 331).

Further characteristic features of the pattern are the positive correlations with "Sensory Qualities" (*Dim* 19b; as in Factors 2, 6, 8, and 11), which correspond to the hypochondriacal and self-centered tendencies. The positive correlation with "Feelings and Emotions" (*Dim* 20b) (see Factors 2 and 11) corresponds to the increased emotionality of high scorers; for example, they were found to be more emotional in comments, more fluent in associations elicited by emotional than by nonemotional stimuli, even more responsive to jokes, more susceptible to annoyances in general and to those involving ego threats in particular, and less willing to do unpleasant activities (Hundleby *et al.*, 1965, pp. 230–232, Items 205, 55, 595, 211a, 211b, and 366).

As might be expected, there were positive correlations with "Cognitive Qualities" (*Dim* 22), which correspond to the findings about the tendencies of high scorers (as in Factors 2, 6, and 11) to worry, brood, and emphasize the inner cognitive world in general, as evidenced, for example, in reporting more daydreams (Singer & Rowe, 1962). Finally, there are indications also of the tendency of high scorers to have "less acceptance of the reality principle" (Hundleby *et al.*, 1965, p. 231, Item 113); a negative correlation with the attributive types of relation, which probably reflect realism; and positive correlations with metaphors and exemplifying instances, which reflect a rather subjective approach. The preference for the personal mode and the deemphasis on the lexical mode seem to be characteristic of psychopathological tendencies.

Factor 18 (loaded on Factors 1, 2, 7, 9, and 11): The major characteristics of the high scorers (Cattell, 1973, p. 186; Cattell & Eber, 1962, p. 22) are an emphasis on functionalism and practical effectiveness (see the positive correlation with "Function," *Dim* 3); emotional coolness and control, as well as low concern with emotionality, thought, daydreaming, and the subtle relationships of life beyond the obvious (see the negative correlations with "Sensory Qualities," *Dim* 19b; "Feelings and Emotions," *Dim* 20; and "Cognitive Qualities," *Dim* 22—all of which are indicative of deemphasis on the inner world). More specific information may be obtained from data presented concerning Factor U.I. 22, with which Factor 18 is correlated (Hundleby *et al.*, 1965, pp. 199–208). The data show that high scorers on Factor 18 tend to have less fluency on emotional than nonemotional themes (Item 55, p. 206; negative correlation with "Feelings and Emotions," *Dim* 20b); less fluency when they talk about themselves (Item 143a, p. 207); fewer eidetic images (Item 79, p. 207); smaller reactions to threat stimuli (Item 95, p.207); larger recovery of galvanic skin response when relaxed from shock (Item 80, p. 206) and greater endurance of difficulties (Item 28, p. 206; negative correlation with "Sensory Qualities," *Dim* 19b); lower speed in reaction time and performance on most of the measures of simple speed, though not on all those that introduce an element of complexity, irregular warning, and so on (pp. 206–208; negative correlation with "Temporal Qualities," *Dim* 16); and less "action impetus," less involuntary muscle tension in the right arm, and lower fidgetometer frequency (Items 475, 78, and 83, pp. 206–207; negative correlation with "Action," *Dim* 4a).

Factor 19 (loaded particularly on Factors 3, 4, and 6): The major characteristic of high scorers is independence, manifested in action, judgments, perceptual performance, and so on. Specifically, the high scorer does not need support from other persons and is not likely to orient his or her behavior toward persons who give such support (Cattell & Eber, 1962, p. 22). The pattern of correlations with the meaning variables includes a negative correlation with "Judgments and Evaluations" (*Dim* 21)

Table 19. Comparisons in the Number of Correlated Meaning Variables between Groups of 16 PF Factors Defined in Terms of Different Criteria

Criterion	Groups		
Heritability index[a]	High $H > .40$	Medium $.40 < H > .30$	Low $H \le .30$
Means	17.86	17.17	14.57
SD	7.00	4.68	7.53
Factors (primary and secondary)	1, 4, 6, 7, 8, 18, 20	2, 5, 9, 14, 16, 17	3, 10, 11, 12, 13, 15, 19
Significance	$F = .36$, $df = 2/17$, n.s.; high vs. low, $t = .78$, n.s.		
Means	19.60	18.25	15.83
SD	7.70	5.06	7.40
Factors (primary only)	1, 4, 6, 7, 8	2, 5, 9, 14	3, 10, 11, 12, 13, 15
Significance	$F = .41$, $df = 2/12$, n.s.; high vs. low, $t = .82$, n.s.		
Rank ordering of heritability indices[b]	High (first eight factors)		Low (last seven factors)
Means	18.88		16.14
SD	6.88		6.90
Factors (primary)	1, 2, 4–9		3, 10–15
Significance		$t = .77$, n.s.	
Rank ordering of heritability indices[b]	High (first two factors)		Low (last three factors)
Means	15.50		11.00
SD	.25		3.61
Factors (secondary)	15, 16		17–19
Significance		$t = 2.15$, n.s.	
Characteristics of age trends[c]	Regular curve (increasing, decreasing, or steady)		Irregular curve (ups and downs)
Means	17.43		16.55
SD	9.30		4.85
Factors	2, 5, 6, 10, 12, 13, 19		1, 3, 4, 7–9, 11, 14–18
Significance		$t = .23$, n.s.	
Characteristic state of factor at age of subjects (20–30 yr.)[d]	Increasing		Decreasing or steady
Means	19.60		13.33
SD	6.38		5.37
Factors	1–3, 5–7, 9, 10, 14, 16		4, 8, 11–13, 15, 17–19
Significance		$t = 2.32$, $p < .05$	
Existence of factor from early childhood or later periods[d]	Factor present clearly and consistently in all age groups from preschool (4–6 yr.) to adulthood (18+ yr.)	Factor present clearly only in some age groups before adulthood (18+ yr.)	Factor present clearly only in adulthood (18+ yr.)
Means	14.67	18.17	22.00
SD	4.91	8.70	3.61
Factors	1, 2, 4, 7, 11, 15	3, 5, 6, 10, 13, 14	8, 9, 12
Significance	$F = 1.27$, $df = 2/12$, n.s.; first vs. last group, $t = 2.54$, $p < .05$		

Table 19. (*Continued*)

Criterion	Groups		
	High $H > .40$	Medium $.40 < H > .30$	Low $H \le .30$
Effect of different life events on factor[e]	No effect		Effect
Means	19.00		17.25
SD	10.82		6.06
Factors	1, 3, 6		2, 4, 5, 7–15
Significance		$t = .39$, n.s.	
Correspondence to factors identified in data of ratings in life situations (*L* data)[f]	High correspondence to factors in ratings		Low correspondence to factors in ratings
Means	18.56		16.17
SD	6.51		7.54
Factors	1–9		10–15
Significance		$t = .63$, n.s.	
Correspondence to factors identified in data of objective tests (*T* data)[g]	Factors with a correspondence index of 3.25		Factors with a correspondence index of 3.00
Means	20.43		14.88
SD	7.43		5.80
Factors	1, 2, 6, 7, 9, 10, 11		3–5, 8, 12–15
Significance		$t = 1.59$, n.s.	
Correspondence to factors identified in data of objective tests (*T* data)[h]	Factors corresponding to 3 or more obj. data factors		Factors corresponding to 2 objective data factors
Means	18.90		14.60
SD	7.56		5.18
Factors	1, 2, 4, 6, 7, 9–12, 15		3, 5, 8, 13, 14
Significance		$t = 1.31$, n.s.	

[a] The indices represent Cattell's summary estimates (1973), based on various studies (p. 147) presented in Table 25 (p. 147) and explained in pp. 156–190. Although Factor 6 has a stated heritability index of .40, it was included in the high-index group because it is the only factor about which Cattell wrote "may have to be revised upward" (p. 167). Also, in a ranking of heritability Cattell (1973, p. 188) placed this factor in the sixth position, higher than factors 5, 9, and 14, to which an index of .40 was assigned, too. H = heritability.

[b] Based on the rank orderings presented by Cattell (1973, p. 188) on the basis of studies by Klein and Cattell (1972). The original list included, in addition, three factors not assessed by the 16 PF. The ranking was split in the middle. The rankings for second-order factors were presented separately.

[c] The information was derived from Cattell (1973, pp. 149–178).

[d] The information is based on Cattell (1973, Chapter 3, in particular Table 10, p. 84) and Hundleby et al. (1965, Chapter 5). The age groups for which information is presented are 4–6 yr., 6–8 yr., 8–12 yr., 12–18 yr., and 18 to adulthood.

[e] Information is based on Cattell (1973, pp. 156–182).

[f] Information is based on Cattell (1973, Chapter 7) and on Hammond (1977). High-correspondence factors are those Cattell listed as strong *L*-data factors (i.e., Factors 1–12) in Table 35 (pp. 251–261); low-correspondence factors are those Cattell listed as weak.

[g] Information is based on the tables specifying the saturation of the 16 PF questionnaire factors on the 36 objective-data factors presented by Hundleby et al. (1965, Chapters 7, 8). Only significant saturations were counted. The correspondence index was constructed so that, for each objective-data factor, when the questionnaire factor was consistently saturated in the same direction in all cited studies one point was assigned; if it was so saturated in more than 50% of the cited studies, .75 point was assigned; if in 50% of the cited studies, .50 point was assigned. The index ranged from 2.00 to 5.75.

[h] Information is based on the same source as g (Hundleby et al., 1965). The number of objective-data factors on which the questionnaire factor was significantly saturated was counted.

as the most salient corresponding finding. Perhaps the negative correlation with the visual subdimension of "Sensory Qualities" (Dim 19a$_1$) is a contributing factor to the field-independence of high scorers (Hundleby *et al.*, 1965, pp. 164ff).

Factor 20: (This neuroticism factor is characterized particularly by negative values on Factors 2, 3, 4, and 6 and by positive values on Factors 7, 8, 9, 11, and 15; in addition, neurotics have higher scores than normals on the second-order factors of Anxiety, Factor 16; Invia, Factor 17; and Pathemia, Factor 18; Cattell & Scheier, 1961, pp. 39–49; Delhees, 1977.) The pattern of correlations corresponds well to these findings. The positive correlations with "Sensory Qualities" (*Dim* 19b), "Judgments and Evaluations" (*Dim* 21), and "Cognitive Qualities" (*Dim* 22) are characteristic of a general focusing on one's inner world, guilt-proneness, worrying, and introversion. The positive correlation with "Feelings and Emotions" (*Dim* 20) corresponds to the findings about the emotionality of neurotics, their emotional immaturity (i.e., they are described as "emotional," "changeable," "excitable," and so on and as having low scores on corticalertia or emotional maturity; Cattell & Scheier, 1961, pp. 66–67), their suspiciousness, jealousy and emotional sensitivity (Cattell & Scheier, 1961, p. 46). They are easily upset and excitable, a finding that corresponds to the positive correlation with "Sensory Qualities" (*Dim* 19b). Again, the consistent findings about neurotics' hypochondriacal tendencies (see loadings on Factors 2, 3, 4, and 6) correspond to the negative correlations with *Dim* 19b and particularly internal sensations (*Dim* 19b$_8$). The recurrent finding that the neurotics tend to turn away from reality (Cattell & Scheier, 1961, pp. 70–73) is perhaps reflected in a series of medium-strength negative correlations with "Domain of Application" (*Dim* 8a; turning away from people?), "Weight" (*Dim* 12), and "Sensory Qualities" (*Dim* 19a). The negative correlations with "Manner of Occurrence" (*Dim* 5) and the number of different types of relation (*TR*) may reflect a higher rigidity (as indicated by findings concerning U.I. 23, to which Factor 20 partly corresponds; Hundleby *et al.*, 1965, pp. 209–219). Finally, the most salient finding is the negative correlation with "Temporal Qualities" (*Dim* 16), which corresponds to a long and consistent list of findings about the relative slowness of neurotics in such different tasks as reading, tapping, memory, calculating, body movement, and perception (Hundleby *et al.*, 1965, pp. 69, 70, 461–467). Slowness is also prominent in the secondaries, like invia and pathemia, characteristic of neurotics (Delhees, 1977).

Factor 21 (characterized particularly by negative values on Factors 2, 3, 24, and 25): Validation of our findings is rendered more difficult by the inconclusiveness of the research results covering this factor (Van Egeren, 1977) and by the nature of our sample, which was so-called normal and not psychotic. The fact that the patterns of correlations for Factors 21 and 20 were similar in many respects (particularly for dimensions) supports Cattell's contention that both neuroticism and psychoticism are multidimensional phenomena and that psychoticism resembles, in some respects, normality and, in others, neuroticism (Van Egeren, 1977). Psychoticism, like neuroticism, has positive correlations with "Sensory Qualities" (*Dim* 19b), "Feelings and Emotions" (*Dim* 20), and "Cognitive Qualities" (*Dim* 22), which reflect an emphasis on the inner life (see also findings about psychotics' lower scores on the objective-data factor U.I. 25, Realism vs. Tensinflexia; Cattell & Tatro, 1966). The positive correlation with "Judgments and Evaluations" (*Dim* 21a) corresponds to the findings about superego strength (Tatro, 1966; Van Egeren, 1971, p. 661). Concerning "Feelings and Emotions" (*Dim* 20), there seems to be an inconsistency: the correlation with "Feelings and Emotions" experienced by the referent (*Dim* 20b) is positive, but with *Dim* 20a+b it is negative, a finding that suggests a slight negative correlation with "Feelings and Emotions" evoked by the referent (*Dim* 20a). This finding would perhaps indicate concern with one's emotions but lower concern with the emotional reactions of others. The objective evidence on this point is also contradictory. The correlated factors U.I. 21 and U.I. 30 suggest restricted emotionality, whereas Factor U.I. 25 suggests increased emotional tensions (Van Egeren, 1977, p. 661). Again, Tatro (1966, Factor 1) reported psychotics as apathetic, as having a blocking on affect, and as being characterized neither by overemotionality nor by isolation of affect.

A great body of data shows that psychotics are slow in reaction and performance, as would be expected in view of the negative correlation with "Temporal Qualities" (*Dim* 16; Cattell & Tatro, 1966, found psychotics to be low on Factors U.I. 16, U.I. 21, and U.I. 30, all of which indicate slowness; see also Tatro, 1966). Again, the negative correlations with "Action" (*Dim* 4) correspond to the findings about the action inhibition of psychotics (Cattell & Tatro, 1966, found them to have high scores on U.I. 17 and U.I. 33, both of which indicate inhibition; see also Tatro, 1966).

However, our most salient findings are the positive correlations with the exemplifying-illustrative (*TR* 3) and metaphoric-symbolic (*TR* 4) types of relation and the different shifts in referent (*SR*), indicative of a tendency to define referents deviating from the presented stimuli, mainly reversing them, overlooking their actual content, or replacing them with idiosyncratic, remotely associated referents. These findings are important not only because they correspond to what is known about the unrealism and subjective shaping of reality by psychotics, but also because they may explain why Cattell and his co-workers found that psychotics differed too little from normals and that only 30%–50% of the differences in clinical conditions were attributable to the standard personality factors (Cattell & Scheier, 1961; Tatro, 1966). Our findings suggest that the reason may be that the "standard" personality factors do not capture enough of the psychotic characteristics on the variables type of relation (*TR*) and shifts in referent (*SR*).

Our detailed exposition of the findings in regard to 15 of the primary factors and five of the second order factors demonstrates that the pattern of correlations with meaning variables corresponds in each case to the major findings relevant to the factor. In no case was a contradiction spotted (when the validation findings themselves were inconsistent, as in regard to time and speed in the case of Factor 4, the correlation was obviously in correspondence with only part of the findings). In several cases, no validation data were available (e.g., notably for "Weight," *Dim* 12, and "Development," *Dim* 18), but these meaning variables did not seem to concern major characteristics of the factors. These results fully support the major hypothesis of the study.

The second hypothesis was also confirmed. The number of correlations with meaning variables was higher for the primary than for the second-order factors ($\bar{X} =$ 21.06 and $\bar{X} = 12.45$, respectively; $t = 2.64$, $p < .02$). The differences were significant also for the means of correlations with meaning dimensions ($\bar{X} = 14.07$ and $\bar{X} = 8.36$) and shifts in referent ($\bar{X} = 2.33$ and $\bar{X} = 1.00$), but not for types of relation ($\bar{X} = 4.33$ and $\bar{X} = 3.09$; $t = 1.61$, n.s.).

Table 19 summarizes the evidence concerning Hypotheses 3–9. It shows that there were no significant differences in the number of correlations with meaning variables between factors high and low in heritability (Hypothesis 3); between factors with a regular and irregular trend across ages (Hypothesis 4); between factors affected or not affected by different life events (Hypothesis 7); between factors that correspond to clearly defined rating-data factors and those that do not (Hypothesis 8); and between factors corresponding to a larger an a smaller number of objective-data factors (Hypothesis 9). Thus, Hypotheses 3, 4, 7, 8, and 9 were disconfirmed because there were no significant differences. Hypothesis 6, however, was disconfirmed in another sense. The result turned out to be the reverse of the one predicted. The factors that were related to more meaning variables were those that occurred with clear manifestations only on the adult level. Hence, it is plausible that the novelty and change that the factor introduced had something to do with the broad range of meaning variables with which these factors were related. A similar assumption seems appropriate in regard to the findings confirming the fifth hypothesis: factors that were increasing in strength in the age range of 20–30 years were related to more meaning variables than those that were steady or decreasing. Again, the dynamic element may have played a role.

Finally, we would like to raise some more general points. First, the findings indicate the advantage of considering the whole pattern of intercorrelations of the factor with meaning variables when interpreting the score on some specific meaning variable. Take a negative correlation with "Judgments and Evaluations" (*Dim* 21a). In the context of the pattern of intercorrelations with Factor 1, it may denote a rejection of judgments and criticism in favor of an accepting and affective response to others. But in the context of the pattern for Factor 2, this negative correlation could be considered together with the negative correlations with "Sensory Qualities" (*Dim* 19a and *Dim* 19b) and "Feelings and Emotions" (*Dim* 20b) as indicating a deemphasis on the internal world of experiencing, which also includes subjective evaluations.

Second, our findings suggest the utility of considering subdimensions of meaning dimensions in order to obtain a finer grained characterization of an individual. Take "Sensory Qualities" characterizing the referent (*Dim* 19a) and "Sensory Qualities" that the referent perceives (*Dim* 19b). Table 17 shows that various combinations of findings are possible. Factor 6 is correlated negatively with both, perhaps indicating a deemphasis on the internal world of experiencing, and the same is true, though to a lesser degree, for Factor 2; Factor 4 is correlated negatively only with *Dim* 19b, thus indicating a deemphasis on one's own sensations but not on sensory qualities in general; Factors 7 and 14 are correlated positively only with *Dim* 19a, a finding indicating an openness to sensory experiencing that is not necessarily self-focused, whereas the converse seems to hold for Factors 8, 9, and 10, which are positively correlated with *Dim* 19b and negatively with *Dim* 19a. Sensitive discriminations due to subdimensions would have to be checked for generality in order to find out whether the effect is generalizable to other subdimensions and to domains of study other than personality.

Third, this study highlights again the important role played in traits by types of relation and shifts in referent. The point is demonstrated clearly in comparing the patterns for neuroticism and psychoticism (Factors 20 and 21). It is noteworthy that differences of major import between the two factors occur mainly in types of relation and shifts in referent. Psychoticism, but not neuroticism, is correlated positively with the use of all subtypes of the exemplifying-illustrative and of the metaphoric-symbolic types of relation (with metaphors specifically) and with shifts in referent of reversal and other loose connections (i.e., stimulus taken as label, a relation of association, or no obvious relation). These findings reflect major characteristics of psychotics in general and schizophrenics in particular: their affinity with the world of metaphors, their reliance on the personal mode of meaning, and their tendency to change features of interpersonally shared reality. It seems plausible to assume that the processes revealed by types of relation and shifts in referent constitute major tools for the implementation of psychotic processes in cognitive molar behavior. The types of relation indicate the transformations to which the meaning values are subjected, and shifts in referent reveal the transformations that underlie the selection of the referents themselves.

Different types of relation (TR) and referent shifts (SR) implement different personality tendencies. Thus, high scorers on Ego Strength (Factor 2; described as "emotionally stable, mature, faces reality," i.e., as sane and nonpsychotic) prefer mainly the use of the attributive types of relation, complemented through only one of the comparative subtypes, and they turn away from the use of the personal mode (negative correlations with both the exemplifying-illustrative, TR 3, and metaphoric-symbolic, TR 4, types of relation). Of the different shifts in referent, they prefer only the most standard and restricted grammatical variation of the stimuli. Thus, analysis of the types of relation and shifts in referent variables involved in this pattern has served to reveal the major mechanisms that enable these subjects to maintain their emotional stability and reality sense. Moreover, it also highlights their major limitations, because in view of the importance of the personal mode for creativity (H. Kreitler & S. Kreitler, 1983, 1989a; Lahav, 1982), the price of ego strength would seem to be lowered creativity.

Incidently, an emphasis on the personal mode that could be supportive of creativity is evident in Factors 4, 7, 12, and 21. In all four cases, objective evidence confirms the occurrence of creativity. Notably, in Factors 4, 7, and 21, the tendency seems to be toward artistic creativity. But in Factor 12, the only factor that correlates positively with both the lexical and the personal modes, there is evidence of scientific creativity (Cattell, 1973; Cattell & Eber, 1964).

Fourth, an analysis of the matrix of intercorrelations reveals that each of the meaning variables was related to personality factors. This finding indicates not only the personological implications of the meaning system, but also the broad basis of the 16 PF as a test. Yet, there are differences among the meaning variables. In the sphere of meaning dimensions, we may divide the variables (not counting additions of subdimensions) into three groups: those correlated with 31%–61% of the factors ($\bar{X}$ of the intercorrelations = 11.5, n of variables = 10), those correlated with 16%–27% of the factors ($\bar{X}$ = 5.2, n = 12), and those correlated with 3.8%–11.5% of the factors ($\bar{X}$ = 1.7, n = 7). The first group includes "Action" and dimensions focused mainly on the so-called inner world of the individual (Dim 16, 19a, 19b, 21a, 22a, and 22b); the second includes mainly dimensions focused on more matter-of-fact aspects of reality (Dim 3, 7, 9–12, 14, 15, and 18); and the third includes dimensions focused on aspects providing circumstantial information (Dim 2b, 6, 8a, 8b, 17a, and 17b). The classification is not perfect, but it is suggestive, especially because a slight indication of a similar trend is evident in the sphere of types of relation (the mean of intercorrelations with the types of relation of the lexical mode is 4.33, whereas with those of the personal mode, it is 6.86; t = 1.62, $p < .10$, one-tailed). The tendency common to the findings in both spheres is toward a slightly greater number of interrelations with meaning variables reflecting subjective experiencing. This tentative conclusion may indicate that emphasis on the more experientially toned dimensions and types of relation is simply a characteristic of the 16 PF or perhaps even of other personality assessment tools, too, and thus reflects a psychologists' bias. Alternately, their emphasis may also indicate a closer affinity or involvement of personality with certain sections of the meaning system than with others, because personality may determine these sections more than others or may be determined by them more than by others or may be reflected in them more than in others. To be sure, these speculative possibilities have to be subjected to experimental studies.

STUDY 7: DIFFERENT KINDS OF MEANING VARIABLES IN JUNGIAN TYPES

Purpose and Hypotheses

The Myers-Briggs Type Indicator has stimulated our interest for two main reasons. One reason was that the labels of some of the measured variables correspond so obviously to certain meaning variables. The indicator consists of four scales: Extroversion-Introversion, Sensation-Intuition, Thinking-Feeling, and Judging-Perceiving. The labels of the scales, as well as the descriptions of the information presumably provided by the scales (Myers, 1962a), strongly suggest the possibility that at least Sensation, Thinking, Feeling, and Judging correspond to the meaning dimensions "Sensory Qualities," "Cognitive Qualities," "Emotions and Feelings," and "Judgments and Evaluations," respectively. The other reason was some discrepancies that showed up between the description of the scales by Myers, which corresponds closely to Jung's conception of the types (Jung, 1923, 1953), and various findings concerning the scales presented particularly by Ross (1961, 1966) and by Stricker and Ross (1964). In regard to Sensation-Intuition, the Jungian conception emphasizes concern with the actuality of the stimulus versus enrichment through unconscious information, whereas empirical findings show that the scale assesses abilities in and attitudes toward intellectual activity. Hence, the unclarity concerns mainly the nature of intuition. Does it entail focusing mainly on unconscious components, as Jung and Myers claim, or is it a matter of interest in abstract ideas, as found by Stricker and Ross (1964)?

In regard to Thinking-Feeling, the Jungian conception emphasizes the dichotomy of rationality versus emotionality, whereas empirical findings failed to show any of the expected relations with intellectuality and revealed instead relations with attitudes toward work, business interest, and so on. In fact, Stricker and Ross (1964) frankly admitted that "very few of the variables investigated in the present studies or previous ones are relevant to an assessment of either the conceptual (viz. Jungian) definition of the item-content interpretation" (p. 639). Their conclusion that "the results for this variable are not at all clear-cut" is indeed fair. Similarly Ross (1966, p. 14) stated that "no interpretation" could be found for the scale.

In regard to Judgment-Perception, the Jungian conception emphasizes the distinction between reaching conclusions and gathering information, whereas empirical correlates suggest an interpretation in terms of careful planning versus spontaneity.

In regard to Extroversion-Introversion, the match between Jung's conception and empirical findings was, in general, good, and the main deviations concerned an absence of the expected correlations with interest in people and concepts and with abilities.

Discrepancies of this kind suggested the possibility of exploring the matter further by examining the patterns of interrelations between the scores of the Myers-Briggs Type Indicator and meaning variables. Strict hypotheses were replaced by a guiding question concerning the major interpretation of each bipolar scale: Are the implications drawn from the meaning variables correlated with the score compatible mainly with the interpretation of Jung and Myers or with the interpretation suggested by Ross and Stricker?

Method

The Myers-Briggs Type Indicator (Modified, Form G; translated into Hebrew) and the standard meaning questionnaire (11 stimulus words) were administered to 47 undergraduates (20 women and 27 men, 22–29 years old) in random order in group sessions on two separate occasions, three to four weeks apart, by different experimenters. On the Myers-Briggs Type Indicator, we used continuous scores rather than type classifications.

Results and Conclusions

The reader should refer to Table 20 for the correlations discussed in this section.

Concerning Extroversion-Introversion, the pattern of intercorrelations supports Stricker and Ross's conclusion (1964) that "this scale is, to a large extent, measuring extroversion-introversion as it is commonly defined" (p. 635). The pattern includes correlations with many of the meaning variables found to be correlated with Eysenck's and Cattell's measures of extroversion (Study 1): positive correlations with "Action" (Dim 4a), "Possessions" (Dim 17), and the attribute type of relation (TR 1a+b), as well as negative correlations with "Temporal Qualities" (Dim 16), "Sensory Qualities" (Dim 19b, and particularly internal sensations), and "Judgments and Evaluations" (Dim 21a). There are, however, three notable differences. First, Myers's extroversion is correlated negatively with "Contextual Allocation" (Dim 1), whereas Eysenckian and Cattellian extroversion is correlated positively with this dimension. This finding is in accord with Jung's and Myers's claim that introverts are concerned with concepts and ideas, a claim for which Stricker and Ross found no empirical confirmation. Second, Myers's extroversion is correlated positively with "Domain of Application" (Dim 8a and Dim 8b), which could indicate concern with people and objects (see Study 2) as was claimed by Myers and was not confirmed by Stricker and Ross, whereas Eysenckian and Cattellian extroversion is not correlated with this dimension. Third, Myers's extroversion is correlated positively with the number of meaning values, a finding that corresponds to Ross's finding (1966) of a correlation with talkativeness (and is not to be confused with the negative correlation with number of meaning dimensions found for Eysenckian and Cattellian extroverts). However, the differences between Myers's extroverts and the standard ones are minor compared to the resemblances in terms of characteristic meaning variables.

Concerning Sensation-Intuition, the pattern of intercorrelations lends support

Table 20. Significant Intercorrelations of Scores on the Myers-Briggs Type Indicator with Meaning Variables

Variables of the Myers-Briggs Type Indicator	Significant correlations with meaning variables
Extroversion–Introversion	Dim 1, −.41**; Dim 4a, .39**; Dim 4b, .32*; Dim 4a + b, .37**; Dim 8a, .37**; Dim 8b, .37**; Dim 8a + b, .37**; Dim 16, −.42**; Dim 17a + b, .35*; Dim 19b, −.46***; (19a$_3$, .31*; 19b$_1$, −.32*; 19b$_4$, −.36**; 19b$_8$, −.50***); Dim 21a, −.32*; TR 1a + b, .34*; TR 3a, .37**; FR 1, .34*; no. of meaning values, .34*.
Sensation–Intuition	Dim 1, −.32*; Dim 3, .44**; Dim 5, .34*; Dim 7, .38**; Dim 9, .31*; Dim 12, .33*; Dim 13, .36**; Dim 15, .32*; Dim 16, .31*; Dim 17a + b, .35*; Dim 19a, .37**; Dim 19b, −.32*; Dim 22a, −.35*; Dim 22b, −.33*; Dim 22a + b, −.33*; TR 1a + b, .32*; TR 2a, .36**; TR 4b, −.38**; TR 4c, −.33*; SR 1, .35*; SR 4, .37**; SR 7, −.39**; SR 10, −.47***.
Thinking–Feeling	Dim 2a, .41**; Dim 2a + b, .37**; Dim 21a, .45**; Dim 21a + b, .32*; TR 1a, .36**; TR 2a, .32*; TR 2b, .40**; TR 2c, .37**; TR 2d, .36**; TR 2a + b + c + d, .34*; TR 3a, −.38**; TR 3b, −.32*; TR 4a, .30*; TR 4b, −.31*; lexical mode, .37**; personal mode, −.34*.
Judging–Perceiving	Dim 3, .41**; Dim 9, .38**; Dim 6, .40**; Dim 7, .37**; Dim 8a + b, .33*; Dim 10, .34*; Dim 16, .33*; TR 2a, .35*; TR 2c, .36**; TR 2d, .35*; TR 2a + b + c + d, .34*; SR 3, −.42**; SR 4, .34*; SR 5, .40**; SR 6, .39**; FR 3, .31*; FR 4, .30*; FR 5, .34*; FR 7, .31*; FR 8, .33*.

Note. For the code of the meaning variables, see Appendix A.
  *$p < .05$.
 **$p < .01$.
***$p < .001$.

both to the Jungian conception and to the findings of Stricker and Ross. The scale is correlated positively with "Sensory Qualities" (*Dim* 19a), different meaning dimensions (i.e., "Function," *Dim* 3; "Manner of Occurrence," *Dim* 5; "Causes," *Dim* 6; "Consequences," *Dim* 7; "Material," *Dim* 9; "Weight," *Dim* 12; "Size," *Dim* 13; "Locational Qualities," *Dim* 15; "Temporal Qualities," *Dim* 16; and "Possessions," *Dim* 17) and the attributive type of relation, all of which indicate a broadly based interest in reality on the part of individuals high in "sensation," as claimed by Jung and Myers. The scale is also correlated positively with the similarity comparative type of relation (*TR* 2a), which may indicate a preference for the known, the familiar, and standard routine (Myers, 1962b, p. 18). Further, the scale is correlated negatively with "Contextual Allocation" (*Dim* 1), "Sensory Qualities (*Dim* 19b), "Cognitive Qualities" (*Dim* 22), and metaphoric-symbolic types of relation. These findings correspond to Stricker and Ross's findings (1964) that subjects high in intuition have an interest in abstract ideas (i.e., *Dim* 1) and show originality (i.e., *TR* 4), and they also support Jung's and Myers's claim that such subjects are attuned to the so-called unconscious (i.e., *Dim* 19b and *Dim* 22 indicate concern with internal inputs, some of which may be unconscious). There does not seem to be any contradiction between these two aspects of intuition.

Moreover, the findings correspond also to those reported by other investigators. Westcott (1968, pp. 122–123), too, found that intuitive subjects have higher scores on theoretical values in the Allport-Vernon-Lindzey Study of Values (see correlation with "Contextual Allocation," *Dim* 1); often collect less information in cognitive tasks (Westcott, 1968, Chapter 5; i.e., do not have high scores on "Sensory Qualities," *Dim* 19a, and dimensions that reveal interest in different aspects of reality); are concerned with internal processes such as daydreaming and thinking about abstract problems (Westcott, 1968, pp. 130–131; see correlations with "Cognitive Qualities," *Dim* 22 and "Sensory Qualities," *Dim* 19b); and have an interest in art (Westcott, 1968, p. 126; see correlations with metaphoric-symbolic types of relation).

Further, our findings indicate additional tendencies of intuitive subjects, some of which have been confirmed in independent research. Intuitive subjects were found to favor risky decisions (Westcott, 1968, pp. 125, 127). Correspondingly, we found that "Consequences" (*Dim* 7) is positively correlated with "sensation" and may be expected to be low when intuition is high. Again, intuitive subjects admitted more often than others that they were less concerned with practical outcomes (Westcott, 1968, p. 130). Correspondingly, we found that, in addition to "Consequences" (*Dim* 7), "Function" (*Dim* 3) is also positively correlated with "sensation" and may be expected to be low when intuition is high. Another characteristic finding is that intuitive subjects do not follow explicit regulations and procedures in tackling cognitive problems and may stray from the task at hand in a manner that seems unaccountable to outside observers and often to themselves, too (Westcott, 1961, 1968, Chapters 1–4). It is plausible that our findings about how subjects high in intuition cope with referents highlight some of the mechanisms implementing these tendencies as well as the famous "intuitive leaps." Specifically, we found that intuitive subjects tend to use referents that are removed from the presented stimuli and previous responses (see, on the one hand, the high frequency of shifts to referents related merely by association, *SR* 7, or unrelated to previous referents, *SR* 10, both of which reflect deviations from the presented stimuli, and, on the other hand, the low frequency of no shift, *SR* 1, and using the previous meaning value as referent, *SR* 4, both of which reflect sticking to the presented stimuli).

In view of Jung's claim that "sensation" and "intuition" are complementary, it is of particular interest to note that the scale is correlated positively with "Sensory Qualities" of the referent (*Dim* 19a) and negatively with "Sensory Qualities" perceived by the referent (*Dim* 19b). This finding highlights an important facet of the complementarity. Another less prominent facet concerns the attributive type of relation, which is more characteristic of "sensation," and the metaphoric-symbolic type of relation, which is more characteristic of "intuition."

Concerning Thinking-Feeling, the pattern of intercorrelations with meaning variables indicates that the two poles of this scale differ primarily in the modes of meaning. "Thinking" is mainly a matter of focusing on the lexical mode of meaning, whereas "feeling" is mainly a matter of focusing on the personal mode of meaning. This finding does not contradict the Jungian claim that the differences are mainly in the mode of processing information, and it explains why Stricker and Ross failed to find relevant correlates for the scale. As the scale primarily assesses modes of meaning that cut across different domains of content and types of input, it is plausible to expect no (or marginal) correlations with variables that capitalize on contents. Notably, the two meaning dimensions correlated positively with this scale support Jung's claim about the analytic "Range of Inclusion" (*Dim* 2a) and judgmental "Judgments and Evaluations" (*Dim* 21a) approach characteristic of subjects high in "thinking."

Judging-Perceiving is the only one of the scores correlated with all four kinds of meaning variables. Again, the evidence supports both claims to some extent. The findings confirm Myers's suggestion that "judging" assesses the tendency to reach conclusions (positive correlation with "Consequences," *Dim* 7) and also Stricker and Ross's findings indicating a concern with planned orderly performance versus more spontaneous activity (positive correlations with "Causes," *Dim* 6, "Structure," *Dim* 10, and "Temporal Qualities," *Dim* 16). It is of interest to note that the correlations of judging with forms of relation seem to reflect tendencies toward cautious (mixed positive and negative, *FR* 3), carefully selected statements (double negative, *FR* 7; combined positive and negative, *FR* 8) that take account of different alternatives (conjunctive, *FR* 4; disjunctive, *FR* 5). In general, judging seems to be related to a practical orientation (positive correlations with "Function," *Dim* 3, and "Material," *Dim* 9), concern with structure (see in Table 20 the positive correlation with "Structure," *Dim* 10; Myers, 1962b, too, found a positive correlation between this scale and a scale of tolerance for complexity), preference for comparisons (positive correlations with the comparative types of relation, *TR* 2a+b+c+d, especially those of similarity, *TR* 2a, and complementarity, *TR* 2c), and a realistic approach (positive correlations with the variables indicating slight shifts of referent to previous meaning values, *SR* 4; combining the input with the previous meaning value, *SR* 5; or combining several meaning values, *SR* 6). Notably, Stricker and Ross (1964) found—and it seemed inexplicable to them—that this scale "is measuring something akin to prudence" (p. 641). It appears that the practical orientation, the realistic approach, and the cautiously balanced judgments based on comparisons spell out the necessary underpinning for "prudence." However, there is no evidence in our data for Myers's claim (1962b) that subjects low in Judging, i.e., high in Perceiving, focus mainly on satisfying curiosity and gathering information.

In sum, the findings of the study lent support to interpretations of the scales suggested both by Jung and Myers and by Stricker and Ross. In some cases, both interpretations were supported, as in regard to intuition, which was shown to be related to concern with abstract ideas, as claimed by Stricker and Ross, and to concern with internal processes, as claimed by Jung and Myers. In other cases, our findings confirmed and extended results reported by Stricker and Ross as "inexplicable" (e.g., the "prudence" characteristic of "judging"). In most cases of discrepancy between the conceptual interpretation (by Jung and Myers) and the empirical interpretation (by Stricker and Ross), our findings showed that it was justified to extend the empirical interpretation along the lines indicated by Jung and Myers. Incidentally, the findings show that, in most cases, the labels of the scales are not reflected in correlations with the meaning dimensions apparently corresponding to them (the exception is "sensation," which correlates with "Sensory Qualities," among other variables).

Our findings also shed light on some new aspects of the Myers-Briggs Type Indicator. In particular, they showed that Thinking-Feeling differs from the other scales because it assesses primarily the differences between the lexical and the personal modes of meaning, whereas the other scales focus primarily on other variables of meaning. Further, our findings revealed specific facets of complementarity between sensation and intuition. Yet, most important, the study showed that meaning provides a common framework for representing the dynamics of the different scores of the Myers-Briggs Type Indicator and hence makes it possible to compare them both with each other and with other correlates in the same meaningful terms.

STUDY 8: MEANING AND THE CONSTELLATION OF APPROVAL MOTIVE, EGO STRENGTH, AND ANALITY[5]

Purpose and Hypotheses

The purpose of this study was to explore the meaning pattern underlying the triad of personality variables—the approval motive, ego strength, and anality—in an attempt to uncover some of their common dynamics. We chose to focus on these three variables because they represent related, though distinct, aspects of a tendency the manifestations of which include, among other things, acquiescence, submission, conformity, "yea-saying" in questionnaires, and attainment of high scores on social-desirability measures. Hence its importance in the different domains of personality theory, social psychology, and research methodology.

The core of the issue is represented by the approval motive, which has been variously conceptualized as a statistically bothersome response style, a need, a defense, or a personality trait (Crowne, 1979, Chapter 6; Strickland, 1977a). Ego strength (Barron, 1953) is a variable that started out independently of the approval motive but has often come to be related to it to the point of actual identification by some (Megargee, 1966, p. 211). Jackson and Messick (1962) found that ego strength was highly loaded on the two primary factors of the response styles they identified in both normal and psychopathological samples as "acquiescence" and endorsement of desirable item content. In their classical study on the agreeing response set, Couch and Keniston (1960) found that ego functioning and ego intergration were basic variables differentiating between yea-sayers and nay-sayers. It was these two investigators who also generated the relation between the approval motive or social-desirability variable and anality. They not only found the two to be related but suggested that anality, or rather the unsuccessful resolution of the anal issue, lies at the core of yea-saying. They speculated that yea-sayers have not acquired impulse control and hence are more impulsive, need external guidance, and have weaker egos.

This suggestion is fully in accord with the psychoanalytic portrayal of the "anal character" as being anxious about displeasing, initially, the parents by relaxing control of the anal sphincter and, later, authority figures in general by being disobedient and aggressive (Abraham, 1927; Fenichel, 1945; Ferenczi, 1955; Freud, 1938, 1950). There are also research findings that suggest that anal subjects lack confidence in their judgments, remain indecisive, and try to avoid specific commitments (Gordon, 1966, 1967). These tendencies, too, would support a yea-saying response. However, the psychoanalytic position is not entirely clear on this point. It is claimed that there is in anality an underlying resentment against control by others that may be expressed overtly or covertly in the form of negativism and stubbornness. It has even been suggested that there may be an anal-compliant and an anal-rebellious character. Again, some research findings support the negativistic stance of anal characters (e.g., Bishop, 1967). In any case, anality is related to yea-saying or nay-saying and probably most often positively to the former.

Finally, because, following psychoanalytic teachings, the anal period is the age during which the ego develops as an independent agent, anality and ego strength are obviously related.

[5]Thanks are due to Talma Lobel who has kindly made available to us the data of the subjects' scores on the approval motive, ego strength, and anality scales.

In view of these tight theoretical and empirical interrelations among the three concepts, our general hypothesis was that the three concepts would share a core of common interrelations with meaning variables and that these common interrelations would shed light on the underlying dynamics of the approval motive. However, because the three concepts are not identical, each would have its specific interrelations with meaning variables, and these, too, should make sense in view of the available information about that variable. Thus, this study was designed also to illustrate the use of the meaning system to tease out the dynamics common to several variables.

Our specific hypotheses about the meaning variables that would be related to all three constructs and those that would be related to only one of the constructs were shaped in line with the major previous findings about these constructs. These findings led us to expect that the two meaning variables that lie at the common core of interrelations would be the meaning dimensions "Feelings and Emotions" (*Dim* 20, a and/or b) and "Cognitive Qualities" (*Dim* 22, a and/or b). Concerning "Feelings and Emotions" (*Dim* 20), we expected this dimension to be correlated positively with the approval motive and anality, and negatively with ego strength. The rationale was findings about the relative lack of emotional control (*Dim* 20b) and the strong preoccupation with evoked emotional responses (*Dim* 20a) characteristic of high scorers on the approval motive and anality (Couch & Keniston, 1960; Crowne, 1979, pp.169–173) and the relatively low emotional tone, absence of fear and anxiety, and emphasis on poise and control characteristic of high scorers on ego strength (Barron, 1953, pp. 328–329). Concerning "Cognitive Qualities" (*Dim* 22), we expected this dimension to be correlated negatively with the approval motive and ego strength and to be correlated positively with anality because low scorers on approval and ego strength and high scorers on anality were found to be concerned with their internal world and with brooding and worrying (Barron, 1953, p. 328; Couch & Keniston, 1960; Crowne, 1979, pp. 169–172).

Further, we expected several intercorrelations specific to each of the examined concepts. First, we expected that the approval motive would be correlated negatively with "Judgments and Evaluations" (*Dim* 21b); second hypothesis) because high scorers on the approval motive readily change their attitudes in line with persuasive efforts of others, "responding uncritically to arguments and to reinforcing comments" (Crowne, 1979, p. 167), and because they endorse so easily positive but improbable items and reject negative but probable items (Crowne, 1979, pp. 157–158).

Second, we expected anality to be correlated with "State" (*Dim* 11), "Possessions" (*Dim* 17b), "Temporal Qualities" (*Dim* 16), and "Quantity" (*Dim* 14; third hypothesis) because, following psychoanalytic claims, anal characters are expected to be concerned with cleanliness, belongings, punctuality, and precise measurements, respectively. Specifically, we expected all these correlations to be positive, although psychoanalytic sources suggest that, because of reaction formation, these correlations could also be negative. Our rationale for expecting positive correlations was, first, the frequent claim in the psychoanalytic literature that the restrained, orderly, clean, and thrifty "anal personality" is found more frequently than its mirror image, the sloppy, disorderly, dirty, and spendthrift anal character. Second, different experimental studies of the anal character indicate that commonly studied anal subjects react positively to monetary rewards (Bishop, 1967), more than to other rewards (Noblin, 1962; Timmons & Noblin, 1963) and, on the whole, tend toward cleanliness and orderliness (Carpenter, 1965; Rapaport, 1963). Specifically concerning the relation to time, we also expected a positive correlation because anal subjects have been shown to have a saving attitude toward time and to overestimate the time it took them to fill out a questionnaire (Campos, 1963, 1966). We expected that anal subjects, who are concerned about not wasting time, would tend to perform speedily. Hence, anality would be correlated positively with "Temporal Qualities" (*Dim* 16), which was found (e.g., in Studies 1 and 6) to indicate speed in performance.

Third, we expected ego strength to be correlated negatively with "Sensory Qualities" (*Dim* 19b), particularly with internal sensations (19b$_8$), and with "Judgments and Evaluations" (*Dim* 21b; fourth hypothesis). The reason for the former was that high scorers may be expected to disregard sensory experiences in line with the definition of the trait as well as with the manifest content of at least 10 of the items on Barron's (1953) ego strength scale. In addition, high scorers on ego strength have been found to score particularly low on hypochondriasis (Barron, 1953), which is correlated positively with "Sensory Qualities" (*Dim* 19b) and particularly with internal sensations (*Dim* 19b; see Studies 6 and 10). Further, we expected a negative correlation with "Judgments and Evaluations" (*Dim* 21b) because many of the items on the scale suggest that high scorers tend to endorse moral permissiveness, and because high scorers have been found to be undogmatic, scoring high on tolerance scales and low on ethnocentrism and authoritarianism (Barron, 1953). Studies 2 and 13 indicate that tolerance is related negatively to "Judgments and Evaluations" (*Dim* 21).

Method

The subjects were 64 undergraduates (44 women and 20 men) in psychology and the social sciences at Tel Aviv University, in the age range of 21–32 years. They were administered, on separate occasions and in random order, the standard meaning questionnaire (11 stimulus words), Barron's ego strength scale (1953), the social desirability scale (Crowne & Marlowe, 1964), and Beloff's self-rating scale of anal character traits (Beloff, 1957). The latter three were administered in pretested Hebrew versions.

Results and Conclusions

The data were analyzed together because no significant differences were found between men and women in the three variables under consideration. The three variables were interrelated: anality with the approval motive ($r = .40$, $p < .01$); anality with ego strength ($r = .39$, $p < .01$); and ego strength with the approval motive ($r = .30$, $p < .05$), the latter being at variance with the finding of no relation between them (i.e., $r = .17$, $n = 39$) by Crowne & Marlowe (1960). Thus, the data made it possible to examine the common and specific interrelations of these variables with meaning variables.

Table 21 shows that interrelations with "Feelings and Emotions" (*Dim* 20) and "Cognitive Qualities" (*Dim* 22) actually form a part of the common core interrelations as stated in the first hypothesis. Specifically, the approval motive was correlated positively with *Dim* 20a (concern over the emotional reactions of others) and negatively with *Dim* 22a, whereas anality was correlated positively with *Dim* 20b and *Dim* 22a, and ego strength negatively with both dimensions.

Table 21. Significant Correlations of the Approval Motive (Social Desirability), Ego Strength, and Anality with Meaning Variables

Meaning variables	Significant correlations		
	Approval motive	Ego strength	Anality
Variables correlated with the three traits			
Dim 13	$-.33^{**}$	$.31^*$	$.36^{**}$
Dim 14	$.29^*$	$.31^*$	$.38^{**}$
Dim 19b		$-.41^{***}$	
Dim 19a + b			$-.31^*$
$19a_0$			$.27$
$19a_2$	$-.42^{***}$		$-.28^*$
$19a_4$			$-.29^*$
$19a_5$	$-.27^*$		
$19a_7$			$-.35^{**}$
$19a_8$		$-.33^{**}$	
$19a_9$			$.34^{**}$
$19b_0$			$.37^{**}$
$19b_7$	$-.30^*$		
$19b_8$		$-.53^{***}$	
Dim 20a	$.51^{***}$		
Dim 20b			$.47^{***}$
Dim 20a + b		$-.40^{***}$	
Dim 22a	$-.38^{**}$		$.47^{***}$
Dim 22a + b		$-.31^*$	
TR 2a			$-.41^{***}$
TR 2b	$-.48^{***}$		
TR 2c	$.37^{**}$	$.51^{***}$	$.30^*$
TR 3a	$-.38^{**}$		
TR 3b			$-.27^*$
TR 3a + b + c	$-.37^{**}$	$-.39^{**}$	$.29^*$
TR 4a	$-.45^{***}$		
TR 4b		$-.33^{**}$	$.35^{**}$
TR 4c	$.29^*$		
TR 4a + b + c + d	$-.39^{**}$	$-.40^{***}$	$.38^{**}$
Variables correlated with one or two of the three traits			
Dim 1	$.29^*$		$.31^*$
Dim 3		$-.31^*$	$.47^{***}$
Dim 4b			$-.41^{***}$
Dim 4a + b			$-.47^{***}$
Dim 8b			
Dim 8a + b	$.41^{***}$	$.35^{**}$	
Dim 10			$-.36^{**}$
Dim 11		$-.30^*$	$.53^{***}$
Dim 16	$-.52^{***}$		$.37^{**}$
Dim 17b			$.62^{***}$
Dim 21a	$-.37^{**}$		
TR 1a		$.42^{***}$	
TR 1a + b	$.43^{***}$	$.49^{***}$	
No. of diff. *TR*		$-.34^{**}$	
SR 5		$-.33^{**}$	
SR 9		$-.32^*$	

Note. For the code of the meaning variables, see Appendix A.

$^*p < .05.$

$^{**}p < .01.$

$^{***}p < .001.$

Yet, Table 21 shows that the common core was larger than predicted. It also includes interrelations with *Dim* 13, *Dim* 14, *Dim* 19, and *TR* 2, *TR* 3, and *TR* 4. The interrelations with "Size and Dimensionality" (*Dim* 13) are hard to account for because there are no validational data. The interrelations of "Quantity and Number" (*Dim* 14) with anality and ego strength are supported by other findings: the relation of anality to precision was noted by Freud (1938) and Abraham (1927), and the relation of ego strength to a robust reality-oriented approach was emphasized by Barron (1953). There are no comparable findings to support the relation of *Dim* 14 to the approval motive, but the result is plausible and fits in adequately with the overall image of the individual scoring high on the approval motive in a particular society.

The interrelations with "Sensory Qualities" (*Dim* 19) reveal a tendency to disregard sensory qualities and experience on the part of individuals scoring high on the approval motive and on ego strength, as well as a mixed selective approach to sensory qualities and experiences on the part of individuals high in anality. These subjects tend to be concerned with specific aspects of sensory qualities (e.g., visual), perhaps because the way things look plays a role in orderliness, but not with other aspects (e.g., smell or tactility), perhaps because these sensations are potentially associated with dirt. In any case, the negative correlation with *Dim* 19a+b is probably due to a tendency toward a negative correlation with *Dim* 19b, which reflects a disregard for internal inputs.

The interrelations with types of relation indicate that subjects high on the approval motive and subjects high in ego strength tend to deemphasize the personal mode of meaning, whereas subjects high in anality prefer it. The positive correlation of conventional metaphors (*TR* 4b) with anality is of particular interest in view of the psychoanalytic claim that the anal character is based on metaphorically substituting possessions and material goods for the original feces.

In the domain of the comparative type of relation, there are both similarities and differences. All three assessed tendencies are correlated positively with the complementary type of relation (*TR* 2c), which probably indicates a preference for complementarity as a smooth adjustment strategy. The correlation is particularly high in subjects high in ego strength. Possibly, concern with complementarity may be part of the secret of their smooth adaptability. This approach is supplemented in high scorers on anality by a deemphasis of similarities (as part of the obstinacy and rebelliousness syndrome?), and in high scorers on the approval motive by a deemphasis of differences (as part of their characteristic reliance on compliance and social desirability). Incidentally, it should not come as a surprise that, in the cognitive sphere, subjects scoring high on the approval motive have been found (Crowne, Holland, & Conn, 1968; Harter, 1975) to have difficulty in tasks of discrimination, that is, tasks that capitalize on the use of *TR* 2b (S. Kreitler & H. Kreitler, 1987b,c).

Concerning the interrelations with meaning variables specific to each of the constructs, the data show all the expected relations (third hypothesis) for anality (with punctuality, possessions, etc.) but only some of the others. Subjects scoring high on anality were found to be concerned with the state of things, functionality, possessions, and punctuality. These intercorrelations, as well as the emphasis on complementarity (*TR* 2d), show the sublimated tendencies of anality. In view of the psychoanalytic assumptions about the unconscious roots of anality, it is of particular interest to note the negative correlations with the sensations of smell and tactility. Again, the negative correlations may indicate an active disregard of the specified content.

Ego strength was found to be negatively related to *Dim* 19b and to internal sensations but not to "Judgments and Evaluations" (fourth hypothesis), whereas the approval motive was found to be related negatively to *Dim* 21a and not *Dim* 21b, as predicted in the second hypothesis. The latter finding is of particular interest because, together with the finding of a positive correlation with *Dim* 20a, it suggests a new interpretation of the approval-seeking phenomenon. What these individuals are after may not be the good opinion of others but the favorable emotional reactions of others. The judgments and evaluations of others are as unimportant to them as their own attitudes, which are therefore subject to change, if necessary, to attain the goal of pleasing others.

As in the case of the common-core interrelations, our findings show more specific interrelations than were predicted. Notable among these are the following. The positive correlations of ego strength and the approval motive with the attributive type of relation (*TR* 1) indicate that subjects high in ego strength or the approval motive are concerned with interpersonally shared reality. Further, anality was found to be correlated positively with "Contextual Allocation" (*Dim* 1) and "Function" (*Dim* 3) and negatively with "Structure" (*Dim* 10). The first of these correlations is in keeping with empirical findings showing that anal subjects perform well on tasks of abstraction, even in content areas related to anality and aggression (Carpenter, 1965), and that they tend to generalize (Gordon, 1966). The correlation with *Dim* 3 suggests a functional approach (see Study 6), whereas the negative correlation with *Dim* 10 suggests a deemphasis on structural whole-qualities that corresponds, perhaps, to the obsessive preoccupation with details, noted as being typical of the anal personality (Freud, 1938, 1950). Finally, the approval motive was found to be correlated with "Range of Application," which suggests (see Study 2) that subjects high in this need tend to be concerned with what is affected by some event and who is involved in a situation. Considerations of this kind seem natural, perhaps even necessary, to responding in line with social desirability.

To sum up, this study provided insights into a general procedure of analyzing pattern of interrelations with meaning variables and into the underlying dynamics of the three studied personality constructs. The general procedure consists in distinguishing between interrelations with meaning variables that are common to the studied constructs and those that are specific to each of them separately. In analyzing common interrelations, the unit is not only every single meaning variable but also groupings (e.g., the subdimensions and manifestations of *Dim* 19 and the different variables of *TR* 2) within the 22 meaning dimensions, the four types of relations, and the three varieties of stimulus–referent relations. These units may be expected to provide a broader overview. The analysis consists in comparing the direction and magnitude of the interrelations of the personality variables with the same meaning variable in an attempt to uncover the underlying dynamics common to the personality variables. The mere fact that the studied set of personality constructs is interrelated with the same meaning variable does not render this variable automatically important. But the fact serves to focus attention on the role of that variable, whose interrelation with the personality construct is probably not spurious, especially if this interrelation has been predicted or is confirmed through other validational findings.

This study showed that the magnitude of the correlation between two or more personality variables does not provide a good estimate of the number of meaning variables that would be involved in the interrelations common to the two personality variables. Though the correlations between the approval motive, anality, and ego strength were not very high, the number of meaning variables in the common core of interrelations seems to be fairly high, both absolutely (eight variables) and relative to the total number of variables interrelated with each of these personality constructs (62%, 57%, and 53% in the case of approval, ego strength, and anality, respectively). We also find it notable that the common-core interrelations involve both meaning dimensions and types of relations. All these observations about this method of analyzing patterns will have to be checked with other personality variables to determine their generality or uniqueness to the present context.

The major insights that this method provided were that the three constructs share some form of interrelation with a certain set of meaning variables, which includes *Dim* 19, 20, 22, 13, and 14 and *TR* 2, 3, and 4, but that they differ in the specific interrelations. Further, the patterns of interrelations with meaning variables indicate that anality resembles the approval motive and hence is a yea-saying, rather than a nay-saying, tendency. However, the patterns of anality and ego strength often present mirror images of positive and negative correlations with the same meaning variables.

An analysis of both common-core and specific interrelations allows for conclusions about the dynamics underlying each of the studied personality constructs (i.e., about major types of inputs emphasized and deemphasized) and hence about the operative aspects of the constructs. Briefly, basic to the approval motive are concern with evoked emotional reactions, deemphasis of external sensory qualities and internal cognitive reactions, turning away from the personal mode of meaning, limiting oneself to the lexical mode, and disregard of differences. Deemphasis of sensory, cognitive, and emotional inputs and disregard of the personal mode of meaning are basic strategies of maintaining the particular kind of ego strength assessed by Barron's ego strength scale. Finally, characteristic of anality are concern with time, state, possessions, an abstract-generalizing approach, and a functional attitude, coupled with an emphasis on emotional inputs and the personal mode of meaning. However, too little is known about anality as measured by Beloff's scale to allow an evaluation of the latter, somewhat surprising, findings without further research.

STUDY 9: CLEANLINESS AND ORDER

Part A: The Patterns of Meaning Variables

Purpose and Hypotheses

The purpose of this study was to explore the pattern of meaning variables related to the tendencies to maintain cleanliness and order. Information about this pattern was designed to enable the second and major part of this study, which focused on exploring relations between a trait and preferences for specific meaning values.

The tendencies to preserve cleanliness and order form a part of the syndrome of anality. In Study 8, we examined the pattern of intercorrelations between meaning variables and anality, but the questionnaire we used seemed to focus on a broader range of tendencies than those specifically involved in a concern with cleanliness and order. However, the results of that study, complemented by further suggestions in the literature (e.g., Abraham, 1927; Couch & Keniston, 1960; Fenichel, 1945; Ferenczi, 1955; Fisher, 1970, Chapters 18, 24; Freud, 1938, 1950; Schilder, 1935; Tausk, 1933), guided our expectations about the interrelations of cleanliness and order tendencies with meaning variables.

First, we expected the tendencies toward cleanliness and order to be related to more meaning variables than anality. The rationale was that the tendencies toward cleanliness and order are more specific than anality and hence would include specific elements in addition to the elements implementing the general tendency toward anality. It may be recalled that Study 6 showed that the primary factors that represent more specific tendencies are related to more meaning variables than the secondary factors that represent more general tendencies.

Second, we expected the pattern of intercorrelations with cleanliness and order to include many of the meaning variables found to be related with anality (Study 8). No quantitative estimate of relative proportion could be made. Instead, we assumed that the pattern for cleanliness and order would include at least those meaning variables that were related to anality in an interpretable manner, that is, that the relation could be interpreted and understood in view of the present information. Specifically, these meaning variables were the following: "Structure" (*Dim* 10), "State" (*Dim* 11), "Quantity" (*Dim* 14), "Temporal Qualities" (*Dim* 16), "Belonging-ness" (*Dim* 17b), "Sensory Qualities" (*Dim* 19a), "Cognitive Qualities" (*Dim* 22a), the comparative types of relation of similarity (*TR* 2a) and complementarity (*TR* 2c), the conventional metaphor (*TR* 4b), and the metaphoric-symbolic type of relation (*TR* 4a+b+c+d). These 11 meaning variables form 52% of the total pattern that included intercorrelations with 21 meaning variables. The rationale was that the interpretable meaning variables were likely to constitute the major meaning variables, which might therefore be expected to recur.

Third, we expected several specific meaning variables to be related to the tendencies toward cleanliness and order. These were (1) "Locational Qualities" (*Dim* 15), because orderliness may often involve putting things in their place; (2) "Judgments and Evaluations" (*Dim* 21a), because we assumed evaluation in line with standards to be involved in preserving cleanliness and order; and (3) "Material" (*Dim* 9), because we assumed that the material qualities of things are of importance when cleanliness is at issue.

Method

The subjects were 37 eighth-grade students in the age range 13.9–14.4 years (17 girls and 20 boys). They were administered, in random order in two group sessions, 19 days apart, the standard meaning questionnaire (11 stimulus words) and a questionnaire designed to assess tendencies toward cleanliness and order. This questionnaire included 15 statements referring to goals (e.g., "I dream about becoming more orderly"), beliefs about oneself (e.g., "I feel miserable the whole day if I know there is a spot on my shift"), norms (e.g., "Cleanliness is the most important virtue"), and general beliefs (e.g., "Most of my friends have very orderly notebooks"). (Concerning the four types of beliefs, see the cognitive orientation theory in H. Kreitler & S. Kreitler, 1982). This questionnaire was pretested for reliability (the internal consistency coefficient was .89) and validity (against information obtained from teachers and counselors familiar with the students) in another sample drawn from the same population. Responses to the items of the questionnaire were given by checking one of five stated response alternatives arranged in a continuum from 1 (low) to 5 (high). The score ranged from a minimum of 15 to a maximum of 75.

Results and Conclusions

Table 22 shows that the number of meaning variables related to the tendencies toward cleanliness and order was almost identical to the number related to anality (22 vs. 21). Thus, the first hypothesis was disconfirmed.

Of the 22 variables, 11 (counting the correspondences *Dim* 19b–*Dim* 19a+b, *Dim* 20b–*Dim* 20a, *TR* 4b–*TR* 4a+b+c+d, and *Dim* 17b–*Dim* 17a+b as half-point correspondences) corresponded to those found in the pattern for anality (hence 50%), and the rest were new variables. However, most of the correlated variables that corresponded to those correlated with anality were among those considered at present "interpretable" (they constituted 9 of the 11 corresponding variables and hence 82% of the corresponding variables, or 41% of the whole pattern). All of the corresponding variables except one (*TR* 3a+b+c, for which we have no explanation) were correlated with cleanliness and order in the same direction as with anality. Because "interpretability" indicates correspondence to independent findings concerning the trait, the high proportion of the "interpretable" variables lends support to the thesis that meaning variables correlated with a trait represent mainly its underlying dynamics. The 50% of corresponding variables were a close approximation to the 52% expected in the second hypothesis.

The 50% of the variables new in this pattern included the three variables (*Dim* 9, *Dim* 15, *Dim* 21a) that were expected in line with the third hypothesis. There were, however, additional unpredicted variables in this pattern. Of these, two groups seem interesting. The positive correlations with "Domain of Application" (*Dim* 8b and *Dim* 8a+b) suggest concern with a kind of conceptual order that differs from strictly locational placement, whereas the correlations with variables of referent shifts in terms of associations (*SR* 7), grammatical variations (*SR* 8), and from content to labels (*SR* 9) imply a potential for deviating from the conventional conception of reality.

Table 22. Significant Correlations of the Tendency toward Cleanliness and Order with Meaning Variables

Personality variable	Significant correlations with meaning variables
Tendency toward cleanliness and order	*Dim* 2a, .36*; *Dim* 4b, −.37*; *Dim* 8a, .35*; *Dim* 8b, .38*; *Dim* 8a + b, .34*; *Dim* 9, .39*; *Dim* 11, .63***; *Dim* 14, .33*; *Dim* 15, .52***; *Dim* 17b, .38*; *Dim* 17a + b, .42**; *Dim* 19a, .32*; *Dim* 19b, −.34*; *Dim* 20a, .33*; *Dim* 21a, .42**; *Dim* 22a, .39*; *TR* 2a, −.36*; *TR* 3a + b + c, −.37*; *TR* 4a + b + c + d, .39*; *SR* 7, .41*; *SR* 8, .39*; *SR* 9, .43**.

Note. For the code of the meaning variables, see Appendix A.
*$p < .05$.
**$p < .01$.
***$p < .001$.

Part B: Preferences for Specific Meaning Values

Purpose and Hypotheses

The purpose of this study was to explore the conditions under which a trait like the concern with cleanliness and order may be related to preferences for specific meaning values in particular meaning dimensions. The expectation that such preferences exist was based on the observation that some manifestations of traits take the form of particular verbalizations or actions that become characteristic of an individual (e.g., the miser who unfailingly asks, "What does it cost?" or the paranoid who may always glance over her or his shoulder to peep at "the enemies"). These observations also suggested to us the two factors on which the manifestation of such preferences may depend: the intensity of the trait and the presence of particular characteristic referents. Hence, our major hypothesis was that high scorers on cleanliness and order would tend more often than low scorers to use specific meaning values in communicating meanings. Our further hypotheses were that this tendency would be more pronounced in regard to referents that are directly relevant to cleanliness and order than in regard to other referents, and that the tendency would be more pronounced within the sphere of meaning dimensions that were found to be related to cleanliness and order than in other meaning dimensions.

Method

The subjects were 76 eighth-graders (32 girls and 44 boys) in the age range 13.9–14.4 years. They were administered, in random order in two group sessions (about 25 participants in each), 10 days apart, the questionnaire assessing tendencies toward cleanliness and order (see "Method," in Part A of this study) and a special forced-choice meaning questionnaire. The meaning questionnaire presented the subjects with eight referents (four related and four unrelated to cleanliness and order). After each referent, there were 10 separate lists, of 10 meaning values each. Each list referred to a different meaning dimension. The same meaning dimensions were used in regard to all eight referents. The 10 meaning values in the list of a specific meaning dimension remained constant across the eight referents. The orders of the referents, of the lists (i.e., the meaning dimensions) following each referent, and of the meaning values within each list were randomized across subjects. The subject's task was to check for each referent one meaning value in each of the 10 lists, that is, 10 meaning values in all. The instructions requested selection of the meaning value in the list that would best communicate the meaning of the term to an hypothetical other person; the instructions also emphasized the lack of connection between the lists and between the referents.

The four referents related to cleanliness and order (i.e., a drawer, clothes, a school bag, and a notebook) were selected as the ones that occurred most frequently in pretests in which subjects of the same population were asked to name the things or the situations to which cleanliness and order (or their absence) best applied. The other four referents (i.e., a curtain, a pocket, a room, and a paper) were selected because they had evoked the 10 meaning dimensions, used in the closed questionnaire, with frequencies comparable to those characteristic of the other four referents. The 10 meaning dimensions used in this study included the five dimensions that had been found to be most highly related (a correlation above .35) to the score on cleanliness and order (see Table 22 of Part A of this study; i.e., *Dim* 11, *Dim* 15, *Dim* 17b, *Dim* 21a, and *Dim* 22a) and five dimensions that were not related to this score (i.e., *Dim* 1, *Dim* 5, *Dim* 12, *Dim* 13, and *Dim* 16). The 10 meaning values in each list were selected on the basis of pretests in which the subjects were requested to write as many meaning values as possible about a certain referent in each of the specified dimensions. An attempt was made to include in the list only meaning values that could apply naturally to more than one referent (e.g., *small, light, clean, torn, is found in a house,* and *belongs to an individual*).

The scoring of responses consisted in noting how often the subject selected the same meaning value in regard to the different referents. An analysis of the data was done in terms of a three-factor repeated-measures design based on combining the designs for a multifactor experiment with the design for a repeated-measures experiment (Winer, 1971, Chapters 3, 6).

Results and Conclusions

Table 23 shows that, of the three main effects involved in the study, only one was significant beyond the .05 level. This was the effect due to the difference between referents related and unrelated to cleanliness and order. The significance of the other two main effects hovered between the .10 and the .05 levels. However, it is notable that, of the four interactions, only two were significant. Both include the two factors of strength of the trait and relevance of the referents. The double interaction shows that subjects scoring high on cleanliness and order tended to check the same meaning values more often in regard to referents related to cleanliness and order than others. The triple interaction, which was significant on the .01 level, shows that this tendency was stronger in the case of meaning dimensions characteristically correlated with cleanliness and order than others.

Table 23. Three-Factor Analysis of Variance with Sameness of Meaning Values
as Dependent Variable

Source of variation	SS		df		MS	F
Between subjects		13.73		75		
Within subjects		16.62		532		
A (score on cleanliness and order: hi vs. lo)	.112		1		.112	3.75 ($p < .10$)
B (referents: near vs. far)	.114		1		.114	3.81*
C Meaning dimensions: in pattern vs. outside pattern)	.111		1		.111	3.69
A × B	.114		1		.147	4.90*
A × C	.142		1		.078	2.59
B × C	.117		1		.087	2.90 ($p < .10$)
A × B × C	.152		1		.213	7.10**
Residual	15.750		525		.030	
Total			607			

*$p < .05$.
**$p < .01$.

Thus, the hypotheses were not confirmed, insofar as it was shown that the trait score alone does not have an impressive significant effect; but they were confirmed, insofar as there is clear evidence of the joint effect of the three factors.

The findings shed light on two related issues important in the study of personality: perseveration and characteristic features. Perseveration was shown to depend on the strength of the tendency, the relevance of the referents, and the nature of the meaning dimensions. Indeed, all three factors are anchored in the meaning system: the strength of the tendency can be assessed in terms of the number of different meaning variables correlated with the trait, the relevance of referents, in terms of meaningful relations of the referents to the main referent (i.e., in our case, cleanliness and order); and the nature of the meaning dimensions, in terms of whether they constitute a part of the pattern of intercorrelations with the trait or not. Perseveration has external manifestations that may impress others. Because repetition tends to be noted by observers, if an individual perseveres in the use of certain meaning values observers are likely to conclude that the repeated meaning values are characteristic of the individual. Hence, the recurrent use of the same meaning values by an individual may be a determinant of the impressions that others form of the individual's trait. Yet, the impression is not haphazard, arbitrary, or completely subjective. Insofar as the occurrence of meaning values is rooted in the individual's meaning system, there is an objective basis for the impression that others form of that individual.

STUDY 10: HYPOCHONDRIASIS, AVARICE, AND IMPULSIVITY

Purpose and Hypotheses

This study had two purposes. The first was to explore the patterns of intercorrelations with meaning variables of the three traits hypochondriasis, avarice, and impulsivity in order to extend the range of information about the meaning patterns characterizing traits, in this case traits whose assessment tools had been prevalidated against reports of friends and relatives. The second purpose was to compare the patterns of intercorrelations of the three traits with the meaning variables characterizing communications of the meaning of these traits. The comparison was designed to examine whether the pattern of intercorrelations corresponds to the meaning that subjects assign directly to the labels of the traits. The comparison is important theoretically because of the claim that traits are identical with observers' views (Cantor & Mischel, 1977; Stagner, 1976) and empirically because of the desirability of using one set of variables instead of two, when the two actually assess the same thing. In testing this problem, we used both the subjects who participated in the study proper and a further sample of subjects who were not administered the other tools of the study. This extension of the comparison to a further sample was designed to ensure that no effects from participating in the study would influence the subjects' communications of the meaning of the traits, and to obtain more reliable information about the common meaning of the three traits in the studied population.

The exploration of the patterns was open-ended, whereas the comparisons were guided by the general assumption that the pattern of intercorrelations between trait scores and meaning variables is not identical with the pattern of meaning variables characterizing meaning communications of the trait labels.

Method

Five questionnaires were administered to 72 undergraduates and students in a teachers' seminary (36 men and 36 women) in the age range of 18–29. These questionnaires were the standard meaning questionnaire (11 stimulus words), a separate meaning questionnaire that included as stimuli the labels of the three traits (hypochondriasis, avarice, and impulsivity), and three distinct questionnaires, one for each of the three studied traits.

There were 14 items in the hypochondriasis questionnaire, 15 in the avarice questionnaire, and 12 in the impulsivity questionnaire. The three questionnaires were constructed by the authors and were prevalidated on a different sample of 48 subjects against reports of friends and relatives. The latter were asked to rate the subjects on the following scales: "On the basis of your acquaintance with X, to what extent is she/he concerned with diseases? . . . stingy? . . . impulsive?" The ratings were made on a 3-point scale and were to be accompanied by freely stated explanations and examples. Only items that were correlated (by tetrachoric correlation) significantly with the criterion were included in the final questionnaires. All the items were of the self-report type and referred partly to beliefs about oneself (e.g., "When I hear about a certain severe illness I tend to think that perhaps I have already contracted it or may do so in the future"), partly to beliefs about norms (e.g., "A person should try to economize on expenses for personal needs"), partly to beliefs about goals (e.g., "I intend in the future to be thoroughly checked by a doctor once every six months"), and partly to general beliefs (e.g., "It is senseless to collect things because they are rarely used"). The four types of beliefs were included in the questionnaires because they reflect major aspects of the motivation to behave in specific ways (see the cognitive orientation theory in H. Kreitler & S. Kreitler, 1982). In each questionnaire, about half the items were positively phrased, and half negatively. The subjects gave their responses on a rating scale from 1 (designating "Untrue about me") to 6 (designating "Always true about me"), or in the case of three items, they checked one of three presented responses with predetermined scoring. The internal reliability of the three questionnaires was .88, .92, and .90 for hypochondriasis, avarice and impulsivity, respectively.

The two meaning questionnaires were administered in random order on one occasion, and the three trait questionnaires were administered in random order on another occasion. The administration was in group sessions (12–19 participants in each session), 14–17 days apart. About half the subjects got the meaning questionnaires first, and the other half got the trait questionnaires first.

A different group of 183 subjects (100 women and 83 men) in the age range of 23–30 years and of varied professions (students, teachers in schools and universities, police officers, shopkeepers, etc.) were administered only the meaning questionnaire of the three labels.

Results and Conclusions

Table 24 shows the patterns of intercorrelations characteristic of each of the traits. The major findings for hypochondriasis were positive correlations with "Causes" (*Dim* 6), "Consequences" (*Dim* 7), "Domain of Application" (*Dim* 8b), and "Sensory Qualities" (particularly internal kinesthetic and thermal sensations, i.e., sensations intimately involved with the body), and the negative correlation with

Table 24. Significant Correlations of the Traits Hypochondriasis, Avarice, and Impulsivity with Meaning Variables

Traits[a]	Significant correlations with meaning variables
Hypochondriasis	Dim 1, $-.25^*$; Dim 2a, $.24^*$; Dim 3, $-.27^*$; Dim 4b, $.31^{**}$; Dim 4a + b, $.30^{**}$; Dim 5, $-.24^*$; Dim 6, $.41^{**}$; Dim 7, $.63^{***}$; Dim 8b, $.38^{***}$; Dim 8a + b, $.29^*$; Dim 9, $-.52^{***}$; Dim 17a, $.28^*$; Dim 17b, $-.24^*$; Dim 18, $-.26^*$; Dim 19b, $.38^{***}$; (19a$_1$, $.30^{**}$; 19a$_6$, $.26^*$; 19b$_1$, $.27^*$; 19b$_4$, $.28^*$; 19b$_6$, $.35^{**}$; 19b$_8$, $.51^{***}$); Dim 21a, $.31^{**}$; TR 1a + b, $-.27^*$; TR 2c, $-.29^*$; TR 2a + b + c + d, $.34^{**}$; TR 3a + b + c, $.33^{**}$; SR 3, $.30^{**}$; SR 7, $.32^{**}$; FR 8, $.37^{**}$.
Avarice	Dim 4b, $.27^*$; Dim 7, $.37^{**}$; Dim 8b, $.45^{***}$; Dim 8a + b, $.33^{**}$; Dim 14, $.49^{***}$; Dim 17a, $.39^{***}$; Dim 17b, $.66^{***}$; Dim 17a + b, $.57^{***}$; Dim 19b, $-.33^{**}$ (19a$_0$, $-.28^*$; 19a$_5$, $-.27^*$; 19b$_1$, $-.35^*$; 19b$_4$, $-.43^{***}$; 19a + b$_4$, $-.40^{***}$; 19a + b$_5$, $-.31^{**}$); TR 1b, $-.25^*$; TR 2b, $.40^{***}$.
Impulsivity	Dim 2a + b, $-.27^*$; Dim 3, $.45^{***}$; Dim 6, $.24^*$; Dim 7, $-.59^{***}$; Dim 10, $-.26^*$; Dim 16, $.52^{***}$; Dim 17a, $.31^{**}$; Dim 17b, $-.28^*$; (19a$_5$, $.31^{**}$; 19b$_7$, $.27^*$; 19a + b$_5$, $.37^{**}$); Dim 20a, $.53^{***}$; Dim 20b, $.49^{***}$; Dim 20a + b, $.48^{***}$; TR 2a, $-.41^{***}$; TR 3b, $.29^*$; TR 4a, $.33^{**}$; TR 4c, $.30^{**}$; TR 4d, $.28^*$; TR 4a + b + c + d, $.29^*$; FR 8, $.41^{***}$.

[a]The intercorrelations between the traits were: Hypoch. & Avarice $.24^*$; Hypoch. & Impulsivity $-.20$ (n.s.); Avarice & Impulsivity $.17$ (n.s.). The means of Hypoch., Avarice, and Impulsivity were 18.38, 17.79, and 22.19, respectively. For the code of the meaning variables, see Appendix A.
$^*p < .05$.
$^{**}p < .01$.
$^{***}p < .001$.

"Material." Further, it is important to note that hypochondriacs preferred the use of the comparative and the exemplifying-illustrative types of relation but do not often use the regular attributive type of relation. The pattern of intercorrelations seems to be meaningfully related to hypochondriasis. Almost all authorities in the field have emphasized that hypochondriasis is a form of narcissistic self-love (Freud, 1925; Kellner, 1986; Ladee, 1966; Masserman, 1946; Schilder, 1935). Our findings show the manifestation of this narcissistic self-preoccupation to be an increased awareness of internal sensations. As there were no correlations with "Feelings and Emotions" (Dim 20), our findings do not support the claim that hypochondriasis is bound with feelings such as not being loved (Grayden, 1958) or demands for admiration from others (Alexander, 1948). But the positive correlation with "Judgments and Evaluations" (Dim 21a) is in keeping with or at least does not contradict the common thesis that hypochondriasis is bound with guilt, self-punishment (Fenichel, 1945; Horney, 1945), and inadequacy (Cameron, 1947), which involve evaluations of oneself in terms of some standard. In view of the frequently stated hypothesis that hypochondriasis involves a displacement of ungratified wishes of some kind (Freud, 1925; Ladee, 1966), it is of interest to note the positive correlations we found with the tendencies to define referents that represent merely a part of the input (SR 3) or that are related to it only by some association (SR 7).

One may attempt an integration of the different findings in the form of a hypothetical reconstruction of the processes typical of hypochondriasis. The hypochondriac seems to concentrate on the possible causes of a symptom, on its results (e.g., "I would become sick, lie in a hospital, etc."), on the attendant bodily sensations, and on the symptom's manifestations, noting minute details (TR 3) and differences

(*TR* 2), while disregarding the symptom's regular contextual allocation and attributive label (e.g., "It is a pimple"), as well as its manner of occurrence (e.g., how the symptom actually occurred) and development (e.g., the symptom's developmental course), which could help in identifying the somatic manifestations as harmless. Further, there may be a tendency to disregard a part of the phenomenon and to produce associations to it uncritically, with the result that another label is substituted for the common one (i.e., a negative correlation with the attributive type of relation, *TR* 1, and a positive correlation with the combined positive and negative form of relation, *FR* 8, which may be manifested, for example, in a conclusion: "It is not a pimple but some small tumor"). Of course, many of the details in this reconstruction have to be tested empirically.

In sum, the pattern of intercorrelations seems to reveal some of the mechanisms that may promote and facilitate hypochondriasis. This demonstration is also of interest because, up to now, hypochondriasis has not been empirically shown to be associated with a specific personality pattern (Kenyon, 1965; Ladee, 1966).

The major findings for avarice included the high positive correlations with "Possessions" (*Dim* 17a and *Dim* 17b) and "Quantity" (*Dim* 14), which correspond very well to expectations about this trait. In addition, there were positive correlations with "Consequences" (*Dim* 7) and "Domain of Application" (*Dim* 8), and negative correlations with different sensory subdimensions.

Finally, particularly characteristic of impulsivity are high positive correlations with "Feelings and Emotions" (*Dim* 20), "Temporal Qualities" (*Dim* 16), and "Function" (*Dim* 3), as well as specific sensory qualities (could it be accidental that smell and taste, in particular, occur here?) and the pronounced negative correlation with "Consequences" (*Dim* 7), which suggests increased risk-taking. These findings are intuitively convincing. Less so at present are the positive correlations with the metaphoric-symbolic type of relation, which need further exploration.

It should, however, be noted that this pattern of intercorrelations with impulsivity diverges from the one that would be expected with a different scale, such as the one developed by Kipnis, which we could not use because many of its items are culture-bound (e.g., Items 21–44; Kipnis, 1971, pp. 120–123). Hence, it should not be surprising that Kipnis (1971) found that impulsive individuals value material possessions (pp. 31–32) and respond less to emotion-arousing stimuli (pp. 36–39), whereas our results imply the reverse. However, concern with functionality is a finding common to both scales (Kipnis, 1971, Chapters 7, 9).

For the sake of comparing the patterns of meaning variables correlated with the scores of the three traits with the meaning variables used for communicating the meanings of the traits themselves, we set up lists of meaning variables used in the communications of the 72 subjects of the study proper and in the communications of the 183 additional subjects. The lists for each trait were separate and included all the variables that were used by at least 50% of the subjects in the group in communicating the meaning of the trait. The lists for the two groups (the 72 subjects and the 183 additional subjects) were combined because they turned out to be almost identical in the case of each of the traits (e.g., for impulsivity, one list comprised 13 variables and the other 11 variables, and 11 variables were common to both lists).

Table 25 shows that, for each of the three traits, the set of meaning variables used in communicating the meaning of the trait differs from the set occurring in the pattern of intercorrelations with the trait score. The mean percentage of difference

Table 25. Comparison of Meaning Variables Correlated with the Traits' Scores ("Pattern") and Meaning Variables Used in Communicating the Meaning of the Traits ("List")

Meaning variables	Traits		
	Hypochondriasis	Avarice	Impulsivity
In "list" but not in "pattern"	Dim 4a, Dim 8a, Dim 11, Dim 14, Dim 16, Dim 20a, Dim 20b, Dim 21b, Dim 22b, TR 2b, TR 3a, SR 8	Dim 4a, Dim 6, Dim 20a, Dim 20b, Dim 20a + b, Dim 21a, Dim 21b, Dim 22b, TR 2c, TR 3a, SR 8	Dim 4a, Dim 5, Dim 8b, Dim 11, Dim 19a, Dim 19b, Dim 21a, Dim 21b, Dim 22b, Dim 22a + b, TR 2b
In "pattern" but not in "list"	Dim 2a, Dim 4b, Dim 4a + b, Dim 6, Dim 7, Dim 8a + b, Dim 9, Dim 17a, Dim 17b, Dim 18, Dim 19b, Dim 21a, TR 1a + b, TR 2c, TR 2a + b + c + d, TR 3a + b + c, FR 8, SR 3, SR 7	Dim 4b, Dim 7, Dim 8b, Dim 8a + b, Dim 17a, Dim 17a + b, Dim 19b, TR 1b, TR 2b	Dim 2a + b, Dim 6, Dim 7, Dim 10, Dim 16, Dim 17a, Dim 17b, Dim 20a, Dim 20a + b, TR 2a, TR 3b, TR 4a, TR 4c, TR 4d, TR 4a + b + c + d, FR 8
In "list" and in "pattern"	Dim 1, Dim 3, Dim 5, Dim 8b	Dim 14, Dim 17b	Dim 3, Dim 20b
Total of variables:			
In "pattern"	24	11	18
In "list"	16	13	13
In "pattern" and "list"	4	2	2
Mean % of overlap:	20.8	14.8	13.2
Sig. of occurrence of overlap:			
In "pattern"	.001	.066	.002
In "list"	.050	.022	.022

Note. For the code of the meaning variables, see Appendix A.

between the sets ranges from 79% to 87%. Only a minority of the meaning variables is shared by both sets, and its occurrence mostly deviates significantly from chance. A comparison of the sets of meaning variables shows that those used exclusively in communicating the meaning of the traits have a characteristic bias: they emphasize "Feelings and Emotions" (e.g., "The stingy person loves money," "The hypochondriac is afraid of death:); "Judgments and Evaluations" (e.g., "An impulsive person does not care what others think about him"); and "Cognitive Qualities" (e.g., "Avarice implies thinking about money all the time"). This emphasis may be expected to reflect the view of the outside naive observer and his or her implicit personality theory, but not the actual pattern of personality. The results support our initial expectation that the two sets of meaning variables would be distinct. They show that the pattern of meaning variables involved in a trait is not identical with the meaning assigned directly to the trait. Contrary to the view of those who would identify trait with the beholder's conception, the realities of behavior and of the meaning that others assign to it appear to differ greatly.

STUDY 11: THE GENERAL MEANING PATTERN OF EXTERNAL-INTERNAL CONTROL[6]

Purpose and Hypotheses

The purpose of this study was to examine the meaning pattern characteristic of the variable external-internal (EI) control. One reason for our interest in this variable was its theoretically unclear status. It started out as an indicator of a certain cognitive manner of interpreting specific inputs (i.e., whether contingencies of reinforcement are attributed to oneself or not), but in the course of its survival in the psychological marketplace, it has increasingly been treated as a trait—yet neither completely nor exclusively so. The cognitive undercurrent of its origin has accompanied it in the form of a constantly hovering question mark: Is it a set of beliefs or, rather, a content-free cognitive-style variable (Crowne, 1979, Chapter 7; Phares, 1976; Strickland, 1977b)? It may be recalled that a general assumption guiding our studies of the interrelations of traits and meaning is that meaning dimensions reflect tendencies in regard to content (i.e., behaviors, beliefs, and attitudes), whereas types of relation and stimulus-referent relations reflect tendencies involved in more content-free variables, such as cognitive style and personal style (see the introductory remarks to Chapter 3). Accordingly, in view of the persisting unclarity about the status of IE, we expected the distribution of its significant correlations with meaning variables to deviate from the chance distribution defined in line with the frequency of the kinds of meaning variables and confirmed in the case of personality traits like Cattell's 16 personality factors (Study 6, Table 18). More specifically, we expected IE to be correlated more with the variables type of relation (TR) and shift of referent (SR) than would be warranted by chance (in accordance with the distribution expected in patterns of meaning variables corresponding to traits, p. 79, adjusted for the fact that no variables of forms of relation were used in this study).

Another reason for our interest in this variable was the specific issue of concern with the external world. The concept of externality implies that the individual tends to view the environment as being responsible for the occurrence of different events and phenomena relevant to himself or herself. It seems logical, therefore, that a high external should be concerned with the state of things in the environment. On the other hand, concern with the environment should be higher in internals because information is indispensable to adequate functioning that promotes one's interests. The majority of research findings support the latter expectation. Internals have been shown to be more vigilant and attentive to external arrangements, to situational cues, to institutional regulations, and to favorable opportunities in general (DuCette & Wolk, 1972; Lefcourt & Wine, 1969; Seeman & Evans, 1962). Internals have also been found to make more accurate judgments, to recall information more adequately, to make better use of information in estimating subsequent performance

[6]Thanks are due to Talma Lobel who has kindly made available to us the data of the subjects' scores on the E-I scale.

(DuCette & Wolk, 1973), and to use denial less than externals (Phares, 1976, pp. 129–143). However, there are deviant findings, too, indicating that externals are receptive at least to cues of a social nature (Baron, Cowan, Ganz, & McDonald, 1974; Baron & Ganz, 1972; Fitz, 1971; Lefcourt, 1976).

These findings suggested the possibility that concern with the external world was not a unitary construct. A similar argument was made by Rodin (1981) concerning the external orientation of obese and normal-weight individuals. Hence, we expected that both externals and internals would be concerned with the external environment but would note different aspects of it. Although all meaning variables are involved in external reality to some extent, those that are more obviously involved include the meaning dimensions that refer to observable qualities of referents: "Sensory Qualities," "Material," "Size," and Weight." However, because of the scarcity of data, we could not formulate hypotheses about the particular meaning variables that would manifest an orientation toward the external world in externals and internals.

More specific hypotheses about the correlations to be expected between IE and meaning variables were based on findings about the correlates and effects of IE. Thus, we expected high scores on externality (1) to be related negatively to "Actions (*Dim* 4), because externals were shown to be less concerned than internals about actions and the possibilities of active changes (e.g., Gore & Rotter, 1963; Strickland, 1965), and to be less interested in active efforts to master their environment, in achievement, and even in behaviors designed to improve their own well-being (Brown & Strickland, 1972; Phares, 1976, Chapters 5–7; Strickland, 1973); (2) to be related negatively to the difference comparative type of relation (*TR* 2b) and to "Judgments and Evaluations" (*Dim* 21b) because externals have been found to be, in general, conforming (Crowne & Liverant, 1963; Odell, 1959; about the relation of *TR* 2b to conformity, see Studies 2 and 6 in this chapter) and specifically to be more ready to change their judgments and evaluations in response to persuasions and external influences (Biondo & MacDonald, 1971; Johnson, Ackerman, Frank, & Fionda, 1968; Ryckman, Rodda, & Sherman, 1972; Sherman, 1973); (3) to be related negatively to "Consequences and Results" (*Dim* 7) because externals have been shown to be less concerned with effecting changes (Strickland, 1977b, pp. 242–245), and with predictable effects like the dangers of smoking (James, Woodruff, & Werner, 1965; Straits & Sechrest, 1963) or probabilities and risks (Liverant & Scodel, 1960; Lefcourt, 1965), although they tend more than internals to believe that the world is unpredictable and ruled by chance (Collins, 1974); and (4) to be related negatively to "Causes and Antecedents" (*Dim* 6) because externals have been shown to be less concerned than internals with assigning blame and responsibility to particular agents or events rather than to general forces like chance or "the government" (Phares, Wilson, & Klyver, 1971; Sosis, 1974).

Method

The subjects were 60 undergraduates in psychology and the social sciences (16 women and 44 men) in the age range 20–28 years. They were administered Rotter's E-I Questionnaire (pretested Hebrew version) and the standard meaning questionnaire (11 stimulus words) on separate occasions and in random order. The coders of each questionnaire were unaware of the purpose of the study.

Results and Conclusions

A comparison between the distribution of significant correlations of EI with meaning variables of the three types (51.14% *Dim*, 22.58% *TR*, 25.81% *SR*) and the distribution expected in traits (51.52% *Dim*, 24.24% *TR*, 11.83% *SR*, adjusted for the absence of *FR*) shows that the difference is significant ($\chi^2 = 16.64$, df = 2, p < .001). Hence, in line with the first hypothesis, EI is correlated with a particularly large number of relatively content-free meaning variables, especially shifts of referent.

Concerning the second hypothesis (see Table 26), the findings show that externals are higher on almost all meaning variables reflecting concern with the perceivable aspects of external reality, that is, "Sensory Qualities" (*Dim* 19), "Material" (*Dim* 9), and "Weight and Mass" (*Dim* 12). "Size and Dimensionality" (*Dim* 13) is the only dimension not involved, but many of the specific categories of sensory qualities are involved, including not only those characterizing the referent (*Dim* 19a) but also those perceivable by the referent (*Dim* 19b). Thus, as was expected, externals were shown to be oriented toward external reality. Further, as was expected, internals, too, were shown to be concerned with reality; yet this tendency was manifested not in the domain of meaning dimensions, but in preferences for types of relation and shifts of referent. In contrast to the externals, internals deemphasized the two types of relations characteristic of the personal mode of meaning, whereas they preferred the comparative type, which belongs to the lexical mode of meaning. It may be assumed that the personal mode of meaning is bound with a lower level of concern with conventional reality than the lexical mode. Moreover, internals deemphasized the use of several referent-shift variables that reflect the tendency to deviate from a strictly interpersonal reality (i.e., *SR* 7, *SR* 9, *SR* 10, and *SR* 2) and emphasized the use of other referent-shift variables that characterize a reality orientation (i.e., *SR* 4— the referent is a previous meaning value; and *SR* 8—the referent is a grammatical variation of the input; both of these are classified as SR_{near}).

Thus, the second hypothesis, about the different reality orientations of externals and internals, was confirmed, though, contrary to expectation, the difference did not consist solely in dimensions of meaning. A comparison of externals and internals revealed two basic kinds of reality orientation, the one based on concern with certain classes of meaning values, and the other based on the salience of specific ways of

Table 26. Significant Correlations of External–Internal Control with Meaning Variables

Personality variable	Significant correlations with meaning variables
Locus of control: External vs. internal ("external" in the positive pole of the scale)	*Dim* 4a, −.46***; *Dim* 4a + b, −.45***; *Dim* 6, −.44***; *Dim* 7, −.39**; *Dim* 8a, −.37**; *Dim* 9, .26*; *Dim* 10, −.33**; *Dim* 11, .28*; *Dim* 12, .30**; *Dim* 15, −.26*; *Dim* 16, −.49***; *Dim* 18, .29*; *Dim* 19a, .46***; *Dim* 19b, .40**; *Dim* 19a + b, .39**; (19a$_1$, .50***; 19a$_3$, .38**; 19a$_4$, .41**; 19a$_6$, .44***; 19a$_7$, .48***; 19a$_8$, .55***; 19b$_8$, .35**); *Dim* 21b, −.41**; *TR* 2a, −.27*; *TR* 2b, −.50***; *TR* 2a + b + c + d, −.31*; *TR* 3a, .48***; *TR* 3c, .38**; *TR* 4b, .37**; *TR* 4c, .43***; *SR* 2, .41*; *SR* 4, −.27*; *SR* 5, .39**; *SR* 6, .29*; *SR* 7, .46***; *SR* 8, −.30**; *SR* 9, .34**; *SR* 10, .40**.

Note. For the code of the meaning variables, see Appendix A.
*p < .05.
**p < .01.
***p < .001.

relating meaning values to referents and of selecting the referent. Externals were found to be high on the former, content-based reality-orientation and low on the latter, cognitive-process reality-orientation. Internals were found to be high on the latter, cognitive-process reality-orientation. Further, internals were not found to prefer content or processes possibly inimical to a reality orientation, whereas externals were found to do so. Thus, one may conclude that the grasp of externals on interpersonal reality is probably somewhat looser than that of internals, as indeed has been shown by previous studies (e.g., DuCette & Wolk, 1972, 1973).

The third hypothesis was confirmed by the negative correlations between EI and "Actions" (*Dim* 4a+b; and particularly *Dim* 4a), the difference comparative type of relation (*TR* 2b), "Judgments and Evaluations" (*Dim* 21b), "Consequences and Results" (*Dim* 7), and "Causes and Antecedents" (*Dim* 6). These findings confirm our expectations about the meaning variables that reflect low concern with activity, readiness to conform in general and in regard to judgments and evaluations in particular, and low concern with causes and consequences.

There are further correlations of EI with meaning variables that were not mentioned in the hypotheses. Among these, the negative correlations with "Structure" (*Dim* 10) and "Temporal Qualities" (*Dim* 16) are of particular interest. The first is highly plausible because of the presumable low concern of externals with the structure of institutions and phenomena (where there is no concern with affecting changes, there may be no concern about the structure). The second is important because it is fully and directly confirmed by independent findings: externals, compared to internals, are less accurate in judging the lapse of a minute (Walls & Smith, 1970), report shorter future-time perspectives (Cross & Tracy, 1971; Platt & Eisenman, 1968; Shybut, 1968), are less capable of "delaying" in tests like Kagan's Matching of Familiar Figures and the Porteus Mazes (Shipe, 1971), and tend less to delay gratification on the classical Mischel task (Mischel, Zeiss, & Zeiss, 1974; Strickland, 1973; Walls & Smith, 1970) and in life situations that involve planning one's future (Erikson & Roberts, 1971). These results demonstrated that the meaning profile indicates domains in which an individual has abilities of particular high or low salience. In this respect, among others, it is a more efficient tool that the self-report questionnaire, which provides no similar indications about domains in which manifestations of the trait(s) may be expected.

In sum, the study revealed the microstructure of meaning variables that underlies external-internal control. The rich validational material that exists about EI enables us to confirm the various personological implications of the meaning variables. The examination of the pattern of intercorrelations with meaning demonstrate that the meaning profile indicates domains in which the individual has tendencies of particularly high or low salience that are not evident from the content of the items in the personality questionnaire (e.g., in the case of EI, "Temporal Qualities"). The pattern of intercorrelations with meaning variables has provided insights into the nature of EI, for example, into the different kinds of reality orientations of externals and internals. Further, EI turned out to differ from the bulk of personality traits in its greater emphasis on the relatively content-free meaning variables, especially referent shifts that enable organizing reality in a variety of ways, more and less conventional. Thus, the constellation of meaning variables corresponding to EI implies that EI is a trait which shapes meaning assignment partly through emphasis on specific contents but mainly through particular styles of organizing reality and the infrastructure of modes of meaning.

STUDY 12: THE MEANING PATTERNS OF SPECIFIC SUBTYPES OF EXTERNAL AND INTERNAL CONTROL

The purpose of this study was to explore the possibility of defining clusters within the total pattern of intercorrelations with meaning variables corresponding to external-internal (EI) control that was presented in Study 11. We intended to define the clusters by means of meaning and to test their psychological reality by examining predictions about the differential responses of high scorers in the different clusters to a standard experimental situation. The first part of this study deals with defining the clusters, and the second deals with testing predictions about the differential responses.

Part A: Defining Four Clusters of Externality and Internality

Purpose and Hypothesis. The possibility that there may be different subtypes within the larger pattern of EI was suggested by previous findings (Mirels, 1970; Paulhus & Christie, 1981; Schneider & Parsons, 1969). Collins (1974), for example, found four clusters of EI beliefs focused on the difficulty, justice, predictability, and political responsiveness of the world; Levenson (1981) distinguished between externals who believe in chance and those who believe in powerful others; and Lefcourt (1981) explored the utility of defining locus of control in terms of a set of goal-specific scales. Our attempt to introduce differentiations into the locus-of-control construct was to be based on meaning, and the clusters were to consist of groupings of meaning variables.

The assumption that meaning would enable us to define clusters of EI got some support from the findings of a pretest conducted with 25 high-school students in the age range of 16–17 years. They were presented with a series of eight brief descriptions of problem domains (e.g., criminality in urban areas, Palestinian terrorism, hostility and war, the lower educational level of certain disadvantaged classes, the gap in understanding between parents and children, and marital problems) and were asked first to state whether they thought these problems could ever be solved definitively, and second, if the answer was negative, to explain the reasons, and if the answer was positive, to describe the solution. Each answer was coded in two ways: one reflected whether the subject thought a solution was possible or not, and the other indicated the meaning dimension that played the major role in the stated reasons for insolubility or in the description of the solutions. For example, when a subject wrote that the gap between parents and children cannot be bridged because there will always be status differences between them, the answer was coded as "No solution/dimension: 'State.'" Comparisons of the answers given by the subjects who suggested solutions and those who did not indicated that there were roughly two kinds of answers in each of these groups of subjects. Thus, one group suggested solutions focused on action, another group suggested solutions focused on circumstantial factors (e.g., time and place), a third group indicated no solution because of "the way things are," and a fourth group indicated no solution because of the specific actions or personalities involved.

We assumed that the dichotomy defined by the responses "solution possible" and "solution impossible" corresponds to the EI variable, and on this basis, we set up the hypothesis of two subtypes of external control and two subtypes of internal control defined by the meaning variables that were used by the pretest subjects and that were found to be related to EI in Study 11. We expected one subtype of external control to consist of high scores on "Sensory Qualities" of the referent (*Dim* 19a), "Sensory Qualities" perceived by the referent (*Dim* 19b), "State" (*Dim* 11), "Material" (*Dim* 9), and "Weight" (*Dim* 12). Another type of external control was to consist of high scores on active "Actions" (*Dim* 4a) and "Domain of Application" (*Dim* 8a). Further, we expected one type of internal control to consist of high scores on "Causes" (*Dim* 6), "Consequences" (*Dim* 7), active "Actions" (*Dim* 4a), and "Domain of Application" (*Dim* 8a). Finally, another type of internal control was to consist of high scores on "Structure" (*Dim* 10), "Development" (*Dim* 18), "Locational Qualities" (*Dim* 15), and "Temporal Qualities" (*Dim* 16). The described subtypes were designed to serve as general guidelines for an exploratory cluster analysis of the intercorrelations among the meaning variables. The four subtypes include all the meaning dimensions found to be related to EI in Study 11. However, the clustering more closely followed suggestions based on the pretests. The subtypes are defined only in terms of meaning dimensions. The main reason is that we assumed that meaning dimensions form the defining core of the subtypes. Another reason is that the described pretests could give us no indications of the role of the other meaning variables in the subtypes.

Method. The subjects were 84 high-school students (48 girls and 36 boys) in the age range of 15.8–17.1 years. They were administered, in two separate group sessions and in random order, the standard meaning questionnaire (11 stimulus words) and Rotter's (1966) E-I Questionnaire (pretested Hebrew version). The whole sample was divided into two groups: those who got an EI score above the mean (i.e., externals) and those who got an EI score below the mean (i.e., internals). A cluster analysis (Holzinger & Harman, 1941) was performed separately for the subgroups of externals and internals. The analysis was based on comparing the mean of intercorrelations within the cluster with the mean of correlations of the clustered variables with those outside the cluster. The ratio yielded a coefficient with 1.30 as the arbitrarily set minimum significant value.

Results and Conclusions. A cluster analysis based on the hypothesized subtypes provided partial confirmation of the hypothesis. Two of the subtypes were supported by the data, whereas the other two were not. One of the supported subtypes was an externality cluster defined by "Sensory Qualities" of the referent (*Dim* 19a), "Sensory Qualities" perceived by the referent (*Dim* 19b), "State" (*Dim* 11), "Material" (*Dim* 9), and "Weight" (*Dim* 12). The other was an internality cluster defined by "Causes" (*Dim* 6), "Consequences" (*Dim* 7), "Action" (*Dim* 4a), and "Domain of Application" (*Dim* 8a). An exploration of the obtained matrices of intercorrelations indicated possibilities of improving the definition of the two nonconfirmed clusters through the addition of meaning variables to each of them. Thus, the total pattern yielded the following four clusters:

1. External, which includes the dimensions "Sensory Qualities" of the referent (*Dim* 19a), "Sensory Qualities" perceived by the referent (*Dim* 19b), "State" (*Dim* 11), "Material" (*Dim* 9), and "Weight" (*Dim* 12); coefficient = 3.75.

2. External, which includes the dimensions "Action" (*Dim* 4a), "Domain of Application" (*Dim* 8a), and "State" (*Dim* 11); coefficient = 1.92.
3. Internal, which includes the dimensions "Causes" (*Dim* 6), "Consequences" (*Dim* 7), "Action" (*Dim* 4a), and "Domain of Application" (*Dim* 8a); coefficient = 4.08.
4. Internal, which includes the dimensions "Causes" (*Dim* 6), "Consequences" (*Dim* 7), "Structure" (*Dim* 10), "Development" (*Dim* 18), "Locational Qualities" (*Dim* 15), "Temporal Qualities" (*Dim* 16), and "Judgments and Evaluations" (*Dim* 21a); coefficient = 2.10.

(Clusters 1 and 3 were predicted; clusters 2 and 4 were improved *post hoc*). These findings support the conception of subtypes of E-I defined in terms of meaning dimensions. One of the externality clusters (1) is focused on perceivable external properties of things, and the other (2) on properties of situations that include specifications of activity and participants. One of the internality clusters is focused on specifying causality and action (3) and the other (4) is focused on specifying causality and the structural properties of situations.

The clusters suggest that four groupings of dimensions are probably involved:

1. A grouping of the dimensions "Causes" (*Dim* 6) and "Consequences" (*Dim* 7), which occurs in the subtypes of internality but not in those of externality.
2. A grouping of the dimensions "Action" (*Dim* 4a) and "Domain of Application" (*Dim* 8a), which cuts across the EI dichotomy.
3. A grouping of the dimensions "Sensory Qualities" of the referent (*Dim* 19a), "Sensory Qualities" perceived by the referent (*Dim* 19b), "Material" (*Dim* 9), and "Weight" (*Dim* 12), which occurs only in one externality subtype.
4. A grouping of the dimensions "Structure" (*Dim* 10), "Locational Qualities" (*Dim* 15), "Temporal Qualities" (*Dim* 16), "Development" (*Dim* 18), and "Judgments and Evaluations" (*Dim* 21a), which occurs only in one internality subtype.

One way to make sense of the clusters (the first list) is to conceive of them as ordered linearly on a continuum from extreme externality (Cluster 1) through intermediate externality (Cluster 2) and intermediate internality (Cluster 3) to extreme internality (Cluster 4). This conception makes it possible to account also for the relatively lower clustering coefficients of clusters 2 and 3 which represent the intermediate region. However, it is to be emphasized that the differences among all four clusters are qualitative in terms of the meaning system.

Further, there is a certain parallelism in the differences between Clusters 1 and 2 and between Clusters 3 and 4. The two clusters of externality indicate the rejection of enterprising action but differ in the reasons for this negative approach to dynamic changes. Cluster 1 indicates rejection on the basis of the perceivable qualities of things, whereas Cluster 2 indicates rejection on the basis of the futility of actions and the nature of the participants in actions. Again, the two clusters of internality indicate the acceptance of enterprising action but differ in the reasons for this positive approach to dynamic changes. Cluster 4 indicates acceptance on the basis of the presumed effects of actions, whereas Cluster 3 indicates acceptance on the basis of the structural and circumstantial properties of things and situations. The parallelism of the difference between Clusters 1 and 2 and Clusters 4 and 3 consists in a reliance on the properties of actions versus a reliance on the static-intrinsic properties of things.

Part B: Testing the Four Clusters of Externality and Internality

Hypothesis. This part of the study was designed to test two hypotheses about the differences between the four clusters of EI (see Part A above). The assumption underlying both hypotheses was that the four clusters form a continuum from the most "external" orientation to the most "internal" orientation (see "Part A, Results and Conclusions"). The first hypothesis was that subjects with meaning profiles reflecting Cluster 1 would have the highest scores on the EI questionnaire, that subjects with meaning profiles reflecting Cluster 4 would have the lowest, and that subjects with meaning profiles reflecting Clusters 2 or 3 would have intermediate scores. The hypothesis was designed to validate the clusters and their ordering against the EI questionnaire. The second hypothesis was that, when confronted with the suggestion to volunteer for a project designed to help disadvantaged children, the highest percentage of volunteers would be subjects with meaning profiles reflecting Cluster 4, the lowest would be subjects with meaning profiles reflecting Cluster 1, and subjects with meaning profiles reflecting Clusters 2 or 3 would occupy middle positions. This hypothesis was designed to validate the clusters and their ordering in terms of a variable that has been amply investigated in regard to EI: commitment to social action (Crowne, 1979, pp. 195–197; Strickland, 1977b, pp. 242–245). Most studies have shown that externals do not tend to volunteer for social action, whereas internals do.

Method. The subjects of the study were 60 high-school students (36 boys and 24 girls) in the age range of 15–16.5 years. They were selected on the basis of their meaning profiles from a larger pool of subjects ($n = 130$) of the same population. The meaning profiles were based on a prior administration of a standard meaning questionnaire. The criteria for the selection of the subjects for the study proper were based on frequencies of specific meaning dimensions in the meaning profiles. A subject was classified in a cluster if his or her meaning profile (1) included a minimum number of the meaning dimensions defining the clusters (3 of 5, 2 of 3, 3 of 4, and 5 of 7 for Clusters 1, 2, 3, and 4, respectively) in a frequency above the group's mean for those variables and (2) included, in a frequency above the group's mean, no more than a given number of the other meaning dimensions involved in defining the clusters (no more that 2 of 9, 3 of 11, 2 of 10, and 2 of 7 for Clusters 1, 2, 3, and 4, respectively). Special care was taken to differentiate between Clusters 2 and 3. The number of subjects was 21, 16, 8, and 15 in Clusters 1, 2, 3, and 4, respectively.

The subjects were administered the EI questionnaire (Hebrew version) in group sessions. Because they were in different schools, the questionnaires were administered in the context of the classes to which the subjects belonged. About a month later, without any apparent connection with the previous questionnaires, the subjects, together with their classmates, were confronted by a disguised experimenter who presented to them an actual national project of volunteering help for disadvantaged children. In order to control for the possibility that the subjects might not volunteer because of lack of time during a specific period, the experimenter emphasized that volunteers were needed for all time periods, even for a year ahead. No persuasion was involved in presenting the case. Complete secrecy of the commitments in regard to school authorities, parents, and peers was pledged. The volunteers were requested to sign their names and to state in writing when they would be free, and how they could be reached. Debriefing took place a week later.

Results and Conclusions. The means of EI scores were 18.3, 16.2, 14.9, and 13.4 for subjects of Clusters 1, 2, 3, and 4, respectively. The differences were found to be significant ($F = 3.06$, $df = 3/56$, $p < .05$). Comparisons between the means by the Newman-Keuls method (an *a posteriori* test that is stricter than the *a priori* tests that would have been justified in this case) showed all the differences except the one between Clusters 2 and 3 to be significant at the .05 level. The findings support the first hypothesis about the continuum of externality-internality.

The percentages of volunteers were 13% (2 out of 15), 25% (2 out of 8), 44% (7 out of 16), and 62% (13 out of 21) in clusters 1, 2, 3, and 4, respectively. This distribution deviates significantly from the chance distribution ($\chi^2 = 38.61$, $df = 3$, $p < .001$). Tests of the differences between the percentages in the two clusters of externality and in the two clusters of internality showed the former not to be significant ($t = 1.15$, $df = 21$, n.s.) and the latter to be significant ($t = 2.19$, $df = 35$, $p < .025$, one-tailed). These findings confirm the second hypothesis. Together with the findings that confirmed the first hypothesis, these findings support the psychological reality of the clusters of EI defined in terms of meaning dimensions.

To summarize, the two parts of this study show that it is possible to define clusters within a larger constellation of meaning variables and that the clusters have psychological reality. They are more specific than the overall constellation. Yet, the question of whether they are autonomous (or individual-bound) or alternating (within the same individual) remains open.

STUDY 13: YOU DON'T HAVE TO BE DOGMATIC TO BE AUTHORITARIAN

Purpose and Hypotheses

The major purpose of this study was to use a comparison of the meaning constellations of dogmatism and authoritarianism in order to suggest resolutions to some controversial issues about the interrelations of these two concepts. One basic issue concerns the essential similarity or difference of authoritarianism and dogmatism. Authoritarianism has been the father of dogmatism in more than one sense. The notions that personality is the source of political attitudes, and that personality types correspond to political typologies were first demonstrated by research in authoritarianism (Adorno, Frenkel-Brunswick, Levinson, & Sanford, 1950) before dogmatism was conceived. The conception of dogmatism occurred under the sign of rebellion. The major idea was that dogmatism is a generalized framework for the organization of belief systems characterized by specific degrees of isolation and differentiation, and that it applies equally to different types of content (Rokeach, 1954, 1960). However, this challenging idea did not stand up well under research. Dogmatic subjects were found to be more likely to espouse a conservative than a left-wing ideology. It seems probable that dogmatism measures a broader range of authoritarian beliefs, but essentially, there are no differences in the content of the attitudes endorsed by high scorers on dogmatism and authoritarianism (Vacchiano, 1977). Further, there are also similarities in the major personality variables found to be associated with the two constructs, mainly defensiveness, conformity, and obedience to authority (Cherry & Byrne, 1977; Vacchiano, 1977). These findings seem to imply a fair amount of overlap in the range of application of these two constructs. Yet, there seem also to be differences, although no systematic comparison of the two concepts has been made. The most salient difference is the stronger emphasis in dogmatism on properties of cognitive structure and processing. Cognitive functioning has been integral to Rokeach's (1954) theory from the very beginning, but has not been widely explored in regard to authoritarianism.

We assumed that if dogmatism and authoritarianism measure the same kind of variable(s), the patterns of their interrelations with meaning variables would overlap to a greater extent than if they measure different variables. This assumption was more like a question than a hypothesis, because so far we have no standard by which to evaluate similarity or difference in meaning patterns. The hypothesis that could actually be stated referred to the relative proportion of significant correlations with meaning dimensions (more content-bound) and other meaning variables (more content-free) of dogmatism and authoritarianism. In line with Rokeach's original formulations, we expected that dogmatism's pattern of interrelations with meaning would include a higher number of correlations with meaning variables that were not meaning dimensions than the pattern of authoritarianism.

The second hypothesis concerned the issue of inconsistency in behavioral correlates, which has implications for both theory and research methodology. (For our general approach to this problem see Chapter 8. The arguments raised in Chapter 8 apply equally to authoritarianism and to dogmatism.) However, research has shown that authoritarianism is probably more subject to fluctuations and inconsistencies than dogmatism. Christie (1952, 1954) raised this issue soon after the introduction of authoritarianism into psychology, and subsequent research has justified his qualms both in regard to the dependence of the high authoritarian's behavior on the situation (Cherry & Byrne, 1977, pp. 124–149; Kirscht & Dillehay, 1967; Titus & Hollander, 1957, p. 62) and in regard to the great effect of questionnaire characteristics on the authoritarian's responses to the F-Scale (Cherry & Byrne, 1977, pp. 114–116). To be sure, dogmatism has also not been spared the charge of inconsistency due to situational factors. Bailes and Guller (1970), for example, claimed that the basic relation between dogmatism and extremity of political opinions has been overshadowed by confounding factors, that is, emotional issues (e.g., draft issues involved in the Vietnam war), peer expectations, and the environments of testing. However, our impression of the literature concerning these two constructs is that the problem of inconsistency has been more acute in regard to authoritarianism than in regard to dogmatism.

The construct that helped us to form the bridge between the authoritarian fluctuation in responses and the meaning system was the concrete structural level of information processing (Schroder, Driver, & Streufert, 1967, pp. 14–18). Some studies (Harvey, 1963; Harvey et al., 1961, Chapters 3, 5, 8) have shown that behavior is maximally controlled by external stimulus conditions and fluctuations in response to external cues when the individual's conceptual system is concrete (Schroder et al., 1967, p. 17). Schroder et al. (1967, pp. 15–16) characterized a concrete structure as being based on a unidimensional "reading" of stimuli, on comparatively few degrees of freedom, and on the use of dichotomous dimensions. Several studies, indeed, have shown that authoritarians tend to be rigid in thinking about people and events, to be intolerant of ambiguities, and to be hasty in avoiding them (Berkowitz, 1960; Harvey, 1963; Kirscht & Dillehay, 1967; Steiner & Johnson, 1963).

Hence, we made an attempt to translate into the terms of the meaning system the particular properties of concreteness mentioned by Schroder et al. This attempt has led to the hypotheses that authoritarianism would be:

1. Correlated negatively with the number of different dimensions used (because in concrete thinking, "at any given time, stimuli are . . . interpreted unidimensionally"—Schroder *et al.*, 1967, p. 15).
2. Correlated negatively with the number of different meaning values (because in concrete thinking, "if a stimulus is categorized in an absolute way . . . alternate resolutions or interpretations fail to arise"—Schroder *et al.*, 1967, p. 17).
3. Correlated negatively with the comparative type of relation *similarity* (because in concrete thinking, "stimuli either fit into a category or are excluded from consideration . . . when conflict is introduced . . . it quickly is minimized and resolved," and there is a "lack of alternate schemata for 'sensing' shades of difference. . . . the discrimination of stimuli along dimensions is minimally graduated" so that there is "a minimum of ambiguity"—Schroder *et al.*, 1967, pp. 16–17).
4. Correlated positively with the obligatory form of relation (*FR* 6; because in concrete thinking, there is a tendency to adhere strictly to rules—Schroder *et al.*, 1967, p. 17).
5. Correlated negatively with the mixed form of relation (*FR* 3; because in concrete thinking, there is a tendency to think in categorial black–white distinctions that allow for no "relativeness of 'greys' and 'degrees'"—Schroder *et al.*, 1967, p. 117).
6. Correlated negatively with "Range of Inclusion: Classes" (*Dim* 2a; because in concrete thinking, categorization schemata are "undifferentiated" and categorization is compartmentalized, proceeding in terms of one rule and independent of other subrules—Schroder *et al.*, 1967, p. 16) so that there is no real hierarchical classification system—Schroder *et al.*, 1967, p. 16).
7. Correlated positively with "Sensory Qualities" (*Dim* 19a) and probably also with "State" (*Dim* 11; because in concrete thinking, there is presumably an emphasis on external conditions—Schroder *et al.*, 1967, p. 17).

Thus, this set of seven expectations is based on two interrelated assumptions, namely, that individuals with a concrete conceptual system fluctuate in responses more than others, and that a concrete conceptual system is manifested in the meaning system in the way outlined above.

Defensiveness is the third issue that was of interest to us. The pronounced tendency of authoritarians toward projection was emphasized by the original investigators of the concept (Adorno *et al.*, 1950). They explained authoritarianism essentially as a projection of repressed hostility. Information about the conceptional system of authoritarianism further reinforces the conception that projection is characteristic of authoritarians. Schroder *et al.* (1967) maintained, "Conflicting attitudes tend to be misperceived or 'warded off' . . . when a person continues to perceive the whole completely in terms of his own schemata . . . he is 'projecting.' Thus, projection may be considered to be a defense mechanism commonly used by individuals low in integrative complexity" (p. 17). In contrast, dogmatism seems to us to be characterized primarily by denial. Rokeach (1960) himself was not very clear when he contended that dogmatism "is nothing more than a total network of psychoanalytic defense mechanisms" (p. 70). Others have maintained that dogmatism itself is a kind of defense mechanism (Bernhardson, 1967; Byrne, Blaylock, & Goldberg, 1966). However, most of the findings concerning the defensiveness of dogmatics highlight the role of denial in this "network" (e.g., Hallenbeck, 1965; Hallenbeck & Lundstedt, 1966; Plant, Telford, & Thomas, 1965; Vacchiano, Strauss, & Schiffman, 1968). In this context, it may be also relevant to mention the rapid decision time of high dogmatics, possibly designed to avoid prolonged exposure to information (Taylor, 1972), their disregard of the anxiety-provoking present and past (Castle, 1971; Rokeach & Bonier, 1960), and their low sensory acuity (Kaplan & Singer, 1963).

This fairly clear distinction in defensive tendencies between authoritarians and dogmatics made it possible for us to examine the manifestations of these tendencies in the meaning profiles. Such an examination was of particular interest in view of our findings about the manifestations in meaning of beliefs orienting toward these and other defenses (S. Kreitler & H. Kreitler, 1989c). We found that the tendency to endorse beliefs orienting toward projection is generally correlated negatively with "Range of Inclusion" (*Dim* 2), "Consequences" (*Dim* 7), "Possessions" (*Dim* 17a), and "Feelings and Emotions" (*Dim* 20) and positively with the exemplifying-illustrative (*TR* 3) and metaphoric-symbolic (*TR* 4) types of relation, as well as with shifts of referent to a part of the presented input (*SR* 3) and to a combination of the input with a previous meaning value (*SR* 10). (The relation of the latter to projection was indicated also by Factor 8 in Study 6). Further, the tendency to endorse beliefs orienting toward denial is generally correlated positively with "Contextual Allocation" (*Dim* 1), "Action" (*Dim* 4a), "Consequences" (*Dim* 7), "Domain of Application" (*Dim* 8b), "Material" (*Dim* 9), "Size" (*Dim* 13), the comparative (*TR* 2) and metaphoric-symbolic (*TR* 4) types of relation, and the grammatical variations of the referents (*SR* 8), but it is correlated negatively with the shift in referent variable of identity (*SR* 1). It should, however, be noted that these two patterns overlap to some extent. The common elements may represent features characteristic of belief tendencies or of defensiveness in general. Indeed, we found that "Consequences" (*Dim* 7), "Domain of Application" (*Dim* 8b), "Possessions" (*Dim* 17a), "Feelings and Emotions" (*Dim* 20), and the metaphoric-symbolic type of relation (*TR* 4) were probably involved in all defense mechanisms in some form. In any case, we took these findings as our guidelines for exploring the manifestations of projection and denial in meaning variables correlated with authoritarianism and dogmatism. We did not, however, expect all the mentioned variables actually to be manifested, first because they were found to be involved in belief tendencies and not trait manifestations, and second because of the possibility of interactions with other meaning variables within the context of the constellation of meaning variables characteristic of the trait.

Method

The subjects were 74 undergraduates in psychology and the social sciences (44 women and 30 men) in the age range 21–29 years. They were administered, in random order on separate occasions, two to four weeks apart, the standard meaning questionnaire (11 stimulus words) and Hebrew versions of Rokeach's Dogmatism Scale Form E, and the F-Scale (Forms 45 and 40, Adorno *et al.*, 1950).

Results and Conclusions

Table 27 allows for computing the ratios of significant correlations with content-free meaning variables out of the total number of significant correlations with mean-

Table 27. Significant Correlations of Dogmatism and Authoritarianism with Meaning Variables

Personality variable	Significant correlations with meaning variables
Dogmatism	*Dim* 1, .27*; *Dim* 2a, .38***; *Dim* 2b, .41***; *Dim* 2a + b, .39***; *Dim* 3, −.32**; *Dim* 5, −.29**; *Dim* 6, .55***; *Dim* 8a, −.31**; *Dim* 8b, −.36**; *Dim* 8a + b, −.33**; *Dim* 13, .28*; *Dim* 15, −.43***; *Dim* 17a, .39***; *Dim* 17b, −.27*; (19b$_0$, −.39***); *Dim* 21a, .42***; *Dim* 22a, .45***; *Dim* 22a + b, .40***; *TR* 2d, .39***; *SR* 1, −.38***; *SR* 8, .33**.
Authoritarianism	*Dim* 2a, −.44***; *Dim* 7, −.38***; *Dim* 9, −.37***; *Dim* 11, .32**; *Dim* 12, .35**; *Dim* 18, .26**; *Dim* 19a, .36**; *Dim* 19a + b, .34**; (19a$_0$, −.31**; 19a$_1$, .42***; 19a$_3$, .37**; 19a$_6$, .40***; 19a$_7$, .42***; 19a$_8$, .45***; 19b$_2$, −.30**); no. of dif. meaning *Dim*, −.26*; *TR* 1b, −.28*; *TR* 2a, −.33*; *TR* 3c, .38***; *TR* 4d, .42***; *FR* 3, −.43***; *FR* 6, .38***; *SR* 1, −.37**; *SR* 2, .45***; *SR* 9, −.31**; *SR* 10, .57***; no. of meaning values, .37**.

Note. For the code of the meaning variables, see Appendix A.
*p < .05.
**p < .01.
***p < .001.

ing variables. If we do not count correlations with the subdimensions of "Sensory Qualities" (*Dim* 19), the percentages are 15% (3 out of 20) for dogmatism and 50% (10 out of 20) for authoritarianism. If we count the separate correlations with the subdimensions of "Sensory Qualities" (*Dim* 19), the percentages are 14% (3 out of 21) for dogmatism and 37% (10 out of 27) for authoritarianism. In both cases, the percentage of authoritarianism is significantly higher ($z = 2.33$, $p < .01$, and $z = 1.77$, $p < .05$ respectively). Moreover, if we compare these distributions with those expected by chance in view of the number of variables involved (by chance, one should get 53.01% correlations with meaning variables that are not meaning dimensions, i.e., types of relation, shifts in referent, and forms of relation), the percentage for authoritarianism does not deviate from chance expectation (when the total does not include the subdimensions of "Sensory Qualities," *Dim* 19, $z = .24$, n.s.; when it includes them, $z = .05$, n.s.), but the percentage for dogmatism is definitely below the expected (when the total does not include the subdimensions of "Sensory Qualities," *Dim* 19, $z = 3.22$, $p < .01$; when it includes them, $z = 2.27$, $p < .05$). In whatever way we look at it, dogmatism does not live up to the requirements of a variable with heavy investments in content-free cognitive processes. Despite initial hopes to the contrary, the pattern of interrelations of dogmatism with meaning reveals it to be a content variable, as its critics have claimed all along.

Our second hypothesis dealt with the issue of the concrete conceptual system presumably involved in authoritarianism. Table 27 shows that, as predicted, authoritarianism is correlated negatively with the number of different meaning dimensions, negatively with the comparative type of relation similarity (*TR* 2a), positively with the obligatory form of relation (*FR* 6), negatively with the mixed form of relation (*FR* 3), negatively with "Judgments and Evaluations" (*Dim* 21), and positively with a whole array of "Sensory Qualities" (*Dim* 19a). Contrary to expectation, it correlated positively instead of negatively with the number of meaning values. It is possible that this deviation occurred because we failed to translate adequately Schroder *et al.*'s reference to "alternate interpretations." In any case, because six of the seven diagnostic symptoms of concreteness did show up in the data, it seems justified to conclude that authoritarians may indeed be more than commonly sensitive to situational cues and subject to fluctuations. Notably, the pattern for dogmatism does not show any of the signs of the "fluctuation syndrome."

Concerning the tendencies toward defense mechanisms, the data are more difficult to evaluate. Of the eight different meaning variables interrelated with the beliefs orienting toward projection, five occurred in the pattern for authoritarianism (i.e., "Range of Inclusion," *Dim* 2a; "Consequences," *Dim* 7; the exemplifying type of relation, *TR* 3; the metaphoric type of relation, *TR* 4; and the shift to an unrelated referent, *SR* 10), and three did not (i.e., "Feelings and Emotions," *Dim* 20; shift to a part of the input, *SR* 3; and "Possessions," *Dim* 17a, perhaps because it was counteracted by the authoritarians' conservative approach to possessions). None of these variables occurred in the pattern for dogmatism. Of the 10 meaning variables interrelated with the beliefs orienting toward denial, six occurred in the pattern for dogmatism (i.e., "Contextual Allocation," *Dim* 1; "Domain of Application," *Dim* 8b; "Size," *Dim* 13," the complementary type of relation, *TR* 2d; the referent being identical with the input, *SR* 1; and grammatical variation of the referent, *SR* 8) and four did not (i.e., "Action," *Dim* 4a; "Material," *Dim* 9; the metaphoric type of relation, *TR* 4; and "Consequences," *Dim* 7, perhaps because it was counteracted by the high correlation of dogmatism with "Causes," *Dim* 6). Again, none of the variables identified as denial signs were correlated with authoritarianism. Although the results are not perfect, there can be no doubt that the findings show authoritarians tending toward projection and dogmatists toward denial.

The overall rate of confirmation for the third hypothesis was about 60%. In order to evaluate this finding adequately, it would be necessary to recognize that we are dealing with a cluster or a vector rather than with single variables. Perhaps, a part of the cluster may represent the whole; perhaps, some of the elements in the cluster are interchangeable and hence redundant. Moreover, it is to be recalled that the complete pattern was characteristic of belief groupings and not traits. Therefore, it is plausible that different subsets of the whole pattern become manifest on different occasions or in the context of different traits. Such contexts may promote a specific selection by strengthening or suppressing different meaning variables. Thus, it is only after the relations of defenses to further traits are investigated that we will know whether the occurrence of five or six meaning variables, or 60% of a cluster, suffices to enable a manifestation of the defensive tendency, and to what extent the same meaning variables recur in each case.

Be that as it may, translating defensive tendencies into meaning variables helps to reveal the manner in which these tendencies operate in the case of different constellations of meaning variables. Take the authoritarian's projection. The emphasis on the personal mode of meaning is complemented through a deemphasis of the lexical mode of meaning. Perhaps the specific types of relation through which these preferences are manifested are not fortuitous. The negative correlation with the comparative type of relation similarity (*TR* 2a) is part of the matrix of the concrete information-processing structure, which was shown to be characteristic of authoritarianism. Similarly, the positive correlation with symbols (*TR* 4d) corresponds to the authoritarian's sensitivity to symbols of power and to figures in authority. Notably, subjects high in *n* Power were also found to prefer the use of metaphors (*TR* 4b), possibly for similar reasons (Study 4). In authoritarianism, the bias toward the personal mode of meaning is accompanied by the tendency to define referents that deviate from the presented inputs and from the common procedures of treating these inputs, for example, by reversing them or by replacing them through associations. These pathogenic tendencies are, however, counterbalanced by a surprisingly broad attentiveness to sensory qualities, which is responsible for the notorious fluctuation in experimental behavior but may account for the manner in which individuals of this kind maintain their hold on reality.

The pattern for dogmatism reveals, in turn, the dynamics of denial. Coupled with the disregard for functionality, location, manner of operation, and domains of application, there is an emphasis on "Judgments" (*Dim* 21a), "Cognitions" (*Dim* 22a, 22a+b), and classifications ("Contextual Allocation," *Dim* 1, and "Range of Inclusion," *Dim* 2a and *Dim* 2b). This concern with cognitive content is remarkable when one recalls that dogmatism originated as a variable that is descriptive of belief systems and attitudes. However, as noted, the concern is rooted in content rather than in structures *per se*. The dogmatist is attentive to judgments, causes, and so on, but not particularly to similarities and differences for their own sake. Our findings are thus in line with the empirical results (Feather, 1969a,b, 1970, 1973) that refuted Rokeach's original hypotheses (1960) about the low dissonance threshold of dogmatic subjects. Moreover, we found that there is in dogmatism an imbalance between concern with more intellectual aspects and disregard of the more concrete and practical facets of reality. Perhaps, it is precisely this imbalance that enables the survival of the dogmatic approach.

STUDY 14: MEANINGS OF COGNITIVE AND MOTOR ACTIVITIES

Purpose and Hypotheses

The object of this study was to explore and compare the patterns of meaning variables associated with the tendencies toward cognitive and motor activities.

The tendencies toward cognitive and motor activities have been shown to be characteristic personality variables that play a role in normal and abnormal individuals, affecting different behaviors (Phillips & Zigler, 1961, 1964; Stein & Craik, 1965). The stability of these tendencies over time (Phillips & Zigler, 1961), their relation to sociocultural variables such as sex-role identification (Keller, 1978, pp. 79–85), and their simultaneous presence in every individual (Stein & Craik, 1965) highlight their status as traits. However, they are more often mentioned as constituents of extroversion-introversion than as independent traits. Extroverts are commonly described as preferring motor actions whereas introverts are conceived as preferring cognitive activities (Wilson, 1977). Hence, it was of special interest to explore the relation of these tendencies to extroversion in terms of the meaning variables with which each of them is correlated. Accordingly, the first hypothesis was that the pattern of meaning variables correlated with preference for motor actions would include many similar correlations to those in the pattern corresponding to extroversion whereas the patterns correlated with preference for cognitive activities would include many opposite correlations to those in the extroversion pattern.

The second hypothesis focused on examining whether the label of a scale and the manifest content of its items correspond to meaning dimensions referred to explicitly in the label and the items. The label and the items of the tendency toward cognitive activities refer to the meaning dimension "Cognitive Qualities" (*Dim* 22), whereas those of the tendency toward motor action refer to the meaning dimension "Actions" (*Dim* 4). If there is actually a correspondence, the tendencies toward cognitive and motor activities can be expected to correlate positively with *Dim* 22 and *Dim* 4, respectively. Indeed, previous studies (Studies 1–13) showed that meaning variables that correlated with a scale reveal the underlying dynamics of the assessed tendencies rather than the face validity of the scale. But because in the present case it seemed to us that concern with cognitive properties or with actions is relevant to the underlying dynamics, too, we expected the assessed tendencies to be correlated positively with the meaning dimensions corresponding to each.

The third hypothesis, closely related to the second, focuses on the reflection of structural features of the overall meaning system in the pattern of intercorrelations with specific tendencies. According to the circular model of meaning dimensions, the dimensions are arranged in a circular structure that enables one to specify the relative distances between them (Chapter 2 and Figure 1). Meaning dimensions located more closely to each other in the model resemble each other in content more than dimensions located further from each other. Thus, it is plausible to expect that scores on the scales may correlate with more meaning dimensions relatively close to the focal meaning dimensions corresponding to the scale than with dimensions located further away in terms of the model. This expectation rests on the assumption that the structural features of the meaning system affect the patterns of intercorrelations of the scales with the meaning variables. An increased number of correlations with the neighboring dimensions can be viewed as a spread of effect (if the scale actually corresponds to the focal meaning dimension—in line with the second hypothesis), or as a replacement phenomenon (if the scale does not correspond to the focal dimension). (In line with the circular model, "Cognitive Qualities," *Dim* 22, is in the neighborhood of "Judgments and Evaluations," *Dim* 21; "Feelings and Emotions," *Dim* 20; "Development," *Dim* 18; and "Possessions," *Dim* 17; and "Action," *Dim* 4, is in the neighborhood of "Function," *Dim* 3; "Manner of Occurrence," *Dim* 5; "Causes," *Dim* 6; and "Consequences," *Dim* 7.)

The fourth hypothesis focused on exploring differences in the maturational level of the two tendencies. Developmental and depth psychological studies have led to the prevalent assumption that an orientation toward action is earlier and more primitive than an orientation toward thought (A. Freud, 1952; Kris, 1950; Lewin, 1936; Piaget, 1951; Rapaport, 1951; Werner, 1948). In keeping with this assumption, psychiatric patients with a thought orientation have been found to have higher premorbid social competence, as assessed by an index of maturational level (Phillips & Zigler, 1961); a broader future time perspective, which may require higher abstraction (Stein & Craik, 1965); and higher frequencies of movement responses to the Rorschach, which may be indicative of a higher developmental level (Kruger, 1954; Misch, 1954).

The testing of this assumption in terms of the meaning system required a translation of the concept of maturational level into indices based on meaning variables. Following Werner (1948), we assumed that the major criteria for maturational level are differentiation and complexity. These criteria may be assessed in terms of the four following indices: (1) the number of different meaning variables correlated with the score; (2) the number of different meaning dimensions correlated with the score; (3) the ratio of the number of meaning values to the number of meaning variables correlated with the score (this ratio may vary from a minimum of 1, when the numerator and the denominator are equal, to any number above 1); (4) dispersion of the correlated meaning dimensions over the circular model of meaning dimensions; if the circle is divided into four equal parts (see Figure 1 in Chapter 2 and in this chapter, Footnote b to Table 30), then the larger the number of quarters of the circle represented by the correlated meaning dimensions, the greater the dispersion of the meaning dimensions; and (5) dispersion of the correlated types of relation over the four types of relation (i.e., attributive, comparative, exemplifying-illustrative, and metaphoric-symbolic).

Indices 1, 2, 4, and 5 are expected to be higher and Index 3 is expected to be lower when maturational level is higher. Each index combines the two criteria of complexity and differentiation by reflecting, in some sense, the greater number of meaning variables and differences between them. If a distinction is nevertheless desired, then it seems that the first two indices reflect complexity to a greater extent, and the last three reflect differentiation to a greater extent. Indices 1 and 2 overlap to some extent but were both included for purposes of exploration. Indices 1 and 2, in particular are based on previous studies (S. Kreitler & H. Kreitler, 1986c, 1989b) that showed that the number of meaning variables—and, in particular, the number of meaning dimensions—is lower in subjects of lower developmental levels than in subjects higher in developmental level (i.e., young children compared with other children, children compared with adults, and retarded individuals compared with nonretarded adults). The fourth hypothesis was that the tendency toward motor actions (as assessed by the Motoric Activity Preference score) would have a lower maturational level in terms of the five indices than the tendency toward cognitive activity (as assessed by the Ideational Activity Preference score and the Cognitive Activity score).

The fifth issue in this study focused on comparing the patterns of intercorrelations with meaning variables of two different measures of thought tendencies: the Jancke-Boucsein Scale (Jancke, 1973), which explores different aspects of the individual's thinking and cognitive activities, and Stein and Craik's (1965) Motoric-Ideational Activity Preference Scale (MIAPS), which investigates only preferences for activities and provides two kinds of scores (direct scores of preferences and a derived index). It was of interest to examine differences in the number and kind of meaning variables related to the Jancke-Boucsein Scale and to each of the two kinds of scores based on the MIAPS. The Jancke-Boucsein Scale and the MIAPS are comparable in number of items, but the variety of themes referred to in the items seems to be greater in the former than in the latter scale. If the variety of items in the scale seriously affected the pattern of intercorrelations with meaning variables, the Jancke-Boucsein Scale could be expected to be related to a broader range of meaning variables than either of the MIAPS scores. Further, we hoped that a comparison of the kind of meaning variables related to the two measures of the tendency toward cognitive activities would shed light on similarities and differences, the former providing a set of common meaning variables assessing the tendency toward cognitive activity across measures, the latter providing features for characterizing idiosyncracies of the scales.

Finally, the sixth hypothesis of the study focused on examining the pattern of intercorrelations with meaning variables of the index Interest Level defined by the MIAPS. Some of Stein and Craik's (1965) findings support the assumption that this index assesses the breadth of the range of interests, irrespective of pathology. Hence, we expected this index to be correlated with more meaning variables than either of the separate scores of preference for motor or ideational activities.

Method

The 78 subjects (42 men and 36 women) included 30 undergraduates and 48 students at teachers' seminars, in the age range of 18–27 years. They were administered, on two separate occasions in group sessions, two to three weeks apart, in random order, the standard meaning questionnaire (11 stimulus words) and two scales: the Jancke-Boucsein Scale for Cognitive Activity (Jancke, 1973) and the MIAPS (Stein & Craik, 1965).

The Jancke-Boucsein Scale included 24 of the 56 original items. They were selected on the basis of pretests as the items most highly intercorrelated with the total score, and as the least redundant. This selection improved the internal consistency of the scale and raised it to .96. Responses were given in terms of six alternatives, ranging from "Is never true of me" (1) to "Is always true of me" (6). On the MIAPS, we included 30 of the original 50 items, selected on the basis of pretests as those most highly intercorrelated with the total score and best discriminating between the motoric and the ideational subgroups. Most of the dropped items were culture-bound and hence inadequate for an Israeli sample (e.g., "shoot pool," "hunting," and "watch horse racing"). Half the items referred to motoric activities and half to ideational ones. The subjects were asked to rate on a 4-point scale their interest in each of the activities at present or in the recent past.

Testing the first hypothesis required comparing the patterns of meaning variables correlated with the preference for motor actions or with the preference for cognitive activities (the Cognitive Activity score and the Ideational Activity Preference score) with the pattern of meaning variables correlated with extroversion (see Table 6, p. 138). Thus, there were three comparisons (i.e., the pattern of each of the preference scores with the extroversion pattern).

For each comparison we counted (1) the number of identical correlations, namely, the number of meaning variables that were correlated in the same direction in the two patterns, and (2) the number of opposite correlations, namely, the number of meaning variables that were correlated in opposite directions in the two patterns. If the two patterns included exactly the same meaning variable the correspondence was counted as 1 point; if however one pattern included the more general variable and the other the more specific one (say, *Dim* 2a+b and *Dim* 2a) the correspondence was counted as $\frac{1}{2}$ point.

Results and Conclusions

Comparing the pattern of the motor activity preference with the extroversion pattern showed that the two patterns included only two identical correlations (10.5% of the motor preference pattern and 8.3% of the extroversion pattern) but also one opposite correlation. Further comparisons showed that the pattern of the Cognitive Activity score and the extroversion pattern included five opposite correlations (13.9% of the preference pattern and 20.8% of the extroversion pattern) but also six identical correlations. Finally, in the Ideational Activity preference pattern and the extroversion score there were 2.5 opposite correlations (10% of the preference pat-

Table 28. Significant Correlations of Tendencies for Cognitive and Motor Activities with Meaning Variables

Personality variable	Significant correlations with meaning variables
Cognitive Activity score (Janke-Boucsein score)	*Dim* 1, .45***; *Dim* 2a, −.33**; *Dim* 2a + b, −.31**; *Dim* 3, .25*; *Dim* 4a, −.29**; *Dim* 4b, −.30**; *Dim* 4a + b, −.26*; *Dim* 7, −.27*; *Dim* 10, .29**; *Dim* 11, .35**; *Dim* 16, −.24*; *Dim* 18, .30**; *Dim* 19a, −.44***; *Dim* 19a + b, −.46***; $(19a_1, −.30^{**}; 19a_3, −.25^*; 19a_5, −.39^{***}; 19a_9, −.28^*; 19a_{10}, −.36^{**}; 19a + b_{0+1+2}, −.31^{**}; 19a + b_2, −.32^{**}; 19a + b_9, −.31^{**}; 19a + b_{10}, −.32^{**})$; ratio of no. of meaning dimensions to no. of meaning values, −.26*; *TR* 1a + b, .25*; *TR* 2c, .25*; *TR* 3a, −.27*; *TR* 3b, −.29**; *TR* 3a + b + c, −.30**; *TR* 4a, .27*; *TR* 4b, .26*; *TR* 4c, .24*; *TR* 4d, −.23*; *TR* 4a + b + c + d, .25*; no. of diff. *TR*, .24*; *SR* 1, −.30*; *SR* 3, −.26*; *SR* 5, .25*; *SR* 8, −.26*; *SR* 9, −.28*; no. of diff. *SR*, −.25*; *FR* 2, .37***; *FR* 3, −.24*; FR_{pos}, −.36**; FR_{neg}, .37***.
Ideational Activity Preference score (Stein & Craik Motoric-Ideational Activity Pref. score)	*Dim* 1, .25*; *Dim* 2a, −.24*; *Dim* 3, .27*; *Dim* 7, −.25*; *Dim* 10, .35**; *Dim* 11, .33**; *Dim* 14, .28*; *Dim* 18, .30**; $(19a_5, .23^*; 19a + b_5, .23^*)$; *Dim* 20a + b, −.25*; *Dim* 21b, .49***; *Dim* 21a + b, .28*; *Dim* 22b, .42***; *Dim* 22a + b, .32**; *TR* 1a, .25*; *TR* 1a + b, .24*; *TR* 2c, .33**; *TR* 2a + b + c + d, .29**; *TR* 3a, −.26*; *TR* 4a, .36**; *TR* 4a + b + c + d, .28*; no. of diff. *TR*, .31**; *SR* 1, −.30**; *SR* 5, .30**; *SR* 7, .26*; *FR* 2, .24*
Motoric Activity Preference score (Stein & Craik Motoric-Ideational Activity Pref. score)	*Dim* 4a, .51***; *Dim* 6, .32**; *Dim* 9, .29**; *Dim* 11, .25*; *Dim* 13, .28*; *Dim* 14, .39***; $(19a_3, .26^*; 19a_{11}, .27^*; 19b_4, −.24^*; 19a + b_{11}, .26^*)$; *Dim* 20a, −.27*; *TR* 2a + b + c + d, .28*; *TR* 3a, −.23*; lexical mode, .26*; *SR* 1, −.26*; *SR* 4, .27*; *SR* 5, .30**; SR_{near}, .25*; no. of diff. *SR*, .23*.
Difference score of the Ideational and Motoric Activities Preference scores (Ideational-Motoric) (Stein & Craik)	*Dim* 6, −27.*; *Dim* 7, −.29**; *Dim* 10, .35**; $(19a_3, −.32^{**}; 19a_8, .24^*; 19a + b_3, −.25^*)$; *Dim* 21b, .54***; *Dim* 22b, .31**; *Dim* 22a + b, .33**; *TR* 2c, .28*; *TR* 3c, −.32**; *TR* 4a, .35**; *TR* 4a + b + c + d, .33**; *SR* 7, .26*.
Sum of Ideational and Motoric Activities Preference scores (Ideational + Motoric) (Stein & Craik)	*Dim* 1, .24*; *Dim* 2a, −.23*; *Dim* 3, .27*; *Dim* 4a, .33**; *Dim* 9, .26*; *Dim* 11, .34**; *Dim* 14, .32**; *Dim* 15, .29**; $(19a_5, .28^*; 19a_{11}, .26^*; 19a + b_5, .29^*; 19a + b_{11}, .27^*)$; *Dim* 20a, −.28*; *Dim* 21b, .31**; *Dim* 22b, .27*; no. of diff. meaning dimensions, .26*; *TR* 1a, .25*; *TR* 1a + b, .26*; *TR* 2c, .31**; *TR* 2a + b + c + d, .30**; *TR* 3a, −.27*; *TR* 3a + b + c, −.25*; *TR* 4a, .27*; no. of diff. *TR*, .26*; lexical mode, .24*; *SR* 1, −.30**; *SR* 4, −.27*; *SR* 5, .41***; SR_{near}, .32**.

Note. For the code of the meaning variables, see Appendix A.
*$p < .05$.
**$p < .01$.
***$p < .001$.

tern and 10.4% of the extroversion pattern) but also 6.5 identical ones. Thus, the expected relations with extroversion were not supported by the data, possibly because the assessed preferences are of a different order than the constituents of extroversion.

An examination of the meaning dimensions to which the Cognitive Activity score and the two MIAPS preference scores are related reveals that only the MIAPS scores are related positively to the directly corresponding meaning dimensions, that is, the Ideational Activity Preference score to "Cognitive Qualities" (*Dim* 22), and the Motoric Activity score to "Action" (*Dim* 4). The Cognitive Activity score (Jancke-Boucsein) was not related to "Cognitive Qualities" (*Dim* 22). However, it was related negatively to "Action" (*Dim* 4a), a finding that may reveal some of the underlying dynamics of the tendency assessed by this scale and the sense in which it differs from the comparable tendency assessed by the MIAPS. Thus, the findings provide partial support for the second hypothesis.

Table 29 shows that two of the patterns of intercorrelations do not show any evidence of including meaning dimensions in the "neighborhood" of the focal dimensions with an above-chance frequency. There is some contrary evidence in the pattern for Motoric Activity Preference, but it is too limited to be interpretable. Hence, contrary to the third hypothesis, it seems justified to conclude that the patterns of intercorrelations of personality traits with meaning variables do not follow the "neighborhood" principle.

Table 30 presents the data relevant to evaluating the fourth hypothesis. It shows that the tendency toward motor activity has a lower maturational level than the tendency toward cognitive activity—definitely according to three indices (the ratio of responses to variables, dispersion of dimensions and of types of relation), partly according to one index (number of different meaning variables), and not at all according to one index (number of meaning dimensions). Essentially, there was no difference in the results when the Motoric Activity Preference score was compared with the Ideational Activity Preference score or the Cognitive Activity score. The two indices that provided weaker or no confirmation were the relatively simpler indices, based only on the number of different variables. Be that as it may, the findings

Table 29. Frequencies of Meaning Dimensions in the "Neighborhood" of the Target Dimensions in the Patterns of Intercorrelations with Three Scores

		Motoric Activity Preference score	Ideational Activity Preference score	Cognitive Activity score
Frequency of "neighbor- hood" meaning dimen- sions[a]	1st degree	1	3	2
	2nd degree	4	1	2
	Total	5	4	4
Proportions out of total meaning dim. in pat- tern[b]	1st degree	.143	.273	.200
	2nd degree	.571	.091	.200
	Total	.714	.364	.400
Comparisons with chance expectations				
$(4/22 = .182)$	1st degree	−.21	.48	.09
$(4/22 = .182)$	2nd degree	2.05*	−.48	−.09
$(8/22 = .364)$	Total	1.59	.00	.16

[a]For *Dim* 4, 1st-degree "neighborhood" meaning dimensions are *Dim* 3, *Dim* 5, *Dim* 6, and *Dim* 7; those of the 2nd degree are *Dim* 11, *Dim* 13, *Dim* 14, and *Dim* 9. For *Dim* 22, 1st-degree "neighborhood" meaning dimensions are *Dim* 20, *Dim* 21, *Dim* 16, and *Dim* 18; those of the 2nd degree are *Dim* 1, *Dim* 17, *Dim* 15, and *Dim* 19.
[b]In computing proportions, each meaning dimension was counted only once (i.e., *Dim* Xa and *Dim* Xb and *Dim* Xa + b were considered equivalent and were counted as one dimension regardless of whether one or more occurred in the pattern). Thus, there were 7, 11, and 10 meaning dimensions in the patterns of Motoric Preference, Ideational Preference, and Cognitive Activity scores, respectively. Target meaning dimensions were included in the proportions. For the code of the meaning variables, see Appendix A.
*$p < .05$, two-tailed.

Table 30. Differences in Indices of Maturational Level between Tendencies
toward Cognitive and Motor Activities

Indices of maturational level	Cognitive Activity score (a)	Ideational Activity Pref. score (b)	Motoric Activity Pref. score (c)	Significance of differences	
				Groups (c) & (a)	Groups (c) & (b)
Number of different meaning variables in the pattern	36	25	15	$z = 2.80^*$	$z = 1.42$
Number of different meaning dimensions in the pattern	14	13	7	$z = 1.31$	$z = 1.12$
Ratio of number of $\bar{X}$ meaning values to SD number of meaning variables[a]	1.12 .85	1.16 .71	2.83 1.06	$t = 5.55^{**}$	$t = 5.42^{**}$
Number of different circle quarters represented by the correlated meaning dimensions[b]	4	4	2	$z = 4.55^{**}$	$z = 4.55^{**}$
Number of different kinds of types of relation represented by the correlated meaning variables[c]	4	4	2	$z = 4.55^{**}$	$z = 4.55^{**}$

[a]The minimum is 1 (see text of Study 14). For the code of the meaning variables, see Appendix A.
[b]*Cognitive Activity score*: In the 1st quarter of the circle of dimensions (circular meaning-dimensional model): *Dim 1, Dim 2a, Dim 2a + b, Dim 3*; in the 2nd quarter: *Dim 4a, Dim 4b, Dim 4a + b, Dim 7, Dim 10, Dim 11*; in the 3rd quarter: *Dim 16, Dim 19a, Dim 19a + b*; in the 4th quarter: *Dim 18*.
Ideational Activity Preference score: In the 1st quarter of the circle of dimensions: *Dim 1, Dim 2a, Dim 3*; in the 2nd quarter: *Dim 7, Dim 10, Dim 11, Dim 14*; in the 3rd quarter: *Dim 20a + b, Dim 21b, Dim 21a + b*; and in the 4th quarter: *Dim 22b, Dim 22a + b*.
Motoric Activity Preference score: In the 1st quarter of the circle of dimensions: none; in the 2nd quarter: *Dim 4a, Dim 6, Dim 9, Dim 11, Dim 13, Dim 14*; in the 3rd quarter: *Dim 20a*; and in the 4th quarter: none.
[c]The four groups of TR are attributional (*TR 1a, TR 1b, TR 1a + b*); comparative (*TR 2a, TR 2b, TR 2c, TR 2d, TR 2a + b + c + d*); exemplifying-illustrative (*TR 3a, TR 3b, TR 3c, TR 3a + b + c*); and metaphoric-symbolic (*TR 4a, TR 4b, TR 4c, TR 4d, TR 4a + b + c + d*). The occurrence of at least one of the subtypes of a TR sufficed for scoring the TR kind as occurring.
$^*p < .01$, two-tailed.
$^{**}p < .001$, two-tailed.

provide sufficient support for the hypothesis to make it at least worthy of further exploration.

The fifth hypothesis led to a comparison of the patterns of intercorrelations with meaning variables of the two measures of cognitive activity. It showed that the pattern for Cognitive Activity does not include significantly more meaning variables than the pattern for Ideational Activity Preference (36 vs. 25, $z = 1.28$, $p < .10$), despite the wider range of content that seems to be tapped by its items. But within the MIAPS itself, the pattern of interrelations with meaning variables formed by the raw score of Ideational Activity Preference comprises more meaning variables than the pattern formed by the difference score, evidently preferred by Steiner and Craik (25 vs. 11, $z = 2.17$, $p < .05$). Whereas the former findings contradict the hypothesis, the latter were unexpected.

More informative, however, is the impressive set of meaning variables that are related to both measures of cognitive activity in the same direction. This set comprises 16 meaning variables (which form 44.4% of the variables in the pattern of Cognitive Activity and 64% of the more restricted MIAPS score pattern), which suggest a larger extent of overlap than would be predicted merely on the basis of the intercorrelation between the two scores ($r = .33$, $p < .01$). The list of common variables includes (1) meaning dimensions: "Contextual Allocation" (*Dim* 1), "Range of Inclusion" (*Dim* 2a; neg.), "Function" (*Dim* 3), "Consequences" (*Dim* 7, neg.), "Structure" (*Dim* 10), "State" (*Dim* 11), and "Development" (*Dim* 18); (2) types of relation: attribution (*TR* 1a+b), complementary (*TR* 2c), exemplifying instance (*TR* 3a, neg.), interpretation (*TR* 4a), and the metaphoric-symbolic (*TR* 4a+b+c+d), as well as the number of different types of relation; (3) shifts in referent: no shift (*SR* 1, negative) and combination of input with previous meaning value (*SR* 5); and (4) forms of relation: negative (*FR* 2).

Most of the findings are at least intuitively convincing. The pattern of meaning variables indicates that the characteristics of individuals preferring cognitive activities include concern with abstractions ("Contextual Allocation," *Dim* 1) and general ideas (interpretation, *TR* 4a), which is balanced neither by differentiations within the abstract categories (negative correlation with "Range of Inclusion," *Dim* 2a) nor by consideration of specific instances (negative correlation with exemplifying instance, *TR* 3a); awareness of structure ("Structure," *Dim* 10) and developments ("Development," *Dim* 18); and the tendencies to use different types of relation, the lexical and the personal, as well as to transform referents, which probably indicates cognitive facility and flexibility. Surprising at present is only the recurrent finding of a negative correlation with "Consequences" (*Dim* 7).

The difference score between Ideational and Motoric Preferences, which was designed to serve as an index measure of ideational preferences, is correlated with 11 meaning variables, 5 of which are common to it and the set of 15 meaning variables shared by the other two cognitive activity measures (i.e., "Consequences," *Dim* 7 neg.; "Structure," *Dim* 10; the complementary type of relation, *TR* 2c; interpretation, *TR* 4a; and the metaphoric-symbolic type of relation, *TR* 4a+b+c+d).

It seems plausible to assume that the 15 meaning variables shared by the two measures for cognitive activity form the common core of meaning variables characteristic of the tendency toward cognitive activity. As we saw, this core suggests some of the particular strengths as well as the weaknesses of individuals who tend toward cognitive activities. The presented image of the pattern of meaning variables characteristic of preferring cognitive activities contrasts sharply with the pattern of meaning variables characteristic of preferring motor activities. The latter is focused on concern with actions; with the causal, material, quantitative, and sensory qualities of things; and with grasping interpersonal reality (high frequencies of lexical mode and of shifts in referent to the previous meaning value, *SR* 4, and to the stimulus combined with the previous meaning value, *SR* 5). Of course, the conclusions concerning the different tendencies would have to be validated against independent findings.

The comparison of the patterns of the two measures of the tendency toward cognitive activities also suggest differences between the measures. The major difference is that high scorers on the Jancke-Boucsein measure admitted an interest in cognitive activities apparently not because they preferred it but because they rejected action (negative correlation with "Action," *Dim* 4) and external reality (negative correlation with "Sensory Qualities," *Dim* 19a), whereas high scorers on the Ideational Activity Preference score stated preferences for cognitive activities because they actually were concerned with "Cognitive Qualities" and "Judgments and Evaluations" without an accompanying rejection of external reality (positive relations with "State," *Dim* 11, and subdimensions of "Sensory Qualities," *Dim* 19a), though with a slight disregard of emotional qualities (negative correlation with "Feelings and Emotions," *Dim* 20). In other words, the high scores on the Jancke-Boucsein measure had turned to cognition from a potentially neurotic background (further suggestive indicators are the positive correlations with metaphors, *TR* 4b and *TR* 4c, and negative correlations with the mixed form of relation, *FR* 3), the high scorers on the scale of the Ideational Activity Preference out of a healthy, nondisplaced interest in the cognitive realm.

The final issue concerns the MIAPS index measure of interest level. Table 28 shows that it was correlated with 25 meaning variables and hence, contrary to expectation (sixth hypothesis), did not differ in this respect from the separate scores for ideational preferences (25 vs. 25, $z = .00$, n.s.) and motoric preferences (25 vs. 15, $z = 1.42$, n.s.). Yet, in keeping with the expectation, this index was correlated with the number of different meaning dimensions that the subject used. According to our findings, breadth-of-interest level is related to a fairly realistic attitude toward reality. This conclusion is based on the positive correlations of the index with the lexical mode of meaning, various procedures of defining referents close to the presented inputs, and several meaning dimensions that manifest interest in the more objective, functional, and actional aspects of reality (i.e., "Function," *Dim* 3; "Action," *Dim* 4a; "Material," *Dim* 9; "Quantity," *Dim* 14; and "Locational Qualities," *Dim* 15) rather than the experiential (negative correlation with "Feelings and Emotions," *Dim* 20). However, this realistic approach seemed to be complemented by a more ideationally oriented approach, too (i.e., "Contextual Allocation," *Dim* 1; "Judgments and Evaluations," *Dim* 21b; "Cognitive Qualities," *Dim* 22b; and interpretation, *TR* 4a).

In sum, this study revealed the major meaning variables underlying the tendencies toward cognitive or motor activities and related derived indices. The major characteristics of the tendency toward cognitive activity were found to be concern with abstractions unbalanced by considering discriminations, instances, and consequences; regard for structure and development; a variety of types of relation and referent shifts reflecting cognitive facility and flexibility; and a fairly realistic approach. The major characteristics of the tendency toward motor activity were found to be concern with actions; interest in the material and perceivable qualities of things; and sticking to interpersonally shared reality. The tendency toward cognitive activities was found, on the basis of most indices, to be on a higher maturational level than the tendency toward motor activities. All three tendencies are not related as expected to extroversion.

The findings also support some conclusions of a more general nature. First, two intercorrelated variables may share intercorrelations with a larger number of meaning variables than is warranted by the value of the correlation coefficient between them. Second, the patterns of intercorrelations may serve to identify differences between two measures that apparently measure the same tendency. A comparison of the patterns of the two measures of the tendency toward cognitive activities showed that, in one case, the high scorers preferred such activities because of a disregard for actions and external reality, whereas in the other case, they preferred them because of actual concern with cognitive qualities, judgments, and evaluations. Third, a larger number of items or even of aspects covered by a scale does not necessarily imply that the scale is correlated with a larger number of meaning variables than another, briefer scale. Fourth, the label of a scale and the manifest content of its items may provide guidelines but are not a guarantee of the prominence of the corresponding meaning dimensions in the dynamics of the trait (see Study 7 for a similar conclusion). Fifth, intercorrelations between a scale score and meaning dimensions do not follow the "neighborhood" principle; that is, when a scale correlates with a dimension, it does not necessarily correlate with other meaning dimensions in the vicinity. Hence, we may conclude that the pattern of intercorrelations with a trait reflects the dynamics of the trait rather than the structure of the meaning system.

STUDY 15: THE DIFFERENT MEANING PATTERNS OF SENSATION SEEKING

Purpose and Hypotheses

This study focused on exploring the patterns of meaning variables associated with sensation seeking. As defined by Zuckerman (1979a), sensation seeking is a general, genetically based personality trait that is assumed to mediate responses to various kinds of stimulation. A broad range of studies have shown the sensation-seeking scale to be correlated with different direct and indirect measures presumably manifesting responsiveness to stimulation (Zuckerman, 1974, 1979b). However, these studies raise problems that apparently cannot be resolved in terms of the sensation-seeking theory in its present form. One of the major problems is the manner in which the sensation-seeking tendency or trait operates within the psychological system of personality. The biological model suggested by Zuckerman (1979b, Chapter 13) deals merely with the biological predisposing factors of sensation seeking but leaves open the question of how the sensation-seeking trait actually operates.

This problem is closely related to the second problem, which concerns the particular expressions of sensation seeking. Criminality, drug abuse, daydreaming, breast-feeding, skydiving, risky decisions, preferences for spicy-sour and crunchy foods, and enhanced sexual interests are some of the responses more characteristic of high scorers than of low scorers on sensation seeking (Zuckerman, 1979a). Because it is inconceivable that high scorers on sensation seeking engage in all these and similar activities, some selectivity has to be postulated. Zuckerman (1979a, pp. 375–378) assumed that general social and specific parental factors determine the particular choices. This assumption is probably true but does not provide the whole of the necessary explanatory mechanism. For example, why should sensation seeking be related more to the seeking of visual than auditory stimulation after a period of sensory deprivation (Zuckerman & Haber, 1965)? Moreover, it has remained unclear how the specific manifestations occur and how, if at all, they are related to constructs like sensory curiosity and cognitive curiosity (Zuckerman, 1979b, p. 375), and especially to the four subscales of sensation seeking (i.e., Thrill and Adventure Seeking, Experience Seeking, Disinhibition, and Boredom Susceptibility), which were defined factorially (Zuckerman, 1971) and were shown to be differentially related to different responses (Zuckerman, 1979b, e.g., pp. 211, 266, 273, 276–277).

The assumption underlying the present study was that sensation seeking is bound with a particular pattern of meaning variables that mediate the individual's response to different kinds of inputs. Further, as the four different subscales were found to be related differentially to other measures, we expected each of them to be bound with a characteristic pattern of meaning variables that would clarify the manner in which the measured trait operates. For example, because "Experience Seeking" was described as reflecting "the seeking of new experiences through the mind and senses," we expected it to be correlated with the meaning dimensions of "Sensory Qualities" (*Dim* 19) and "Cognitive Qualities" (*Dim* 22).

In exploring the patterns of meaning variables bound with sensation seeking, we also adopted another approach, based on the explicit content of the items in the sensation-seeking scale. The items lent themselves to classification in terms of "Feelings and Emotions" (e.g., Items 21 and 72); "Cognitive Qualities" (e.g., Items 12, 17, and 65); "Temporal Qualities," specifically speed (e.g., Items 40, 44, and 71); and "Sensory Qualities" (e.g., Items 1, 5, 11, and 51), even specific sensory qualities like temperature (Items 5 and 44), odor (Item 11), and auditory stimuli (Items 39 and 45). Because the items of the Sensation Seeking Scale (SSS) were constructed with the intention of directly reflecting the presumed needs, desires, and interests of sensation-seeking subjects (Zuckerman, 1979b, p. 98), it was likely that the explicit content of the items would be related to meaning variables that are assumed to reflect underlying dynamics. Therefore, we expected that the scores on these different classifications would be related to the particular meaning dimensions corresponding to the manifest content of the items.

In addition, for the purpose of explaining the relation of specific items to meaning variables, we examined the meaning correlates of two further kinds of manifest content: items that refer explicitly to sex and an item that refers to harmony in art.

In sum, the major expectations guiding the study were (1) that the specific factors of sensation seeking and the total score on the Sensation Seeking Scale would be related to patterns of meaning variables corresponding to the dynamics and the validational findings of sensation seeking, and (2) that specific groupings of items would be correlated with the meaning variables corresponding to their manifest content. Each of these expectations was designed to serve as a framework for examining specific issues bound with each of the scores and explaining aspects of their underlying dynamics.

Method

The standard meaning questionnaire (11 stimulus words) and the SSS (Form IV, translated into Hebrew and pretested on another sample) were administered in group sessions in random order on two separate occasions, six to seven weeks apart, to a sample of 62 undergraduates in the social sciences at Tel Aviv University (29 women and 33 men) in the age range of 19–32 years.

The grouping of the items of the SSS in terms of manifest content was done by two judges (a physician and a psychologist) separately, in line with a set of criteria. The criteria specified the different meaning dimensions and the kinds of content in items that refer to these dimensions. For example, when the item deals with odors, auditory experiences, sensations of cold, and so on, it refers to "Sensory Qualities"; when it deals with speeding, racing, and so on, it refers to "Temporal Qualities." The judges could add categories on their own or leave empty any of the presented categories. The groupings of items finally selected (see Table 31) are based on unanimous agreement of the two judges. No item was classified in more than one category. Only a part of the items of the SSS were classified in this manner.

Results and Conclusions

Table 31 presents the constellations of meaning variables correlated with the scores on the different factors and other subgroupings of items on the SSS, as well as the total score.

The groupings of the intercorrelations with the scores on the four factors of sensation seeking are remarkably different but seem to conform to the various findings concerning these four factors. The factor of *Thrill and Adventure Seeking* was described as expressing "a desire to engage in outdoor sports or other activities involving elements of speed or danger" (Zuckerman, 1971, p. 47). It was found to be related to physical risk-taking (Zuckerman, 1979b, pp. 206–209) and often to be unrelated to different cognitive measures, mainly of cognitive achievement (Zuckerman, 1979b, e.g., pp. 234, 237, 243). Major characteristics of the pattern of intercor-

Table 31. Significant Intercorrelations of Sensation Seeking with Meaning Variables

Variables of sensation seeking	Significant correlations with meaning variables
Sensation seeking: Thrill and adventure seeking	*Dim* 3, .39**; *Dim* 6, −.29*; *Dim* 7, −.42***; *Dim* 9, −.26*; *Dim* 10, −.27*; *Dim* 14, .34**; ($19a_{10}$, −.28*; $19b_8$, .30*; $19a + b_{10}$, −.28*); *Dim* 20b, −.29*; *Dim* 21a, −.31*; *Dim* 21a + b, −.31*; *Dim* 22b, −.32*; *Dim* 22a + b, −.35**; *TR* 1b, .25*.
Sensation seeking: Experience seeking	*Dim* 2b, −.26*; *Dim* 2a + b, −.26*; *Dim* 3, .27*; *Dim* 4b, −.28*; *Dim* 8b, .27*; *Dim* 11, .29*; *Dim* 12, .34**; *Dim* 13, .29*; *Dim* 14, .28*; *Dim* 15, .40**; *Dim* 16, .30*; *Dim* 19b, .29*; ($19a_3$, .33**; $19b_1$, .34**; $19b_3$, .26*; $19a + b_3$, .33**); *Dim* 21b, .33**; *TR* 4d, −.26*; *TR* 4a + b + c + d, .31*; *SR* 2, −.27*; *SR* 5, .29*; *SR* 6, .26*; *SR* 7, .29*; *FR* 8, .35**
Sensation seeking: Disinhibition	*Dim* 4a, .53***; *Dim* 4a + b, .49***; *Dim* 11, −.31*; *Dim* 17a, .28*; *Dim* 17a + b, .28*; *Dim* 18, −.30*; *Dim* 19a, .31*; ($19a_3$, .31*; $19a_{11}$, −.29*; $19a + b_{11}$, −.28*); *SR* 2, −.31*; *SR* 7, .33**; *FR* 2, .34**; *FR* 8, .39**; FR_{pos}, −.32*; FR_{neg}, .39**.
Sensation seeking: Boredom susceptibility	*Dim* 4a, .31*; *Dim* 4b, −.29*; *Dim* 17b, −.30*; *Dim* 19b, .42***; ($19a_{10}$, −.25*; $19a_{11}$, −.27*; $19b_0$, .37**; $19b_8$, .45***); *TR* 2c, .29*; *TR* 3a, −.28*; *TR* 4d, −.27*; *SR* 1, −.25*; *SR* 2, −.32*; *SR* 4, .27*.
Sensation seeking: Total score	*Dim* 2b, −.26*; *Dim* 2a + b, −.33**; *Dim* 3, .36**; *Dim* 4a, .38**; *Dim* 7, −.33**; *Dim* 17b, .29*; ($19a_3$, .28*; $19b_6$, .29*; $19a + b_8$, .39**); *Dim* 21b, .30*; *TR* 3a, −.28*; *TR* 4d, −.27*; *SR* 2, −.28*; *SR* 3, .32*.
Score on items referring to sensory qualities: Total score (Items 5, 11, 19, 37, 39, 44, 45, 63 on SSS IV)	*Dim* 13, .29*; *Dim* 14, .31*; *Dim* 15, .37**; *Dim* 16, .38**; *Dim* 17a, −.27*; *Dim* 19a, .49***; *Dim* 19a + b, .54***; ($19a_0$, .26*; $19a_1$, .37**; $19a_8$, .38**; $19a_{10}$, −.29*; $19a + b_{0+1}$, .27*; $19a + b_7$, −.32*; $19a + b_{10}$, −.29*); *Dim* 21a, .33**; *Dim* 21b, .31*; *Dim* 21a + b, .32*; *Dim* 22a, .37**; *Dim* 22b, −.29*; *TR* 1a + b, .28*; *TR* 2a, .30*; *TR* 2d, .28*; *TR* 4a, .29*; *TR* 4b, .34**; *TR* 4d, −.27*; *TR* 4a + b + c + d, .31*; *SR* 1, −.27*; *SR* 5, .33**; *SR* 6, .35**; *SR* 7, .26*; *FR* 2, .27*; *FR* 8, .30*.
Subscore: Items referring to temperature (Items 5, 44 on SSS IV)	*Dim* 2a + b, −.28*; *Dim* 14, .30*; *Dim* 16, .30*; *Dim* 17a, −.32*; ($19a_6$, .41***; $19a_8$, .27*; $19a_{10}$, −.28*; $19b_3$, −.39**; $19b_6$, .49**; $19a + b_7$, −.29*; $19a + b_8$, .33**; $19a + b_{10}$, −.29*); *TR* 1a + b, .31*; *TR* 2a, .33**; *TR* 3a, −.36**; *TR* 3a + b + c, −.31*; *TR* 4a, .28*; *SR* 1, −.27*; *SR* 8, .30*; no. of different *SR*, .25*; *FR* 5, .29*.

Table 31. (*Continued*)

Variables of sensation seeking	Significant correlations with meaning variables
Subscore: Items referring to auditory sensations (Items 39, 45 on SSS IV)	$Dim\ 1$, $-.33^{**}$; $Dim\ 9$, $-.28^*$; $Dim\ 15$, $.44^{***}$; $Dim\ 19b$, $.31^*$; $(19a_0, .27^*$; $19a_3, .41^{***}$; $19a_4, .29^*$; $19a_{10}, -.26^*$; $19b_3, .45^{***}$; $19a + b_3, .40^{**}$; $19a + b_4, .30^*$; $19a + b_{10}, -.27^*$); $Dim\ 22a$, $.35^{**}$; $TR\ 2a$, $.32^*$; $TR\ 2b$, $-.34^{**}$; $TR\ 4c$, $-.30^*$; $SR\ 6$, $.29^*$; $FR\ 5$, $.27^*$.
Subscore: Item referring to smell (Item 11 on SSS IV)	$Dim\ 1$, $-.27^*$; $Dim\ 6$, $.29^*$; $Dim\ 16$, $.28^*$; $(19a_0, -.28^*$; $19a_3, -.26^*$; $19a_5, .29^*$; $19a_7, .36^{**}$; $19a_{11}, .32^*$; $19b_0, -.26^*$; $19b_3, .30^*$; $19b_5, .31^*$; $19b_5, .43^{**}$; $19b_8, .36^{**}$; $19b_9, -.28^*$; $19b_{11}, .31^*$; $19a + b_0, -.27^*$; $19a + b_5, .28^*$; $19a + b_7, .33^{**}$; $19a + b_8, .38^{**}$; $19a + b_{11}, .31^*$); $TR\ 4b$, $.28^*$; no. of different TR, $.29^*$.
Score on items referring to temporal qualities (Items 40, 44, 71 on SSS IV)	$Dim\ 3$, $.28^*$; $Dim\ 6$, $-.31^*$; $Dim\ 14$, $.45^{***}$; $(19a_0, -.28^*$; $19a_{12}, -.30^*$); $Dim\ 20b$, $-.30^*$; $Dim\ 21a$, $-.30^*$; $Dim\ 21a + b$, $-.29^*$; $Dim\ 22b$, $-.31^*$; $TR\ 4d$, $-.27^*$.
Score on items referring to emotions (Items 21, 42, 47, 72 on SSS IV)	$Dim\ 1$, $-.34^*$; $Dim\ 2$, $-.38^{**}$; $Dim\ 2b$, $-.31^*$; $Dim\ 2a + b$, $-.27^*$; $Dim\ 3$, $.36^{**}$; $Dim\ 4b$, $-.27^*$; $Dim\ 4a + b$, $-.26^*$; $Dim\ 5$, $-.29^*$; $Dim\ 6$, $-.42^{***}$; $Dim\ 10$, $-.28^*$; $Dim\ 11$, $.36^{**}$; $Dim\ 13$, $-.31^*$; $Dim\ 15$, $-.32^*$; $Dim\ 19a$, $.25^*$ $(19a_4, -.39^{**}$; $19a_5, -.30^*$; $19a_6, -.27^*$; $19a_7, -.26^*$; $19a_8, -.28^*$; $19a_{10}, -.29^*$; $19a_{11}, -.25^*$; $19b_6, .35^{**}$; $19b_7, .31^*$; $19b_8, .44^{***}$; $19a + b_4, -.37^{**}$; $19a + b_5, -.28^*$; $19a + b_8, .30^*$; $19a + b_{10}, -.27^*$; $19a + b_{11}, -.26^*$); $Dim\ 20a + b$, $.42^{***}$; $Dim\ 21a$, $-.27^*$; $Dim\ 21b$, $.47^{***}$; $Dim\ 21a + b$, $-.27^*$; $Dim\ 22a + b$, $-.27^*$; no. of diff. meaning dimensions, $-.25^*$; ratio of no. of meaning dim. to no. of meaning values, $-.26^*$; $TR\ 1a$, $-.33^{**}$; $TR\ 1b$, $-.25^*$; $TR\ 1a + b$, $-.33^{**}$; $TR\ 2a$, $-.31^*$; $TR\ 2d$, $-.30^*$; $TR\ 2a + b + c + d$, $-.34^{**}$; $TR\ 4c$, $.28^*$; $TR\ 4a + b + c + d$, $.25^*$; lexical mode, $-.33^{**}$; $SR\ 1$, $-.27^*$; $SR\ 3$, $-.26^*$; $SR\ 4$, $-.28^*$; $SR\ 6$, $-.43^{***}$; $SR\ 8$, $-.32^*$; SR_{near}, $-.28^*$; no. of different SR, $-.28^*$; $FR\ 2$, $-.25^*$; no. of meaning values, $-.30^*$.
Score on items referring to cognitive qualities (Items 7, 16, 17, 32, 46, 61, 65, 70 on SSS IV)	$Dim\ 1$, $.31^*$; $Dim\ 4a$, $.26^*$; $Dim\ 12$, $.29^*$; $Dim\ 16$, $-.27^*$; $(19a_0, -.27^*$; $19a_3, .26^*$; $19a_7, -.26^*$; $19b_0, .29^*$; $19b_4, -.28^*$; $19a + b_4, -.27^*$); $Dim\ 20b$, $-.27^*$; $Dim\ 20a + b$, $-.29^*$; $Dim\ 21a$, $-.30^*$; $Dim\ 21b$, $-.27^*$; $Dim\ 21a + b$, $-.28^*$; $Dim\ 22a$, $.49^{***}$; $Dim\ 22a + b$, $.50^{***}$; $TR\ 2c$, $.29^*$; $TR\ 4a$, $.29^*$; $SR\ 1$, $-.27^*$; $FR\ 2$, $-.28^*$; $FR\ 3$, $-.27^*$.
Score on items referring to sexual experiences (Items 26, 38, 54, 59, 64 on SSS IV)	$Dim\ 8a + b$, $-.28^*$; $Dim\ 11$, $-.41^{***}$; $Dim\ 14$, $-.29^*$; $Dim\ 17b$, $.40^{**}$; $Dim\ 17a + b$, $.30^*$; $Dim\ 18$, $-.27^*$; $(19a_3, .26^*$; $19a_8, .46^{***}$; $19a_{11}, -.28^*$; $19b_6, .42^{***}$; $19b_8, .46^{***}$; $19a + b_8, .43^{***}$; $19a + b_{12}, -.26^*$); $Dim\ 22b$, $.25^*$; $Dim\ 22a + b$, $.28^*$; $TR\ 2b$, $-.27^*$; $SR\ 3$, $-.28^*$; $SR\ 7$, $.30^*$; $SR\ 5$, $-.26^*$; SR_{far}, $.27^*$; $FR\ 8$, 29^*.
Score on item referring to harmony in painting (Item 51 on SSS IV)	$Dim\ 15$, $.31^*$; $(19a_2, .46^{***}$; $19b_2, .30^*$; $19a + b_2, .34^{**}$); $Dim\ 19b$, $.28^*$; $Dim\ 21b$, $.29^*$; $Dim\ 22a$, $.36^{**}$; $TR\ 4a$, $.31^*$; $FR\ 2$, $.30^*$; FR_{pos}, $-.29^*$.

Note. For the code of the meaning variables, see Appendix A.
$^*p < .05.$
$^{**}p < .01.$
$^{***}p < .001.$

relations with meaning are the negative correlations with "Feelings and Emotions," "Judgments and Evaluations," and "Cognitive Qualities," all of which suggest that this factor may reflect not merely a neutral stance but perhaps an active disregard of the inner world of experiencing. One notable exception is the positive correlation with "Internal Sensations" (Dim 19b$_8$), which may be expected of individuals intent on exposing themselves to danger for the sake of the thrill. Remarkably, this scale was found to correlate positively with degree of heterosexual activities (Zuckerman, 1979b, p. 174) and the use of drugs and alcohol (pp. 281, 288) but not with smoking (p. 295), perhaps because the first three affect internal sensations more markedly than smoking. Further, there is evidence of a functional-utilitarian approach (positive correlations with "Function," Dim 3, and "Quantity," Dim 14) and of a disregard of "Causes" (Dim 6) and "Consequences" (Dim 7), which conforms with the findings about risk taking.

Experience Seeking was defined as reflecting a desire to have a variety of experiences through external or internal sensations (Zuckerman, 1979b, p. 102). It was found to be correlated with measures of novelty seeking by cognitive means, volunteering for experiments and so on (Zuckerman, 1979b, e.g., pp. 141, 184). The pattern for Experience Seeking is richer and more diverse than that for Thrill and Adventure Seeking. It includes positive correlations with "Sensory Qualities," "Judgments and Evaluations," and "Cognitive Qualities," which reflect an emphasis on internal-experiential aspects, though not specifically emotional aspects; positive correlations with "Function," "Domain of Application," "State," "Weight," "Quantity," "Temporal Qualities," and "Locational Qualities," all of which seem to reflect a relatively broad interest in reality; positive correlations with variables of shifts in referent that show reality-preserving manipulations of the input; and finally, positive correlations with the metaphoric-symbolic type of relation, which are consistent with the finding about an openness to experiences of fantasy, daydreams, and night dreams (Zuckerman, 1979b, pp. 245ff).

In sum, the pattern of intercorrelations suggests that the Experience Seeking factor is more complex than may be immediately evident. Its particular characteristics are the balancing of an openness to reality and the availability of reality-testing procedures, on the one hand, and concern with the internal world and the symbolic-metaphoric type of relation, on the other hand. This combination indicates both interest in the internal world and the psychological strength to be exposed to it without succumbing to its dangers or withdrawing from reality. Thus, the pattern of intercorrelations may explain why the Experience Seeking factor is the one that was found to be most highly correlated with "inner experiences," "tolerance for unusual sensations or 'irrational' ideas," "openness to experience," and "regression in the service of the ego" (Zuckerman, 1979a, p. 176). Further, the particular pattern of intercorrelations indicates that the factor of Experience Seeking is probably the major element that accounts for the relations detected between Sensation Seeking and creativity (Zuckerman, 1979b, pp. 238–240).

The *Disinhibition* factor describes the tendency to seek release and social disinhibition through the more traditional means of drinking, partying, gambling, and sex. Zuckerman (1979b, p. 103) assumed that it is more closely allied to biological traits and is less dependent on sociocultural conditions than the other factors. Two findings stand out in the pattern of intercorrelations with meaning: a positive correlation with "Actions" and with forms of relation that are based on negation. The former indicates a preference for dynamism, and the latter, probably for negativism.

Both tendencies together are consistent with the dynamic, nontraditional behavior characteristic of Disinhibition. Because the dimension "Action" is correlated with this factor, but not the dimension "Judgments and Evaluation," it may be assumed that the unconventional approach of the high scorers is manifested in a kind of style of living rather than through outright rebellion.

Boredom Susceptibility was defined as "an aversion for repetitive experience of any kind, routine work, or dull and boring people and extreme restlessness under conditions when escape from constancy is impossible" (Zuckerman, 1979b, p. 103). The major findings in the pattern of intercorrelations with meaning are the positive correlations with "Sensory Qualities" (*Dim* 19b) and, in particular, with "Internal Sensations," and with "Action" (*Dim* 4a). The correlations suggest that high scorers on this factor are attuned to internal sensations and dynamism, and that these may be the sources of their susceptibility to constancy.

As may be expected in view of the distinctiveness of the four patterns of inter-correlations, the pattern for the total score on the SSS presents a kind of noncharac-teristic combination of the different patterns. It includes a positive correlation with "Function" (*Dim* 3) and a negative one with "Consequences" (*Dim* 7), which repre-sent mainly the first factor and partly the second; positive correlations with sub-dimensions of "Sensory Qualities" (including internal sensations) and "Judgments and Evaluations," which represent the second and fourth factors; and a positive correlation with "Actions," which represents the third and fourth factors. This com-posite pattern reflects the different elements of the sensation-seeking orientation: concern with functionality, action, certain sensory qualities (referring to sound, temperature, and internal sensations), and evaluative aspects of experiencing, cou-pled with a disregard of consequences. This pattern reveals major elements in the dynamics of sensation seeking. It indicates that, overall, actions and certain sensory inputs play a more important role in sensation seeking than cognitive and emotional experiences. This conclusion corresponds to the main bulk of the findings, which show high sensation-seekers to be attuned to certain sensory inputs (the relative salience of auditory and internal body sensations is remarkable; see Rao, 1978; Zuckerman, Neary, & Brustman, 1970) and related phenomena like vivid imagery and hallucinatory experiences (e.g., Belcher, Bone, & Walker, 1972; Blankstein, 1976; Rao, 1978), but less, if at all, to more purely cognitive and emotional experiences (Segal & Singer, 1976; Zuckerman, 1979b, Chapter 8, see especially pp. 247–248).

Further, there is a lot of evidence in support of the specific positive correlation with "Action" (*Dim* 4a) and the negative correlation with "Consequences" (*Dim* 7). The former indicates concern with physical action, the latter, a disregard of possible results. Findings consistent with the salience of "Action" (*Dim* 4a) include the con-cern of high scorers on the SSS with traveling (Zuckerman, 1979a), mobility (Jacobs and Koeppel, 1974), sports (Zuckerman, 1979b, pp. 206–207), opportunities for physical movement (Hocking & Robertson, 1969), and so on. Findings consistent with the negative correlation with "Consequences" (*Dim* 7) include the tendency of high scorers on the SSS to appraise many situations as less risky than low scorers (Zuckerman, 1979a), to be more adventurous in situations that evoke fear in low scorers (Mellstrom, Cicala, & Zuckerman, 1976), and to engage in risky behavior, such as drug taking, sexual-variety seeking, and gambling (Zuckerman, 1979b, Chapters 7, 10). Together, the tendencies toward action and risk taking suggest that high SSS scorers have a particular propensity for physical actions that involve risk. Indeed, studies showed that high SSS scorers engage more than low scorers in risky activities such as parachuting, scuba diving, fire fighting, speeding and reckless driving, race-car driving, fighting on antiriot squads, and traveling in dangerous areas (Hymbaugh & Garrett, 1974; Zuckerman, 1979b, pp. 206–209). Again, the tendency toward risk taking, together with the concern with possessions (positive correlation with "Belongingness," *Dim* 17b), corresponds to the finding that high scorers on the SSS are interested in gambling, particularly when monetary profits are involved (Zuckerman, 1979b, pp. 211–212).

The pattern of intercorrelations with meaning variables also has implications relevant to the major issue of the relation of sensation seeking to arousal. The SSS was originally designed to account for individual differences in the responses of subjects under sensory-deprivation conditions (Zuckerman, 1979b, p. 59). Although the SSS has proved useful in accounting for many different psychological phenomena, the results of applying the scale to responses to sensory deprivation were disappointing and inconclusive (Zuckerman, 1979b, pp. 196–203). The pattern of interrelations with meaning variables provides some suggestions about the reactions that were not observed and those that were observed. For example, the pattern does not include a correlation with "Sensory Qualities" (*Dim* 19a), and hence, there is no reason to assume that high scorers on the SSS would be particularly sensitive to reduced external stimulation. Indeed, they did not report the situation as stressful (Zuckerman, 1979b, pp. 196–203). Further, after sensory deprivation, they did not have particularly high rates of exposure to sensory stimuli, especially not to the visual (there is in the pattern no correlation with the visual subdimension of "Sensory Qualities"), and their arousal level was not appreciably affected. However, there is clear evidence that, when given the choice of visual, auditory, or kinesthetic stimulation during a 3-hour sensory-deprivation period, high scorers on the SSS responded relatively more to the kinaesthetic stimulation, which allowed them to move on and off the bed for 15 seconds, than to visual or auditory stimuli (Hocking & Robertson, 1969). This finding clearly shows that the source of stress for high SSS scorers is a low level of activity and the related internal sensations, as would be predicted from the positive correlations with "Action" (*Dim* 4a) and "Sensory Qualities: Internal Sensations" (*Dim* $19a+b_8$).

Again, in another study that compared high and low SSS scorers on various physiological indices during an 8-hour period of confinement, only one variable showed a relationship to the SSS: restless body movements that increased more in the high than in the low scorers (Zuckerman *et al.*, 1966). This finding, too, corresponds clearly to the correlation of the SSS with "Action" (*Dim* 4a). Thus, the pattern of interrelations with meaning variables indicates that sources of stress and stimuli are potent as reinforcers.

Table 31 also presents the findings concerning groupings of items in line with specific content that corresponds to particular meaning dimensions. The findings show in all cases (except the case of speed) a high and significant correlation between the manifest content of the items and the meaning dimension(s) to which this content corresponds. Specifically, the score on items that refer to sensory qualities is highly correlated with "Sensory Qualities" (*Dim* 19a and *Dim* 19b); moreover, the items that refer to temperature, sound, and olfactory sensations are correlated with the subdimensions of temperature, sound, and olfactory sensations, respectively. The score on items that refer to temporal qualities is correlated mainly with "Quantity" (*Dim* 14) but not with "Temporal Qualities" (*Dim* 16), a finding that suggests that at least speed may be a matter of quantity rather than time. The score on items that refer to emotions is correlated with "Feelings and Emotions" (*Dim* 20). Finally, the score on items that refer to cognitive qualities is correlated with "Cognitive Qualities" (*Dim* 22).

However, each of these scores is correlated not merely with the mentioned corresponding meaning dimension but with a whole pattern of meaning variables. An examination of these patterns reveals information that is of potential interest for studying the different scores. For example, the score on sensory qualities is correlated positively also with the evaluative (*Dim* 21) and cognitive (*Dim* 22) dimensions and with the metaphoric-symbolic type of relation (*TR* 4), which is anchored partly in sensations. Further, the score on emotional items is correlated positively with "State" and "Internal Sensations," and negatively with "Causes" and with "Judgments and Evaluations" (these findings correspond to findings about meaning variables that are correlates of emotional experiencing; see H. Kreitler & S. Kreitler, 1983b and S. Kreitler & H. Kreitler, 1985a). Finally, the score on cognitive items is correlated negatively with "Feelings and Emotions" (*Dim* 20) and "Judgments and Evaluations" (*Dim* 21), a finding that indicates the purely cognitive, rather than generally experiential, nature of the underlying tendency.

Accordingly, the findings about the patterns characteristic of dimensionally defined clusters of items show that the manifest content of items in a scale is of crucial importance in itself, and that it may affect the surplus information that the items are expected to provide about underlying personality traits.

Finally, the last two items of Table 31 present the patterns for sexual items and the item testing for sensitivity to harmony in painting. The main importance of these findings is that they demonstrate the use of patterns of correlations with meaning variables for the purpose of exploring underlying dynamics. The salient findings in the pattern for sexual items are the high positive correlations with "Possessions" and the subdimensions of "Sensory Qualities," especially temperature and internal sensations. The main findings for the item of harmony in painting are the correlations with form ("Sensory Qualities," *Dim* $19a_2$, $19b_2$, and $19a+b_2$), "Locational Qualities" (*Dim* 15), "Judgments and Evaluations" (*Dim* 21b), and "Cognitive Qualities" (*Dim* 22a), and the absence of a correlation with the dimension "Structure" (*Dim* 10).

In sum, the major findings of this study are that the meaning variables related to the scores on the four separate factors and to the total score on the SSS correspond to the basic findings about these scores and may contribute to the resolution of issues produced by various apparently inconsistent or unexpected findings. Hence, the personological manifestations of meaning variables have empirical validity in view of the findings in this domain, as well as theoretical value for unraveling the dynamics underlying the assessed tendencies. Some of the suggested interpretations of the four factors of the SSS will be tested in Study 16.

STUDY 16: MEANINGFUL CHOICES OF SUBTYPES OF SENSATION SEEKERS

Purposes and Hypotheses

The purpose of this study was to test the validity of some of the interpretations of the four subfactors of sensation seeking suggested in Study 15 on the basis of the patterns of intercorrelations of these factors with meaning variables. Specifically, the patterns indicated that the factor of Thrill and Adventure Seeking reflects a functional approach coupled with a disregard of consequences; the factor of Experience Seeking reflects an emphasis on experiencing coupled with an interest in the external world; the factor of Disinhibition reflects concern with action; and the factor of Boredom Susceptibility is bound with attentiveness to sensations, particularly internal ones.

We tested these conclusions in the domain of volunteering for psychological experiments. We chose volunteering as the dependent variable, because it is merely a commitment and hence may be expected to be more directly affected by meaning variables than an actual action would be. Previous work showed that sensation seeking is related to volunteering for experiments, particularly unusual ones, and that the different subfactors of sensation seeking are related differentially to different types of suggested experiments (Bone, Cowling, & Choban, 1974; Myers & Eisner, 1974; Stanton, 1976; Zuckerman, 1974, pp. 112–113; Zuckerman, Schultz, & Hopkins, 1967). Our hypothesis was that subjects relatively high in any one of the four factors of sensation seeking and relatively low in the other three factors would volunteer more for the type of experiment that corresponds to the major meaning variables found to be correlated with that factor (see Study 15 Results and Conclusions) than they would volunteer for other types of experiments. Specifically, we expected that subjects high only in the factor Thrill and Adventure Seeking would prefer experiments described as useful but not completely predictable in all specifics; subjects high only in the factor of Experience Seeking would prefer experiments described as providing the opportunity for exceptional experiences of reality; subjects high only in the factor of Disinhibition would prefer experiments described as providing the possibility of some unusual action; and subjects high only in the factor of Boredom Susceptibility would prefer experiments described as providing the opportunity for unusual sensory experiences.

Method

The Sensation Seeking Scale (SSS, Form IV) was administered to an unselected sample of 259 undergraduates at Tel Aviv University (in the age range 19–32 years). They were given the questionnaire for completion at home, and 248 (134 women and 114 men) returned it. Upon handing in this questionnaire, the subjects were presented with a sheet of paper on which four different kinds of experiments were listed. It was emphasized that the presented descriptions referred to kinds of experiments and not to any specific experiment. They were asked to check the one (and only one) kind of experiment in which they would like to participate in the framework of completing their duties as subjects in psychological experiments. The subjects were urged to check their choices only on the basis of their real preferences without considering credit points, the time and duration of the experiments, and so on. The experimenter explained that the subjects' choices would provide information important to researchers in the department who scheduled experiments, but that he or she could not promise that the subjects would actually be invited to participate in experiments of the kind they had checked as most desirable.

The four types of experiments were (1) an experiment that would involve the subject in some useful but not completely predictable procedure; it was emphasized that "of course, it is not actually dangerous, but not all details of the outcome can be specified"; (2) an experiment that would provide the subject with the opportunity to experience some unusual aspect of reality, or plain reality in some exceptional manner; (3) an experiment that would require some actual action on the part of the subject, which would itself be unusual or would be performed under unusual circumstances; and (4) an experiment that would provide the subject with the opportunity to undergo some experience involving exceptional sensations. We expected Experiments 1, 2, 3, and 4 to be selected by subjects high in Thrill and Adventure Seeking, Experience Seeking, Disinhibition, and Boredom Susceptibility, respectively.

Out of the 248 subjects, 90 subjects were identified as being high (above the mean) in one of the four factors of sensation seeking and low (below the mean) in the other three factors. Table 32 presents the number of subjects in each subgroup as well as the means of the factors and the intercorrelations between them.

Results and Conclusions

Table 32 shows that, as expected, subjects high in any one of the factors of sensation seeking and low in the others chose predominantly to participate in the type of experiment that corresponded to the meaning variables with which their characteristic scores had correlated. The results are significant for each subgroup separately as well as for all subjects together. The findings indicate that the patterns of intercorrelations with meaning variables allow the prediction of preferences and choices made by subjects.

Table 32. Choices of Subjects Scoring High in Any One of the Four Sensation-Seeking Factors and Low in the Others[a]

Subjects high only in:	N	No. of subjects choosing experiment with				z^b
		Useful but unpredictable	Experience of excep. reality	Unusual action	Experience with excep. sensations	
A. Thrill and adventure seeking	26	21	1	2	2	2.94**
B. Experience seeking	25	2	18	0	5	2.00*
C. Disinhibition	19	3	0	16	0	2.75**
D. Boredom susceptibility	20	4	0	1	15	2.01*
Total	90	Ss choosing predicted experiment ($n = 70$) vs. others ($n = 20$)				5.17***

[a]Correlations between the factors of the Sensation Seeking Scale (SSS): A & B, .38**; A & C, .37**; A & D, .21 ($p = .055$); B & C, .43***; B & D, .48***; C & D, .43***. The means of the factors were 21.9, 26.1, 19.7, and 27.4 for factors A, B, C, and D, respectively.
[b]The z values represent the differences between the number of subjects who chose the predicted type of experiment and all those who chose the other types.
*$p < .05$.
**$p < .01$.
***$p < .001$.

STUDY 17: THE MEANING PATTERNS OF SEX-ROLE CONCEPTIONS (BEM SCALE)

Purpose and Hypotheses

Sex-role conceptions may not constitute full-fledged traits in the conventional sense of the term, but most sex-role conceptions probably reflect underlying traits that may characterize "masculine," "feminine," and "androgynous" individuals. This is particularly true when one accepts Bem's definition (1974) of these concepts in terms of self-descriptions. Accordingly, "masculine" describes an individual who applies to himself or herself descriptive terms viewed in the culture as being characteristic of males, "feminine" describes an individual who applies to himself or herself descriptive terms considered characteristic of females, and "androgynous" would apply to a person who describes himself or herself in terms of both kinds of terms. The major assumption underlying Bem's inventory is that the three types of self-descriptions represent distinct personality dimensions, which may be expected to mediate sex-typed behavior. Concepts about oneself are clusters of beliefs that may be expected to be affected by meaning (see "Meaning Preferences and Beliefs" in Chapter 3). Hence, an exploration of the patterns of interrelations with meaning variables corresponding to the different concepts about the self could deepen our understanding of these concepts and their manifestations. This expectation is rendered particularly plausible in view of the more recent conception of sex typing as deriving from the cognitive processing of information in terms of gender-specific schemas (Bem, 1981).

The first hypothesis of the study was that the patterns of intercorrelations with meaning variables would be different for masculinity and femininity. This general hypothesis was based on the finding that masculinity and femininity are two independent variables (see Bem, 1981). The second hypothesis was that masculinity would be related negatively to the dimensions "Feelings and Emotions" (*Dim* 20), "Judgments and Evaluations" (*Dim* 21), and "Sensory Qualities" (particularly those perceived by the referent, *Dim* 19b). The rationale was the findings reported by Olds and Shaver (1980) showing that masculinity was correlated with self-reports about emotions ("worry" and "guilt" in both genders, "tension" and "fears" only in females), about decreased evaluation of the self ("worthlessness" and self-deprecation in both genders), and about different bodily symptoms (general psychosomatic index and tiredness in both genders). Finally, the third hypothesis was designed to examine the relation between the meaning variables correlated with the constructs and the connotation of the descriptive terms in the inventory assessing the constructs. Accordingly, we expected masculinity to be related to, among other meaning variables, the meaning dimension "State" (*Dim* 11) and femininity to the meaning dimension "Feelings and Emotions" (*Dim* 20). The rationale was that, out of the 20 "masculine" items in the Sex-Role Inventory (Bem, 1974), 7 seemed to refer to "State" (i.e., Items 10, 37, 19, 7, 52, 40, and 34), whereas out of the 20 "feminine" items, 8 seemed to refer to "Feelings and Emotions" (i.e., Items 11, 5, 32, 14, 56, 8, 23, and 41). No other meaning variables were represented in the inventory to the same extent.

Method

Bem's (1974) Sex-Role Inventory (in a pretested Hebrew version) and the standard meaning questionnaire (11 stimulus words) were administered, in random order on two separate occasions in group sessions three to four weeks apart, to 82 undergraduates (40 females and 42 males) in the social sciences in the age range 20–29 years. The inventory yielded the four standard separate scores of masculinity, femininity, androgyny (i.e., femininity minus masculinity multiplied by 2.322), and social desirability (based on the neutral items of the Sex-Role Inventory).

Results and Conclusions

Table 33 shows that the patterns of intercorrelations for masculinity and femininity were very different. Indeed, of the 19 correlations in the masculinity pattern and the 20 in the femininity pattern, not a single one was shared by both patterns, but 3 (about 15%) involved the same meaning variables (i.e., "Judgments and Evaluations," *Dim* 21a and *Dim* 21a+b, and the comparative difference type of relation, *TR* 2d), though in reversed direction of correlation. The data confirm the first hy-

Table 33. Intercorrelations of Variables Assessed by Bem's Sex-Role Inventory with Meaning Variables

Variables based on Bem's inventory	Significant correlations with meaning variables
A. Masculinity score	*Dim* 2a, $-.22^*$; *Dim* 3, $.36^{***}$; *Dim* 9, $.29^{**}$; *Dim* 11, $.32^{**}$; *Dim* 19a, $-.37^{***}$; *Dim* 19a + b, $-.41^{***}$; $(19a_4, -.36^{***}; 19a_5, -.25^*; 19a_{11}, -.28^{**}; 19b_1, -.27^*; 19b_3, -.33^{**}; 19b_4, -.36^{***}; 19a + b_4, -.49^{***}; 19a + b_5, -.29^{**})$; *Dim* 20a, $-.54^{***}$; *Dim* 21a, $-.31^{**}$; *Dim* 21a + b, $-.35^{**}$; *Dim* 22a, $-.39^{***}$; *Dim* 22a + b, $-.47^{***}$; *TR* 2d, $-.27^*$; *TR* 4a, $.37^{***}$; *TR* 4c, $.26^*$; *TR* 4a + b + c + d, $.39^{***}$; *SR* 3, $-.34^{**}$; *SR* 8, $-.35^{**}$; SR_{far}, $-.40^{***}$; *FR* 5, $-.42^{***}$.
B. Femininity score	*Dim* 4a, $-.27^*$; *Dim* 4b, $.29^{**}$; *Dim* 6, $.29^{**}$; *Dim* 8b, $.26^*$; *Dim* 10, $.35^{**}$; *Dim* 16, $.26^*$; *Dim* 17a, $-.28^*$; *Dim* 17b, $.31^{**}$; $(19a_0, .25^*)$; *Dim* 21a, $.27^*$; *Dim* 21b, $.26^*$; *Dim* 21a + b, $.27^*$; *Dim* 22b, $.25^*$; *TR* 2a, $-.30^{**}$; *TR* 2d, $.35^{**}$; *TR* 3a, $.31^{**}$; no. of diff. *TR*, $.24^*$; *SR* 4, $.26^*$; SR_{near}, $.27^*$; *FR* 2, $.26^*$; no. of meaning values, $.29^{**}$.
C. Social desirability score	*Dim* 3, $.29^{**}$; *Dim* 9, $.29^{**}$; *Dim* 18, $.25^*$; *Dim* 19a, $-.28^*$; *Dim* 19a + b, $-.27^*$; $(19a_0, .24^*; 19a_6, .26^*)$; *Dim* 20a, $-.36^{***}$; *Dim* 20a + b, $-.35^{**}$; *TR* 3b, $-.33^{**}$; *SR* 5, $.34^{**}$; *FR* 2, $.25^*$.
D. Androgyny score	*Dim* 2a, $.29^{**}$; *Dim* 2a + b, $.28^*$; *Dim* 3, $-.29^{**}$; *Dim* 4b, $.27^*$; *Dim* 6, $.28^*$; *Dim* 8b, $.24^*$; *Dim* 9, $-.28^*$; *Dim* 11, $-.30^{**}$; *Dim* 16, $.27^*$; *Dim* 17a, $-.27^*$; *Dim* 17b, $.34^{**}$; *Dim* 19a, $.33^{**}$; $(19a_4, .35^{**}; 19a_{11}, .41^{***}; 19b_1, .26^*; 19a + b_4, .31^{**}; 19a + b_{11}, .44^{***}; 19a + b_{0+1}, .24^*)$; *Dim* 20a, $.31^{**}$; *Dim* 21a, $.34^{**}$; *Dim* 21b, $.25^*$; *Dim* 21a + b, $.30^{**}$; *Dim* 22b, $.31^{**}$; ratio of no. of meaning dimensions and no. of meaning values, $.24^*$; *TR* 1a, $.24^*$; *TR* 1b, $.23^*$; *TR* 1a + b, $.24^*$; *TR* 2a, $.25^*$; *TR* 2d, $.42^{***}$; *TR* 2a + b + c + d, $.28^*$; *TR* 3a, $.32^{**}$; *TR* 4c, $-.25^*$; *TR* 4a + b + c + d, $-.26^*$; lexical mode, $.28^*$; *SR* 3, $.36^{***}$; *SR* 4, $.27^*$; *SR* 8, $.31^{**}$; SR_{near}, $.27^*$; *FR* 1, $.24^*$; *FR* 2, $.25^*$; no. of meaning values, $.24^*$.

[a] The correlations between variables A through D are: A & B, $-.02$; A & C, $.10$; A & D, $-.80^{***}$; B & C, $.38^{**}$; B & D, $.61^{***}$; C & D, $.14$. The means are: 91.57, 93.23, 100.27, and 3.87 for variables A, B, C, and D, respectively. For the code of the meaning variables, see Appendix A.
$^*p < .05.$
$^{**}p < .01.$
$^{***}p < .001.$

pothesis. They support the "dualistic" approach to masculinity and femininity as largely orthogonal factors rather than the traditional "bipolar" conception of masculinity and femininity as attributes on the opposite ends of one continuum (Spence & Helmreich, 1978).

Concerning the second hypothesis, the findings show, as expected, negative correlations of masculinity with "Feelings and Emotions" (particularly those evoked by the referent, *Dim* 20a), "Judgments and Evaluations," and "Sensory Qualities." Concerning the third hypothesis, the findings show that masculinity is indeed correlated positively with "State" but that, contrary to expectation, femininity is not correlated with "Feelings and Emotions." These findings indicate that the manifest content of items is not an infallible basis for drawing conclusions about related meaning variables, particularly when the items are merely adjectives and not sentences clearly anchored on some referent. In the present context, there may be a further reason that the hypothesis was not confirmed. Because the dimension "Feelings and Emotions" is correlated negatively with masculinity and social desirability, a positive correlation with "Feelings and Emotions" would require adopting an antimasculinity and anti-social-desirability stance that presumably is incompatible with the stereotyped conception of femininity, particularly in Israel.

An examination of the patterns shows that the major characteristics of the pattern of masculinity are negative correlations with "Feelings and Emotions," "Sensory Qualities," "Judgments and Evaluations," and "Cognitive Qualities"; positive correlations with "Function" and "Material"; and positive correlations with the metaphoric-symbolic type of relation. The first two clusters of findings correspond fully to the cultural stereotypes of the tough, unemotional, and functionally oriented male who disregards the internal world. The last finding deviates from expectation and is hard to explain without further data.

The pattern of intercorrelations with femininity is less clear. The correlations are, on the whole, lower, and the clustering of the variables is less obvious. (Is this a reflection of the ambiguities of feminism in the present age?). Some of the more readily interpretable findings are the negative correlation with "Actions" (*Dim* 4a), which may be bound with the passivity and lower assertiveness expected of women; the positive correlation with passive "Action" (*Dim* 4b), which may indicate dependence and concern with nurturant reactions of others toward oneself (as in Study 6, Factor 7); the positive correlation with "Domain of Application" (*Dim* 8b), which may indicate sociability and a concern with interpersonal relations (as in studies 2, 4, and 20); the positive correlations with "Judgments and Evaluations" and "Cognitive Qualities," which may be bound with the expected emphasis on the internal world; the positive correlations with the variables of shifts in referents, which suggest sticking to interpersonally defined reality; and the positive correlation with the number of meaning values, which is consistent with the verbal facility expected of women. The pattern of femininity is also interesting because of the variables it does not contain, mainly those indicating a subjective approach (the personal mode of meaning). Some of the findings that are less readily interpretable at present include the positive correlations with "Possessions," "Structure," "Causes," "Temporal Qualities," and the form of relation of negation (*FR* 2), and the negative correlations with the comparative type of relation similarity(*TR* 2a).

Thus, the pattern for femininity includes several salient elements of the social stereotype for women, just as the pattern for masculinity includes dominant features of the masculine stereotype. Yet, the two stereotypes are not mirror images. The only aspect in the patterns that reveals a tendency toward reversed directionality concerns the variables indicative of relations to the internal world, that is, "Judgments and Evaluations" (*Dim* 21) and "Cognitive Qualities" (*Dim* 22). They are negatively correlated with the masculinity score and positively with the femininity score.

The pattern of intercorrelations with the social-desirability score is biased in favor of masculinity. Of the 10 correlations in the pattern, almost 6 (counting *Dim* 20a+b as a half-point correspondence), all referring to major variables, are identical with those in the masculinity pattern; 1, referring to a relatively minor variable in this context, is identical with a meaning variable in the femininity pattern; and 3 are meaning variables that did not appear in either of the other patterns. This finding indicates that the social-desirability scale is geared to the particular issue of gender in the particular present social situation.

The androgyny pattern is richer ($n = 35$) than either the masculinity ($z = 2.04$, $p < .05$) or the femininity ($z = 1.89$, $p < .06$) patterns. This may support Bem's claim (1974, 1975) about the larger flexibility and adaptability of androgynous subjects. Also, it seems to be the most interesting pattern. All the meaning variables in the pattern (except the positive form of relation, *FR* 1) fall into one of the following three groups: (1) variables that are also correlated with the femininity score in the same direction (i.e., passive "Action," *Dim* 4b; "Causes," *Dim* 6; "Domain of Application," *Dim* 8b; "Temporal Qualities," *Dim* 16; "Possessions," *Dim* 17a; "Belongingness," *Dim* 17b; "Judgments and Evaluations" about the referent, *Dim* 21a; "Judgments and Evaluations" of the referent, *Dim* 21b; "Cognitive Qualities," *Dim* 22b; the exemplifying instance, *TR* 3a; the shifts to close referents, SR_{near}; the negative form of relation, *FR* 2; and the number of meaning values); (2) variables that are correlated with the femininity score in an opposite direction (i.e., the comparative type of relation similarity, *TR* 2); and (3) variables that are correlated with the masculinity score in an opposite direction (i.e., "Range of Inclusion," *Dim* 2a; "Function," *Dim* 3; "Material," *Dim* 9; "State," *Dim* 11; "Sensory Qualities," *Dim* 19a; "Feelings and Emotions," *Dim* 20a; metaphor, *TR* 4c; the metaphoric-symbolic type of relation, *TR* 4a+b+c+d; the shift of the referent to a part of the input, *SR* 3; shifts to far-removed referents, SR_{far}; and the disjunctive form of relation, *FR* 5). Four of the latter variables occur with a reversed sign in the pattern of the social-desirability score (i.e., "Function," *Dim* 3; "Material," *Dim* 9; "Sensory Qualities," *Dim* 19a; and "Feelings and Emotions," *Dim* 20a). The three groups of variables indicate that the androgyny score is unbalanced in favor of femininity in a double sense: it includes 13 "femininity variables" and no "masculinity variables," and it includes many more antimasculinity variables (i.e., 11 variables) than antifemininity variables (only 1).

These findings are interpretable in a broader social context. In view of the lower social status of women in many countries, the obstacles to the development of genuine androgyny are mainly posed by the still disparaged conception of femininity. Hence, at the present stage, androgyny may require a positive adoption of many "femininity variables," a negative stance against many "masculinity variables," and, in addition, a readiness not to succumb to "social-desirability variables." Bem (1977) also found that androgyny is a complex concept. Our conclusions, based on analyzing the pattern of intercorrelations with meaning variables, indicate in which particular respects androgyny consists of femininity, antimasculinity, and anti-social-desirability. Moreover, the underlying dynamics of meaning suggest that, at least at present, androgyny is not merely a combination of the two independent variables of femininity and masculinity but a specific entity, distinct from the other two. Yet, if our interpretation is valid, then we should expect the pattern of meaning-assignment variables corresponding to androgyny to vary in line with the prevalent status of women (see Olds & Shaver, 1980).

In sum, the study showed that, in terms of the pattern of meaning variables, masculinity, femininity, and androgyny are distinct constructs. The patterns do not reflect primarily the content of the items in the inventory but are more akin to the schemata assumed by Bem (1981) to mediate information processing. Indeed, the patterns indicate how the schemata function and which domains of content are likely to be affected by them. Moreover, the study showed the possibilities inherent in using patterns of intercorrelations with meaning variables to explore the personality manifestations of social stereotypes.

STUDY 18: THE THREE MEANINGFUL FACES OF INTOLERANCE OF AMBIGUITY

Purpose and Hypotheses

The purpose of this study was to explore the characteristic meaning variables related to intolerance of ambiguity. This exploration was of interest for two reasons. First, intolerance of ambiguity has been one of the first and most persistently studied traits that reflect the convergence of cognition and personality (Frenkel-Brunswick, 1948a,b). Because the study of meaning carries a similar message, it was of interest to us to examine whether intolerance of ambiguity is related to a pattern of meaning variables as are other personality traits that we have studied. Second, because a previous study (Kreitler, Maguen, & Kreitler, 1975) showed that distinguishable subtypes of intolerance of ambiguity exist, this trait lent itself well to the study of interrelations between subtypes of a trait and individual meaning profiles (Study 19).

Previous research has shown recurrently that subjects high in intolerance of ambiguity prefer simple and habitual conceptions, as well as fast resolutions of uncertainties such as those posed by problems and figures with incomplete closure (Budner, 1962; Smock, 1955; Thurstone, 1944). We expected scores on intolerance of ambiguity to be correlated with those meaning variables that seemed relevant to these tendencies. Specifically, we expected the pattern of intercorrelations with intolerance of ambiguity to include positive correlations with "Contextual Allocation" (*Dim* 1), "Structure" (*Dim* 10), and the comparative type of relation similarity (*TR* 2a), and negative correlations with the comparative type of relation difference (*TR* 2b).

Method

The standard meaning questionnaire (11 stimulus words) and Rydell and Rosen's Tolerance of Ambiguity Scale (1966) were administered in random order on two occasions, in group sessions five to six weeks apart, to 40 subjects, undergraduates in the age range 22–31 years (21 women and 19 men). We selected the scale by Rydell and Rosen because a previous study (Kreitler, Maguen, & Kreitler, 1975) showed that it was related to all three types of intolerance of ambiguity that we found. Thus, it seemed more adequate for our purposes at this first stage than a measure of this trait that is more limited in scope (like Budner's, 1962, or Walk's [O'Conner, 1952] scales, which were each related to two of the three kinds of intolerance of ambiguity). Notably, Rydell and Rosen's scale was based on a multifactored approach to intolerance of ambiguity and was designed to tap mainly the tendencies toward premature closure and reduction of situations to black-and-white dichotomies (Rydell, 1966).

Results and Conclusions

Table 34 presents the pattern of intercorrelations of intolerance of ambiguity with meaning variables. It shows that the pattern includes meaning variables of the four kinds. In view of the claim that intolerance of ambiguity is a cognitive style (Goldstein & Blackman, 1978, p. 40) it is of interest to examine in the pattern of its correlations with meaning variables the relative proportions of meaning variables focused more on contents (i.e., meaning dimensions) and those relatively content-free (i.e., types of relation, forms of relation and referent shifts). It is noteworthy that the proportions of the four kinds of meaning variables in the pattern did not deviate significantly from those expected in traits in general (see p. 79, p. 304: $\chi^2 = .503$, df = 3, n.s.). More specifically, nor did the proportion of content-free meaning variables in the pattern (57.69%) exceed significantly that expected in traits in general (45.25%; CR = 1.09, n.s.). Hence, at least from this point of view, intolerance of ambiguity is a "regular" trait.

The pattern of intercorrelations is interesting both because of the variables it does not contain and because of those it does contain. There are no correlations at all with "Contextual Allocation" and "Structure," the dimensions we expected to be salient in subjects presumably intent on attaining a tight categorization of items or a univocal closure of incomplete drawings. However, there are indications of concern with more concrete content that may help in resolving ambiguities about the identity of a referent and that thus may act as substitutes for categorization. These are "Domain of Application" and "Belongingness," which serve to answer questions like "To whom or to what does the thing apply?" and "To whom does it belong?"

Table 34. Significant Correlations of Intolerance of Ambiguity with Meaning Variables

Personality variable	Significant correlations with meaning variables
Intolerance of ambiguity	*Dim 2b*, .36*; *Dim 5*, −.35*; *Dim 6*, −.37*; *Dim 8b*, .44**; *Dim 8a + b*, .43**; *Dim 11*, −.36*; *Dim 15*, .60***; *Dim 17a*, .37*; (*19a₃*, −.33*); *Dim 19b*, −.38*; *Dim 20b*, −.53***; no. of different meaning dimensions, −.49**; *TR 2a*, .51***; *TR 2b*, −.44**; *TR 2c*, −.35*; *TR 3a*, .47**; *TR 4a*, −.38*; *TR 4b*, .33*; no. of different *TR*, .34*; *SR 1*, .39*; *SR 4*, .41**; *SR 7*, −.45**; *SR 10*, −.47**; no. of different *SR*, −.42**; *FR 3*, −.40**; *FR 4*, −.45**; *FR 5*, −.53***.

Note. For the code of the meaning variables, see Appendix A.
*p < .05.
**p < .01.
***p < .001.

Questions of this kind can be answered with relatively concrete specifications, without recourse to more inclusive and perhaps more abstract contexts. Perhaps, also the meaning dimensions "Locational Qualities" and "Range of Inclusion" are applied in these concretized procedures of identification.

Further, there is information about domains of content that tends to be disregarded by subjects high in intolerance of ambiguity. The most obvious is the triad of meaning dimensions "State" (*Dim* 11), "Sensory Qualities" (*Dim* 19b), and "Feelings and Emotions" (*Dim* 20), which were found to be related to concern with emotional experiences (S. Kreitler & H. Kreitler, 1986a, 1987b,c). It is plausible that this triad would be avoided by individuals intolerant of ambiguity, first because emotional cues in general and internal cues in particular are potentially ambiguous, and second because they may introduce considerations of a personal kind and about inherently unstable qualities that threaten to upset any strict system of categorization and routine planning.

Further, Table 34 shows that subjects intolerant of ambiguity tend to deemphasize "Manner of Occurrence" (*Dim* 5) and "Causes" (*Dim* 6). It seems plausible to suggest that these two dimensions are deemphasized because they are likely to provide information that may be ambiguous or disruptive of any rigid categorizations. In regard to "Manner of Occurrence" (*Dim* 5), we may be more specific because previous findings have suggested that the frequent use of this dimension corresponds to mental flexibility (Study 6, Factor 10), and that the infrequent use of this dimension corresponds to rigidity and a reduced ability to shift from one conception to another (Study 6, Factor 20). Because intolerance of ambiguity has been shown to be typically related to rigidity (Leach, 1967), perhaps in this context, too, the negative correlation with "Manner of Occurrence" (*Dim* 5) denotes rigidity.

More informative about the possible cognitive sources of intolerance of ambiguity is the negative correlation with the number of different meaning dimensions. It indicates that subjects intolerant of ambiguity tend to consider very few cognitive alternatives and ways of categorizing, perhaps as a strategy designed to minimize the possibility of incompatible categorizations. But regardless of the cause or the motive, the restricted range of dimensions renders the task of guarding against ambiguities more difficult. A novel way of categorizing may often resolve stubborn ambiguities.

Of particular interest are the interrelations with types of relation, shifts in referent, and forms of relation, which reveal some of the clearest manifestations of intolerance of ambiguity, as well as some of the strategies used by individuals intolerant of ambiguity to reduce ambiguity or to maintain it at a minimum. The distinction between manifestations and strategies tends to be blurred because, at the borderline of the normal and the abnormal, the manifestation of a tendency often serves to resolve the issue to some extent. The forms of relation with which intolerance of ambiguity is correlated negatively are such clear manifestations of the assessed tendency that they could almost serve to define it. They show that individuals intolerant of ambiguity avoid the use of the mixed form of relation (*FR* 3; e.g., "sometimes," "to some extent"), the conjunctive form of relation (*FR* 4; e.g., "It could be both X and Y"), and the disjunctive form of relation (*FR* 5; e.g., "It is either X or Y").

Further, the types of relation and referent shift variables correlated with intolerance of ambiguity reveal some of the most characteristic strategies that can be used to minimize ambiguity: (1) emphasizing similarities between inputs, including similarities of the kind that have been sanctioned as conventional metaphors (see the positive correlations with the types of relation comparative similarity, *TR* 2a, and conventional metaphors, *TR* 4b); (2) disregarding differences between referents (see negative correlation with the comparative type of relation difference, *TR* 2b); (3) concentrating on concrete instances as examples that may serve to identify standard schemata (see the positive correlation with the type of relation exemplifying instance, *TR* 3a); (4) avoiding an interpretive approach to inputs that could introduce ambiguous cues (see the negative correlation with interpretation, *TR* 4a); and (5) sticking to the presented stimuli as closely as possible (see the positive correlation with the identity shift in referent, *SR* 1), deviating from them only to the extent that is common and probably necessary for comprehension (see the positive correlation with the shift of referent to a previous meaning value, *SR* 4), but avoiding transformations that may introduce associations and referents tenuously related to the presented stimuli (see the negative correlations with shifts to referents related merely by association, *SR* 7, or unrelated, *SR* 10), and thus potentially threatening to the maintenance of the familiar categories.

To the best of our knowledge, only some of these strategies have been tested directly in validating studies. So far, the widest support can be cited for the first two strategies. Common to the first two strategies is the attempt to include as many referents as possible within the same schemata or categories in order to uphold the familiar categories and to avoid awareness of incongruities between referents and categorizing principles. These strategies underlie the well-known tasks (e.g., identifying a cat through a series of its transformations to a dog) devised by Frenkel-Brunswick (1948a,b) for assessing intolerance of ambiguity. The third and fourth strategies are related to the concrete approach, which has often been found to be characteristic of ambiguity-intolerant subjects (Schroder, Driver, & Streufert, 1967, Chapter 1). The fifth strategy is related to the rigidity that typically accompanies intolerance of ambiguity (Leach, 1967).

Of course, the availability of several strategies does not imply that all are applied by every ambiguity-intolerant individual to the same task or to the same extent. Rather, it is more plausible to assume that they constitute alternate procedures that can be applied in line with the requirements of different problem situations and personal tendencies.

Indeed, even the procedures themselves are probably affected to some extent by the larger context of the other tendencies bound with the assessed trait. The data provide one suggestive example. The first and second procedures are, in a sense, complementary and may even seem partly redundant. However, when one recalls that a negative correlation with the comparative type of relation difference (*TR* 2b) is related to conformity (see Studies 2, 6, 8, and 11), and that individuals high in intolerance of ambiguity tend toward conformity (Adorno *et al.*, 1950; Frenkel-Brunswick, 1948a; Leach, 1967), it becomes clear that the choice of the strategy of deemphasizing differences is not accidental. Indeed, it is likely that the comparative type of relation difference (*TR* 2b) fulfills a double role in the pattern of meaning variables correlated with intolerance of ambiguity: as a strategy that is facilitating in combating ambiguities, and as a procedure that promotes conformity (see Study 13 for another example of this kind of dual role of a meaning variable).

In sum, although the pattern of intercorrelations with intolerance of ambiguity includes meaning dimensions and other meaning variables in a balanced proportion, which approximates the expected distribution, we were able to detect, on the basis of external data, more indications and manifestations of intolerance of ambiguity in the relatively content-free meaning variables than in the meaning dimensions. Further studies will have to examine whether this finding is due to restrictions on the validating data, to the characteristics of intolerance of ambiguity, or to the typical functions of the different meaning variables.

STUDY 19: THE THREE CLUSTERS OF INTOLERANCE OF AMBIGUITY

Purpose and Hypotheses

The purpose of this study was to identify and test clusters of meaning variables that correspond to the three kinds of intolerance of ambiguity detected in a previous study (Kreitler, Maguen, & Kreitler, 1975). The first kind of intolerance of ambiguity arises when there are multiple interpretations of a given situation (e.g., in regard to a Rorschach card or a TAT plate); the second kind arises when it is not clear how to identify or categorize a situation in terms of distinct or familiar conceptions (e.g., the stimulus is too vague to be identified as a jar); and the third arises when there are contradictory or conflicting cues (e.g., a person is perceived as an enemy and as lovable). Kreitler *et al.* (1975) showed that these kinds of intolerance of ambiguity can be identified in terms of behavioral measures and on the level of cognitive orientation clusters, which reflect motivational tendencies. Further, the prediction of the behavioral measures of the three kinds of intolerance of ambiguity was better when the cognitive orientation cluster corresponding specifically to each of the types was used, rather than the other cognitive orientation clusters.

This study focused on identifying, within the comprehensive pattern of intercorrelations of intolerance of ambiguity with meaning variables, clusters of meaning variables corresponding to the three kinds of intolerance of ambiguity. It was hoped that this attempt might deepen our understanding of intolerance of ambiguity in general and of clusters within traits in particular. Our expectations were guided by information about the three kinds of intolerance of ambiguity and about the meaning variables related to them (Study 18). Thus, we assumed that the first kind (ambiguity of multiple interpretations) would correspond to low values on "Manner of Occurrence" (*Dim* 5), "Causes" (*Dim* 6), "State" (*Dim* 11), "Feelings and Emotions" (*Dim* 20b), the type of relation interpretation (*TR* 4a), and a low number of different meaning dimensions. Further, we assumed that the second kind (ambiguity of identifying and categorizing) would correspond to high values on "Range of Inclusion" (*Dim* 2b), "Domain of Application" (*Dim* 8b or *Dim* 8a+b), "Locational Qualities" (*Dim* 15), "Possessions" (*Dim* 17a), exemplifying instance (*TR* 3a), no shift in referent (*SR* 1), and shift to previous meaning value (*SR* 4) and low values on shifts to referents related merely by association (*SR* 7) or unrelated to the previous referent (*SR* 10). Finally, we assumed that the third kind (ambiguity of contradictions) would correspond to high values on the similarity (*TR* 2a) and the metaphoric types of relation (*TR* 4c) and low values on the difference type of relation (*TR* 2b), the complementary type of relation (*TR* 2c), and the mixed (*FR* 3), conjunctive (*FR* 4), and disjunctive (*FR* 5) forms of relation. They include all the meaning variables of Table 34 (Study 18) except two (i.e., number of different types of relation, *TR*, and number shifts in referent, *SR*), which were deleted because their significance in regard to the clusters was unclear to us.

The assignment of meaning variables to kinds of intolerance of ambiguity reflects our assumptions that the first kind of intolerance is manifested largely in attempts to control ambiguity by minimizing the use of content that is likely to produce multiple interpretations; the second kind is manifested largely in attempts to identify inputs by sticking to the presented stimuli and relying on concrete cues in the given situation; and the third kind is manifested largely in attempts to control ambiguities by using strategies that reduce the likelihood of contradictions. It will be noted that the first hypothetical cluster includes mainly low values on certain meaning dimensions, the second mainly variables of shifts in referents and high values on certain meaning dimensions, and the third only variables of types and forms of relation (*TR* and *FR*). The number of meaning variables allocated to the three clusters was not equal, but it was comparable (i.e., 6, 9, and 7). However, there was no reason to assume that the three kinds of intolerance of ambiguity are equally strong or equally frequent in the population at large. On the contrary, to judge by the number of studies devoted to the three kinds and by the prevalence of common conceptions about intolerance of ambiguity, the second kind seems to be the most frequent or salient one.

In order to test the correctness of our assumptions about the correspondence of meaning variables to kinds of intolerance of ambiguity, it was necessary to examine the way in which subjects high in any one of the clusters of meaning variables responded in ambiguous situations. Therefore, on the basis of previous findings (Kreitler *et al.*, 1975), we selected three behavioral measures of intolerance of ambiguity, each of which was shown to correspond most closely to only one of the three kinds of intolerance of ambiguity. Thus, the degree of readiness to expose oneself voluntarily to information contradicting one's attitudes and opinions was chosen as a manifestation of the first kind of intolerance of ambiguity; the number of trials up to the first guess in a sequence of Smock's figures (1955) was chosen as a manifestation of the second kind of intolerance of ambiguity; and the number of adjective pairs with similar social-desirability values crossed out in presented pairs of adjectives (Steiner, 1954) was selected as a manifestation of the third kind of intolerance of ambiguity (see "Method"). Our hypotheses were that subjects whose meaning profile included the characteristics of the first (or second or third) cluster of meaning variables would manifest more intolerance of ambiguity on the first (or second or third) measures of intolerance of ambiguity, respectively.

Method

In order to select adequate groups of subjects for the study, it was first necessary to administer the standard meaning questionnaire to a larger sample (160 subjects). These were eighth-graders (72 girls and 88 boys) in the age range of 13–14.7 years, students in two schools in two towns near Tel Aviv.

In order to identify subjects in the first cluster, the meaning profile of the subjects had to include at least 3 of the 6 characteristics of meaning variables specified for that cluster and no more than 7 of the characteristics specified for the other two clusters. For the second cluster, the numbers were at least 4 of the 9 identifying characteristics of the cluster and no more than 6 of the 13 characteristics of the other two clusters; and for the third cluster, the numbers were at least 3 of the 7 identifying characteristics of the cluster and no more than 7 of the other 15 characteristics. In order to be identified as a subject high in any cluster, the subject's meaning profile had to show the specified meaning variables in the specified high or low frequency. High and low frequency were defined as being above or below the group's mean for that variable. In each case, the characteristics of the other clusters had to be distributed between the two clusters so as to sharpen the distinction among the three groups of subjects. The selection turned up 26 subjects (16 boys and 10 girls) for the first cluster; 17 (9 girls and 6 boys) for the second cluster; and 29 (14 boys and 15 girls) for the third cluster.

Three measures of intolerance of ambiguity were administered to the subjects:

1. Exposure to contradicting information. The subjects were first asked to check their pro or contra opinion on eight stated issues (establishment of a Palestinian state, changing the election system in Israel, instituting capital punishment for terrorists, extending the duty of military service to Arabs, abolishing final exams at the end of secondary school, extending obligatory education, including work as a part of the student's duties, and self-rule of students in schools). A half hour later, they were asked to state their preference for reading material supporting one or another opinion on the same issues during a break in the experiment. Intolerance of ambiguity was measured by the number of discrepancies between stated opinions and reading preferences (range: from a minimum of 0 to a maximum of 8).

2. Smock's Ambiguity Task (1955). Five series, each comprising 8 cards reflecting a progressively more complete presentation of a specific object, were projected to the subjects. The 8 cards were selected, on the basis of pretests, from the 15 in the original series as representing approximately equally spaced steps in the sequence. The subject's task was to identify the presented object as early in the series as possible. In order to minimize group pressure effects, all the subjects were required to write something after each projection, even if it was merely "I don't know." Intolerance of ambiguity was measured by the mean number of trials up to the trial in which the subject wrote down the first identification for the series.

3. Steiner's Trait Discrepancy Scale (1954). The scale consists of 15 items, each comprising two pairs of traits, one of which is characterized by similar values of social desirability and the other by discrepant values. (The scale was cross-validated for Israeli samples.) The subject's task was to cross out the pair of traits less likely to occur together in the same person. The score for intolerance of ambiguity was the number of crossed-out pairs characterized by dissimilar social-desirability values.

All three tasks were administered on the same occasion. The first part of the first task was always administered first in order to allow for an interval before the administration of the second part of this task. The second and third tasks were administered in random order. The tasks were administered in a group session in the classroom, and the participants included all the students in the class, in addition to the subjects proper, who did not know that they were the target subjects.

Results and Conclusions

Table 35 shows that there were significant differences between the mean scores of the subjects in the three groups on the three measures of intolerance of ambiguity. On the Smock task, the overall F was significant only on the $p < .10$ level. The crucial test, however, consists in comparing the target group of subjects (i.e., the group with the specific cluster of meaning variables in their meaning profiles) with the other groups on the specific measure in which it was expected that they would manifest intolerance of ambiguity. Five of the six comparisons (bottom rows of Table 35) turned out to be significant and in the expected direction. The sixth comparison was in the expected direction but failed to pass the .05 significance level. This failure might have been due to a number of factors, such as a lower degree of differentiation between the second and third clusters in terms of meaning variables or the intervention of factors other than intolerance of ambiguity in determining closure (e.g., Westcott, 1968, pp. 161–165). In any case, the bulk of the findings confirm the existence of clusters of meaning variables characteristic of different subtypes of the trait intolerance of ambiguity. We venture to suggest the possibility that the clusters represent the convergence between the individual's meaning profile and the overall pattern of meaning variables characteristic of a certain trait. It is as if the individual's meaning profile is a filter for the selection of specific sections from the total schema, which serves as an idealized blueprint of different possibilities of a certain kind.

Table 35. Responses of Subjects with Meaning Profiles
Corresponding to the Three Clusters of Intolerance of Ambiguity

Subjects with meaning variables		Mean responses		
Above mean cluster	Below mean clusters	Exposure to contradicting information	Mean no. of trials up to first-guess (Smock series)	Trait Discrepancy Scale (Steiner)
I	II & III	2.0	3.5	5.3
	$n = 26$			
II	I & III	4.3	1.8	3.4
	$n = 17$			
III	I & II	6.2	2.7	9.4
	$n = 20$			
F		3.18*	2.20	3.28*
$df = 2/60$			$(p < .10)$	
Mean comparisons		I vs. II*	II vs. I*	III vs. I
(by Newman-Keuls)		I vs. III*	II vs. III	III vs. II

*$p < .05$.

STUDY 20: THE MEANING PROFILES OF LEADERSHIP STYLES

Purpose and Hypotheses

The purpose of this study was to explore the constellation of meaning-assignment tendencies characteristic of leadership styles. We chose to assess leadership style by means of descriptions of the least-preferred co-worker (LPC scores; Fiedler, 1967) because this measure has been tested for reliability and validity, has been used widely in research, has theoretical value, and is closely related to the traditional classifications of autocratic and democratic leadership. LPC scores were found to distinguish between two major types of leaders: those who are concerned more with interpersonal relations in the group and those who are rather task-oriented. The major problem that Fiedler (1967) noted concerning this variable is its low correlations with "other personality, intellectual and personal-background variables" (p. 277). Fiedler concluded that "these scores do not measure attributes which correlate with the usual personality and ability tests or with attitude scales. Nor is there a one-to-one relationship between these scales and behaviors" (p. 45). Hence, he assumed that the LPC is "relatively unique" (p. 277) and admitted that "it has been extremely difficult to develop an adequate and readily supportable interpretation" of these scores (p. 45).

To our mind, the major challenge was to find a framework that could not only account for the diverse and disparate findings that have accumulated about LPC scores but that would also allow us to integrate the two conceptions that have been developed about the LPC scores: the motivational and the cognitive. On the one hand, Fiedler (1967) concluded, in view of some studies (e.g., Burke, 1965), that LPC scores "reflect the individual's motivational structure" (p. 59), "the underlying need-structure . . . which motivates his behavior in various leadership situations" (p. 36). On the other hand, Fiedler (1971) suggested, on the basis of other studies (Fishbein, Landy, & Hatch, 1965; Mitchell, 1970), that the LPC score must be seen as a measure that, at least in part, reflects "the cognitive complexity of the individual" (p. 129) and that is an index of attitudes. The two views stay side by side uncombined and in no position to interact.

Our assumption was that the meaning system would provide the framework that is called for in this case. Accordingly, our major hypothesis was that LPC scores would be correlated with a pattern of meaning-assignment variables. The diverse findings about LPC scores led us to expect particular correlations. Our main expectations were that (1) LPC scores would be positively correlated with "Feelings and Emotions" (both those evoked by the referent, *Dim* 20a, and those experienced by the referent, *Dim* 20b) because high LPC scorers in contrast to low LPC scorers have been found to be concerned with the emotional responses of others and with the emotional atmosphere of the group, and to be, in general, sensitive to emotional cues (Fiedler, 1967, Chapter 3); (2) LPC scores would be positively correlated with the number of different meaning dimensions because high LPC scorers have been found to be more complex cognitively in their thinking about groups than low LPC scorers (Mitchell, 1970); (3) LPC scores would be positively correlated with "Domain of Application" (particularly concerning the subject, *Dim* 8a) because high LPC scorers have been found to be more concerned than low LPC scorers with interpersonal relations and to have a co-worker orientation (Bass, Fiedler, & Krueger, 1964);

(4) LPC scores would be positively correlated with "Contextual Allocation" (*Dim* 1) because, in contrast to low scorers, high LPC scorers seem concerned with classifications (e.g., they distinguish between the co-worker as a group member and the co-worker as a person—Fiedler, 1967, p. 44; they use various categories—Bass *et al.*, 1964). We expected, however, further correlations with different meaning variables.

Method

The subjects were 34 elementary-school teachers (6 men and 28 women). They were in the age range of 29–54 years and had been teaching 6–31 years. At the time of the study, all the subjects were practicing teachers. The rationale for selecting teachers as subjects was that teachers serve as leaders of classes that function as groups. This is a widely shared viewpoint (Charters, 1963; Withall & Lewis, 1963).

The subjects worked in different schools and did not know who the other participants of the study were. The material for the study was collected over a period of a year and a half.

At his or her convenience, each teacher individually filled out the questionnaires, which were administered separately in random order. The questionnaires were the standard meaning questionnaire and a measure of LPC. The former included, besides the standard stimulus words, two further stimulus words (*classroom* and *teacher*) added at the end for exploration, but the responses to these stimuli were not included in the meaning profile. The LPC measure was administered with the instructions presented by Fiedler (1967, pp. 40–41). The only difference was that, instead of referring to "the person with whom you can work least well," our measures referred to "the student with whom you can work least well," "someone you work with now or someone you knew in the past." It was emphasized that it need not be "the student you like least well, but should be the student with whom you had the most difficulty in getting a project (e.g., an assignment or teaching some subject matter) done." The teacher was reminded not to mention any names or to give any suggestive cues about the identity of the student whom he or she had in mind. The measure included the 16 bipolar scales used by Fiedler (e.g., cold-warm, pleasant-unpleasant, helpful-frustrating, cooperative-uncooperative, and quarrelsome-harmonious) after a pretest showed that, in the Hebrew translation, the adjectives defining the scales expressed positive or negative evaluations, as they did in the original measure.

The scoring was based on assigning the higher value to the positive evaluation. The LPC scores were the summed item scores (range: 22.3–113.5). Thus, a low LPC score indicates that the subject evaluated low and rejected the least preferred student, whereas a high LPC score indicates that the subject evaluated the least preferred student positively and did not reject him or her, although the student had performed poorly on the required tasks. Accordingly, the lower the LPC score, the greater the emphasis of the subject on task performance as the major determinant in evaluating the student.

Results and Conclusions

Table 36 shows that LPC scores are correlated with a broad range of meaning-assignment tendencies. The obtained correlations support the four specific hypoth-

Table 36. Significant Correlations of LPC Score with Meaning Variables

Significant correlations of LPC scores with:					
Meaning dimensions		Types of relation		Forms of relation	
Dim 1	.35*	TR 2a	.43**	FR 3	.37*
Dim 3	−.36*	TR 2b	.51**		
Dim 5	.34*	TR 2c	.66***		
Dim 7	−.36*	TR 2d	−.34*		
Dim 8a	.59***	TR 3a	.56***		
Dim 8b	.48**	TR 3b	.49**		
Dim 8a + b	.55***	Total no. of	.45**		
Dim 9	.37*	dif. TR			
Dim 11	.69***				
Dim 20a	.89***				
Dim 20b	.85***				
Dim 20a + b	.86***				
Dim 21a	−.46**				
Dim 21b	−.44**				
Total no. of dif. m. dim.	.57***				

Note. For the code of the meaning variables, see Appendix A.
*p < .05.
**p < .01.
***p < .001.

eses that were presented about the relation of LPC scores to "Feelings and Emotions," the number of meaning dimensions, "Domain of Application," and "Contextual Allocation." In addition, they reveal a fairly broad constellation of meaning-assignment tendencies, anchored particularly on meaning dimensions and types of relation.

The findings indicate that the high LPC scorers were concerned, as noted, with emotional aspects (positive correlations with "Feelings and Emotions," Dim 20a, 20b, and 20a+b) and social aspects (positive correlations with "Domain of Application," Dim 8a, 8b, and 8a+b) and were attentive to the manner of operation (positive correlation with "Manner of Occurrence," Dim 5), material elements (positive correlation with "Material," Dim 9), and the state (positive correlation with "State," Dim 11) of the situation, as well as to concrete instances in general (positive correlations with exemplifying instances, TR 3a, and exemplifying situations, TR 3b). However, they tended to disregard consequences, evaluations, and utilitarian functionality (negative correlations with "Consequences," Dim 7; "Judgments and Evaluations," Dim 21a; and "Function," Dim 3). Particularly notable was their cognitive flexibility, manifested in their concern with multiple aspects (positive correlations with number of different meaning dimensions and number of different types of relation), consideration of both similarities and differences (positive correlations with the comparative types of relation of similarity, TR 2a, and difference, TR 2b), abstract classifications (positive correlation with "Contextual Allocation," Dim 1), and concrete instances (positive correlations with exemplifying instances, TR 3a, and exemplifying situations, TR 3b), while emphasizing a balance, noncategorical approach (positive correlation with the mixed form of relation, FR 3) and avoiding comparisons with standards (negative correlation with the relational comparative type of relation, *TR* 2d).

The findings correspond well with the information available about LPC scores (see "Purpose and Hypotheses") and contribute to their deepening, extension, and integration. Further, in view of the general hypothesis about the distinction between meaning dimensions and other meaning variables (see "Introducing the Studies" at the beginning of this chapter), it is plausible to assume that the so-called motivational component of LPC scores corresponds to the salience of particular meaning dimensions, whereas the cognitive component corresponds to specific types of relation, forms of relation, and content-free characteristics like the number of different dimensions or types of relation. Comparing the proportions of meaning variables of the two classes—meaning dimensions versus types of relation, forms of relation and shifts of referent—in the LPC pattern with the expected proportions, shows that the proportions observed in the LPC pattern (65.22% versus 34.78%, respectively) do not deviate significantly from those expected in line with the distribution of variables in the system of meaning (see pp. 92–93; 46.99% versus 53.01%, respectively; $\chi^2 = .601$, df = 1, n.s.) or from those expected in patterns corresponding to traits in general (see p. 79, p. 304; 54.75% versus 45.25%, respectively; $\chi^2 = 1.188$, df = 1, n.s.). Thus, the findings indicate that the motivational and cognitive aspects are represented in the LPC pattern in proportions characteristic of traits and hence may be expected to act and interact as integral constituents of the total pattern.

For the sake of exploration we also compared the meanings of specific key concepts in high and low LPC scorers (i.e., above and below the mean of 63.8). In communicating the meaning of *classroom*, high LPC scorers used, more frequently (on the .05 level of significance) than low LPC scorers, "Manner of Occurrence" (*Dim* 5) and "Feelings and Emotions" (*Dim* 20a and 20b) and less frequently "Function" (*Dim* 3); in communicating the meaning of *teacher*, they more frequently used "Manner of Occurrence" (*Dim* 5) and less frequently "Judgments and Evaluations" (*Dim* 21a and 21b). These findings show, as expected, that, in communicating specific meanings, individuals often use a selection out of their preferred meaning dimensions, presumably if these dimensions provide relevant meaning values. The limited range of findings suggests that a larger pool of stimulus words is necessary if one is to obtain more comprehensive information. However, the obtained findings may well be used to summarize major aspects of groups with which high LPC scorers are likely to be concerned: emotional reactions and manner of operation, but not functionality and evaluations.

In sum, the pattern of meaning variables found to be correlated with LPC scores reveals the meaning-assignment tendencies that mediate two particular leader orientations. One (assessed by high LPC scores) is based on attending to emotional cues, persons, state, manner of operation, and different concrete instances in the flow of events, disregarding evaluations, utility, and consequences, and it is characterized by cognitive richness, complexity, and flexibility. The other orientation (assessed by low LPC scores) is based on a narrow concentration on evaluation, utility, and consequences, emphasizing comparison with standards, while avoiding a consideration of multiple aspects of the situation and the participating persons. Accordingly, high LPC scores seem to indicate an orientation toward the person in the situation, whereas low LPC scores indicate a clear-cut task orientation.

STUDY 21: MEANING AND THE EYE OF THE BEHOLDER[7]

Purpose and Hypotheses

The major purpose of the study was to examine the relation between the meaning profiles of individuals and ratings of various properties of these individuals by external observers. More specifically, we wanted to know whether individuals rated by observers in a specific way share certain characteristics in their meaning profiles and what these characteristics are. Thus, the question underlying the study is interactional in an unconventional sense; it focused on the network of relations between the meaning-assignment tendencies of subjects and the ratings of these subjects by others. Because judges have often been found to be wrong or inaccurate in their judgments of others' behavior (Cline, 1964; Krech, Crutchfield, & Ballachey, 1962; Sarbin, Taft, & Bailey, 1960), we did not assume that the judged traits would actually be characteristic of the judged subjects. Rather, we assumed that if the ratings of behavior were found to be related to particular meaning variables in the subjects' meaning profiles, then one might conclude that the meaning variables characteristic of a subject are manifested in the subject's reactions in a way that impresses observers in a certain manner.

The studied traits were reliability (or dependability), leadership, ability to decide, sociability, ability to withstand stress, intellectual ability, and mental health. Our major hypothesis was that the ratings by observers would be correlated with specific meaning variables in the meaning profiles of the rated subjects. The rationale was that we expected particularities of meaning profiles to be manifested in the subjects' behavior in some form. However, at that stage of our ignorance, it was not possible to hypothesize about the specific meaning variables that would be involved in each rated trait. This general hypothesis was amended by two more specific hypotheses. One was that, if correlations were found at all, they would be relatively low (i.e., would not exceed the range of .30 to .35, which indicates 9%–12.25% common variance). The reason was the indirect relation we assumed to exist between subjects' meaning profiles and observers' ratings of the subjects' behavior. We expected the intervention of different variables in each of the different stages of the process to lower the correlations.

The other hypothesis was that, of the three types of meaning profiles (the lexical, the personal, and the unspecified), the personal would be the least correlated with the observers' ratings, whereas the lexical and the unspecified would be more highly correlated with the observers' ratings and would probably not differ from each other in this respect. There were two reasons for this expectation. First, we assumed that the subjects' lexical and unspecified meaning profiles would be manifested in responses more readily available to and discernible by external observers than the personal meaning profile, particularly in the case of the behaviors studied in the present context, which were largely of the interpersonal kind. Further, we thought it likely that, in the military framework, the subjects might tend to provide richer responses to a questionnaire calling for lexical or unspecified meaning than to a personal meaning questionnaire.

---

[7]Thanks are due to Shmaryahu Sheppes for his help in collecting the data.

Method

The subjects were 87 males, all soldiers enlisted in the Israeli army. Their mean age was 20.5 years. They were being examined in the framework of the personnel-selection services of the army. The subjects were administered, in three separate group sessions, three different meaning questionnaires: one requested the subjects to provide lexical meaning, one requested personal meaning, and one included merely the standard instructions without further specification (see Chapter 2). The order of the three questionnaires was random and differed across subjects. The number of stimuli in each questionnaire was 10: 2 concrete nouns, 2 abstract nouns, 2 adjectives, 2 adverbs, and 2 verbs; 4 of these (1 concrete noun, 1 abstract noun, 1 adjective, and 1 verb, all randomly selected) were repeated across the three questionnaires in order to provide the possibility of comparison.

The comparisons between the lexical and the personal meaning of responses to the same stimuli were made in terms of two separate scales. One referred to comparisons in content and consisted of 14 levels, increasing in distance from Level 1 (denoting responses identical in content and wording) to Level 14 (denoting responses unrelated in content). Levels 1–6 were used to denote highly similar responses with different variations; Levels 7–11 were used to denote different responses related to each other in different ways (dimensionally or by content); and Levels 12–14 were used to denote different responses unrelated to each other. The other scale referred to comparisons in types of relation and consisted of nine levels. Levels 1–3 denoted minimal gap (i.e., differences in subtypes of the same type of relation); Levels 4–6 denoted intermediate degrees of gap (i.e., differences in types of the same mode of meaning); and Levels 7–8 denoted larger degrees of gap (i.e., differences in types of different modes of meaning). In addition, each subject got two further scores reflecting the degree of distinction between the lexical and personal meaning profiles: one score was the percentage of responses in the personal mode given in the lexical meaning questionnaire, and the other was the percentage of responses in the lexical mode given in the personal meaning questionnaire.

The ratings were made in a military framework that dealt with personnel selection designed to identify candidates for officer's training. The ratings of reliability (dependability), leadership, ability to decide, sociability, ability to withstand stress, intellectual ability, and mental health were made by trained psychologists on the basis of individual interviews conducted with the subjects (each interview lasted about 20–30 minutes, and each subject was interviewed only once) and a file of biographical and psychometric data prepared by trained personnel. The psychologist who acted as judge in a specific case was selected randomly from a pool of 10 psychologists. The ratings were made on 7-point scales. For the sake of increased clarity, the ratings on mental health were split at the median into high and low, equivalent roughly to mentally adjusted and mentally disturbed, respectively. An additional measure of leadership was available in the form of sociometric choices by peers who had spent at least five weeks with the subject in some military framework, such as a course. The group of peers generally included 20–30 individuals. Each individual in the group chose three of his peers as best suited to serve as officers. The sociometric measure represents the percentage of peers who selected the subject as suited to be an officer. This measure could range from a minimum of zero to a maximum of 99.

The ratings of sociometric choices were made by individuals who had no connection whatsoever with the administration, the scoring, and the findings of the meaning questionnaire. Again, the meaning questionnaires were obtained and scored by individuals who knew nothing about the ratings and the sociometric choices.

The ratings and the sociometric choices assigned to the subjects were correlated with each of the three meaning profiles of the subjects representing the responses to the lexical, personal, and unspecified meaning questionnaires.

A comparison was made of the three patterns of intercorrelations in terms of the meaning variables included in each. For this purpose, the number of identical meaning variables in any two of the patterns was counted and then turned into a proportion of the total number of meaning variables in the pattern (the results of this analysis are presented in Table 39).

Results and Conclusions

Table 37 shows that all the rated traits were highly and positively intercorrelated. The correlations were particularly high in the cluster of reliability, leadership, ability to decide, sociability, ability to withstand stress, and intellectual ability. Correlations within this cluster were in the range of .68–.98. Correlations of this cluster with mental health were in the range of .36–.60, and with sociometric choices in the range of .20–.46. Not knowing what the elements common to the different ratings were, we can only assume that they were probably one or more qualities that made the difference between "good" and "bad" evaluations.

Thus, in examining the findings in Table 38, an attempt must be made to distinguish between correlations with meaning variables expressing the halo effect of good-bad evaluations and correlations with meaning variables that are more specific to the rated qualities. This attempt will be facilitated by the clear-cut findings. For lexical meaning, the patterns of correlations with the highly interrelated cluster of six traits included positive correlations with "Causes" (*Dim 6*; in six traits), "Consequences" (*Dim 7*; in six traits), and the number of different meaning dimensions (in six traits), and negative correlations with "Domain of Application: Object" (*Dim* 8b; in six traits), "Domain of Application: Subject and Object" (*Dim* 8a+b; in six traits), and "Feelings and Emotions" (*Dim* 20b; in five traits). For personal meaning, the patterns of correlations with the mentioned cluster of six traits included a positive correlation with "Manner of Occurrence" (*Dim* 5; in six traits) and negative correlations with "Function" (*Dim* 3; in five traits), and with the percentage of lexical types of relation used in personal meaning. Notably, the patterns for unspecified meaning included the correlations mentioned above for lexical and personal meanings.

These findings seem to warrant the conclusion that, for the sample of psychologists-observers who participated in this study, positive evaluations correlated positively with "Manner of Occurrence" (*Dim* 5), "Causes" (*Dim* 6), "Consequences" (*Dim* 7), and the number of different meaning dimensions, and negatively with "Domain of Application" (particularly concerning the object, *Dim* 8b), "Feelings and Emotions" (particularly those experienced by the referent, *Dim* 20b), "Function" (*Dim* 3), and the frequent use of attributive and comparative types of relation in personal meaning. At least some of these findings are highly suggestive. It seems sensible that, in the military context, there would be positive evaluations for

Table 37. Intercorrelations between the Rated Traits

Traits	Reliability	Leadership	Ability to decide	Sociability	Ability to withs. str.	Intellectual ability	Mental health	Sociom. choices
Reliability	—							
Leadership	.68***	—						
Ability to decide	.67***	.94***	—					
Sociability	.69***	.97***	.91***	—				
Ability to withstand stress	.69***	.97***	.93***	.97***	—			
Intellectual ability	.72***	.98***	.94***	.98***	.98***	—		
Mental health[a]	.36***	.57***	.58***	.56***	.58***	.60***	—	
Sociometric choices	.46***	.35***	.36***	.28**	.34***	.37***	.20*	—

[a]Biserial correlations.
*$p < .05$.
**$p < .01$.
***$p < .001$.

Table 38. Significant Relations between Ratings of Traits by Observers and Subjects' Meaning Variables[a]

Personality variables	Lexical meaning	Personal meaning	Unspecified meaning	Other meaning variables
Reliability	Dim 4a .19* Dim 6 .27** Dim 7 .25* Dim 8b −.23* Dim 8a + b −.26** Dim 17b .17* Dim 20a .26** Dim 22b .20* No. of dif. m. dim. .38***	Dim 3 −.18* Dim 5 .27** Dim 22a .17* No. of dif. m. dim. .18*	Dim 3 −.19* Dim 4a .20* Dim 5 .23* Dim 6 .26** Dim 7 .24* Dim 8b −.20* Dim 8a + b −.23* Dim 20a .24* Dim 22b .23* Dim 22a + b .20* No. of dif. m. dim. .21*	% of lex. in pers., −.19* Gap in content: Hi reliab. $\bar{X}$ = .23 Lo reliab. $\bar{X}$ = 3.23 t = 2.18*
Leadership	Dim 6 .31** Dim 7 .32** Dim 8b −.26** Dim 8a + b −.29** Dim 20a .17* Dim 20b −.19* No. of dif. m. dim. .27** TR 1a + b .19*	Dim 3 −.17 Dim 5 .24* Dim 6 .24* Dim 7 .17* Dim 20b −.17* Dim 20a + b −.17*	Dim 5 .25* Dim 6 .36*** Dim 7 .35*** Dim 8b −.25* Dim 8a + b −.28** Dim 16 .23* Dim 20b −.24* Dim 20a + b −.22*	% of lex. in pers. −.19*
Ability to decide	Dim 6 .22* Dim 7 .26** Dim 8b −.22* Dim 8a + b −.24* Dim 20b −.20* Dim 20a + b −.17* Dim 22b .20* No. of dif. m. dim. .35*** TR 1a + b .22*	Dim 5 .32*** Dim 16 .17* No. of dif. m. dim. .17*	Dim 5 .28** Dim 6 .25* Dim 7 .27** Dim 8b −.24* Dim 8a + b −.25* Dim 16 .21* Dim 20b −.24* Dim 20a + b −.21* Dim 22b .18* Dim 22a + b .17* No. of dif. m. dim. .22*	% of lex. in pers. −.21*

Sociability

Dim 5	.19*	Dim 3	−.18*	Dim 5	.26**	% of lex. in pers. −.26**
Dim 6	.26**	Dim 5	.22*	Dim 6	.29**	Gap in TR .17*
Dim 7	.34***	Dim 6	.19*	Dim 7	.36***	Gap in content .17*
Dim 8b	−.24*	Dim 7	.17*	Dim 8b	−.23*	
Dim 8a + b	−.28**	Dim 16	.19*	Dim 8a + b	−.27*	
Dim 20a	.19*	Dim 18	.17*	Dim 16	.27*	
Dim 20b	−.19*			Dim 20b	−.24*	
Dim 21a	−.21*			Dim 20a + b	−.21*	
Dim 22b	.17*			No. of dif. m. dim.	.19*	
No. of dif. m. dim.	.31**					
TR 1a + b	.17*					

Sociometric choices

No. of dif. m. dim.	.17*	Dim 5	.19*	Dim 22b	.22*	
TR 1a + b	.18*	Dim 21b	.24*	Dim 22a + b	.17*	
		Dim 22b	.19*	TR 1a + b	.18*	
				TR 3a + b + c	−.20*	

Ability to withstand stress

Dim 5	.20*	Dim 3	−.18*	Dim 5	.31**	% in lex. in pers. −.21*
Dim 6	.29**	Dim 5	.27**	Dim 6	.29**	Gap in content .17*
Dim 7	.34***			Dim 7	.36***	
Dim 8b	−.22*			Dim 8b	−.23*	
Dim 8a + b	−.26**			Dim 8a + b	−.26**	
Dim 20b	−.18*			Dim 16	.22*	
No. of dif. m. dim.	.29**			Dim 20b	−.23*	
TR 1a + b	.18*			Dim 20a + b	−.20*	
TR 3a + b + c	−.20*			No. of dif. m. dim.	.17*	

Intellectual ability

Dim 1	.19*	Dim 3	−.18*	Dim 1	.18	% of lex. in pers. −.23*
Dim 2a	.17*	Dim 5	.27**	Dim 5	.29**	Gap in content .22*
Dim 3	.17*	Dim 6	.18*	Dim 6	.29**	
Dim 5	.18*	Dim 16	.19*	Dim 7	.36***	
Dim 6	.26**	No. of dif. m. dim.	.18*	Dim 8b	−.23*	
Dim 7	.35***	Total no. of m. values	.18*	Dim 8a + b	−.27**	
Dim 8b	−.25*			Dim 16	.26**	
Dim 8a + b	−.28**			Dim 20b	−.22*	
Dim 20a	.18*			Dim 20a + b	−.20	
Dim 20b	−.18*			No. of dif. m. dim.	.20*	
Dim 22b	.18*					
No. of dif. m. dim.	.32***					
TR 1a + b	.19*					

(continued)

Table 38. (*Continued*)

Personality variables	Lexical meaning	Personal meaning	Unspecified meaning	Other meaning variables
Mental health[b]	*Dim 2b* .010 vs. .036 $t = 3.40$**	*Dim 2a* .001 vs. .007 $t = 1.97$*	*Dim 2a* .030 vs. .050 $t = 2.16$*	Gap in content 2.33 vs. .80 $t = 2.22$*
	Dim 2a + b .02 vs. .04 $t = 3.71$**	*Dim 2b* .001 vs. .010 $t = 3.31$**	*Dim 2b* .010 vs. .023 $t = 3.78$**	
	Dim 6 .144 vs. .080 $t = 2.58$*	*Dim 2a + b* .001 vs. .018 $t = 3.80$**	*Dim 2a + b* .010 vs. .043 $t = 4.58$**	
	Dim 8b .113 vs. .010 $t = 6.59$**	*Dim 3* .001 vs. .016 $t = 3.40$**	*Dim 6* .128 vs. .078 $t = 2.92$*	
	Dim 8a + b .166 vs. .044 $t = 3.73$**	*Dim 11* .058 vs. .013 $t = 2.80$*	*Dim 8b* .101 vs. .026 $t = 4.17$**	
	Dim 17a .001 vs. .007 $t = 1.99$*	*Dim 16* .02 vs. .06 $t = 3.05$*	*Dim 8a + b* .144 vs. .053 $t = 3.55$*	
	Dim 17a + b .001 vs. .007 $t = 2.18$*	*Dim 19b* .043 vs. .010 $t = 2.09$	*Dim 10* .006 vs. .001 $t = 1.94$*	
	Dim 19b .099 vs. .001 $t = 5.81$**	*Dim 19a + b* .072 vs. .020 $t = 2.03$*	*Dim 11* .054 vs. .003 $t = 7.23$**	

Dim 19a + b
.124 vs. .011
t = 2.68**

Dim 20a
.042 vs. .085
t = 2.99*

Dim 20b
.051 vs. .021
t = 2.56*

Dim 21b
.023 vs. .001
t = 3.82**

No. of dif. m. dim.
6.70 vs. 4.77
t = 3.11*

TR 2a + b + c + d
.029 vs. .005
t = 3.00**

TR 4a + b + c + d
.08 vs. .001
t = 4.53**

Dim 14
.034 vs. .084
t = 2.73**

Dim 16
.03 vs. .08
t = 3.42*

Dim 19b
.071 vs. .020
t = 3.23**

Dim 19a + b
.084 vs. .030
t = 3.34**

Dim 20a
.031 vs. .114
t = 3.36**

Dim 20b
.065 vs. .025
t = 3.19*

Dim 20a + b
.035 vs. .120
t = 3.32**

TR 4a + b + c + d
.100 vs. .002
t = 4.58**

aVariables that are specific to rated traits and do not recur across most traits are underlined. For the code of the meaning variables, see Appendix A.
bThe first and second means characterize subjects high and low in mental health, respectively.
*p < .05.
**p < .01.
***p < .001.

the flexibility (reflected by the "Manner Of Occurrence," *Dim* 5), for the awareness of multiple alternatives (reflected by the use of many meaning dimensions), and for concern with implications (reflected by "Consequences," *Dim* 7). Similarly, it is reasonable that there would be negative evaluations for concern with emotional cues and for a blurring of the distinction between the lexical and personal modes of meaning. However, further studies will be needed to clarify whether this set of findings is peculiar to the specific context of the study (i.e., the military), or perhaps to the specific subjects of the study (i.e., males), the specific observers (i.e., psychologists), the specific cluster of traits that were rated (i.e., interpersonal), or some combination of these variables. However, the very finding that general evaluations of observers corresponded to specific meaning dimensions in the subjects' profiles is of great significance for increasing our understanding of the interaction between the subject's behavior and "the eye of the beholder."

An important implication of these findings for the present study is that the meaning variables characteristic of the rating of the specific traits were different from those meaning variables that were involved in the correlations with nonspecific evaluations. In the present study, the former were generally fewer than the latter. Table 38 shows that the meaning variables occurring most frequently in relation to specific traits (they are underscored in Table 38) were limited to "Feelings and Emotions" (*Dim* 20a), "Cognitive Qualities," "Temporal Qualities," and the attributive type of relation. The limited range again indicates that there is more variety in reality than in the eye of the beholder. However, the specific meaning variables that were related to the different traits suggest that the relations are not accidental. For example, the ability to decide was related positively to "Temporal Qualities"; sociability was related negatively to "Judgments and Evaluations" (*Dim* 21a; see Study 2 for a similar finding in regard to the CPI scale of Tolerance); leadership was related positively to emotions that the referent evoked in others (*Dim* 20a); and sociometric choices as a leader were correlated positively with concern with cognitive qualities (*Dim* 22), as well as with the two complementary meaning dimensions "Contextual Allocation: (*Dim* 1) and "Range of Inclusion: Classes" (*Dim* 2a), which have been found to be involved in the cognitive operations classifying and analyzing (S. Kreitler & H. Kreitler, 1986c,d, 1987b,c, 1988a, 1989b,c).

The specific character of the relations is particularly evident in regard to mental health ratings. The notable features here are the positive relation with "Feelings and Emotions" (those experienced by the referent, *Dim* 20b), "Sensory Qualities" (particularly those perceived by the referent, *Dim* 19b), and "State" (*Dim* 11), and the negative correlations with "Feelings and Emotions" (those evoked by the referent in others, *Dim* 20a), "Range of Inclusion," "Possessions," "Quantity," and "Temporal Qualities." Notably, independent studies (e.g., S. Kreitler & H. Kreitler, 1985a) have shown that the three meaning dimensions "Sensory Qualities" perceived by the referent (*Dim* 19b), "State" (*Dim* 11), and "Feelings and Emotions" experienced by the referent (*Dim* 20b) are related to the scope and intensity of emotional experiencing. Also highly interesting is the positive relation of mental health to the variable of the gap in content between personal and lexical meaning. It may be noted that dependability was related negatively to this variable. It is plausible to assume that this variable reflects a low degree of integration between lexical and the personal meanings. Hence, it seems that observers (and they were psychologists) tend to diagnose low mental health in subjects who are concerned with their own emotions, have a metaphoric tendency, and are not concerned with such worldly aspects as possessions, quantity, and temporal qualities.

When the content-focused examination of the interrelations of the traits with meaning variables is complemented by a more quantitative content-free analysis, two further characteristics become evident. The first concerns the number of inter-correlations with the different traits. When we average across the three question-naires, it turns out that six of the variables (all the rated traits) are intercorrelated with a number of meaning variables that lie in a closely defined range (6.7–9.7; $\bar{X} =$ 6.67, $SD = 3.43$), whereas one of the variables (sociometric choices) is correlated with an appreciably lower number (about half) of meaning variables (i.e., 3), and one (mental health) with an appreciably larger number (about double) of meaning vari-ables (i.e., 13). These data suggest that ratings of traits share many features with each other that they do not share with sociometric choices, or alternatively, that sociometric choices differ from rated traits. Concerning mental health, no conclusion can be drawn because the method of analysis was not correlational, as it was in regard to the other variables.

The second characteristic concerns the relative frequency of meaning variables of different kinds. All three questionnaires provided significantly more significant correlations with meaning dimensions than could be expected by chance (67.00 vs. 35.71, $z = 7.08$, $p < .001$; 37.00 vs. 17.38, $z = 6.30$, $p < .001$; and 75.00 vs. 36.65, $z = 8.59$, $p < .001$ for lexical, personal, and unspecified meanings, respectively); all provided significantly fewer significant correlations with types of relation than could be expected by chance (9.00 vs. 18.32, $z = 2.26$, $p < .01$; 0 vs. 8.92, $z = 3.11$, $p < .01$; and 3.00 vs. 18.80, $z = 3.70$, $p < .01$; for lexical, personal, and unspecified meanings, respectively); and all provided significantly fewer significant correlations with the content-free kinds types of relation, shifts in referent, and forms of relation than expected (9.00 vs. 40.29, $z = 7.31$, $p < .001$; 0 vs. 19.62, $z = 6.63$, $p < .001$; and 3.00 vs. 41.35, $z = 8.81$, $p < .001$, for the three meanings, respectively).

These findings indicate that the patterns of intercorrelations with ratings of traits are characterized by a preponderance of aspects of content manifested through the subjects' characteristic use of meaning dimensions and a paucity of the relatively more content-free aspects of the other kinds of meaning variables; types of relation, shifts in referent, and forms of relation. Indeed, these patterns consist mainly of correlations with meaning dimensions (88.2%, 100%, and 96.15% for the lexical, personal, and unspecified meaning questionnaires, respectively; the rest are correla-tions with types of relation variables). A comparison with the findings characteristic of patterns typical for traits in general (i.e., 54.75% correlations with meaning dimen-sions, 25.75% with types of relation, 5.9% with forms of relation, and 12.57% with shifts in referent; see Table 5) suggests that the patterns for ratings differ from the patterns for traits in their focus on meaning dimensions and disregard of the other kinds of meaning variables. However, it seems intuitively plausible that meaning dimensions, which express content more directly, would be more clearly manifested in the subjects' reactions than the other kinds of meaning variables.

Table 38 presents data that also support our further two specific hypotheses. First, it shows that most of the correlations are in the expected range and that none exceed .38 (i.e., 14% of common variance). Second, it shows that there are more correlations with the lexical and unspecified meaning profiles than with the personal meaning profile. In terms of sheer numbers, for the seven traits—excluding mental health, which was analyzed in terms of t tests—the number of meaning variables correlated with lexical meaning was 61 ($\bar{X} = 8.71$, $SD = 3.41$) and with personal meaning, 30 ($\bar{X} = 4.29$, $SD = 1.69$; $t = 3.07$, $df = 5$, $p < .05$). When mental health is included, the numbers are 76 ($\bar{X} = 9.5$, $SD = 3.85$) and 38 ($\bar{X} = 4.75$, $SD = 2.05$), respectively ($t = 3.08$, $df = 6$, $p < .05$). These findings show that about twice as many meaning variables were related to the ratings in lexical meaning than in personal meaning. The number of meaning variables of unspecified meaning that correlated significantly with the seven traits ($\bar{X} = 8.86$, $SD = 2.22$) or the eight traits ($\bar{X} = 9.75$, $SD = 3.37$) did not differ significantly from the number of meaning variables of lexical meaning that correlated with the seven traits ($\bar{X} = 8.71$, $SD = 3.41$) or the eight traits ($\bar{X} = 9.50$, $SD = 3.85$; $t = .10$, $df = 5$, n.s.; and $t = .14$, $df = 6$, n.s., respectively). Thus, in purely quantitative terms, the questionnaires of lexical or unspecified meaning provided a greater number of meaning variables related to the rated traits than the personal meaning questionnaire. This finding was expected, first, because of the interpersonal nature of the rated behaviors and, second, because of the possible uneasiness of the subjects about expressing personal meaning in a military framework.

Table 39 sheds light on another aspect of the above conclusion. It shows that the questionnaires of unspecified and of lexical meanings provided patterns of intercorrelations that shared 71% of identical meaning variables. This percentage is significantly higher than the percentages of meaning variables shared by each of them and the personal meaning questionnaire (29% on the average). As expected, the pattern based on the questionnaire of personal meaning resembles the two other patterns to the same degree (about 50%; see Table 39, first row). It may be suggested tentatively that the pattern of intercorrelations based on a questionnaire of personal meaning represents a more limited aspect of the sphere of meaning that is focused largely on personal meaning, whereas the other two patterns represent both sections of personal meaning and probably aspects of interpersonally shared meaning. This tentative conclusion, coupled with the finding that the patterns with lexical and unspecified meanings were more extensive than the pattern with personal meaning, indicates that, from the viewpoint of the provided information, the use of lexical or unspecified meaning questionnaires is preferable and more advantageous. This conclusion will have to be tested in further studies.

Table 39. Comparisons of Proportions of Identical Correlated Meaning Variables in the Three Types of Meaning Questionnaires

Type of meaning questionnaire	Proportions of identical correlated meaning variables shared with				
	Lexical meaning	Unspecified meaning	t	Personal meaning	t
Personal meaning	$\bar{X} = .44$ $SD = .21$	$\bar{X} = .66$ $SD = .19$	2.20	—	—
Lexical meaning	—	$\bar{X} = .71$ $SD = .16$	—	$\bar{X} = .21$ $SD = .14$	6.65**
Unspecified meaning	$\bar{X} = .71$ $SD = .18$	—	—	$\bar{X} = .37$ $SD = .15$	4.09*

*$p < .01$.
**$p < .001$.

In sum, the different findings presented indicate that explorations of relations between meaning profiles and impressions of observers define a fruitful and rewarding interactional domain of research that may shed light on the trait of biases in ratings, on ratings of traits, and on the involvement of the meaning profile in both.

STUDY 22: TRAITS IN INTERACTION

Purpose and Hypotheses

The purpose of this study was to explore the possibility of studying the interactions among traits in terms of the patterns of meaning variables underlying the traits. The major assumption of the study was that the pattern of meaning variables that is interrelated with a trait may provide cues suggesting with which other traits the assessed trait will interact in a specific way in regard to a specific task. The general hypothesis guiding the study was that, if two traits are correlated with the same meaning variable, these traits will interact and produce a stronger effect than only one of the traits alone. We expected that the effect would become manifest only in a task or a phenomenon likely to be affected by the meaning variable shared by the traits.

We tested this hypothesis in regard to two separate trait combinations. The choices of traits were dictated by the nature of the patterns of intercorrelations with meaning that were available to us (Studies 1–20) and the intercorrelations among these traits that made it more-or-less likely that we would find subjects who had the desired combination of traits (see "Method"). Eventually, we worked with one set of trait combinations focused on the meaning dimension "Feelings and Emotions," and with another focused on the meaning dimension "Judgments and Evaluations." The trait combinations were selected so that, in one group of subjects, both traits were correlated positively with the target meaning dimension; in another group, one trait was correlated positively, whereas the other was not; and in another group, one trait was correlated positively, whereas the other was correlated negatively. Thus, there were three groups in each set of combinations. The task that provided the dependent measures consisted of assigning descriptive terms to pictures of people (see "Method"). The specific hypotheses were that subjects who have high scores in two traits both of which are correlated positively with "Feelings and Emotions" will assign more emotional descriptive terms than the other subjects; and that subjects who have high scores in traits both of which are correlated positively with "Judgments and Evaluations" will assign more value-oriented descriptive terms than the other subjects. The two hypotheses were partial because it was not possible to set up specific predictions about the magnitude of the differences between the subgroups in each set.

Method

The patterns of intercorrelations of traits with meaning variables (Studies 1–20) were examined with the purpose of selecting traits correlated positively with only one of a set of meaning dimensions. The final selection of traits and their interrelations with meaning variables is presented in Table 40. Table 40 shows that there were two sets of traits, one focused on the dimension "Feelings and Emotions" (the

Table 40. Characterization of Experimental Groups

Target dimension	Traits	N	Dim 20a, 20b, 20a + b	Dim 21a, 21b, 21a + b	Dim 22a, 22b, 22a + b	Dim 4a, 4a + b	Characterization of group
"Feelings and emotions"	Machiavellianism (High)	15 (7M, 8W)	High (pos. cor.)	No cor.	No cor.	No cor.	+
	Impulsivity (High)		High (pos. cor.)	No cor.	No cor.	No cor.	+
	Machiavellianism (High)	16 (7M, 9W)	High (pos. cor.)	No cor.	No cor.	No cor.	+
	Authoritarianism (High)		No cor.	No cor.	No cor.	No cor.	0
	Machiavellianism (High)	16 (8M, 8W)	High (pos. cor.)	No cor.	No cor.	No cor.	+
	Intolerance of ambiguity (High)		Low (neg. cor.)	No cor.	No cor.	No cor.	−
"Judgments and evaluations"	Thinking (Myers-Briggs) (High)	15 (6M, 9W)	No cor.	High (pos. cor.)	No cor.	No cor.	+
	Factor 5 (16 PF) (High)		No cor.	High (pos. cor.)	No cor.	No cor.	+
	Thinking (Myers-Briggs) (High)	18 (6M, 12W)	No cor.	High (pos. cor.)	No cor.	No cor.	+
	Authoritarianism (High)		No cor.	No cor.	No cor.	No cor.	0
	Thinking (Myers-Briggs) (High)	14 (6M, 8W)	No cor.	High (pos. cor.)	No cor.	No cor.	+
	Factor 6 (16 PF) (High)		No cor.	Low (neg. cor.)	No cor.	No cor.	−

Note. For the code of the meaning variables, see Appendix A. M = men, W = women.

first three) and the other on the dimension "Judgments and Evaluations" (the last three). The three groups in each set differed by whether both traits were correlated positively with the target dimension, one positively and one not at all, or one positively and the other negatively. In the set focused on "Feelings and Emotions," Machiavellianism (Studies 3–5) was the trait positively correlated with "Feelings and Emotions" that remained constant in the three groups. In the set focused on "Judgments and Evaluations," the Thinking scale of the Myers-Briggs Type Indicator (Study 7) was the trait positively correlated with "Judgments and Evaluations" that remained constant in the three groups.

Table 40 shows that the selected traits were characterized not only by their correlation with the target dimension, but also through absence of correlations with three other meaning dimensions, which were included for the purpose of control. Moreover, this fact also enabled us to expand the original three-group design of the study to include a further group characterized by traits that had no correlations with the target dimension. This fourth group consisted, in fact, of the three subgroups of the set other than the one focused on the target dimension. Thus, two separate analyses were made, one based on a three-group design (i.e., $++$, $+0$, $+-$), and one based on a four-group design (i.e., $++$, $+0$, $+-$, 00).

The measures administered to the subjects included the scales of the relevant traits and a test of character interpretation. The administered measures were the scales of *Mach IV* (see Studies 3 and 4), impulsivity (see Study 10), authoritarianism (see Study 13), intolerance of ambiguity (see Study 19), the Myers-Briggs Type Indicator (for the scale of Thinking; see Study 7), and Cattell's 16 PF (for the measures of Factors 5 and 6; see Study 6).

The character interpretation test was modeled after the test with the same name devised by Freeman (1951). The test included four photographs of people—two adult males and two adult females—and a set of 24 descriptive terms appended to each of them, the same set for all photographs. The descriptive terms included six terms denoting emotions (e.g., *capable of love* or *tends to fear*), six denoting values and moral qualities (e.g., *honest* or *corrupt*), six denoting cognitive qualities (e.g., *clever* or *has good memory*), and six denoting actions (e.g., *drives a car* or *plays soccer*). The terms denoting emotions and values were designed to test the hypotheses of the study, whereas the other terms were included for the sake of control. The terms were selected from a larger pool on the basis of pretest judgments by subjects who were asked to specify the major meaning of the term. Only terms about which the judgments of 90% of the pretest subjects ($n = 30$) were in agreement were selected. In order to control for the effect of positive and negative connotations of terms, we presented each term together with a 5-point scale labeled at its positive and negative poles (e.g., "Honest" and "Dishonest"). The subject's task was to select only four terms that seemed to him or her "most adequate for describing the person in the photograph" and to check the selected point on the scale appended to these terms. The score of the subject was the number of terms referring to each of the four meaning dimensions that the subject selected. These numbers were summed across the photographs. The sums were treated as raw data but were also converted to proportions of the total of responses.

All the trait measures and the character interpretation test were administered to a large sample of subjects ($n = 210$; 90 men and 120 women) from which the subjects of the study proper were selected. The original sample included first- and second-year students in psychology and social sciences at Tel Aviv University, enlisted soldiers, students in an art school, and students in a teacher's seminary. The mean age of the students was 24.3 years, and the range was 18.2–31.1 years. The subjects of the study proper were selected on the basis of their responses to the measures of the traits. Subjects whose scores on the specified traits met the criteria (see Table 40) were selected. High scores on a trait were defined as scores above the group's mean for that trait. The number of selected subjects was 94, that is, 47 (22 men and 25 women) for the set focused on "Feelings and Emotions" and 18 men and 29 women for the set focused on "Judgments and Evaluations." Table 40 shows the distribution of the subjects in the different subgroups.

The questionnaires were given to each subject personally or in small groups. The experimenter explained the tasks and pointed out the instructions. The subjects filled out the questionnaires at their convenience and returned them about a week later. All except two of the subjects of the original sample returned the questionnaires. About 5% were incomplete in several items and were deleted.

Results and Conclusions

Tables 41 and 42 show that, as predicted, in both sets of data, the subjects in Group A (the group high in two traits correlated positively with the target dimension) selected, more frequently than the subjects in the other groups, descriptive terms that corresponded with the target dimension. This effect is highly significant regardless of whether group means are compared with each other (Table 41) or whether the obtained frequencies are tested against those expected by chance (Table 42). Table 42 shows that the effect was limited to the target dimension. In both sets of data, five of the six different groups of subjects selected terms corresponding to the three nontarget meaning dimensions in comparable degrees. The one exception was Group A on the second target dimension, in which there were significant differences in the use of terms of the three nontarget dimensions, apparently because of the lower-than-chance use of action terms.

The differences between the groups are highly significant. Most marked are the differences between the subjects of Group A and subjects of Groups D (who had no

Table 41. Comparisons of Groups in the Two Target Dimensions

| Groups[a] | Proportions in target groups of | | z | Mean of the two target groups (standard deviation in parentheses) |
	"Feelings and emotions"	"Judgments and evaluations"		
A	112/144 (.78)	44/80 (.55)	3.59*	2.79 (.70)
B	64/176 (.36)	48/112 (.43)	1.19	1.56 (.39)
C	20/128 (.16)	28/112 (.25)	1.74	.80 (.20)
D	72/304 (.24)	88/448 (.20)	.23	.85 (.21)

[a]For the definition of the groups, see Table 40.
*$p < .001$.

Table 42. Frequencies of the Four Kinds of Descriptive Terms in the Different Groups of Subjects

Target dimension	Groups[a]	Frequency of words denoting:[b]				Total	X^2 df = 3	z Target vs. expected	X^2 No. of target df = 2
		Emotions	Evaluations	Cog.	Q. actions				
"Feelings and emotions"	A	112 (.78)	12 (.08)	13 (.09)	7 (.05)	144	214.49***	7.57***	1.94
	B	64 (.36)	40 (.23)	36 (.20)	36 (.20)	176	12.35**	1.57	.27
	C	20 (.16)	36 (.28)	32 (.25)	40 (.31)	128	7.00	1.50	.89
"Judgments and evaluations"	A	8 (.10)	44 (.55)	20 (.25)	8 (.10)	80	43.20***	4.29***	7.99*
	B	28 (.25)	48 (.43)	20 (.18)	16 (.14)	112	21.72***	2.57*	3.50
	C	36 (.32)	28 (.25)	20 (.18)	24 (.21)	112	5.15	.00	5.08

[a] See Table 40 for definition of groups and number of subjects in each.
[b] The numbers in parentheses below each frequency denote proportions.
*p < .05.
**p < .01.
***p < .001.

traits correlated with the target dimensions) and Group C (who had one trait correlated positively with the target dimension, and one correlated negatively). Table 41 shows that, in both sets, the groups were ordered in a linear decreasing order: the subjects of Group A (both traits correlated positively with the target dimension) selected terms in the target dimensions more often than the subjects of Group B (only one trait correlated positively), and the latter more often than subjects in Groups C (one trait correlated positively and one negatively) and D (no trait correlated with the target dimensions). Groups C and D hardly differed from each other. In quantitative terms, the subjects of Group A concentrated about 70% of their choices on the target dimensions; the subjects of Group B, about 39%; and the subjects of Groups C and D, only 20% (Table 41). Thus, the subjects in Group A selected more than three times as many terms in the target dimensions than the subjects in Groups C and D.

Hence, it is obvious that the two traits interact in the expected manner, that is, in terms of the meaning dimensions with which the traits are correlated. Further, the interaction seems to be regularly linear. When the meaning dimension is supported by a positive correlation with two traits, the effect is 1.79 stronger than when it is supported by a positive correlation with only one of the traits. Again, when the meaning dimension is supported by a positive correlation with only one trait, the effect is 1.86 stronger then when it is not supported by any correlation with traits or by a positive correlation with one trait and a negative correlation with another. Incidentally, the last two cases correspond to chance conditions, and so does the percentage of responses in the target dimension under these conditions. Hence the addition of a trait correlated with the target dimension seems to strengthen the response corresponding to the target dimension by a factor of 1.8.

The conclusions stated above are based on the two sets of data. However, the effect tended to be stronger when the target dimension was "Feelings and Emotions" than when it was "Evaluations and Judgments." Table 42 shows that, though on the level of Group B the differences were not significant, on the level of Group A, they were. Such differences may have been due to a variety of factors, such as the strength of the correlations between the traits and the dimension, the content of the specific descriptive terms included in the test to represent the different dimensions, or perhaps the appropriateness of these terms to the pictures. The impact of factors like these would have to be studied before any conclusions could be drawn about the difference in the strength of the interaction.

In sum, this study showed that traits interact in line with the meaning dimensions with which they are correlated. The effect should be further studied in regard to other meaning variables, other dependent variables, and a greater number of traits.

How to Work with the New Trait Concept

Assessment of Personality Traits

ASSESSING ALL TRAITS BY MEANS OF THE MEANING QUESTIONNAIRE

The purpose of this and the following chapters is to illustrate, through concrete examples and detailed procedures, some of the uses to which the suggested new concept of traits can be put.

One of the reasons for studying personality is to improve personality assessment techniques, which are a main application in the field of psychology. Thus, the first and possibly the most important of the uses of the new trait concept concerns the assessment of traits. The only instrument used for the assessment is the standard meaning questionnaire. The scoring and interpretation of this single questionnaire may provide information about any number of traits, which would regularly require the administration of many different scales. Indeed, it could provide information about all of the traits if the patterns of meaning variables corresponding to all traits had been studied.

Besides being a most economical way of assessing personality traits, assessing traits by means of the meaning questionnaire has several additional advantages. But it is preferable to present them only after we have explained and illustrated the procedure of assessing traits through the meaning questionnaire.

THE PROCEDURE OF ASSESSING PERSONALITY TRAITS BY MEANS OF THE MEANING QUESTIONNAIRE

The procedure is based on assessing the subject's personality traits by means of the subject's responses to the meaning questionnaire. Applying the procedure requires two things: the subject's meaning profile and information about the patterns of the meaning variables corresponding to the different traits to be assessed. In a nutshell, the procedure consists of identifying, in the subject's meaning profile, the patterns of the meaning variables corresponding to the different traits. It includes four steps: (1) administering and scoring the meaning questionnaire; (2) identifying the subject's positively and negatively preferred meaning variables; (3) counting correspondences between the subject's preferred meaning variables and the trait's pattern; and (4) interpreting the findings.

The first step is administering the standard meaning questionnaire and scoring the responses according to the usual procedure, so as to obtain the individual's meaning profile. As explained earlier (see "The Meaning Profile" in Chapter 2), the subject's responses (i.e., communications of meaning) are divided into meaning units, each of which consists of a referent and a meaning value. Each of the meaning units is coded on the four sets of meaning variables (for coding instructions, see Appendix C). The sums of the codings yield the subject's meaning profile, which consists, in fact, of the frequencies with which the subject has applied each of the meaning variables, including those to which the subject gave no (i.e., zero) re-

Table 43. Meaning Profiles and Preferences (Positive and Negative) of Subjects A and B

Meaning var.	Response frequencies		Meaning var.	Response frequencies	
	Subject A	Subject B		Subject A	Subject B
Dim 1	10	16	No. of dif. meaning dim.	25	27
Dim 2a	10	4	TR 1a	92	100
Dim 2b	14	3	TR 1b	27	82
Dim 2a + b	24	7	TR 1a + b	119	182
Dim 3	4	18	TR 2a	1	3
Dim 4a	11	6	TR 2b	1	2
Dim 4b	8	2	TR 2c	1	2
Dim 4a + b	19	8	TR 2d	4	0
Dim 5	9	6	TR 2a + b + c + d	7	7
Dim 6	2	7	TR 3a	15	2
Dim 7	3	6	TR 3b	0	2
Dim 8a	8	10	TR 3c	0	2
Dim 8b	16	10	TR 3a + b + c	15	6
Dim 8a + b	24	20	TR 4a	3	2
Dim 9	3	3	TR 4b	2	0
Dim 10	3	0	TR 4c	0	1
Dim 11	9	1	TR 4d	0	0
Dim 12	0	0	TR 4a + b + c + d	5	3
Dim 13	5	1	No. of dif. TR	13	14
Dim 14	4	16	Lex. mode	126	190
Dim 15	4	17	Pers. mode	20	9
Dim 16	2	5	FR 1	126	178
Dim 17a	2	2	FR 2	7	6
Dim 17b	0	19	FR 3	2	8
Dim 17a + b	2	21	FR 4	3	0
Dim 18	0	3	FR 5	6	1
Dim 19a	4	7	FR 6	2	4
Dim 19b	2	1	FR 7	0	1
Dim 19a + b	6	8	FR 8	0	0
Dim 20a	0	10	FR_{pos}	139	191
Dim 20b	3	10	FR_{neg}	7	7
Dim 20a + b	3	20	No. of dif. FR	8	8
Dim 21a	3	10	SR 1	53	88
Dim 21b	5	1	SR 2	0	5
Dim 21a + b	8	11	SR 3	0	1
Dim 22a	0	0	SR 4	90	89
Dim 22b	2	4	SR 5	1	4
Dim 22a + b	2	4			

Table 43. (*Continued*)

Meaning var.	Response frequencies		Meaning var.	Response frequencies	
	Subject A	Subject B		Subject A	Subject B
SR 6	1	6	SR_{near}	145	188
SR 7	1	3	SR_{far}	1	10
SR 8	0	0	No. of diff. SR	5	8
SR 9	0	2	Total no. of resp.	146	198
SR 10	0	0			

Meaning var.	Subject A	Subject B	Meaning var.	Subject A	Subject B
Highly frequent (positively pre-ferred)	($Q_1 = 8$)	($Q_1 = 10$)			SR 4
	Dim 2b	Dim 1			SR_{near}
	Dim 2a + b	Dim 3	Highly infrequent (negatively pre-ferred)	($Q_3 = 1$)	($Q_3 = 1$)
	Dim 4a	Dim 8a		Dim 12	Dim 10
	Dim 4b	Dim 8b		Dim 17b	Dim 11
	Dim 4a + b	Dim 8a + b		Dim 18	Dim 12
	Dim 5	Dim 14		Dim 20a	Dim 13
	Dim 8a	Dim 15		Dim 22a	Dim 19b
	Dim 8b	Dim 17b		TR 2a	Dim 21b
	Dim 8a + b	Dim 17a + b		TR 2b	Dim 22a
	Dim 11	Dim 20a		TR 2c	TR 2d
	Dim 21a + b	Dim 20b		FR 7	TR 4b
	TR 1a	Dim 20a + b		FR 8	TR 4c
	TR 1b	Dim 21a		SR 5	TR 4d
	TR 1a + b	Dim 21a + b		SR 7	FR 4
	TR 3a	TR 1a		SR 8	FR 5
	Lex. mode	TR 1b		SR_{far}	FR 7
	FR 1	TR 1a + b			FR 8
	FR_{pos}	Lex. mode			SR 3
	SR 1	FR 1			SR 8
	SR 4	FR_{pos}			SR 10
	SR_{near}	SR 1			

Note. For the code of the meaning variables, see Appendix A.

sponses. Table 43 presents the meaning profiles of two subjects: A is a female, and B is a male; both are students at an American university and are 19–20 years old.

The second step consists in identifying the subject's positive and negative prefer-ences for meaning variables. These preferences are defined operationally in terms of the frequencies of the meaning variables in the meaning profile. Thus, positive preferences are defined as meaning variables with high frequency, and negative preferences are defined as meaning variables with low frequency. In our work, we have settled on more specific criteria and have identified high and low frequencies as those above and below the first (Q_1) and third (Q_3) quartiles in the frequency distribu-tion of the subject's meaning profile, respectively. Thus, meaning variables with high frequencies are those in the upper 25% of the distribution, and meaning variables with low frequencies are those in the lower 25% of the distribution. Quartiles seemed to us preferable to measures of variability based on means and standard deviations, because (1) they are less sensitive to the impact of extreme scores, which are not rare in meaning profiles; (2) they enable specifying an equal number of high- and low-frequency meaning variables in the profiles; and (3) they enable keeping the numbers of variables identified as high and low in frequency constant across subjects.

The third-mentioned advantage is important for controlling the chance of identifying in the meaning profiles patterns corresponding to the different traits. In numerical terms, there are 79 meaning variables (38 meaning dimensions, 17 types of relations, 2 meaning modes, 10 forms of relations, and 12 shifts of reference; see Appendix A). Hence, there are 20 variables above the first quartile and 20 variables below the third quartile. The former are those of high frequency corresponding to the positive preferences, and the latter are those of low frequency corresponding to the negative preferences. This leaves 39 variables in the middle, interquartile range. In practice, the number may deviate slightly from 20 in either direction because of ties in frequencies. Thus, in Subject A, Q_1 was equal to 8, and this yielded 21 "frequent" variables. Excluding the variables of frequency 8 would have left us with 18 "frequent" variables. We chose the former alternative because it constitutes a smaller deviation from the preestablished limit of 20. Again, in Subject B, Q_1 was equal to 10, a frequency at which there were five variables, so that the overall number of "frequent" variables was 22. This alternative was preferred to the alternative of 17 "frequent" variables. Table 43 lists for each subject the meaning variables of high frequency (i.e., those positively preferred) and of low frequency (i.e., those negatively preferred).

The third step consists in establishing the correspondences between the positively and negatively preferred meaning variables of the subject and the patterns of meaning variables that represent the different traits.

Let us first describe the procedure for a single trait. The correspondence between the subject's preferences and the trait's pattern is established in the following way: one compares separately each positively and each negatively preferred meaning variable in the subject's meaning profile with the pattern of meaning variables representing the specific trait. There is a correspondence of 1 point if the pattern includes the subject's positively preferred meaning variable as a variable based on a positive correlation, or if the pattern includes the subject's negatively preferred meaning variable as a variable based on a negative correlation. When all the subject's positively and negatively preferred meaning variables have been checked in this way, the number of correspondence(s) is added up. This sum represents the total of correspondences between the subject's preferences for meaning variables and the meaning variables included in the trait's pattern. This number represents, in fact, the strength of the particular trait in a particular subject. However, the number of meaning variables in the patterns of different traits varies. Therefore, in order to obtain a measure of the trait's strength in a certain subject, which is stable across different traits, it is necessary to transform the number of correspondences into a percentage of the total number of meaning variables in the pattern of the trait.

Let us illustrate the procedure concerning the pattern for extroversion as defined by Eysenck (see Table 6 or the second column in Table 1). The positively correlated variables in this pattern include "Contextual Allocation" (*Dim* 1), "Action" (*Dim* 4a), "Size" (*Dim* 12), "Possessions and Belongingness" (*Dim* 17b and 17a+b), "Sensory Qualities" (*Dim* 19a and 19a+b), the number of different meaning dimensions, the substance–quality attributive type of relation (*TR* 1a), the complementariness comparative type of relation (*TR* 2c), the associative shift in referent (*SR* 7), the shift to apparently unrelated referents (*SR* 10), and the number of different shifts in the referent.

The negatively correlated variables in the pattern include "Range of Inclusion" (*Dim* 2a), "Consequences" (*Dim* 7), "Locational Qualities" (*Dim* 15), "Temporal

Qualities" (*Dim* 16), "Sensory Qualities" by referent (*Dim* 19b), "Judgments and Evaluations" (*Dim* 21a, 21b, and 21a+b), conventional metaphors (*TR* 4b), and shifts to previous meaning variables (*SR* 4). Let us check now how many of the positively preferred meaning variables in the meaning profile of Subject A (see Table 43) correspond to the meaning variables in the pattern based on positive correlations, and how many of the negatively preferred meaning variables in the meaning profile of Subject A correspond to the meaning variables in the pattern based on negative correlations. We find correspondences only for the positively preferred meaning variables "Action" (*Dim* 4a) and the attributive type of relation (*TR* 1a), and for none of the negatively preferred meaning variables. Hence, the total number of correspondences is 2, which constitutes 9.09% of the total number of meaning variables in the extroversion pattern (*n* = 22). In the case of Subject B (Table 43), there are somewhat more correspondences: for the positively preferred "Possessions and Belongingness" (*Dim* 17b and 17a+b) and the attributive type of relation (*TR* 1a), and for the negatively preferred "Judgments and Evaluations" (*Dim* 21b) and conventional metaphors (*TR* 4b). These amount to 5 correspondences, which constitute 22.73% of the meaning variables in the extroversion pattern. The results of these countings and computations for the two subjects can be read in Table 43 in the row that corresponds to extroversion (see the second row).

The comparisons can be done with any pattern of meaning variables representing a trait that has been established following the standard procedure described in Part II of this book. The patterns established by means of Studies 1–20 are summarized in Table 1. In this table, each meaning variable that was found to be correlated positively with the trait score is represented by a plus (+) sign, and each meaning variable that was found to be correlated negatively with the trait score is represented by a minus (−) sign. This form of representing the pattern of the trait facilitates the procedure of comparing the subject's preferences with the meaning variables in the trait's pattern. Further trait patterns can be found in Chapters 11 and 12, which present the patterns of the Minnesota Multiphasic Personality Inventory (MMPI) scales (Table 47) and the scales of the Personality Research Form (PRF; Table 50).

The process that has been exemplified in regard to one trait (extroversion) can be repeated in regard to any number of traits. The only limitation is the availability of information about the patterns of traits. The comparisons between the preferred meaning variables according to the subjects' profiles and the meaning variables in the traits' patterns can be made simultaneously for a great number of traits by checking each preferred meaning variable of a subject against all trait patterns before proceeding to the next preferred meaning variable. The comparison can be made by hand or by a computer into which the meaning profiles and the trait patterns have been fed. Thus, Table 44 presents the results for Subjects A and B in regard to all 76 traits examined in Studies 1–20 (see the columns labeled "Trait").

An interesting possibility, which has not yet been pursued further, is applying the procedure to a collective meaning profile based on the means of a large number of individual meaning profiles of subjects in a certain group. In that case, applying the procedure would result in a set of trait scores characterizing the group as a whole. This procedure is of great potential importance for social psychology.

Applying the procedure allows one to assign to subjects scores reflecting their standing on traits. At this stage, many psychologists dealing with personality assessment for diagnostic or research purposes would consider their task at an end. Our

Table 44. Meaning-Based Trait Scores and Antitrait Scores of Subjects A and B[a]

Traits	Subject A		Subject B		Traits	Subject A		Subject B	
	Trait	Antitrait	Trait	Antitrait		Trait	Antitrait	Trait	Antitrait
Exvia[b]	14.29	14.29	28.57	35.71	PF 18	10.00	30.00	40.00	20.00
Extroversion	9.09	36.36	22.73	31.82	PF 19	16.67	50.00	0.00	50.00
CPI: Do	9.09	33.33	11.11	22.22	PF 20	14.28	35.71	14.29	35.71
Cs	20.00	50.00	20.00	33.33	PF 21	0.00	39.13	4.35	39.13
Sy	8.33	33.33	25.00	25.00	PF 22	18.18	9.09	45.45	18.18
Sp	18.18	18.18	27.27	9.09	PF 23	14.29	28.57	57.14	28.57
Sa	26.67	33.33	13.33	26.67	PF 24	12.50	12.50	25.00	37.50
Wb	36.36	0.00	45.45	18.18	PF 25	10.00	20.00	40.00	20.00
Re	33.33	0.00	58.33	8.33	PF 26	0.00	33.33	33.33	16.67
So	50.00	0.00	50.00	0.00	PF 27	0.00	50.00	0.00	25.00
Sc	20.00	20.00	30.00	40.00	M.-B.: Extro.	53.85	0.00	46.15	15.38
To	33.33	0.00	66.67	16.67	M.-B.: Sens.	26.09	8.70	43.48	17.39
Gi	8.33	50.00	16.67	25.00	M.-B.: Thinking	31.25	18.75	18.75	12.50
Cm	21.43	35.71	21.43	21.43	M.-B.: Judg.	15.00	30.00	30.00	30.00
Ac	12.50	37.50	12.50	50.00	Approval	25.00	18.75	43.75	12.50
Ai	25.00	50.00	50.00	0.00	Ego strength	18.75	12.50	43.75	18.75
Ie	0.00	25.00	25.00	0.00	Anality	20.00	20.00	30.00	20.00
Py	0.00	0.00	50.00	50.00	Cleanliness	23.81	23.81	47.62	14.28
Fx	0.00	0.00	50.00	0.00	Hypochondr.	30.44	13.04	13.04	30.43
Fe	75.00	0.00	25.00	25.00	Avarice	27.27	27.27	54.54	9.09
Mach IV	9.09	9.09	72.73	9.09	Impulsivity	11.11	33.33	27.78	27.78
n Power	29.17	16.67	70.83	20.83	EI	9.68	38.71	9.68	29.03
PF 1	20.00	20.00	50.00	20.00	Authoritar.	11.11	38.89	0.00	33.33
PF 2	27.78	11.11	33.33	22.22	Dogmatism	15.00	30.00	10.00	60.00
PF 3	18.75	12.50	43.75	12.50	Cog. activity	12.12	30.30	18.18	18.18
PF 4	18.75	12.50	18.75	25.00	Ideat. pref.	16.67	25.00	25.00	20.83
PF 5	18.18	18.18	54.54	9.09	Mot. act. pref.	42.86	14.28	21.43	28.57
PF 6	25.81	6.45	25.81	16.13	SSS: Total	27.27	36.36	36.36	9.09
PF 7	21.74	30.43	13.04	21.74	SSS: Thrill	8.33	8.33	33.33	25.00
PF 8	43.75	18.75	18.75	12.50	SSS: Exp. seek.	16.67	41.67	20.83	33.33
PF 9	33.33	12.50	25.00	16.67	SSS: Disinhib.	30.77	30.77	15.38	23.08
PF 10	41.67	4.17	25.00	16.67	SSS: Boredom	50.00	20.00	20.00	30.00
PF 11	18.18	27.27	36.36	36.36	Bem: Mas.	26.32	10.53	31.58	31.58
PF 12	36.36	27.27	27.27	22.73	Bem: Fem.	33.33	11.11	33.33	16.67
PF 13	0.00	57.14	0.00	28.57	Bem: Androg.	36.36	18.18	39.39	18.18
PF 14	17.65	17.65	11.76	29.41	Bem: Soc. des.	20.00	20.00	10.00	20.00
PF 15	11.11	44.44	11.11	33.33	Int. of ambig.	34.78	17.39	43.48	8.69
PF 17	6.67	26.67	13.33	40.00	LPC	23.80	28.57	42.85	19.05

[a]The scores are percentages. For the labels of the traits see Part II or Table 1. The list of traits includes all the traits investigated in Part II, Studies 1–20.
[b]Exvia corresponds to PF 16.

procedure, however, includes a fourth step, which is optional, and which depends on the interests of the person who applies the procedure. *The fourth step* is interpreting the obtained numbers. There are two forms of interpretation. One concerns the relative magnitudes of the assigned numbers. Of course, it is possible to treat them as they stand, located on a scale (which, at the very least, is on the level of an interval scale), extending from a minimum of zero to a maximum of 100. In addition, it is also possible to interpret the numbers in verbal-evaluative terms. At present, our validational studies (see "Validation" later in this chapter) and previous experience (see Studies 12, 13, 16, and 19) support the following rough correspondences: Trait scores in the range of 0%–20% may be considered "very weak"; those in the range of 21%–40% "weak"; those in the range of 41%–60%, "moderate"; those in the range of 61%–80%, "strong"; and those in the range of 81%–100%, "very strong."

The second form of interpretation concerns noting the particular content of the traits in the case of the specific subject, that is, noting which meaning variables of the trait's pattern constitute the trait in the case of that subject, and specifying the manifestations of those meaning variables. This form of interpretation would be more suitable in regard to traits of at least moderate strength. One may note the content of the trait in the case of the subject by simply reading off the comparisons that have been made before. Thus, in the case of Subject B, who is extroverted to a moderate degree, extroversion consists of a positive concern with "Possessions" and a negative concern with "Judgments and Evaluations," but it does not include those aspects of extroversion that concern overinclusion (a positive preference for *Dim* 1 and a negative one for *Dim* 2a), activity (a positive preference for *Dim* 4a), or impulsiveness (a negative preference for *Dim* 7). Naturally, in another subject who may be extroverted to the same moderate degree, extroversion may include other aspects of the total pattern of extroversion. Differences of this kind between subjects who may all have a trait to a comparable degree may account for the variations in the responses and performance of these subjects when they are expected to respond more uniformly.

After having noted the constitution of the trait in the case of the subject, we may now focus on the manifestations of these meaning variables. We do this by reading the manifestations of each of these positively or negatively preferred meaning variables in Appendix B. Please note that Appendix B lists different manifestations for positively and for negatively preferred meaning variables. Thus, for example, among the manifestations of a positive preference for "Belongingness" (*Dim* 17b), we read "concerned with possessions and saving money . . . as a part of a conservative outlook . . . or of a selective obsessive orientation," and among those of a positive preference for "Possessions and Belongingness" (*Dim* 17a+b), we read in addition, "practical, . . . concerned with facts . . . respond well to monetary rewards," and so on. The resulting image becomes richer when we proceed to amplify it in line with the manifestations of the other meaning variables.

ANTITRAITS

In addition to the straight trait scores, the procedure may also yield information about a further aspect of traits, which we call *antitraits*. Antitraits consist of the reversed correspondences between the subject's preferred meaning variables and the meaning variables included in the trait's pattern. A reversed correspondence exists if the subject has a positive preference for a meaning variable in the pattern that is based on a negative correlation with the trait, or if the subject has a negative preference for a meaning variable in the pattern that is based on a positive correlation with the trait. Each case of a reversed correspondence counts as 1, and all cases can be summed. The sum has to be converted into a percentage of the total number of meaning variables in the trait's pattern. This percentage constitutes the score of the antitrait. The higher the score, the stronger the antitrait. The scores of antitraits, like those of traits, are located on a scale (at least, interval) from 0 to 100. Table 44 presents the antitrait scores of Subjects A and B for all 76 traits.

Antitraits are correlated negatively with traits ($r = -.48$ and $-.45$ in the case of Subjects A and B, respectively). Yet, this negative correlation does not determine

Table 45. Strength of Traits and Relative Strength of Traits
and Antitraits in Subjects A and B

	Number (and percentage) of traits	
Strength of traits[a]:	Subject A	Subject B
Very weak (0–20)	44 (57.89%)	25 (32.89%)
Weak (21–40)	25 (32.89%)	29 (38.16%)
Moderate (41–60)	6 (7.89%)	19 (25.00%)
Strong (61–80)	1 (1.32%)	3 (3.95%)
Very strong (81–100)	0 (0.00%)	0 (0.00%)
Relative strength of traits and antitraits:		
Trait stronger than antitrait	27 (35.53%)	39 (51.32%)
Trait and antitrait equal	16 (21.05%)	9 (11.84%)
Antitrait stronger than trait	33 (43.42%)	28 (36.84%)

[a]The numbers in parentheses are trait scores (for definition and description, see text, Chapter 10).

fully the relative relations between trait and antitrait scores in regard to each trait. Thus, the trait may score higher, or the antitrait may score higher, or both may be equal. The distributions of these relations for the two Subjects A and B (Table 45) differ significantly ($\chi^2 = 7.27$, $df = 2$, $p < .05$), although the correlation coefficients between the traits and the antitraits do not.

We have introduced the concept of antitraits although at present we are just beginning to form a conception of their likely function and impact. Our preliminary explorations suggest that, in the case of bipolar traits (such as external-internal control or most of the 16 PF traits), antitraits may reflect the strength of the pole contrasted to the regular trait. This conclusion indicates that, even in the case of bipolar traits, a subject may have each pole of the trait to some extent. In other words, being high on internal control does not necessarily mean being low on external control. Similarly, a subject may be a little extrovert and a little introvert in different senses or in different domains. The concept of antitraits seems to do justice to his possibility.

Further, in the case of all traits, antitraits seem to provide a measure of the degree to which a specific trait in a specific subject may be changed, that is, strengthened or weakened by a manipulation of the trait's meaning variables. At present, it seems likely that it is easier to weaken the pattern of a trait whose antitrait is higher than it is to weaken a trait whose antitrait is lower.

VALIDATION

In this case, *validation* refers to the results of checking the correlations between the trait scores obtained on the meaning questionnaires and the trait scores of the same traits obtained by means of the conventional scales. Up to now, three validation studies of this kind have been carried out. The first dealt with the validity of meaning-based trait scores on the California Psychological Inventory (CPI); see Study 2); the second with the validity of meaning-based trait scores for the 16

Personality Factors Test (16 PF; see Studies 1 and 6); and the third with the validity of meaning-based trait scores on the Myers-Briggs Type Indicator (see Study 7). The number of subjects in the first was 48, in the second 50, and in the third 36. In each case, half were men and half women. They were all students, in the age range 21–28 years. In the first study, the subjects were administered the meaning questionnaire and the CPI; in the second, the meaning questionnaire and the 16 PF; and in the third, the meaning questionnaire and the Myers-Briggs Type Indicator. The meaning-based trait scores were computed by use of the procedure described in this chapter. The correlations between the meaning-based and the regular scale-based trait scores were in the range of $r = .20$ (n.s.) to $r = .94$ ($p < .001$) (see Table 46). The lowest coefficients (including the only nonsignificant one for the So scale of the CPI) were obtained for the five CPI scales with the lowest number of meaning variables in their pattern. The mean of the correlations (based on z transformations) for all the CPI scales was .50, and it was .59 for the 13 CPI scales whose patterns included more than four meaning variables. The mean of the correlations for the 16 PF was .74 and for the Myers-Briggs .76. A possible explanation for the lower mean of correlations for the CPI than for the other scales is the lower number of meaning variables in the patterns of the CPI. The mean is 8.5 for all CPI scales, 10.5 for the 13 CPI scales whose patterns included more than four meaning variables, 16.8 for the 16 PF, and 18 for the Myers-Briggs. Be that as it may, the findings of the validation studies support the procedure for deriving meaning-based trait scores.

Table 46. Correlations between Meaning-Based and Scale-Based Trait Scores[a]

Study 1: CPI scales ($n = 48$)		Study 2: 16 PF scales ($n = 50$)		Study 3: Myers-Briggs ($n = 36$)	
Scale	Correlation	Scale	Correlation	Scale	Correlation
Do	.52***	PF 1	.66***	Extroversion	.69***
Cs	.56***	PF 2	.69***	Sensing	.82***
Sy	.64***	PF 3	.73***	Thinking	.75***
Sp	.58***	PF 4	.74***	Judging	.80***
Sa	.79***	PF 5	.58***	Mean	.76***
Wb	.65***	PF 6	.87***		
Re	.61***	PF 7	.81***		
So	.20	PF 8	.69***		
Sc	.54***	PF 9	.94***		
To	.47**	PF 10	.76***		
Gi	.71***	PF 11	.56**		
Cm	.69***	PF 12	.76***		
Ac	.42**	PF 13	.53**		
Ai	.49**	PF 14	.83***		
Ie	.27*	PF 15	.59***		
Py	.28*	PF 16	.63***		
Fx	.31*	Mean	.74***		
Fe	.34*				
Mean	.50**				

[a]The means of correlations are based on z transformations. For the code of the CPI scales, see Table 8, and for the code of the 16 PF, see Table 16.
  *$p < .05$.
 **$p < .01$.
***$p < .001$.

ADVANTAGES OF THE MEANING-BASED TRAIT SCORES

The assessment of traits through meaning-based trait scores seems preferable to assessment through the regular trait scales. One reason has already been mentioned. It is the most evident gain: assessing any number of traits through one questionnaire (the meaning questionnaire). The gain is economical in the time and resources involved in administering a great number of trait scales, and also in reliability, which declines, because of boredom and the increasing impact of response set, if a subject responds to many questionnaires. A single meaning questionnaire provides trait scores without these difficulties.

But there are further advantages that deserve to be mentioned:

1. Even when they concern a single trait, meaning-based trait scores provide, even now, more information than the regular run-of-the mill trait scale, and at least as much information as an especially widely investigated trait scale. The information available through the meaning-based trait scores relates to the manifestations of each of the meaning variables in the pattern and, in many cases, also to their interactions. The lists available at present (see Appendix B) provide a summary of major findings concerning the personological (including motivational, emotional, attitudinal, and social) manifestations of each meaning variable. The lists will undoubtedly be complemented in the future by additional information derived from further research. New studies reveal ever newer domains of manifestations of preferred meaning-assignment tendencies. For example, it was shown that when an item in a questionnaire is judged to be true or false, the checked response is more extreme in the positive or negative sense when the content of the item corresponds to the individual's preferred meaning dimension than when it does not (S. Kreitler & H. Kreitler, 1984b). In addition to the manifestations in domains conventionally related to personality, meaning variables were shown to have manifestations also in the domains of perception, memory, concept formation, and problem solving, beyond those mentioned in Appendix B (S. Kreitler & H. Kreitler, 1984a, 1987b,c, 1989b). Thus, an important advantage of using this system of assessment is the possibility of obtaining both information about the personality dynamics and the cognitive functioning of the individual and insights into the manner in which these two facets are interrelated structurally and dynamically.

2. Even when they concern a single trait, meaning-based trait scores provide more personalized information than scale-based trait scores. Meaning-based trait scores indicate precisely which positively and negatively preferred meaning variables constitute the trait in the case of the specific subject. This precise indication allows a much finer and more precise evaluation of the individual's tendencies than the more global, scale-based trait, which provides no information about the microstructural constituents of the trait in the single subject. The microstructural constituents enable specifying the manifestations of the particular meaning variables in the case of each subject, and thus, they increase the precision of individual predictions and reduce the amount of unaccounted-for variation in the responses of subjects with similar trait scores. Moreover, information about the constituents of the trait in the particular subject allows insights into and predictions about interactions among traits in that subject (see Study 22).

3. Meaning-based trait scores may be used to obtain information about any number of the individual's traits. The point to be emphasized is that not only does

the procedure yield a great number of trait scores, but these trait scores are all expressed in the same quantitative terms and hence may be compared with each other in the same individual and across individuals. Thus, the meaning-based trait score tells us not only what the strength of a certain trait is in a certain individual, but also what is its strength relative to that of other traits of that individual. Therefore, knowing that Trait X is weak implies different things, depending on the overall distribution of traits in the individual. Let us examine, for example, Subject A, in whom 91% of the assessed traits are weak or very weak, and Subject B, in whom only 71% of the assessed traits are weak or very weak. In Subject A, the finding of a weak trait is more to be expected than it is in Subject B. Further, it would be important to examine what is the strength of other similar traits in that individual. For example, if the weak trait is intolerance of ambiguity, whereas anthoritarianism and dogmatism are moderate or strong, it is possible to conclude that, in that individual, the latter two traits probably have a more ideological than obsessive flavor.

In other words, information about many comparable traits in the individual is not merely additive but may provide insight into the overall structure of the personality and into the role and status of any particular trait in this structure. Thus, we may learn what the total distribution of trait scores in the individual is, for example, how many of the traits are strong or weak, and which are the strong and salient traits, such as, Femininity (CPI) in Subject A versus *n* Power and Machiavellianism in Subject B. Further, we may also learn about the distribution of antitraits and of their relation to traits. For example, it is noteworthy that Subject B has not only more strong and medium traits and fewer weak and very weak traits than Subject A, but also fewer traits whose trait scores are equal to their antitrait scores (Table 45). Do these observations constitute criteria for concluding that Subject B has a more sharply outlined personality than Subject A? Information of this kind about the distribution and structuring of traits in the individual provides the outlines for a new approach to personality typology.

4. The assessment procedure of meaning-based trait scores appears to be preferable to that of scale-based scores. The meaning questionnaire is a more direct measure of the trait than scales that consist of responses to self-report items that are merely one manifestation of the meaning variables in the trait's pattern. Further, the information provided by the meaning questionnaire is most probably more reliable than that provided by scale-based scores. The reason is that subjects would be unable to figure out the relation between communications of meaning and traits, whereas they are more likely to guess or infer, to some extent, the relation between responses to self-report items and traits.

Identifying Personality Traits

IMPORTANCE OF IDENTIFYING TRAITS

This chapter focuses on a special application of the new conception of traits: identifying constructs that are personality traits or differentiating between constructs that are personality traits and those that are not. This application is important because, on the one hand, there are so many personality variables and so many different kinds of them, and, on the other hand, the term *personality trait* is used very loosely, often interchangeable with other terms, such as *personality constructs, personality tendencies,* or *personality variables.* The lack of distinctions and the absence of a tool for checking distinctions result in confusion. It is possible that personality traits have qualities that other constructs in this domain do not have; for example, they may be related more closely than, say, temperamental constructs to cognitive content, cognitive maps, systems of values, and program-oriented schemata, and/or they may play a smaller role in regard to behavior (Strelau, 1987). If traits are to be included as constructs in a future theory of personality, it is necessary for them to be distinguishable from other constructs by means of a systematic procedure. It is the purpose of this chapter to present such a procedure and to exemplify its application.

THE PROCEDURE FOR IDENTIFYING TRAITS

The procedure for identifying traits or for distinguishing between traits and nontrait constructs rests on examining whether a given personality variable resembles the majority of what are called personality traits or not. This examination requires two kinds of information: (1) information about the pattern of meaning variables corresponding to the construct to be examined and (2) information about the meaning pattern of meaning variables corresponding to a representative group of personality traits, like the information that was examined in Studies 1–20.

The procedure is based on comparing the pattern of meaning variables of the construct to be examined with the pattern of a representative group of personality traits. The comparison is made in terms of the features that have been identified before as characteristic of patterns of meaning variables corresponding to personality traits. In Chapter 5, seven characteristics of trait patterns were described. Even

303

though all are important, not all of them have, at present, an equally sharp operational definition. Specificity, structure, and coherence, for example, are defined operationally less well than the other characteristics. Therefore, for the present, we have selected as criteria only those characteristics that are operationally well defined. The list includes the following criteria (for the numerical values see Chapter 5 and Tables 2, 3, and 4): (1) the number of different kinds of meaning variables in the pattern, which for traits is 3 to 4; (2) the proportion of the different kinds of meaning variables in the pattern, which for traits is 54.75% meaning dimensions, 25.75 types of relation, 12.57 referent-shift variables, and 5.9 forms of relation; (3) the relative proportion of negative components in the pattern of meaning variables, which for traits is .38; (4) the number of meaning variables in the pattern, which for traits is in the range of the mean ± 1 *SD*, that is, 13.81 ± 6.50 (i.e., 7–20); and (5) the proportion of meaning dimensions and types of relation in the pattern representing general meaning variables (e.g., *Dim* 1, *Dim* 22a+b, and *TR* 1a+b) in contrast to more specific subvariables (e.g. *Dim* 4a, *Dim* 22a, and *TR* 1b), which for traits is .44

Thus, the procedure for identifying personality traits includes the following seven steps:

1. Administering to a sample of subjects the trait scale(s) to be examined and the standard meaning questionnaire. (The sample should be random unless otherwise indicated.)

2. Scoring the trait scale and meaning questionnaire to obtain for each subject the trait score(s) and the meaning profile.

3. Intercorrelating the trait score(s) and the meaning profiles.

4. Extracting from the intercorrelations matrix the meaning variables correlated with the trait score(s) significantly, either positively or negatively. These meaning variables constitute the pattern of meaning variables of the trait to be examined.

5. Establishing for the pattern (defined in Step 4), the values for the five abovementioned criteria. The number of kinds of meaning variables (Criterion 1) is simply counted. Its range is 1–4. The distribution of the proportions of kinds of meaning variables (Criterion 2) is determined by first counting the number of meaning variables of each kind in the pattern and then turning it into a percentage of the total number of meaning variables in the pattern. The proportion of negative constituents in the pattern (Criterion 3) is determined by counting in the pattern the number of meaning variables of all kinds that were correlated negatively with the trait score, and by turning this number into a proportion of the total number of variables in the pattern. The number of variables in the pattern (Criterion 4) is established by counting. The proportion of several meaning variables in the pattern (Criterion 5) is established by counting in the pattern the number of general meaning dimensions (i.e., *Dim* 1, 3, 4a+b, 5, 6, 7, 8a+b, 9 to 16, 17a+b, 18, 19a+b, 20a+b, 21a+b, and 22a+b) and general types of relation (*TR* 1a+b, *TR* 2a+b+c+d, *TR* 3a+b+c, and *TR* 4a+b+c+d), and by turning the number into a proportion of the total of meaning dimensions and types of relations in the pattern.

6. Comparing the values of the pattern to be checked (as established in Step 5), with the values for personality traits. The comparison is done for each criterion separately. If the values of the checked pattern do not conform to those characteristic for personality traits, a deviation is registered for that criterion. In order to check whether there is conformity to the values of trait patterns in regard to Criterion (1), it is necessary only to count how many of the four different kinds of meaning variables

are represented in the checked pattern. Conformity requires three or four kinds, whereas deviation is registered if there are one or two kinds only. In the case of Criterion (4), it is merely necessary to determine whether the number of meaning variables in the checked pattern falls within the specified range of meaning variables, which is 7 to 20. There is conformity if the number falls within the range, and deviation if it falls outside it. In the case of Criteria 2, 3, and 5, it is necessary to examine the significance of the differences between the value established for the checked pattern and those characteristic of personality traits. In regard to Criterion 2, the differences between the percentages in the checked pattern and those in the patterns of personality traits are examined by the chi-square test. In regard to Criteria 3 and 5, the differences between the proportions are examined by z values. In regard to each of these criteria, deviation is registered if the difference is significant.

7. Summing up the number of deviations between the checked pattern and the patterns of personality traits. Checking each of the five criteria (Step 6) yields either "deviation" or "no deviation." All criteria get the same weight. Thus, in order to determine whether the pattern of the checked construct conforms to that of personality traits, it is necessary to sum up the number of "deviations" of that pattern from the pattern of personality traits. The number of "deviations" could range from 5, in which case the construct's pattern is totally dissimilar from that of traits, to 0, in which case the construct's pattern is totally similar to that of traits. In view of the variabilities observed in the patterns of personality traits, we suggest regarding a construct's pattern as trait-similar if it deviates from that of personality traits on no more than two criteria. If it deviates on three to five criteria, it can be considered trait-dissimilar.

THE CASE OF THE MMPI: AN EXAMPLE OF APPLYING THE PROCEDURE

We will illustrate the procedure for identifying traits by applying it to the basic scales of the Minnesota Multiphasic Personality Inventory (MMPI): The 10 clinical scales and the three validity scales (F, K, and L). We chose the MMPI for this purpose because there is a persistent unclarity about the function of these famous scales and about what they actually assess.

The major issue is whether the MMPI is a psychodiagnostic tool designed to provide differential diagnoses among abnormal groups of patients or whether it is a "personality inventory or test," "an objective instrument for the multiphasic assessment of personality" (Hathaway, 1960, p. vii). Even the test's manual does not clearly present the MMPI's objectives. In the opening section (Hathaway & McKinley, 1983, p. 1.), we read that the MMPI "is designed to provide an objective assessment of some of the major personality characteristics that affect personal and social adjustment," to assess "traits that are commonly characteristic of disabling psychological abnormality," and to measure "the personality states of literate adolescents and adults." An obscure reference to the Social Introversion Scale states that it was added soon after the publication of the MMPI, an assertion that raises some questions concerning its relation to the diagnostic scales. To top the confusion, it is expressly stated, "The scales were not expected to measure pure traits or to represent discrete etiological or prognostic entities." Another "practical guide" (Graham, 1977, p. 5) refers openly to the fact that the MMPI has no validity as a clinical

Table 47. Significant Correlations of the MMPI Scales with Meaning Variables

Scale	Significant correlations with meaning variables
Hypochondriasis (*Hs*)	*Dim* 4b, .27**; *Dim* 12, .24*; *Dim* 19b, .34***; *TR* 2a, .33***; *TR* 2b, .39***; *TR* 2d, .28**; *TR* 2a + b + c + d, .38***.
Depression (*D*)	*Dim* 9, −.27**; (*Dim* 19a + b₂, −.32***); *TR* 2a, .32***; *TR* 2d, .31**; *TR* 2a + b + c + d, .34***; *TR* 3c, −.31**; *TR* 4d, .28**; no. of different *FR*, .30**.
Hysteria (*Hy*)	*Dim* 4b, .30**; *Dim* 19a + b₈, −.26**; *TR* 2a, .37***.
Psychopathic Deviate (*Pd*)	*Dim* 4b, .36***; *Dim* 5, .41***; *Dim* 9, −.27**; *Dim* 14, −.29**; *Dim* 21a, −.26**; *Dim* 21b, −.28**; *Dim* 21a + b, −.31**; *TR* 2a, .39***; *TR* 4d, .32**; no. of different *FR*, .28**.
Masculinity–Femininity (*Mf*)	*Dim* 9, −.30**; (*Dim* 19a + b₂, −.32***); *TR* 2a, .42***; *TR* 4c, .27**; *TR* 4d, .31**; *SR* 2, −.29**.
Paranoia (*Pa*)	*Dim* 4b, −.37***; *Dim* 4a + b, .24*; *Dim* 8b, −.27**; *Dim* 16, −.29**; *TR* 1a + b, −.26**; *TR* 2a, .42***.
Psychoasthenia (*Pt*)	*Dim* 7, .32***; *Dim* 9, −.27**; *Dim* 12, .24*; *TR* 2a, .31**; *TR* 2b, .25*; *TR* 2a + b + c + d, .37***; no. of different *FR*, .33***.
Schizophrenia (*Sc*)	*Dim* 1, .36***; *Dim* 2a, −.26**; *Dim* 4a, .39***; *Dim* 4a + b, .39***; *Dim* 5, .38***; *Dim* 7, .36***; *Dim* 8b, .34***; *Dim* 8a + b, .37***; *Dim* 22a, .38***; *Dim* 22a + b, .33**; *TR* 2a, .33***; *TR* 4d, .31**; *TR* 4a + b + c + d, .36***; no. of different *FR*, .41***; *FR* 8, .32**; *SR* 3, .35***; *SR* 4, .42***.
Hypomania (*Ma*)	*Dim* 18, .83***; *Dim* 19a + b, .31**; (*Dim* 19a + b₂, .27**); *TR* 2b, −.26**; *TR* 2a + b + c + d, −.26**.
Social Introversion (*Si*)	*Dim* 1, .38***; *Dim* 3, .30**; (*Dim* 19a + b₀, .25*; *Dim* 19a + b₃, −.26**; *Dim* 19a + b₆, −.38***; *Dim* 19a + b₇, .44***; *Dim* 19a + b₈, .35**); *TR* 2d, .34***; *TR* 2a + b + c + d, −.44***; *TR* 3c, −.25*; no. of different *FR*, .30**.
Lie (*L*)	*Dim* 4b, −.33***; *Dim* 7, −.34***; *Dim* 8b, .36***; *Dim* 8a + b, −.35***; *Dim* 12, −.29**; *Dim* 15, −.33***; *Dim* 18, .26**; *Dim* 19b, −.34***; (*Dim* 19a + b₈, −.27**); *TR* 2a, −.34***; *SR* 8, −.37***; no. of different *SR*, −.32***.
Infrequency (*F*)	*Dim* 2a, −.26**; *Dim* 4a, .43***; *Dim* 4b, .34***; *Dim* 4a + b, .41***; *Dim* 5, .40***; *Dim* 6, .39***; *Dim* 7, .45***; *Dim* 8a, .39***; *Dim* 8b, .35***; *Dim* 8a + b, .40***; *Dim* 11, .35***; *Dim* 13, .36***; *Dim* 15, .35***; *Dim* 22a, .44***; *Dim* 22a + b, .37***; no. of different meaning dimensions, .29**; *FR* 4, .37***; *FR* 8, .27**; no. of different *FR*, .40***; *SR* 4, .42***.
Defensiveness (*K*)	*Dim* 7, −.33***; *Dim* 22a, −.22a; *TR* 2b, −.29**; *FR* 4, −.33***; *SR* 3, −.31**.

Note. For the code of the meaning variables, see Appendix A.
*p < .05.
**p < .01.
***p < .001.

psychodiagnostic tool. Nevertheless, "it is assumed that the clinical scales are measuring something" and "the new approach treats each MMPI scale as an unknown" whose correlates are to be identified.

It is likely that the problem depends at least partly on the unclarity concerning the status of psychopathological manifestations: Are they temporary or personality-characteristic responses? Are they actually personality traits, or do they only depend on traits?

The situation is even more blurred, if possible, in regard to the validational scales. On the one hand, they are viewed as test-bound specific measures designed merely to detect deviant test-taking attitudes; on the other hand, they are viewed as "related to personality and other characteristics" (Lanyon, 1968, p. 6), assessing personality tendencies just as the clinical scales do (Dahlstrom, Welsh, & Dahlstrom, 1972, Chapters 4, 5; Graham, 1977, Chapter 3).

In view of this situation, it seemed both important and interesting to apply to the MMPI our procedure for identifying traits. For this purpose the MMPI (the standardized translation by Montag, published by Ramot, Tel-Aviv) and the standard meaning questionnaire were administered in random order on two separate occasions to 100 students (50 males and 50 females, mean age 24.3 years), who according to self-reports had never suffered from any mental symptoms and had never had psychiatric help. The meaning questionnaire was scored according to the standard procedure, and so was the MMPI. Table 47 presents the significant correlations between the scores on the MMPI scales (10 clinical scales and three validational scales) and the meaning variables. We may now apply to these data the procedure for identifying traits.

First, let us check the findings for all 10 clinical scales together and for the three validational scales together, according to each of the five criteria (see above, p. 304) separately. Table 48 shows that the patterns of the 10 MMPI clinical scales deviate from the patterns characteristic of personality traits on three of the five criteria (i.e., 1, 2, and 3). Hence, as a set of scales, they cannot be considered scales that assess personality traits. It may be of interest to note that the pattern of meaning variables in the 10 clinical scales deviates also from the pattern specifically characteristic of mental-health traits (see Tables 2 and 3; there are deviations in Criteria 1, 2, 4, and 5). On the other hand, the validity scales do not deviate from the patterns characteristic of personality traits on any of the criteria and may be considered personality traits.

However, an examination of the set as a whole cannot replace an examination of each scale separately. Table 49 presents the results of the checking of each scale. It shows that the patterns of four of the clinical scales resemble those of personality traits. These are Scales 2 (Depression), Scale 4 (Psychopathic Deviate), Scale 7 (Psychoasthenia), and Scale 10 (Social Introversion). Of the validity scales, only Scale L (Lying) has a pattern that resembles those of personality traits. Our attempts to discover distinctions between the MMPI trait-similar and trait-dissimilar scales led to no positive findings: they do not differ in the mean number of scale items or in the number of meaning variables in the patterns or in the number of presumed correlates (see Graham, 1977, Chapter 4). On the other hand, our finding may not be accidental. The scale of Social Introversion is a kind of deviate in the set and was designed from the very beginning to assess a personality type akin to the trait introversion (Dahlstrom & Walsh, 1960, pp. 77–79). Further, Scale 7 (Psychoasthenia) assesses obsessive-compulsive tendencies, which have often been consid-

**Table 48. Results of Applying the Procedure for Identifying Traits to the Scales
of the MMPI and the PRF[a]**

Criteria	MMPI (10 scales)	MMPI (valid. scales)	PRF (20 scales)	PRF (22 scales)
(1) Number of different kinds of meaning variables	$\bar{X}$ = 2.7 [Dev.]	4 [No dev.]	4 [No dev.]	4 [No dev.]
(2) Proportion of different kinds of meaning variables	Dim 45.26% TR 45.26% FR 6.32% SR 3.16% χ^2 = 23.501 p < .001 [Dev.]	Dim 57.45% TR 25.53% FR 8.51% SR 8.51% χ^2 = 2.601 not sig. [No dev.]	Dim 59.18% TR 27.35% FR 4.49% SR 8.57% χ^2 = 2.067 not sig. [No dev.]	Dim 55.33% TR 28.67% FR 5.00% SR 9.67% χ^2 = 1.143 not sig. [No dev.]
(3) Proportion of negative components in the pattern	.24 z = 2.00 p < .05 [Dev.]	.36 z = .056 Not sig. [No dev.]	.49 z = .917 Not sig. [No dev.]	.53 z = 1.256 Not sig. [No dev.]
(4) Number of meaning variables in the pattern	$\bar{X}$ = 9.5 SD = 5.85 [No dev.]	$\bar{X}$ = 15.67 SD = 12.89 [No dev.]	$\bar{X}$ = 12.25 SD = 5.48 [No dev.]	$\bar{X}$ = 13.64 SD = 8.20 [No dev.]
(5) Proportion of general meaning dimensions and types of relation in the pattern	.38 z = 1.20 Not sig. [No dev.]	.49 z = .625 Not sig. [No dev.]	.38 z = 1.50 Not sig. [No dev.]	.39 z = .833 Not sig. [No dev.]
Total number of deviations	3	0	0	0

[a]Dim = meaning dimensions; TR = types of relation; FR = forms of relation; SR = shifts of referent.

ered a personality configuration (Carr, 1974; Sullivan, 1947; Shapiro, 1965). The same could be claimed about psychopathy (Cleckly, 1964). Yet, emphasizing the "personality" characteristics of the trait-similar scales raises the problem of why Scale 3 (Hysteria) was not found to be trait-similar.

The application of our method for identifying traits to the MMPI led to the following conclusions. As a set, the MMPI is trait-dissimilar, but it includes four trait-similar scales. Further, as a set, the validity scales are trait-similar, but two of the three scales are trait-dissimilar. Notably, according to their patterns of meaning variables, the validity scales differ from the clinical scales on three of the criteria (1, 2, and 4; for Criterion 4, $\bar{X}$ = 21.699, p < .001). This finding accords with the common treatment of the validity scales as a separate part of the test. These conclusions have been reached on the basis of data obtained from a normal sample. Before final conclusions about the MMPI are drawn, it would be necessary to check data obtained from a sample of abnormal subjects.

Even though the MMPI as a set and six of its scales are trait-dissimilar, the meaning variables in the profiles corresponding to each of the scales can be interpreted in terms of their manifestations exactly as the constituents of trait-similar patterns are. Thus, the meaning variables have to be located in Appendix B, and their manifestations can be read off. The validity of the process can be illustrated through examples that obviously correspond to the expected: high scorers on Scale 1 (Hypochondriasis) are concerned with sensory experiences, including internal sensations (see positive correlation with "Sensory Qualities" of the referent, Dim 19b); high scorers on Scale 4 (Psychopathic Deviate) have low concern with "Judgments

Table 49. Evaluating the MMPI Scales in Terms of the Five Criteria for Identifying Traits[a]

MMPI scale	No. of dif. kinds of meaning var. (Crit. 1)	Proportion of dif. kinds of meaning var. (Crit. 2)	Relative prop. of neg. components (Crit. 3)	No. of meaning var. in the pattern (Crit. 4)	Prop. of general m. dim. and TR (Crit. 5)	No. of deviations from traits
Hypochondriasis	2	$\chi^2 = 59.317$***	.00	7	.28	3
	(D)	(D)	(D)			
Depression	3	$\chi^2 = 113.516$***	.30	10	.30	1
		(D)				
Hysteria	2	$\chi^2 = 23.296$***	.33	3	.00	4
	(D)	(D)		(D)	(D)	
Psychopathic Deviate	3	$\chi^2 = 18.289$***	.33	15	.40	1
		(D)				
Masculinity–Femininity	3	$\chi^2 = 38.455$***	.33	6	.17	3
		(D)		(D)	(D)	
Paranoia	2	$\chi^2 = 23.519$	.50	6	.33	3
	(D)	(D)		(D)		
Psychoasthenia	3	$\chi^2 = 60.038$***	.11	9	.55	2
		(D)	(D)			
Schizophrenia	4	$\chi^2 = 11.789$**	.04	23	.43	3
		(D)	(D)	(D)		
Hypomania	2	$\chi^2 = 26.859$***	.40	5	.40	3
	(D)	(D)		(D)		
Social Introversion	3	$\chi^2 = 15.828$**	.36	11	.18	2
		(D)			(D)	
Infrequency	4	$\chi^2 = 43.319$	1.00	5	.20	3
		(D)	(D)		(D)	
Defensiveness	4	$\chi^2 = 26.512$***	.83	12	.42	2
		(D)	(D)			
Lie	4	$\chi^2 = 11.909$**	.10	30	.43	3
		(D)	(D)	(D)		

[a] In the second row for each MMPI scale, (D) signifies deviation and a blank signifies no deviation.
**$p < .01$.
***$p < .001$.

and Evaluations" about the referent (*Dim* 21a), of the referent (*Dim* 21b), and in general (*Dim* 21a+b); and high scorers on Scale 8 (Schizophrenia) are concerned with the personal mode of meaning.

THE CASE OF THE PRF

In view of the conclusions about the MMPI, the reader may wonder whether similar results would not also be obtained with any other set of scales. In order to check whether the procedure for identifying traits is a sufficiently valid tool for clarifying the nature of psychological scales, we also applied the procedure to the set of scales of the Personality Research Form (PRF). This is a relatively new personality test (Jackson, 1984), which, because of its careful construction and psychometric qualities, is widely considered the best personality test on the market. Therefore, it seemed to us a good specimen for demonstrating the validity of the procedure. We expected that the patterns of meaning variables corresponding to the PRF would not deviate from those of personality traits. Table 50 presents the patterns of the 22 scales, based on the responses of 100 students (50 males and 50 females; mean age 28.2 years) who were administered the standard meaning questionnaire and the PRF in a pretested Hebrew translation.

An analysis of the whole matrix of interrelations of the PRF scales with meaning variables showed that there were no deviations from the patterns of personality traits on any of the five criteria, either for the 20 scales of traits or for the 22 scales, including the validation scales, Infrequency and Desirability (see Table 48, last column). Hence, as expected, the total set can be regarded as having trait-identical patterns of meaning variables.

As in the case of the MMPI, we also applied the procedure to each of the 22 scales separately. Table 51 shows that the patterns of 17 scales deviated from the patterns of personality traits on fewer than three criteria. These 17 scales can be considered personality traits in the accepted sense of the term. In the case of 5 scales, there were three or more deviations from the modal characteristics of personality traits (i.e., the four trait scales Abasement, Affiliation, Autonomy, and Play, and the validity scale Desirability). Hence, 80% of the PRF trait scales conform in their patterns to personality traits, in contrast to 30% of the MMPI scales. The number of deviant scales is low and does not seem to be exceptional (see the distribution of trait patterns in Table 1).

Thus, in view of the results both for the total matrix of intercorrelations and for the scales separately, the PRF conforms to the characteristics of personality traits. This conclusion demonstrates the validity of the procedure for identifying personality traits.

OTHER APPLICATIONS OF THE METHOD FOR IDENTIFYING TRAITS

In order to illustrate the potential of the method for identifying traits, we will describe briefly two further applications of this method. One study dealt with personal styles in individual planning (S. Kreitler & H. Kreitler, 1986a). *Style* was defined as the tendency to apply particular content to plans, for example, to consider

Table 50. Significant Correlations of the PRF with Meaning Variables

Scale	Significant correlations with meaning variables
Abasement (*Ab*)	*Dim* 2a, $-.28^{**}$; (*Dim* 19a + b$_2$, $.26^{**}$; *Dim* 19a + b$_7$, $.24^*$); *TR* 3c, $.28^{**}$; *TR* 4a, $.29^{**}$; no. of different *TR*, $.27^{**}$
Achievement (*Ac*)	*Dim* 14, $-.25^*$; *Dim* 22b, $.36^{***}$; *Dim* 22a + b, $.30^{**}$; *FR* 1, $.29^{**}$; *FR*, 2, $.36^{***}$; FR_{pos}, $.29^{**}$; FR_{neg}, $.36^{***}$; *SR* 8, $-.33^{***}$.
Affiliation (*Af*)	*Dim* 4b, $.25^*$; *Dim* 17a, $-.25^*$; (*Dim* 19a + b$_{10}$, $-.30^{**}$; *Dim* 19a + b$_6$, $-.27^{**}$; *Dim* 19a + b$_7$, $-.27^{**}$; *Dim* 19a + b$_8$, $-.27^{**}$); *TR* 2c, $.25^*$; *TR* 4a, $-.35^{***}$.
Aggression (*Ag*)	*Dim* 4b, $.28^{**}$; *Dim* 6, $.25^*$; *Dim* 7, $.34^{***}$; *Dim* 8b, $.24^*$; *Dim* 9, $.34^{***}$; x(*Dim* 19a + b$_6$, $-.24^*$); *TR* 2d, $-.24^*$; *TR* 4a, $-.37^{***}$; *TR* 4a + b + c + d, $-.32^{***}$; *FR* 6, $-.27^{**}$; *FR* 8, $-.30^{**}$; *SR* 3, $.24^*$.
Autonomy (*Au*)	*Dim* $-.26^{**}$; (*Dim* 19a + b$_3$, $-.25^*$); *Dim* 20a, $-.25^*$; *Dim* 21a, $-.31^{**}$; *Dim* 22b, $.32^{***}$; *TR* 2a, $-.29^{**}$; *TR* 2c, $-.30^{**}$; *TR* 2a + b + c + d, $-.34^{***}$; *TR* 3c, $.34^{***}$.
Change (*Ch*)	*Dim* 3, $-.27^{**}$; *Dim* 6, $-.28^{**}$; *Dim* 7, $-.28^{**}$; (*Dim* 19a + b$_0$, $.27^{**}$; *Dim* 19a + b$_1$, $.37^{***}$; *Dim* 19a + b$_3$, $.30^{**}$); *TR* 2d, $-.27^{**}$; *TR* 3c, $.25^*$; *SR* 5, $-.30^{**}$.
Cognitive Structure (*Cs*)	*Dim* 2b, $-.26^{**}$; *Dim* 3, $.31^{***}$; *Dim* 6, $-.26^{**}$; *Dim* 7, $-.26^{**}$; *Dim* 12, $-.29^{**}$; *Dim* 17b, $-.30^{**}$; *Dim* 17a + b, $-.34^{***}$; (*Dim* 19a + b$_0$, $-.27^{**}$; *Dim* 19a + b$_6$, $-.24^*$; *Dim* 19a + b$_{10}$, $.30^{**}$); *TR* 1a, $.35^{***}$; *TR* 1a + b, $.27^{**}$; *TR* 2d, $.25^*$; *TR* 2a + b + c + d, $.25^*$; *TR* 3a, $-.34^{***}$; *TR* 3a + b + c, $-.29^{**}$; *Lex Mode*, $.30^{**}$; *Pers Mode*, $-.30^{**}$; *FR* 3, $-.24^*$; *SR* 3, $-.23^*$.
Defendence (*De*)	*Dim* 4a, $.30^{**}$; *Dim* 7, $-.24^*$; *Dim* 9, $-.24^*$; (*Dim* 19a + b$_1$, $.30^{**}$); *TR* 1a, $-.25^*$; *SR* 8, $-.24^*$; *SR* 9, $-.29^{**}$; SR_{far}, $-.25^*$.
Dominance (*Do*)	*Dim* 8b, $.26^{**}$; *Dim* 8a + b, $.33^{***}$; *Dim* 9, $.34^{**}$; *Dim* 12, $-.27^{**}$; (*Dim* 19a + b$_1$, $.25^*$); *Dim* 20a, $.24^*$; *TR* 2a, $-.39^{***}$; *TR* 2d, $-.28^{**}$; *TR* 2a + b + c + d, $-.34^{***}$; *TR* 3a, $.24^{***}$; *TR* 4a, $-.39^{***}$; *TR* 4a + b + c + d, $-.31^{**}$.
Endurance (*En*)	*Dim* 8b, $.42^{***}$; *Dim* 8a + b, $.34^{***}$; *Dim* 9, $.29^{**}$; *Dim* 18, $-.28^{**}$; (*Dim* 19a + b$_7$, $-.27^{**}$); *TR* 2a, $-.30^{**}$; *TR* 4a, $-.26^{**}$; *FR*2, $.26^{**}$; *FR* 7, $.24^*$; *SR* 1, $-.28^{**}$; *SR* 3, $.27^{**}$; *SR* 4, $.31^{**}$; *SR* 7, $-.24^*$.
Exhibition (*Ex*)	*Dim* 1, $-.29^{**}$; *Dim* 3, $-.36^{***}$; *Dim* 4b, $.25^*$; *Dim* 7, $.32^{**}$; *Dim* 9, $.25^*$; (*Dim* 19a + b$_0$, $.27^{**}$; *Dim* 19a + b$_1$, $.49^{***}$; *Dim* 19a + b$_3$, $.25^*$; *Dim* 19a + b$_6$, $-.32^{**}$; *Dim* 19a + b$_7$, $-.27^{**}$); *TR* 2a + b + c + d, $-.30^{**}$; *TR* 3c, $.31^{**}$; no. of different *TR*, $-.31^{**}$.
Harmavoidance (*Ha*)	*Dim* 1, $.30^{**}$; *Dim* 2b, $-.27^{**}$; *Dim* 3, $.32^{***}$; *Dim* 8a + b, $-.26^{**}$; *Dim* 10, $-.45^{***}$; *Dim* 17a, $.29^{**}$; *Dim* 19a, $-.28^{**}$; *Dim* 19a + b, $-.28^{**}$; (*Dim* 19a + b$_0$, $-.32^{***}$; *Dim* 19a + b$_6$, $.26^{**}$); *Dim* 21a, $.28^{**}$; *Dim* 21a + b, $.30^{**}$; *TR* 2b, $.32^{***}$; *TR* 2d, $.32^{***}$; *TR* 2a + b + c + d, $.46^{***}$; *TR* 3c, $-.31^{**}$; *TR* 3a + b + c, $-.29^{**}$; *Lex Mode*, $.27^{**}$; *Pers Mode*, $-.27^{**}$; *SR* 9, $-.25^*$.
Impulsivity (*Im*)	*Dim* 1, $-.32^{***}$; *Dim* 2b, $.30^{**}$; *Dim* 2a + b, $.26^{**}$; *Dim* 4b, $.37^{***}$; *Dim* 7, $-.25^*$; *Dim* 10, $.33^{***}$; *Dim* 19a, $.27^{**}$; *Dim* 19a + b, $.26^{**}$; (*Dim* 19a

(*continued*)

Table 50. (*Continued*)

Scale	Significant correlations with meaning variables
	+ b_0, .35***; *Dim* 19a + b_1, .30**; *Dim* 19a + b_2, .25*; *Dim* 19a + b_6, −.35***; *Dim* 19a + b_{10}, .25*); *TR* 1a, .25*; *TR* 2d, −.26**; *TR* 2a + b + c + d, −.28**; *TR* 3a, .30**; *TR* 3a + b + c, .25*; *Pers Mode*, .25*; *FR* 5, .27**; *SR* 1, .28*; *SR* 7, −.30**; SR_{near}, .28**.
Nurturance (*Nu*)	*Dim* 8b, .34***; *Dim* 10, −.27**; *Dim* 11, .25*; *Dim* 17a, −.25*; *Dim* 19b, −.26**; (*Dim* 19a + b_8, −.34***); *Dim* 20a, .25*; *Dim* 22b, −.30**; *TR* 2a, −.25*; SR_{far}, −.29**.
Order (*Or*)	*Dim* 2a, −.29**; *Dim* 2b, −.29**; *Dim* 2a + b, −.26**; *Dim* 3, .27**; *Dim* 10, −.27**; *Dim* 15, .29**; *TR* 2a, −.29**; *TR* 2c, .25*; *TR* 2a + b + c + d, .23*; *TR* 3a, −.25*; *TR* 3a + b + c, −.24*; *TR* 4b, −.24*; SR_{far}, −.24*.
Play (*Pl*)	*Dim* 7, .24*; (*Dim* 19a + b_1, .26**; *Dim* 19a + b_6, −.32***; *Dim* 19a + b_7, −.31**); *TR* 2b, −.29**.
Sentience (*Se*)	*Dim* 10, .26*; *Dim* 19a, .38***; *Dim* 19b, .36***; *Dim* 19a + b, .42***; (*Dim* 19a + b_0, .28**; *Dim* 19a + b_1, .30**); *TR* 3c, .25*; *SR* 7, −.30**.
Social Recognition (*Sr*)	*Dim* 2b, −.24*; *Dim* 10, −.32***; *Dim* 11, .24*; *Dim* 19a, .24*; (*Dim* 19a + b_0, −.26**; *Dim* 19a + b_{10}, −.27**); *Dim* 20b, .25*; *Dim* 20a + b, .27**; *Dim* 21a, .27**; *Dim* 21a + b, .28**; *Dim* 22b, −.25*; *TR* 1a, .26**; *TR* 1a + b, .30**; *TR* 2b, .26**; *TR* 3c, −.29**; *TR* 3a + b + c, −.26**; *TR* 4c, −.26**; *TR* 4a + b + c + d, −.25*; *Lex Mode*, .33***; *Pers Mode*, −.33***; *FR* 4, −.33***.
Succorance (*Su*)	*Dim* 1, .26**; *Dim* 3, .29**; *Dim* 17b, −.30**; *Dim* 17a + b, −.31**; *Dim* 19a, .37***; (*Dim* 19a + b_7, .36***); *Dim* 20a, .31**.
Understanding (*Un*)	*Dim* 1, .33***; *Dim* 3, −.25*; *Dim* 13, −.30**; *Dim* 20a, −.33***; *Dim* 21a, .29*; *Dim* 22a, .28**; *Dim* 22b, .30**; *Dim* 22a + b, .32***; *TR* 2b, .24**; *TR* 2a + b + c + d, .26**; *TR* 4a, .27**; *TR* 4d, .30**; *SR* 2, −.34***; *SR* 8, −.31**; *SR* 9, −.26**.
Infrequency (*In*)	*Dim* 2a, −.27**; *Dim* 6, .31**; (*Dim* 19a + b_1, .33***; *Dim* 19a + b_5, −.27**); *TR* 3b, .30**; *TR* 3c, .49***; *TR* 3a + b + c, .34***; *Lex Mode*, −.25*; *Pers Mode*, .25*; *FR* 4, −.27**; *SR* 1, −.29**; SR_{near}, −.28**.
Desirability (*Dy*)	*Dim* 5, .34***; *Dim* 6, .33***; *Dim* 8a, .34***; *Dim* 8b, .32***; *Dim* 8a + b, .37***; *Dim* 10, −.27**; *Dim* 12, −.28**; *Dim* 13, −.31**; *Dim* 14, .29**; *Dim* 16, −.31**; (*Dim* 19a + b_0, −.27**; *Dim* 19a + b_7, −.24*); *Dim* 20a, .25*; *Dim* 21a, −.30**; *Dim* 22a, −.31**; *Dim* 22b, −.34**; *Dim* 22a + b, −.37***; *TR* 1a, .36***; *TR* 1b, .27**; *TR* 1a + b, .34***; *TR* 2a, −.30**; *TR* 2b, −.44***; *TR* 2c, .26**; *TR* 3a, −.30**; *TR* 3a + b + c, −.32***; *TR* 4a, −.26**; *TR* 4b, −.40***; *TR* 4c, −.34***; *TR* 4d, −.278*; *TR* 4a + b + c + d, −.35***; *Pers Mode*, −.33***; *FR* 4, −.34***; *FR* 8, −.25*; FR_{pos}, −.37***; no. of different *FR*, −.34***; no. of different meaning dimensions, −.29**; *SR* 2, −.34***; *SR* 3, −.34***; *SR* 4, −.35***; *SR* 8, −.36***; SR_{near}, −.29**; SR_{far}, −.30**; no. of different *SR*, −.36***.

Note. For the code of the meaning variables, see Appendix A.
*p < .05.
**p < .01.
***p < .001.

the emotional state and the reactions of the involved persons or to emphasize administrative and formal aspects.

Using particular content in plans may be viewed as situation-bound and task-dependent or as characteristic of the individual. Only in the latter case is it of interest to the personality or clinical psychologist. Yet, even if the uses of content are characteristic of the personality, how should we score them so as to unravel their personality-characteristic nature? In order to answer this question, we asked each of 50 subjects who were students in the social sciences (of both genders and with a mean age of 23 years) to form 10 plans in different domains of activity. The content of the plans was scored in terms of two systems. One consisted of five categories based on a factor analysis of the content responses. The five categories were concern with formal-administrative arrangements, with normative aspects (with rules, laws, and prohibitions), with aesthetics and external appearance, with psychological and mental reactions or states, and with functional-financial content. The other system consisted of eight categories based on scoring the material in terms of meaning dimensions: content referring to functional aspects, time, location, quantity, sensory qualities, feelings and emotions, judgments and evaluations, and cognitive qualities. The categories of both systems were correlated with the subjects' meaning profiles.

The resulting correlation matrices were subjected to analysis in terms of the procedure for identifying traits. The analysis showed that the patterns of all five factorially based categories deviated from those of personality traits on three or more criteria and hence that none of them can be considered trait-similar. In contrast, of the eight categories based on meaning dimensions, only two (i.e., those that dealt with temporal aspects and locational aspects) had patterns that deviated from those of personality traits in three or more of the five criteria.[1] Thus, six of the meaning-based categories can be considered trait-similar.

These findings show that the tendency to use particular content in plans reflects a characteristic trail-like tendency on the part of the individual. This tendency also has manifestations in other domains in line with the meaning variables in the pattern. Further analyses showed that these tendencies did not particularly resemble cognitive traits despite their apparent cognitive nature. Moreover, the data suggested that the factorially based categories were probably subclusters within the more encompassing constructs based on meaning. For example, "concern with psychological states" turned out to be a subcluster of "concern with emotional contents," and "normative concerns" was found to be a subcluster of "concern with judgments and evaluations." Finally, the application of the procedure for identifying traits to planning styles revealed candidates for new forms of traits, based on concern with particular kinds of content. Traits of this kind could enrich the sphere of traits and add a new facet to the concept of personality traits.

Another example of the application of the procedure for identifying traits concerns anxiety (S. Kreitler & H. Kreitler, 1985a). The issue of whether anxiety is a personality trait or a mood state has provoked a heated controversy that has not been fully resolved through the introduction of the distinction between trait and state anxiety (Spielberger, 1975). There remain the problems of whether the so-called trait-anxiety questionnaire actually assesses a trait, and which of the many different

---

[1]The same conclusions were reached in the published study on the basis of deviation in two out of the three criteria: Criteria 2, 3, and 4.

Table 51. Evaluating the PRF Scales in Terms of the Five Criteria for Identifying Traits

PRF scale	No. of dif. kinds of meaning var. (Crit. 1)	Proportion of dif. kinds of meaning var. (Crit. 2)	Relative prop. of negative components (Crit. 3)	No. of meaning var. in the pattern (Crit. 4)	Prop. of general m. dim. and TR (Crit. 5)	No. of deviations from traits
Abasement	2 (D)	$\chi^2 = 21.11^{***}$ (D)	.16 (D)	6 (D)	.00 (D)	5
Achievement	3	$\chi^2 = 360.81^{***}$ (D)	.25	8	.66 (D)	2
Affiliation	2 (D)	$\chi^2 = 34.07^{***}$ (D)	.72 (D)	8	.09 (D)	4
Aggression	4	$\chi^2 = 21.52^{***}$ (D)	.50	12	.44	1
Autonomy	2 (D)	$\chi^2 = 32.04^{***}$ (D)	.78 (D)	9	.22 (D)	4
Change	3	$\chi^2 = 9.15^{*}$ (D)	.55	6	.12 (D)	2
Cognitive Structure	4	$\chi^2 = 12.99^{**}$ (D)	.65	20	.55 (D)	2
Defendence	3	$\chi^2 = 62.57^{***}$ (D)	.75 (D)	8	.40	2
Dominance	2 (D)	$\chi^2 = 35.99^{***}$ (D)	.46	12	.42	2
Endurance	4	$\chi^2 = 50.61^{***}$ (D)	.46	10	.43	1
Exhibition	2	$\chi^2 = 27.73^{***}$	.38	11	.39	

Scale		χ²				
Harmavoidance	3	14.28**	.50	12	.53	2
	(D)	(D)				
Impulsivity	4	1.23	.35	23	.43	1
		(D)				
Nurturance	3	27.69***	.70	10	.40	1
		(D)	(D)	(D)		
Order	3	43.89***	.54	13	.58	2
		(D)				
Play	2	31.40***	.60	5	.20	1
	(D) 3	(D)		(D)		
Sentience	3	20.21	.12	8	.29	3
		(D)	(D)			
Social Recognition	3	24.26**	.53	21	.45	2
		(D)		(D)		
Succorance	1	81.62***	.28	7	.29	2
	(D) 3	(D)				
Understanding	3	10.36**	.40	15	.27	2
		(D)				
Infrequency	4	23.26***	.46	12	.40	1
		(D)				
Desirability	4	48.41***	.74	43	.43	3
		(D)	(D)	(D)		

[a] In the second row for each PRF scale, (D) signifies deviation and a blank signifies no deviation.
*$p < .05$.
**$p < .01$.
***$p < .001$.

anxiety scales does or does not. In order to deal with these questions by means of the procedure for identifying traits, seven samples, each of 70 subjects, were administered the standard meaning questionnaire and one of seven anxiety scales, a different one in each sample. The scores on the anxiety scales and the meaning profiles were intercorrelated.

In order to increase the generalization and stability of the results, we first applied the procedure of identifying traits to the matrix based on the intercorrelations with all seven scales. The analysis showed that the total matrix differed from that of personality traits on three criteria (Criteria 2, 3, and 5). Hence, on the basis of the total matrix, the seven anxiety scales cannot be regarded as having patterns identical to those of personality traits. Because the deviations were found on only three criteria, one could conclude that "anxiety corresponds not to a trait-identical but to a trait-like pattern of meaning assignment tendencies" (S. Kreitler & H. Kreitler, 1985a, p. 133).[2]

Because applying the procedure for identifying traits to the whole matrix led to a borderline conclusion, it may be expected that several of the scales probably have trait-identical patterns, whereas others do not. Separate analyses of each of the seven scales showed that the patterns of four scales did not deviate on more than two criteria from those of personality traits. These included, for example, the Self-Rating Anxiety Scale (Zung & Cavenar, 1980), the Test Anxiety Scale (Sarason, 1978), and the Zuckerman Inventory of Personal Reactions (Zuckerman, 1977), but, by some stroke of irony, did not include the Trait Anxiety Inventory (STAI-Y2—Spielberger, Gorsuch, Lushene, & Vagg, 1977). Hence, the analyses of the individual scales show that, when one picks an anxiety scale, there is about a 50% chance that its pattern will be trait-similar and a 50% chance that its pattern will be trait-dissimilar. The theoretical implication is that the construct of anxiety still has fuzzy edges. The practical implication is that, in order to be sure that the anxiety scale has a traitlike pattern, one should either check previous findings (if the scale has been examined) or proceed to check the scale oneself.

---

[2]Please note that the analysis in the text is based on criteria somewhat different from those used in the cited study, which was done before the new set of criteria had been defined.

Characterizing Trait Scales and Factors

This chapter deals with procedure for characterizing trait scales. *Characterizing* includes identifying the general class of traits to which a set of traits or a particular trait belongs, comparing traits, or specifying the nature of a factor.

IDENTIFYING THE GENERAL CLASS OF TRAITS

The new conception of traits has made it possible to integrate within one framework traits that have often been considered different, and to specify the distinctions among them, if any. Thus, we showed that it is possible to distinguish four kinds of traits: mental-health traits, emotional-temperamental traits, social traits and cognitive traits (see Chapter 7, Question 5, and Tables 2, 3 and 5). Each type is defined structurally in terms of specific values along the same five criteria that were presented in Chapter 10 for identifying the whole class of personality traits: i.e., (1) the number of different kinds of meaning variables; (2) the distribution of the proportions of meaning variables of the four kinds; (3) the proportion of negative constituents in the patterns; (4) the number of meaning variables in the pattern; and (5) the proportion of general variables out of the meaning dimensions and types of relations in the pattern. Table 52 presents the characteristic values that were reached by summarizing the data for patterns of the relevant traits obtained in Studies 1–20.

The four types of personality traits may be used to examine the nature of particular trait scales. This is done by comparing the patterns of meaning variables of the traits to be examined with the patterns of one or more of the relevant trait types, in terms of the five mentioned criteria. Thus, the procedure includes the following steps:

1. Administering to a sample of subjects the relevant trait scale(s) and the standard meaning questionnaire. (The sample should be random unless otherwise indicated.)
2. Scoring both so as to obtain for each subject the trait score(s) and the meaning profile.
3. Intercorrelating the trait score(s) and the meaning profiles.

Table 52. Criteria for Identifying Different Kinds of Traits[a]

Criteria		Personality traits	Mental-health traits	Emotional traits	Social traits	Cognitive traits
(1) No. of different kinds of meaning variables		4	3	4	4	4
(2) Proportion of different kinds of meaning var.	Dim	54.75%	65.98%	58.60%	51.46%	50.36%
	TR	25.75%	24.74%	24.19%	33.89%	28.47%
	SR	12.57%	9.28%	12.56%	6.69%	15.69%
	FR	5.90%	0.00%	4.65%	7.95%	5.47%
(3) Relative prop. of neg. components		.38	.42	.47	.18	.48
(4) No. of meaning var. in the pattern	M	13.85	19.60	15.50	12.92	17.43
	SD	6.50	3.44	5.82	5.68	9.47
(5) Proportion of general meaning dim. and TR		.44	.51	.44	.38	.47

[a]The column "Personality traits" includes information about personality traits in general, without specification. Dim = meaning dimensions; TR = types of relation; SR = shifts of referents; FR = forms of relation.

4. Extracting from the intercorrelation matrix the meaning variables that correlated significantly, which constitute the pattern of meaning variables of the trait(s).
5. Establishing for the pattern extracted in Step 4 the values of the above-mentioned five criteria (for detailed instructions for establishing these values, see Chapter 11, "The Procedure for Identifying Traits," Step 5).
6. Comparing the values established for the pattern in Step 5 with those of the relevant type or types of personality traits.

The comparison is made for each criterion separately. The results of the comparison can be either "deviation" or "no deviation." In the case of the number of kinds of meaning variables (Criterion 1), either the numbers are identical (i.e., "no deviation"), or a "deviation" is registered. In regard to the percentages of the different kinds of meaning variables (Criterion 2), the differences are checked by the chi-square test. A significant value denotes a "deviation." In regard to the number of meaning variables in the pattern (Criterion 4), a "deviation" is registered if the number of the checked pattern does not fall within the range of $M \pm 1\ SD$ of the pattern of the relevant type of traits. In regard to the proportion of negative constituents (Criterion 3) and general meaning variables (Criterion 5), the differences are checked by z values. Significant values denote "deviations." The total number of deviations is summed, so that each deviation is accorded the same weight. If the number of deviations equals 3 or more, the checked trait(s) differ from the relevant type of trait to which it was compared. If the number of deviations is lower than 3, the checked trait resembles the type of trait to which it was compared. The cutting point 3 was established in view of the characteristic variations in the values of patterns in each type of personality trait.

Our first example concerns the Personality Research Form (PRF) (see also Chapter 11). This carefully constructed test was designed expressly to assess the normal personality rather than psychopathology and to "describe personality comprehensively, if not exhaustively" (Jackson, 1984, p. 4). These goals suggest that the 20 PRF scales should differ from mental-health traits but should resemble the three other types of traits (emotional, social, and cognitive), which provide a wide coverage of various personality aspects. In order to check this expectation, we used the same patterns of meaning variables of the PRF scales presented in Chapter 11, Table 50. In regard to these patterns we applied the above-described method of identifying the general class of traits. Table 53 shows the values of the PRF patterns on the five criteria and the comparisons of these patterns, in terms of the five criteria, with the patterns of the four types of personality traits. The results show that the PRF patterns differ from mental-health traits on four of the five criteria. In contrast, they do not differ from emotional or cognitive traits on any of the criteria and differ from social traits only on one criterion. These findings fully confirm the expectation. The traits measured by the PRF scales may be regarded as different from psychopathological traits and as belonging to the general classes of emotional, social, and cognitive traits. The conclusion is that the test conforms to its goals and description.

Our second example concerns another aspect of the PRF. Jackson (1984) offered several groupings of the PRF scales, "suggested in part on the basis of theoretical considerations and in part upon the results of a number of factor analytic studies." Jackson may not have been sure of the groupings because he added, "All of the groupings do not, strictly speaking, define specific factors. Certain of the groupings are based on conceptual categories" (pp. 4–5). In cases of unclarity of this kind it is advisable to apply the procedure for identifying the general class of traits. We did so in regard to two sets of scales. One set included three of Jackson's groupings that relate to interpersonal relations: "Measures of orientation toward direction from other people" (Succorance and Autonomy), "Measures of degree of ascendancy" (Dominance and Abasement) and "Measures of degree and qualities of interpersonal orientation" (Affiliation, Nurturance, Exhibition, Social Recognition, Aggression, and Defendence). The second set included two scales (Understanding and Sentience), which Jackson called "Measures of intellectual and aesthetic orientations." It is reasonable to expect that the former 10 PRF scales would resemble the general type of social traits, whereas the latter two PRF scales would resemble the general type of cognitive traits.

In order to test these expectations, we used the same patterns of meaning variables of the PRF scales that were presented in Chapter 11, Table 50. We computed for each of the two groupings separately (for the so-called social scales and the so-called cognitive scales) the values of the five criteria that serve for comparisons with types of traits. Table 53 presents these values as well as the results of the comparisons of each of the two tested groupings with the four types of traits, that is, the target type and the three others that served as controls. The findings show that the "social" PRF scales do not differ from the social type traits (number of deviations = 2), but that they also do not differ from the cognitive or from the emotional types of traits, whereas they do differ from the mental-health traits. The conclusion is that the "social" PRF scales resemble social traits, and that they also resemble emotional and cognitive traits. Hence, they are not pure social traits and could at best be characterized as socially oriented general personality traits. A similar conclusion applies to the two "cognitive" PRF scales. They do not differ from the cognitive type of traits and also not from the social and emotional trait types, whereas they differ from mental-health traits. Accordingly, they could at best be characterized as cog-

Table 53. The Results of Comparing PRF Scales to Various Kinds of Traits

Criteria	Values of compared scales	Results of the comparisons to			
		Mental-health traits	Emotional traits	Social traits	Cognitive traits
(1) No. of diff. kinds of meaning variables	Scales: 20 PRF 4	Dev.	No dev.	No dev.	No dev.
(2) Prop. of diff. kinds of meaning variables	Dim^c 59.18% TR 27.35% FR 4.49% SR 8.57%	$\chi^2 = 27.83$*** Dev.	$\chi^2 = 1.79$ No dev.	$\chi^2 = 3.45$ No dev.	$\chi^2 = 2.74$ No dev.
(3) Relative prop. of neg.	.49	$z = 1.17$ No dev.	$z = .40$ No dev.	$z = 6.33$*** Dev.	$z = .25$ No dev.
(4) No. of meaning var.	M 12.25 SD 5.48	Dev.	No dev.	No dev.	No dev.
(5) Prop. of general dim. and TR	.38	$z = 2.60$* Dev.	$z = 1.20$ No dev.	$z = 0.00$ No dev.	$z = 1.85$ No dev.
Total dev.		4	0	1	0
(1) No. of diff. kinds of meaning variables	Scales: Social PRF scales^a 4	Dev.	No dev.	No dev.	No dev.
(2) Prop. of diff. kinds of meaning variables	Dim 63.64% TR 26.36% FR 2.73% SR 4.54%	$\chi^2 = 5.34$ No. dev.	$\chi^2 = 6.54$ No dev.	$\chi^2 = 8.67$* Dev.	$\chi^2 = 12.95$** Dev.
(3) Relative prop. of neg.	.55	$z = 1.88$ No. dev.	$z = 1.33$ No dev.	$z = 4.75$*** Dev.	$z = 1.46$ No dev.
(4) No. of meaning var.	M 11.10 SD 4.33	Dev.	No dev.	No dev.	No dev.
(5) Prop. of general dim. and TR	.33	$z = 2.57$** Dev.	$z = 1.83$ No dev.	$z = .73$ No dev.	$z = 2.33$* Dev.
Total dev.		3	0	2	2
(1) No. of diff. kinds of meaning variables	Scales: Cognitive PRF scales^b 3	Dev.	No dev.	No dev.	No dev.
(2) Prop. of diff. kinds of meaning variables	Dim 60.87% TR 21.74% FR 00.00% SR 17.39%	$\chi^2 = 7.85$* Dev.	$\chi^2 = 6.84$ No dev.	$\chi^2 = 27.16$*** Dev.	$\chi^2 = 9.44$* Dev.
(3) Relative prop. of neg.	.30	$z = 1.09$ No dev.	$z = 1.54$ No dev.	$z = 1.00$ No dev.	$z = 1.22$ No dev.
(4) No. of meaning var.	M 11.50 SD 4.95	Dev.	No dev.	No dev.	No dev.
(5) Prop. of general dim. and TR	.28	$z = 1.77$ No dev.	$z = 1.23$ No dev.	$z = 0.91$ No dev.	$z = 0.76$ No dev.
Total dev.		3	0	1	1

^{a}Includes the following scales: Abasement, Affiliation, Aggression, Autonomy, Defendence, Dominance, Nurturance, Exhibition, Social Recognition, and Succorance.
^{b}Includes the following scales: Sentience and Understanding.
^{c}Dim = meaning dimensions; TR = types of relation; SR = shifts of referent; FR = forms of relation.
*$p < .05$.
**$p < .01$.
***$p < .001$.

nitively oriented general personality traits. In view of the results of the comparisons with the four trait types, it appears that the two groups of scales do not differ from each other. Indeed, a comparison between them in terms·of the five criteria showed only two deviations (namely, in the percentages of the four kinds of meaning variables and in the proportion of negative elements in the patterns). Moreover, the comparisons show that these two groups also do not differ from the whole set of PRF scales (see above). Hence, it seems doubtful whether the groupings mentioned by Jackson have psychological reality.

Our final example is focused on a single trait, again selected from the PRF. It is "Cognitive Structure," a scale described in terms suggestive of both cognitive aspects (e.g., "clarifying," "explicit," and "defining") and emotional needs (e.g., "needs certainty" and "needs structure") (Jackson, 1984, p. 6). It was therefore of interest to examine whether this trait would actually resemble both the cognitive and the emotional types of traits. The data were the pattern of meaning variables of this trait presented earlier (Chapter 11, Table 50). We established the values of this pattern for the five criteria and compared these values with those of cognitive and emotional traits (Table 52). The comparison showed that the trait deviated from emotional traits and from cognitive traits only on one criterion (i.e., the distribution of the percentages of the kinds of meaning variables, $\chi^2 = 16.172$ and $\chi^2 = 11.989$, respectively). Hence, as expected, the scale assesses a cognitive-emotional trait.

COMPARING TRAITS

Trait comparison is important in clarifying the nature of specific trait scales, in characterizing traits, and in selecting traits for specific diagnostic or research purposes. Trait comparison was discussed earlier in theoretical terms (Chapter 7, Question 3) and was exemplified in several studies (e.g., Studies 1, 7, 8, 13, 14, and 15). However, these applications dealt with content comparisons of the patterns of meaning variables of different traits, and they consisted in determining the elements common to the patterns of meaning variables of two or more traits. The present section is designed to complement the theme of comparison through the procedure for comparing the structural characteristics of traits. By means of this procedure, one can compare groups of traits, single traits, or single traits with groups of traits.

The procedure of comparison resembles that for identifying the general class of traits. It, too, rests on the five criteria specified earlier, with the difference that the values of the criteria are those not of the general type(s) of traits but of one of the compared traits or group of traits. Thus, the comparing procedure requires administering to subjects the scales of the two traits or sets of traits and the standard meaning questionnaire, scoring them so that each subject is assigned the traits' scores and a meaning profile, intercorrelating each of the trait scores with the meaning variables, and extracting from the intercorrelation matrices for each trait or trait set the meaning variables correlated significantly (positively or negatively) with that trait or trait set. These meaning variables constitute the pattern of the trait or trait set. Then, the values of the five criteria are established for each pattern separately. These values may then be compared, in line with the procedure described in detail in "Identifying the General Class of Traits," above. When single traits are compared, the number of meaning variables in the patterns is compared not by the t test, that is based on means comparisons, but by the binomial test. The traits or trait sets may be considered different if there are deviations between them on at least three of the five criteria.

But the procedure also allows for an assessment of the relative degree of similarity between the compared traits. There are two techniques for doing this: (1) the technique of summed deviations, which consists in comparing the number of deviations (in terms of the five criteria) for each pair of traits, so that the traits that yielded the comparison with more deviations are more distant or less similar, and (2) the technique of summed ratings, which consists in rating for each criterion the degree of relative similarity of the target trait to each of the traits with which it is compared, starting with the most similar (rated as 1), and then summing the ratings, so that the trait that yielded the comparison with the lowest rating is the most similar. Both techniques are exemplified in Table 54.

Table 54. Determining by Two Techniques the Relative Degrees of Similarity of the PRF Scale Exhibition to Three CPI Scales Correlated Positively with It

			Values of and results of comparisons to		
Technique	Criteria	Values of exhibition	Social presence	Self-acceptance	Sociability
	(1) No. of diff. kinds of meaning variables	2	4	4	2
Deviations			No dev.	No dev.	No dev.
Ratings			2.5	2.5	1
	(2) Prop. of diff. kinds of meaning variables	Dim 76.9% TR 23.1% FR 0.0% SR 0.0%	45.4% 9.1% 36.4% 9.1% $\chi^2 = 66.81^{***}$	12.5% 43.7% 25.0% 18.7% $\chi^2 = 116.14^{***}$	50.0% 0.0% 50.0% 0.0% $\chi^2 = 87.57^{***}$
Deviations			Dev.	Dev.	Dev.
Ratings			1	3	2
	(3) Prop. of neg.	.38	.27 $z = .58$	0.0 $z = 2.71^*$	0.0 $z = 1.05$
Deviations			No dev.	Dev.	No dev.
Ratings			1	2.5	2.5
	(4) No. of meaning variables[a]	13	11 $z = .43$	17 $z = .92$	2 $z = 3.33^{***}$
Deviations			No dev.	No dev.	Dev.
Ratings			1	2	3
	(5) Prop. of general dim. and TR	.39	.33 $z = .25$	0.0 $z = 1.77$	1.00 $z = 1.20$
Deviations			No dev.	No dev.	No dev.
Ratings			1	2.5	2.5
Summed deviations			1	2	3
Summed ratings			6.5	12.5	11.0
Ranked ratings			1	3	2

[a]The binomial test was used because there are no means for t-test comparisons as, for example, in Table 53. *Dim* = meaning dimensions; *TR* = types of relation; *SR* = shifts of referent; *FR* = forms of relation.
*$p < .05$.
**$p < .01$.
***$p < .001$.

The example deals with the comparison of the trait Exhibition (from the PRF) with three traits from the CPI: Social Presence (*Sp*), Self Acceptance (*Sa*), and Sociability (*Soc*). This triad was selected because Exhibition was found to be correlated with these three traits to almost the same degree both by Jackson (1984, p. 50), who reported the correlation coefficients .68, .69, and .67, respectively, and by us (r = .54, .52, and .55, respectively). It was therefore of interest to apply the procedure of comparison to the relations of Exhibition to each of the three traits so as to determine the relative degrees of similarity, which are not revealed by the correlations. The pattern of Exhibition was taken from Table 50, the patterns of the three CPI traits from Table 8. Table 54 shows that, by the technique of summed deviations, Exhibition is most similar to Social Presence, then to Self Acceptance, and least to Sociability. The table also shows the rating of similarity for each criterion, based on relative distances from the target trait, regardless of whether the difference counts as a deviation or does not. In the case of Criterion 2, the rating was done in line with the magnitude of the chi-square values, which are measures of distance. Summing the ratings shows that Exhibition is most similar to Social Presence (*Sp*), then to Sociability (*Soc*) and least to Self Acceptance (*Sa*). The two methods yielded similar findings concerning the most similar of the traits. One could venture the interpretation that commanding attention is a relatively more salient element in Exhibition than either socializing with others or satisfaction with oneself.

CHARACTERIZING FACTORS

This section briefly describes the extension of the procedure for comparing traits to the issue of characterizing factors, in this case factors representing scales of traits. The procedure is designed to help in systematizing the process of interpreting factors, which is notoriously subjective and nonsystematic.

Implementation of the procedure requires, first, establishing the patterns of meaning variables of all the traits involved in the factor analysis (the involved steps are described in "Identifying the General Class of Traits," above). The procedure consists in comparing the patterns of the traits highly saturated on a factor, extracting the common elements, and stating their common manifestations. The procedure is based on the assumption that the nature of the factor is reflected in the meaning variables common to the patterns of the traits saturated on that factor. Common meaning variables are identified as meaning variables correlated significantly in the same direction (i.e., positively or negatively) with at least 33.3% of the traits highly saturated on the factor (i.e., above an arbitrarily determined cutting-off point, such as .30 or .50 or even .70).

Naturally, this criterion would lead to selecting only a part of the meaning variables in the patterns. Those that are not selected are considered idiosyncratic for the different traits rather than characteristic of the factor as a whole. After the common elements are identified, their manifestations are to be read off from the lists in Appendix B. Manifestations of different meaning variables that are similar or that reinforce each other are accepted; those that contradict each other are dropped. Thus, the meaning of the factor may be viewed as the similar and noncontradictory manifestations of the meaning variables common to the patterns of the traits highly saturated on a factor. (For an example of this procedure in the domain of curiosity, see S. Kreitler & H. Kreitler, 1986c.)

Meaning-Based Validation of Personality Traits

TRAITS AND MANIFESTATIONS

The new trait conception presented in this book claims that a trait is a pattern of positively and negatively preferred meaning-assignment tendencies, each of which represents a set of manifestations. The manifestations, many of which are summarized in Appendix B, are the storehouse of information about the trait. In the course of the book, we showed how the manifestations have been specified (Part II), along with the advantages that accrue to the trait construct from the information they provide. For example, the manifestations of the meaning variables of which the trait pattern consists enabled us to provide answers about the structure of traits, or their manner of functioning (Chapter 7), and to resolve different problems that have arisen concerning specific traits (Studies 1–22, Part II). The manifestations include cognitive, perceptual, experimental, attitudinal, and even actional responses and thus allow the integration within one system of all the different aspects of traits and their correlates. This integration is important theoretically for the sake of unifying the domain of traits. It is important practically because the manifestations allow us to interpret the trait score by simply reading off the lists of manifestations presented in Appendix B (see, for example, Chapter 10, The Procedure of Assessing Personality Traits by Means of the Meaning Questionnaire, last paragraph). It is also important methodologically for the validation of trait constructs, as will be shown in this chapter.

VALIDATING BY MEANING

Trait scores are important only because of what we expect them to tell us beyond themselves. Information about the correlates of the trait score is the major, if not the only, rationale for assessing a trait. Manuals of trait scales are supposed to specify the known correlates of the scales or at least the sources where they can be obtained. The act of proceeding from the trait score to its known correlates is called *interpretation* of the trait score or scale. One of the major functions of research into personality traits is to specify the correlates of trait scores. In research, the act of proceeding from the trait score to its yet unknown correlates is called *construct validation*. The main question is: How does the researcher know where, in which domain, to look for correlates of the trait?

Up to now, there has existed no systematic way to identify the domains in which one is likely to find the trait's correlates. In the absence of clear-cut guidelines, investigators relied on their (often creative) intuition, buttressed by interpersonal experience, analogical reasoning based on other traits, and disparate theoretical considerations.

In their classic paper about construct validity, Cronbach and Meehl (1955) dwelt at length on methods for collecting and evaluating data concerning construct validity but hardly discuss the major problem of what data to collect. At one point, they mentioned the content of the items in the test (particularly when the content is common to many items) as a cue: "If a trait such as dominance is hypothesized, and the items inquire about behaviors subsumed under this label," and when interitem correlations are high, "the general quality would have power to predict behavior in a variety of situations represented by the specific items" (p. 288). If one recalls that items in scales assessing traits are mostly beliefs about the self, which constitute only one of four types of beliefs, all of which are required for the prediction of overt actions (Chapter 8), one could hardly wonder about the sad fate of the attempts to predict dominance from a scale whose items refer to dominance.

Indeed, beliefs about the self may turn out to be correlated with measures of behaviors other than overt actions, but they do not provide clues to how to detect these behaviors. In his basic text on measurement in personality, Fiske (1971) summarized the scientific state of construct validity in a succinct statement: "The notion of construct validity is a case in which methodology is ahead of empirical research and much current theory" (p. 169).

The absence of a systematic and reliable method of identifying manifestations of traits has led, on the one hand, to a plethora of unintegrated findings, that often accumulate without promoting any advance in theory or understanding, and, on the other hand, to a decrease of interest in traits in general. The pattern of meaning-assignment tendencies corresponding to a trait constitutes the set of systematic principles that is required to detect the trait's manifestations. The pattern provides straightforward directives about the domains in which manifestations of the trait can be found. *The manifestations are found in domains of content and processes defined by the meaning variables included in the pattern corresponding to the trait.*

In evaluating this conclusion, it is important to recall that we showed the pattern of meaning variables corresponding to a trait to be correlated neither with the meaning that subjects assigned directly to the trait or its label (Study 10), nor with the manifest content of the questionnaire commonly used to assess the trait (e.g., Study 15) (unless the latter happens to represent the underlying dynamics, which is a rare and unpredictable case). Thus, the directives for detecting the trait's manifestations embodied in the pattern of meaning variables corresponding to the trait represent the trait's dynamics specifically and uniquely.

Studies 1–22 include many examples illustrating the relations of a trait to responses in different domains that could not be deduced from the trait's questionnaire or label or even theory, but that were clearly indicated by the meaning variables correlated with the trait score. For example, various studies (see Study 11) showed that subjects high in external control are less accurate than subjects high in internal control in judging the lapse of time, have shorter future-time perspectives, and are less able to delay test performance and need gratification. There are no indications in the external-internal questionnaire and no specific assumptions in the accompanying theory that would lead one to deduce these behaviors, but they are clearly indicated through the negative correlation of externality with the meaning dimension "Temporal Qualities" (*Dim* 16).

THE PROCEDURE OF MEANING-BASED VALIDATION

What we present here forms the core of an entirely new principle of validating trait measures. Because it is based on the pattern of meaning variables corresponding to a trait, we suggest calling it *meaning-based validation*. Essentially, it consists in examining whether the manifestations indicated by the meaning variables that are correlated positively or negatively with the trait are actually characteristic of subjects who score high on the trait as compared with those who score low on it.

The procedure involves several steps: (1) administering to subjects both the trait measure (which need not be a verbal scale, although it usually is) and the standard meaning questionnaire; (2) scoring both so that we obtain trait scores and the subject's meaning profiles; (3) intercorrelating the trait scores and the meaning profiles; (4) extracting from the matrix of intercorrelations the significant correlations, both positive and negative (these constitute the pattern of meaning variables corresponding to the trait); and (5) setting up one or more studies to check the manifestations of the particular trait in domains defined by the meaning variables correlated positively or negatively with that trait. For example, if the trait score was found in Steps 3 and 4 to be correlated positively with the meaning dimension "Temporal Qualities" (*Dim* 16), the trait would have manifestations in the sphere of time. The manifestations would be enhanced if the correlation with the meaning variable is positive and reduced if it is negative. The search for manifestations may also be guided by hypotheses about interactions between meaning variables in the pattern.

In Step 5, one need not start from scratch, because many manifestations of meaning variables have already been identified (see Appendix B). One may use the available information either in order to explore responses not yet described or in order to elaborate on the described manifestations by investigating responses more precisely defined or more specific to particular contexts than those described.

If the pattern of meaning variables correlated with a trait score is already known from previous studies (such as those in this book), one may proceed directly to Step 5. However, it is always necessary to make sure that the pattern has been obtained from a sample representing the population in which one is interested. To increase the reliability of the findings, two techniques for obtaining the pattern are recommended. One is the multisample technique: it consists in repeating Steps 1–4 in several comparable samples, and then including in the pattern that serves as basis for Step 5 only those meaning variables that were correlated with the trait score in the same direction and with a comparable magnitude in a certain number of the samples, or even in all. The second is the multimeasure technique. It consists in administering in Step 1 not one but several trait measures (if available) and including in the pattern that serves as basis for Step 5 only those meaning variables that were correlated in the same direction and in a comparable magnitude with a certain number of the trait measures, or even with all. (For an example of the multimeasure technique, see S. Kreitler & H. Kreitler, 1985a.)

MEANING-BASED VALIDATION AND OTHER VALIDATION METHODS

The described procedure of validation differs from other procedures used to implement construct validity, for example, deducing behavioral manifestations on the basis of the questionnaire's items (i.e., from content validity) or on the basis of theoretical assumptions that have preceded the construction of the questionnaire (Cronbach & Meehl, 1955). Our thesis is that meaning-based validation is a more reliable, theoretically justified, and systematic procedure.

Let us illustrate the difference between the validation methods in regard to Eysenckian extroversion. Many items of the standard Eysenckian questionnaire refer to social situations and attitudes toward people. So does the accompanying theory. When one is guided by these clues, validating this trait questionnaire against behavior would involve looking for correlations between the behaviors indicated explicitly in the items and equivalent actual behaviors in social contexts. Validating the questionnaire in terms of clues provided by the pattern of meaning variables correlated with it (Table 6) orients us toward completely different behaviors. For example, extroversion was correlated negatively with the meaning dimension "Sensory Qualities," particularly bodily sensations. This correlation indicates that extroversion should be validated by examining its relation to behaviors dependent on attending to internal sensations (e.g., hypochondriasis, reactivity to drugs, pain tolerance, and sensitivity to temperature). Indeed, research findings fully support the latter set of deductions but tend to disconfirm those based on the former clues (Study 1).

It is noteworthy that meaning-based validation constitutes a unification of the different procedures applied to establishing the various kinds of psychometrically defined types of validity. It is based on determining the pattern of intercorrelations of the trait measure with the variables of meaning that represent a system with an established content validity, in the sense that its items are a representative sample of a clearly specified universe of content. This pattern constitutes a means of establishing the trait's concurrent validity, which requires correlation with some test or variable of established validity, mostly at the same point in time. As noted, the pattern of intercorrelations with meaning variables constitutes the basis for a theory about the nature and functioning of the trait and hence serves as a guide to specifying the manifestations that will form the trait's construct validity. The testing of these manifestations will provide the trait scale with criterion (or predictive) validity by showing that the trait correlates with specific present or future variables external to the trait scale. Thus, validation by meaning enables integration between the traditionally distinct "theoretically based" construct validity and "empirically based" criterion validity. In fact, it shows that they are two facets of the same procedure.

VALIDATION AS A CONTINUING PROCESS

One may, however, wonder whether validation by meaning is at all necessary if manifestations corresponding to the different meaning variables have already been established, as is evident, in part, from Appendix B. As stated above, there can be little doubt that the already-established manifestations facilitate future applications, but they do not cancel the need for further efforts at validation. There are five main reasons. One is that, so far, only a part of the manifestations of meaning variables have been established. Another reason is that the manifestations of meaning variables may differ in samples of different ages, mental states, cultures, and socioeconomic levels. In this book, we have presented only manifestations established in samples of normal individuals, adolescents and adults. A third reason is that, as psychological research proceeds, more information and more precise information become available about the different spheres of content and processes denoted by meaning variables, for example, about the spheres of time perception and time estimation, which we already know are denoted by the meaning dimension, "Temporal Qualities" (*Dim* 16). A fourth reason is that manifestations of meaning variables also depend on interactions among meaning variables, which so far have been investigated only very little. Finally, manifestations also interact within the context of the individual subject in a manner that is still barely understood, but that is probably responsible to no small degree for the unique character of each individual.

In sum, meaning-based validation is a continuous process dependent on the characteristics of different populations, the progress of knowledge, and the dynamics of interactions among meaning variables across and within individuals.

Postscript

We add this postscript not only because we do not want to take chances by ending a book with a chapter numbered 13. The main purpose of the postscript is to state the good and bad news resulting from this book. The good news is that personality traits are alive and well. Indeed, this may be bad news for some, but it is hoped that they, too, will eventually recognize that, so far, no better building blocks or units of personality have been identified. Thus, the really bad news is that we still do not have a new theoretically viable and empirically sturdy conception of personality. Traits are one kind of unit of personality. It is an important unit, but it is not identical with personality. The newly envisaged conception of personality would require information about how the meaning of situations is grasped and how it affects the individual; about motivational tendencies and behavioral forms characteristic of the individual; about how traits interact with the meanings of situations, motivational tendencies, and behavioral forms; and about how all these dynamic elements are integrated structurally and functionally. Then again, the good news is that we expect in the near future to make another step in the direction of this new conception of personality, which we hope will be a big step not only for the authors but also for others who care about understanding not just people but *the individual*.

Appendixes

The Meaning Variables: List and Code

MEANING DIMENSIONS

Dim 1	Contextual Allocation
Dim 2a	Range of Inclusion: Classes, Members
Dim 2b	Range of Inclusion: Parts
Dim 2a+b	Range of Inclusion
Dim 3	Function, Purpose, and Role
Dim 4a	Actions and Potentialities for Action (referent does)
Dim 4b	Actions and Potentialities for Action (done to, with referent)
Dim 4a+b	Actions and Potentialities for Action
Dim 5	Manner of Occurrence and Operation
Dim 6	Causes and Antecedents
Dim 7	Consequences and Results
Dim 8a	Domain of Application (subject of the referent)
Dim 8b	Domain of Application (object of the referent)
Dim 8a+b	Domain of Application
Dim 9	Material of Referent
Dim 10	Structure
Dim 11	State and Potential Changes in State
Dim 12	Weight and Mass
Dim 13	Size and Dimensionality
Dim 14	Quantity and Number
Dim 15	Locational Qualities
Dim 16	Temporal Qualities
Dim 17a	Possessions (of referent)
Dim 17b	Belongingness (of referent)
Dim 17a+b	Possessions and Belongingness
Dim 18	Development
Dim 19a	Sensory Qualities (characterizing the referent)

Owing to the specific requirements of research into traits, the list of meaning variables, as applied in other research domains, has been extended by subdividing many of the meaning variables.

Dim 19b	Sensory Qualities (referent may perceive)
Dim 19a+b	Sensory Qualities
	Specifications of *Dim* 19a, *Dim* 19b, *Dim* 19a+b: 0, visual; 1, color and brightness; 2, form and shape; 3, auditory sensations; 4, tactility; 5, taste sensations; 6, temperature; 7, smell sensations; 8, internal sensations (incl. pain); 9, transparency; 10, pressure and elasticity (or rigidity); 11, moisture
Dim 20a	Feelings and Emotions (evoked by referent)
Dim 20b	Feelings and Emotions (experienced by referent)
Dim 20a+b	Feelings and Emotions
Dim 21a	Judgments and Evaluations (concerning the referent, about the referent, or evoked by the referent)
Dim 21b	Judgments and Evaluations (held by the referent)
Dim 21a+b	Judgments and Evaluations
Dim 22a	Cognitive Qualities and Actions (in regard to the referent, or evoked by the referent)
Dim 22b	Cognitive Qualities and Actions (by or of the referent)
Dim 22a+b	Cognitive Qualities and Actions
No. of different meaning dimensions	
Ratio of meaning values per meaning dimensions	

TYPES OF RELATION

TR 1a	Attributive: Quality to substance (Substantive)
TR 1b	Attributive: Action to agent (Actional)
TR 1a+b	Attributive
TR 2a	Comparative: Similarity, identity
TR 2b	Comparative: Difference, contrast
TR 2c	Comparative: Complementary
TR 2d	Comparative: Relational
TR 2a+b+c+d	Comparative
TR 3a	Exemplifying-illustrative: Exemplifying instance
TR 3b	Exemplifying-illustrative: Exemplifying situation
TR 3c	Exemplifying-illustrative: Exemplifying scene
TR 3a+b+c	Exemplifying-illustrative
TR 4a	Metaphoric-symbolic: Interpretation
TR 4b	Metaphoric-symbolic: Metaphor (conventional)
TR 4c	Metaphoric-symbolic: Metaphor
TR 4d	Metaphoric-symbolic: Symbol
TR 4a+b+c+d	Metaphoric-symbolic
No. of different *TR*	

MODES OF MEANING

Lex Mode	Lexical mode (*TR* 1a+b + *TR* 2a+b+c+d)
Pers Mode	Personal mode (*TR* 3a+b+c + *TR* 4a+b+c+d)

FORMS OF RELATION

FR 1	Positive (assertion)
FR 2	Negative (denial)
FR 3	Mixed positive and negative (or, positive-restrictive, e.g., sometimes, to some extent)
FR 4	Conjunctive (both . . . this and this)
FR 5	Disjunctive (either/or)
FR 6	Obligatory
FR 7	Double negative (neither/nor)
FR 8	Combined positive and negative (not this but this)
$FR_{pos.}$	Positive forms of relation ($FR\ 1 + FR\ 3 + FR\ 4 + FR\ 5 + FR\ 6$)
$FR_{neg.}$	Negative forms of relation ($FR\ 2 + FR\ 7$)

No. of different *FR*

SHIFTS IN REFERENT

SR 1	Actual referent is identical with presented referent
SR 2	Actual referent is the negation (or opposite) of the presented referent
SR 3	Actual referent is a part of the presented referent
SR 4	The referent is the whole or a part of a previous meaning value
SR 5	Actual referent is the presented referent combined with a previous meaning value
SR 6	The referent is a combination of several previous meaning values
SR 7	The actual referent is related to the presented or previous referent by some association only
SR 8	Actual referent is a grammatical variation of the presented referent
SR 9	Actual referent is the presented referent viewed as a label
SR 10	The actual referent is not related in any obvious way to the presented or previous referent
SR_{near}	Relatively small shifts in referent ($SR1 + SR3 + SR4 + SR5 + SR6 + SR8$)
SR_{far}	Relatively large shifts in referent ($SR9 + SR7 + SR2 + SR10$)

No. of different *SR*

No. of meaning values

Note. In the interests of brevity, the names of the variables are often mentioned in the text in an abbreviated form, for example, *Dim* 4a+b is mentioned as "Actions," *Dim* 11 as "State," and *Dim* 22a+b as "Cognitive Qualities."

Summary of Manifestations of Meaning Variables

MEANING VARIABLE: CONTEXTUAL ALLOCATION (*DIM* 1)

Manifestations:

Positive. Overinclusion, confabulatory tendency, good short-term recall (perhaps specifically when combined with a negative correlation with *Dim* 2a) (Study 1); awareness of organizations and superordinate structures (Study 4); unconventionality, intellectual independence (perhaps particularly when combined with a positive correlation with *Dim* 5 and *TR* 4c) (Study 6, Factors 3 and 4); ability to suggest classifications (Study 6, Factor 6); tendency toward analytical thought (Study 6, Factor 12); concern with general concepts and ideas (Study 7, extroversion, intuition); concern with theoretical values (Study 7, intuition); good ability for abstraction (Study 8); tendency to generalize (Study 8, anality); in subjects who score high on dogmatism, probably because of their concern with general conceptions (Study 13); concern with abstractions, tendency toward and preference for cognitive activities (Study 14); concern with classifications (Study 20); in subjects rated by others as having high intellectual ability (Study 21).

Negative. Flexibility, tolerance of ambiguities, perhaps mainly in the abstract sense (Study 2, Scale *Fx*); concentration on specific concrete instances (perhaps particularly when coupled with a preference for *TR* 3a+b+c) (Study 10, Hypochondriasis).

Throughout Appendix B "positive" manifestations refer to manifestations of meaning variables that are correlated positively with the trait score, or alternately, are preferred positively by the subject according to his or her meaning profile; "negative" manifestations refer to manifestations of meaning variables that are correlated negatively with the trait score, or alternately, are negatively preferred by the subject (namely, are used very infrequently or not at all by him or her) according to his or her meaning profile. No positive or negative manifestations are listed if none were found or none were sufficiently supported by the data to be included in the Appendix. Under "negative" we list explicit findings concerning the relevant manifestations and not merely findings implied by those listed under "positive" that can be supplied by the reader. The listed manifestations are based on Studies 1–22, Part II. An attempt was made to stick to interpretations supported by research, preserving as much as possible the wording of the original investigators. Hence the occasional redundancy. The appendix can be used together with Table 1 which lists all the correlations obtained for each meaning variable, including those that cannot yet be fully interpreted. For the code of the meaning variables see Appendix A. For the code of the CPI scales see Table 8, and for the code of the 16 *PF* see Table 16.

Additional Remarks. In view of the above information and the additional findings about the positive correlations of *Dim* 1 with Factors 1, 3, 4, and 5 of the 16 PF (which diagnose individuals who are "adaptable, easy-going," "independent, rebellious," "happy-go-lucky, alert, impulsive," and "adventurous, carefree, responsive," respectively) (Study 6), the approval motive (Study 8), and co-worker orientation (Study 20), it is likely that the facility with abstractions and generalizations indicated by *Dim* 1 enables the individual to be flexible, to switch classifications, and to be open and responsive to people, reality and changing situations.

MEANING VARIABLE: RANGE OF INCLUSION: CLASSES, MEMBERS (*DIM* 2A)

Manifestations:

Positive. Analytic approach (Study 7, thinking); in subjects who score high on cleanliness and order (Study 9); in subjects who score high on dogmatism, probably because of their concern with precise distinctions between classifications (Study 13); in subjects rated by others as having high intellectual ability (Study 21).

Negative. Overinclusion, particularly when coupled with a positive correlation with *Dim* 1 (Study 1); low performance on vigilance tasks, not disturbed by competing responses (Study 1); categorization schemata are undifferentiated, categorization is compartmentalized, and there is no hierarchical classification system (Study 13, authoritarianism); in subjects who do not tend toward or prefer cognitive activities (Study 14).

MEANING VARIABLE: RANGE OF INCLUSION: PARTS (*DIM* 2B)

Manifestations:

Positive. Analytical approach (Study 6, Factor 10); person has exact, calculating mind, is smart, and is insightful regarding herself or himself and others (Study 6, Factor 10); analytical thought (Study 6, Factor 12); in subjects scoring high on dogmatism, perhaps because of their concern with the membership of particular categorizations (Study 13); in subjects high in intolerance of ambiguity (Studies 18 and 19).

Negative. Person has no tendency toward sensation seeking, and particularly not toward experience seeking (Study 15).

MEANING VARIABLE: FUNCTION, PURPOSE, AND ROLE (*DIM* 3)

Manifestations:

Positive. Emphasis on functionality and promoting one's interests even if one appears to react inconsistently with or counter to one's values (Study 3, Machiavellianism); reacting to cues suggesting functionality (Study 5); in subjects scoring high on *n* Power (Study 4); preference for efficient people and for success at tasks that require a functional approach (Study 6, Factor 5); adventurous, not considerate or careful (Study 6, Factor 6); acts on practical, logical evidence, keeps to the point, and is hard to the point of cynicism (Study 6, Factor 7); concerned with personal gain, "cuts corners," and is calculating, astute, worldly, and artful (Study 6, Factor 10); alert to practical needs, prosaic, concerned with immediate issues, guided by objective realities, dependable in practical judgment (Study 6, Factor 9); aloof, practical, not imaginative, emphasizing functionality and practical effectiveness (Study 6, Factor 18); practical orientation (Study 7, judging); practicality, realism, concentration on facts (Study 7, sensing); in subjects high in anality (Study 8); in subjects high in social desirability (Study 8); concern with functionality (Study 10, impulsivity); functional-utilitarian approach (Study 15, Factor thrill and adventure seeking); in subjects high in masculinity; task-oriented rather than co-worker-oriented (Study 20); low on hypochondriasis (Study 6, Factor 7; Study 10).

Negative. Careful, considerate (Study 6, Factor 6); impractical, strays from the point, imaginative, fanciful, interested in art, theory, inner creations (Study 6, Factors 6, 7, 9, and 18); trusting, vague, lacks insight in regard to others (Study 6, Factor 10); not concerned with practical outcomes (Study 7, intuition).

MEANING VARIABLE: ACTION AND POTENTIALITIES FOR ACTION (*DIM* 4A)

Manifestations:

Positive. Concern with actions and activity in general (Study 1, in subjects high in extroversion; see also Study 7); concern with motor actions, manifestations of energy and dynamism (Study 2, CPI scale *Sa*); concern with actions like sports (Study 4, in subjects high in *n* Power); person is active, tends to act out; there is evidence of a physiological pattern of high activity that decreases in periods of low physical activity (Study 6, Factor 4); activity, responsiveness (Study 6, Factor 6); person is active (Study 6, Factor 9); high rate of participation in groups (Study 6, Factor 12); interest in and preference for motoric action rather than cognitive actions (Study 14); emphasis on dynamism and activities (Study 15, disinhibition factor); person feels stress when possibility of physical movement is restricted (Study 15); under conditions of restricted physical movement, possibility of moving is reinforcing (Study 15).

Negative. Tendency to remain inactive, inhibited in acting (Study 6, Factor 15); inhibition in action (Study 6, Factor 17); person is blocked in action (Study 6, Factor 21); low concern with actions and possibilities of active change, low interest in active efforts to master the environment, in achievement, and even in behaviors designed to improve one's well-being (Study 11, in subjects higher in external control); disregard of and low preference for motoric actions (Study 14, in subjects who do not prefer motor activities but cognitive activities); in subjects high in femininity (Study 17).

MEANING VARIABLE: ACTIONS AND POTENTIALITIES FOR ACTION (*DIM* 4B)

Manifestations:

Positive. Adjusts to given restraints (Study 6, Factor 2); person is dependent, seeks help, clinging, insecure, indulgent to oneself and others (Study 6, Factor 7); tense, driven (Study 6, Factor 15); swayed, does not control oneself and circumstances (Study 6, Factors 18, 20, 21); person is blocked in action (Study 6, Factors 20, 21); concerned, cautious, reflective (Study 6, Factor 4); avoids the farfetched (Study 6, Factor 6); is conservative, accepts traditional difficulties (Study 6, Factor 12); adjusting (Study 6, Factor 18); low on creativity (Study 6, Factor 23); in subjects scoring high on hypochondriasis, avarice

(Study 10), and femininity (Study 17); low tendency toward sensation seeking, and particularly low boredom susceptibility (Study 15).

Negative. Relative freedom from caution and restraints in action (Study 6, Factors 4, 6, 7, 12, 18, 20, 21); more controlling than controlled (Study 6, Factors 15, 17, 20, 21); preference for cognitive activities rather than motor activities (Study 14).

MEANING VARIABLE: ACTIONS AND POTENTIALITIES FOR ACTION (*DIM* 4 A + B)

Manifestations:

Positive. Bold in action, adventurous, carefree, responsive, sees no danger signals (Study 6, Factor 6); no blocks in action (Study 6, Factors 20, 21); has energy, is active (Study 6, Factor 15); fidgety, insecure (Study 6, Factor 7); irritable (Study 6, Factor 8); does not prefer cognitive activities to motor activities (Study 14); in subjects high in internal control (Study 11); emphasis on dynamism, activities (Study 15, sensation seeking factor disinhibition factor); in subjects high in hypochondriasis (Study 10); extroversion (Study 7).

Negative. Low level of energy, cautious, blocked in action (Study 6, Factors 6, 7, 8, 15, 17, 21); low in extroversion (Study 7) and sensation seeking (Study 15); preference for cognitive activities rather than motor activities (Study 14).

Additional Remarks. The manifestations of *Dim* 4a+b include the manifestations of the constituent subdimensions; hence the apparent contradictions. Which of the manifestations are actually revealed depends on further factors.

MEANING VARIABLE: MANNER OF OCCURRENCE AND OPERATION (*DIM* 5)

Manifestations:

Positive. Creativity, unconventionality, cognitive independence (perhaps particularly when coupled with preference for *TR* 4c) (Study 6, Factors 3, 4); creativity, unconventionality, tendency to be cognitively and imaginatively fascinated by inner creations, art, theory, ideas (Study 6, Factor 9); mental flexibility (Study 6, Factor 10); keeps trying to solve a problem even when difficult (Study 6, Factor 14); imaginative, independent in approach (Study 6, Factor 19); self-reliant, acts on evidence, independent-minded (Study 6, Factor 7); realistic, observant, concentrating on facts (Study 7, sensing); low in dogmatism (Study 13); high in tolerance of ambiguities (Studies 18, 19).

Negative. Conventionality, low creativity (Study 6, Factors 3, 4, 7, 9, 19); rigidity, low ability to shift (Study 6, Factor 20); dogmatism (Study 13); intolerance of ambiguities (Studies 18, 19).

Additional Remarks. The evidence points to two trends: creative imaginativeness and coping with facts. Although they are not necessarily mutually exclusive, one may predominate. Which trend predominates depends on other factors, and the unconventional viewpoint remains common to both. The latter may be responsible for the correlation with LPC scores (i.e., shifting away from the conventional task orientation, Study 20).

MEANING VARIABLE: CAUSES AND ANTECEDENTS (*DIM* 6)

Manifestations:

Positive. Person is skeptical and inquiring regarding ideas (Study 6, Factor 12), experimenting with problem solutions (Study 6, Factor 12); effective in raising and solving problems (Study 6, Factor 14); tends toward logical, consistent thinking, impersonal analysis of causes, concerned with planned performance (Study 7, judging); tolerance of ambiguities (Studies 18, 19); preference for motor activities (Study 14); in subjects scoring high on dogmatism (Study 13); in high scorers on hypochondriasis (Study 10); in high scorers on femininity and androgyny (Study 17); tendency toward internal control, regarding oneself as an active agent in occurrences (Study 11).

Negative. Low concern with assigning blame and responsibility to specific rather than general agents (Study 11, in subjects higher in external control); high in subjects scoring high on the sensation-seeking factor, thrill and adventure seeking (Study 15); in subjects high in intolerance of ambiguity, perhaps as a means of reducing ambiguities by minimizing the use of content that may give rise to multiple interpretations (Studies 18, 19).

MEANING VARIABLE: CONSEQUENCES AND RESULTS (*DIM* 7)

Manifestations:

Positive. Person is calculating, shrewd, artful, devious (Study 6, Factor 10); person is skeptical and inquiring concerning ideas, is sensitive concerning inconsistencies (Study 6, Factor 11); experimenting with solutions (Study 6, Factor 12); analytical, precise in thinking (Study 6, Factors 12, 14); guided by objective realities, dependable in practical judgment, alert to practical implications (Study 6, Factor 9); has foresight, considerateness, ability to set up a *consistent* set of standards (Study 6, Factor 14); tends to logical, objective, consistent thinking, tends to draw conclusions and implications, concerned with logical results of actions, tends to impersonal analysis of effects, including all the consequences of the alternate solutions, pleasant as well as unpleasant (Study 7, judging); realistic, practical, observant of facts and works well with facts (Study 7, sensing); tendency toward internal control, i.e., concern with effecting changes (Study 11); in subjects high in avarice, hypochodriasis (Study 10).

Negative. Person has disregard for implications and consequences, is impulsive, tends toward risk taking, is low in reflectiveness and in fearfulness (Study 1, in subjects high in extroversion); tendency toward risk taking, lack of concern over discrepancies between opinions and behaviors and over refutations of one's own position (Study 3); lack of concern about possible consequences of actions and events (Study 6, Factor 9); in subjects high in impulsivity (Study 10); lack of concern with predictable effects, e.g., dangers of smoking, probabilities, and risks (Study 11); lack of concern with bringing about changes (Study 11, in subjects high in external control); person tends to believe that the world is unpredictable and is ruled by chance (Study 11); in subjects with preference for cognitive activities rather than motor activities (Study 14); person has tendency toward physical risk taking and toward exposing himself or herself to activities involving danger (Study 15, in subjects high in the sensation-seeking factor, thrill and adventure seeking); person appraises situations as low in risk, is adventurous in situations that evoke fear in others, engages in risky behaviors such as drug taking, gambling, and seeking of sexual variety (Study 15); when coupled with preference for *Dim* 4a, person engages in dangerous physical activities such as scuba diving, skydiving, fire fighting, and riot fighting (Study 15).

MEANING VARIABLE: DOMAIN OF APPLICATION (SUBJECT OF THE REFERENT) (*DIM* 8A)

Manifestations:

Positive. Sociability, interest in people, concern with social occasions (Study 2, CPI scales *Do, Sy, Sp, So, Cm*); concern with the identity of the specific individuals involved in different situations (Study 4, in subjects scoring high in *n* Power); open to people (Study 6, Factor 20); in subjects scoring high in extroversion (Study 7); in high scorers on cleanliness and order (Study 9); tend toward external control (Study 11); are low in dogmatism (Study 13); concern with interpersonal relations, prominence of co-worker orientation rather than task orientation (Study 20).

Negative. Active lack of concern in people (Study 2, CPI scale *Ie*); turning away from people (Study 6, Factor 20); tendency toward internal control (Study 11); tendency toward dogmatism (Study 13).

MEANING VARIABLE: DOMAIN OF APPLICATION (OBJECT OF REFERENT) (*DIM* 8B)

Manifestations:

Positive. Concern with the identity of individuals involved in the situations and the nature of the things collected or owned (Study 4, in subjects scoring high on *n* Power); in subjects scoring high on cleanliness and order (perhaps a reflection of concern with objects) (Study 9); in subjects scoring high on hypochondriasis, or avarice (Study 10); in high scorers on the sensation seeking scale, experience seeking (Study 15); in high scorers on femininity and androgyny (Study 17); concern with interpersonal relations (Study 20); in subjects scoring high in intolerance of ambiguity (Study 18) (perhaps in a concrete sense) but low on dogmatism (Study 13) (perhaps in an abstract sense); accepting social values and status quo (Study 2, *Cs*).

MEANING VARIABLE: DOMAIN OF APPLICATION (SUBJECT AND OBJECT) (*DIM* 8A + B)

Manifestations:

Positive. Concern with the identity of individuals and things involved in situations (Study 4, in subjects scoring high on *n* Power); in subjects high in the approval motive, perhaps implementing responsiveness in line with social desirability (Study 8); realistic, orderly, matter-of-fact (Study 7, judging); tendency toward cleanliness and order (Study 9); concern with interpersonal relations, co-worker orientation (Study 20); extroversion

(Study 7); high in intolerance of ambiguities (Studies 18, 19) (concrete sense?) but low in dogmatism (abstract sense?) (Study 13); in subjects scoring high on hypochondriasis, avarice (Study 10).

MEANING VARIABLE: MATERIAL (*DIM* 9)

Manifestations:

Positive. Practical, down-to-earth attitude toward life that combines realism with openness to life and readiness for enjoyment (Study 2, CPI scales *Sy, Sp, Sc*); analytical, believes in facts, in science and technology, admits that occasionally is afraid of ideas because they are so unreal (Study 6, Factor 12); careful and calculated approach to life, programmed, orderly (Study 6, Factor 14); restrained, rule-bound, cautious, realistic, sees danger signals (Study 6, Factor 6); practical, matter-of-fact, realistic, tries to analyze situations impersonally and to count the full costs of everything (Study 7, judging); in subjects high in internal control, concerned with getting things done in reality (Study 11); interest in the material aspects of things in subjects with preference for motor rather than cognitive activities (Study 14); in subjects scoring high on masculinity and social desirability (Study 17).

Negative. Lack of concern with practical aspects of things, low realism and openness to reality (Study 2, CPI scales *Wb, Re*).

MEANING VARIABLE: STRUCTURE (*DIM* 10)

Manifestations:

Positive. Good performance on tasks that require awareness of structural qualities (Study 1); awareness of situational interrelations in subjects high in *n* Power (Study 4); good performance in mathematics and perceptual closure tasks, in finding embedded and hidden words and pictures (Study 6, Factor 6); interest in science, technology, social issues (Study 6, Factor 12); mathematical skill, interest in science (Study 6, Factor 14); preference for administration (Study 6, Factor 14); high in creativity and academic achievement (Study 6, Factors 23, 24); tendency toward planned and orderly performance, toward considering all aspects and costs of action (Study 7, judging); concern with structure, tolerance for complexity (Study 7, judging); preference for cognitive activities (Study 14); low in subjects who tend toward impulsivity (Study 10), toward anality (Study 8), and toward the sensation seeking factor, thrill and adventure seeking (Study 15).

Negative. Low concern with structure of institutions (Study 11, in subjects high in external control); in subjects high in anality, perhaps reflecting preoccupation with details (Study 8).

MEANING VARIABLE: STATE AND POTENTIAL CHANGES IN STATE (*DIM* 11)

Manifestations:

Positive. Interest in science (Study 6, Factor 12); socially precise, controlled, tendency toward rigidity, even compulsivity (Study 6, Factors 14, 21); concern with cleanliness (high in anality, Study 8, and cleanliness and order, Study 9); sensitivity to external cues (Study 13, authoritarianism); scoring high in intolerance of ambiguity (Study 18), authoritarianism (Study 13), and n power (Study 4); high in masculinity (Study 17); preference for motor activities (Study 14); experience seeking, probably reflecting interest in external cues (Study 15); tendency toward internal control (Study 11).

Additional Remarks. There is evidence of two trends: sensitivity to external cues and concern with status, both of which form part of state.

MEANING VARIABLE: WEIGHT AND MASS (*DIM* 12)

Manifestations:

Positive. Acts on practical, logical evidence, keeps to the point (Study 6, Factor 7); pliant to changes, tolerant in view of reality (Study 6, Factor 8) realistic, conventional, practical, prosaic, avoids the farfetched (Study 6, Factor 9); unskilled in analysis, has simple tastes, content with the existing (Study 6, Factor 10); bound to facts (Study 6, Factor 20); accepting of reality, observant of facts, and works well with facts (Study 7, sensing); responsive to external cues (extroversion, Study 1; authoritarianism, Study 13; experience seeking, Study 15).

Negative. Turning away from reality (Study 6, Factor 20).

MEANING VARIABLE: SIZE AND DIMENSIONALITY (*DIM* 13)

Manifestations:

Positive. Realistic, practical, observant, focusing on facts and good at working with them (Study 7, sensing); preference for motor activities rather than cognitive activities (Study 14); in subjects who score high on the sensation seeking factor experience seeking, probably reflecting responsiveness to external cues (Study 15); in subjects who score high on anality, perhaps reflecting concern with details and aspects of measurement (Study 8).

Additional Remarks. It may be of interest to note that *Dim* 13 correlates with low academic achievement (Study 6, Factor 24), low conformity (Study 6, Factor 25), low correspondence to the norms (Study 6, Factor 26), low approval motive (Study 8), low acceptance of social norms and low sensitivity to others (Study 2, CPI scales *Sc*, *Py*), which indicate a tendency toward turning away from common norms, which may accompany the above-noted narrow-ranged concentration on "facts."

MEANING VARIABLE: QUANTITY (*DIM* 14)

Manifestations:

Positive. Concern with standards—personal, legal, etc. (Study 2, CPI scales *Wb*, *Re*); reality orientation (Study 6, Factor 3); tendency toward calm, stability, expediency, adjustment to facts, placidity (Study 6, Factors 3, 11, 21); person is precise, calculating (Study 6, Factor 10); concern with quantitative precision (Study 8, in subjects high in anality); a robust reality-oriented approach (Study 8, in subjects scoring high on ego strength); in subjects concerned with cleanliness and order (Study 9); precision concerning numbers and quantities, in subjects high in avarice (Study 10); interest in reality, concern with activity—motor or cognitive (Study 14); functional-utilitarian approach (Study 15, sensation seeking factor thrill and adventure seeking); concern with speed (Study 15, in subjects who check on the SSS items dealing with speed).

Negative. Rejection of fixed standards, resilience (Study 2, CPI scales *Sy*, *Sc*); low numerical ability (Study 6, Factor 10).

Additional Remarks. The positive correlations with *Mach*, *n* Power, and approval motive reflect, perhaps, a reality orientation and a focus on functionality.

MEANING VARIABLE: LOCATIONAL QUALITIES (*DIM* 15)

Manifestations:

Positive. Reality orientation (Study 6, Factor 3); realistic, practical, observant, good at handling facts (Study 7, sensing); in subjects who admit they prefer harmony in painting (Study 15); tendency toward cleanliness and order (Study 9); in subjects high in intolerance of ambiguities (Studies 18, 19).

Negative. Mistakes on tasks requiring attention to locational qualities (Study 1).

Additional Remarks. It may be interesting to note that *Dim* 15 is preferred by subjects scoring high on variables suggesting concern with power and assertiveness (*Mach*, *n* Power, 16 PF Factor 3) and is not preferred by subjects scoring low on on variables suggesting tolerance of ambiguities, reserve, caution (16 PF Factors 4, 6; CPI scale *Sp*; dogmatism).

MEANING VARIABLE: TEMPORAL QUALITIES (*DIM* 16)

Manifestations:

Positive. Speedy reactions (Study 6, Factor 11, 17); concern with punctuality and being on time (Study 8, in subjects high in anality); concern with saving time (Study 8); subjects overestimate length of time it took to answer a questionnaire (Study 8); in subjects who score high on impulsivity (Study 10); in subjects rated by observers as being able to decide (Study 21).

Negative. Difficulties in tasks that require attention to temporal qualities and aspects (Study 1); slowness (Study 1); subject is placid, tends to renounce immediate satisfaction (Study 6, Factor 4); subject is slow in reaction time when warning about signal is given irregularly (Study 6, Factor 4); not particularly or consistently fast (Study 6, Factor 6); low speed in different tasks that measure simple reaction time and speed but not necessarily when complexity and irregularities in forewarning are introduced (Study 6, Factor 18); slowness in many different cognitive and performance tasks (Study 6, Factor 20); slowness in many different tasks, psychomotor retardation (Study 6, Factor 21); low accuracy in judging lapse of time (Study 11, in subjects high on external control); subjects report short future-time perspectives (Study 11, in subjects scoring high on external control); poor capability of delaying in the Matching of Familiar Figures Test) and Porteus Mazes

(Study 11); weak tendency to delay gratification in the lab, and in life, when planning is involved (Study 11, in subjects high in external control).

Additional Remarks. It may be of interest to note that *Dim* 16 is preferred by subjects who tend toward anxiety, insecurity, depression, withdrawal, worrying, and introversion (16 PF Factors 2–6, 10, 11, 17; CPI scale *So;* introversion in Studies 1, 7).

MEANING VARIABLE: POSSESSIONS (*DIM* 17A)

Manifestations:

Positive. Concern with possessions as part of a functional-exploitive orientation (Study 3, in high *Mach* scorers); concern with possessions as a source of power, status, and prestige (Study 4, in high scorers on *n* power); concern with possessions and saving money, in subjects scoring high in avarice (Study 8); in subjects who score high on dogmatism (Study 13) and on intolerance of ambiguity (Study 18); in subjects scoring high on femininity (Study 17); in subjects who tend to be conventional, cautious, fearful, withdrawn (Study 2, CPI scale *Sp*); cautious, rigid, conservative, defensive (Study 2, scale *Fx*); unrealistic, immature, low in achievement via independence (Study 2, scale *Ai*); submissive, dependent, conventional, conforming (Study 6, Factor 3).

MEANING VARIABLE: BELONGINGNESS (*DIM* 17B)

Manifestations:

Positive. Concern with possessions and saving money, in subjects high in avarice (Study 10); concern with possessions as a source of power, status, and prestige (Study 4, in subjects scoring high on *n* Power); concern with possessions as part of a conservative outlook (Study 1, in extroverts); concern with possessions and belongingness in subjects scoring high on Anality (Study 8), and on cleanliness and order (Study 9), perhaps as part of a retentive-obsessive orientation; in subjects who tend to be disciplined, conscientious, responsible (Study 6, Factor 5); high in femininity (Study 17); low in impulsivity (Study 10).

MEANING VARIABLE: POSSESSIONS AND BELONGINGNESS (*DIM* 17A + B)

Manifestations:

Positive. Concern with possessions as part of a conservative outlook (Study 1, 7, in Extroverts); concern with possessions as part of a functional-exploitive orientation (Study 3, in high *Mach* scorers); concern with possessions as a source of power, status, and prestige (Study 4, in high scorers on *n* Power); concern with possessions and saving money in subjects high on avarice (Study 10); concern with possessions in subjects high in anality (Study 8), and in cleanliness and order (Study 9), perhaps as part of a retentive-obsessibe orientation; in subjects described as conscientious, consistently ordered, disciplined, concerned with duty (Study 6, Factor 5); practical, observant, concerned with facts (Study 7, sensing); when there is also low preference for *Dim* 7, subjects engage in gambling, particularly for monetary profits (Study 15, SSS); subjects respond well to monetary rewards, better than to other rewards (Study 8, anality).

MEANING VARIABLE: DEVELOPMENT (*DIM* 18)

Manifestations:

Positive. No specific information is available. Preference for *Dim* 18 is found in subjects who tend to be shy, cautious, withdrawn (Study 6, Factor 6); insecure, attention-seeking (Study 6, Factor 7); tolerant, conciliatory, permissive (Study 6, Factor 8); earnest, concerned, worried (Study 6, Factor 9); trusting (Study 6, Factor 10); score high on internal control (Study 11), social desirability (Study 17), and authoritarianism (Study 13), perhaps as part of a conservative past-oriented approach; prefer cognitive activities (Study 14).

MEANING VARIABLE: SENSORY QUALITIES (OF REFERENT) (*DIM* 19A)

Manifestations:

Positive. Attention to external cues, "stimulus hunger" (Study 1, in extroverts); noting sensory qualities of things, as opposed to focusing on experiencing sensations (Study 1); unstable, changeable, reacting to externals (Study 6, Factors 2, 3); acts on "sensory impression", flighty (Study 6, Factor 7); interested in immediate issues, alert to practical needs, guided by realities (Study 6, Factor 9); vague, injudicious mind, simple tastes, no self-insight or analytical approach, distractible (Study 6, Factor 10); openness to reality (Study 6, Factor 14); interested in reality, in the sensory qualities of things, attentive to sensory information about what is "actually there" and what is "actually happening," noticing observable facts, observant, realistic, good at dealing with facts (Study 7, sensing); changeable in response to external cues, unstable (Study 2, CPI scale *Fx*); concern with certain sensory qualities (i.e., visual) but not others (i.e., taste, touch) (Study 8, anality); sensitivity to and dependence on external cues, changing in response to external cues (Study 13, authoritarianism); concern with cleanliness and order (Study 9); low preference for cognitive activities (Study 14); (when *Dim* $19a_3$ preferred) low thresholds for auditory stimuli (Study 15); concern with sensory experiences, and specifically with sound ($19a_3$), smell ($19a_7$), and temperature ($19a_6$) (Study 15, SSS).

Negative. Stable, unruffled (Study 6, Factor 2; withdrawn from reality (Study 6, Factors 8, 20), unaffected by distractions (Study 6, Factors 6, 10); does not stick to reality (Study 6, Factors 8, 9); when low preference for $19a_0$, field-independent (Study 6, Factor 19); collects less information in cognitive tasks, relies on "meanings and relationships and possibilities that are beyond the reach of your senses" (Study 7, intuition); high on internal control (Study 11); high on masculinity (Study 17); prefers cognitive activities (Study 14).

MEANING VARIABLE: SENSORY QUALITIES (BY REFERENT) (*DIM* 19B)

Manifestations:

Positive. Concern with internal sensations (Study 1); concern with experiencing sensations as opposed to noting sensory qualities (Study 1); tendency to suffer from physical symptoms, to note them, to report them (Study 4, in subjects scoring high on *n* Power); inclination toward hypochondriasis, sleep disturbances, psychosomatic complaints (Study 6, Factor 2); hypochondriasis (particularly $19b_8$) (Study 6, Factors 2, 3, 4, 9, 10, 11,

17, 20, 21); shy, withdrawn, easily fatigued by the wear and tear of dealings with people and situations (Study 6, Factor 6); high in inner tension (Study 6, Factor 8); high arousal level ($19b_8$) (Study 6, Factor 9); heightened arousal (Study 6, Factor 17); worrying, introspective, easily upset, changeable (Study 6, Factors 2, 3, 4, 6, 9–11, 17, 18, 20, 21); self-centered (Study 6, Factors 20, 21); tends toward anxiety (Study 6, Factor 17); centered on internal world (Study 6, Factors 9, 20, 21); fatigue, insomnia, sensitivity to health and internal reactions (Study 6, Factor 11); physical complaints (Study 6, Factor 20, 21); concern with internal inputs and the inner world, reliance on intuition (Study 7, intuition); concentration on oneself, narcissistic preoccupation with one's body, tendency toward hypochondriasis (especially $19b_8$) (Study 10, hypochondriasis); introversion (Studies 1, 7); high arousal level (Study 1); tendency toward depression, anxiety (in subjects high on external control, Study 11); tendency to respond to threatening stimuli (externals, Study 11; Study 6, Factors 6, 9); interest in internal experiences (especially $19b_8$) (Study 15, sensation seeking factor thrill and adventure seeking); aversion to constancy (especially $19b_8$) (Study 15, sensation seeking factor boredom susceptibility); correlates with the use of drugs and alcohol (not smoking) and degree of heterosexual activities (specifically $19b_8$) (Study 15); sensitivity to internal stimulation (specifically $19b_8$) (Study 15); in subjects rated as low in mental health (Study 21).

Negative. Deemphasizing experiential aspects of sensations (Study 1, in extroverts); high pain tolerance, high thresholds for internal stimulation and for changes in arousal (particularly $19b_8$) (Study 1); unaffected by threats and danger signals (Study 6, Factor 6); relative freedom from excessive physical symptoms, no hypochondriasis, no preoccupation with body and oneself, relative stability (Study 6, Factors 2, 3, 4, 6, 9, 10, 11, 17, 18, 20, 21); low or no tendency toward hypochondriasis and psychosomatic complaints (Study 1, Study 4); only weak fluency in regard to the self, few eidetic images, only a small reaction to threat stimuli, large recovery of GSR after release from shock, great endurance of difficulties (Study 6, Factor 18); low on hypochondriasis, disregard of sensory experiences (Study 8, ego strength); only low interest in internal experiences, low sensitivity to internal stimulation (Study 15); in subjects high in intolerance of ambiguity, perhaps because internal cues are potentially ambiguous (Study 18).

MEANING VARIABLE: SENSORY QUALITIES (OF AND BY REFERENT) (*DIM* 19A + B)

Manifestations:

Positive. Attention to external stimulation (Study 1, in extroverts); attention to internal stimulation, narcissistic preoccupation with body, hypochondriasis (Study 6, Factors 3, 7, 19, 10); shy, withdrawn, easily upset (Study 6, Factors 3, 8); reacting to external stimuli, changeable, flighty (Study 6, Factors 3, 8, 7); practical, attentive to reality (Study 6, Factor 9); observant of facts, good at handling facts, dependent on the senses for information about what is actually happening, interest in reality, practical (Study 7, sensing); sensitivity to particular aspects of sensory stimuli in subjects scoring high on anality (see *Dim* 19a), and in subjects scoring high on cleanliness and order (Study 9); attention to details in subjects scoring high on dogmatism (Study 13); no preference for cognitive activities (Study 14); low on masculinity (Study 17); high in external control (Study 11).

Additional Remarks. Information is available about certain combinations of positive and negative preferences for *Dim* 19a and *Dim* 19b. Positive for *Dim* 19a and negative for

Dim 19b: openness toward external inputs relatively greater than for internal inputs (Study 7, sensing vs. intuiting). Negative for *Dim* 19a and positive for *Dim* 19b: self-absorbed, greater intensity of images relative to sensory stimuli (Study 6, Factors 9, 10, 20).

MEANING VARIABLE: FEELINGS AND EMOTIONS (EVOKED BY REFERENT) (*DIM* 20A)

Manifestations:

Positive. Concern with evoking emotions in others, concern with the emotional reactions of others (Study 4, in high *n* Power scores); warm emotional responses, concern with affective interpersonal relations, attentive to emotional reactions of others (Study 6, Factor 1); gregarious, gets warmly and emotionally involved (Study 6, Factor 10); sensitive to people's approval and disapproval (Study 6, Factor 11); concern with people's responses (interest in leading people) (Study 6, Factor 12); concern with emotional responses of others (Study 8, approval motive); in subjects high in impulsivity (Study 10); low interest in motor activities (Study 14); scoring low on masculinity, perhaps because the stereotype of masculinity is "non-emotional" (Study 17); concern with emotional responses of others, sensitivity to emotional cues and emotional atmosphere in group (Study 20, co-worker orientation); in subjects rated by others as high in leadership, perhaps because leaders tend to pick up cues indicative of emotional responses (Study 21).

Negative. Lack of concern with the emotional reactions of others, perhaps because of egocentric preoccupation with oneself (Study 2, CPI scale *Fe*); emotional detachment (Study 6, Factor 1); emotional detachment, lack of sentimentality, emotional discipline, shrewdness (Study 6, Factor 10); placidity, lack of sensitivity to people's approval or disapproval, does not care (Study 6, Factor 11); in subjects high in masculinity (Study 17); in subjects who are task-oriented rather than co-worker-oriented (Study 20); in subjects rated as low in mental health (perhaps particularly when coupled with a preference for *Dim* 20b) (Study 21).

MEANING VARIABLE: FEELINGS AND EMOTIONS (FELT BY REFERENT) (*DIM* 20B)

Manifestations:

Positive. Awareness of feelings and emotions (Study 2, CPI scale *Wb*); concern with controlling one's emotions (Study 4, high *n* Power scorers); becomes easily emotional and annoyed, worrying, emotionally unstable, gets emotional when frustrated, easily perturbed, gets into fights (Study 6, Factor 2); emotionally sensitive, lives by feelings, expects affection, anxious, acts on sensitive intuition (Study 6, Factor 7); generally enthused, occasional hysteric swings (Study 6, Factor 9); moody, cries easily, overcome by moods, brooding, phobic symptoms, easily touched (Study 6, Factor 11), uncontrolled, follows emotional urges, lets emotions run away with her or him (Study 6, Factor 14); increased emotionality, tendency to get annoyed, responds more to emotional than to nonemotional stimuli, etc. (Study 6, Factor 17); emotional, more fluency on emotional than nonemotional cues (Study 6, Factor 18); worrying, emotional, changeable, excitable, low on emotional maturity, suspicious, jealous, emotionally sensitive (Study 6, Factor 20); increased emotional tension (according to most criteria but not all, Study 6, Factor

21); preoccupation with emotional responses (Study 8, anality); in subjects high in impulsivity (Study 10); concern with emotional responses of others, sensitivity to emotional cues and to emotional atmosphere in group (Study 20, co-worker orientation); in subjects rated as low in mental health (particularly when coupled with a negative preference for *Dim* 20a) (Study 21).

Negative. Denial of one's emotions (Study 2, CPI scale *Wb*); emotionally restrained, calm, emotionally mature, unruffled, stable, "does not let emotional needs obscure realities of a situation" (Study 6, Factor 2), placid, does not care, has no fears (Study 6, Factor 11); unsentimental, hard to the point of cynicism, acts on evidence and not on feeling (Study 6, Factor 7), earnest, unemotional, prosaic (Study 6, Factor 9); emotional self-control (Study 6, Factor 14); low concern for emotionality, not sentimental, emotions cool and under control, less fluency on emotional than nonemotional stimuli (Study 6, Factor 18); unruffled, emotionally thick-skinned (Study 6, Factor 20); apathy, emotional block, restricted emotionally (according to most criteria) (Study 6, Factor 21); in subjects scoring high in the sensation seeking factor thrill and adventure seeking (Study 15, SSS); in subjects high in intolerance of ambiguity, perhaps because emotional cues are potentially ambiguous or inimical to rigid categorizations (Studies 18, 19).

MEANING VARIABLE: FEELINGS AND EMOTIONS (BY AND OF REFERENT) (*DIM* 20A + B)

Manifestations:

Positive. Concern with controlling one's emotions (Study 4, *n* Power); uncontrolled, follows emotional urges, lets emotions run away with him or her (Study 6, Factor 14); emotional, more fluency on emotional than nonemotional cues (Study 6, Factor 18); increased emotional tension (according to most criteria) (Study 6, Factor 21); low emotional control, tendency toward fears and anxiety (Study 8, ego strength); in subjects high in impulsivity (Study 10); in subjects who admit to be concerned with emotional experiences (Study 15); in subjects with tolerance for ambiguity (perhaps because emotional cues are potentially ambiguous) (Studies 18, 19); concern with emotional responses of others, sensitivity to emotional cues and atmosphere in group (Study 21).

Negative. Emotional self-control (Study 6, Factor 14); low concern for emotionality, not sentimental, emotions cool and under control, less fluency on emotional than non-emotional stimuli (Study 6, Factor 18); apathy, emotional block, restricted emotionality (according to most criteria) (Study 6, Factor 21); low emotional tone, absence of fear and anxiety, emphasis on poise and control (Study 8, ego strength).

MEANING VARIABLE: JUDGMENTS AND EVALUATIONS (ABOUT REFERENT) (*DIM* 21A)

Manifestations:

Positive. Concern about evaluation by others, about reputation (Study 4, *n* Power); critical, stands by her or his own ideas, skeptical, critical-judgmental attitude, emphasis on evaluations (Study 6, Factor 1); fulfills responsibilities, does not give up, stable in attitudes and values, shows restraint in avoiding fights and problem situations, stable in accepting group's evaluations (Study 6, Factor 2); responsible, conscientious, dominated by sense of duty, concerned about moral standards and rules, dependable, superego strength, regard for moral standards, governed by strict rules, accepts moral standards unquestioningly (Study 6, Factor 5); sticks to inner values (Study 6, Factor 4); high standards of conformity to rules, strong sense of duty, sensitive to people's approval and disapproval, scrupulous, feels guilty, emphasizes value judgments, claims others are not as moral as they should be (Study 6, Factor 11); sensitive to approval and disapproval, is critical, has certain (i.e., radical) attitudes on political and social issues (Study 6, Factor 12); conscientious, concern for social approval (Study 6, Factor 14); inhibited (Study 6, Factor 15); uses high evaluative standards, is critical about oneself and others, adopts moral view, clear attitudes, extreme viewpoints (Study 6, Factor 17); looks to others for approval (Study 6, Factor 19); guilt-proneness (Study 6, Factor 20); strong super-ego (Study 6, Factor 21); judgmental approach, impersonal analysis (Study 7, thinking); scoring high in cleanliness and order, perhaps reflecting consideration for others' evaluations (Study 9); evaluating oneself, sense of inadequacy, guilt (Study 10, hypochondriasis); upholding a certain ideology (Study 13, dogmatism); scoring high in femininity, perhaps because the stereotype of femininity includes dependence on others' evaluation, considerateness, etc. (Study 17); in subjects who are co-worker-oriented, sensitive to responses of group members (Study 20); sensitivity to evaluations of others (Study 1, in introverts).

Negative. Disregard of evaluations of others (Study 1, extroverts); does not care much for ideas and attitudes, changes them for cooperating (Study 6, Factor 1); changeable in attitudes, evasive of responsibilities, gets into fights and problem situations, insensible to social approval (Study 6, Factor 2); disregards obligations to people, irresponsible, undependable, does not care about duties, frivolous (Study 6, Factor 5); impervious to social suggestion, happy-go-lucky (Study 6, Factor 4); uninhibited, unworried about the judgments of others (Study 6, Factor 6); devious, "cuts corners," complacent (unconcerned about others' evaluations) (Study 6, Factor 10); opportunistic, impenitent, does not care about duties, insensitive to people's approval or disapproval (Study 6, Factor 11); discounts public opinion, has no need for others' agreement or approval (Study 6, Factor 13); does not need support of others for thinking or action (Study 6, Factor 19); in subjects with sociopathic tendencies (to the point of delinquency) (Study 6, Factors 2, 4, 5, 6, 11); in subjects high in the sensation seeking factor thrill and adventure seeking, perhaps because free of constraints and dependence on others' approval (Study 15); in subjects high in masculinity, perhaps because masculine stereotype is ruthless, independent (Study 17); task-oriented rather than co-worker-oriented (Study 20).

MEANING VARIABLE: JUDGMENTS AND EVALUATIONS (OF REFERENT) (*DIM* 21B)

Manifestations:

Positive. Interiorization of values, strong superego (Study 1, introverts); prudish, appreciative, cautious, mannerly (Study 2, CPI scale *Sp*); tends to be dogmatic in attitudes and values, holds explicit views (Study 2, scale *To*); accepts conventional values, concern with values and judgments, has social conscience (Study 2, scale *Cs*); critical, stands by his or her own ideas, skeptical, critical-judgmental attitude, emphasis on evaluations (Study 6, Factor 1); responsible, conscientious, dominated by sense of duty, concerned about moral standards, strong superego (Study 6, Factor 5); genuine, critical of others (Study 6, Factor 10); sticks to her or his values, tends to behave in line with her or his values, does not change attitudes in response to social pressure and subtle suggestibility

(Study 11, in internals); prefer ideational activities (Study 14); interest in internal experiences (sensation seeking factor experience seeking, Study 15); co-worker orientation (Study 20).

Negative. Low interiorization of values, disregarding one's own values (Study 1, extroverts); manipulates and uses people, rejects Protestant ethic with its emphasis on duty and conformity, rejects social rules and prohibitions, tendency toward criminality (Study 2, CPI scale *Sp*); low social conscience (Study 2, scale *Cm*); low concern with values manifested in permissive, nonjudgmental social beliefs and attitudes (Study 2, scale *To*); does not care much for attitudes, changes them for the sake of cooperation (Study 6, Factor 1); disregards obligations to people, irresponsible, frivolous, neglects duties, sociopathic even delinquent tendencies (Study 6, Factor 5); independent in thinking and action, does not need support of others (Study 6, Factor 19); ready to change attitudes in response to persuasion, respond uncritically to arguments and reinforcing comments, endorse easily positive but improbable items (Study 8, approval motive); ready to change one's evaluations and judgments in response to persuasions, does not care if there is a gap between values and behavior (Study 11, external control); task-oriented (Study 20).

MEANING VARIABLE: JUDGMENTS AND EVALUATIONS (ABOUT AND OF REFERENT) (*DIM* 21A + B)

Manifestations:

Positive. Interiorization of values, high superego strength (Study 1, introverts); critical, stands by her or his own ideas, skeptical, critical-judgmental attitude, emphasis on evaluations (Study 6, Factor 1); stable in attitudes, accepts group's evaluations, fulfills responsibilities, restraints in avoiding fights and problem situations (Study 6, Factor 2); responsible, conscientious, dominated by sense of duty, sticks to moral standards (Study 6, Factor 5); high standards of conformity to rules, strong sense of duty, morality (Study 6, Factor 11); critical of oneself and others, high morality, extreme viewpoint (Study 6, Factor 17); judgmental approach, impersonal analysis (Study 7, thinking); preference for ideational activities (Study 14); co-worker orientation (Study 20).

Negative. Low interiorization of values, disregards own values (Study 1, extroverts); disregard for evaluations (Study 6, Factor 1); changeable in attitudes, evades responsibilities, insensible to social approval, gets into problem situations (Study 6, Factor 2); disregards obligations, irresponsible (Study 6, Factor 5); uninhibited, impulsive, unworried about judgment of others (Study 6, Factor 6); opportunistic, impenitent, no sense of duty, does not care about approval (Study 6, Factor 11); sociopathic tendencies (Study 6, Factors 2, 4, 5, 6, 11); score high on masculinity, perhaps because stereotype of masculinity is ruthless, inconsiderate (Study 17); score high in the sensation seeking factor thrill and adventure seeking, perhaps reflecting freedom from social constraints (Study 15); task rather than co-worker orientation (Study 20).

MEANING VARIABLE: COGNITIVE QUALITIES (EVOKED BY REFERENT) (*DIM* 22A)

Manifestations:

Positive. Stable in attitudes and interests (Study 6, Factor 2); unconventional in approach and thinking (Study 6, Factor 3), cognitive alertness (Study 6, Factor 4); imaginative in inner life and conversation, artistically inclined, tends toward daydreams, acts on intuition (Study 6, Factor 7); a rich and intense internal and imaginative internal life, absorbed in ideas, interested in art, theory and basic beliefs, "enthralled by inner creations, when frustrated increases daydreaming" (Study 6, Factor 9); tends toward brooding and fantasy (Study 6, Factor 11); fretful, worried (Study 6, Factors 12, 15); brooding over internal problems (Study 6, Factors 15, 17); report many daydreams (Study 6, Factor 17); worrying, introverted (Study 6, Factor 20); emphasis on inner life (Study 6, Factor 21); concern with internal inputs, turning away from the senses and reliance rather on intuition "for meanings and possibilities beyond the reach of the senses," daydreaming, thinking about problems (Study 7, intuition); turning away from the external world, brooding, worrying (Study 8, low approval motive); concern with internal problems, brooding (Study 8, anality); concern with belief systems (Study 13, dogmatism); interest in internal experiences (Study 15, sensation seeking factor experience seeking); subjects admit to be interested in cognitive qualities (Study 15); low in subjects high in masculinity, probably because stereotypical image of masculinity is action-directed, free from brooding (Study 17).

Negative. Denial, no concern with cognitive qualities and reactions of oneself and others (Study 2, CPI scale *Fe*); does not care about intellectual qualities, impulsive and self-centered (Study 2, scale *Sc*); bland, shallow approach (Study 2, scale *Cm*); changeable in attitudes and interests (Study 6, Factor 2); conventional, rigid (Study 6, Factor 5); no fantasy, no artistic responses, cynical, hard, to-the-point (Study 6, Factor 7); prosaic, practical, no fantasy, avoidance of anything farfetched (Study 6, Factor 9); low concern with thought and internal life, no daydreaming (Study 6, Factor 18); reliance mainly on sensory information (Study 7, sensing); in subjects high in masculinity, perhaps reflecting stereotype of action-oriented nonbrooding male (Study 17).

MEANING VARIABLE: COGNITIVE QUALITIES (OF REFERENT) (*DIM* 22B)

Manifestations:

Positive. Related to a broad range of intelligence tests and cognitive aptitude tests, high giftedness, high creativity (mostly), concern with one's cognitive functioning, emphasis on efficiency with which intellectual endowment is used, commitment to intellectual and cultural pursuits (Study 2, CPI scale *Ie*); stable in attitudes and interests (Study 6, Factor 2); cognitive alertness (Study 6, Factor 4); acts on intuition, daydreams, rich inner life, imaginative in inner life and conversation, artistically inclined (Study 6, Factor 7); brooding, suspicious (Study 6, Factor 8); brooding over internal problems, worried (Study 6, Factor 12, 15); emphasis on inner life (Study 6, Factor 21); concern with internal inputs, reliance on intuition, daydreaming, thinking about problems (Study 7, intuition); preference for ideational activities (Study 14); in subjects rated by others as having high intellectual ability (Study 21); in subjects nominated by many peers as suitable for military leadership (Study 21); in subjects high in femininity, probably reflecting the stereotypical image of woman as hesitating, brooding (Study 17).

Negative. Denial, no concern for cognitive properties and reactions of self and others (Study 2, CPI scale *Fe*); changeable in attitudes and interests (Study 6, Factor 2); no internal life, no fantasy (Study 6, Factor 7); concentrating on facts, turning away from internal inputs, fantasy, thinking (Study 7); in subjects high in sensation seeking factor thrill and adventure seeking, which is unrelated to cognitive measures and especially to cognitive achievements (Study 15).

MEANING VARIABLE: COGNITIVE QUALITIES (EVOKED BY AND OF REFERENT) (*DIM* 22 A + B)

Manifestations:

Positive. Stable in attitudes and interests (Study 6, Factor 2); cognitive alertness (Study 6, Factor, 4); rich inner imaginative life, daydreams, absorbed in ideas and thinking (Study 6, Factor 7); daydreaming, inner life, artistically inclined (Study 6, Factor 9); fantasy, brooding, worrying, introverted (Study 6, Factors 11, 17, 20, 21); concern with internal inputs, thinking, daydreaming, reliance on intuition (Study 7, intuition); preference for ideational activities (Study 14); subjects admit to be interested in cognitive properties (Study 15); subjects low in masculinity, probably because stereotypical image of men is action-oriented, nonbrooding (Study 17).

Negative. Changeable in attitudes and interests (Study 6, Factor 2); no fantasy, no artistic interests, cynical, hard, to-the-point (Study 6, Factor 7); prosaic, practical, no fantasy, nothing farfetched (Study 6, Factor 9); low concern for thought and internal life, no daydreaming (Study 6, Factor 18); reliance on facts, turning away from intuition and thinking (Study 7); low concern with internal world (Study 8, ego strength); in subjects high in the sensation seeking factor thrill and adventure seeking, which is unrelated to cognitive measures, especially cognitive achievements (Study 15); in subjects high in masculinity, probably because the stereotype of men is action-oriented, turning away from fantasy (Study 17).

MEANING VARIABLE: ATTRIBUTIVE TYPE OF RELATION—SUBSTANTIVE (*TR* 1A)

Manifestations:

Positive. Realism (Study 1); adherence to accepted reality (Study 2, CPI scales *Re, Ai, To, Wb*); realism (Study 6, Factor 12); emphasis on objective impersonal approach (Study 7, thinking); emphasis on interpersonally shared reality in subjects scoring high on *Mach* (Study 3) and ego strength (Study 8); preference for cognitive activities (Study 14).

MEANING VARIABLE: ATTRIBUTIVE TYPE OF RELATION—ACTIONAL (*TR* 1B)

Manifestations:

Positive. Sticks to the realities of a situation (Study 6, Factor 2); careful, notices cues in situations (Study 6, Factor 6); realism (Study 6, Factor 12); high in accepting conventional rules (Study 6, Factor 25); attention to external cues (Study 15, the sensation seeking factor thrill and adventure seeking); particularly attentive to external cues (Study 13, authoritarianism).

Negative. Deemphasis on interpersonal reality (Study 13).

MEANING VARIABLE: ATTRIBUTIVE TYPE OF RELATION—SUBSTANTIVE AND ACTIONAL (TR 1A + B)

Manifestations:

Positive. Realism (Studies 1 and 7); sticks to the realities of a situation (Study 6, Factor 2); careful, notices cues in situations (Study 6, Factor 6); realistic (Study 6, Factor 12); realistic, practical, interest in reality, observant of facts (Study 7, sensing); emphasis on interpersonally shared reality in subjects high in ego strength (Study 8); concern with conventional reality (Study 8, approval motive); preference for cognitive activities (Study 14); in subjects who got many sociometric choices as suitable for military leadership (Study 21).

Negative. Nonacceptance of the reality principle, absorbed in private internal world (Study 6, Factor 17); interested more in internal than external world (Study 8, approval motive, ego strength; Study 1, introversion); preoccupation with one's body (Study 10, hypochondriasis); concerned with internal intuitions rather than observed facts (Study 7).

MEANING VARIABLE: COMPARATIVE TYPE OF RELATION—SIMILARITY (TR 2A)

Manifestations:

Positive. Emphasis on similarities in status (Study 2, CPI scale Cs), in personality characteristics (Study 2, scale Gi); vague and injudicious mind, unskilled in analysis (perhaps due to emphasis on similarities) (Study 6, Factor 10); lack of shades of difference between stimuli, all-or-nothing categorization with minimum graduation of stimuli, ambiguity, or conflict (Study 13, authoritarianism); intolerance of ambiguity, perhaps subserved by emphasis on similarities (Studies 18, 19); preference for the known, the familiar and the standard routine (Study 7, sensing); concern with comparisons (?) (Study 7, thinking, judging); a tendency not to yield to conformity pressures (Study 2, CPI scales Ai, Cs, and partly Gi); stands by his or her own ideas (Study 6, Factor 1); independent (Study 6, Factor 13); resistant to attempts at persuasion and conformity pressures (Study 11, internal control), low scores an anality (Study 8) and cleanliness and order (Study 9), perhaps reflecting tendency to overlook small differences at the expense of similarities; co-worker orientation, perhaps reflecting interpersonal similarity (Study 20).

MEANING VARIABLE: COMPARATIVE TYPE OF RELATION—DIFFERENCE (TR 2B)

Manifestations:

Positive. Tendency not to yield to conformity pressures (Study 2, CPI scales Sp, Sa, Ai), defiance or contrariness (Study 2, scales Sp, Sa, Gi, Ai, Cs); does not conform (Study 6, Factor 4); competitive (Study 6, Factor 10); tends not to agree to suggestions of authority, is not suggestible to indirect information (Study 6, Factor 11); nonconformist, tends not to agree to authority (Study 6, Factor 12); goes about his or her own way independently, without conforming or seeking support (Study 6, Factor 13); low approval motive (Study 8); low conformity, low susceptibility to persuasion and attitude change pressures

(Study 11, internal control); analytic thought, concern with comparing and weighting different alternatives (Study 7, thinking); good in tasks that require discrimination (Study 8, ego strength); tolerance of ambiguities, which may result from comparisons (Studies 18, 19).

Negative. Conformity, agreement responses, suggestibility (Study 6, Factors 4, 11, 12); compliance, concern with social desirability, difficulty in tasks of discrimination (Study 8, low approval motive); suggestibility, conformity (Study 11, external control).

MEANING VARIABLE: COMPARATIVE TYPE OF RELATION— COMPLEMENTARITY (*TR* 2C)

Manifestations:

Positive. Tendency not to yield to conformity pressures (Study 2, CPI scales *Do, Cs, Sy, Sa, Ai*); social poise, ascendancy, assertiveness, social activity, and participation, leadership (Study 2, all the scales loaded on the factors of extroversion, interpersonal effectiveness, person orientation); stable, adjustive, self-control (Study 6, Factor 2, 5, 18, qualities that may facilitate social interaction), independence (nonconformity) (Study 6, Factor 13); leadership (Study 6, Factor 22); social participation, adjustment (Study 1, in extroversion); adjustment, participation (Study 8, approval motive, ego strength); not concerned with oneself (low on hypochondriasis, Study 10); dependent on external stimulation (Study 15, sensation seeking factor boredom susceptibility); co-worker orientation, which reflects social participation (Study 20); analytic thought, concern with comparing and weighing different alternatives (Study 7, thinking, judging); high tolerance of ambiguity (Studies 18, 19); preference for cognitive activities (Study 14).

MEANING VARIABLE: COMPARATIVE TYPE OF RELATION—RELATIONALITY (*TR* 2D)

Manifestations:

Positive. Tendency not to yield to conformity pressures (Study 2, scales *Do, Cs, Sy, Sa*); social poise, ascendancy, assertiveness, social activity and participation, leadership (Study 2, all the scales loaded on the factor of extroversion, interpersonal effectiveness, person orientation); concern with moral and social standards (Study 2, scales *Wb, Re, To, Cm, Ac*), which may require relational comparisons; analytic thought, concern with comparing and weighing different alternatives (Study 7, thinking, judging); analytic thought (Study 13, dogmatism).

MEANING VARIABLE: COMPARATIVE TYPE OF RELATION—SIMILARITY, DIFFERENCE, COMPLEMENTARITY, AND RELATIONALITY (*TR* 2A + B + C + D)

Manifestations:

Positive. Low conformity, low suggestibility, low susceptibility to persuasion (Study 11, internal control); independence in thinking and action (Study 6, Factor 13); realism, practicality (Study 6, Factor 6, 9); analytic thought, concern with comparing and weighing different alternatives (Study 7, thinking, judging); preference for cognitive activities and for motor activities (Study 14).

MEANING VARIABLE: EXEMPLIFYING-ILLUSTRATIVE TYPE OF RELATION—EXEMPLIFYING INSTANCE (*TR* 3A)

Manifestations:

Positive. Focus on the concrete here-and-now case, judging everything by personal value, "concentration on other people's viewpoint sometimes makes them lose sight of the value of their own" (Study 7, feeling and extroversion); emphasis on subjective-personal approach to reality (Study 6, Factor 17, 20); subjective approach to reality, bound to concrete case without synthesizing information (Study 11, externals); changeable, easily perturbed, perhaps because focused on concrete cases (Study 6, Factor 2); do not prefer cognitive or ideational activities (Study 14); accommodating, conventional (Study 6, Factor 3; Study 2, CPI scales *Cm*, *Ac*); isolating the particular case of broader contexts and implications, and hence a certain amount of tolerance of human frailties (Study 2, *Sa*); socializing with people considered not moral (Study 2, *Sy*); attending to reality even when distateful (Study 2, *Do*); intolerance of ambiguity (Studies 18, 19), probably due to focus on concrete instance.

MEANING VARIABLE: EXEMPLIFYING-ILLUSTRATIVE TYPE OF RELATION—EXEMPLIFYING SITUATION (*TR* 3B)

Manifestations:

Positive. Social poise, ascendancy, assertiveness, social confidence (Study 2, scales *Do*, *Cs*, *Sy*, *Sa*, all the scales loaded on the factor on interpersonal effectiveness, extroversion, reflecting good command of social situations); acceptance of conventional rules in regular action (Study 2, scales *Gi*, *Cm*, *Ac*; Study 6, Factors 9, 12, 21); personal approach, enjoy the present moment, without dwelling on broader implications (Study 7, high on feeling, low on thinking); no preference for cognitive activities (Study 14); high on sensation seeking factor experience seeking, openness to reality (Study 15); co-worker orientation (Study 20).

Negative. Unconcerned over daily matters, oblivious of particular people and physical realities (Study 6, Factor 9).

MEANING VARIABLE: EXEMPLIFYING-ILLUSTRATIVE TYPE OF RELATION—EXEMPLIFYING SCENE (*TR* 3C)

Manifestations:

Positive. Changeable, perturbable (Study 6, Factor 2); pliant to changes (Study 6, Factor 8); flighty (Study 6, Factor 7); loves dramatics, is theatrical, artistic tendency (Study 6, Factor 7); vague injudicious mind (Study 6, Factor 10); certain degree of creativity (Study 6, Factor 14); subjective approach (Study 6, Factor 2; Study 13; Study 11, external control); do not tend to synthesize information (Study 11, external control); changing response in line with external cues (Study 13, authoritarianism); conventional, prosaic (?) (Study 6, Factors 6, 9).

Negative. Unconcerned over daily matters, oblivious of particular people and physical realities (Study 6, Factor 9); careless of details (Study 6, Factor 6); cynical, hard-headed (Study 6, Factor 10).

MEANING VARIABLE: EXEMPLIFYING-ILLUSTRATIVE TYPE OF RELATION— EXEMPLIFYING INSTANCE, EXEMPLIFYING SITUATION, AND EXEMPLIFYING SCENE (*TR* 3A + B + C)

Manifestations:

Positive. Changeable, easily perturbed (Study 6, Factor 2); flighty (Study 6, Factor 4), perhaps because of focus on concrete situation; personal-subjective approach (Study 6, Factors 17, 21; low approval motive, low ego strength, Study 8); narcissistic self-occupation, turning away from reality (Study 10, hypochondriasis); no preference for cognitive activities (Study 14).

Negative. Worldly, experienced, hardheaded, shrewd (Study 6, Factor 10); reality orientation (high ego strength, high approval motive, Study 8); in subjects who got many sociometric choices as suitable for military leadership (Study 21).

MEANING VARIABLE: METAPHORIC-SYMBOLIC TYPE OF RELATION— INTERPRETATION (*TR* 4A)

Manifestations:

Positive. Subjective, personal approach, not bound by rules (Study 6, Factors 5, 10); seems to be simpleminded because not shrewd or worldly (Study 6, Factor 10); preferences for cognitive and ideational activities (Study 14); focus on thinking, weighing all possibilities, concern with implications (Study 7, thinking); openness to unusual experiences (Study 15, sensation seeking factor experience seeking); not concerned about others' approval (Study 8); emphasis on conceptual clarity (Studies 18, 19).

MEANING VARIABLE: METAPHORIC-SYMBOLIC TYPE OF RELATION— METAPHOR (CONVENTIONAL) (*TR* 4B)

Manifestations:

Positive. Tendency to deal with symbols of power and prestige as well as other vicarious satisfactions (Study 4, *n* Power); introversion (Study 1); withdrawal from interpersonal relations, emotional cautiousness, introspection, internal tension, emphasis on inner life, imagination (Study 6, Factors 4, 6, 15, 17, 21); experimenting in thought, tendency toward new, nonconventional ideas (Study 6, Factor 12); emphasis on achievement within the bounds of conventional rules (Study 2, CPI scales *Cs, Gi, Ac*); tendency toward creativity, perhaps when coupled with preferences for *Dim* 1 and *Dim* 5 (Study 6, Factor 4) or *TR* 1a and/or 1b (Study 6, factor 12); focus on internal inputs, intuition rather than sensing, on personal feeling-tinged appraisal rather than thinking rationally (Study 7, intuition, feeling); focus on internal reality (Study 8, low ego strength); interest in art (Study 7, intuition); good utilization of information, cognitive synthesis (internal control, Study 11).

MEANING VARIABLE: METAPHORIC-SYMBOLIC TYPE OF RELATION—METAPHOR (*TR* 4C)

Manifestations:

Positive. Independence, nonconventionality (Study 6, Factors 3, 19); intense inner life, self-absorbed, tendencies of withdrawal from interpersonally shared reality (Study 6, Factors 7, 9, 21); intense imagination, artistic orientation (Study 6, Factors 7, 9); creativity (Study 6, Factors 3, 9, 12, 23); "imaginatively enthralled by inner creations" (Study 6, Factor 9); interested in ideas, theories, cognitive creations (Study 6, Factors 7, 9, 12, 23, 24), experimenting, free thinking (Study 6, Factor 12); focus on intuition, concerned with internal inputs rather than external ones, artistically inclined, originality (Study 7, intuition); subjective personal rather than realistic approach (Study 6, factors 3, 7, 9, 12, 21; Study 7; Study 8; Study 11); turning away from the sensory world (Study 7, low sensing); focus on inner life (Study 8, low ego strength); openness to unusual experiences (Study 15, sensation seeking factor experience seeking); preference for cognitive activities (Study 14); individualized synthesis of information in the cognitive sense (Study 11, internal control); in subjects high in intolerance of ambiguity (perhaps together with preference for *TR* 2a, part of strategy to minimize ambiguities by emphasizing similarities (Studies 18, 19).

MEANING VARIABLE: METAPHORIC-SYMBOLIC TYPE OF RELATION—SYMBOL (*TR* 4D)

Manifestations:

Positive. Rich internal life, subjective approach to reality, artistically inclined, interested in ideas, acts on sensitive intuition (Study 6, Factor 7); self-control, productivity, creativity (Study 6, Factor 14); withdrawn, emotionally cautious (Study 6, Factor 6); pliant, simple, spontaneous (Study 6, Factors 9, 10); low on sensation seeking (Study 15); low preference for cognitive activities (?) (Study 14): sensitivity to symbols of power and figures in authority, subjectivity (coupled with preference for *TR* 3c and negative preference for *TR* 1a and *TR* 2a) (Study 13, authoritarianism).

MEANING VARIABLE: METAPHORIC-SYMBOLIC TYPE OF RELATION—INTERPRETATION, CONVENTIONAL METAPHOR, METAPHOR, AND SYMBOL (*TR* 4A + B + C + D)

Manifestations:

Positive. Rich inner world, affected emotionally, easily perturbed, unstable, tense, worrying (Study 6, Factors 2, 10, 21); emotional sensitivity, fantasy, imagination, subjectivity (Study 6, Factor 19); low conformity (Study 6, Factor 25); creativity (Study 6, Factor 4); expressive, unrestrained (Study 6, Factor 4); focus on internal life, turning away from interpersonally shared reality (Study 8, low on ego strength, low on approval motive); high on impulsivity (Study 10); openness to unusual experiences (Study 15); emphasis on internal personal problems (Study 8, anality); in subjects rated as low in mental health (Study 21); preference both for ideational activities and motor activities (?) (Study 14).

Negative. Worldly, shrewd, hard-headed (Study 6, Factor 10); realism (Study 8, ego strength).

MEANING VARIABLE: FORM OF RELATION—POSITIVE (ASSERTION) (*FR* 1)

Manifestations:

Positive. Good adjustment to reality by social conformity (Study 2, 7 of the 10 scales loaded on the main recurrent factor of conformity, adjustment, and reality adaptation: *Wb, Re, So, To, Gi, Ac, Ai*); interpersonal effectiveness and assertive self-assurance (Study 2, 3 of the 5 scales loaded on the factor of extroverted social confidence: *Cs, Sp, Sa*); conformity to conventional standards or contented normativism (Study 2, all the scales loaded on this factor: *So, Cm*); adaptation to conventional reality (Study 7, extroversion).

MEANING VARIABLE: FORM OF RELATION—NEGATIVE (DENIAL) (*FR* 2)

Manifestations:

Positive. Tendency toward anticonformity (Study 2, preference for five of the six scales correlated with an anticonformity stand, i.e., *Do, Sy, Sp, Sa, Sc,* and low preference for two of the seven pro-conformity scales, i.e., *Wb, Re*); self-assurance, ascendancy, assertiveness in interpersonal relations (Study 2, scales *Do, Sy, Sa,* that are three of the five scales loaded on the CPI factor "assertive self-assurance" or "dominance adjustment by control of external reality"); low concern with conventional standards (Study 2, scales *Wb, Re*); thinking about problems, concern with pro and con arguments (Study 7, judging); preference for cognitive and ideational activities (Study 14); nonconformity (Study 15, sensation seeking factor disinhibition).

MEANING VARIABLE: FORM OF RELATION—MIXED POSITIVE AND NEGATIVE (*FR* 3)

Manifestations:

Positive. Tendency toward anti-conformity (Study 2, preference for five of the six scales correlated with an anticonformity stand, i.e., *Do, Sy, Sp, Sa, Sc,* and low preference for two proconformity scales: *Wb, Re*); ascendancy, assurance, and participation interpersonally (Study 2, three of the four scales loaded on the corresponding CPI factor: *Do, Sy, Sa*); low concern with fixed standards (Study 2, *Wb, Re*); low preference for cognitive activities (Study 14); high tolerance of ambiguities (a mixed positive and negative form of relation is, by definition, ambiguous) (Studies 18, 19); low authoritarianism, that is, low tendency to think in categorical black–white dichotomies allowing for no relativeness of degrees and graduations (Study 13).

MEANING VARIABLE: FORM OF RELATION—CONJUNCTIVE (*FR* 4)

Manifestations:

Positive. Concern with all implications of all conceptually conceivable alternatives (Study 7, judging); low intolerance of ambiguities, probably because considering several implications and possibilities may entail discovering contradictions among them (Studies 18, 19).

MEANING VARIABLE: FORM OF RELATION—DISJUNCTIVE (*FR* 5)

Manifestations:

Positive. Tendency toward anticonformity (Study 2, preference for five of the six scales correlated with anticonformity: *Do, Sy, Sp, Sa, Sc,* and low preference for two proconformity scales: *Wb, Re*); self-assurance, ascendancy, assertiveness in interpersonal relations (Study 2, four of the five scales loaded on the corresponding CPI factor *Do, Sy, Sp, Sa*); cognitive abilities that enable success in academic contexts (Study 2, scales *Ac, Py,* e.g., ability to see different sides of a problem, to distinguish between alternatives); concern with the pro and con of different alternatives and weighing possibilities (Study 7, judging); high tolerance of ambiguities that are often involved in considering mutually exclusive possibilities (Study 18).

MEANING VARIABLE: FORM OF RELATION—OBLIGATORY (*FR* 6)

Manifestations:

Positive. Tendency to appeal to norms that reflect the way things should or should not be (Study 13, authoritarianism).

MEANING VARIABLE: FORM OF RELATION—DOUBLE NEGATIVE (*FR* 7)

Manifestations:

Positive. Concern with all alternatives and their relations and implications (Study 7, judging).

MEANING VARIABLE: FORM OF RELATION—COMBINED POSITIVE AND NEGATIVE (*FR* 8)

Manifestations:

Positive. Concern with all alternatives, the pros and cons, implications and relations (Study 7, judging); unrestrained, perhaps low deliberation and lack of choice between alternatives (high on impulsivity, Study 10, and on sensation seeking factor disinhibition, Study 15).

MEANING VARIABLE: FORMS OF RELATION—POSITIVE (*FR*$_{pos}$)

Manifestations:

Positive. No preference for cognitive activities (Study 14); high on sensation seeking factor disinhibition (Study 15).

MEANING VARIABLE: FORMS OF RELATION—NEGATIVE (FR_{neg})

Manifestations:

Positive. Preference for cognitive activities (Study 14); high on sensation seeking factor disinhibition (Study 15).

MEANING VARIABLE: SHIFTS IN REFERENT—ACTUAL REFERENT IDENTICAL WITH PRESENTED REFERENT (SR 1)

Manifestations:

Positive. Conservative, respecting established ideas (Study 6, Factor 12); intolerant of ambiguities, pedantic (Study 6, Factor 8); unlikely to yield to an erroneous group judgment (Study 2, scale *Ai*); observant, notes facts, sticks closely to facts, relies on senses for information about what is actually there (Study 7, sensing); high in intolerance of ambiguities, which may be a reason for nondeviance from presented referents (Studies 18, 19); low scores in authoritarianism (Study 13), and dogmatism (Study 13), perhaps reflecting emphasis on facts at the expense of general conceptions; low preference for cognitive and ideational activities (Study 14).

MEANING VARIABLE: SHIFTS IN REFERENT—ACTUAL REFERENT IS NEGATION OF PRESENTED REFERENT (SR 2)

Manifestations:

Positive. Schizoid tendencies, withdrawal, restricted interests, rule-bound (Study 6, Factor 6); harsh, no imagination (Study 6, Factor 7); dogmatic, suspicious, paranoid trend (Study 6, Factor 8); avoids anything farfetched (Study 6, Factor 9); lack of insight (Study 6, Factor 10); cautious, rigid, exacting (Study 6, Factor 14); obsessive and rigid (Study 6, Factors 8 *and* 14); high on neuroticism (Study 6, Factor 20); low in sensation seeking, perhaps reflecting deemphasis on presented stimuli (Study 15, low on three factors); high in authoritarianism, perhaps because of tendency to think in dichotomies (Study 13); prone to change evaluation of stimuli under conditions of threat or stress (Study 11, external control).

MEANING VARIABLE: SHIFTS IN REFERENT—ACTUAL REFERENT IS PART OF PRESENTED REFERENT (SR 3)

Manifestations:

Positive. Conventional, conforming, submissive (Study 6, Factor 3); noncreative (Study 6, Factor 23); changeable, easily perturbed (Study 6, Factor 2); strong tendency toward denial (Study 2, scales *Sc, Gi, Cm, Sa*); tendency toward displacement (Study 10, high on hypochondriasis); low tendency toward careful examination of possibilities and all implications (Study 7, low judging); low preference for cognitive activities (Study 14).

MEANING VARIABLE: SHIFTS IN REFERENT—REFERENT IS THE WHOLE OR A PART OF A PREVIOUS MEANING VALUE (SR 4)

Manifestations:

Positive. Acceptance of social reality (Study 2, *Cs, Sa*); worldly, realistic (Study 6, Factor 10); good grasp of reality, efficient information-processing (Study 11, internal control); observant, notices facts, realistic (Study 7, sensing); considers all possibilities and implications (Study 7, judging); open to reality (Study 15, sensation seeking factor boredom susceptibility); realistic approach (Study 14); intolerant of ambiguities (Studies 18, 19).

MEANING VARIABLE: SHIFTS IN REFERENT—ACTUAL REFERENT IS THE PRESENTED REFERENT COMBINED WITH A PREVIOUS MEANING VALUE (SR 5)

Manifestations:

Positive. Adaptability (Study 6, Factor 1); realistic, conservative, respecting established ideas (Study 6, Factor 12); scans and weighs conceptual possibilities and implications (Study 7, judging); good grasp of reality and efficient information-processing (Study 11, internal control); preference for cognitive and ideational activities (Study 14); grasp of social reality (Study 17, social desirability).

MEANING VARIABLE: SHIFTS IN REFERENT—REFERENT IS A COMBINATION OF SEVERAL PREVIOUS MEANING VALUES (SR 6)

Manifestations:

Positive. Unconventional in thinking and values (Study 6, Factors 3, 19); independent, nonconformist approach to social attitudes and values (Study 2, *Sa, Wb, Re*); openness to reality (Studies 1, 15); scans and weighs conceptual possibilities and implications (Study 7, judging); good grasp of reality and efficient information processing (Study 11, internal control).

MEANING VARIABLE: SHIFTS IN REFERENT—ACTUAL REFERENT RELATED TO PRESENTED OR PREVIOUS REFERENT ONLY BY ASSOCIATION (SR 7)

Manifestations:

Positive. Schizoid tendencies, withdrawal, restricted interests (Study 6, Factor 6); affected, imagination, rich inner life (Study 6, Factor 7); suspicious, paranoid trend, projections (Study 6, Factor 8); lack of insight (Study 6, Factor 10), cautious, rigid, exacting (Study 6, Factor 14); tendency toward subjective shaping of reality, unrealistic (Study 6, Factors 7, 9, 21); tendency toward displacement (Study 10, hypochondriasis); imposes one's own conception on reality (Study 11, internal control); turning away from facts and sensory information, preferring "intuitive leaps" (Study 7, low sensing); preference for ideational activities (Study 14); tolerant of ambiguities, which may be reflected in deviating from presented referents (Studies 18, 19).

MEANING VARIABLE: SHIFTS IN REFERENT—ACTUAL REFERENT IS GRAMMATICAL VARIATION OF PRESENTED REFERENT (*SR* 8)

Manifestations:

Positive. Accepts rules of reality and particularly social reality (Study 2, *Gi, Cm*); realistic, reflects group values (Study 6, Factors 2, 4) but would not let oneself be bound by rules and regulations (Study 1, extroversion: low degree of interiorization; Study 2, low on *Re* but high on *Fx)*; bold, assertive, adventurous and independent (Study 6, Factors 3, 6, 19); good grasp of reality yet preserving one's own conceptualizations about occurrences (Study 11, internal control); high in dogmatism, perhaps reflecting analytical thinking (Study 13); low preference for cognitive activities (Study 14).

MEANING VARIABLE: SHIFTS IN REFERENT—ACTUAL REFERENT IS THE PRESENTED REFERENT CONSIDERED AS A LABEL (*SR* 9)

Manifestations:

Positive. Unrealistic, subjective approach to reality (Study 6, psychoticism); turning away from interpersonal reality, absorption in inner reality (Study 8, low ego strength); not attentive to external cues (Study 13, low authoritarianism); low efficiency in information processing and attention to reality cues (Study 11, external control); no preference for cognitive activities (Study 14).

MEANING VARIABLE: SHIFTS IN REFERENTS—ACTUAL REFERENT NOT RELATED IN ANY OBVIOUS WAY TO PREVIOUS OR PRESENTED REFERENT (*SR* 10)

Manifestations:

Positive. Schizoid tendencies, withdrawal, restricted interests (Study 6, Factor 6); imagination, inner life (Study 6, Factor 7); dogmatic, paranoid trend, projections (Study 6, Factor 8); lack of insight (Study 6, Factor 10), rigid (Study 6, Factor 14); subjective grasp of reality, unrealistic (Study 6, psychoticism, Factor 7); turning away from facts and sensory information, preferring internal cues and inputs (Study 7, low sensing); low efficiency in information processing and low attentiveness to external cues (Study 11, external control); tolerant of ambiguities (Studies 18, 19).

MEANING VARIABLE: SHIFTS OF REFERENT—RELATIVELY SMALL SHIFTS (*SR$_{near}$*)

Manifestations:

Positive. Concern with reality (Study 14, preference for motor activities); conservative, respecting established ideas, sticking close to reality, admission that one is occasionally afraid of one's own ideas because they are so unreal (Study 6, Factor 12), restrained, rule-bound, quick to see dangers (Study 6, Factor 6).

MEANING VARIABLE: NUMBER OF DIFFERENT MEANING DIMENSIONS

Manifestations:

Positive. Cognitive richness and flexibility (Study 1); absorbed in inner life and problems, has fantasy, uncontrolled in thinking and cognitive activities, schizoid tendencies (Study 6, Factors 6, 11, 18); adaptable to changing circumstances (Study 17, androgyny); tolerance of ambiguities (Studies 18, 19); tendency to think about groups in relatively complex ways (Study 20, LPC scores).

Negative. Conservatism and limited range of cognitive alternatives (Study 1); tendency to interpret stimuli unidimensionally, mainly in a fixed and restricted manner (Study 13, authoritarianism); intolerance of ambiguities (Studies 18, 19).

MEANING VARIABLE: NUMBER OF DIFFERENT TYPES OF RELATION

Manifestations:

Positive. Facility for varying cognitive forms of approach; tendency not to conform (Study 2, five of the six anti conformity scales: *Do, Cs, Sy, Sa, Ie*); ascendancy and assertiveness in interpersonal relations (Study 2, all scales saturated on corresponding CPI factor: *Do, Cs, Sy, Sa*); intellectual competence, cognitive achievements (Study 2, *Ie, Ac*); creativity (Study 2, scales correlated with creativity: *Ie, Sa, Sy, Do*); experimenting, free thinking, analytical (Study 6, Factor 12); independent in thinking (Study 6, Factor 19); controlled by intellect (Study 6, Factor 18); controlled, exacting (Study 6, Factor 14); has academic achievements (Study 6, Factor 24); preference for cognitive and ideational activities (Study 14); tends to think in a complex way about groups (Study 20); tendency toward realism, no subjectivistic approach to reality (Study 6, low neuroticism, low psychoticism).

MEANING VARIABLE: NUMBER OF DIFFERENT SHIFTS IN REFERENT

Manifestations:

Positive. Variability in responses, high alternation (Study 1); does not necessarily keep to the point, relies on intuition (Study 6, Factor 7); precise, objective (Study 6, Factor 1); ordered, thorough (Study 6, Factor 5); rule-bound (Study 6, Factor 6), cognitively efficient (Study 6, Factor 14); no preference for cognitive activities (Study 14); openness to stimuli, realistic (Study 14); tolerance of ambiguities (Studies 18, 19).

MEANING VARIABLE: LEXICAL MODE (*LEX MODE*)

Manifestations:

Positive. Concern with thinking; predicting the logical results of events; impersonally examining implications, causes, and results; considering the evidence logically, objectively, and consistently; and so on (Study 7, thinking); realistic, openness to external cues (Study 14, preference for motor activities).

MEANING VARIABLE: PERSONAL MODE (*PERS MODE*)

Manifestations:

Positive. Creativity (Study 2); reliance on feeling rather than thinking, "taking into account anything that matters or is important to you or to other people (without requiring that it be logical)," deciding on the basis of "personal values" (Study 7, feeling).

MEANING VARIABLE: TOTAL NUMBER OF MEANING VALUES

Manifestations:

Positive. Cooperation, sense of duty and obligation (Study 2, scales *Do, Cs, Sa, Cm Ac*); flexibility (?) (Study 2, *Fx*); conforming to group standards, complying (Study 6, Factors 6, 14); rule-bound, considerate (Study 6, Factor 6); flighty, attention-seeking, insecure, seeks help and sympathy, which may facilitate rich responsiveness in a test situation (Study 6, Factor 7); pliant, trusting, permissive, divulges information about self, accepts personal unimportance (Study 6, Factor 8); earnest, concerned, perseveres in task, alert to immediate interests and issues (Study 6, Factor 9); controlled, exacting, precise, good working habits (Study 6, Factor 14); talkative, responsive (Study 7, extroversion); conforming to requirements and rules (Study 13, authoritarianism); adaptability (Study 17, androgyny); verbal facility, perhaps corresponding to stereotype of women (Study 17, femininity).

Negative. Inhibited, restricted (Study 6, Factor 6); does not give information about oneself in a test situation (Study 6, Factor 8); does not care about social rules and conventions (Study 6, Factor 14).

SPECIAL COMBINATIONS OF MEANING VARIABLES*

Combination: Dim 19a, *Dim* 19b, *Dim* 19a+b, *Dim* 20a, *Dim* 20b, *Dim* 21a, *Dim* 21b, *Dim* 21a+b, *Dim* 22a, *Dim* 22b, *Dim* 22a+b—Positive preferences for at least three of the above listed 11 meaning variables indicate concern with the internal world of experiencing (Study 15, sensation seeking factor experience seeking, for variables 2, 7, 9 of above; Study 17, femininity, for variables 6–8, 10 of above). Negative preferences for five or more indicate turning away from internal reality, internal experiencing (Study 15, sensation seeking factor thrill and adventure seeking, for variables 5, 6, 8, 10, 11 of above; Study 17, masculinity, for variables 1, 3, 4, 6, 8, 9, 11 of above list).

Combination: Positive preference for *Dim* 4a and negative for *Dim* 7 indicate tendency to engage in dangerous physical activities (Study 15).

Combination: Positive preference for *Dim* 17b and negative for *Dim* 7 indicate tendency to engage in gambling for monetary profit (Study 15).

---

*Concerning the "Combinations," the higher the number of meaning variables preferred in the indicated direction (according to the subject's meaning profile), the higher the likelihood that the specified tendency would be sufficiently strong to be manifested and, beyond this threshold, be salient. Unless otherwise indicated, the threshold is usually preferences for at least 50% of the specified meaning variables.

Combination: Negative preferences for number of different meaning dimensions, *Dim* 2a, *Dim* 19a (and its dimensions), *TR* 2a, or *TR* 2b indicate a tendency toward concreteness in thinking (Study 13, authoritarianism).

Combination: Negative preferences for *Dim* 2a and *Dim* 7 and positive preferences for *TR* 3c, *TR* 4d and *SR* 10 indicate a tendency toward projection (Study 13, authoritarianism).

Combination: Positive preferences for *Dim* 1, *Dim* 13, and *SR* 8 and negative for *Dim* 8b and *SR* 1 indicate a tendency toward denial (Study 13, dogmatism).

Combination: Positive preferences for *Dim* 3, *Dim* 4a, *Dim* 9, *Dim* 11, *Dim* 13, and *Dim* 14 indicate concern with and interest in external reality, from the viewpoint of practical action (Study 14, Motor Activity Preference).

Combination: Positive preferences for *Dim* 8b, *Dim* 11, *Dim* 12, *Dim* 13, *Dim* 14, *Dim* 15, and *Dim* 16 indicate openness to external reality, from the viewpoint of information and/or experiencing (Study 15, experience seeking).

Combination: Negative preferences for *Dim* 5, *Dim* 6, *Dim* 11, *Dim* 19b, *Dim* 20b, and *TR* 4a indicate intolerance of ambiguity (Studies 18, 19).

Combination: Positive preference for *Dim* 20b and negative for *Dim* 20a as well as *Dim* 2a, *Dim* 2b, *Dim* 17a, *Dim* 14, and *Dim* 16 are characteristic of subjects rated as having low mental health (Study 21).

Combination: Different *TR* of the lexical mode and different *TR* of the personal mode—The more *TR* of the personal mode are preferred, the greater the tendency toward a subjectivistic approach to reality, in line with personal evaluations and subjective meanings (Study 6, especially Factors 4, 7, 9, 12, 21). Preferences in particular for *TR* 4a, *TR* 4c, and *TR* 4d may be manifested in concern with unusual experiences (Study 15, sensation seeking factor experience seeking). Preferences for the *TR* of the lexical mode and in particular *TR* 1a, *TR* 1b, and *TR* 1a+b indicate a realistic, impersonal, objectivistic approach to reality, emphasizing interpersonal reality. Positive preferences for one or more of the types of relation of the *Lex Mode* coupled with negative preferences for one or more of the types of relation of the *Pers Mode* indicate a restricted, especially bolstered, realism (Study 21, sociability, positive preference for *TR* 1a+b, negative for *TR* 3a+b+c). Positive preferences for one or more of the types of relation of the *Pers Mode* coupled with negative preferences for one or more of the types of relation of the *Lex Mode* indicate upholding the subjectivistic viewpoint at the expense of the more objective approach to interpersonal reality (Study 13, authoritarianism, positive preference for *TR* 3c and *TR* 4d, negative for *TR* 2a and *TR* 1b).

Combination: The more *TR* of the comparative type of relation are preferred (*TR* 2a, *TR* 2b, *TR* 2c, *TR* 2d), the stronger the tendency not to yield to pressures toward conformity (Study 2).

Combination: Positive preferences for *TR* 4b and/or *TR* 4c and *Dim* 1, *Dim* 5 suggest tendency toward creativity in the sciences (Study 6).

Combination: Positive preferences for *FR* 2, *FR* 3, and *FR* 5 indicate a general disposition to manipulate one's environment, change it by some actual active or cognitive transformation (Study 2); negative preferences for above variables indicate tendency for leaving things as they are and adapting oneself to them (Study 2).

Combination: Negative preference for FR_{pos} and positive preference for FR_{neg} probably indicate a tendency toward a nonconventional approach (Study 15).

Combination: Negative preferences for SR 2, SR 7, SR 9, and SR 10 and positive for SR 4, SR 8 indicate sticking to inputs from reality without deviating unduely from the presented situation (Study 11).

General Instructions for Coding the Meaning Questionnaire

Coding the meaning questionnaire consists in analyzing, in terms of the meaning system, the subject's responses provided as communications of the meanings of the presented stimuli. For the sake of coding, it is first necessary to identify the meaning unit(s) in the subject's response. The response to one stimulus may include one or more meaning units. A meaning unit consists of a referent and a meaning value. For example, when the stimulus is *Street* and the response is "It is for cars," we have one meaning unit (i.e., *street* —it is for cars); when the response is "It is wide and has two lanes," there are two meaning units: (1) *street*—it is wide; and (2) *street*—has two lanes.

Dividing a response into meaning units is done by determining (1) the referent, and (2) the meaning value, that is, the information provided in regard to that referent. The referent is the stimulus or the expression closest to it in content and form. The coder may identify it by asking herself or himself, "*About what* does the subject talk or write here?" For example, when the stimulus was *Life* and the response was "Living is the most wonderful thing," then the referent is *living* because it is closest to the stimulus in content and form. Again, when the stimulus was *life* and the response was "I love life," the referent is *life* because it is identical to the stimulus, and not *I*, which happens to be merely the syntactical subject of the sentence.

The meaning value may be best identified by means of the question "*What* does the subject tell us about the referent?" The answer should specify information that refers to the referent and that is homogeneous. For example, when the stimulus is *bicycle* and the response is "It has two wheels and a seat and can carry you far," there are three meaning units: the first consists of *bicycle* as referent and "has two wheels" as meaning value; the second consists of *bicycle* as referent and "(has) a seat" as a meaning value; and the third consists of *bicycle* as referent and "can carry you far" as meaning value.

There are four major rules for coding meaning responses. The first is that one codes the response as it has been presented by the subject, as closely as possible to its literal meaning, without interpreting the subject's intended, covert, or implicit meaning. Thus, if the response to the stimulus *justice* is "nowhere" the coding should reflect the fact that the meaning value is along the dimension "Locational Qualities" and not "Judgment and Evaluations" or "State."

The second rule is that, in coding, one has to ignore the veridicality of the presented contents. Thus, regardless of whether the subject refers to the stimulus *sun* as "blue" or "yellow," the meaning value is coded on the dimension "Sensory Qualities."

The third rule is that the means of expression are irrelevant to coding. The same content may be conveyed verbally or graphically (through a drawing), or through a description of a drawing, and so on.

The fourth rule is that each meaning unit gets one coding, and only one, in each of the four sets of meaning variables, that is, one coding for referent-shift variables, one for meaning dimensions, one for types of relation, and one for forms of relation. One could add a coding also for forms of expression (which may be verbal, graphic, both verbal and graphic, descriptive of drawing, showing or pointing, descriptive of movements or pantomime, etc.), but these are optional and do not form part of the meaning profile.

For the sake of convenience, the codings are arranged in the form of a table. The standard table used for coding meaning responses is to be found at the end of this appendix. The coding can be done by hand or directly on a computer. Thus, coding a meaning unit consists in placing one code in each column of the table. A full coding of a meaning unit is represented by one line in the table.

The coding placed in each column should refer to one of the meaning variables appropriate to that column; that is, in the column headed "Meaning dimensions," the coder should place a code representing one of the meaning dimensions; in the column headed "Types of relation," the coder should place a code representing one of the types of relation; and so on. The meaning variables that may be used for coding are listed in Appendix A. Out of those listed, coding uses only the simple variables and not those that represent additions of simpler ones. Thus, in meaning dimensions, one uses Dim 2a and Dim 2b, Dim 4a and Dim 4b, but not Dim 2a+b or Dim 4a+b; in types of relation, one uses TR 1a or TR 1b, but not TR 1a+b, or TR 2a+b+c+d or the modes of meaning; in forms of relation, one uses FR 1 to FR 8, but not the sums of FR_{pos} or FR_{neg}; and in shifts of referent, one uses SR 1 to SR 10, but not the sums SR_{near} or SR_{far} (concerning the computation of the summed variables see last paragraph of this appendix). In order to facilitate counting and summation, it is advisable to use the codes instead of the descriptive titles of the meaning variables. (See Appendix A for the list of meaning variables and their codes).

Each response given by the subject is coded except those remarks that refer to the meaning-assignment process itself, such as "I find it difficult to think of something to say," "I am not sure I am correct," "This was a very personal response," or "I love this questionnaire." A response that constitutes an exact repetition of a previous response (and also gets exactly the same coding in all columns) is not coded twice.

As noted, the coding of each meaning unit consists in assigning to it one code in each set of meaning variables (or placing one code in each cell in the coding table). However, sometimes the coder—invariably the inexperienced one—may feel that more than one meaning variable should be used to code one meaning unit. There may be three reasons for this. One reason is that the meaning unit actually includes two meaning values in a sequence, which were somehow connected or interrelated by the coder. In such cases, the solution is to separate what seemed to be one meaning unit into two. For example, to the stimulus *ocean*, the response is "deep, dangerous." The two words *deep* and *dangerous* may seem to an inexperienced coder to convey one meaning and hence to constitute one response. He or she may then wonder whether the response should be coded on the meaning dimension "Size and Dimensionality" or "Judgments and Evaluations." Yet, as a matter of fact, this response includes two meaning values: one is "deep" and should be coded along the meaning dimension of "Size and Dimensionality," and the other is "dangerous" and should be coded along the meaning dimension "Judgments and Evaluations."

A second reason for the impression that two meaning variables may be necessary to code one meaning unit is that the two meaning values do not refer to the same referent.

For example, when the stimulus is *computer* and the response is "It is used by many people for writing," inexperienced coders may wonder whether they should code the response on the meaning dimension "Function" or "Domain of Application." Here again, we have two meaning units: one has *computer* as referent and "used for writing" as meaning value, coded on the dimension "Function"; the other has *used for writing* as referent and "by many people" as meaning value, coded on the meaning dimension "Domain of Application." Further, it is possible to disentangle here a third meaning unit, whose referent is *people* and whose meaning value is "many," coded on the meaning dimension "Quantity and Number." The referent of the second meaning unit (i.e., *used for writing*) is a second-order referent, in contrast to the referent *computer*, which is called a first-order referent because it is identical to the presented stimulus. Again, by the same logic, the referent *people* in the third meaning unit is a third-order referent. Incidentally, the second-order and third-order referents are examples of a shift in referent (see the variable *SR*4, Appendix A). The coding of the meaning questionnaire refers to first-, second-, and third-order referents, but in coding, it is not necessary to specify to which level these subtypes of referents belong.

The third and last reason for the erroneous impression that two meaning variables are necessary to code the same meaning unit is that the coder is not sure which of two meaning variables actually applies. A doubt of this kind can refer only to meaning dimensions or forms of relation. If the doubt refers to meaning dimensions, then it is most often a case of deciding between two meaning dimensions placed adjacent to each other on the circle of dimensions (see Figure 1). The adjacent placement reflects the fact that the dimensions are similar in content, so that there are meaning values sharing the characteristics of both. "Boring" is a case in point. In some respects, it belongs to "Judgments and Evaluations," and in other respects, to "Feeling and Emotions." If the subject is no longer available for inquiry to clarify the doubt, the coder's best bet is to code the response in terms of the meaning dimension that has appeared more often in the subject's meaning questionnaire.

If the difficulty of deciding between meaning variables arises in regard to forms of relation, then it is most probably due to the difficulty of deciding in the following cases: between the positive (*FR* 1) or mixed (*FR* 3) or obligatory (*FR* 6), on the one hand, and the conjunctive (*FR* 4) or disjunctive (*FR* 5) or combined (*FR* 8), on the other hand; or between the negative (*FR* 2), on the one hand, and the double negative (*FR* 7) or the combined positive and negative (*FR* 8), on the other hand. The solution of these problems is in line with the following convention: Whenever both a simpler and a more complex form of relation apply, two meaning units are involved anyhow, and thus, the notation of the simpler of relation is used (that is, *FR* 1, *FR* 2, *FR* 3, or *FR* 6) for one of the meaning units and the notation of the more complex *FR* (that is, *FR* 4, *FR* 5, *FR* 7, or *FR* 8) for the other meaning unit.

After all responses to the questionnaire have been coded, the notations in each column are summed separately; that is, a count is made of the frequency with which each of the variables in that column was used across all meaning units. Because each meaning unit gets one notation in each column, the totals of the frequencies for each column should be identical to those of the other columns and to the overall number of meaning units. For purposes of research, assessment, or diagnosis, the compound variables (that is, the sums such as *Dim* 4a+b, the meaning modes, *TR* 1a+b, FR_{pos}, etc.) are computed. For the sake of statistical uses, all meaning variables—namely, the original ones and the computed ones—are turned into proportions of the total of meaning units in the individual's questionnaire. A computer program is available that counts the notations of the meaning units in each column, places them in appropriate locations according to a specified format, adds the computed variables, and turns all the variables into proportions.

An example of the coding table and the coded response follows. The stimulus is *street*. The response is "There are avenues and highways. Cars drive in it. In cities, there are many streets. There are houses in it. Some streets are small, some are noisy. Sometimes dangerous. I am scared of them."

Stimulus	Referent shifts	Meaning dimensions	Types of relation	Forms of relation	Coded response[a]
Street	1	2a	1a	1	there are avenues
	1	2a	1a	1	(there are) highways
	1	4b	1b	1	drive in it
	4	8a	1a	1	cars
	8	15	1a	1	streets—in cities
	8	14	1a	1	streets—many
	1	2b	1a	1	there are houses in it
	8	13	1a	1	streets—small
	8	19a	1a	1	streets—noisy
	1	21a	1a	3	sometimes dangerous
	8	20a	1a	1	scared of them
	4	8a	3a	1	I

[a]The "coded response" is not a part of the standard coding table and has been added here as help for the reader. For the code of the meaning variables, see Appendix A.

Standard table for coding meaning

Stimulus	Referent shifts	Meaning dimensions	Types of relation	Forms of relation

References

Abraham, K. The influence of oral eroticism on character formation. In *Selected papers of Karl Abraham*. London: Hogarth, 1927.

Abraham, K. Contributions to the theory of the anal character. In D. Bryan, & A. Strachey (trans.), *Selected papers of Karl Abraham, M.D.* New York: Basic Books, 1954. (Originally published in 1921).

Adler, A. *Social interest: A challenge to mankind.* New York: Capricorn Books, 1964. (Originally published in 1933)

Adorno, T. W., Frenkel-Brunswik, E., Levinson, D. J., & Sanford, R. N. *The authoritarian personality.* New York: Harper & Row, 1950.

Aiken, L. R., Jr. Personality correlates of the attitude toward mathematics. *Journal of Educational Research*, 1963, *56*, 476–480.

Albert, H. *Treatise on critical reason.* Princeton, NJ: Princeton University Press, 1985.

Alexander, F. *Fundamentals of psychoanalysis.* New York: W. W. Norton, 1948.

Alker, H. A. Is personality situationally specific or intrapsychically consistent? *Journal of Personality*, 1972, *40*, 1–16,

Allport, G. W. *Personality: A psychological interpretation.* New York: Holt, 1937.

Allport, G. W. *Pattern and growth in personality.* New York: Holt, Rinehart & Winston, 1961.

Allport, G. W. Traits revisited. *American Psychologist*, 1966, *21*, 1–10.

Allport, G. W., & Odbert, H. S. Trait-names: A psycho-lexical study. *Psychological Monographs*, 1936, *47*, (211), 1–171.

Allsopp, J. F., & Feldman, M. P. Extraversion, neuroticism, psychoticism and antisocial behavior in schoolgirls. *Social Behavior and Personality*, 1974, *2*, 184–190.

Alston, W. P. Traits, consistency, and conceptual alternatives for personality theory. *Journal for the Theory of Social Behavior*, 1975, *5*, 17–47.

Altrocchi, J. Dominance as a factor in interpersonal choice and perception. *Journal of Abnormal and Social Psychology*, 1959, *59*, 303–308.

Anderson, B. F. *Cognitive psychology: The study of knowing, learning and thinking.* New York: Academic Press, 1975.

Argyle, M., & Little, B. R. Do personality traits apply to social behavior? *Journal for the Theory of Social Behavior*, 1972, *2*, 1–35.

Arnon, R., & Kreitler, S. Effects of meaning training on overcoming functional fixedness. *Current Psychological Research and Reviews*, 1984, *3*, 11–24.

Attneave, F. Some informational aspects of visual perception. *Psychological Review*, 1954, *61*, 183–194.

Bailes, D. W., & Guller, I. B. Dogmatism and attitudes toward the Vietnam war. *Sociometry*, 1970, *33*, 140–146.

Bakan, P. Extraversion-introversion and improvement in an auditory vigilance task. *British Journal of Psychology*, 1959, *50*, 325–332.

Baron, R. M., & Ganz, R. L. Effects of locus of control and type of feedback on the task performance of lower-class black children. *Journal of Personality and Social Psychology*, 1972, *21*, 124–130.

Baron, R. M., Cowan, G., Ganz, R. L., & McDonald, M. Interaction of locus of control and type of performance feedback: Correlations of external validity. *Journal of Personality and Social Psychology*, 1974, *30*, 285–292.

Barron, F. An ego-strength scale which predicts response to psychotherapy. *Journal of Consulting Psychology*, 1953, *17*, 327–333.

Barron, F. The psychology of creativity. In F. Barron *et al.*, *New Directions in Psychology* (Vol. 2). New York: Holt, Rinehart & Winston, 1965.

Bass, A. R., Fiedler, F. E., & Krueger, S. *Personality correlates of assumed similarity (ASo) and related scores*. Urbana, IL: Group Effectiveness Research Laboratory, University of Illinois, March 1964. (Mimeographed)

Beck, A. Cognitive therapy: Nature and relation to behavior therapy. *Behavior Therapy*, 1970, *1*, 184–200.

Belcher, M. M., Bone, R. N., Walker, T. D. *The relationship of various components of Zuckerman's sensation seeking scale to dream report ratings*. Paper presented at the Association for the Psychophysiological Study of Sleep, New York, April 1972.

Beloff, H. The structure and origin of the anal character. *Genetic Psychology Monographs*, 1957, *55*, 141–172.

Bem, S. L. The measurement of psychological androgyny. *Journal of Consulting and Clinical Psychology*, 1974, *42*, 155–162.

Bem, S. L. Sex role adaptability: One consequence of psychological androgyny. *Journal of Personality and Social Psychology*, 1975, *31*, 634–643.

Bem, S. L. On the utility of alternate procedures for assessing psychological androgyny. *Journal of Consulting and Clinical Psychology*, 1977, *45*, 196–205.

Bem, S. L. Gender schema theory: A cognitive account of sex typing. *Psychological Review*, 1981, *88*, 354–364.

Bendig, A. W., & Klugh, H. E. A validation of Gough's *Hr* scale in predicting academic achievement. *Educational and Psychological Measurement*, 1956, *16*, 516–523.

Berkowitz, L. Judgmental processes in personality functioning. *Psychological Review*, 1960, *67*, 130–142.

Bernhardson, C. S. Dogmatism, defense mechanisms, and social desirability responding. *Psychological Reports*, 1967, *20*, 511–513.

Bierwisch, M. Some semantic universals of German adjectivals. *Foundations of Language*, 1967, *3*, 1–36.

Biondo, J., & MacDonald, A. P. Internal-external locus of control and response to influence attempts. *Journal of Personality*, 1971, *39*, 407–419.

Bishop, F. V. The anal character: A rebel in the dissonance family. *Journal of Personality and Social Psychology*, 1967, *6*, 23–36.

Blankstein, K. R. *Sensation seeking and vividness of imagery*. Unpublished Manuscript, 1976. (reported in Zuckerman, 1979a).

Block, J. The equivalence of measures and correction for attenuation. *Psychological Bulletin*, 1963, *60*, 152–156.

Block, J. Recognizing attenuation effects in the strategy of research. *Psychological Bulletin*, 1964, *62*, 214–216.

Block, J. Some reasons for the apparent inconsistency of personality. *Psychological Bulletin*, 1968, *70*, 210–212.

Block, J. *Lives through time*. Berkeley, CA: Bancroft Books, 1971.

Block, J. Advancing the psychology of personality: Paradigmatic shift or improving the quality of research. In D. Magnusson & N. S. Endler (Eds.), *Personality at the crossroads: Current issues in interactional psychology*. Hillsdale, NJ: Erlbaum, 1977.

Block, J. Some enduring and consequential structures of personality. In A. I. Rabin, J. Aronoff, A. M. Barclay, & R. A. Zucker (Eds.), *Further explorations in personality*. New York: Wiley, 1981.

Bloom, B. S. *Stability and change in human characteristics*. New York: Wiley, 1964.

Bogart, K., Geis, F., Levy, M., & Zimbardo, P. No dissonance for Machiavellians. In R. Christie & F. L. Geis. *Studies in Machiavellianism*. New York: Academic Press, 1970.

Bolinger, D. *Aspects of language*. New York: Harcourt Brace Jovanovich, 1968.

Bone, R. N., Cowling, L. W., & Choban, M. C. Sensation seeking and volunteering for experiments. Personal communication, 1974 (reported in Zuckerman, 1979b).

Bouchard, T. J., Jr. Personality, problem solving procedure, and performance in small groups. *Journal of Applied Psychology Monograph*, 1969, *53*, 1–29.

Bowers, K. S. Situationism in psychology: An analysis and a critique. *Psychological Review*, 1973, *80*, 307–336.

Brandt, R. B. Traits of character: A conceptual analysis. *American Philosophical Quarterly*, 1970, *7*, 23–37.

Bridgeman, P. W. *The logic of modern physics*. New York: Macmillan, 1927.

Brim, O. G. Jr., & Kagan, J. (Eds.), *Constancy and change in human development*. Cambridge: Harvard University Press, 1980.

Broadbent, D. E. *Perception and communication*. New York: Macmillan, 1958.

Brown, J. C., & Strickland, B. R. Belief in internal-external control of reinforcement and participation in college activities. *Journal of Consulting and Clinical Psychology*, 1972, *38*, 148.

Budner, S. Intolerance of ambiguity as a personality variable. *Journal of Personality*, 1962, *30*, 29–50.

Burke, W. Leadership behavior as a function of the leader, the follower, and the situation. *Journal of Personality*, 1965, *33*, 60–81.

Buss, D. M., & Craik, K. H. Acts, dispositions, and personality. In B. A. Maher & W. B. Maher (Eds.), *Progress in experimental personality research: Vol. 13. Normal personality processes* (pp. 241–301). New York: Academic Press, 1984.

Byrne, D. Repression-sensitization as a dimension of personality. In B. Maher (Ed.), *Progress in experimental personality research*. New York: Academic Press, 1964.

Byrne, D., & Holcomb, J. The reliability of a response measure: Differential recognition threshold scores. *Psychological Bulletin*, 1962, *59*, 70–73.

Byrne, D., Blaylock, B., & Goldberg, J. Dogmatism and defense mechanisms. *Psychological Reports*, 1966, *18*, 739–742.

Cameron, B., & Myers, J. L. Some personality correlates of risk taking. *Journal of General Psychology*, 1966, *74*, 51–60.

Cameron, N. *The psychology of behavior disorders*. New York: Houghton Mifflin, 1947.

Campbell, D. T., & Fiske, D. W. Convergent and discriminant validation by the multitrait-multi-method matrix. *Psychological Bulletin*, 1959, *56*, 81–105.

Campos, L. P. *The relationship between "anal" personality traits and temporal experience*. Presented at the Annual Meeting of the California State Psychological Association, San Francisco, 1963.

Campos, L. P. Relationship between time estimation and retentive personality traits. *Perceptual and Motor Skills*, 1966, *23*, 59–62.

Canestrari, R. Sindromi psichiatriche e rigidita percettiva. *Riv. exp. di Freniatria.*, 1957, *81*, 1–10.

Canter, F. M. Simulation on the California Psychological Inventory and the adjustment of the simulator. *Journal of Consulting Psychology*, 1963, *27*, 253–256.

Cantor, N. A cognitive-social approach to personality. In N. Cantor & J. F. Kihlstrom (Eds.), *Personality, cognition, and social interaction*. Hillsdale, NJ: Erlbaum, 1981.

Cantor, N., & Kihlstrom, J. Cognitive and social processes in personality: Implications for behavior therapy. In E. M. Franks & G. T. Wilson (Ed.), *Handbook of behavior therapy*. New York: Guilford, 1982.

Cantor, N., & Mischel, W. Traits as prototypes: Effects on recognition memory. *Journal of Personality and Social Psychology*, 1977, *35*, 38–48.

Cantor, N., & Mischel, W. Prototypes in person perception. In L. Berkowitz (Ed.), *Advances in Experimental Social Psychology*. New York: Academic Press, 1979.

Carpenter, S. *Psychosexual conflict, defense, and abstraction*. Unpublished doctoral thesis, University of Michigan, 1965.

Carr, A. T. Compulsive neurosis: A review of the literature. *Psychological Bulletin*, 1974, *81*, 311–319.

Carrigan, P. M. Extraversion-introversion as a dimension of personality: A re-appraisal. *Psychological Bulletin*, 1960, *57*, 329–360.

Carson, G. L., & Parker, C. A. Leadership and profiles on the MMPI and CPI. *Journal of College Student Personnel*, 1966, *7*, 14–18.

Cassirer, E. *The philosophy of symbolic forms* (Vol. 1). New Haven, CT: Yale University Press, 1953.

Castle, T. J. Temporal correlates of dogmatism. *Journal of Consulting and Clinical Psychology*, 1971, *36*, 70–81.

Cattell, R. B. *Personality: A systematic, theoretical, and factual study*. New York: McGraw-Hill, 1950.

Cattell, R. B. *The scientific analysis of personality*. Baltimore: Penguin Books, 1965.

Cattell, R. B. *Personality and mood by questionnaire*. San Francisco: Jossey-Bass, 1973.

Cattell, R. B. A more sophisticated look at structure: Perturbation, sampling, role and observer trait—New theories. In R. B. Cattell & R. M. Dreger (Eds.), *Handbook of modern personality theory*. Washington, DC: Hemisphere Publishing, 1977.

Cattell, R. B., & Eber, H. W. *Manual for forms A and B: Sixteen Personality Factor Questionnaire*. Champaign, IL: Institute for Personality and Ability Testing, 1962.

Cattell, R. B., & Eber, H. W. *The Sixteen Personality Factor Questionnaire Test* (rev. ed.). Champaign, IL: Institute for Personality and Ability Testing, 1964.

Cattell, R. B., & Scheier, I. H. *The meaning and measurement of neuroticism and anxiety*. New York: Ronald Press, 1961.

Cattell, R. B., & Tatro, D. F. The personality factors, objectively measured, which distinguish psychotics from normals. *Behavioral Research Therapy*, 1966,4, 39–51.

Cattell, R. B., Eber, H. W., & Delhees, K. H. A large sample cross-validation of the personality trait structure of the 16 P.F. with some clinical implications. *Multivariate Behavioral Research*, (Special Issue), 1968, 107–132.

Cattell, R. B., Eber, H. W., & Tatsuoka, M. M. *Handbook for the Sixteen Personality Factor Questionnaire* (16 P.F.). Champaign, IL: Institute for Personality and Ability Testing, 1970.

Chafe, W. L. *Meaning and the structure of language*. Chicago: University of Chicago Press, 1970.

Charters, W. W., Jr. The social background of teaching. In N. L. Gage (Ed.), *Handbook of research on teaching*. Chicago: Rand McNally, 1963.

Cherry, F., & Byrne, D. Authoritarianism. In T. Blass (Ed.), *Personality variables in social behavior* (pp. 109–133). Hillsdale, NJ: Erlbaum, 1977.

Christie, R. Changes in authoritarianism as related to situational factors. *American Psychologist*, 1952, 7, 307–308. (Abstract)

Christie, R. Authoritarianism re-examined. In R. Christie & M. Jahoda (Eds.), *Studies in the scope and method of "The Authoritarian Personality."* Glencoe, IL: Free Press, 1954.

Christie, R. The person in the person x situation paradigm: Reflections on the (P)erson in Lewin's B = f(P,E). In H. London (Ed.), *Personality: A new look at metatheories*. New York: Hemisphere Publishing, 1978.

Christie, R., & Geis, F. L. The ten dollar game. In R. Christie & F. L. Geis, (Eds.), *Studies in Machiavellianism*. New York: Academic Press, 1970.

Claridge, G. S. *Personality and arousal*. London: Pergamon, 1967.

Claridge, G. S., & Herrington, R. N. Excitation-inhibition and a theory of neurosis: A study of the sedation threshold. In H. J. Eysenck (Ed.), *Experiments with drugs*. New York: Pergamon, 1963.

Cleckley, H. *The mask of sanity* (4th ed.). St. Louis, MO: Mosby, 1964.

Cline, V. B. Interpersonal perception. In B. Maher (Ed.), *Progress in experimental personality research* (Vol. 1). New York: Academic Press, 1964.

Cohen, C. E. Goals and schemata in person perception: Making sense from the stream of behavior. In N. Cantor & J. F. Kihlstrom (Eds.), *Personality, cognition, and social interaction*. Hillsdale, NJ: Erlbaum, 1981.

Cohen, R. H., & Oziel, L. J. Repression-sensitization and stress effects on Maudsley Personality Inventory scores. *Psychological Reports*, 1972, 30, 837–838.

Collins, B. E. Four components of the Rotter Internal-External scale: Belief in a difficult world, a just world, a predictable world, and a politically responsive world. *Journal of Personality and Social Psychology*, 1974, 29, 381–391.

Costello, C. G., & Eysenck, H. J. Persistence, personality and motivation. *Perceptual and Motor Skills*, 1961, 12, 169–170.

Couch, A., & Keniston, K. Yeasayers and naysayers: Agreeing response set as a personality variable. *Journal of Abnormal and Social Psychology*, 1960, 60, 151–174.

Craik, K. H. Personality unvanquished. *Contemporary Psychology*, 1969, 14, 147–148.

Craske, S. A study of the relationship between personality and accident history. *British Journal of Medical Psychology*, 1968, 41, 325–326.

Crites, J. O. The CPI: 2. As a measure of client personalities. *Journal of Counselling Psychology*, 1964, 11, 229–306.

Crites, J. O., Bechtoldt, H. P., Goodstein, L. D., & Heilbrun, A. B., Jr. A factor analysis of the California Psychological Inventory. *Journal of Applied Psychology*, 1961, 45, 408–414.

Cronbach, L. J., & Meehl, P. E. Construct validity in psychological tests. *Psychological Bulletin*, 1955, 52, 281–302.

Cross, H. J., & Tracey, J. J. Personality factors in delinquent boys: Differences between blacks and whites. *Journal for Research in Crime and Delinquency*, 1971, 8, 10–22.

Crowne, D. P. *The experimental study of personality*. Hillsdale, NJ: Erlbaum, 1979.

Crowne, D. P., & Liverant, S. Conformity under varying conditions of personal commitment. *Journal of Abnormal and Social Psychology*, 1963, 66, 545–547.

Crowne, D. P., & Marlowe, D. A new scale of social desirability independent of psychopathology. *Journal of Consulting Psychology*, 1960, 24, 349–354.

Crowne, D. P., & Marlowe, D. *The approval motive: Studies in evaluative dependence*. New York: Wiley, 1964.

Crowne, D. P., Holland, C. H., & Conn, L. K. Personality factors in discrimination learning in children. *Journal of Personality and Social Psychology*, 1968, 10, 420–430.

Crutchfield, R. S. Conformity and character. *American Psychologist*, 1955, 10, 191–198.

Dahlstrom, W. G., & Welsh, G. S. *An MMPI handbook: A guide to use in clinical practice and research*. Minneapolis: University of Minnesota Press, 1960.

Dahlstrom, W. G., Welsh, G. S., & Dahlstrom, L. E. *An MMPI handbook: Vol. 1. Clinical interpretation* (rev. ed.). Minneapolis: University of Minnesota Press, 1972.

Dana, R. H., & Cocking, R. R. Repression-sensitization and Maudsley Personality Inventory scores: Response sets and set effects. *British Journal of Social and Clinical Psychology*, 1969, *8*, 263–269.

D'Andrade, R. G. *Cognitive structure and judgment.* Paper prepared for C. O. B. R. E. Research Workshop on Cognitive Organization and Psychological Processes, Huntington Beach, CA, August 1970.

Deese, J. *The structure of associations in language and thought.* Baltimore: John Hopkins Press, 1965.

Delhees, K. H. The abnormal personality: Neurosis and delinquency. In R. B. Cattell & R. M. Dreger (Eds.), *Handbook of modern personality theory.* Washington, DC: Hemisphere Publishing, 1977.

Dicken, C. F. Convergent and discriminant validity of the California Psychological Inventory. *Educational and Psychological Measurement*, 1963, *23*, 449–459.

DuCette, J., & Wolk, S. Locus of control and extreme behavior. *Journal of Consulting and Clinical Psychology*, 1972, *39*, 253–258.

DuCette, J., & Wolk, S. Cognitive and motivational correlates of general expectancy of control. *Journal of Personality and Social Psychology*, 1973, *26*, 420–426.

Dudycha, G. J. An objective study of punctuality in relation to personality and achievement. *Archives of Psychology*, 1936, *204*, 1–319.

Durflinger, G. W. Academic and personality differences between students who do complete the elementary teaching credential program and those who do not. *Educational and Psychological Measurement*, 1963, *23*, 775–783. (a)

Durflinger, G. W. Personality correlates of success in student teaching. *Educational and Psychological Measurement*, 1963, *23*, 383–390. (b)

Dzendolet, E. Sinusoidal electrical stimulation of the human vestibular apparatus. *Perceptual and Motor Skills*, 1963, *17*, 171–185.

Edelstein, R. Risk-taking, age, sex and Machiavellianism. Unpublished manuscript, New York University, 1966. Summarized by J. Macperson in R. Christie & F. L. Geis, *Studies in Machiavellianism.* New York: Academic Press, 1970.)

Edwards, A. L. *Edwards Personal Preference Schedule.* New York: Psychological Corporation, 1959.

Ekehammar, B. Interactionism in personality from a historical perspective. *Psychological Bulletin*, 1974, *81*, 1026–1048.

Elliott, L. L. *WAF performance on the California Psychological Inventory.* Wright Air Development Division Technical Note 60-218, Lackland AFB, Air Research and Development Command, 1960.

Endler, N. S., & Magnusson, D. Interactionism, trait psychology, psychodynamics and situationism. *Reports from the Psychological Laboratories*, The University of Stockholm, 1974, No. 418.

Endler, N. S., Hunt, McV., & Rosenstein, A. J. An S-R Inventory of Anxiousness. *Psychological Monographs*, 1962, *76* (17, Whole No. 536), 1–33.

Ensenberg, M. *The expansion of meaning and its effect on classification, creativity and curiosity of children.* Unpublished master's thesis, Tel Aviv University, 1976.

Epstein, S. Traits are alive and well. In D. Magnusson & N. S. Endler (Eds.), *Personality at the crossroads: Current issues in interactional psychology.* Hillsdale, NJ: Erlbaum, 1977.

Epstein, S. Explorations in personality today and tomorrow: A tribute to Henry A. Murray. *American Psychologist*, 1979, *34*, 649–653.

Erikson, E. H. *Childhood and society.* New York: Norton, 1950.

Erikson, R. V., & Roberts, A. H. Some ego functions associated with delay of gratification in male delinquents. *Journal of Consulting and Clinical Psychology*, 1971, *36*, 378–382.

Evans, R. Gordon Allport: A conversation. *Psychology Today*, 1971(April), 55–59, 84, 86, 90, 94.

Eysenck, H. J. *Dimensions of personality.* London: Kegan Paul, 1947.

Eysenck, H. J. *The structure of human personality.* New York: Wiley, 1953.

Eysenck, H. J. *Psychology of politics.* London: Routledge & Kegan Paul, 1954.

Eysenck, H. J. Personality and problem solving. *Psychological Reports*, 1959, *5*, 592.

Eysenck, H. J. *Crime and personality.* New York: Houghton Mifflin, 1965.

Eysenck, H. J. *The biological basis of personality.* Springfield, IL: Charles C Thomas, 1967.

Eysenck, H. J. A dimensional system of psychodiagnostics. In A. H. Mahrer (Ed.), *New approaches to personality classification.* New York: Columbia University Press, 1970.

Eysenck, H. J. *The inequality of man.* London: Temple Smith, 1973.

Eysenck, H. J. *Sex and personality.* London: Open Books, 1976.

Eysenck, H. J., & Eysenck, S. B. G. *Manual of the Eysenck Personality Inventory.* London: London University Press, 1964.

Eysenck, H. J., & Eysenck, S. B. G. *Personality structure and measurement.* London: Routledge & Kegan Paul, 1969.

Eysenck, H. J., & Wilson, G. *Know your own personality.* New York: Harper & Row, 1976.

Eysenck, H. J., Hendrickson, A., & Eysenck, S. B. G. The orthogonality of personality structure. In H. J. Eysenck & S. B. G. Eysenck, *Personality structure and measurement*. London: Routledge & Kegan Paul, 1969.

Eysenck, M. W. Extraversion, arousal, and retrieval from semantic memory. *Journal of Personality*, 1974, *42*, 319–331. (a)

Eysenck, M. W. Individual differences in speed of retrieval from semantic memory. *Journal of Research in Personality*, 1974, *8*, 307–323. (b)

Eysenck, M. W. *Human memory: Theory, research and individual differences*. Oxford, England: Pergamon Press, 1977.

Eysenck, S. B. G., & Eysenck, H. J. Rigidity as a function of introversion and neuroticism: A study of unmarried mothers. *International Journal of Social Psychiatry*, 1962, *8*, 180–184.

Farber, I. E. Anxiety as a drive state. In M. R. Jones (Ed.), *Nebraska Symposium on Motivation*. Lincoln: Nebraska University Press, 1954.

Feather, N. T. Attitude and selective recall. *Journal of Personality and Social Psychology*, 1969, *12*, 310–319. (a)

Feather, N. T. Cognitive differentiation, attitude strength, and dogmatism. *Journal of Personality*, 1969, *37*, 111–126. (b)

Feather, N. T. Balancing and positivity effects in social recall. *Journal of Personality*, 1970, *38*, 602–628.

Feather, N. T. Cognitive differentiation, cognitive isolation, and dogmatism: A rejoinder and further analysis. *Sociometry*, 1973, *36*, 221–236.

Feiler, J. *Machiavellianism, dissonance, and attitude change*. Unpublished Manuscript, New York University, 1967 (summarized by Macperson, 1970, see below).

Fenichel, O. *The psychoanalytic theory of neurosis*. New York: Norton, 1945.

Ferenczi, S. Stimulation of the anal erotogenic zone as a precipitating factor in paranoia (1911). In *Selected papers of Ferenczi*. New York: Basic Books, 1955.

Fiedler, F. E. *A theory of leadership effectiveness*. New York: McGraw-Hill, 1967.

Fiedler, F. E. Validation and extension of the contingency model of leadership effectiveness: A review of empirical findings. *Psychological Bulletin*, 1971, *76*, 128–148.

Fillmore, C. J. The case for case. In E. Bach & R. T. Harms (Eds.), *Universals in linguistic theory*. New York: Holt, Rinehart, & Winston, 1968.

Fishbein, M., Landy, E., & Hatch, G. *Some determinants of an individual's esteem for his least preferred coworker: An attitudinal analysis*. Urbana, Ill.: Group Effectiveness Research Laboratory, University of Illinois, 1965. (Mimeograph)

Fisher, R., Griffin, F., & Rockey, M. L. Gustatory chemoreception in man: Multi-disciplinary aspects and perspectives. *Perspectives in Biological Medicine*, 1966, *9*, 549–577.

Fisher, S. *Body experience in fantasy and behavior*. New York: Appleton-Century-Crofts, 1970.

Fiske, D. W. *Measuring the concepts of personality*. Chicago: Aldine, 1971.

Fiske, D. W. The limits of a conventional science of personality. *Journal of Personality*, 1974, *42*, 1–11.

Fiske, D. W. *Strategies for personality research*. San Francisco: Jossey-Bass, 1978.

Fitz, R. J. The differential effects of praise and censure on serial learning as dependent on locus of control and field dependency. *Dissertation Abstracts International*, 1971, *31*, 4310.

Flaherty, M. R., & Reutzel, E. Personality traits of high and low achievers in college. *Journal of Educational Research*, 1965, *58*, 409–411.

Forgus, R., & Shulman, B. H. *Personality: A cognitive view*. Englewood Cliffs, NJ: Prentice-Hall, 1979.

Forrest, D. W. Relationship between sharpening and extraversion. *Psychological Reports*, 1963, *13*, 564.

Foulds, G. A. Temperamental differences in maze performance: 1. Characteristic differences among psychoneurotics. *British Journal of Psychology*, 1951, *42*, 209–217.

Foulds, G. A., & Caine, T. M. Psychoneurotic symptom clusters, trait clusters and psychological tests. *Journal of Mental Science*, 1958, *104*, 722–731.

Frenkel-Brunswick, E. Intolerance of ambiguity as an emotional and perceptual personality variable. *Journal of Personality*, 1948, *18*, 104–141. (a)

Frenkel-Brunswick, E. Tolerance towards ambiguity as a personality variable. *American Psychologist*, 1948, *3*, 268. (b)

Freud, A. Mutual influences in the development of ego and id: Introduction to the discussion. *Psychoanalytic Study of the Child*, 1952, *7*, 42–50.

Freud, S. On narcissism: An introduction. In *Collected papers* (Vol. 4). London: Hogarth Press, 1925. (Originally published in 1914.)

Freud, S. *Collected Papers* (Vols. 1–4). London: Hogarth Press, 1938.

Freud S. Character and anal eroticism. In J. Riviere (trans.), *Collected papers* (Vol. 2). London: Hogarth Press, 1950. (Originally published in 1908.)

Frijda, N. H. *The emotions*. New York: Cambridge University Press, 1986.

Fromm, E. *Man for himself*. Greenwich: Fawcett Publications, 1967. (Originally published in 1947.)

Gale, A. "Stimulus hunger": Individual differences in operant strategy in a button-pressing task. *Behavior Research and Therapy*, 1969, *7*, 265–274.

Gale, A. Individual differences: Studies of extraversion and EEG. In P. Kline (Ed.), *New approaches in psychological measurement*. London: Wiley, 1973.

Gardner, R. W. Cognitive controls and adaptation: Research and measurement. In S. Messick & J. Ross (Eds.), *Measurement in personality and cognition*. New York: Wiley, 1962.

Gardner, R. W., & Long, R. I. Control, defense, and centration effect: A study of scanning behavior. *British Journal of Psychology*, 1962, *53*, 129–140.

Gardner, R. W., Holzman, P. S., Klein, G. S., Linton, H. B., & Spence, D. P. Cognitive control: A study of individual consistencies in cognitive behavior. *Psychological Issues*, 1959, *1* (4, Whole No. 8).

Garwood, D. S. Personality factors related to creativity in young scientists. *Journal of Abnormal and Social Psychology*, 1964, *68*, 413–419.

Geen, R. G. *Personality: The skein of behavior*. St. Louis: Mosby, 1976.

Geis, F. L. The con game. In R. Christie & F. L. Geis, *Studies in Machiavellianism*. New York: Academic Press, 1970.

Geis, F. L. The psychological situation and personality traits in behavior. In H. London (Ed.), *Personality: A new look at metatheories*. New York: Hemisphere, 1978.

Geis, F. L., & Christie, R. Overview of experimental research. In R. Christie & F. L. Geis. *Studies in Machiavellianism*. New York: Academic Press, 1970.

Geis, F. L., & Levy, M. The eye of the beholder. In R. Christie & F. L. Geis, *Studies in Machiavellianism*. New York: Academic Press, 1970.

Geis, F. L., Weinheimer, S., & Berger, D. Playing legislature: Cool heads and hot issues. In R. Christie & F. L. Geis, *Studies In Machiavellianism*. New York: Academic Press, 1970.

Gendre, F. Évaluation de la personalité et situation de sélection. *Bulletin D'Études et Recherches Psychologiques*, 1966, *15*, 259–361.

Gibson, H. B. *Manual of the Gibson Spiral Maze*. London: University of London, 1965.

Gill, L. J., & Spilka, B. Some non-intellectual correlates of academic achievement among Mexican-American secondary school children. *Journal of Educational Psychology*, 1962, *53*, 144–149.

Golding, S. L. The problem of construal styles in the analysis of person-situation interactions. In D. Magnusson & N. S. Endler (Eds.), *Personality at the crossroads: Current issues in interactional psychology*. Hillsdale, NJ: Erlbaum, 1977.

Golding, S. L. Toward a more adequate theory of personality: Psychological organizing principles. In H. London (Ed.), *Personality: A new look at metatheories*. New York: Hemisphere, 1978.

Goldstein, K. M., & Blackman, S. *Cognitive style*. New York: Wiley, 1978.

Goodstadt, B. E., & Hjelle, L. A. Power to the powerless: Locus of control and the use of power. *Journal of Personality and Social Psychology*, 1973, *27*, 190–196.

Goodstein, L. D., Crites, J. O., Heilbrun, A. B., Jr., & Rempel. P. P. The use of the California Psychological Inventory in a university counseling service. *Journal of Counseling Psychology*, 1961, *8*, 147–153.

Gordon, C. M. Some effects of information, situation, and personality on decision-making in a clinical setting. *Journal of Clinical Psychology*, 1966, *30*, 219–224.

Gordon, C. M. Some effects of clinician and patient personality on decision-making in a clinical setting. *Journal of Consulting Psychology*, 1967, *31*, 477–480.

Gore, P. M., & Rotter, J. B. A personality correlate of social action. *Journal of Personality*, 1963, *31*, 58–64.

Gorsuch, R. L., & Cattell, R. B. Second stratum personality factors defined in the questionnaire realm by the 16 P. F. *Multivariate Behavioral Research*, 1967, *2*, 211–224.

Gottesman, I. I. Genetic variance in adaptive personality traits. *Journal of Child Psychology and Psychiatry*, 1966, *7*, 199–208.

Gough, H. G. A short social status inventory. *Journal of Educational Psychology*, 1949, *40*, 52–56.

Gough, H. G. The development of a rigidity scale. Unpublished mimeographed manuscript, Institute of Personality Assessment and Research, Berkeley, California, 1951,

Gough, H. G. The construction of a personality scale to predict scholastic achievement. *Journal of Applied Psychology*, 1953, *37*, 361–366. (a)

Gough, H. G. A nonintellectual intelligence test. *Journal of Consulting Psychology*, 1953, *42*, 242–246. (b)

Gough, H. G. *Manual for the California Psychological Inventory* (rev. ed). Palo Alto, California: Consulting Psychologists Press, 1960.

Gough, H. G. *Factors related to differential achievement among gifted persons.* Unpublished Manuscript, Institute of Personality Assessment and Research, University of California, Berkeley, 1963.

Gough, H. G. A cross-cultural analysis of the CPI-Femininity Scale. *Journal of Consulting Psychology,* 1966, *30,* 136–141.

Gough, H. G. An interpreter's syllabus for the California Psychological Inventory. In P. McReynolds (Ed.), *Advances in psychological assessment* (Vol. 1). Palo Alto, CA: Science and Behavior Books, 1968.

Gough, H. G. A leadership index on the California Psychological Inventory. *Journal of Consulting Psychology,* 1969, *16,* 283–289. (a)

Gough, H. G. *Manual for the California Psychological Inventory* (rev. ed.). Palo Alto, CA: Consulting Psychologists Press, 1969. (b) (Edition of 1975).

Gough, H. G., Chun, K., & Chung, Y. E. Validation of the CPI Femininity Scale in Korea. *Psychological Reports,* 1968, *22,* 155–160.

Graham, J. R. *The MMPI: A practical guide.* New York: Oxford University Press, 1977.

Gray, J. A. Causal theories of personality and how to test them. In J. R. Royce (Ed.), *Multivariate analysis and psychological theory.* London: Academic Press, 1973,

Gray, J. A. A neuropsychological theory of anxiety. In C. E. Izard (Ed.), *Emotions in personality and psychopathology.* New York: Plenum Press, 1979.

Grayden, C. *The relationship between neurotic hypochondriasis and three personality variables: Feeling of being unloved, narcissism and guilt feelings.* Unpublished doctoral dissertation, New York University, 1958.

Grooms, R. R., & Endler, N. S. The effect of anxiety on academic achievement. *Journal of Educational Psychology,* 1960, *51,* 299–304.

Guilford, J. P. *Personality.* New York: McGraw-Hill, 1959.

Guilford, J. S., Zimmerman, W. S., & Guilford, J. P. *The Guilford-Zimmerman Temperament Survey handbook.* San Diego: EdITS Publishers, 1976.

Hall, C. S., & Lindzey, G. *Theories of personality.* (2nd ed.). New York: Wiley, 1957.

Hallenbeck, P. A study of the effects of dogmatism on certain aspects of adjustment to severe disability. *Dissertation Abstracts,* 1965, *25,* 6759–6760.

Hallenbeck, P. N., & Lundstedt, S. Some relations between dogmatism, denial and depression. *Journal of Social Psychology,* 1966, *70,* 53–58.

Hamilton, V. *The cognitive structures and processes of human motivation and personality.* New York: Wiley, 1983.

Hammond, S. B. Personality studied by the method of rating in the life situation. In R. B. Cattell & R. M. Dreger (Eds.), *Handbook of modern personality theory.* Washington, DC: Hemisphere, 1977.

Harkins, S., & Geen, R. G. Discriminability and criterion differences between extraverts and introverts during vigilance. *Journal of Research in Personality,* 1976, *9,* 335–340.

Harper, F. B. W. The California Psychological Inventory as a predictor of yielding behavior in women. *Journal of Psychology,* 1964, *58,* 187–190.

Harris, T. M. *Machiavellianism, judgment independence and attitude toward teammate in a cooperative judgment task.* Unpublished doctoral dissertation, Columbia University, 1966 (summarized by Macperson, 1970, p. 393, see below).

Harter, S. Mastery motivation and need of approval in older children and their relationship to social desirability response tendencies. *Developmental Psychology,* 1975, *11,* 186–196.

Hartshorne, H., & May, M. A. *Studies in the nature of character: Studies in deceit* (Vol. 1). New York: Macmillan, 1928.

Hartshorne, H., & May, M. A. *Studies in the nature of character: Studies in service and self-control* (Vol. 2). New York: Macmillan, 1929.

Hartshorne, H., May, M. A., & Shuttleworth, F. K. *Studies in the nature of character: Studies in the organization of character* (Vol. 3). New York: Macmillan, 1930.

Harvey, O. J. Authoritarianism and conceptual functioning in varied conditions. *Journal of Personality,* 1963, *31,* 462–470.

Harvey, O. J., Hunt, D. E., & Schroder, H. M. *Conceptual systems and personality organization.* New York: Wiley, 1961.

Hase, H. D., & Goldberg, L. R. Comparative validity of different strategies of constructing personality inventory scales. *Psychological Bulletin,* 1967, *67,* 231–248.

Haslam, D. R. *Individual differences in pain threshold and the concept of arousal.* Unpublished Ph.D. thesis, University of Bristol, 1966.

Hathaway, S. R. Foreword. In W. G. Dahlstrom & G. S. Welsh, *An MMPI handbook: A guide to use in clinical practice and research.* Minneapolis: University of Minnesota Press, 1960.

Hathaway, S. R., & McKinley, J. C. *MMPI: Manual for administration and scoring.* Minneapolis: University of Minnesota Press, 1983.

Heider, F. *The psychology of interpersonal relations.* New York: Wiley, 1958.

Helson, R. Personality characteristics and developmental history of creative college women. *Genetic Psychology Monographs*, 1967, *76*, 205–256. (a)

Helson, R. Sex differences in creative style. *Journal of Personality*, 1967, *35*, 214–233. (b)

Helson, R., & Crutchfield, R. S. Mathematicians: The creative researcher and the average Ph.D. *Journal of Consulting and Clinical Psychology*, 1970, *34*, 250–257.

Higgins, E. T., Herman, C. P., & Zanna, M. P. (Eds.), *Social cognition: The Ontario symposium.* Hillsdale, NJ: Erlbaum, 1982.

Hill, A. B. Extraversion and variety seeking in a monotonous task. *British Journal of Psychology*, 1975, *66*, 9–13.

Hill, R. E., Jr. Dichotomous prediction of student teaching excellence employing CPI scales. *Journal of Educational Research*, 1960, *53*, 349–351.

Hirschberg, N. A correct treatment of traits. In H. London (Ed.), *Personality: A new look at metatheories.* New York: Hemisphere, 1978.

Hocking, J., & Robertson, M. The sensation seeking scale as a predictor of need for stimulation during sensory restriction. *Journal of Consulting and Clinical Psychology*, 1969, *33*, 367–369.

Hogan, R. A dimension of moral judgment. *Journal of Consulting and Clinical Psychology*, 1970, *35*, 205–212.

Holland, J. L., & Astin, A. W. The prediction of the academic, artistic, scientific and social achievements of undergraduates of superior scholastic aptitude. *Journal of Educational Psychology*, 1962, *53*, 132–143.

Holzinger, K. J., & Harman, H. H. *Factor analysis: A synthesis of factorial methods.* Chicago: University of Chicago Press, 1941.

Horn, J., Plomin, R. A., & Rosenman, R. Heritability of personality traits in adult male twins. *Behavior Genetics*, 1976, *6*, 17–30.

Horney, K. *Our inner conflicts.* New York: Norton, 1945.

Howarth, E. Extraversion and increased interference in paired-associates learning. *Perception and Motor Skills*, 1969, *29*, 403–406.

Humphreys, L. G. Note on the multitrait-multimethod matrix. *Psychological Bulletin*, 1960, *57*, 86–88.

Hundleby, J. D., Pawlik, K., & Cattell, R. B. *Personality factors in objective test devices.* San Diego: Robert R. Knapp, 1965.

Hymbaugh, K., & Garrett, J. Sensation seeking among skydivers. *Perceptual and Motor Skills*, 1974, *38*, 118.

Icheiser, G. Misunderstanding in human relations: A study in false social perception. *American Journal of Sociology*, 1949, *55*(Part 2), 1–70.

Ishikawa, A. Trait description and measurement through discovered structure in objective tests (T data). In R. B. Cattell & R. M. Dreger (Eds.), *Handbook of modern personality theory.* Washington, DC: Hemisphere, 1977.

Jacobs, K. W., & Koeppel, J. C. Psychological correlates of the mobility decision. *Bulletin of the Psychonomic Society*, 1974, *3*, 330–332.

Jackson, D. N. *Personality research form manual.* Port Huron, MI: Research Psychologists Press, 1984.

Jackson, D. N., & Messick, S. Response styles and the assessment of psychopathology. In S. Messick & J. Ross (Eds.), *Measurement in personality and cognition.* New York: Wiley, 1962.

James, W. H., Woodruff, A. B., & Werner, W. Effect of internal and external control upon changes in smoking behavior. *Journal of Consulting Psychology*, 1965, *29*, 184–186.

Jancke, W. Skala "Geistige Aktivität." In W. Boucsein, *Analyse einiger psychologischer Testverfahren zur Erfassung von Persönlichkeitsmerkmalen.* Bericht aus dem Psychologischen Institut der Universität Düsseldorf, Düsseldorf, W. Germany, 1973.

Jensen, A. R. Authoritarian attitudes and personality maladjustment. *Journal of Abnormal and Social Psychology*, 1957, *54*, 303–311.

Johnson, R. C., Ackerman, J. M., Frank, H., & Fionda, A. J. Resistance to temptation and guilt following yielding and psychotherapy. *Journal of Consulting and Clinical Psychology*, 1968, *32*, 169–175.

Johnson, R. T., & Frandsen, A. N. California Psychological Inventory profile of student leaders. *Personnel and Guidance Journal*, 1962, *41*, 343–345.

Jones, E. Anal-erotic character traits. In E. Jones. *Papers on psychoanalysis* (3rd ed.). New York: William Wood, 1923. (a) (Originally published in 1918.)

Jones, R. Hate and anal eroticism in the obsessional neurosis. In E. Jones. *Papers on psychoanalysis* (3rd ed.). New York: William Wood, 1923. (b) (Originally published in 1918.)

Jones, E. E., & Davis, K. E. From acts to dispositions: The attribution process in person perception. In L. Berkowitz (Ed.), *Advances in experimental social psychology* (Vol. 2). New York: Academic Press, 1965.

Jones, E. E., & Nisbett, R. E. The actor and the observer: Divergent perceptions of the causes of behavior. In E. E. Jones, *et al.*, *Attribution: Perceiving the causes of behavior*. Morristown, NJ: General Learning Press, 1971.

Jones E. E., Kanouse, D. E., Kelley, H. H., Nisbett, R. E., Valins, S., & Weiner, B. *Attribution: Perceiving the causes of behavior*. Morristown, NJ: General Learning Press, 1971.

Jung, C. G. *Psychological types*. London: Routledge & Kegan Paul, 1923.

Jung, C. G. Two essays on analytical psychology. In *Collected works of Jung* (Vol. 7). New York: Pantheon, 1953.

Jung, C. G. *Man and his symbols*. Garden City, NY: Doubleday, 1964.

Kagan, J. Developmental studies in reflection and analysis. In A. H. Kidd & J. L. Rivoire (Eds.), *Perceptual development in children*. London: University of London Press, 1966.

Kaplan, M. F., & Singer, E. Dogmatism and sensory alienation: An empirical investigation. *Journal of Consulting Psychology*, 1963, *27*, 486–491.

Karni, E. S., & Levin, J. The use of Smallest Space Analysis in studying scale structure: An application to the California Psychological Inventory. *Journal of Applied Psychology*, 1972, *56*, 341–346.

Karson, S., & O'Dell, J. W. *A guide to the clinical use of the 16 PF*. Institute for Personality and Ability Testing, Champaign, IL, 1976.

Kay, E. J., Lyons, A., Newman, M., Mankin, D., & Loeb, R. C. A longitudinal study of the personality correlates of marijuana use. *Journal of Consulting and Clinical Psychology*, 1978, *46*, 470–477.

Keller, H. *Männlichkeit Weiblichkeit*. Darmstadt, W. Germany: Dr. Dietrich Steinkopff Verlag, 1978.

Kelley, H. H. Attribution theory in social psychology. In D. Levine (Ed.), *Nebraska Symposium on Motivation*. Lincoln: University of Nebraska Press, 1967.

Kellner, R. *Somatization and hypochondriasis*. New York: Praeger, 1986.

Kelly, G. A. Man's construction of his alternatives. In G. Lindzey (Ed.), *Assessment of human motives*. New York: Rinehart, & Co., 1958.

Kendon, A., & Cook, M. The consistency of gaze patterns in social interaction. *British Journal of Psychology*, 1969, *60*, 481–494.

Kenyon, F. E. Hypochondriasis: A survey of some historical, clinical and social aspects. *British Journal of Medical Psychology*, 1965, *38*, 117.

Kipnis, D. *Character structure and impulsiveness*. New York: Academic Press, 1971.

Kirscht, J. P., & Dillehay, R. C. *Dimensions of authoritarianism: A review of research and theory*. Lexington: University of Kentucky Press, 1967.

Klein, G. S. *Perception, motives and personality*. New York: Knopf, 1970.

Klein, T., & Cattell, R. B. Heritabilities of high school personality questionnaire factors from intraclass correlations on twins and sibs. Paper presented at Behavior Genetics Association meeting, 1972.

Kogan, N., & Wallach, M. A. *Risk taking: A study in cognition and personality*. New York: Holt, Rinehart, & Winston, 1964.

Kohfeld, D. L. & Weitzel, W. Some relations between personality factors and social facilitation. *Journal of Experimental Research in Personality*, 1969, *3*, 287–292.

Köhler, W. *Gestalt psychology*. New York: Liveright, 1947.

Krech, D., Crutchfield, R. S., & Ballachey, E. L. *Individual in society*. New York: McGraw-Hill, 1962.

Kreitler, S. *Symbolschöpfung und Symbolerfassung: Eine experimentalpsychologische Untersuchung* (The production and perception of symbols). Munich-Basel: Reinhardt, 1965.

Kreitler, S., & Chemerinski, A. The cognitive orientation of obesity. *International Journal of Obesity*, 1988, *12*, 471–482.

Kreitler, S., Drechsler, I., & Kreitler, H. How to kill jokes cognitively? The meaning structure of jokes. *Semiotica*, 1988, *68*, 297–319.

Kreitler, H., & Kreitler, S. *Die weltanschauliche Orientierung der Schizophrenen* (The cognitive orientation of schizophrenics). Munich-Basel: Reinhardt, 1965.

Kreitler, H., & Kreitler, S. *Die kognitive Orientierung des Kindes*. (The cognitive orientation of the child). Munich-Basel: Reinhardt, 1967.

Kreitler, H., & Kreitler, S. *Cognitive orientation and defense mechanisms*. Princeton, NJ: Educational Testing Service, Research Bulletin 23, 1969.

Kreitler, H., & Kreitler, S. *Cognitive orientation, achievement motivation theory, and achievement behavior*. Princeton, NJ: Educational Testing Service, Research Memorandum 1, 1970.

Kreitler, H., & Kreitler, S. The cognitive determinants of defensive behavior. *British Journal of Social and Clinical Psychology*, 1972, *11*, 359–372. (a)

Kreitler, H., & Kreitler, S. The model of cognitive orientation: Towards a theory of human behavior. *British Journal of Psychology*, 1972, *63*, 9–30. (b)

Kreitler, H., & Kreitler, S. *Psychology of the arts*. Durham, NC: Duke University Press, 1972. (c)

Kreitler, H., & Kreitler, S. *Cognitive orientation and behavior.* New York: Springer, 1976.

Kreitler, H., & Kreitler, S. *Cognitive rehabilitation by meaning of aphasic patients and imbecile children.* Paper presented at the Johan Gutenberg University, Mainz, W. Germany, at its 500th anniversary, June 1977.

Kreitler, H., & Kreitler, S. The cognitive determinants of curiosity. In H. G. Voss & H. Keller (Eds.), *Neugierforschung: Grundlagen, Theorien, Anwendungen.* Weinheim and Basel: Belz Verlag, 1981.

Kreitler, H., & Kreitler, S. The theory of cognitive orientation: Widening the scope of behavior prediction. In B. A. Maher & W. B. Maher (Eds.), *Progress in experimental personality research: Normal personality processes* (Vol. 11, pp. 101–169). New York: Academic Press, 1982.

Kreitler, H., & Kreitler, S. Artistic value judgments and the value of judging the arts. *Leonardo,* 1983, *16,* 208–211.

Kreitler, H., & Kreitler, S. The cognitive effects of art (in German). *Manuskripte,* 1984, *23,* 89–92.

Kreitler, H., & Kreitler, S. Schizophrenic perception and its psychopathological implications: A microgenetic study. In U. Henschel, G. Smith, & J. G. Draguns (Eds.), *The roots of perception* (pp. 301–330). Amsterdam and New York: Elsevier Science Publishers, 1986.

Kreitler, H., & Kreitler, S. Psychosomatic foundations of creativity. In K. J. Gilhooly, M. Keane, R. Logie, & G. Erdos (Eds.), *Lines of though: Reflections on the psychology of thinking.* Chichester, England: Wiley, 1989. (a)

Kreitler, H., & Kreitler, S. Cognitive primacy, cognitive behavior guidance and their implications for cognitive therapy. *Journal of Cognitive Psychotherapy,* 1989. (b)

Kreitler, S., & Kreitler, H. Dimensions of meaning and their measurement. *Psychological Reports,* 1968, *23,* 1307–1329.

Kreitler, S., & Kreitler, H. *Perception and meaning assignment.* Paper presented at International Conference on Microgenesis, Mainz, W. Germany, 1977.

Kreitler, S., & Kreitler, H. Item content: Does it matter? *Educational and Psychological Measurement,* 1981, *41,* 635–641.

Kreitler, S., & Kreitler, H. The consistency of behavioral inconsistencies. *Archives of Psychology,* 1983, *135,* 199–218.

Kreitler, S. & Kreitler, H. Meaning assignment in perception. In W. D. Fröhlich, G. J. W. Smith, J. G. Draguns, & U. Henschel (Eds.), *Psychological processes in cognition and personality* (pp. 173–191). Washington, DC: Hemisphere, 1984. (a)

Kreitler, S., & Kreitler, H. Test item content versus response style. *Australian Journal of Psychology,* 1984, *36,* 255–266. (b)

Kreitler, S., & Kreitler, H. Traits and situations: A semantic reconciliation in the research of personality and behavior. In H. Bonarius, G. van Heck, & N. Smid (Eds.), *Personality psychology in Europe: Theoretical and empirical developments* (pp. 233–251). Lisse, The Netherlands: Swets & Zeitlinger, 1984. (c)

Kreitler, S., & Kreitler, H. The psychosemantic determinants of anxiety: A cognitive approach. In H. van der Ploeg, R. Schwarzer, & C. D. Spielberger (Eds.), *Advances in Test Anxiety research* (Vol. 4) (pp. 117–135). Lisse, The Netherlands & Hillsdale, NJ: Swets & Zeitlinger/Erlbaum, 1985. (a)

Kreitler, S., & Kreitler, H. The psychosemantic foundations of comprehension. *Theoretical Linguistics,* 1985, *12,* 185–195. (b)

Kreitler, S., & Kreitler, H. Individuality in planning: Meaning patterns of planning styles. *International Journal of Psychology,* 1986, *21,* 565–587. (a).

Kreitler, S., & Kreitler, H. The psychosemantic structure of narrative. *Semiotica,* 1986, *58,* 217–243. (b)

Kreitler, S., & Kreitler, H. Types of curiosity behaviors and their cognitive determinants. *Archives of Psychology,* 1986, *138,* 233–251. (c).

Kreitler, S., & Kreitler, H. Modifying anxiety by cognitive means. In R. Schwarzer, H. M. van der Ploeg, & C. D. Spielberger (Eds.), *Advances in Test Anxiety research* (Vol. 5) (pp. 195–206). Lisse, The Netherlands and Hillsdale, NJ: Swets and Zeitlinger/Erlbaum, 1987. (a)

Kreitler, S., & Kreitler, H. The motivational and cognitive determinants of individual planning. *Genetic, Social and General Psychology Monographs,* 1987, *113,* 81–107. (b)

Kreitler, S., & Kreitler, H. Plans and planning: Their motivational and cognitive antecedents. In S. L. Friedman, E. K. Scholnick, & R. R. Cocking (Eds.), *Blueprints for thinking: The role of planning in cognitive development* (pp. 110–178). New York: Cambridge University Press, 1987. (c)

Kreitler, S., & Kreitler, H. Psychosemantic aspects of the self. In T. M. Honess & K. M. Yardley (Eds.) *Self and identity: Individual change and development* (pp. 338–358). London: Routledge and Kegan Paul, 1987. (d)

Kreitler, S., & Kreitler, H. Solution to the problem of horizontal decalage as a paradigm for research in cognitive development. *Eighth Conference on Developmental Psychology,* Bern, Switzerland, 1987 (invited address). (e)

Kreitler, S., & Kreitler, H. The cognitive approach to motivation in retarded individuals. In N. W. Bray (Ed.), *International Review of Research in Mental Retardation* (Vol., 15, pp. 81–123), 1988. (a)

Kreitler, S. & Kreitler, H. Meanings, culture, and communication. *Journal of Pragmatics*, 1988, *12*, 135–152. (b)

Kreitler, S., & Kreitler, H. Horizontal decalage: A problem and its resolution. *Cognitive Development*, 1988, *4*, 89–119. (c).

Kreitler, S., & Kreitler, H. The circle of meaning dimensions: Applications of Guttman's methodology to studies in cognition and personality, 1989 (in press). (a)

Kreitler, S., & Kreitler, H. Cognitive enrichment cf mentally retarded children. Unpublished book manuscript, 1989. (b)

Kreitler, S., & Kreitler, H. The cognitive foundations of personality. Unpublished book manuscript, 1989. (c)

Kreitler, S., Kreitler, H., & Carasso, R. Cognitive orientation as predictor of pain relief following acupuncture. *Pain*, 1987, *28*, 323–341.

Kreitler, S., Kreitler, H., & Zigler, E. Cognitive orientation and curiosity. *British Journal of Psychology*, 1974, *65*, 45–52.

Kreitler, S., Maguen, T., & Kreitler, H. The three faces of intolerance of ambiguity. *Archiv fuer Psychologie*, 1975, *127*, 238–250.

Kreitler, S., Shahar, A., & Kreitler, H. cognitive orientation, type of smoker, and behavior therapy of smoking. *British Journal of Medical Psychology*, 1976, *49*, 167–175.

Kreitler, S., Schwartz, R., & Kreitler, H. The cognitive orientation of expressive communicability in schizophrenics and normals. *Journal of Communication Disorders*, 1987, *20*, 73–91.

Kreitler, S., Kreitler, H., & Carasso, R. Cognitive styles and personality traits as predictors of response to therapy in pain patients. *Personality and Individual Differences*, 1989, *10*, 313–322.

Kreitler, S., Kreitler, H., & Wanounou, V. Cognitive modification of test performance in schizophrenics and normals. *Imagination, Cognition, and Personality*, 1987–1988, *7*, 227–249.

Kris, E. Notes on the development and on some current problems of psychoanalytic child psychology. *Psychoanalytic Study of the Child*, 1950, *5*, 34–62.

Kruger, A. *Direct and substitute modes of tension-reduction in terms of developmental level: An experimental analysis by means of the Rorschach test*. Unpublished doctoral dissertation, Clark University, 1954.

Krupski, A., Raskin, D. C, & Bakan, P. Physiological and personality correlates of commission errors in an auditory vigilance task. *Psychophysiology*, 1971, *8*, 304–311.

Ladee, G. A. *Hypochondriachal syndromes*. New York: Elsevier, 1966.

Lahav, R. *The effects of meaning training on creativity*. Unpublished master's thesis, Tel Aviv University, 1982.

Landfield, A. W., & Leitner, L. M. (Eds.), *Personal construct psychology: Psychotherapy and personality*. New York: Wiley, 1980.

Lanyon, R. I. *A handbook of MMPI group profiles*. Minneapolis: University of Minnesota Press, 1968.

Lazarus, R. S. *Personality* (2nd ed.). Englewood Cliffs, NJ: Prentice-Hall, 1971.

Leach, P. J. A critical study of the literature concerning rigidity. *British Journal of Social and Clinical Psychology*, 1967, *6*, 11–22.

Lefcourt, H. M. Risk-taking in negro and white adults. *Journal of Personality and Social Psychology*, 1965, *2*, 765–770.

Lefcourt, H. M. *Locus of control: Current trends in theory and research*. Hillsdale, NJ: Erlbaum, 1976.

Lefcourt, H. M. The construction and development of the multidimensional-multiattributional causality scales. In H. M. Lefcourt (Ed.), *Research with the locus of control construct: Vol. 1. Assessment methods* (pp. 245–277). New York: Academic Press, 1981.

Lefcourt, H. M., & Wine, J. Internal versus external control of reinforcement and the development of attention in experimental situations. *Canadian Journal of Behavioral Science*, 1969, *1*, 167–181.

Leith, G. O. M. Individual differences in learning: Interactions of personality and teaching. *Association of Educational Psychologists 1974 Conference Proceedings*, London, 1974.

Lessinger, L. M., & Martinson, R. A. The use of California Psychological Inventory with gifted pupils. *Personnel and Guidance Journal*, 1961, *39*, 572–575.

Lester, D. The relationship between some dimensions of personality. *Psychology*, 1976, *13*, 58–60.

Leton, D. A., & Walters, S. A factor-analysis of the California Psychological Inventory and Minnesota Counseling Inventory. *California Journal of Educational Research*, 1962, *13*, 126–133.

Levenson, H. Differentiating among internality, powerful others, and chance. In H. M. Lefcourt (Ed.), *Research with the locus of control construct: Vol. 1. Assessment methods*. (pp. 15–63). New York: Academic Press, 1981.

Levin, J., & Karni, E. Demonstration of cross-cultural invariance of the California Psychological Inventory in America and Israel by the Guttman-Lingoes smallest space analysis. *Journal of Cross-Cultural Psychology*, 1970, *1*, 253–260.

Lewin, K. *Principles of topological psychology.* New York: McGraw-Hill, 1936.

Liebert, R. M., & Spiegler, M. D. *Personality: Strategies and issues* (3rd ed.). Homewood, IL: Dorsey Press, 1978.

Liverant, S., & Scodel, A. Internal and external control as determinants of decision making under conditions of risk. *Psychological Reports,* 1960, *7,* 59–67.

Lobel, T. E. The prediction of behavior from different types of beliefs. *Journal of Social Psychology,* 1982, *118,* 213–223.

Loehlin, J. C., & Nichols, R. C. *Heredity, environment, and personality: A study of 850 sets of twins.* Austin and London: University of Texas Press, 1976.

London, H. Personality paradigms and politics. In H. London (Ed.), *Personality: A new look at metatheories.* New York: Hemisphere, 1978.

London, H., & Exner, J. (Ed.). *Dimensions of personality.* New York: Wiley, 1978.

Lorei, T. W. Prediction of length of stay out of the hospital for released psychiatric patients. *Journal of Consulting Psychology,* 1964, *28,* 358–363.

Lorenz, K. Innate bases of learning. In K. Pribram (Ed.), *On the biology of learning.* New York: Harcourt Brace Jovanovich, 1969.

Ludvigh, E. J., & Happ, D. Extraversion and preferred level of sensory stimulation. *British Journal of Psychology,* 1974, *65,* 359–365.

Lynn, R., & Butler, J. Introversion and the arousal jag. *British Journal of Social and Clinical Psychology,* 1962, *1,* 150–151.

Lynn, R., & Eysenck, H. J. Tolerance for pain, extraversion and neuroticism. *Perceptual and Motor Skills,* 1961, *12,* 161–162.

Maccoby, E. E., & Jacklin, C. N. *The psychology of sex differences.* Stanford, CA: Stanford University Press, 1974.

MacKinnon, D. W. The creativity of architects. In D. W. Taylor & F. Barron (Eds.), *Widening horizons in creativity.* New York: Wiley, 1964.

Maddi, S. R. *Personality theories: A comparative analysis.* Homewood, IL: Dorsey Press, 1968.

Maddi, S. R. The uses of theorizing in personality. In E. Staub, (Ed.), *Personality: Basic aspects and current research* (pp. 334–375). Englewood Cliffs, NJ: Prentice-Hall, 1980.

Magnusson, D., Duner, A., & Zetterblom, G. *Adjustment: A longitudinal study.* Stockholm: Almquist & Wiksell; New York: Wiley, 1975.

Mahoney, M. J. *Cognition and behavior modification.* Cambridge, MA: Ballinger, 1974.

Mann, R. D. A review of the relationships between personality and performance in small groups. *Psychological Bulletin,* 1959, *56,* 241–270.

Masserman, J. H. *Principles of dynamic psychiatry.* Philadelphia: Saunders, 1946.

McClelland, D. C. *Power: The inner experience.* New York: Irvington Publishers, Halsted Press, Division of John Wiley, 1975.

McClelland, D. C. Is personality consistent? In A. I. Rabin, J. Aronoff, A. M. Barclay, & R. A. Zucker (Eds.), *Further explorations in personality.* New York: Wiley, 1981.

McClelland, D. C. & Jemmott, J. B., III. Power motivation, stress and physical illness. *Journal of Human Stress,* 1980, *6,* 6–15.

McClelland, D. C., Locke, S. E., Williams, R. M., & Hurst, M. W. *Power motivation, distress and immune function.* Unpublished manuscript, Harvard University, 1982.

McDermid, C. D. Some correlates of creativity in engineering personnel. *Journal of Applied Psychology,* 1965, *49,* 14–19.

McGuire, W. J. Contextualist theory of knowledge: Its implication for innovation and reform in psychological research. In L. Berkowitz (Ed.), *Advances in experimental social research* (Vol. 16) (pp. 1–47). New York: Academic Press, 1983.

Megargee, E. I. Problems of structured tests: Response sets and biases. In E. I. Megargee (Ed.), *Research in clinical assessment.* New York: Harper & Row, 1966.

Megargee, E. I. *The California Psychological Inventory handbook.* San Francisco: Jossey-Bass, 1972.

Meichenbaum, D. *Cognitive-behavior modification: An integrative approach.* New York: Plenum Press, 1977.

Meili, R. The structure of personality. In J. Nuttin, P. Fraisse, & R. Meili. *Experimental psychology, its scope and method: Vol. 5. Motivation, emotion, and personality.* New York: Basic Books, 1968.

Mellstrom, M., Jr., Cicala, G. A., & Zuckerman, M. General versus specific trait anxiety measures in the prediction of fear of snakes, heights, and darkness. *Journal of Consulting and Clinical Psychology,* 1976, *44,* 83–91.

Miller, A. G. (Ed.), *In the eye of the beholder: Contemporary issues in stereotyping.* New York: Holt, Rinehart & Winston, 1980.

Miller, G. A., Galanter, E., & Pribram, K. *Plans and the structure of behavior.* New York: Holt, Rinehart & Winston, 1960.

Miller, J. G. Living systems: Basic concepts. *Behavioral Science*, 1965, *10*, 193–237.

Mirels, H. L. Dimensions of internal versus external control. *Journal of Consulting and Clinical Psychology*, 1970, *34*, 226–228.

Misch, R. *The relationship of motoric inhibition to developmental level and ideational functioning: An analysis by means of the Rorschach test*. Unpublished doctoral dissertation, Clark University, 1954.

Mischel, W. *Personality and assessment*. New York: Wiley, 1968.

Mischel, W. Continuity and change in personality. *American Psychologist*, 1969, *24*, 1012–1018.

Mischel, W. Processes in delay of gratification. In L. Berkowitz (Ed.), *Advances in experimental social psychology* (Vol. 7). New York: Academic Press, 1974.

Mischel, W. *Introduction to personality* (2nd ed.). New York: Holt, Rinehart & Winston, 1976. (Originally published in 1971)

Mischel, W. The interaction of person and situation. In D. Magnusson & N. S. Endler (Eds.), *Personality at the crossroads: Current issues in interactional psychology*. Hillsdale, NJ: Erlbaum, 1977.

Mischel, W. On the interface of cognition and personality: Beyond the person-situation debate. *American Psychologist*, 1979, *34*, 740–754.

Mischel, W., Zeiss, R., & Zeiss, A. Internal-external control and persistence: Validation and implications of the standard pre-school internal-external scale. *Journal of Personality and Social Psychology*, 1974, *29*, 265–278.

Mitchell, J. V., Jr., & Pierce-Jones, J. A factor analysis of Gough's California Psychological Inventory. *Journal of Consulting Psychology*, 1960, *24*, 453–456.

Mitchell, T. R. Leadership complexity and leadership style. *Journal of Personality and Social Psychology*, 1970, *16*, 166–174.

Mohan, J., & Mohan, V. Personality and variability in esthetic evaluation. *Psychological Studies*, 1965, *10*, 57–60.

Moos, R. H. Differential effects of psychiatric ward settings on patient change. *Journal of Nervous and Mental Disease*, 1970, *5*, 316–321.

Morgan, H. H. A psychometric comparison of achieving and nonachieving college students of high ability. *Journal of Consulting Psychology*, 1952, *16*, 292–298.

Morris, L. W. *Extraversion and introversion: An interactional perspective*. New York: Hemisphere, Halsted Press, Wiley, 1979.

Myers, I. B. *Introduction to type* (2nd ed.). Gainesville, FL: Center for Applications of Psychological Type, 1962 (Third printing, 1979). (a)

Myers, I. B. *Manual, the Myers-Briggs Type Indicator*. Princeton, NJ: Educational Testing Service, 1962. (b)

Myers, T. I., & Eisner, E. J. *An experimental evaluation of the effects of karate and meditation (Report No. 42800 [P-391X-1-29])*. Washington, DC: American Institues for Research, 1974.

Nelsen, E. N., Grinder, R. E., & Mutterer, M. L. Sources of variance in behavioral measures of honesty in temptation situations: Methodological analyses. *Developmental Psychology*, 1969, *1*, 265–279.

Newcomb, T. M. *Consistency of certain extrovert-introvert behavior patterns in 51 problem boys*. New York: Columbia University, Teachers College, Bureau of Publications, 1929.

Nichols, R. C., & Schnell, R. R. Factor scales for the California Psychological Inventory. *Journal of Consulting Psychology*, 1963, *27*, 228–235.

Noblin, C. D. *Experimental analysis of psychoanalytic character types through the operant conditioning of verbal responses*. Unpublished doctoral dissertation, Louisiana State University, 1962.

Norman, W. T. Toward an adequate taxonomy of personality attributes: Replicated factor structure in peer nomination personality ratings. *Journal of Abnormal and Social Psychology*, 1963, *66*, 574–583.

O'Conner, P. Ethnocentrism, "intolerance of ambiguity," and abstract reasoning ability. *Journal of Abnormal and Social Psychology*, 1952, *47*, 526–530.

Odell, M. *Personality correlates of independence and conformity*. Unpublished master's thesis, Ohio State University, 1959.

Ogden, R. M., & Richards, I. A. *The meaning of meaning*. London: Routledge & Kegan Paul, 1949.

Oksenberg, L. *Machiavellianism and emotionality*. Unpublished master's thesis, Columbia University, 1964 (summarized by Macperson, 1970) p. 396).

Olds, D. E., & Shaver, P. Masculinity, femininity, academic performance, and health: Further evidence concerning the androgyny controversy. *Journal of Personality*, 1980, *48*, 323–341.

Olmstead, D. W., & Monachesi, E. D. A validity check on MMPI scales of responsibility and dominance. *Journal of Abnormal and Social Psychology*, 1956, *53*, 140–141.

Osgood, C. E. *Method and theory in experimental psychology*. New York: Oxford University Press, 1964.

Osgood, C. E., Suci, G. J., & Tannenbaum, P. H. *The measurement of meaning.* Urbana: Illinois University Press, 1958.

Parloff, M. B., & Datta, L. E. Personality characteristics of the potentially creative scientist. In *Science and psychoanalysis* (Vol. 3). New York: Grune & Stratton, 1965.

Parloff, M. B., Datta, L. E., Kleman, M., & Handlon, H. H. Personality characteristics which differentiate creative male adolescents and adults. *Journal of Personality,* 1968,36, 528–552.

Paulhus, D., & Christie, R. Spheres of control: An interactionist approach to assessment of perceived control. In H. M. Lefcourt (Ed.), *Research with the locus of control construct: Vol. 1. Assessment methods* (pp. 161–188). New York: Academic Press, 1981.

Pavlov, I. P. *Conditioned reflexes.* Oxford, England: Clarendon Press, 1927.

Payne, R. W. Cognitive abnormalities. In H. J. Eysenck (Ed.), *Handbook of abnormal psychology* (2nd ed.) (pp. 420–483). San Diego: Robert R. Knapp, 1973.

Pervin, L. A. Performance and satisfaction as a function of individual-environment fit. *Psychological Bulletin,* 1968, *69,* 56–68.

Pervin, L. A. *Personality: Theory, assessment, and research* (3rd ed.). New York: Wiley, 1980.

Pervin, L. A. The stasis and flow of behavior: Toward a theory of goals. In R. A. Dienstbier & M. M. Page (Eds.), *Nebraska Symposium on Motivation 1982: Personality—Current theory and research.* Lincoln: University of Nebraska Press, 1983.

Phares, E. J. *Locus of control in personality.* Morristown, NJ: General Learning Press, 1976.

Phares, E. J., Wilson, K. G., & Klyver, N. W. Internal-external control and the attribution of blame under neutral and distractive conditions. *Journal of Personality and Social Psychology,* 1971, *18,* 285–288.

Phillips, L., & Zigler, E. Social competence: The action-thought parameter and vicariousness in normal and pathological behaviors. *Journal of Abnormal and Social Psychology,* 1961, *63,* 137–146.

Phillips, L., & Zigler, E. Role orientation, the action–thought parameter and outcome of psychiatric disorders. *Journal of Abnormal and Social Psychology,* 1964, *63,* 381–389.

Piaget, J. *Language and thought of the child.* London: Routledge & Kegan Paul, 1948.

Piaget, J. Principal factors in determining evolution from childhood to adult life. In D. Rapaport (Ed.), *Organization and pathology of thought.* New York: Columbia University Press, 1951.

Piaget, J. *Structuralism.* New York: Basic Books, 1970.

Pierce-Jones, J., Mitchell, J. V., Jr., & King, F. J. Configurational invariance in the California Psychological Inventory. *Journal of Experimental Education,* 1962, *31,* 65–71.

Pinneau, S. R., & Milton, A. The ecological veracity of the self-report. *Journal of Genetic Psychology,* 1958, *93,* 249–276.

Plant, W. T., Telford, C. W., & Thomas, J. A. Some personality differences between dogmatic and non-dogmatic groups. *Journal of Social Psychology,* 1965, *67,* 67–75.

Platt, J. *Grammatical form and grammatical meaning.* Amsterdam: North-Holland, 1971.

Platt, J. J., & Eisenman, R. Internal-external control of reinforcement, time perspective, adjustment, and anxiety. *Journal of General Psychology,* 1968, *79,* 121–128.

Porter, E. R., Argyle, M., & Salter, V. What is signalled by proximity? *Perceptual and Motor Skills,* 1970, *30,* 39–42.

Purkey, W. W. Measured and professed personality characteristics of gifted high-school students and analysis of their congruence. *Journal of Educational Research,* 1966, *60,* 99–103.

Rao, P. V. K. *Mental imagery and sensation seeking.* Unpublished manuscript, 1978 (reported in Zuckerman, 1979a).

Rapaport, C. *Character, anxiety, and social affiliation.* Unpublished doctoral dissertation, New York University, 1963.

Rapaport, D. Toward a theory of thinking. In D. Rapaport (Ed.), *Organization and pathology of thought.* New York: Columbia University Press, 1951.

Rim, Y. Machiavellianism and decisions involving risks. *British Journal of Social and Clinical Psychology,* 1966, *5,* 30–36.

Rim, Y., & Seidendross, H. Personality and response to pressure from peers vs. adults. *Personality,* 1971, *2,* 35–43.

Rodin, J. The current status of the internal-external obesity hypothesis: What went wrong? *American Psychologist,* 1981, *36,* 361–372.

Rogers, T. B. A model of the self as an aspect of the human information processing system. In N. Cantor & J. F. Kihlstrom (Eds.), *Personality, cognition, and social interaction.* Hillsdale, NJ: Erlbaum, 1981.

Rokeach, M. The nature and meaning of dogmatism. *Psychological Review,* 1954, *61,* 194–204.

Rokeach, M. *The open and closed mind.* New York: Basic Books, 1960.

Rokeach, M., & Bonier, R. Time perspective, dogmatism, and anxiety. In M. Rokeach, *The open and closed mind*. New York: Basic Books, 1960.

Rosenberg, L. A., McHenry, T. B. Rosenberg, A. M., & Nichols, R. C. The prediction of academic achievement with the California Psychological Inventory. *Journal of Applied Psychology*, 1962, *46*, 385–388.

Ross, J. *Progress report on the College Student Characteristics study: June, 1961*. Princeton, NJ: Educational Testing Service, 1961. (Res. Memo. 61-11)

Ross, J. The relationship between a Jungian personality inventory and tests of ability, personality and interest. *Australian Journal of Psychology*, 1966, *18*, 1–17.

Ross, L. The intuitive psychologist and his shortcomings: Distortions in the attribution process. In L. Berkowitz (Ed.), *Advances in experimental social psychology* (Vol. 10). New York: Academic Press, 1977.

Rotter, J. B. Generalized expectancies for internal versus external control of reinforcement. *Psychological Monographs*, 1966, *80* (1, whole no. 609).

Rotter, J. B., & Mulry, R. C. Internal versus external control of reinforcement and decision time. *Journal of Personality and Social Psychology*, 1965, *2*, 598–604.

Ryckman, R. M., Rodda, W. C., & Sherman, M. F. Locus of control and expertise relevance as determinants of changes in opinion about student activism. *Journal of Social Psychology*, 1972, *88*, 107–114.

Rydell, S. T. Tolerance of ambiguity and semantic differential ratings. *Psychological Reports*, 1966, *19*, 1303–1312.

Rydell, S. T., & Rosen, E. Measurement and some correlates of need-cognition. *Psychological Reports*, 1966, *19*, 139–165.

Sainsbury, P. Psychological disorders and neurosis in outpatients attending a general hospital. *Journal of Psychosomatic Research*, 1960, *4*, 261–273.

Sapir, E. Grading: A study in semantics. *Philosophy of Science*, 1944, *2*, 93–116.

Sarason, I. G. The Test Anxiety Scale: Concept and research. In C. D. Spielberger & I. G. Sarason (Eds.), *Stress and anxiety* (Vol. 5). Washington, DC: Hemisphere, 1978.

Sarbin, T. R., Taft, R., & Bailey, D. E. *Clinical inference and cognitive theory*. New York: Holt, Rinehart & Winston, 1960.

Schachter, S. The interaction of cognitive and physiological determinants of emotional states. In L. Berkowitz (Ed.), *Advances in experimental social psychology* (Vol. 1). New York: Academic Press, 1964.

Schalling, D., & Levander, S. Ratings of anxiety-proneness and responses to electrical pain stimulation. *Scandinavian Journal of Psychology*, 1964, *5*, 1–19.

Schilder, P. *The image and appearance of the human body*. London: Kegan, Paul, Trench, Trubner, & Co., 1935.

Schlesinger, J. M., & Guttman, L. Smallest space analysis of intelligence and achievement tests. *Psychological Bulletin*, 1969, *71*, 95–100.

Schneider, J. M. & Parsons, O. A. *Categories on the Locus of Control scale and cross-cultural comparisons in Denmark and the United States*. Unpublished master's thesis, University of Oklahoma, 1969.

Schroder, H. M., Driver, M. J., & Streufert, S. *Human information processing*. New York: Holt, Rinehart & Winston, 1967.

Schwartz, S. Individual differences in cognition: Some relationships between personality and memory features. *Journal of Research in Personality*, 1975, *9*, 217–225.

Seeman, M., & Evans, J. W. Alienation and learning in a hospital setting. *American Sociological Review*, 1962, *27*, 772–783.

Segal, B., & Singer, J. L. Daydreaming, drug, and alcohol use in college students: A factor analytic study. *Addictive Behaviors*, 1976, *1*, 227–235.

Shagass, C. Sedation threshold. *Psychosomatic Medicine*, 1956, *18*, 410–419.

Shapiro, D. *Neurotic styles*. New York: Basic Books, 1965.

Sheldon, W. H. *The varieties of temperament: A psychology of constitutional differences*. New York: Harper & Row, 1942.

Sherman, S. J. Internal-external control and its relationship to attitude change under different social influence techniques. *Journal of Personality and Social Psychology*, 1973, *23*, 23–29.

Shipe, D. Impulsivity and locus of control as predictors of achievement and adjustment in mildly retarded and borderline youth. *American Journal of Mental Deficiency*, 1971, *1*, 12–22.

Shure, G. H., & Rogers, M. S. Personality factor stability for three ability levels. *Journal of Psychology*, 1963, *55*, 445–456.

Shweder, R. A. How relevant is an individual difference theory of personality? *Journal of Personality*, 1975, *43*, 455–484.

Shybut, J. Time perspective, internal versus external control and severity of psychological disturbance. *Journal of Clinical Psychology*, 1968, *24*, 312–315.

Singer, J. *Daydreaming*. New York: Random House, 1966.

Singer, J. L., & Rowe, R. An experimental study of some relationships between daydreaming and anxiety. *Journal of Consulting Psychology*, 1962, *26*, 446–454.

Singh, S. D., Gupta, V. P., & Manocha, S. N. Physical persistence, personality and drugs. *Indian Journal of Applied Psychology*, 1966, *3*, 92–95.

Sinha, A. K. P., & Ojha, H. An experimental study of the operation of prestige suggestions in extraverts and introverts. *Journal of Social Psychology*, 1963, *61*, 29–34.

Skinner, B. F. *Verbal behavior*. New York: Appleton-Century-Crofts, 1957.

Smelser, W. T. Dominance as a factor in achievement and perception in cooperative problem-solving interactions. *Journal of Abnormal and Social Psychology*, 1961, *62*, 535–542.

Smith, S. The effect of personality and drugs on auditory threshold when risk-taking factors are controlled. 1966. Quoted in H. J. Eysenck, *The biological basis of personality* (pp. 102, 384). Springfield, IL: Charles C Thomas, 1967.

Smock, C. D. The influence of psychological stress on the "intolerance of ambiguity." *Journal of Abnormal and Social Psychology*, 1955, *50*, 177–182.

Snider, J. G., & Linton, T. E. The predictive value of the California Psychological Inventory in discriminating between the personality patterns of high school achievers and underachievers. *Ontario Journal of Educational Research*, 1964, *6*, 107–115.

Sokolov, E. N. The orienting reflex, its structure and mechanisms. In L. G. Voronin, A. N. Leontiev, A. R. Luria, E. N. Sokolov, & O. S. Vinogradova (Eds.), *Orienting reflex and exploratory behavior*. Moscow: Publishing House of the Academy of Pedagogical Sciences of RSFSR, 1958.

Sosis, R. H. Internal-external control and the perception of responsibility of another for an accident. *Journal of Personality and Social Psychology*, 1974, *30*, 393–399.

Southern, M. L., & Plant, W. T. Personality characteristics of very bright adults. *Journal of Social Psychology*, 1968, *75*, 119–126.

Spence, J. T., & Helmreich, R. L. *Masculinity and femininity: Their psychological dimensions, correlates and antecedents*. Austin, University of Texas Press, 1978.

Spielberger, C. D. Anxiety: State-trait process. In C. D. Spielberger & I. G. Sarason (Eds.), *Stress and anxiety* (Vol. 1). Washington, DC: Hemisphere, 1975.

Spielberger, C. D., Gorsuch, R. L., Lushene, R. E., & Vagg, P. R. *The state-trait anxiety inventory: Form Y*. Tampa: University of South Florida, 1977.

Springob, H. K., & Struening, E. L. A factor analysis of the California Psychological Inventory on a high school population. *Journal of Counseling Psychology*, 1964, *11*, 173–179.

Stagner, R. Traits are relevant: Theoretical analysis and empirical evidence. In N. S. Endler & D. Magnusson (Eds.), *Interactional psychology and personality*. Washington, DC: Hemisphere, 1976.

Stanton, H. E. Hypnosis and encounter group volunteers: A validational study of the Sensation-Seeking Scale. *Journal of Consulting and Clinical Psychology*, 1976, *44*, 692.

Stein, K. B., & Craik, K. H. Relationship between motoric and ideational activity preference and time perspective in neurotics and schizophrenics. *Journal of Consulting Psychology*, 1965, *29*, 460–467.

Steiner, I. D. Ethnocentrism and tolerance of trait "inconsistency." *Journal of Abnormal and Social Psychology*, 1954, *49*, 349–345.

Steiner, I. D., & Johnson, H. H. Authoritarianism and conformity. *Sociometry*, 1963, *26*, 21–34.

Stephenson, G. M., & Barker, J. Personality and the pursuit of distributive justice: An experimental study of children's moral behavior. *British Journal of Social and Clinical Psychology*, 1972, *11*, 207–219.

Stewart, L. H. Social and emotional adjustment during adolescence as related to the development of psychosomatic illness in adulthood. *Genetic Psychology Monographs*, 1962, *65*, 175–215.

Straits, B., & Sechrest, L. Further support of some findings about the characteristics of smokers and non-smokers. *Journal of Consulting Psychology*, 1963, *27*, 282.

Strelau, J. The concept of temperament in personality research. *European Journal of Personality*, 1987, *1*, 107–117.

Stricker, L. J., & Ross, J. Some correlates of a Jungian personality inventory. *Psychological Reports*, 1964, *14*, 623–643.

Strickland, B. R. The prediction of social action from a dimension of internal-external control. *Journal of Social Psychology*, 1965, *66*, 353–358.

Strickland, B. R. Delay of gratification and internal locus of control in children. *Journal of Consulting and Clinical Psychology*, 1973, *40*, 338.

Strickland, B. R. Approval motivation. In T. Blass (Ed.), *Personality variables in social behavior* (pp. 315–356). Hillsdale, NJ: Erlbaum, 1977. (a)

Strickland, B. R. Internal-external control of motivation. In T. Blass (Ed.), *Personality variables in social behavior* (pp. 219–279) Hillsdale, NJ: Erlbaum., 1977. (b)

Sullivan, H. S. *Conceptions of modern psychiatry*. Washington, DC: William Alanson White Psychiatric Foundation, 1947.

Tatro, D. F. *The interpretation of objectively measured personality factors in terms of clinical data, and concepts*. Unpublished doctoral dissertation, University of Illinois, 1966.

Tausk, V. On the origin of the influencing machine in schizophrenia. *Psychoanalytic Quarterly*, 1933, *2*, 519–556.

Taylor, H. F. *Balance in small groups*. New York: Van Nostrand Reinhold, 1970.

Taylor, J. A. A personality scale of manifest anxiety. *Journal of Abnormal and Social Psychology*, 1953, *48*, 285–290.

Taylor, R. N. Risk taking, dogmatism, and demographic characteristics of managers as correlates of information-processing and decision making behavior. Proceedings of the Annual Convention of the American Psychological Association, 1972 (Part I), 443–444.

Thackray, R. A., Jones, K. N., & Touchstone, R. M. Personality and physiological correlates of performance decrement on a monotonous task requiring sustained attention. *British Journal of Psychology*, 1974, *65*, 351–358.

Thorndike, R. L. Review of the California Psychological Inventory. In O. K. Buros (Ed.), *Fifth mental measurements yearbook*. Highland Park, NJ: Gryphon Press, 1959.

Thurstone, L. L. A factorial study of perception. *Psychometric Monographs*, 1944, No. 4.

Timmons, E. O., & Noblin, C. D. The differential performance of orals and anals in a verbal conditioning paradigm. *Journal of Consulting Psychology*, 1963, *27*, 383–386.

Tinbergen, N. *The study of instinct*. Oxford: Clarendon, 1951.

Titus, H. E., & Hollander, E. P. The California F scale in psychological research. *Psychological Bulletin*, 1957, *54*, 47–64.

Tizard, J., & Venables, P. H. The influence of extraneous stimulation on the reaction time of schizophrenics. *British Journal of Psychology*, 1957, *48*, 299–305.

Trickett, E. J., & Moos, R. H. Generality and specificity of student reactions in high school classrooms. *Adolescence*, 1970, *5*, 373–390.

Trites, D., Kurek, A., & Cobb, B. Personality and achievement of air traffic controllers. *Aerospace Medicine*, 1967, *38*, 1145–1150.

Tuddenham, R. Correlates of yielding to a distorted group norm. *Journal of Personality*, 1959, *27*, 272–284.

Tune, G. S. Errors of commission as a function of age and temperament in a type of vigilance task. *Quarterly Journal of Experimental Psychology*, 1966, *18*, 358–361.

Vacchiano, R. B. Dogmatism. In T. Blass (Ed.), *Personality variables in social behavior* (pp. 281–314). Hillsdale, NJ: Erlbaum, 1977.

Vacchiano, R. B., Strauss, P. S., & Schiffman, D. C. Personality correlates of dogmatism. *Journal of Consulting Psychology*, 1968, *32*, 83–85.

Van Egeren, L. F. Multivariate research on the psychoses. In R. B. Cattell & R. M. Dreger (Eds.), *Handbook of modern personality theory*. Washington, DC: Hemisphere, 1977.

Vaughan, G. M. Personality and small group behavior. In R. B. Cattell, & R. M. Dreger (Eds.), *Handbook of modern personality theory*. New York: Hemisphere, Halsted, Wiley, 1977.

Venables, P. H. Psychophysiological aspects of schizophrenia. *British Journal of Medical Psychology*, 1966, *39*, 289.

Venables, P. H., & O'Connor, N. Reaction time to auditory and visual stimulation in schizophrenics and normals. *Quarterly Journal of Experimental Psychology*, 1959, *11*, 175–179.

Vernon, P. E. *Personality assessment*. London: Methuen, 1964.

Vernon, P. E. Multivariate approaches to the study of cognitive styles. In J. R. Royce (Ed.), *Multivariate analysis and psychological theory*. London: Academic Press, 1973.

Vestewig, R. E. Extraversion and risk preference in portfolio theory. *Journal of Psychology*, 1977, *97*, 237–245.

Vygotsky, L. S. *Thought and language*. Cambridge: MIT Press, 1962.

Wachtel, P. L. Psychodynamics, behavior therapy and the implicable experimenter: An inquiry into the consistency of personality. *Journal of Abnormal Psychology*, 1973, *82*, 324–334.

Walls, R. T., & Smith, T. S. Development of preference for delayed reinforcement in disadvantaged children. *Journal of Educational Psychology*, 1970, *61*, 118–123.

Watson, D. L. Introversion, neuroticism, rigidity, and dogmatism. *Journal of Consulting Psychology*, 1967, *31*, 105.

Weiner, B. *Theories of motivation: From mechanism to cognition*. Chicago: Markham, 1972.

Welsh, G. S. An anxiety index and an internalization ratio for the MMPI. *Journal of Consulting Psychology*, 1952, *16*, 65–72.

Werner, H. *Comparative psychology of mental development* (rev ed.). Chicago: Follett, 1948.

Werner, H., & Kaplan, B. *Symbol formation*. New York: Wiley, 1963.

Westcott, M. R. On the measurement of intuitive leaps. *Psychological Reports*, 1961, *9*, 267–274.

Westcott, M. R. *Toward a contemporary psychology of intuition: A historical, theoretical, and empirical inquiry*. New York: Holt, Rinehart & Winston, 1968.

Westhoff, K., & Halbach-Suarez, C. Cognitive orientation and the prediction of decisions in a medical examination context. *European Journal of Personality*, 1989, *3*, 61–71.

White, K. Anxiety, extraversion-introversion and divergent thinking ability. *Journal of Creative Behavior*, 1968, *2*, 119–127.

White, P. O., Eysenck, H. J., & Souief, M. I. Combined analysis of Cattell, Eysenck and Guilford factors. In H. J. Eysenck & S. B. G. Eysenck, *Personality structure and measurement* (pp. 194–217). London: Routledge & Kegan Paul, 1969.

Wiggins, N. Individual differences in human judgment: A multivariate approach. In L. Rappoport & D. Summer (Eds.), *Human judgment and social interaction*. New York: Holt, Rinehart & Winston, 1973.

Wilde, J. G. S. Trait description and measurement by personality questionnaires. In R. B. Cattell & R. M. Dreger (Eds.), *Handbook of modern personality theory*. Washington, DC: Hemisphere, 1977.

Wilson, G. Introversion/extraversion. In T. Blass (Ed.), *Personality variables in social behavior*. Hillsdale, NJ: Erlbaum, 1977.

Wilson, G. Introversion/extraversion. In H. London & J. Exner (Eds.), *Dimensions of personality* (pp. 217–261). New York: Wiley, 1978.

Wilson, G. D., & Nias, D. K. B. Sexual types. *New Behavior*, 1975, *2*, 330–332.

Winer, B. J. *Statistical principles in experimental design* (2nd ed.). New York: McGraw-Hill, 1971.

Winter, D. G. *The power motive*. New York: Free Press, A Division of Macmillan, 1973.

Winter, D. G., & Stewart, A. J. The power motive. In H. London & J. E. Exner (Eds.), *Dimensions of personality* (pp. 391–447). New York: Wiley, 1978.

Withall, J., & Lewis, W. W. Social interaction in the classroom. In N. L. Gage (Ed.), *Handbook of research on teaching*. Chicago: Rand McNally, 1963.

Witkin, H. A., Lewis, H. B., Hertzman, M., Machover, K., Meissner, P. B., & Wapner, S. *Personality through perception*. New York: Harper, 1954.

Witkin, H. A., Dyk, R. B., Faterson. H. F., Goodenough, D. R., & Karp, S. A. *Psychological differentiation*. New York: Wiley, 1962.

Wittgenstein, L. *Philosophical investigations*. Oxford: Basil, Blackwell, 1953.

Young, R. K., Benson, W. N., & Holzman, W. H. Change in attitudes toward the Negro in a Southern university. *Journal of Abnormal and Social Psychology*, 1960, *60*, 131–135.

Zakay, D. *Decision by meaning: A decision making model based upon the cognitive orientation theory*. Unpublished doctoral dissertation, Tel Aviv University, 1976. (In English)

Zakay, D., Bar-El, Z., & Kreitler, S. Cognitive orientation and changing the impulsivity of children. *British Journal of Educational Psychology*, 1984, *54*, 40–50.

Ziv-Av, Y. *Slowness in different types of action as a function of cognitive structures and contents*. Unpublished master's thesis, Tel Aviv University, 1978.

Zivin, G. (Ed.), *The development of self-regulation through private speech*. New York: Wiley, 1979.

Zuckerman, M. Dimensions of sensation-seeking. *Journal of Consulting and Clinical Psychology*, 1971, *36*, 45–52.

Zuckerman, M. The sensation seeking motive. In B. A. Maher (Ed.), *Progress in experimental personality research* (Vol. 7). New York: Academic Press, 1974.

Zuckerman, M. Development of a situation-specific trait-state test for the prediction and measurement of affective responses. *Journal of Consulting and Clinical Psychology*, 1977, *45*, 513–523.

Zuckerman, M. Sensation seeking and risk taking. In C. E. Izard (Ed.), *Emotions in personality and psychopathology*. New York: Plenum, 1979. (a)

Zuckerman, M. *Sensation seeking: Beyond the optimal level of arousal*. Hillsdale, NJ: Erlbaum, 1979. (b)

Zuckerman, M., & Haber, M. M. Need for stimulation as a source of stress response to perceptual isolation. *Journal of Abnormal Psychology*, 1965, *70*, 371–377.

Zuckerman, M., Persky, H., Hopkins, T. R., Murtaugh, T., Basu, G. K., & Schilling, M. Comparison of stress effects of perceptual and social isolation. *Archives of General Psychiatry*, 1966, *14*, 356–365.

Zuckerman, M., Schultz, D. P., & Hopkins, T. R. Sensation seeking and volunteering for sensory deprivation and hypnosis experiments. *Journal of Consulting Psychology*, 1967, *31*, 358–363.

Zuckerman, M., Neary, R. S., & Brustman, B. A. Sensation-Seeking Scale correlates in experience (smoking, drugs, alcohol, "hallucinations" and sex) and preference for complexity (designs). *Proceedings of the 78th Annual Convention of the American Psychological Association*, 1970.

Zung, W. W. K., & Cavenar, J. O. Jr. Assessment scales and techniques. In L. L. Kutash, L. B. Schlesinger, & Associates (Eds.), *Handbook on stress and anxiety*. San Francisco: Jossey-Bass, 1980.

Index